Arcades

The MIT Press
Cambridge, Massachusetts
London, England

Arcades

The History of a Building Type

Johann Friedrich Geist

Based on a translation by Jane O. Newman and
John H. Smith

© 1983 by Massachusetts Institute of Technology

Originally published in German under the title
Passagen—Ein Bautyp des 19. Jahrhunderts, third
edition © 1979 by Prestel-Verlag, Munich

This book was set in VIP Sabon by Achorn
Graphic Services, Inc. and printed and bound by
Halliday Lithograph in the United States of
America.

Library of Congress Cataloging in Publication Data
Geist, Johann Friedrich, 1936–
  Arcades, the history of a building type.

  Bibliography: p.
  "Based on a translation by Jane O. Newman and
John H. Smith."
  1. Arcades. 2. Architecture, Modern—19th cen-
tury. I. Title.
NA6218.G4313 1983   725'.21   82–10014
ISBN 0–262–07082–0   AACR2

Contents

Preface

I conceived this project while designing an arcade for the Kurfürstendamm in Berlin. Questions of public space, its function, and its regulation as they are realized in the arcade led me to focus my attention on examples from the past; they also tempted me to investigate more closely one of the many blank spots in the architectural picture of the nineteenth century. The arcade was the creation of the private sector of speculative building; it was thus one of the few architectural types which both grew out of and disappeared with the nineteenth century. The existence of the arcade is clearly defined by the period between the French Revolution and World War I; the century is reflected in the development of the arcade. In its fate are revealed both the external virtuosity and the inner abyss of the century's still unresolved social conditions.

The first building which deserves the designation "arcade" stood in Paris at the Palais Royal. Its commercial success and legendary fame as the promenade of an emancipated, urban society of the postrevolutionary era made the arcade a fashionable trend. The arcade endowed the pedestrian once again with his full import and became the driving force behind a reorganization of public space. It became the unmistakable index of urban life. The arcade was the exotic flower of a civilization whose public life reached its peak in the nineteenth century.

There are numerous questions about the heritage of the arcade's architectural form and its relation to other structures of the era. Is the arcade a street, a building, or only a variation of the colonnade? Is it the connecting link between earlier forms of the marketplace and the warehouses of advanced capitalism? Or is it something of a greenhouse, serving also as a quasi-foyer for an aristocratic public? Was the arcade, as a space of transition and movement, in some ways a forerunner of the train station? Were the built-up bridges of the Renaissance and the London exchanges, the Eastern bazaars, and the rows of shops at the great markets and fairs also early forms? Is the arcade not as well a tenement house, an open-air exercise yard for the jail, and a secularized sacred space, which instead of an altar has only an additional exit? These are startling parallels. It seemed to me that the task of the volume at hand was to investigate the architectural form of the arcade in all its aspects, from its suitability as a bordello to its function as a commune hall of the social revolution. The development of the arcade as an object of private speculation into one with a public purpose was also important to me. Finally, I sought to portray the reasons for the disintegration of its spatial form at the beginning of the twentieth century and for its more recent rebirth. Certainly some areas will remain inextricably complex. Of the many arcades cataloged here only a few remain standing, and of those only a few in their original form. The overwhelming number have been either torn down or modernized. They exist in an environment which no longer accounts for them. The urban centers of the nineteenth century are now either decaying or being destroyed, insofar as the air raids of World War II left any standing. The arcades are vanishing with them. Perhaps this study will work on behalf of those few examples which may still be salvaged. My project was conceived in a period when it had become clear that the public realm was no longer intact as a controlling force and architecture failed at precisely that point where it should make way for the public. The arcade, developed in the nineteenth century as a systematic forum for a communication free from interruptions and interference, could, once freed from the taint of private speculation, become again an element of urban organization.

Johann Friedrich Geist

Introduction

The Architectural History
of the Arcade

A Definition of the Arcade

The word "arcade" is used here to translate the German *Passage,* a word which expresses the transitional nature of this building type. The German term comes from the French *passage,* which was used as early as the eighteenth century to refer to the narrow private streets which divided and connected the interiors of larger building blocks. The root is *passus,* the Latin word for step, conveying the element of movement, of passage through a space. It has numerous meanings in common linguistic usage: street, roadway, thoroughfare, alley, transit, crossing, part of a book or musical composition, measured gait of a horse, or, in French, the sense of *passage de la vie.* All these meanings, either spatial or temporal in emphasis, have one element in common: they express transition, threshold, passing, measured distance, or disappearance. Something occurs, comes to pass; movement becomes an event.

In architectural history, the arcade is primarily a pedestrian thoroughfare, a space with a beginning and an end. But this space is bordered or covered by a building which serves its own function. Therefore the function of the arcade itself varies. While foreign terms for the arcade often characterize these various specific applications, they generally designate the same building type. They are listed below in alphabetical order.

1. *Arcade*—in all English speaking countries
2. *Bazar*—in Germany and countries along the Danube
3. *Boulevard*—in Australia only
4. *Cité*—in Belgium only
5. *Colonnade*—in England
6. *Corridor*—in England
7. *Durchgang*—in Switzerland
8. *Galeria*—in Spanish speaking countries
   Galerie—in France, Belgium, and Germany; used for arcades of architectural pretensions; related to the palace gallery
   Galleria—in Italy, also used for tunnel
9. *Halle*—in Germany only
10. *Passage*—in Germany, France, and the Benelux countries. In France, one differentiates between the opened and the closed arcade (*passage ouvert* and *passage couvert*)
    Passaje—in Spain
    Pasaz—in Czechoslovakia
    Pasaji—in Turkey
11. *Stoa*—in Greece
12. *Walk*—in England

Many arcades are called simply "passage," "the arcade," or "the corridor." Commonly, however, another name is added which stems from a completely different sphere. Arcades may be named after (1) streets, squares, and buildings which are located in the vicinity or which stand in some direct connection to the arcade; (2) cities or countries in which they are built; (3) structures which once stood on the site; (4) builders, architects, and famous local or national personalities; and (5) historical events. Examples of these five possibilities follow:

1. Passage du Pont Neuf, Galerie Vivienne, Passage de l'Opéra, Galerie du Parlement
2. Cleveland Arcade
3. Galerie Colbert, Passage du Saumon
4. Sillem's Bazar, Passage Lemonnier, Lowther Arcade, Galleria Mazzini, Kaisergalerie
5. Passage du Caire, Sedanbazar

From these usages, we may construct a general definition of arcade as a glass-covered passageway which connects two busy streets and is lined on both sides with shops. Stores, offices, workshops, or dwellings may be located in the upper stories. The arcade is the organizing force of retail trade. It offers public space on private property as well as an easing of traffic congestion, a short cut, protection from the weather, and an area accessible only to pedestrians. These advantages suggest financial success for the renters of the sites and finally for their owners. The arcade is, then, an object of building speculation. Its prosperity depends to a considerable extent on the urban context in which it is located. It can thrive only if it lies in the main commercial district and connects two streets which are equally heavily frequented.

The arcade can be an independent structure built on its own piece of land. The illusory element of the arcade is the space within its confines: an intended exterior is made interior; the facade with exterior architecture is drawn into the enclosed space. The space of the arcade differs from the street only in its glass roof, symmetrical facades, and exclusively pedestrian walkway. These three elements are present in each example and differentiate the building type of the arcade from all analogous architectural forms.

I have organized the material here into several topics to (1) elucidate the many historical facets of the arcade; (2) depict it as a building type in the context of architectural history; (3) show its derivation from other related building types; and (4) relate it to other building types of its century—the prison, railway station, exhibition hall, department store, and conservatory. I also attempt to illuminate the social and economic background of its conception. These topics isolate specific aspects and give a better impression of the intricate connection of the arcade to other products created to fulfill the needs of the nineteenth century.

The Eastern Bazaar
All general studies of the arcade refer to the model of the Eastern bazaar. I have been unable to establish any direct architectonic influence of the Oriental model on the structure of the arcade. I therefore presume that the influence was actually of a more literary nature, stemming from the countless travelogs of the eighteenth and nineteenth centuries, many of which included sketches. Napoleon's campaign and scientific expedition in Egypt and the political events connected with the collapse of the Turkish empire formed the background of the new interest in the "Oriental question" and the cultural history of the Eastern countries. Lady Montagu's letters from the Orient appeared in 1784; Charles Pertusier published his *Promenades Pittoresques dans Constantinople* in 1815–1817; Sonnini published the three volumes of his travels through Egypt in 1798–

1799; Cassas reported on Syria and Phoenicia in 1799; Forbin's work, *Voyage en Orient,* appeared in Paris in 1819; and Coste produced his magnificent volumes on Arabian architecture in Cairo and Isfahan in 1824 and 1840. These are only a few titles from a list which could be extended indefinitely; it would be impossible to know them all. These reports by travelers demonstrate how the East had become a center of interest for the great powers. Russia, France, and England were searching for new markets and resources, and were dividing the territory among themselves.

In 1798–1799 Napoleon waged his Egyptian campaign as a challenge to the British monopoly on Mediterranean trade. From 1804 to 1828 feudal Persia fought against the Russians, and the vassal states of Turkey began the battle for independence. "Passage du Caire" is the name of one of the first Parisian arcades, built in 1799. It was part of the Egyptian fashion which swept France in the period following the Napoleonic campaign. Obelisks were erected and pyramids built. Charles Percier and Pierre Fontaine designed interiors with Egyptian motifs. The name *bazaar* was commonly used for retail marketplaces, department stores, and world exhibitions. The word appears in connection with arcades only as a descriptive term. Bazaar actually characterized a completely different building type. Its distinctive feature is the open vending stand, a feature which never appears in the arcade. The arcade always contains closed stores with glass fronts.

In order to explain why the arcade is not a simple continuation of the tradition of the Eastern bazaar, it will be necessary to analyze the function of the bazaar in Moslem life and its situation in the Islamic city. In the cities bordering the Mediterranean, in Persia and the Islamic portions of Russia, there are countless bazaars, differing widely in form and origin. Some stem from the Middle Ages, others are more modern. Many, destroyed by fire, were later replaced by a new building on the same site. It is hardly possible to achieve a coherent image, although as far as I can ascertain no systematic study of the Islamic bazaar has even been attempted. Therefore a detailed consideration of some important examples will reveal the astounding structural similarities, although the direct lines of influence cannot be demonstrated.

The Islamic City   The Islamic city is organized differently from the European medieval town.[1] It consists of a loose community of familial clans, each with its own housing units. No one group unites the entire community.[2] Hence the city does not play an essential role in Moslem life. The one element unifying the believers in Islamic society is the mosque. Dwellings revolve around the clan, the family, and blood relations. Only the Koran supersedes the family unit. This explains the urban structure. The city, the public buildings, and the dwellings are closed against the steppes, with their sandstorms and hot winds. As life turns inward, the architecture can unfold only in the courtyards. The facades, the public space in European terms, are virtually nonexistent. Few streets traverse the entire city. Most avenues serve to demarcate living quarters. Only those streets built by the Romans have a regular pattern. Branching off these streets are innumerable alleys which provide access to the living quarters. Whoever does not live here is considered not a visitor but an invader, an enemy.

The inhabited alleys gradually flow together and meet in the center of collective life: a building complex consisting of a mosque, madrasa (school), bazaar (for retail trade), chan (for wholesale trade), bath, and other smaller institutions. These buildings for public use are often bequests from rich Moslems and are administered by their own officials. The money received from the rents is used to maintain the buildings. These buildings appear wherever there are residential districts. There is never one city center.

Types of Bazaars   Within the building complex, there is an especially close architectonic relationship between the bazaar and the chan. The chan is the point from which the caravan departs and returns, is the resting place, the exchange center, and the warehouse. Normally it has the form of a large courtyard with a multileveled circle of niches, stalls, and rooms. It can be located either in the city or in the country, where it serves as a stopping place for caravans. The bazaar develops in the city around the chan. Both are illuminated from above by overhead lights in the form of small domes. The bazaar is the center of retail trade and is ideally situated next to the wholesale businesses. It is the only place in the Arabian city where trade is conducted.

The following types of bazaars can be distinguished:

1. Bazaars in the form of irregular streets lined on both sides with booths. Protection from the sun is guaranteed by temporary wooden structures covered with straw mats.

2. Bazaars in the form of a covered archway. Small openings cut into the side of the archway provide illumination. The archway can be either a barrel vault or a series of individual domes. The course of such a bazaar-street can often be irregular.

3. Bazaars in the stricter form of segmental shops radiating out of the central chan. The simplest manifestation consists of two intersecting streets. The actual point of intersection may be furnished with a dome and fountain.

4. Bazaars in the form of domed colonnades which spread out as conglomerates of smaller units. This type resembles a market hall.

5. Bazaars that occupy an entire district of the town. The area is sectioned into open and covered bazaar-streets. These streets form blocks of shops which stand back to back. This type developed gradually by expanding around an older center which became too small to service the community.

An essential feature of all bazaars is the strict regularity of the interior, the spatial subdivision according to merchandise and artisan groups. The bazaar is subdivided into smaller bazaars, such as the clothier's, the coppersmith's, the jeweler's, and the carpetmaker's. Each shop has a business room above street level which can be locked at night. In front of this room is a walled estrade where the merchandise is displayed and bargaining takes place. The shops of the wealthier bazaars generally contain additional back rooms, including the workshop and storage area. I doubt that the rooms on the upper levels served as apartments, as Borrmann claims,[3] since the bazaars were locked and patrolled at night.

The bazaars that developed out of the classical colonnades of the Roman colonial cities were often used during the numerous sieges as the last line of defense since they offered limited means of access. The largest bazaar in Damascus still follows the course of such a columned street and is partially covered. Five bazaars from five different cities will illustrate the principal types.

Example 1: Isfahan
Under Shah Abbas I (1585–1629), Isfahan was made the capital of the Persian empire. The city expanded, thanks to an extensive city planning program, comparable only to the building of New Delhi.[4] A rectangle measuring 385 by 140

1
Isfahan, fabric
bazaar, after Coste

meters with continuous two-storied galleries and radiating bazaar streets occupies the middle of the irregularly built city. It serves as a kind of forum for the
Meidan-i-Shah. A 30-meter-wide avenue lined with plane trees and canals runs
due south along the western side of the forum. A double structure consisting of
a madrasa and caravan post is connected to the boulevard (see fig. 1). The inn
for the caravans was built in 1710, during the late period of Islamic architecture. Along the northern side of both courtyards runs a 222-meter bazaar covered by domes and ogee arches.[5] The ground plan resembles the plan of an
arcade. Entering from the main street one encounters first the entrance gate,
then the café, and finally the series of shops. These are interrupted only by the
fountains at the wider points of intersection from which one can enter the
madrasa and chan.

Another bazaar in Isfahan is the fabric bazaar.[6] It is attached to the Meidan-i-
Shah on the north side and has the form of a cross. In fig. 2 one can see the octagonal domed room at the crossing, the tiled brick architecture, the wooden
screen in front of the shops, the estrade, and the balconies on the upper level,
which are closed off by wooden gates. The bazaar is illuminated by the round
openings at the apex of the dome.

The bazaars of Isfahan are the most beautiful in Persia. Chardin[7] wrote of them
in 1811: "I have already observed that the word bazaar means sale and that this
word is then also used for the great covered streets which are filled with shops.
The majority consist of brick buildings covered by vaults, though some have
domes. Light enters through large air-holes in the ceiling and through the entrances for the intersecting streets. Hence, one can walk through all of Isfahan
in any weather and remain dry under the covered ways."

Example 2: Istanbul
The bazaars of Istanbul date from the period of the Turkish conquest. They
demonstrate the Islamic influence on Byzantine architecture. In the eighteenth
century Istanbul was almost more significant than London or Paris. Its one million inhabitants consisted of a mixture of all peoples. In the bazaars were sold
wares from three continents. Nearby stood the slave market, famous for its
beautiful Georgian women. Charles Morazé[8] characterized the significance of
the city in that era: ". . . it arose from the intermixing of trades, peoples, customs and religions on this thin stretch of the Bosporus, where world history
seems to be gradually decaying."

Two bazaars are worth describing:

1. The Great Bazaar (Büyük Carsi): The Great Bazaar is itself a separate quarter
of the city. It has eleven gates, a wall, and a surface area of 200,000 square meters. Mehmet II had it constructed in 1461 out of wood. A Byzantine marketplace was supposed to have been located on the site. In 1631 and 1701 the
Great Bazaar was destroyed by fire, then rebuilt of stone and vaulted. It was destroyed by an earthquake in 1894, reconstructed in 1898, and leveled by fire
once again in 1954.

Fig. 3 gives an outline of the bazaar district.[9] In the middle are two large, domed
colonnades which serve today as copper and furniture bazaars. Surrounding
them are numerous shops subdivided according to different crafts. Large sections of the bazaar streets were, and are once again, vaulted, occasionally with
two or three naves.

2
Isfahan, bazaar, plan

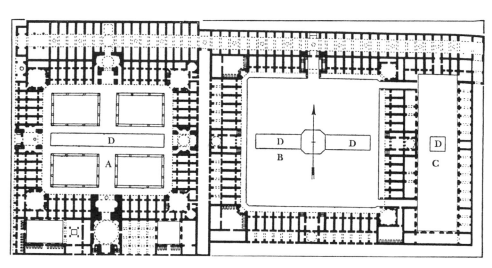

3
Istanbul, the Great
Bazaar, site plan

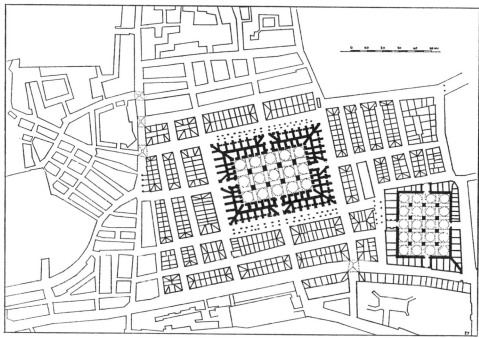

2. The Egyptian Bazaar (Misir Carsi): In 1660 the Sultan Tarhan Hadice replaced an older construction with the Egyptian spice market. Gurlitt, from
whom I have reprinted the plan,[10] believes that the one wing of the L-shaped
structure was built in 1470. The plan (fig. 4) depicts a bazaar with a right-angle
bend. The street running through it is covered by a barrel vault 6 meters wide.
A dome rests on four massive pillars at the corner. The bazaar was replaced in
1944.

In her *Letters from the Orient,* Lady Montagu described the Istanbul bazaars at
a time predating the first arcades:[11] "The bazaars are superb buildings, filled
with beautiful covered passages, most of which rest on pillars. They are all well
maintained. Each business has its own hall, where the merchandise is presented
in the same order as in the New Exchange in London. The bedestan or jeweler's
hall displays so many treasures and such an abundance of diamonds and precious stones that one is practically blinded. . . . The embroiderer's hall is also
magnificent. Visitors come for entertainment as well as for business." Here one
should note the reference to the New Exchange; it was one of the important
prototypes of the English arcade, directly influencing Samuel Ware's conception
of the Burlington Arcade.

Example 3: Fez
In the thirteenth century Fez was, after Mecca, one of the holiest Islamic cities.
At that time, it had 400,000 inhabitants. We can observe two kinds of bazaars,[12] as indicated in fig. 5: the continuous street lined on both sides with
shops of different sizes, and the Quissariya, the old bazaar of the sacred quarter,
in which animals were prohibited. Narrow alleys, covered with grass mats and
lined on both sides with booths, form a grid. They house the perfume dealer,
candlestick maker, tailor, jeweler, and clothier. The exits have gates which are
locked and patrolled at night by guards. Additional markets are commonly set
up in front of the city gates. This type of bazaar is found in nearly every city in
the Orient.

Example 4: Damascus
The Long Bazaar in Damascus is an ancient street mentioned in the Acts of the
Apostles. Its colonnade crosses the city along an east-west axis.[13] It extends 1.7
kilometers although only the western third, called "Souk Midhat Pascha," is
covered. Countless smaller bazaars branch off the main street into the separate
city quarters.

Example 5: Bokhara
In Bokhara, in the middle of the Transcaspian desert, stands one of the most fascinating urban developments produced by Islamic culture.[14] The old city is structured on an irregular system of coordinates consisting of a series of independent
and hardly related buildings: mosques, madrasas, baths, chans, mausoleums,
private palaces, and open or closed bazaars (fig. 6). At the intersection of the
axes stands the domed tomb of Zargavo. The profile of the streets changes constantly, sometimes enclosed by walls, lined by open shops, or engulfed in large,
vaulted bazaars. The streets wind their way between closed blocks constructed
in symmetrical and asymmetrical patterns. This example demonstrates that the
bazaar need not be a simple building but can also be a main thoroughfare with
vehicular traffic.

From these examples we see how the Eastern bazaar differs from the arcade.
The most essential difference is that the bazaar makes up a part of the public

4
Istanbul, Egyptian
Bazaar, plan

5
Fez, bazaars

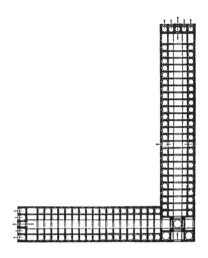

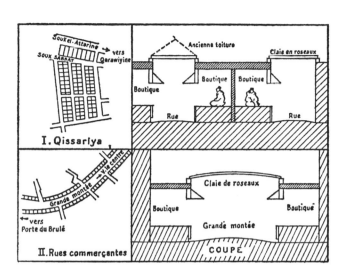

6
Bokhara, inner city

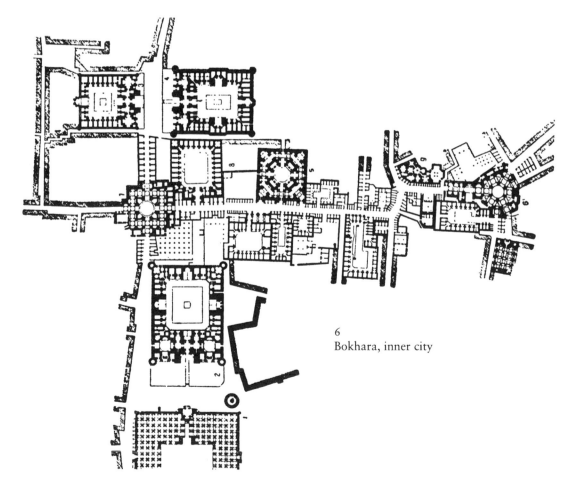

street system and is open not only to people but to animals and carts. Significantly, the bazaar offers the only shopping opportunity to the inhabitants of an Islamic city. It is therefore more similar to the booths and trading halls of medieval markets, generally the only centers granted retail trade privileges. Both the medieval market and the bazaar were strictly organized and regulated according to trades, guilds, and commercial associations. Even though they arose under different circumstances, both served the same functions as public institutions and became indispensable parts of urban life. In all these aspects they differ from the arcade.

The Characteristics of the Arcade

From antiquity to the eighteenth century there were a wide variety of structures seemingly related to the arcade. However, one must not conclude that they were its immediate predecessors. The arcade remains an invention which responded to the specific needs and desires of a society in a specific era of its cultural and industrial development—namely, the need for a public space protected from traffic and weather and the search for new means of marketing the products of a blossoming luxury goods industry. The examples that could be listed in connection with the arcade display such variety that no common denominator can be found. Classical colonnades, markets, basilicas, medieval market squares, and trading halls are all examples of this wider context. The symmetrically constructed bridges of the Renaissance, the London Exchanges, the "rows," the open buildings of the trade cities, the *foires* (fairs), colonnades, *cours*, and *cités* are related to the arcade, but do not constitute necessary phases of its development. Rather, these earlier forms served as models during the development of this building type. In the Passage Choiseul the model was the early Christian basilica; in the Burlington Arcade the Exchange; in the Passage des Panoramas probably the avenues of the Foire St. Germain. The arcades were also influenced by other more recent forms and methods of access. The interior galleries in Paxton's Crystal Palace were not without their effect on the arcades of the British industrial cities. Furthermore, the arcade itself served as a model for other building types, for example, the means of access in prisons, the railway station, and the collective dwellings of social utopias.

In order to organize the repertoire of earlier forms and to depict the role of the arcade in differentiation of the building types of the nineteenth century, I have arranged examples according to seven characteristics of the arcade:

1. As access to the interior of a block
2. As public space on private property
3. As a symmetrical street space
4. As a skylit space
5. As a system of access
6. As a form of organizing retail trade
7. As a space of transition.

Access to the Interior of a Block   Of all methods of opening up the unused interior of a block, the arcade is the most ingenious. The provision of access to the inside of a block of buildings developed around its borders always follows from the demands of outside circumstances: Such was the case in medieval cities with defensive walls which limited space and compelled the growing populace to exploit interior sites. This was also the case in the large cities of the late eighteenth century where real estate markets began to prosper. The urban area was divided into industrial quarters, residential areas for both the wealthy bourgeoisie and the proletariat, and commercial districts for individual trades. The great process of differentiation began with the trend toward class isolation: the wealthy separated themselves from the lower classes. Real estate became merchandise, an object of speculation. Profit became dependent on the measure of use to which land was put. This process led to conditions which were inhuman and asocial by present standards because of the liberal, that is, laissez-faire, economic system. There was no disinterested public regulation. There was no satisfactory source of action to deal with the growth of population and subsequent impoverishment of the industrial proletariat. No institution existed in the nineteenth century to undertake the difficult task of long-range planning free of private interests. Urban planning went no farther than advancing the formation and technology of public space. The construction of living quarters was left to private initiative and hence to unscrupulous building speculation. It was this speculation which made nineteenth-century urban planning so suspect.

The arcade was a part of this general building speculation. Its systems of spatial access enabled construction of great numbers of apartments and shops on inexpensive land. In this function the arcade has predecessors which are worth discussing. In the Middle Ages, for example, the cities of the Hanseatic League included arcade-like areas which made narrow and hidden pieces of land accessible. However, these were used only as residential districts.

Example 1: Lübeck, Der Durchgang
Der Durchgang was one of the 150 alleyways in Lübeck,[15] of which nearly 100 still exist on the lower slope of the city's hill. The entrance is a low, barely passable opening in the side of the gabled houses. Rows of small one- or two-storied booths fill the recessed areas, formerly used as gardens. Fig. 7 demonstrates how two such passages can be united to form a kind of arcade.

These passages date from the fourteenth century and were built out of the older sections of the buildings to increase the living area or the source of income of the owners. A few, of regular construction, are religious institutions. Today a total of nearly 3000 people still live in these passages in the center of the old town.

A more advanced form of this means of making space accessible is the magnificent symmetrical housing development in London, The Albany.

Example 2: London, The Albany
The Albany[16] is situated between Burlington Gardens and Piccadilly, parallel to the Burlington Arcade on the other long side of Burlington House. It is a housing development for bachelors which was built inward off the street with an entrance through pergolas. The three-storied rows of houses are separated by a distance of 11 meters. They were built in 1770 by William Chambers for Lord Melbourne and converted to apartments in 1812. Lords Byron, Gladstone, and Bulwer and, more recently, Edward Heath are just a few of the prominent men who have lived there.

In the late eighteenth and early nineteenth centuries, there were numerous, often luxurious private streets in London, Paris, and other capitals that were constructed as open courtyards in a block interior. They can be found in the newer, western suburbs which became fashionable in the eighteenth century. They replaced and opened up the gardens which once occupied the oversized blocks. These "buildings" in London resemble the *cités* and *passages couverts* which Eduard Kolloff describes as follows:

In Paris there are many people who attach their interest or their fancy to the more populated quarters of the city. These people must live amid the din of the city, yet do not want to hear it in their homes. They are wealthy enough to pay a considerable rent, but not wealthy enough to afford a whole house. The Passage Violet, the Passage Sannier, and the Passage Cendrier were built for them— three imposing streets complete with guards who lock the iron gates at night. The so-called *cités* were constructed for the same purpose and according to the same principle. *Cité* used to refer exclusively to the old island town, but now one speaks of the Cité Bergère, Cité Trévise, Cité d'Antin, Cité Berryer, Cité Vindé, etc. These *cités* are either streets closed off by gates and guarded at each entrance by a porter, in which case they are merely derivative of other arcades; or they are groups of individual buildings architectonically united as a single structure and enclosing one or more courtyards. Such building aggregates are usually constructed and leased by entrepreneurs. They therefore resemble the ancient Roman *insulae*.[17]

Some of these *cités*, actually built after the first arcades, have been included in the catalog in the overview of the Parisian arcades.[18]

Besides these examples, which were used solely for housing, there is another variation of the arcade which serves to give access to the interior of a city block. These are the walk-through buildings in convention and fair cities like Vienna and Leipzig. They were not only used for housing but were also leased during fairs and conventions as storage space and meeting places. Auerbachs Hof in Leipzig was the famous predecessor of these walk-through houses.

Example 3: Auerbachs Hof
In 1530 Dr. Heinrich Stromer von Auerbach built this courtyard on the Grimmaischen Strasse in Leipzig. One corner opens up into the Neumarkt (New Market) and thereby provides a site for a hundred stands during a fair.[19] This court, the Palais Royal of Leipzig, was famous in the eighteenth century as the meeting place of Saxon high society. Thanks to its wine cellar it even found its way into world literature [Goethe's *Faust*, part 1]. An etching by Rossmässler brings the bustling fair in the courtyard to life. However, this courtyard, like the walk-through house in general, lost its significance in the nineteenth century since the emphasis of the fairs changed from actual goods to model wares.

The walk-through houses developed out of the particular shape of the blocks of the old city of Leipzig.[20] They were private houses connected by passageways and made accessible to the rear by building wings. Rentable shops were situated on the ground floor of the wings while the upper stories contained smaller apartments and storage rooms for the participants in the fair.

Example 4: Leipzig, Koch's Hof
The first walk-through houses planned according to a unified scheme were built in the eighteenth century. The most impressive example, Koch's Hof, no longer exists today. A view of the courtyard is shown in fig. 8. In the plan of this walk-through house (figs. 9, 10), at 3 Market Square, one can distinguish the two frontal buildings (facing the market and Reichsstrasse), a transverse building, and the four connecting wings, which enclose the paved arcade.[21] The frontal buildings each contained two shops while the wings held fourteen vaulted bays used during the fairs. The detail of the facades calls the arcade to mind.

Example 5: Vienna, Seitzer Hof[22]
Walk-through houses are common in the cities of Czechoslovakia. They probably provided the major source of inspiration for the architects who built the arcades there in the twentieth century.

7
Lübeck, Der
Durchgang

8
Leipzig, Koch's Hof,
1732

In the countries along the Danube the walk-through building also influenced a kind of tenement building which made the space more accessible by means of a continuous gallery. Seitzer Hof is an example of a Viennese walk-through building. Later, with the addition of shops, it came to resemble an arcade without a glass roof.

Although most of the walk-through buildings fulfilled only temporary commercial needs connected to fairs and conventions, the *cours* (courts) or *passages ouverts* (open passages) in Paris provided a place for trading, living, and manufacturing all year round. The earliest of these *cours* dates from the eighteenth century. The Cour du Commerce St. André, which has now been made shorter by the Boulevard St. Germain, was established in 1776. The hundreds of ordinary passageways related to the *passages couverts* (covered passages) are narrower and more regular in shape than the *cours*.

Kolloff[23] described these *cours:* "At the same time different Parisian businesses employed this same method in order to bring together their dispersed branches in one larger unit. They organized similar arrangements which were, however, more rectangular. They were called 'cours,' like the Cour Batave (so named because it was built by a Dutchman during the Revolution), the Cour des Coches, the Cour de la Trinité, etc. All these passages and courtyards formed self-contained populations of artisans and manufacturers producing those objects which became known throughout the world as 'articles de Paris.'" This description demonstrates that the *passage couvert* was at the time of its conception a special form of passageway or courtyard. It served trade in luxury items and had its unique public. The *passage ouvert, cour,* and *cité* were all parallel methods of making the interior of a block accessible. The walk-through building, however, was a particular form which eventually led to the construction of arcades in Prague and Leipzig in the twentieth century.

Public Space on Private Property The interior facades of the arcades have one motif which occurs again and again: the arcade. It appears in various transformations, as arches on supports, on pillars, alternating with pillar-borne supports and engaged columns, or simply as arches cut into the wall. The colonnade openings are glazed and define the shop unit. The galleries of the Palais Royal and the Rue de Rivoli, the porticoes of the public buildings in Rome (like the halls of the Colosseum or the Basilica Julia) provided the prototype. Many architects of the empire knew these buildings firsthand. Parallel to the motif of the arcade is that of the colonnade, as in the Lower Arcade in Bristol. There the arcade space is a covered, column-lined passage. The classical colonnade was almost literally transposed into the building type of the modern arcade. The multistoried covered way or arbored walk can be considered a third motif. It occurs predominantly in the British arcades built after 1850. Local models of the arbored walk, which provided protection less from the rain than from the sun, had a particularly strong influence. Examples of these are the row houses in Chester (fig. 11), the walks in the spas, and the cast-iron galleries in front of multistoried houses.

All of these motifs found in the interior facades of the arcade were originally structures which functioned as covers over private property that was accessible to the public. Loggias, porticoes, colonnades, arbored or covered walks, and archways all served the pedestrian, offered protection from sun, rain, and traffic. These structures could be attached to individual private houses, could form a continuous chain (determining the image of an entire street or city, as in Turin,

Bern, and Bologna), or could be localized in one monumental edifice, as in a market or place of public justice.

As early as the Hellenistic period, the peristyle of the temple was copied for the passages along streets and squares. In the Roman colonial cities in the eastern provinces, the colonnades and column-lined streets became the main proces sional avenues—the architectural showpieces of the city. They were later used to house the bazaars.

Example 1: Palmyra, Street of Columns
The backbone of the Roman city of Palmyra, conquered by the Arabs in 634, is the massive street of columns, Decumanus.[24] It is broken at two points by street intersections decorated with a tetrapylon and triumphal arch. In the middle of the street is an 11-meter-wide roadway. It is flanked by two 6-meter-wide colonnades with Corinthian columns. They connect in turn to the walls of the bordering shops and buildings. Market life took place under these colonnades. There was room between the columns for booths and stands. The structure was, therefore, just one step from a bazaar.

In Rome the colonnade exists only in connection with the public markets, the forums. Arcades in front of private houses first appeared in Constantinople where they were called "emboloi." Some were freestanding while others formed part of the house, sometimes even taking up two stories. From Constantinople, if one can thus simplify the historical development, the arcade wandered first to northern Italy, where it dominated the street profile of Padua and Bologna, and then to the southern Alps, Switzerland, and the Southern Tyrol.[25] Bern is the most impressive example from this last group. There the level of the covered way becomes independent, so that the cellar is directly accessible from the street while the covered way must be reached by a stairway. This same development can be found in the row houses of Chester in central England. During the late Middle Ages, the phenomenon of arcaded private houses finally reached as far north as the main market in Münster.

In the Renaissance the arcade motif was a strictly codified means of providing uniformity to facades, courtyards, and squares. During the Baroque period the play of colonnades created a stage-set effect. In the eighteenth century Victor Louis built the galleries of the Palais Royal in Paris.[26] A wide colonnade that would have connected both sides of the garden and separated the public from the private parts of the palace was never executed. Instead the first arcade, the Galeries de Bois, arose in its place.

The Rue de Rivoli (begun in 1803 by Percier and Fontaine), the Quadrant in London (built by Nash in 1813), and the total arcading of the Kaiserstrasse in Karlsruhe (designed by Weinbrenner in 1808) are three examples of monumental designs for arcades along city streets of the nineteenth century. In all three cases arcades proper eventually appeared. The arcaded sidewalk and the colonnade provide the pedestrian protection and the opportunity for promenading. While the arcade proper cuts through the buildings, the arcaded walk—a kind of half-arcade—merely surrounds the block. It is a precursor of the modern sidewalk, dependent on the street and not yet a separate building like the arcade.

A Symmetrical Street Space   The arcade strives to be like a street. It must not deny the pedestrian his anonymity. Its facades are exterior facades, but both sides are symmetrical. This is the fundamental difference between the arcade

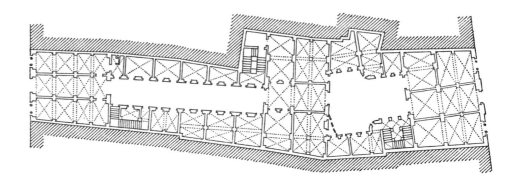

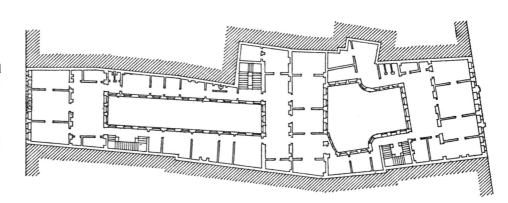

9
Koch's Hof, ground
floor plan, showing
shops and vaulting

10
Koch's Hof, second
floor plan, three
dwelling units

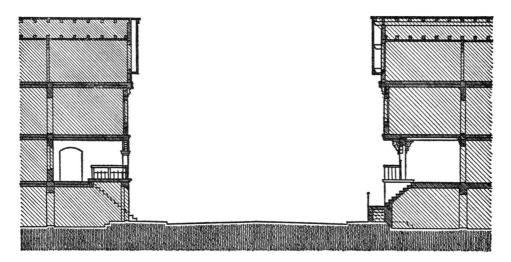

11
Chester, Rows, cross
section

and the normal commercial street. Any symmetrical development of the street space tends necessarily toward an arcade-like structure. The sensation of the opposition of two facing and competing sides gives way to the sensation of an accessible public space. All that is needed to convert this space into an arcade is a glass roof. There are many examples of such symmetrical streets; some of them illustrate a specific phenomenon of the arcade. The most impressive example is the Uffizi in Florence.

Example 1: Florence, The Uffizi
The cul-de-sac enclosed within the Uffizi (fig. 12) creates a spatial effect suggestive of the arcade. The administrative building, built by Vasari, was converted by Francesco de' Medici in 1580 into a museum for the Medici art collection. The ground floor is largely arcaded. The extended roof increases the sense of an interior space, out of which one can look onto the Arno.

Symmetrical streets serve a function in the urban planning of absolutism. The Via Po in Turin, the Rue Royale in Paris, the streets of Richelieu, and the uniform street facades conceived by Haussmann are all attempts to construct streets in such a way that individual expression is subordinated to a grand scheme. Only one undisturbed perspective is offered: the view of a state symbol, a public building, or the center of power.

Bridges lined with shops and apartments are also important precursors of the arcade. They are symmetrical, forced passages. Some are covered bridges like those described by Alberti[27] or like Swiss wooden bridges. Others include houses and shops, like the Ponte Rialto in Venice, the Ponte Vecchio in Florence, the fifteenth-century bridges in Paris, or the even older London Bridge. Some bridges, like those built in Berlin during the seventeenth and eighteenth centuries, developed colonnades for aesthetic reasons, namely, to block the view of unsightly buildings on the riverbanks.[28] Only a few examples of this building type of the developed bridge still exist; most have been sacrificed to increasing traffic and a changed attitude toward the value of the river for the city. I will discuss three bridge-arcades in more detail.[29]

Example 2: London, London Bridge
London Bridge was the oldest bridge in London. Until 1794 it was the only one in the city. It was built of stone in 1176. Over the centuries it was gradually covered with buildings. Such development began without any uniform plan. In an etching by Johannes Kip (circa 1715), however, one can see the introduction of regular three-storied buildings with spaces in between which give a view of the river. The center arch could be raised by means of a drawbridge. Interestingly, the street space of the bridge was divided into sections by transverse buildings which could be entered through gateways. The whole bridge was demolished in 1832 and then rebuilt by John Rennie.

Example 3: Paris, Pont Notre Dame
In Paris the Pont Notre Dame, Pont au Change, Pont Marie, and Pont St. Michel were all covered with buildings.[30] The Pont Notre Dame is of Roman origin. After its destruction by the Normans, it was reconstructed in 1413 of wood. A flood destroyed it again in 1499. In 1507 the Italian architect Fra Giacondo undertook its reconstruction in stone. This is the first urban structure in Paris built according to a plan.[31] Giacondo lined the bridge with two rows of thirty-four arcaded, identical buildings. The brick buildings, with sculptural decoration and sawtooth gables, were numbered and created a completely sym-

metrical street space. Two small towers and a triumphal arch at the bridge's beginning close off the ends. The etching by Jean Marot (fig. 13) offers a fascinating view.

This bridge exploited the confines of the passageway to create a shop street; art galleries, bookstores, secondhand shops, and jewelers became established there. But more importantly, the street was a festive area for the city, a *via triumphalis,* where kings were received. For the procession of Henry II on June 16, 1549, the bridge was spanned by a fine net, under which thousands of birds were set free to fly. The buildings were removed in 1786.

Example 4: Venice, Ponte Rialto
In the second half of the sixteenth century, Vignola, Sansovino, Scamozzi, and Palladio took part in the competition for the Ponte Rialto, which was to span the Grand Canal. Since the bridge was intended only for pedestrians, new and imaginative solutions could be proposed. Palladio envisioned in his design three parallel shop-lined streets raised up above the water by outside staircases.[32] The entrances and center of the bridge were embellished by gates and porticoes. This design must have inspired Sir John Soane's Triumphal Bridge.[33] The bridge was actually constructed by Giovanni da Ponte in 1588–1592. He spanned the Grand Canal with two series of shops separated at the center by two arches giving a view of the river.

Bridges with permanent structures are hence related to the building type of the arcade not only in their symmetrical organization but also in their use of two independent rows of shops. The bridge exploits the linear passage to sell merchandise.

A Skylit Space If one defines the arcade as a skylit space, one places it in a different context of architectural history. It becomes one aspect of the historical development of overhead lighting. In antiquity there were already three methods of illumination from above:

The light of the atrium, an opening cut out of the roof

The round skylight in the center of a dome

Light coming from openings placed high up along a wall (essentially windows), sometimes in semicircular formation.

Illumination from above is employed in totally enclosed rooms. It is the sole source of light, isolating the space from its natural environment and preventing other perspectives and distractions. Well into the eighteenth century it was still employed in the basilica and central rooms of sacred and secular buildings. In the 1770s, however, the first attempts were made to break away from the traditional spatial schemes. Deeper ground plans and new formulations were developed to answer the challenge of new building types like the museum, gallery, market hall, stock exchange, library, bank, department store, and orangerie. Such projects were designed by Soane in England, by Ledoux and the architects of the revolution in France.

The goal was even and subdued lighting for exhibition rooms and for spaces whose depth renders side lighting inadequate (as in convention halls, reading rooms, department stores, and banks). Lighting from all sides was needed for the cultivation of plants and tropical flowers. In arcades, exhibition halls, and railway stations the two requirements of adequate lighting and protection from the weather had to be fulfilled simultaneously. Three methods of construction can be differentiated:

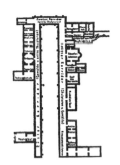

12
Florence, Uffizi, plan,
upper story

13
Paris, Pont Notre
Dame, engraving by
Jean Marot

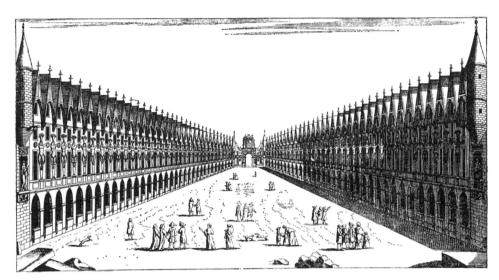

14
Ducerceau, arbor,
Montargis

1. The opening without glazing. The climate of the northern countries precludes application of this method.

2. The opening covered by a glass roof. This method was used for small apertures as early as the eighteenth century. However, problems of construction discouraged using glass to cover larger openings. In particular, no large, transparent, and sturdy sheets of glass could be produced. Moreover, the only available methods of supporting and sealing the glass plates were inadequate: wood rotted too quickly and bronze framing was too expensive and too short. It was not until the introduction of iron that these problems could be solved.

3. A skylight with two layers: an exterior glass roof and an interior dust cover. This method solved numerous problems. It permitted ornamental fixtures, prevented too great a loss of heat, admitted even light, hid the dirt which accumulated on the exterior glass roof, and avoided overloading of the construction from condensed water. Furthermore, the dust cover hid the main load-bearing construction, and hence allowed for the spanning of greater distances.

Although skylights exceeding the dimensions of small holes were common as academic designs before 1800, no such construction was, to my knowledge, executed that early.[34] The first example of a larger glass skylight was probably the temporary connection between the Galeries de Bois and the unfinished Palais Royal, the so-called Galerie Vitrée (Glass Gallery).[35] It consisted of a wooden roof framework with small glass panes between the rafters. It was said to be so leaky that the floor became a veritable swamp on rainy days. It was not until the invention of the industrially manufactured glass plate and the milled iron skeleton that a technically flawless skylight, free of the problems of leakage and poor ventilation, became possible.

The glass skylight developed during the nineteenth century to fantastic dimensions. It became an indispensable part of almost all building types, eliminated direct contact between the interior spaces and the outer world, and transformed the atmosphere of the space. Sunlight, the play of sharp shadows and reflections, gave way to a softer, more neutral light—studio lighting. Northern exposures became fashionable. Nature was replaced by the artificially created mood of the "indoor Orient." As an extension of this trend, branches of the applied arts, interior decoration, and plant cultivation thrived as never before.

The following methods of overhead illumination were employed in the nineteenth century:

The skylight set to the sides
The central skylight
The oblong skylight
The continuous skylight
Space-defining lighting from all sides
The ceiling skylight.

Each is related to many different building types. The central skylight is found in the early English arcades above stairwells, in the corner rooms of Klenze's Glyptothek (1816–1830), in the Halle au Blé in Paris, in the Royal Pavilion in Brighton, in the London Coal Exchange (fig. 15), and in the central spaces of arcades, where it takes the form of a monumental glass dome.

15
London, Coal
Exchange

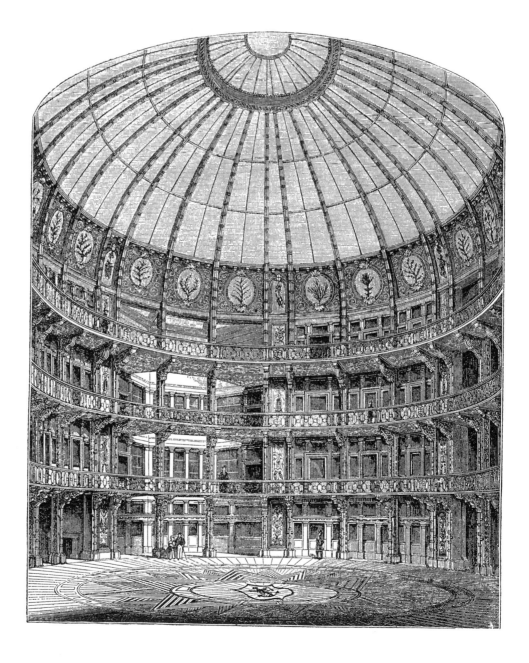

The oblong skylight appears for the first time in an arcade in the Passage des Panoramas in Paris (1800) and for the first time in a museum in the Grande Galerie of the Louvre. Between 1805 and 1810, after numerous changes of plan, Percier and Fontaine installed skylights in the vault of the long gallery to provide better lighting for the public art collection.[36] This method was also employed in the Dulwich Gallery by Soane (1811–1814); in the Braccio Nuovo of the Vatican Museum (1821), where long sections of the barrel vault were cut out; and in the British Museum (1823). In 1826 a popular variation of this method was used in the Pinakothek in Munich: mirror vault and two-layered glass skylights.

The continuous skylight is the method appropriate for the arcade as a transitional passageway. The first arcade covered in this way seems to have been the Passage Delorme in Paris (1809). The symmetrical saddle roof then dominated until circa 1830. The first vaulted glass roof was built by Fontaine for the Galerie d'Orléans in the garden of the Palais Royal. This kind of glass roof relates the arcade to garden and greenhouse architecture by transforming the vaulted arbors and wooden gates into iron and glass constructions.[37] The arbor in Montargis can be mentioned for comparison; it is shown here in a reproduction from Durcerceau's *Les Plus Excellents Bâtiments de France* (fig. 14). A conservatory, orangerie, or hothouse could not have served as the model since all comparable forms of these structures date from a later period. After the Galerie d'Orléans, we find the glass barrel vault again in the great arcades in Brussels, Hamburg, The Hague, Milan, and Moscow. All these examples are related.

The continuous glass skylight appears as well in other building types, for example in the great halls of libraries and museums, in railway stations, exhibition halls, and factories. Two examples can be mentioned here which represent countless others: the Patent Office in Washington, D.C. (fig. 16), and a little-known exhibition hall proposed for an international exhibition in Berlin by the architects of the Berlin Kaisergalerie, Kylmann and Heyden, in 1876, shortly after the opening of the arcade (fig. 17).[38]

The orangerie, greenhouse, winter garden, and palm conservatory, leading to the Crystal Palace and the Great Victorian Way, are all building types with lighting from all sides, fully glazed. One cannot demonstrate direct influence of these building types on the arcade. The conservatory and the arcade have parallel developments just as the bazaar and the arcade do, each following its own laws. However, the conservatory can eventually become an expanded form with monumental proportions, as an exhibition palace and finally as an endless glass tube which directs all traffic and solves all traffic problems. At least, so were the visions of one man, Sir Joseph Paxton. In his designs the building type of the conservatory meets the building type of the arcade in a utopian structure.

England is the country in which the climatic and architectural problems of the conservatory were being systematically approached in the early eighteenth century. The orangeries and conservatories,[39] luxuries accessible only to the landed nobility and courts of the eighteenth century, had been illuminated by vertical glass windows. However, as early as the eighteenth century, proposals had been made for glass roofs. Unfortunately, the required heavy wood frames admitted little light. The writings of Henry Repton, James Anderson, George Mackenzie, and Thomas Knight were the first to investigate scientifically improved methods for constructing glass buildings. In 1815 Mackenzie established that "the form of glass roof best calculated for the admission of the sun's rays is a hemispherical figure."[40]

Knight, the president of the Horticultural Society, was evidently the first to construct a vaulted conservatory out of iron in Downton Castle. Loudon, the inventor of the ridge and furrow system (1817) employed by Paxton in Chatsworth and the Crystal Palace, also experimented with vaulted glass roofs. In 1827 he constructed a conservatory in Bretton Hall in the form of a glass dome 30 meters in diameter and 18 meters high.[41] Five years later Charles Rohault de Fleury, architect of the Passage du Saumon, built the great conservatories of the Jardin des Plantes in Paris. They consisted of square pavilions linked by vaulted structures. The next stages are familiar: 1837, the Great Conservatory in Chatsworth by Paxton; 1842, the Palm House at Kew by the architect Decimus Burton and the engineer Richard Turner (fig. 18). Erich Schild writes of the Great Conservatory:[42] "With this 20-meter-tall structure Paxton covered a surface area which was fantastically large for the time (37 by 83 meters). The space he created corresponded to the dimensions of the largest railway stations of those years. . . . Although the shape of the exterior profile was in part determined by earlier conservatories, the building as a whole must be considered a new conception: the floor plan and construction were conceived from a strictly functional point of view. The inner division of the hall, for example, was determined by the concentration and heights of the plants. The form and execution of the outer covering were also completely functional, and incorporated all of the results of Paxton's investigations of conservatory glazing."

The year 1850 saw the conclusion of this phase in the development of the conservatory building and its variations. This building type is now divided into different subcategories: hothouses employed in botanical gardens for scientific purposes; the winter garden, used as an exotic decorative background for the social scene (the Jardin d'Hiver, Paris, 1847, and the Flora in Berlin); and the exhibition building, which takes advantage of the developments of the conservatory, for it is easily dismantled, consists of light, prefabricated parts, and provides illumination from all sides.

The ceiling skylight is a method of illumination used in centralized, completely enclosed interior spaces. It consists of a double layered overhead light of the kind found in skylight rooms of museums, light wells of department stores, reception halls of public buildings, cashier halls of banks, and the halls of parliamentary buildings. Two Parisian examples point out the distances which can be spanned by ceiling skylights: the semicircular ceiling light of the Salle des Séances in the Palais Royal, which is a smaller copy of the semicircle of the parliamentary room and probably dates from Jules de Joly's reconstruction in 1830, and the light well of the Musée d'Histoire Naturelle, whose ceiling light measures 12 by 35 meters. The girders necessary to bridge such distances are hidden by a dust cover.

The glass roofs of nineteenth-century arcades never mask their own structure. This is of course always possible when smaller distances are spanned. The few arcades built in the early twentieth century are characterized by dust covers,[43] an indication that the feeling for the external structure of the arcade space has totally disappeared.

16
Washington, D.C.,
Patent Office, gallery

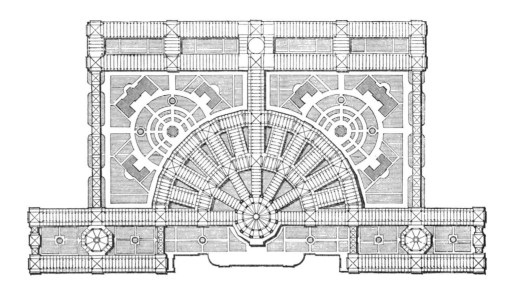

17
Berlin, exhibition
hall, design

18
Kew, Palm House

A System of Access   The open space of an arcade resembles that of a street
with houses on both sides. This is obvious from the plans of early arcades. They
consist of narrow, self-sufficient units brought together by the interior facades.
The sum of these units defines the arcade as a building. If a building serves a
public purpose and its open space is structured according to the system of the
arcade, it can become a department store, market hall, bath house, or prison. Indeed, one of the most exciting perspectives on this area of architectural history
is that the arcade system of access revolutionized the prison building. This was
the achievement of an architect who had built an arcade and was inspired by the
Burlington Arcade in London.

Until the eighteenth century prisons were merely rooms, cellars, and chambers
in which the prisoners were left to themselves.[44] John Howard in England was
the first to propose the reform idea that cells have minimum legal dimensions.[45]
In 1786 a society to improve conditions in prisons was founded in Philadelphia.[46] The society defended the idea of the individual cell, large enough to allow the prisoner to perform productive work. The prisons built according to
this penitentiary system became the models for those of the nineteenth century. Later, so many variations in plan developed that one can hardly gain an
overview.[47]

Between 1822 and 1825 John Haviland built the Eastern Penitentiary in Philadelphia according to the radial system as an experimental building for the society.[48] The individual wings had one story with a long corridor illuminated from
above and lined on both sides with indefinitely extendable cells. Each wing
ended in a walled courtyard. The cross section of these wings resembled that of
an arcade. The radial arrangement was probably inspired by Bevan's radiating
plan for the London asylum (fig. 19).[49]

Haviland built two more prisons in 1836: one in Trenton, New Jersey and another in New York.[50] The latter was in the Egyptian style and had a separate
section in the courtyard for prisoners held for interrogation. The cross section of
this courtyard shows a multistoried system of access which resembles that of the
early American arcades. Fig. 19 shows this building, which was demolished in
1900.

The history of prison building is one of the most fascinating chapters in
nineteenth-century architecture. Graul compiled much of the important information in his book *Der Straffvollzugsbau einst und heute*, unfortunately without illustrations. The book describes a variety of prisons with arcade-like
arrangements of cells which can be reached from continuous multistoried iron
galleries. Most prisons have skylights and central spaces at the crossing, from
which all of the wings and corridors can be watched simultaneously. A perfect
example of such an arrangement is the men's penitentiary of the criminal court
in Moabit near Berlin (fig. 20).[51] The domed space here is not, as in churches,
the place of the gods; not, as in arcades, the meeting place of urban public life;
but the space of total control by a single uniformed guard. He stands on a platform raised on a cast-iron column and stares incessantly down the five long arcades of cells, each leading to a dead end. The prison as arcade—this is the
logical conclusion of the search for a system in which the greatest number of
cells can be located in the smallest possible area. The prisoners then can be
served and patrolled by a limited staff. Paxton's Great Victorian Way can be
considered the utopia of the arcade, the ultimate extension of the concept to a

total traffic system which transforms a city street into a building. The prison as arcade is the ultimate reduction of this concept (fig. 21).

A completely different, even opposite course of development was to apply the arcade's method of accessibility to housing projects. Almost every continental arcade contains dwellings. Yet the housing units are all oriented toward the arcade space; they have no direct contact with the outside world but are instead twice removed from it by glass layers. However, the arcade conceived as a system of access to the interior of a freestanding building leads inhabitants to residences facing the outside.

This purely residential arcade was a part of early nineteenth century social utopianism. Such utopias were drawn up on paper down to the last detail of execution and administration. A French merchant, Charles Fourier,[52] one of the three great social reformers before Marx and Engels (the others being Saint-Simon and Owen), wanted to house mankind in phalansteries—not individual houses like those envisioned by Robert Owen but large units for 2000 people. Fourier was not a socialist and did not want to abolish private property; he wanted to create a community system free of the amorality of the free market. Its guiding principle would be the spontaneity of the nine passions, which for him were the expression of reason: the five senses and the four social passions of friendship, pride, love, and familial instinct. In his system there were subdivisions into many "series," each forming a relationship of associated groups dedicated to different human activities but to the same basic impulses. The rich and the poor were to live directly next to one another, according to the principle of pleasure.

Already in his first work of 1808, the *Théorie des quatre mouvements et des destinées générales*,[53] he paints a general picture of these phalansteries, a picture which he makes more precise in his later work.

The palaces or castles of neighboring clans are to be linked by covered passageways which provide protection from inclement weather. In this way one is protected during meetings, business and entertainment from the influence of the unfriendly seasons under which civilized man presently suffers. It must be possible to wander, by day and by night, from one palace to another through heated and ventilated corridors. In this way one would not run the danger, as one does under the present order, that by leaving one's room one will become dirty or wet or catch a cold or pneumonia. At the end of a ball or party, men and women who have to spend the night away from their clan must be able to wander without boots or furs and without having to take a cab. Instead of having to walk three or four blocks, as one does in present civilization, one merely proceeds through the covered passages of three or four neighboring castles, without experiencing the extremes of heat and cold, wind and rain. These protected connecting passageways are only one of the thousand amenities which the new social order has in store and which distinguish the new social group of the clan.

Behind this vision stands the model of the Palais Royal. Fourier transposes this model into his phalansteries, which he conceives of as massive palaces, similar to the Hôtel des Invalides, the Louvre, and Versailles.[54] Fourier is the first to strive for communal housing, not on a small scale, not in the form of the small private house but as a grand scheme, a commune, which is organized with a self-sufficient economy on a small scale as the city is organized on a large scale. His phalansteries are the forefathers of the Unité d'Habitation of Le Corbusier, who refers specifically to Fourier. They undoubtedly influenced the urban conceptions of Varentsov,[55] the designs of the building committee of the economic council of the RSFSR for housing communes during the creative phase of revo-

19
Prisons designed by
John Haviland: Tren-
ton, New Jersey State
Prison, plan; Eastern
Penitentiary, plan
and sections; New
York, Hall of Justice,
section

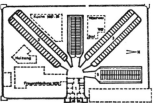
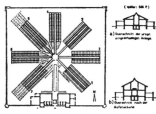
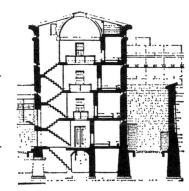

20
Berlin, Moabit,
Prison for Men, de-
tail of plan

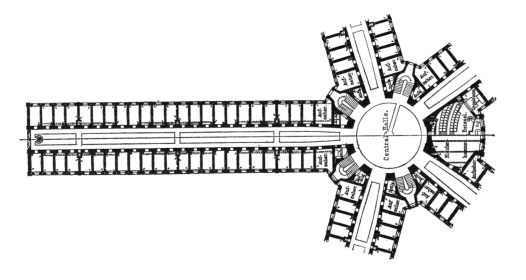

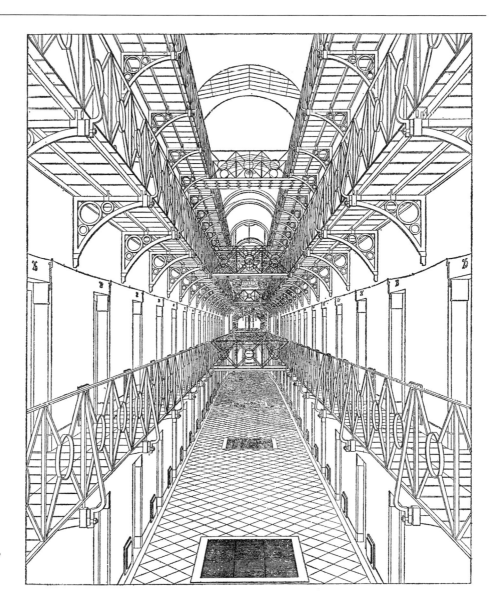

21
Stein an der Donau,
prison, central
corridor

lutionary Russia, and the most recent attempts of the international avant-garde to transcend the cement-block style of official urban architecture. All of those on this list, dating back to the nineteenth century, strove to solve the housing problems of a socialist society founded on the principle of free choice.

Fourier came upon the idea of the phalanstery from a simple consideration:[56] "A town or village of 300 people would be better provided for with one well maintained attic and cellar than with 300 poorly maintained ones. One kitchen would suffice to produce a variety of quality meals instead of 300 individual stoves. One protective wall, or even none at all, would replace 300 individual fences. One shop for buying and selling goods would replace the 300 parasitic and competitive businesses. In short, a uniform economic plan would be applied on a large scale as on a small scale."

In his biography of Fourier, August Bebel describes the bird's-eye view of a phalanstery, drawn according to Fourier's specifications and shown in fig. 22 in the version from the collected works of Fourier's interpreter, Victor Considérant.[57]

Just as the cross determines the form of medieval cathedrals and churches, so the series or row determines the form of the dwellings and factories of the phalanx. More specifically, a central area has two middle or main wings, to which are attached further wide wings. Each architectural structure is only the external reflection of social conditions and the connoisseur can always deduce the social state of a period from its architecture. . . .

The communal economy, whatever its specific form, requires of course completely different buildings from those built for a private economy. . . . The center must contain rooms where about 2000 people can come together numerous times over the course of the day, in particular dining halls, meeting clubs, bazaars, libraries, etc. The two main wings branch off perpendicularly to the middle building and form the central area of the whole phalanx. The two farthest wings extend to the left and right and join the main avenues. These wings contain the different workshops, the noisiest on the extreme ends. Dwellings take up the upper stories of the whole complex. . . .

The administrative building, factories, stalls, etc. would be located opposite the phalanx and the central square, parallel to the main street [not shown in the drawing]. . . . The phalanx building extends ca. 2000 feet or 600 meters from one end of the wing to the other. In order to prevent too long an extension, the row of individual units is doubled. These parallel rows enclose courtyards and gardens. . . . A wide covered gallery running along the interior walls facing the courtyard connects all sections of the building and functions as the main traffic artery.

This description does not mention several features: the apartments are arranged as in a hotel along the inner galleries; all roofs are walkways; the phalanstery has central heating; and the central tower houses the observatory and telegraph office. Fourier himself described the inner galleries in great detail:[58]

The "street-gallery" is situated on the first [second] floor; it could not be on the ground floor, which is crossed at various points by passages for vehicles.

The street-gallery does not receive light from both sides, because one side of it adjoins the building; throughout the phalanstery there are two series of rooms, one getting its light from the outside, the other from the street-gallery, which must be as high as the three floors that look on to it. The doors to the apartments on the first, second and third floors open on to the street gallery, which has stairs leading to the second and third floors. The main stairs, as is customary, lead only to the first floor; but two lateral stairways will lead to the fourth floor. . . .

Fourier believed intensely in the realization of his system of phalansteries. He even stayed home every day until noon in case someone should appear to answer his repeated appeals for money to construct an experimental structure. He never received any response, and died impoverished and bitter in 1837. Heine described him as follows:[59] "How often I saw him as he strode hastily in his worn gray suit through the pillars of the Palais Royal. Both jacket pockets were always weighed down, the one by a bottle of wine, the other by a long loaf of bread." His ideas live on, disseminated through the publication of his complete works in 1841 and through the work of a man named Godin,[60] the owner of a radiator factory in Guise. Between 1859 and 1883 he constructed a *familistère*, or "familial phalanstery," the only attempt to realize the conception of the phalanstery.

Godin wanted to create a collective, home-like environment for his factory workers. He wrote in his *Solutions Sociales*:[61] "Any attempted reform of the labor situation will remain ineffective and insufficient as long as a building reform of the dwellings of the working class is not undertaken simultaneously. Such a reform must answer their needs and supply the pleasures of social life to which every human being has a claim."

The three-storied social palace (fig. 23), which Godin had built on a river island near his factory, had a central space with two wings. Disposed in the manner of a palace, these elements enclosed three inner glass-covered courtyards with continuous galleries. The entire structure was 180 meters long and contained 487 individual apartments of widely varying sizes but all with the same decor. Rents were scaled according to the income of the inhabitants, the floor space, and the story. Heating, ventilation, maintenance, gas lighting, and fresh water were provided centrally by the community. Community institutions were housed in separate buildings. The store, bath, laundry, theater, offices, schools, and day care center for children were all located in a row opposite the apartment palace. In 1896, 1625 people inhabited the *familistère*. It still functions as a housing cooperative. Indeed, the massive glass-covered connecting spaces still astonish visitors.

Godin's attempts to dissolve the nuclear family, to introduce self-government, and to implement profit sharing according to Fourier's conceptions were never fully carried out. This is not the place, however, to present or criticize Fourier's theories or to compare the bourgeois and visionary elements, even though such an analysis would reveal the architectural advances represented by the phalanstery. Elizabeth Lenk wrote in the introduction to the German translation of *Théorie des quatre mouvements*:[62] "Fourier is sometimes criticized as a fantasist, sometimes celebrated as an ingenious inventor, and sometimes ridiculed as a petit bourgeois utopian. And yet today we still cannot classify his system precisely, this mixture of realistic observation, fantasy, and calculation."

There are other building types of the nineteenth century besides the prison and phalanstery which employ the arcade's method of spatial access. Market halls and the stacks of large libraries are two examples. In 1863 Baltard built the Halles Centrales in Paris.[63] These market halls (fig. 24), whose construction had originally been ordered by Napoleon I, replaced a loose conglomeration of market stands and united them in a system of equal-sized blocks, subdivided and made accessible by covered delivery streets. Others also designed a system of arcades as an organizing structure to link the market halls to the network of streets. In a design by Charles Duval[64] the saddle-roofed arcade—a more direct

22
Charles Fourier,
phalanstery,
bird's-eye view

23
Guise, Familistère,
wing, cross section

24
Paris, Halles
Centrales

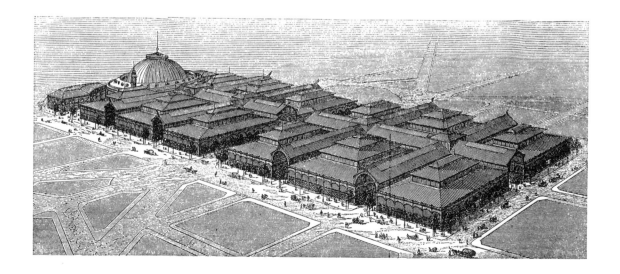

application of the principle than in Baltard's construction—appears as the means of access and illumination. Baltard's system of market halls is based on the Marché du Temple[65] and perhaps even more clearly on the Foire St. Germain.

Baltard also designed the "Entrepôt pour les Sels, Graines, Farines, et Denrées Coloniales" (Depot for Salt, Grains, Meals, and Colonial Wares) built in Lyon in 1828.[66] A large domed central hall with skylights provides access to the deep storage rooms which extend to both sides and are linked on the upper stories by continuous galleries. The Butcher Market and Vegetable Market in Newcastle, built in 1834 by John Dobson (the architect of the Royal Arcade[67]), and the Covent Garden Market by Charles Fowler should also be mentioned. They have arcades containing open stands rather than closed shops. Other markets of this kind were built in London at the end of the nineteenth century, for example, the Leadenhall Market.

The examples in this chapter demonstrate how the arcade from the time of its conception inspired architects to use its system of spatial access in completely different programs for which no clear formal tradition existed in architecture.

Form of Organizing Retail Trade   The arcade is a conglomeration of individual shops; it therefore occupies a specific place in the development of the organizational forms of retail trade. It arose at the beginning of high capitalism. The overproduction caused by technological advances made it imperative for the manufacturers of luxury goods to discover new methods of distribution, faster turnover, and easier promotion. The success of the arcade resulted from the combination of two factors: a supply of goods in department-store variety and a supply of public space for undisturbed promenading, window shopping, and display of merchandise.

The arcade is only an association of shops. The bazaar, the *magasin de nouveauté*, and the department store, on the other hand, are extended shops, the concentrated form, the capitalistic form of retail trade. The arcade must therefore be distinguished from these forms. One must first investigate whether large formations of retail trade from past centuries, i.e., rows of shops and booths, resembled the structure of the arcade. The arcade remained a site for retail trade throughout the nineteenth century as has been seen. It never lost this characteristic through its numerous transformations. This consistency lies in the connection of the arcade to a specific branch of retail trade. The architectural programs were extended and reinterpreted, but the foundation of the row of shops never changed. At the beginning of its development, the arcade was an object of private speculation, an imitation of the Palais Royal; then it became the symbol of cultural progress, the showpiece of newly established nations, like Italy and Germany, which were seeking recognition.

The Shop
The formless original state of the retail shop was the market in which goods were spread out on the ground. The next stages of the market structure included carts, trading stands with a table and protective covering, movable stands, sturdy booths with locks, and finally rows of shops divided according to the branches of artisans. These steps were taken toward a marketing system institutionalized by guilds, class structure, and urban authorities.

The predecessor of the shop is the booth with two large wooden chests[68] and two flaps which open up; the one served as a table, the other as a protective eave. Customer and dealer stand opposite each other, maintaining the direct contact common in markets. The land for the fixed booth is leased. With the passing of generations, the lease becomes ownership, and the former privilege becomes permission to replace the booth with a building. The one-room booth is transformed into a series of rooms—storage room, shop, and apartment. Yet the shop, in spite of all the new variations, remains a large open box which can be locked by a wooden flap.

The next decisive step in the development is the provision of entry into the shop. The shop table is taken inside and the site of trade is shifted to the interior. As a consequence, the merchandise cannot be placed directly before the shopper's eyes; he cannot be addressed directly. Advertising—in the form of written material, shop sign, and display of goods—must be employed to attract the attention of the passerby. The open shop is closed, the wooden flaps become the door and show window. The invention of cast glass by the Frenchman Lucas de Neheon in 1688, however, soon made it possible to manufacture larger and, most important, transparent glass plates which granted a better view into the shop. Such rolled poured glass was first used for the manufacture of mirrors, one of the main luxury industries of the eighteenth century. Mass production finally brought about a decrease in the high price and thereby made such glass available outside of courtly circles.

The first glass show windows appeared near the beginning of the eighteenth century in the distinguished luxury businesses. Not until the middle of the century, however, were shops widespread, with show windows which not only offered a view of the shop but also an exhibition of the products on a table behind the windowpane. The panes became ever larger,[69] allowing fewer subdivisions into small frames and thereby a freer view. About 1850 the panes produced had finally become large enough so that show windows could be made of only one sheet. The interior facades of the arcades, viewed as an ensemble, illustrate this development.

While this solution granted increased comfort, it also meant a loss of variety, subdivision, and ornamental design of the facades. The show window defines the retail store in its simple form: the product is protected from the weather and can be viewed through the window after the shop has closed. Fixed prices replace bargaining, variety of goods replaces individual production, and competition replaces mutual support. The show window itself undergoes a development. About 1800 it was still a large opening divided into square fields by wooden frames. Along the streets of London and Paris they were arranged in irregular patterns; in other cities they were lined up uniformly in arcaded porticoes and arcades. Some were curved, like English bow windows, and others were connected by showcases which covered the wall areas to form a continuous glass front.[70]

In the nineteenth century the area of the glass window took on a life of its own; the shop entrance was drawn into the shop to increase the size of the show window. The depth of the show window attained an architectural quality and became separate from the shop itself. The presentation of merchandise developed from a mere pile of goods to a collection of displays and finally to window dressings which were the responsibility of a special decorator. About 1800 the decor and facade of a shop became an aspect of official architecture. The architects of the Empire gave the shop a strict classical front.[71] Small temples of luxury were built into the ground floors of buildings with mirrors, marble facing, bronze fittings and mouldings. The street was transformed into the image we have today: a battlefield of competitive advertising. This new business street still lacked an essential element, however—the sidewalk. Yet in its systematic form, as a speculative whole, it is the arcade.

Early in the nineteenth century, however, a different process began to unfold: the individual shop expanded to the department store. With increased consumer demand and variety of goods, the shop had to become wider, deeper, taller. Its architectural program had now to differentiate among the sales rooms, offices, storage space, display space, and workshops. This expansion of the shop within one building was made possible by the new application of iron as a construction material. It was used to make thin columns, supports, girders, and cantilever constructions, all pieced together to form a skeleton which dispensed with walls and arches and thereby offered a greater command of the view over larger series of spaces. A special house of business with numerous employees developed out of the expanded shop. This development ended about 1860. It still awaits systematic analysis.

All these stages of the development of the shop still exist today side by side, for each fulfills a specific need. The arcade developed at precisely that moment when the shop reached its finished form while the increased production of goods necessitated the search for forms of increased marketing and new methods of creating demand.

Stages of Organization

The development of the shop must be understood against the background of the differentiation of retail trade. It begins with the closed concessionary system of the guilds, which excluded advertising, competition, and increased rates of exchange; it ends with the capitalist methods of marketing, creation of demand, and quick turnover of goods. This change was made possible by mass production, mobility of consumers and commodities, and public transportation systems. The arcade occupies a unique place in this development. Many building types are related to it in plan, but it came into its own thanks to the appearance of a particular type of shop, the fashion and luxury item store. The social changes that parallel this architectural process create the expanded bourgeois public which seeks out the commodities sold in these shops.

In the Middle Ages there were three social groups involved in retail trade:[72]

1. The hawker. He is the traveling retail dealer; his shop is the basket on his back. He trades with all in the smallest quantities and must seek out his customers.

2. The shopkeeper. He is the settled retail dealer; he trades in cloth, spices, drugs, metal and iron wares. His business is located in a booth, an open shop. The location and extent of his business are strictly prescribed by the guilds. He receives his supplies from merchants and wholesalers.

3. The handworker or artisan. He too can have his own shop in front of his workshop. He works on commission or keeps articles in stock. He is part of a strictly regulated association.

A market can be formed by these three groups. An example, the Ring in Breslau, is described in detail later.

The oldest type of retail trade is the trade in sundry articles as it still exists today in rural areas.[73] It satisfies the daily needs of its customers, selling many different kinds of goods without any specialization. Specialization begins with the end of the Middle Ages; the retail market has four subdivisions: (1) grocery (épicerie), (2) dry goods (mercerie), (3) iron mongery (quincaillerie), and (4) secondhand goods (friperie).

The subdivision of merchandise depends, therefore, on compatibility. The dealer has to meet growing demand with an expertly administered supply. Goods from foreign countries and luxury items by famous manufacturers require a special knowledge of the goods, a more detailed awareness of the market, and hence a larger staff. This results in even greater specialization.

The franchise[74] fulfills this need of differentiating merchandise by separating it first according to the four classes just mentioned, then according to the origin of the goods and the location of the workshops (silk from Lyon, lace from Belgium, and glass from Venice). The class of dry goods, for example, is further subdivided into categories like cotton goods, silk, linens, and knitwear, each with its own shop. Sombart includes lists of these specialty businesses from the eighteenth century.[75] About the middle of the eighteenth century a new type of shop arises from this broad spectrum of retail franchises. Sombart calls it the "consumption-goods" business.[76]

There are three different types:

The fashion business. It developed out of the shop of the mercer—that is, the silk trade. It purveys not only material but also all kinds of accoutrements—everything belonging to a fashionable outfit.

The interior decorating business. It developed out of the shop of the tapestry maker (tapissier) and grew to a large supply business capable of furnishing an apartment or salon. The goods offered range from mirrors, candelabras, and sofas, to carpets, paintings, and etchings.

The luxury-item business. It provides costly and superfluous objects, exotic curiosities, knickknacks, and gifts. Its clientele consists of browsers, people of leisure.

All three of these types of shops contain the seeds of the department store. They cater to a mixed public from courtly society, wealthy nobility, and the *nouveaux riches* of the bourgeoisie. Their clientele is not yet the masses but an extensive, even if limited, section of the privileged class that wants to be treated differently. Its wishes are to be acted upon as commands, and it possesses the unlimited credit to get what it wants. Customer service, the decor of the shop, and the enticement of the customer become a science for these shops. The extensive supply requires large inventories, high investments, and large premises, all of which expand their former boundaries. An army of employees, assistants, and errand boys is needed to satisfy the customers.

Common to these three types of shops is trade in luxury items. Sombart[77] attempts to demonstrate the rise of capitalism from the luxury goods trade.

The rise of luxury businesses had a deeper, more permanent and exclusive effect on retail trade than on wholesale trade. In the early stage of capitalism there did exist some branches of wholesale trade which were capitalist without being involved with luxury items. However, I believe that not a single even remotely capitalist retail dealership can be found before the nineteenth century which did not deal in luxury goods. In the decades around 1700 one can observe how the demand for luxury and the necessity or desire of the trader to satisfy it are both connected to the increased tendency toward an extravagant lifestyle among the wealthy. These were the decades in which Brazilian gold began to fill the pockets of the speculators in Paris, Amsterdam and London. The endeavor to answer the demand of the wealthy for luxury items shook the trader out of his artisan's routine and radically advanced the development of capitalism.

Mercier, the merciless biographer of prerevolutionary Paris, described the social condition underlying luxury trade:[78]

Feelings are no longer satisfied, but dulled. Instead of interesting diversions there arise bizarre extravagances which can only attract the tasteless. This is the reason why everything changes so radically and senselessly: fashions, dress, customs, language. The wealthy will soon reach the point where they will no longer feel anything at all. Their institutions are ever-changing decorations, their clothes a drudgery, their meals a parade. Luxury becomes a torture for the wealthy, I believe, just as hardship is for the poor. . . .

If one compares the mentioned retail branches and the three specialized types of luxury shops with the list of rentals for the Passage des Panoramas and Passage de l'Opéra in Paris (1810 and 1826; see the catalog), one can easily see that luxury trade was concentrated in the arcades.[79] Almost without exception, one finds fashion goods, luxury items, culinary delicacies, paintings, and furniture all sold side by side. The arcade has become, therefore, a luxury department store by 1800. However, it still consists of individual retail shops. It is similar to the department store because one can purchase a large variety of goods without leaving the building. In addition to the close proximity of different franchises, the arcade also offers an undisturbed situation for window shopping and a variety of additional amusements and attractions. The arcade becomes a social center.

The inclusion of many shops under one roof and the grouping of these shops in a space free of disturbance also aid retail trade in its effort to increase sales. However, the arcade is only one of the capitalist methods of organizing retail trade. About 1800 other forms of organization arise which are more capable of development: the bazaar, the *magasin de nouveauté*, and later the department store. The reasons for this trend toward reorganization can be found in growing industrialization,[80] which results in mass production of identical merchandise, uniform pricing, great capital demand, rapid turnover, reduction of stock, and anonymity of the customer. Overproduction causes competition, lower pricing, quicker turnover. These in turn cause expansion of the shopping area, increased supply, and sophisticated methods of advertising. The retail business becomes an enterprise which employs capital investment from many sources.

The arcade is a collection of rentable shops in a street-like area. The bazaar is a structure which consists of numerous courtyards or halls with skylights; it has numerous entrances and rents open stands.

The *magasin de nouveauté* is the expanded version of the eighteenth-century fashionable shop. It has many rooms and several stories; it employs many people and offers a complete selection of the goods available in its line of business.

The *department store* is a massive sundry-article shop. All branches are represented in one building. The business principle is high turnover and low pricing. While the arcade attracts a classifiable clientele, the department store appeals to the masses. They are treated as anonymous consumers.

The *franchise* and *mail-order house* treat the customer like a file card. They are the final stages of the capitalist development of retail trade into big business, a development which ends about the middle of the nineteenth century.

All of these stages of organization will now be illustrated by a series of examples which emphasize on the one hand those forms which could have served as a model for the arcade and on the other those which were influenced by it.

Example 1: Rome: Mercatus Trajani (Antiquity)
On the way to the Torre delle Milizie with its great view over Rome, one encounters suddenly a high, arcade-like, vaulted space, the Aula Trajani.[81] It is a part of the Mercatus Trajani, which was built in encapsulated levels into the side of the Quirinal and which is traversed by the winding Via Biberatica. Today it contains 170 rooms. They are connected by stairs to the Forum Trajani, forming shop-lined streets in semicircles, tangents, and radials. These streets flow into the forum in the form of galleries. The Aula Trajani (drawn in figs. 25 and 26 after the MacDonald plan) is, to my knowledge, the only ancient market street with a covering vault. It was probably a market hall, although its actual extent is unknown. For centuries, it was also used for religious functions. There is no model for this space, whose section so closely resembles that of an arcade.

The main hall, oblong in its present state, has two stories (figs. 27–29). The upper story is set back by a walkway from the vault, thereby admitting light into the central space. The vault rests on pillars placed away from the walls, offering an obstructed view of the galleries. The Mercatus Trajani was built at the same time as the Forum Trajani, about 110 A.D. It was just one of the many great building complexes, markets, and storage spaces which Trajan had built to serve the capital of the empire.

Example 2: Breslau, The Ring (Middle Ages)
The site of all trade in the medieval city was the market. In Germany, its activities were strictly regulated by marketing ordinances and staple rights (official storage and transit rights). This led to the institutionalization of market structures: the series of booths, the market building, the basilica, and the archways of the town halls. The Ring, shown in figs. 30 and 31, represents famous market structures, inasmuch as its organization is remarkably like that of an arcade.

The plans, which are taken from the book by Rudolf Stein,[82] show the site: the large market square is situated in an open space in the middle of the city, which was rebuilt after a fire in 1241. On the Ring stands an easily overlooked block that consists of an arcade-like series of structures. The plan of the area shows the Ring as it was about 1275. Today only the more recent town hall is still standing: the other buildings were demolished after the introduction of free trade in Prussia in 1811.

The block is pieced together, from south to north, out of the following market structures:

1. The market house, called the *Tuchhaus* (cloth house). Originally serving wholesale dealers, it was an open courtyard bordered on both sides by 100-meter-long, three-storied storage buildings with a saddle-roof construction. Later the roofs were extended in the center and supported by a series of double columns, thereby creating a double-naved hall. The *Tuchhaus* housed forty salesrooms with exclusive wholesale privileges and two chambers for the city officials who controlled the merchandise.

2. The imperial shops (*Reichkrame*). The forty (later forty-seven) shops in the double row occupied by the imperial shopkeepers (the second estate of trade) had the privilege of retail trade. The maximum amount of goods sold there was precisely prescribed. The imperial shopkeepers traded groceries and dry goods. A lesser category of "subretailers" (*Partkrämer*) sold their goods by the piece from their double row of booths. They did not have a fixed roof and were located beyond the block to the east.

3. The garment hall (*Gewandreissergang*). The linen draper, with only a wooden, one-story booth, had the right to sell linen by the yard. This hall was bordered on the west by the *Hopfenamt*, the authority controlling hops, on which the city had a trade monopoly.

4. The *Schmetterhaus*. This two-storied, double-naved hall sheltered the artisans and craftspeople. The only ones who could obtain the privilege of installing themselves on its three rows of benches were craftspeople and merchants.

5. The leather goods row (*Riemerzeile*). The block of buildings ends with the saddlery which consists of multileveled, narrow shop buildings attached to the *Schmetterhaus*. These shops were originally one-storied wooden structures. Straps, belts, saddles, and other goods were made here.

6. The linen house. In the sixteenth century the linen house was established in front of the cloth house. It held the stock exchange and scale. The scale, later moved into a separate building, was essential for the exercise of staple rights, the main source of Breslau's prosperity. Traveling merchants were legally required to have their goods weighed on the large scale. They also had to offer their merchandise at the market for three days and to pay a fee before continuing their journey.

To sum up, the town hall, initially one of the houses on the Ring, the later city guardhouse, the fish market, and the smaller series of booths around the market halls all come together to complete the image of this exemplary medieval market.

Example 3: London, The Exchanges (Seventeenth Century)
The stock exchange grows out of the town hall, market hall, guild house, and loggia as a further differentiation of the general activity of the market. Together with banking and insurance, the notion of a stock exchange introduces world trade as a new style of doing business. Credit and shares are its new means. K. H. Schreyl investigated the types of stock exchanges.[83] In one, the court hall exchange,[84] the upper story had rows of open stands called variously *pand*, *pawn*, or *baan*. These bazaars already served trade in luxuries and influenced not only the London Exchanges but also, at least in Great Britain, the arcade building type. The architect Samuel Ware refers to the prototypical Exeter Change in his report on the first project for the Burlington Arcade (London, 1815).

The path that eventually leads to the London Exchanges can be traced back to the court hall exchanges of Antwerp and Amsterdam. These possessed on the upper floor a kind of bazaar, the *pant*, which consisted of open stands. Since these exchanges were used as markets and commodity exchanges simultaneously, they cannot be compared to contemporary ones.

Between 1566 and 1568 Sir Thomas Gresham, a private entrepreneur, built in London a copy of the Antwerp Exchange, the Royal Exchange.[85] The two-

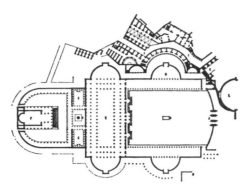

25
Rome, Mercatus Tra-
jani, ca. 110 A.D.,
site plan

26
Mercatus Trajani,
plan, upper story

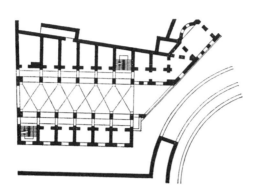

27
Mercatus Trajani

28
Mercatus Trajani,
view into upper
gallery

29
Mercatus Trajani,
view of ground floor

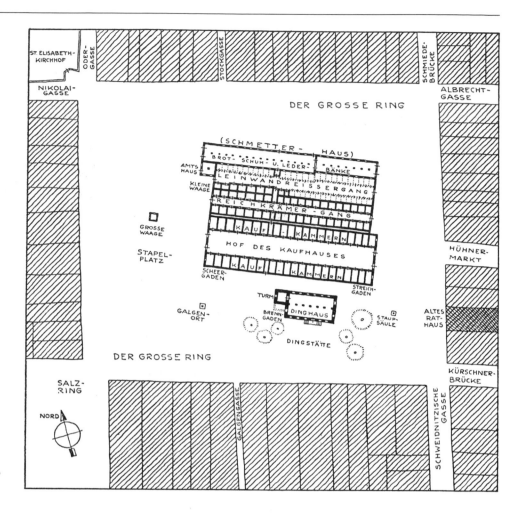

30
Breslau, the Ring,
site plan

31
The Ring, market
buildings, ground
plan

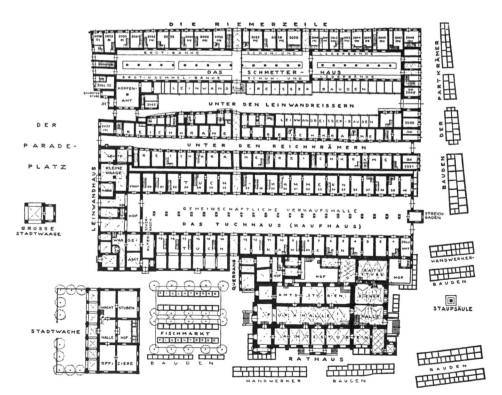

storied building enclosed an arcaded courtyard where the actual exchanges took place. On the ground floor was the Lower Pawn, on the upper story, the Upper Pawn. These were corridors lined with "stalls," open stands which Gresham leased to traders. In 1570 the queen visited the Pawn. She was so impressed that she granted Gresham permission to call the building the "Royal Exchange." It was destroyed in the great fire of 1666, then reconstructed; demolished again in 1838 and finally rebuilt in 1840 in its present form.

The commercial success of the Royal Exchange led as early as 1606 to a competitive project. The New Exchange (see fig. 32) was built to the west of the Royal Exchange, on the southern side of the Strand. It is, however, a simpler construction, consisting merely of a long, two-storied hall with a lower and upper walk. A tavern was located in the cellar. Here too, until 1737, one could find open stalls lining the sides of the hall.

A third building of this kind—the Exeter Change (1676)—exists in London, even further to the west near the later Lowther Arcade. Its position demonstrates the trend in high society to move westward toward Covent Garden. Exeter Change closely resembled the New Exchange, except for its upper floor, which housed Mr. Cross's Menagerie starting in 1773. Its prize possession was London's only elephant. Robert Southey wrote of the building in 1807 in his *Letters from England*:[86] "Exeter Change is precisely a bazaar, a sort of street under cover or large long room, with a row of shops on either hand, and a thoroughfare between them; the shops being furnished with such articles as might tempt an idler, or remind a passenger of his wants. At the further end was a man in splendid costume who proved to belong to a menagerie above stairs. A maccaw was swinging on a perch above him. . . ."

In 1829 the Exeter Change had to yield to the grading of the Strand. The most remarkable aspect of these exchanges, besides the arrangement of the shops, is probably their two stories. This kind of construction can be considered a precursor of the gallery, the specifically British method of making the space of the arcade accessible.

The Parisian counterpart of the London exchange is the Galerie des Marchands in the old royal palace on the Ile de la Cité. It was built by the order of Louis IV.[87] The Parisian *merciers*, the first estate of luxury traders, received permission to display their goods in the palace when the king was in residence. Some of the stands show in Abraham Bosse's etching (fig. 33). Well into the eighteenth century the Galerie des Marchands remained a gathering place of fashionable Parisians.

Example 4: Paris: Foire St. Germain (Eighteenth Century)
After the Middle Ages the weekly farmers' market,[88] the annual country fair, and the wholesale fairs thrived for a limited period before the larger fairs were gradually subdivided into specialty fairs.[89] Originally, commodities were actually traded at the fairs; then in the eighteenth century the fair became transformed into an exhibition of models. It developed its own special site, complete with houses, booths, and halls. The most famous of the French fairs was the Foire St. Germain, located at the gates of Paris. Fig. 34 gives a bird's eye view. I have ascribed the Foire St. Germain to the eighteenth century because in its role in the social life of the city it was an immediate predecessor of the Palais Royal. This gigantic fair had been established by the Abbé of Saint Germain in 1462; it

32
London, New Ex-
change, engraving by
Gravelot

33
Paris, Galerie des
Marchands

34
Paris, Foire St. Germain, detail from an
engraving

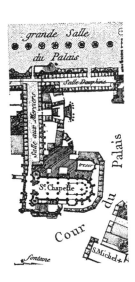

was renovated in 1511, then destroyed by fire and rebuilt in 1762. The etching represents the state of the fair in 1786. It was later totally disbanded.

The fair was located near the church of St. Sulpice on a large rise of ground which is now unrecognizable.[90] It was laid out on a grid with alleyways. Each square is surrounded by a wall which houses uniform two-storied shops facing the interior courtyard. Each shop can be locked at night by means of a wooden board which is raised during the day and used as an eave. Each alley bears the name of the trade which it houses. The shop facades along one alley have an astonishing resemblance to the interior facades of the Passage des Panoramas (to name just one example). The alleys are even reserved exclusively for pedestrian traffic. The Foire enjoyed special privileges and was not regulated by the guilds because it was located outside of the city. Up until the revolution the great luxury market included establishments for entertainment as well. One could dance, gamble in salons, visit all kinds of exhibitions, attend performances of traveling theater companies, and listen to singers and musicians. It was here in 1670 that the first Parisian café was opened. Following reconstruction after the fire of 1762 pleasure gardens were added on the British model. Today the Marché St. Germain, built by Blondel on a section of the old fairgrounds at the beginning of the nineteenth century, is the only reminder of the Foire.

In 1805 N. L. Durand published a plan for a completely different kind of fair in his *Précis de Leçons d'Architecture*[91] (see fig. 35). Durand's mania for systematization, his attempt to force every structure into a symmetrical pattern—which Gottfried Semper called, ironically, "Durand's paper money which the chessboard chancellor circulated for want of hard ideas"[92]—led him to a design which had no immediate prototype. However, many of its individual features were influenced by other buildings. The wall that closes the fair off from the world is derived from the Foire St. Germain; the open spaces and the broad alleys decorated with sculptures and fountains recall the Jardin du Palais Royal.

In Durand's design the fair hall is round because he regarded the endless concourse as the ideal organizational principle for a fair. It has a basilica-like cross section; the ground floor is arcaded on the exterior for the shops and the upper story is arcaded on the interior for the dwellings and storage rooms of the traders. This design may very well have been the basis of the building for the Paris Exposition of 1867. Durand refers to the Eastern bazaar in his description and explanation of the cross section. In the center of the structure are the pleasure gardens, which were also a part of the Foire St. Germain. The small pavilions housing the cafés, small restaurants, and the four semicircular theaters complete the image of a fair according to the conceptions of that period.

It is clear that the Foire St. Germain and the Palais Royal played a role in this design. However, Durand's idea of housing fair activities in an arcade-like space suggests that he was influenced by the first Parisian arcades.

Example 5: London and Paris: The Bazaars (Nineteenth Century)
While searching for arcades in London and Paris, I constantly came across buildings which were called *bazaar, exchange,* or *gallery* but which could not be classified under the arcade building type. These buildings, which I will group together under the term *bazaar,* have been treated in architectural history as an independent building type. Alison Adburgham is the only one to have treated it in any detail.[93]

The bazaar is a series of courtyards and rooms with skylights, light wells, and multileveled, continuous galleries. It resembles the arcade in that it serves retail trade, is built into already developed sites, possesses numerous exits to different streets, and lacks the arcade's transitional nature. The bazaar is a predecessor of the department store because of its spatial organization, the arrangement of the open sales booths around a light well, and the extensive variety of goods. Bazaars existed in the neighborhood of arcades: in London between Oxford Street, Piccadilly, and the Strand, and in Paris on the boulevards. To my knowledge not a single bazaar is still standing; the life of the bazaar was limited to the period between 1816 and 1840. Like the arcade, it represents an effort to create higher forms of organization for retail trade, places where anything can be bought. It gives way to the department store and exhibition hall.

London takes precedence over Paris with the bazaar; yet with the arcade, the situation is reversed. Knight writes in his *Curiosities of London*:[94] "The bazaar is an adaption from the East, the true principle of which is the classification of trades. Thus, Paternoster Row, with its books; Newport Market, with its butcher shops; and Monmouth Street with its shoes, are more properly bazaars than the miscellaneous stalls assembled under cover, which are in London designated by this name. Exeter Change was a great cutlery bazaar; and the row of attorneys' shops in the Lord Mayor's Court Office, in the second Royal Exchange, was a kind of legal bazaar, the name of each attorney being inscribed upon a projecting signboard. The Crystal Palace of 1851 and the Great Exhibition of 1862 were vast assemblages of bazaars."

I have discovered twenty examples of such bazaars—fifteen in London, one in Manchester, and four in Paris. A complete list follows because the bazaar is important as a parallel development to the arcade:

London:
Soho Bazaar. It was the first bazaar ever built. Designed by John Trotter, it opened in Soho Square in 1816.

The Western Exchange. It opened in 1817 between Bond Street and Burlington Arcade.

Queen's Bazaar. Located on Oxford Street, it burned down in 1829.

Pantheon Bazaar. The Pantheon on Oxford Street was built in 1772 by James Wyatt for "the nocturnal adventures of the British aristocracy" (namely, for balls and masquerades). It was rebuilt as a bazaar in 1834 by Sydney Smirke. The schematic plan (fig. 36) shows how smaller rooms—a round one for refreshments and a conservatory built of iron—were linked to the vaulted main room to provide a rear exit to a parallel street. The Pantheon was the most famous bazaar in London. At one time it even housed picture exhibitions.

Baker Street Bazaar. Originally it was located in Portman Square and served as a horse market. A large portion of the bazaar was replaced by Madame Tussaud's museum.

Pantechnicon Bazaar. Built in 1830 between Halkin Street and Belgrave Square, it served as a specialty market for carriages and furniture and later as a site for auctions.

Lowther Bazaar. Located across from the Lowther Arcade on the Strand, it was famous for its Magic Cave, the Cosmorama.

St. James's Bazaar. It was built in 1832 between King Street and St. James's Street. As in many bazaars, diorama presentations took place here.

35
J. N. Durand, design
for a market, 1805

36
London, Pantheon
Bazaar, plan

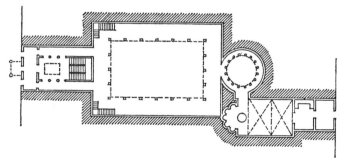

37
Paris, Galerie de Fer,
structural details

38
Paris, Bazar de l'In-
dustrie Française,
plan and section

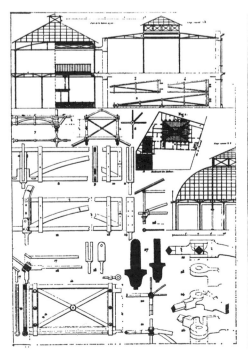

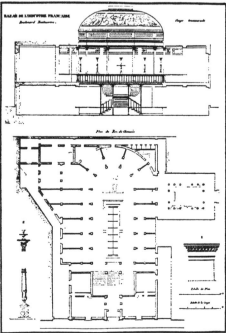

Cosmorama, later the Prince of Wales Bazaar. On Regent Street, it was originally an exhibition hall.

Anti-Corn-Law League. This bazaar was temporarily located in the Covent Garden Theater.

Portland Bazaar, Langham Palace

Crystal Palace Bazaar, Oxford Street

Corinthian Bazaar, Argyle Street

St. Paul's Bazaar, St. Paul's Churchyard

Royal London Bazaar, Liverpool Street.

Manchester:
The Bazaar.[95] It grew out of a small drapery shop and was opened in 1831. Adburgham reprints the text of the prospectus, which contains the house rules and the conditions for tenants of the stands. The prospectus bears the title, *The Bazaar and the Exhibition of Works of Art, including Diorama, Physiorama, etc. Deansgate and Police Street, King Street.*

Paris:
Galerie de Fer (fig. 37). This bazaar was built in 1829 by Tavernier, the architect of the Passage Choiseul, as a replacement for the Galerie de Bouffles, which had burned down. Therefore it is alternatively called "Bazar de Bouffles." It was located between the Rue de Choiseul and the Boulevard des Italiens in the block which is now occupied by the central office of the Crédit Lyonnais. The Galerie de Fer was probably, with the Marché Madeleine, one of the first large halls in Paris built of cast and wrought iron.[96] The bazaar consisted of three two-storied rooms with glass roofs. The rooms contain, among other things, a curiosity shop and a menagerie.

Bazar de l'Industrie Française (fig. 38). Built in 1830 by Le Long between the Boulevard Montmartre and the Rue Montmartre, it consists of a large semicircular room with continuous galleries. It is illuminated by a glass skylight inserted into a mirror vault. Thiollet published the plan of this bazaar.[97]

Galeries du Commerce et de l'Industrie. Built in 1838 by Grisart and Froehlicher on the Boulevard Nouvelle, it was destroyed by fire in 1848.[98] This bazaar had no single owner who rented the stands but belonged to a corporation of small boutique proprietors.

Bazar. I was unable to discover the name of this small bazaar on the Boulevard des Italiens. It is mentioned, however, in the *Petit Atlas Pittoresque de la Ville de Paris* of 1834.

Example 6: Paris: The Department Store (Nineteenth Century)
In the cosmopolitan cities of London and Paris, the department store has come to replace the arcade and the bazaar. Zola, in his novel *Au Bonheur des Dames,* called the department store "the cathedral of modern commerce, built for a population of consumers." Paul Göhre provides the following definition:[99] "The department store is a collection of miscellaneous businesses under one roof and one management. It is limited to the sale of very marketable, consistently popular merchandise."

The department store has its organizational origins in the *magasin de nouveauté* and the drapery shop. For a long time Boucicaut, founder of the Bon Marché, was considered the inventor of the department store. However, Adburgham has demonstrated that shops existed in the 1830s and 1840s in Manchester and Newcastle which must be termed "department stores."[100] They were run according to the principles of a fixed price, the lack of pressure on the shopper, and the law of greatest exchange—low prices and large selection.

The first *magasin de nouveauté,* the Pygmalion, was opened in 1793 in the Rue St. Denis in Paris. It still exists today,[101] although it has grown to a complex comprising a number of the surrounding buildings. In 1801 the famous Petit St. Thomas was opened, in which Boucicaut began his career as an assistant. About 1850 there were already nearly 400 businesses of this kind in Paris. All the *magasins* began small and then expanded gradually into the surrounding buildings thanks to the new architectural possibilities offered by iron. They acquired light wells, galleries, and whole new floors; the sales rooms were decorated with paneling and mirrors; extravagant gas lighting was introduced. Artists designed the show windows; advertisements, notices, and pamphlets were used to attract customers; an army of employees waited on the shoppers. The *magasins* outdid each other with their fantastic names: Le Masque de Fer, Le Mystère de Paris, Nouvelle Héloïse, Le Pauvre Diable. The development of these shops into department stores and large commercial complexes was inseparable from the development of the office building. Iron made possible the required transparency; skeleton construction replaced the massive stone building.

In 1852 Aristide Boucicaut entered the shop of his friend Videau with some saved capital. Together they developed specific business principles, those of the department store, they offered free inspection of goods, the possibility of exchange, and reduced prices for slow-moving items. But they demanded—the real sensation in Paris—cash payment. These were completely different customs from those of the arcade, and harsher ones. In 1854 twelve employees worked in the shop, which was hardly 30 square meters in size; in 1862 many buildings were already in the hands of the two partners; and in the 1870s arose a gigantic new building, the first of the great Parisian department stores. It filled a whole block with continuous show windows, countless light wells, galleries, staircases, and levels. L. C. Boileau was the architect, Eiffel the engineer. They created a skeleton construction which permitted a continuous subdividable space with holes left for the light shafts. Woodcuts from contemporary journals[102] capture the tremendous lighted spaces on the Bon Marché and show the glass-covered interior—for which the arcade had prepared the way. However, here the arcade space is transformed; its facades are now the galleries. From the free-hanging staircases, one can experience the space in all dimensions (fig. 39).

The store is no longer for the privileged class of idle shoppers but for the members of all social classes, the masses. Great expenditures for architectural and decorative features are made to seduce the consumer, to generate the desire to consume. Capitalism has mastered its methods by which buying is converted in the consciousness of the public into a festival.[103] The arcade, the bazaar, and the great exhibition halls were the forerunners of these department-store spaces. This final form of retail trade was created by the railroad, which increased the mobility of customers and goods; the expansion of the market worldwide; and the concentration of capital in the hands of a few men.

39
Paris, Bon Marché,
woodcut, ca. 1880

These six examples illustrating the development of retail trade demonstrate that the arcade, both in architectural and in economic history, forms a link in the chain of attempts by capitalism to discover new forms of marketing. In the case of the arcade it was the combination of luxury trade with publicly accessible space which guaranteed temporary favor with the public and financial success.

A Space of Movement   In this, the last of the seven defining characteristics of the arcade, the arcade appears as a transitional passageway or space in which movement takes place. If one building is connected to another the result is a gallery or pergola; if one street is connected to another the result is an arcade; if a part or a whole city is connected to another the result is the railway station, which terminates the new mode of technologically accelerated movement. Historically, then, the arcade can be placed between the palace gallery (as it still existed well into the eighteenth century) and the railway station (as it appeared in the 1840s with its expansive halls).

The long galleries with lighting from both sides were a necessary ingredient of the palace. They made it possible to build around large courtyards and to expand the size of the palace to create the desired shape. The gallery is a passage or corridor which becomes independent of the other rooms and comes to be used as a family portrait or art gallery in which the lord of the palace can hold receptions and balls, and present his art treasures. In Florence, for example, there are the long corridors which connect the Uffizi to the Pitti Palace over the Arno; in Rome the long galleries of the Vatican museum; in Dresden the Zwinger, and in Paris the Grande Galerie of the Louvre. The Grande Galerie, a vaulted, 250-meter-long room, was famous as a public promenade when the Louvre Museum opened.[104]

The plan for the palace at Ludwigsburg demonstrates most clearly the function of the gallery:[105] galleries are used in pairs to connect the corner pavilions and to enclose a courtyard between the old and new main buildings. The two longer galleries, which are located on the second floor to enable free passage, are called the Picture Gallery and the Family Gallery. The galleries are indoor promenades. This element of palace architecture continues into the nineteenth century in the form of picture galleries, halls with skylights, and freestanding promenades in spas. Bad Kissingen, Marienbad, Wiesbaden, Baden-Baden, and Vichy, to name just a few spas, have large pump rooms which are in part open-air, covered promenades, often with neighboring shops.

The arcade is, of course, always a promenade. The name "gallery" is reserved for the more elegant arcades.[106] Bandmann describes this tendency as follows: "In this response to a building type we see a common tendency of architectural history—a representative genre, which had once been bound to a specific social class, is taken over by a rising emancipated class. Following the great French Revolution the bourgeoisie lays claim to the aristocratic gallery." In the case of the Parisian arcades, the name *galerie* is used for the vaulted promenades which include shops, like the Galeries of the Palais Royal. In this way such structures are differentiated from the ordinary arcades which have little in common with palatial architecture. I have discovered no arcade with strictly interior architecture—in Paris only the Grande Galerie of the Louvre could be considered in this way—but this does not exclude the application of architectural experience to a completely different context. The Galerie d'Orléans, the only arcade which stands on its own and functions as a connecting link like a palace gallery, was built by the same architect who had earlier taken part in the reconstruction with the addition of skylights of the Grande Galerie—and yet it is difficult to see here any direct dependence of the one structure on the other.[107] Has the aristocratic gallery been transformed into an urban arcade, or is the arcade an interiorized street? The transitional character of the passageway, exploited for commercial purposes, determines the building type. In its fully developed form, the structure attempts to legitimate its function and hide its orientation toward profit and exploitation by striving to be a gallery. Precisely from this point on the arcade receives its vaulted roof.

The vault is now the translation into iron and glass of an older method of covering rooms and spaces. It is also the static principle by which larger spaces can be spanned without tall supporting members, because the curvature approximates the direction of thrust. The vault is used to cover the arcade when the arcade space becomes wider, that is, when a simple saddle roof with self-supporting ribs is no longer adequate. But in order to maintain the aesthetic appeal of the street, the glass roof must be as light and thin as possible. The example of the Galeries St. Hubert in Brussels supports this observation.

The glass vault is furthermore the initial stage of a systematic development of a space of transition and movement, a kind of space which originates in the arcade, continues in the railway station, and ends in the subway tubes, where, freed from the street level and historical conditions, it attains an aerodynamically ideal cross section and a technologically refined form which makes fantastic velocities possible. While the arcade is still bound to the street level, the railway demands its own undisturbed plane; the tubes are freely movable and independent of level.

In the period from 1840 to 1855 the following building types were developed through the use of the vaulted glass roof:

The conservatory: Palm Stove in Kew Gardens (1845–1847)

The arcade: Sillem's Bazar in Hamburg (1843); Galeries St. Hubert in Brussels (1839–1847)

The railway station: Central Station in Newcastle (1846–1850); Paddington Station in London (1852–1854); Kings Cross Station in London (1850–1852; fig. 40).

The exhibition hall: Crystal Palace I and II (1850–1854); Crystal Palace in Dublin (1852–1853); Industrial Exhibition in Paris (1855)

The engineer Richard Turner, who had built the Palm Stove in Kew Gardens with Decimus Burton, later built the low-vaulted hall of the second Lime Street Station in Liverpool. John Dobson, architect of the Royal Arcade in Newcastle, built years later the three-naved, slightly curved Central Station. J. P. Cluysenaar, architect of the great arcade in Brussels, built the railway stations for whole stretches in Belgium. Finally, Joseph Paxton built conservatories and the Crystal Palace and planned the Great Victorian Way, which was to be an arcade, railway station, and street in one. The list could be extended; the interconnections are evident. In many places architects and engineers were simultaneously engaged in a search for a new form and structure for a transitional space.

The building type of the railway station developed in this period. It proceeded through a spatial development guided by the production possibilities of an already existing heavy industry. These possibilities themselves were owing to progress in the area of static methods, which had advanced from empirical observation to scientific circulation. The railway station was financed by capital which had been earned and reinvested in railroad speculation.[108] It became the expression or embodiment of the significance of railroad travel and the international expansion of trade.

There were three general phases of the architectural development of railway stations. The first stations,[109] like Euston Station in London by Philip Hardwich (1835–1837), were still aggregates of loosely connected structures—gate, reception building, post office, and platforms. The last were still covered by saddle roofs either with heavy wooden support structures, as in the first Lime Street Station in Liverpool, or with iron girder construction, as in Euston Station. Widths up to 30 meters could be spanned by trusses (French girders) and by parallel trussed girders (as in Manchester Station). In the second phase, in the 1840s, the first vaulted railway station halls were constructed. They were still multinaved and covered with many rows of wrought iron arched girders. These girders gave the halls an arcade-like effect because of the division and directed series of identical elements, both of which suggested movement. The system of arched girders, which carried the templates, which in turn carried the glass framing running parallel to the girders, constitutes glass-roof construction as employed in the Galleria Vittorio Emanuele in Milan and many Victorian arcades.[110]

In the third and final phase, monumental railway station architecture was introduced by extending the arched supports to arched truss beams. These new supports can be non-articulated arches, arches with spreaders (Zugstangen), or two- or three-jointed arches capable of spanning 75 meters, thereby covering all the platforms. The Anhalter station in Berlin, the first Grand Central Station in New York, and St. Pancras in London exemplify this phase. Parallel to the development in construction, the growth of dimensions, and the establishment of the transitional character of the railway station, occurred another development, which drew the many parts of the station into one building with a symmetrical, arcade-like cross section.[111] The architecture of the hall was the same as that of the surrounding parts—the dispatch and delivery agencies, the post office, the ticket windows, the offices, and the restaurants. The railway station became a building attached to an urban-architectural canon: the Gare de l'Est became a kind of city gate on the Boulevard de Sébastopol, an arcade or passage into faraway places. The pedestrian arcade played a subservient role within the large railway stations—as underpass, entranceway, or exit.

We encounter now a flood of projects and visions at the end of the nineteenth century which await systematic investigation. Their boldness can be compared only to the utopian London projects from the 1850s. They all strive radically to technologize and expand the metropolis, to raise traffic above the street level, and to cut across various planes. Long-distance railroads, subways, elevated cable cars, conveyor belts, escalators, elevators, tubes, and ramps were all new elements which met in a transitional point of intersection superseding the railway station. The 1963 sketch by Chalk and Harron for a city interchange (fig. 42) gives one conception of such a point of intersection.[112]

The discussion of the seven defining characteristics of the arcade should demonstrate that conceptions from the Orient, antiquity, the Middle Ages, and contemporary local models come together to create the arcade building type. This

40
London, King's
Cross Station

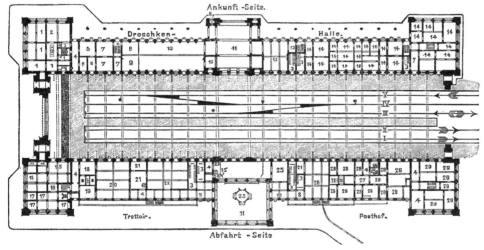

41
Berlin, Lehrter Bahn-
hof, plan

42
City interchange, de-
sign by Chalk and
Harron

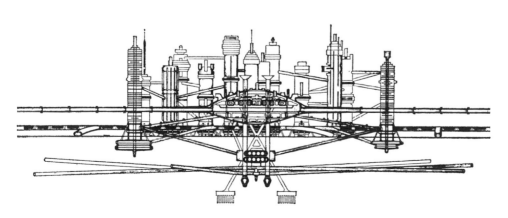

building type is therefore enmeshed in an almost inextricable web of historical relationships. Yet the character of the arcade remains constant throughout the nineteenth century. It expands its dimensions and its position in the public space of a city. It adapts to the stylistic currents of the time. It forms a part of the crystal world, the artificial city of glass and iron, of which Paul Scheerbart, at once epigone and prophet, dreamed in 1914:[113] ". . . and we would then have more precious things on the earth than the gardens from A Thousand-and-One Nights. We would then have paradise on earth and would not have to look up to the paradise in heaven with longing eyes." Thus he dreamed from the basement of his home in Zehlendorf; in reality the topic was long since outdated, for building officials had prohibited exposed iron in interior spaces because of the fire hazard, thereby signaling the death of the arcade.[114]

The French Revolution and the Model of the Palais Royal

The Revolution was in 1788 still a social and economic confrontation between the privileged and nonprivileged classes, between the nobility and clerisy on the one hand and the third estate on the other. However, after 1789 it was transformed into a "merciless confrontation between aristocracy and democracy,"[115] between the nobility, fiercely defending its privileges, and the new front of liberal theoreticians and politicians, representing not just the third estate but, so they believed, the whole nation. In these historically far-reaching confrontations, the public, in the form of public opinion, criticism, and pressure from the streets, played an ever greater role which is difficult to grasp. This well articulated public opinion created centers of activity in the countless salons, circles, secret societies, literary and political clubs, and cafés in and around the Palais Royal.[116] The discussion of the constitution and the temporary suspension of censorship of the press unleashed a flood of pamphlets, handbills, and political journals which were dispersed in the streets, placed in all the reading rooms, and passed around in cafés.

Jürgen Habermas describes this historical process as follows:[117]

The Revolution created the institutions which the politically conscious public had lacked. It created them overnight, and they were therefore less stable than those in England which were the result of a gradual development over centuries. There arise political clubs, from which the parliamentary factions are recruited, and a political daily press. The States General held their deliberations in public. Starting in August the daily *Journal des Débats et des Décrets* appears in order to give reports on parliamentary discussions. Just as important as this institutionalization of the political public is the legal normalization: the revolutionary process is interpreted and defined according to constitutional law. This is undoubtedly related to the fact that on the continent the bourgeois public becomes acutely aware of its actual or possible political functions. A terminological consciousness arises here which is better defined than its counterpart in contemporary England. The political functions of the public change quickly from the codification of the French revolutionary constitution to the mottos which spread across all of Europe. . . .

The pamphlets of 1788 and 1789 were dominated by three demands: declaration of human rights, formulation of the sovereign people, and creation of a new constitution. Those by Sieyès had the greatest impact.[118] He demonstrated in his pamphlet, *What Is the Third Estate?*, that the clergy was actually only an occupational class; that, because of its privileges, the nobility had become separate from the community of the people; and that therefore the third estate alone constituted the French nation. The years following the storming of the Bastille and the Declaration of Human Rights were dominated by attempts to prevent financial crisis. Hence all church property was expropriated and *assignats* were introduced. The ideal political and constitutional form was sought amidst constant threats from the other European powers and the ideological struggle within France.

A crucial conception for the formation of bourgeois society crystallized out of the discussions, reforms, and constitutional proposals: the distinction between active citizens, who were granted political rights, and passive citizens, who possessed only civil rights. The third estate, which for the first time conceived of itself as representative of the whole nation, procured for itself unique new rights that guaranteed ownership of private property. The third estate alone could vote and determine the political situation. The principle of equality was falsified as the principle of mere identity of interest.[119] Bakunin's maxim, that "the freedom of each is realized only in the freedom of all," points out the part of the French Revolution which is to this day unfulfilled.

The third estate consisted of wealthy bourgeois, businessmen, lawyers, and bankers, that is, those who had amassed their wealth through wars, monetary speculation, and food monopolies. It acquiesced in the end to a dictatorship of one man, the successful general, Napoleon. It saw in the dictatorship the escape from the Reign of Terror of the Jacobeans and the rising danger of the royalist reactionaries. The fourth constitution, which was chosen by the whole nation in a plebiscite, offered the appearance of a republic, but was in reality a military monarchy.[120] The constitution, and the laws that were based on it, institutionalized a liberal system of rights and guaranteed the profits of those who gained most from the Revolution and ensuing wars. It created the basis of the capitalist economy in France, free of governmental directives, and was regulated strictly according to the system of open competition. "Camille Desmoulins, Danton,

Robespierre, St. Juste, Napoleon, the heroes, as well as the parties and the masses of the old French Revolution, carried out the task of their time in Roman dress and with Roman phrases, the unleashing and setting up of bourgeois society. The former shattered the feudal turf and lopped off the feudal heads which grew upon it. Napoleon then created within France the conditions for the free development of competition, for the exploitation of parceled private property, and for the application of unbridled industrial productivity. . . ." Such is Karl Marx's characterization from his *Eighteenth Brumaire of Louis Bonaparte*.[121]

And so the arcade had its beginning in France, in Paris, in the Palais Royal, which had already played a role in the growth of public opinion. Desmoulins issued his great call to arms in its garden (fig. 43). This extensive palace, owned by the disreputable intriguer, the Duc d'Orléans, was an economically self-sufficient world, with its endless galleries, gardens, courtyards, avenues, fountains, cafés, theaters, gambling salons, clubs, brothels, shops, and apartments (rented by the Duke as a source of income for the maintenance of the palace). The Palais Royal was the first public urban space removed from the disturbances of traffic. It served as a site of political agitation, a promenade, luxury market, and place of learning and entertainment. It was, in short, a model of the arcade.

In the center of the Palais stood the prerevolutionary wooden structure, the "Champ des Tartares."[122] It was the first arcade with shops on both sides and illumination from above. It was a popular attraction of the city. According to Balzac's descriptions, every night it drew a public of legendary diversity and frivolity, a public consisting of members of each estate and social class. The Palais Royal, boulevards, and arcades united in a system of public space which was well protected for long stretches from all disturbances. Salons, foyers, promenades, cafés, galleries, and arcades combined to offer the postrevolutionary, emancipated urban public a place to convene. This place possessed a mag-

43
Paris, Camille Des-
moulins in the Palais
Royal, December 7,
1789, engraving by
Berthault

ical power of attraction for the rest of Europe, men of leisure, and the literati. It erased the distinction between interior and exterior, and made a new type of person possible, the predecessor of the "man of the crowd,"[123] the *flâneur*. Walter Benjamin has shown how this personality is related to the phenomenon of the arcade.[124]

After this brief sketch of the political background, the economic and social function of the arcade in this epoch can be partially explained by:

The need for public, undisturbed space

The search for new marketing possibilities for the luxury industry which blossomed as a result of the liberal legal system

The real estate that became available in the inner city as a result of expropriation and which was purchased and parceled by private speculators

The lack of sidewalks in Paris.

These four factors provide the prerequisites for the construction of the arcade and explain its popularity until the end of the Restoration.

The need for public, undisturbed space was recognized by speculators and exploited by industry. Arcades could be constructed because large connected plots of land in the inner city became available at low prices as a result of the expropriation of church property and the palaces of the nobility.[125] Land use was unaffected by governmental regulations, for the few regulations which did exist pertained only to facades and were therefore of little import to the construction of arcades.

The arcade came into fashion because the street still existed in its medieval state. It had no sidewalk, was dirty, and was too dangerous for promenading and window shopping. Hence, around 1800 society was more developed than the public space at its disposal. The amount of traffic on the narrow Parisian streets took on dangerous and threatening proportions at this time. Carriages and carts battled pedestrians. This unequal conflict was fought on poorly paved streets without drainage which were transformed by rain into a sea of mud. This theme and its particulars, which belong in every description of Paris of that period, is so important for the development of the fashion of the arcade that I will now provide a more detailed account of the development of the sidewalk.

The Sidewalk Although the sidewalk was a natural structure for the Romans, it disappeared when Rome was conquered from the north. Apart from Venice, where canals replace the street as the carrier of traffic, the sidewalk remained an unknown amenity for centuries. In 1606 Henry IV had the Pont Neuf built across the Seine.[126] On both sides of the road were higher levels separated by a wall and curbstones. These were promenades for pedestrians, which could be reached by stairs at the ends of the bridge. They were lined by small booths and vending stands. After the great fire of 1666 in London, sidewalks were provided on all reconstructed streets. Not until the middle of the eighteenth century were private attempts made to construct *trottoirs*[127] in Paris. Such sidewalks were, of course, only for exclusive streets, the Rue de l'Odéon, Rue Lafayette, Chaussée d'Antin, and Rue de Tournon. Yet, constantly traversed by driveways and generally built at different levels, they were nothing more than unconnected, protruding limestone curbs, serving to hold off carts. This kind of sidewalk was quite dangerous at night because one could easily stumble over its uneven path. On the old streets, which were too narrow for the construction of sidewalks, the only hope—indeed, sometimes the only salvation—for the pedestrian was the *borne,* which consisted simply of a few raised stones onto which one or two people could jump in order to avoid wagons. A first attempt to ameliorate the situation came with the boulevards.[128] In the middle was a walkway (*chaussée*) flanked by ditches and tree-lined promenades. Under the Consulat the ditches were filled and replaced by wooden barriers to separate the different portions. In 1811 these barriers were in turn replaced by round border stones.

The normal Parisian street of the eighteenth century was paved with square flat stones from Fontainebleu. A small gutter in the middle of the street provided drainage. It was supposed to carry the water to the Seine but in heavy rains it swelled to an impassable stream. In the Rue St. Honoré an attempt was made to place these gutters at the sides along the buildings, with the result that the water overflowed up to the shops and the doors could not be opened. The old system was quickly reinstated. Mercier gives a wonderful picture of the Parisian drains:[129] "Nothing could give a foreigner more pleasure than the sight of a Parisian with his elaborate wig, white stockings, and lace-trimmed suit, as he wades through or jumps over a muddy stream, runs through the filthy streets on tiptoe, and defends himself from the dripping roof gutters with his taffeta umbrella. How he jumps into the air when he leaves the Faubourg St. Honoré to eat and must dance around the dripping eaves! Piles of dirt, slippery pavement, greasy cart axles—so many dangers to avoid! And yet he reaches his destination. On each corner he summons a shoe-cleaner and arrives safely, with the exception of a few spots on his stockings. . . ."

In the Middle Ages the streets of Paris were no less congested, but the traffic consisted of slow cargo vehicles, riders, and pedestrians. In the seventeenth and eighteenth centuries, however, the decorative and faster variations of the carriage, the cabriolet, and the gig, were used as mass transportation. Their velocity increased the inequality between riders and pedestrians; accidents become as common as in the twentieth century, with the important difference that no form of ambulance service or insurance existed. Louis XV is quoted as saying:[130] "If I were the head of the police I would abolish these miserable cabriolets." And Pinkerton comments:[131] "The adventurers who recently have attained wealth and position in society, mimic with their carriages the former nobility in their craze to burn up the pavement (*brûler de pavé*). They race along like the wind and leave the cries of the crushed and run down pedestrians echoing in vain. . . ."

What must the pedestrian have been like who dared to move on these streets? What must his qualities have been? Here is a contemporary portrait:[132]

I have perfected my eyes to such a high degree that I can precisely measure the course of a 5½-foot horse which is bearing down on me with its head held high. Twenty paces in advance I can calculate the number of paces he will take to reach me. I see the point where the fateful wheel will sweep by, even taking into account a possible deviation from its course. I see that spot from which I depart and that spot, which the wheel must cross as a mid-point from which two divergent rays are sent . . . I am known throughout Paris by my head movements; I hold my head high and turn it around and around. In this way I avoid the cabriolets with lackeys galloping before. I do this with a precision which, I might well add, is one of my natural gifts. Have you, Sir, ever walked near the Palais Royal along the Rue Vivienne when the stock exchange is open? You will then be able to get an idea of the capabilities of my head in this matter. Actually, the capabilities of my legs are even greater. One can hardly believe the skill with which I dodge the wheels. Like a streak of lightning I skip over the drain canals; I slink by the boundary stones; push an idiot toward the mud; press, even paste myself to the wall to the shock of 20 ladies who envy my sense of security. Occasionally I must act quickly to escape a racing gig and save myself by a neck-breaking leap. How I have to laugh at the dressed up doll in the carriage as she stares with amazement at my fearlessness and my art in rescuing myself from thousands of dangers.

One can now easily appreciate the great enthusiasm that arose at the end of the eighteenth century with the construction of the new arcades of the Palais Royal, providing a completely interior promenade. Even before the first attempts at a uniform network of sidewalks under Napoleon, experiments were made with arcades. They were among the first areas of Paris accessible only to pedestrians. Others were the Pont Neuf, the Quais, the Tuileries, the Palais Royal, the first section of the Rue de Rivoli, the Rue des Colonnes, and the promenades along the boulevards.

Under the prefects of the Seine, Frochot and his successor, the Comte de Chabrol, the first comprehensive effort to construct a sidewalk system was begun;[133] but the program was plagued with indecision. Not until 1838 were the gutters removed from the middle of the streets. Then the streets acquired the profile which they have maintained to the present day.[134] In 1849 Kolloff gave a precise account of the condition of the sidewalks in Paris:[135] "The footpaths are, by the way, an essential improvement of the Parisian street system, although they are not as widespread as one would wish. The present combined length amounts to 181,500 meters, while the total length of the streets is 420,000 meters. Each year new stretches of sidewalks are added. The building owners are involved in their construction since pedestrians will thereby be drawn closer to their shops." Finally, Baron Haussmann and Alphand provided all of Paris with a subterranean sewage system and sidewalks. Precisely in this period the Parisian arcades began their decline.

The Arcade in the Nineteenth Century
The arcade was never an object of instruction. It was never chosen as the theme for the Prix de Rôme. It cannot be found in contemporary textbooks as an architectural exercise. The architectural concept of the arcade is promulgated anonymously, through travelogues, word-of-mouth reports, direct observation, and study of the arcade site itself. It is difficult to reconstruct an unambiguous, demonstrable course for the development of the arcade through the century. We lack, especially for the first stages, records, names of architects, building plans, and any statement of the builders concerning their motives. However, further into the century it becomes easier to establish the lines of development and mutual influences. Illustrated journals, architectural magazines, travel guides, prints, and albums disseminated the architectural concept over the whole world.

The developmental scheme shown in fig. 44 attempts to assemble the established connections into one picture. The scheme is vertically divided into chronological periods of twenty years, a division which proved very effective. The circle represents the place of origin, the larger rectangles represent the chain of models, and the smaller rectangles the arcades influenced by these prototypes. In general, only the names of the cities where the arcades are located are given. The connecting lines indicate the line of influence. Much in this scheme is doubtful and can probably never be cleared up because the arcades were private buildings, and hence clarifying records can usually no longer be found.

This section is divided into the following periods, corresponding to the vertical subdivision of the scheme:

1. The Period of Invention: up to 1820
2. The Period of Fashion: 1820–1840
3. Expansion: 1840–1860
4. The Monumental Phase: 1860–1880
5. The Movement toward Giganticism and Imitation: 1880–1900
6. The Decline of the Architectural Concept: Post-1900

As orientation for these topics, a chronological list of the most important arcades is given in the accompanying table.

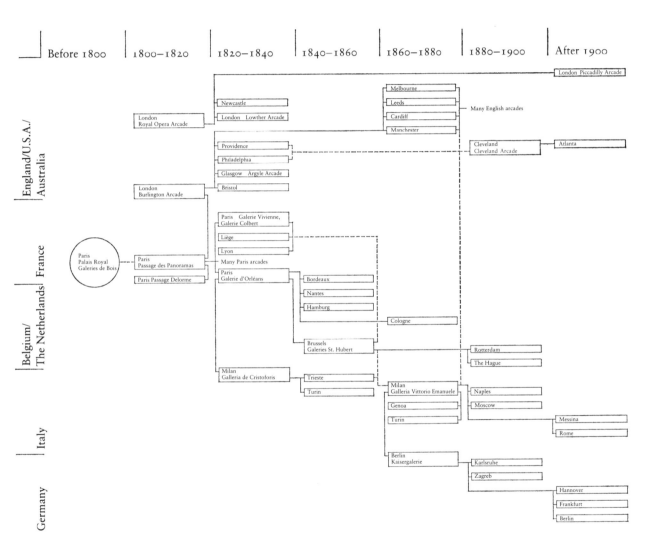

44
Developmental
schema of the arcade

Period	Arcade	City	Built
Pre-1820	Galeries de Bois	Paris	1786–1788?
	Passage Feydeau	Paris	1791?
	Passage du Caire	Paris	1799
	Passage des Panoramas	Paris	1800
	Passage Delorme	Paris	1808
	Passage Montesquieu	Paris	1811
	Royal Opera Arcade	London	1816–1818
	Burlington Arcade	London	1818–1819
	Passage de la Monnaie	Brussels	1820
1820–1840	Passage de l'Opéra	Paris	1823
	Galerie Vivienne	Paris	1825
	Passage Choiseul	Paris	1825
	Upper and Lower Arcade	Bristol	1825
	Galerie Colbert	Paris	1826
	Galerie Véro-Dodat	Paris	1826
	Passage du Saumon	Paris	1827
	Philadelphia Arcade	Philadelphia	1826–1827
	Argyle Arcade	Glasgow	1827?
	Passage de l'Argue	Lyon	1825–1828
	Weybosset Arcade	Providence	1827–1829
	Galerie d'Orléans	Paris	1828–1829
	Lowther Arcade	London	1829–1831
	Royal Arcade	Newcastle	1831–1832
	Galleria de Cristoforis	Milan	1831–1832
	Galerie Bordelaise	Bordeaux	1831–1834
	Passage Lemonnier	Liège	1837–1839
1840–1860	Passage Pommeraye	Nantes	1840–1843
	Exeter Arcade	London	1842–1843
	Sillem's Bazar	Hamburg	1842–1845
	Passage Jouffroy	Paris	1845
	Galeries St. Hubert	Brussels	1846–1847
	Queens' Arcade	Melbourne	1853
1860–1880	Königin Augusta Halle	Cologne	1863
	Galleria Vittorio Emanuele II	Milan	1865–1877
	Royal Arcade	Melbourne	1869
	Barton Arcade	Manchester	1871
	Kaisergalerie	Berlin	1869–1873
	Lancaster Avenue	Manchester	1873
	Galleria Subalpina	Turin	1874
	Great Western Arcade	Birmingham	1875
	Thornton's Arcade	Leeds	1878
	Passage	Rotterdam	1878–1879
	Royal Arcade	London	1879
1880–1900	Galleria Mazzini	Genoa	1880?
	Galleria Principe	Naples	1878–1882
	Passage du Nord	Brussels	1882
	Passage	The Hague	1883–1885
	Kaiser Passage	Karlsruhe	1887
	Queen's Arcade	Leeds	1888
	Cleveland Arcade	Cleveland	1888–1890
	Alexandra Arcade	Swansea	1890
	Galleria Nazionale	Turin	1890

Period	Arcade	City	Built
	Galleria Umberto I	Naples	1887–1891
	New Trade Halls	Moscow	1888–1893
	County Arcade	Leeds	1897
	City Arcades	Birmingham	1899
1900 and Post-1900	Kaiser Wilhelm Passage	Frankfurt am Main	1900
	Georgs Passage	Hannover	1901
	Central Arcade	Wolverhampton	1904
	Friedrichstraßenpassage	Berlin	1907
	Pariser Hof	Budapest	1909–1911
	Piccadilly Arcade	London	1912
	Mädler Passage	Leipzig	1914
	Peachtree Arcade	Atlanta	1916
	Galleria Piazza Colonna	Rome	1925?

The Period of Invention: up to 1820   I have found only one author who deals with the origins of the arcades in Paris: Kolloff. Many of his comments confirm the interpretation given in the last section:[136]

One can divide the arcades into two broad categories: open arcades and covered arcades, the latter being an improved version of the former. All are children of the same mother: industry; and all are still young. As long as the streets remained somewhat accessible to pedestrians and as long as the wagons left enough room for them, arcades were superfluous and unknown. However, luxury soon spread across the entire city like an oil slick, and the old gods fell to pieces, leaving just one symbol of belief, the franc, on the altar. Money, the only blood which filled the veins of the city, pumped faster and faster. Soon the streets of Paris offered their frightful spectacle, a spectacle of constant pushing, shoving, crushing—it almost would seem as if one-half of the population were paid to gallop incessantly behind the other. Retail trade withdrew from the center toward the great line of the northern boulevards where the traffic was not as congested and the pedestrian at least had side streets at his disposal. Then, so that the inner city could compete with the boulevards, speculation hit upon the arcade, which immediately found a favorable response. Large aggregates of buildings between two or three heavily populated streets were selected and cut through in such a way that the pedestrian could escape the terrible bustle of the street and shorten his way. The passageway was filled with two rows of nice open booths where the merchant's goods and the merchant's women noticeably take on their attractive forms. . . . The arcades mentioned so far, with the exception of a few newer structures, represent the old order of arcades. After invention comes perfection; after open arcades come closed arcades. The main purpose had not yet been fulfilled. It was not enough to save the pedestrian from the distress and anxiety of the street tumult; one had to attract him positively to the arcade so that once he put his foot in the faithless arcade he would feel himself caught by its magic and forget everything else. It all depended on the ability to build an arcade as bright as an open space, warm in winter, cool in summer, always dry and never dirty and dusty. . . .

What Kolloff depicts here as a sequence was not one in fact. Open and closed arcades appeared simultaneously. Their difference lies in their function: the former served manufacturing and were located in the industrial districts while the latter served luxury businesses.

In the period until 1820 few arcades were built: six in Paris, two in London, and a small one in Brussels. The two arcades listed first in the table have no overhead illumination but only a high side light (the original form of the roof of the third arcade on the list, the Passage du Caire, is uncertain). The Passage des Panoramas had a wooden saddle roof in which skylights were cut out, a method which can still be seen today in the Burlington Arcade in London. A Monsieur Delorme, the designer and builder of the Passage Delorme, is considered the inventor of the arcade;[137] he was perhaps the first to provide the arcade with a continuous glass roof. Unfortunately I have never been able to discover any material in Paris, not even a picture or plan, which could prove this claim.

All of these Parisian arcades are simple; that is, they have no architectural pretensions. They are merely the first attempts at a new building type. Narrow buildings with shops and apartments are lined up symmetrically and allow fewer than 3 meters for the promenade. Wood, plaster walls, skylights with small panes, show windows divided by square panes, and wooden doors are the ingredients; iron plays no role yet. The last in this group of Parisian arcades is the Passage Montesquieu near the Palais Royal. It originated in the reconstruction of a number of buildings. It was the site of the first experiment with public gas lighting by a method that unfortunately was banned by the police because of its strong odor.[138] The second attempt with an improved system took place in Paris in 1816 when Winsor, who had fled to Paris from London, illuminated a salon in the Passage des Panoramas. In 1817 he extended it to the entire arcade and to the boutiques of the Palais Royal.[139]

Between 1811 and 1823 no more arcades were built in Paris because the Napoleonic wars absorbed the country's energies. After Waterloo, Blücher and Wellington entered Paris, Louis XVIII and the emigrés returned to France, and all of Europe descended on the Palais Royal to celebrate the victory. I mention this because precisely in these years the first arcades outside of Paris were built in London. They were of the first type. Although Samuel Ware, the architect of the Burlington Arcade, referred to the local model of the Exchange, he employed a roof construction similar to that of the Passage des Panoramas.[140] Even the location and cross section proportions resembled those of the Parisian arcade: both cut through the side of a garden of a noble palace which, because of urban development, now lies in the middle of a business district and is used by the owners for profit.

The Royal Opera Arcade in London seems to have been a product of chance; it was a section of a colonnade which cut across a block interior and provided the older opera house with a continuous facade. The Royal Opera Arcade had only one row of small shops. The arcade space was illuminated by round skylights after the style of the Eastern bazaar. It was the prototype of a unique British variation of the arcade.

Two features were common to all these arcades from the period around the turn of the nineteenth century and from the two European capitals which were constantly competing in fashion, life-style, and form: their dimensions and the method of interior organization. A narrow, independently accessible, two- or three-storied building with a shop and apartment formed a unit which was then repeated in two parallel rows, rows which opened up into the still inadequately illuminated arcade space.

The Period of Fashion: 1820–1840 Ten years passed without the construction of a single arcade in either Paris or London. The reasons are undoubtedly to be found in the economic stagnation caused by the continental blockade, which resulted in the paralysis of private construction and general political uncertainty.

In France the Restoration followed the collapse of the Napoleonic Empire. The nobility and church won back much of their former influence. The suspension of the continental blockade opened the way for the liberal economic system (which already had a legal foundation), for the consolidation of markets, and for the unfolding of capitalist means of production. In the period 1820–1840 the arcade became once again the object of real estate speculation by wealthy citizens. In Paris fifteen new arcades were built before the July Revolution. At the same time the building type was imitated in other wealthy mercantile cities possessing a well developed public sphere—Milan, Lyon, Bordeaux, Brussels, Liège, Bristol, Glasgow, and Newcastle. Travels and travelogs made the building type known throughout the world and led famous architects to occupy themselves with this new cultural and architectural problem.

Debret built the Passage de l'Opéra in Paris as a double arcade in connection with the temporary home of the opera. J.-F. Delannoy, winner of the Prix de Rôme, extended the galleries of the Palais Royal on the north by constructing the sculptural, richly decorated Galerie Vivienne. Billaud built its great rival, the Galerie Colbert, with the first great rotunda at the angle in the concourse of the arcade. Rohault de Fleury took over the construction of the great Passage du Saumon. Tavernier executed one of the largest of the Parisian arcades, the Passage Choiseul. Pierre Fontaine, as the state architect who was involved in the restoration of the Palais Royal, had the old Galeries de Bois torn down and replaced by the first expansive vaulted arcade in the world.

These Parisian arcades, sometimes remarkable in their architectural execution, influenced the architecture of the provinces. Vincent Farges built the Passage de l'Argue in Lyon; Durand designed the Galerie Bordelaise in Bordeaux, which cuts through a block diagonally; Lemonnier built the arcade in Liège which crosses two blocks of buildings. Andrea Pizzale, after making an educational journey to Paris and England, built the first arcade on Italian soil, the Galleria de Cristoforis in Milan. Its interior facades are evidence of the impression left on the young architect by the Galerie d'Orléans, which had just been completed at the time of his visit. The arcade was built to satisfy the need expressed by upper-class Milanese citizens for a covered public promenade.[141]

In London, the Lowther Arcade was built in connection with the Strand improvements by John Nash. Newcastle received its formal counterpart, the Royal Arcade, which was built by the multitalented John Dobson. Both were based on the model of the Royal Opera Arcade in London; only the dimensions were altered. In Bristol, a commercial city which had prospered from the slave trade, James Foster constructed the Upper and Lower Arcades in the Greek Revival style. After studying and working in London, John Haviland left England in 1817 and built the first American arcades in Philadelphia and New York. While the facades show the influence of the Burlington Arcade, the structure of the interior strikes out in a new direction. The American as well as the later Victorian arcades were not used for housing. Hence all floors had to have galleries with rentable shops. This variant appeared for the first time in Philadelphia.

In American architectural history there are plenty of examples of continuous galleries and loggias in front of buildings.[142] Haviland certainly saw and employed them for his graduated organization of the arcade space. Russell Warren followed a few years later with the construction of the Weybosset Arcade in

Providence. The exterior facade of this arcade was systematically developed into a temple facade for the three-storied shopping center. All subsequent arcades on American soil are mere variations of this basic plan.

The galleries of the Palais Royal, the Passage des Panoramas, the Burlington Arcade, and the Royal Opera Arcade influenced the arcade fashion of this second period and brought about the international dissemination of this building concept. In the period 1820–1840 the arcade was varied and acquired a variety of appendage structures, like the temple, colonnade, bazaar, gallery, and promenade, all of which adorned the serious function and created a kind of canon. The uncommon demands placed on the architect by the ground plan, spatial profile, construction of the glass roof, and facades led to a variety of new conceptions. Parallel to this development, the structural possibilities of iron and glass expanded so greatly in this period that all kinds of glass-roof constructions could be erected.

By 1830 the arcade was complete; all its parts were fully developed. Longitudinal space, central space, frontal house, inner and exterior facades, continuous glass vault, and glass dome were established as the characteristics of a building type which itself became an indispensable means of opening up public space. Appearing in cities other than London and Paris, the arcade became a symbol of cultural modernity. It was no longer a part of the private sphere of speculation but was integrated into the larger interests of urban life.

The Expanded Dimension: 1840–1860 The Galerie d'Orléans in Paris, of all the arcades mentioned so far, was the one which exercised the most lasting influence on the next stage of the development of the building type. This was owing to its larger dimensions, its vaulted glass roof, and its interior facades, which were reproduced both in copies and variations.

The arcades of the second period were still exclusively private speculations. The landlords were bankers, land-owning nobility, lawyers, real estate entrepreneurs, and occasionally also *sociétés*, small corporations of investors. Many of these arcades had poorly chosen locations. If they did not serve any real function in regulating traffic, their success lasted only as long as the arcade was in fashion. The tragic fate suffered by many arcades brought the building type into disrepute; it seemed to be a risky enterprise. This explains, perhaps, why we find few arcades constructed in the third period.

Building speculation turned to railroad construction and urban expansion. A new style began to replace classicism and the Empire style. It permitted more extravagant decor and was more flexible and more appropriate for new, unsolved architectural problems. The arcade became old-fashioned. However, the new phenomenon of tourism, brought into being and to France by Baedeker and Thomas Cook, created a new public for the arcades. The Parisian arcades, for example, are mentioned in every mid-century depiction of Paris. Indeed, at no other time were the arcades described in greater detail.

After the July Revolution only a few arcades were built in Paris because retail trade found other, more effective forms of concentration and marketing. Furthermore, uniformly laid out sidewalks made them superfluous. The Passage Jouffroy with its northern extension, the Passage Verdeau, is the only new construction worth mentioning. It extended the Passage des Panoramas out beyond the boulevard. Later the Musée Grévin, the great Parisian wax-figure collection, was attached to it.

In 1847, the year of construction of the Passage Jouffroy, the prefect of police in Paris issued an ordinance which replaced and stiffened the 1811 ordinance for the galleries of the Palais Royal. Article 7 was the most important clause; it stated that in the future no arcade on private property could be made accessible to the public without permission of the prefect of police. In 1847, then, one year before Prince Louis Napoleon was elected president for ten years, and six years before Haussmann became the prefect of the Seine, the arcade was virtually forbidden. In the thorough reshaping of Paris by Haussmann, the now too narrow arcades completely lost their function—the city, striving toward wide perspectives and long avenues, entered a new dimension of public space.

Therefore, the third stage of arcade building took place neither in Paris nor London (where only the small Exeter Arcade was built) but in the second order of cities—Brussels, Hamburg, Nantes, and Trieste. Each of these cities introduced in its own way a new dimension to the arcade. All four of them considered the arcade in the context of the city as a whole and as part of an urban renewal program, and they engaged in lengthy planning before starting construction.

In Trieste, which was still under Austrian rule, the architect Buttazoni planned El Tergesteo, the first arcade with a cruciform plan and the first to occupy a whole block. The interior plan was undoubtedly influenced by the Galleria de Cristoforis in Milan. El Tergesteo was constructed in 1840–1842 by F. Bruyn in reduced form, that is, without the vaulted glass roof planned by Buttazoni. The construction was commissioned by an association of Trieste merchants. In this example, one can observe another fundamentally new element: the arcade stands on its own, acts as a downtown public building, connects two squares, and is flanked by the theater and stock exchange. This siting and the cruciform plan recur twenty years later in Milan; it is therefore likely that Mengoni, the architect of the great Galleria Vittorio Emanuele, was familiar with El Tergesteo.

In Hamburg the great fire of May 5–8, 1842, reduced the old city to ashes and opened up the center for a magnificent plan of reconstruction. The plans by Semper and Châteauneuf created the basis for a radical modernization of the old city, which had been a maze of alleys and canals. Sillem's Bazar, by Averdieck, is one of the first buildings which arose out of these plans. Moreover, it was the first arcade on German soil, and, for many years, the largest in existence—as was proudly pointed out in Hamburg. Averdieck must have seen the Galerie d'Orléans in Paris on one of his numerous journeys, for the resemblance in interior plan and glass roof construction is readily apparent. The spatial profile, however, is quite new. It no longer has the dimensions of an alley but of a regular street. The citizens of Hamburg promenaded with amazement through the splendrously illuminated bazaar. Unfortunately, it was located between two unequally frequented streets and was therefore fully populated only during the great Christmas bazaar. It stood until 1881.

Sillem's Bazar was surpassed a few years later by the Galeries St. Hubert in Brussels's old city. The architect, Cluysenaar, had made the initial proposals in 1838, but construction did not commence until 1846. This project must be viewed against the background of the Belgian revolt of 1830. Belgium seceded from the Kingdom of the Netherlands (created by the Congress of Vienna), made Leopold I the King of the Belgians, and continued to fight with Holland until 1839. Brussels, the capital of the new nation, searched for an expression of national independence. This is the function of the Galeries St. Hubert. The project is without its like anywhere. The arcade was supposed to introduce the modernization of the old city and symbolize the new role of Brussels as capital. For a decade Cluysenaar waged a campaign in his writings and speeches for his idea of providing Brussels with a Palais Royal. Behind him stood a consortium of financiers under the directorship of the city administration. Even Leopold I supported the project and was the first to walk through the arcade. The dimensions of the arcade can be compared only with those of the Crystal Palace, which was built some years later. In the Galeries St. Hubert the arcade became a street. The building complex of the Galeries was so massive that it could not be undertaken by private initiative alone. The idea of giving the city a cosmopolitan flavor led directly to government intervention in both the financing and the design of the project. Parliament became involved, since it had to approve the extensive and unpopular expropriations.

Cluysenaar, a follower of Fourier, was a multitalented architect.[143] He had experimented in Antwerp with a smaller arcade and had spent a long time in Paris analyzing the arcades in detail and learning from their fates. He also was familiar with the arcades in nearby Liège, and their siting and arrangement—two arms separated by a street—may have influenced his own project. He placed great emphasis on the function of the arcade as a traffic artery. He understood the model of the Palais Royal and therefore incorporated into his own arcade a theater, vaudeville, restaurants, and club rooms, thereby guaranteeing a continuous flow of visitors who considered the arcade the meeting place of the city. It was Cluysenaar's declared intention to surpass all existing structures. For nearly a decade he struggled against private and public objections and intrigues for the realization of his conceptions. He finally erected the building in one year with an army of workers. The Galeries St. Hubert form the connecting link between the Parisian arcades and the great arcade of Milan, whose architect, Mengoni, is said to have consulted Cluysenaar in person.[144]

The fourth arcade to be treated in this section is located in Nantes. There the architects Durand-Gosselin and Buron built the Passage Pommeraye with the capital of a wealthy lawyer from Nantes. It was their goal to surpass the Parisian arcades. The result was an architectural panopticon. With guards at the doors, it would be a complete museum of the nineteenth century. The arcade is divided into two stylistically heterogeneous parts which are connected by a more than 9-meter-tall stairway. The stairway is extended to a glass-covered arcade space by means of continuous, column-borne galleries. This arcade space is perhaps the best illustration of what Sternberger, in relation to the interior, calls the "indoor Orient,"[145] which begins with the use of forms from the Renaissance and the Orient. The Passage Pommeraye still exists, with all the paraphernalia of the period: the advertising tablets, signs, and decorations. It is a veritable treasure which had been nearly forgotten until its rediscovery by the surrealists.[146]

In England, Queen Victoria ascended to the throne in 1837 and a new period of architectural history began. Although, to my knowledge, no arcades were built in the period 1840–1860, a number of utopian projects were formulated to solve London's traffic problems, solutions that employed arcade-like structures. Gye, Moseley, and later Paxton proposed the radical solution of multileveled arcades, each level for a different mode of transportation. The passages connect the most important points of intersection in the city: railway stations, squares,

RÈGLEMENT

DES GALERIES SAINT-HUBERT

Le Conseil d'Administration de la Société Civile des Galeries St-Hubert,

A arrêté le règlement suivant :

ENTRÉE DE CHARBONS, BOIS, PROVISIONS VOLUMINEUSES, MARCHANDISES, MEUBLES, etc.

ARTICLE PREMIER. — Le déchargement des charbons, bois, marchandises, meubles et tous objets arrivant par voiture, devra avoir lieu de la manière suivante :

Pour la Galerie de la Reine.

Au Marché-aux-Herbes, vers la rue de la Montagne, pour les maisons et entrées d'appartements portant les numéros 1 à 15 inclusivement.

Au Marché-aux-Herbes, vers le Marché-aux-Poulets, pour les numéros 2 à 20.

Grande Rue des Bouchers, vers la rue de la Montagne, pour les numéros 17 à 31.

Grande Rue des Bouchers, vers la rue de la Fourche, pour les numéros 22 à 36.

Pour la Galerie du Roi.

Grande Rue des Bouchers, vers la rue de la Montagne, pour les numéros 1 à 15.

Grande Rue des Bouchers, vers la rue de la Fourche, pour les numéros 2 à 18.

Rue de l'Ecuyer, vers la rue d'Arenberg, pour les numéros 17 à 33.

Rue de l'Ecuyer, vers la rue Léopold, pour les numéros 20 à 36.

Dans la grande Rue des Bouchers, les voitures devront toujours stationner du côté le plus proche des maisons auxquelles les objets sont destinés.

Pour le Passage du Prince.

Rue des Dominicains, du côté des maisons auxquelles les objets à décharger sont destinés, de manière à ne point obstruer l'entrée du Passage.

Pour les maisons ayant une entrée à la rue.

Les déchargements devront avoir lieu devant cette entrée.

ART. 2. — Le déchargement des objets susmentionnés, ainsi que le nettoyage des Galeries, devra être terminé au plus tard à 8 heures du matin.

ART. 3. — Le charbon menu et celui dit gailletteries ne pourront être amenés, pesés et transportés qu'en sacs ou en paniers. Le gros charbon ne pourra être déversé sur le sol des Galeries et aucun charbon ne pourra être rentré par les soupiraux des caves donnant dans les Galeries.

Les porteurs ne pourront pas passer sur le trottoir voisin du lieu de déchargement.

ART. 4. — Si la rue ou les Galeries se trouvent salies par le déchargement ou par le transport des objets susmentionnés, le destinataire devra immédiatement faire opérer le nettoyage nécessaire.

ART. 5. — Les marchandises arrivant par les voitures des chemins de fer ou messageries sont seules exceptées des dispositions de l'Article deux, aucune autre dérogation ne pourra avoir lieu sans l'autorisation préalable et écrite de l'Administration de la Société.

ENLÈVEMENT DES CENDRES, IMMONDICES, etc.

ART. 6. — Les cendres, immondices, etc., devront être versés dans le tombereau de la ferme des boues, qui stationnera, à cet effet, sous le péristyle de la grande Rue des Bouchers, pendant une demi-heure de 6 1/2 heures jusqu'à 7 heures du matin depuis le 1er Avril jusqu'au 31 Octobre et de 7 à 7 1/2 heures depuis le 1er Novembre jusqu'au 31 Mars.

ART. 7. — Les gardes interdiront l'approche du tombereau des Galeries aux chiffonniers, et un des gardes devra assister au transfert des immondices dans le tombe-

reau de la ferme des boues ; il devra prévenir toute poussière au moyen d'un arrosage continue.

ART. 8. — Aucun bac, seau, etc., renfermant des cendres, ordures, ou tout autre objet, ne pourra être déposé dans les Galeries, dans les entrées des escaliers d'appartements, ou dans les corridors et paliers qui en dépendent, ainsi que dans les couloirs de caves.

LAVAGE DU SOL DES GALERIES

ART. 9. — Les locataires qui feront laver le dallage des Galeries, devant leur maison, devront le faire effectuer jusqu'à la moitié de la largeur de la Galerie, en se conformant aux heures prescrites à l'article deux.

RASSEMBLEMENT DEVANT LES ÉTALAGES DES MAGASINS.

ART. 10. — Les rassemblements nombreux devant les vitrines des magasins, étant nuisibles aux voisins et contraires à l'Ordonnance de police les locataires devront, sur l'invitation de l'Administration de la Société, faire cesser l'exhibition qui serait la cause des rassemblements.

ENTRÉE DES ESCALIERS D'APPARTEMENTS, SERVICES DES CONCIERGES, etc.

ART. 11. — Il est interdit aux locataires, aux concierges et aux domestiques des locataires de stationner aux portes.

ART. 12. — Les concierges doivent laver et tenir dans un parfait état de propreté les entrées, marches, paliers, rampes et murs d'escaliers Ils doivent épousseter de plus toutes les parties des cages d'escaliers, en se conformant aux heures de l'article deux.

Ils doivent recevoir les commissions, lettres et paquets, francs de port, destinés aux locataires, et leur en faire la prompte et fidèle remise.

Ils doivent allumer le gaz de l'escalier à la chute du jour.

Il est prescrit aux concierges d'être de la plus grande politesse à l'égard des locataires et des personnes qui viennent chez eux.

ART. 13. — Les locataires des appartements sont invités à monter avant 9 heures du matin, l'eau ou les objets susceptibles d'être répandus sur les escaliers.

Il est interdit de faire le lavage des planchers de manière à tacher les plafonds inférieurs : les dommages occasionnés par les locataires contrevenants seront à leur charge.

Il ne pourra être déposé ni charbon, ni coke, ni copeaux, ni paille dans les chambres ou dans les greniers et mansardes.

ART. 14. — Il est interdit aux locataires occupant les étages, de rien jeter ou laisser tomber par les croisées, soit des cours, soit des Galeries, ni de rien secouer ou battre aux dites croisées ou portes d'appartements.

ATTRIBUTIONS DES GARDES PRÉPOSÉS AU NETTOYAGE

ART. 15. — Le service des gardes chargés du nettoyage des Galeries comprend :

A. La tenue dans un état permanent de propreté des voies publiques des Galeries, ainsi que des colonnes des péristyles d'entrée.

Ce travail doit se faire de manière à éviter toute poussière, et être terminé la première fois de la journée à 7 1/2 heures du matin.

B. L'arrosage des mêmes voies et de leurs abords, lorsqu'il est prescrit par l'Administration de la Société.

C. La surveillance et l'arrosage journalier des cendres et immondices, conformément aux dispositions de l'article sept.

D. Le nettoyage des appareils d'éclairage, leur allumage et la surveillance du luminaire, qui doit être maintenu d'une manière régulière jusqu'à son extinction.

E. Il est prescrit aux gardes de répondre avec politesse aux observations que les locataires croiraient devoir leur faire au sujet de leur service.

ART. 16. — Les agents des Galeries St-Hubert sont chargés de veiller à l'exécution du présent règlement.

ARTICLE GÉNÉRAL

Les locataires sont priés de vouloir bien donner avis à l'Administration de la Société des infractions, négligences, infidélités, etc., qui viendraient à leur connaissance dans le service des gardes, concierges et agents.

Un exemplaire du présent règlement sera délivré à chaque locataire des Galeries et sera affiché dans les loges des concierges et des gardes.

Arrêté par le Conseil d'Administration de la Société à Bruxelles, le 3 Décembre 1898.

Au nom du Conseil d'Administration.

L'Administrateur-Délégué :
Guillaume HOORICKX

L'Administrateur-Président :
Émile DE MOT

VILLE DE BRUXELLES

Ordonnance de Police pour les Galeries St-Hubert.

ART. 1. — Il est interdit de former des rassemblements ou de stationner en groupes de manière à gêner la circulation à l'intérieur ou à l'entrée des Galeries St-Hubert.

Les personnes faisant partie des rassemblements ou des groupes devront se disperser à la première injonction qui leur en sera faite par les agents de la police locale.

ART. 2. — Tout colportage ou distribution d'objets quelconques est interdit dans les Galeries St-Hubert, ainsi que sur les trottoirs des façades.

Le stationnement des commissionnaires y est également interdit.

ART. 3. — Les contraventions aux dispositions qui précèdent seront punies de peines de simple police.

ART. 4 — La présente ordonnance sera publiée en la forme ordinaire.

Ainsi arrêté en séance du Conseil communal, le 9 Janvier 1899.

Par le Conseil :

Le Secrétaire
A. DWELSHAUVERS

Le Conseil
BULS.

Extrait de l'Ordonnance de Police sur la voirie

ART. 44. — Il est défendu de faire circuler ou stationner sur les trottoirs des chevaux, voitures, charrettes, brouettes, etc., d'y faire rouler des tonneaux, d'y placer des caisses, etc., d'y circuler avec des échelles, civières et autres fardeaux analogues et d'y déposer, même momentanément, aucun objet qui puisse gêner la circulation.

ART. 46. — Les Galeries St-Hubert sont assimilées aux trottoirs, en ce qui concerne les prohibitions reprises en l'Article 44. Toutefois les charbons, bois, provisions volumineuses, marchandises, meubles, etc., destinés à l'approvisionnement des habitants des Galeries, pourront y être transportés jusqu'à huit heures du matin.

Ainsi arrêté en séance du Conseil communal le 5 Juillet 1897.

Par le Conseil :

Le Secrétaire
A. DWELSHAUVERS

Le Conseil
BULS

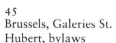

45
Brussels, Galeries St. Hubert, bylaws

the City, and the West End. The plans, which were all presented to the Committee for Metropolitan Improvements, were simply put on file, not only because of the enormous expenditures, but also because of the threat such enterprises posed to the network of small private interests that was embodied in the London city plan. These gigantic projects must be seen in the light of the euphoria which arose with the world's fairs. For the first time, the arcade was conceived of as a carrier of traffic on an independent plane.

The Monumental Phase: 1860–1880   The next development of the arcade building type occurred in Milan. Here the arcade developed into monumentality, into the emancipation of the public building, into a promenade in the manner of Roman baths, and into the secular counterpart of the cathedral. The reason for building was, even more clearly than in Brussels, political—the unification of Italy.

With the support of France, the liberation of Northern Italy from Austrian domination began in Sardinia. The battle of Solferino on June 24, 1859, decided the struggle. Turin became the provisional capital, and one of its residents, the later Vittorio Emanuele II, became King of Italy. The Galleria in Milan is named after him, as the arcade in Genoa is named after Mazzini, and the arcade in Naples after Umberto I. This is the building that nearly everyone associates with the term arcade. It resulted from a long series of competitions for the monumental development of the cathedral square. The first of these competitions was opened to the public by the city on July 27, 1860. There followed a number of smaller competitions with a limited number of participants. Gradually the idea of a public covered promenade crystallized out of the numerous plans to build a major new structure between the cathedral and the Scala. The Bolognese architect Mengoni received the commission.

Mengoni's original proposal consisted of an arcade with a polygonal, dome-covered space in the middle. In the final version, however, he extended this plan into a figure of a cross, even though the traffic pattern did not warrant this form. He sought symbolic forms, based on historical models, which could legitimize the new nation: the Roman triumphal arch as gateway; the inferior spatial proportions of ancient baths; the dome above a cross, the diameter of which was exactly that of the dome of St. Peter's in Rome (see the catalog). If the nearby cathedral represents the body of Christ, then the arcade represents a kind of pantheon of bourgeois society. It is decorated with four allegorical frescoes depicting Science, Art, Industry, and Agriculture, and twenty-four statues of famous Italians; it is filled with the noise of the crowd that incessantly moves through it.

The Galleria Vittorio Emanuele II incorporates an arsenal of historical references. It represents an attempt to give the city and the society, with its rising national consciousness, a new center. This is the first time in the history of the arcade building type that a competition was held and that the city was the landlord. The arcade was built by an English consortium called the City of Milan Improvement Company, Ltd. A French engineer provided the specifications for the iron construction and an Italian architect designed the building. Hence, the arcade was the product of international cooperation. On May 7, 1865, the King laid the cornerstone in the center of the octagonal rotunda; two years later the arcade was dedicated; not until a decade later was the triumphal arch on the piazza completed, from which the architect fell to his death. The effect of the Galleria Vittorio Emanuele was extraordinary and not to be compared with the response to any earlier arcade. To my knowledge, for example, the Galeries St. Hubert in Brussels has never been mentioned in an architectural journal.

The arcade was widely publicized—from the daily press, which celebrated the opening as a national event, to the illustrated magazines, which viewed it as a fairy-tale building. Thanks to detailed accounts in the many new architectural journals, the arcade was known to architects in the farthest provinces. Three levels of architectural-historical influences can be distinguished:

1. An immediate, national effect in other competing cities within Italy, which was still being unified in stages
2. A long-term effect in the English speaking countries—England, Australia, and America—through publications in *The Builder*
3. A direct effect on the Kaisergalerie in Berlin, which was built a few years later with similar political motives.

When the Galleria Vittorio Emanuele was completed, the Kingdom of Naples, Venice, and parts of the Papal States had not yet joined the union. The rest of Italy was composed of independent city-states with old traditions and old feuds. Even after the crowning of Vittorio Emanuele as King of Italy, these cities continued their competition for economic and political leadership of the country. This struggle for the leading role was expressed in the declared intention of other cities to match Milan's arcade with their own buildings.

Turin, which was mourning the end of its reign as provisional capital, built the Galleria Nazionale and the Galleria Subalpina; Genoa built one of the most voluminous arcades, the Galleria Mazzini, named after its freedom-fighter; Naples built first the Galleria Principe di Napoli and then the Galleria Umberto I, named after the successor of Vittorio Emanuele. The great arcade of Naples was also the product of various proposals and financial arrangements. It even surpasses its Milanese counterpart in some of its dimensions. The competition between the two buildings was taken very seriously; the reports argued about every centimeter. The Neopolitan arcade is short and imitates the cross form, but it is taller and wider, and its dome has a slightly larger diameter. Much later and farther to the south, in Messina, another arcade was built. It was dedicated to Vittorio Emanuele III. The series of competing arcades set off by the Milanese monument ended with the project for an arcade on the Piazza Colonna in the middle of Rome's old city. An army of architects participated in the task, some of them offering plans of gigantic dimensions but they ultimately burned themselves out in the process. The solution, finally constructed in the 1920s, was petty, the distilled result of too many discussions and participants; it was already an anachronism. And yet it is this series of great Italian arcades, each striving for a monumentality on the Roman scale, which has become permanently connected in our minds with the concept of the arcade. This series, one might say, represents the arcade.

The arcade in Milan also led to a development in a completely different direction. In 1868 a photographically illustrated article on the Galleria Vittorio Emanuele appeared in *The Builder*. It introduced the English architectural community to one of the great continental arcades. By 1871 the Burton Arcade had been built in Manchester, one of the first larger arcades of the Victorian period.

It was undoubtedly influenced by the Milan arcade. More than one hundred arcades followed the one in Manchester in the decades between 1840 and 1870. Almost all were built, not in old cities with historic centers, but in the countless new urban centers—products of the Industrial Revolution. These new areas were the nodal points of the English trade network, a system which dominated the world as a result of its duty-free products. Asa Briggs characterizes these Victorian industrial and commercial cities:[147] "These Cities are the cities of the railway and tramway age, of the age of steam and of gas, of a society sometimes restless, sometimes complacent, moving, often fumblingly and falteringly, toward greater democracy. The building of the cities was a characteristic Victorian achievement, impressive in scale but limited in vision, creating new opportunities but also providing massive new problems."

In these cities the nineteenth century showed its other side, the darker side which Engels unmasked without mercy. These cities exemplified most forcibly the social condition of the crass and stark contrast between dominating and dominated classes. No urban planning, no social balance regulated or softened the contrast. Liverpool, Manchester, Birmingham, Leeds, Bradford, and Huddersfield; the cities of the coal district of Wales; the centers of steel manufacturing and textile trade; and the centers of colonial expansion like Sydney and Melbourne—these are the cities in which, during the three decades between 1840 and 1870, many arcades were built to serve purely commercial functions—a phenomenon that can be explained by examining the structure of the centers of these cities.

The impression that the celebrated arcade in Milan made on the small architectural firms which joined together in commercial undertakings is just one of the reasons for the construction of the arcades. Other impulses probably came from national models, like Paxton's Crystal Palace and the Coal Exchange in London, with its open spaces formed by continuous galleries. All Victorian arcades served commercial functions. They no longer served luxury trade and promenades, but the normal needs of expanded classes of consumers who flowed daily into the crowded, fully developed downtown area, no longer used as a residential district. The continuous galleries on all floors were the typical feature of all Victorian arcades. They enabled a commercial use of all floors and easy accessibility for the public. The arcades were a part of the unlimited prosperity, the optimism, and the resulting building speculation which characterized the Victorian era. The popularity of these covered promenades in rainy climates led to imitation in smaller cities as well.

The structure of the Victorian city was precisely described as early as 1845. The following is from Engels's description of Manchester, where one of the first arcades of this period was built:[148]

The city itself is uniquely built, so that one could live in it for years and go in and out of it every day without ever coming in contact with a workers' district, indeed without seeing a single worker—so long, namely, as one keeps to one's business or promenades. This is chiefly a result of the fact that, through unconscious, unspoken agreement, as well as through conscious, declared intention, the working quarters have been sharply separated from the quarters left to the middle class. Where the separation is not complete, they are covered with the cloak of charity. Manchester contains in its center a somewhat extended commercial district, about a half mile square. It consists almost exclusively of factories and warehouses. Almost the entire district is uninhabited and during the night desolate and barren—only the watchful policemen slink with their lanterns through the narrow, dark alleyways. This neighborhood is crossed by a few major avenues which bear the enormous mass of traffic and are lined with bright shops on the ground floor. Here and there these streets also have apartments in the upper stories. These areas usually have quite a lot of street life well into the night. With the exception of this commercial district, the entirety of Manchester is a workers' quarter which circles the commercial district like a one-and-a-half-mile-wide belt. Beyond this belt are the residences of the upper class and middle bourgeoisie. . . . The picture which Engels paints of Manchester is typical for these cities. It is still valid today to some extent.

The third influence of the Milanese Galleria Vittorio Emanuele is in the north, where Germany was being formed into a national state under Prussian leadership. The very active architectural firm Kyllmann and Heyden built the Kaisergalerie (1869–1873) in Berlin on the most prominent intersection of the time: the corner of the Friedrichstrasse and Unter den Linden. In Germany, as opposed to Italy, political unification followed economic union. The motivating force was the Zollverein, the tariff union, founded in 1833. The trade agreements with neighboring states, the industrial rise of Prussia thanks to its farsighted and liberal laws, the systematic construction of the transportation network, including the railroads, and the nationalization of foreign capital all required economic union. The way for Bismarck's political efforts had already been prepared by Rudolf von Delbrück, who created a unified German economy. His means were the guarantee of free competition, introduction of a uniform weights and measures system, institution of new trade rights, and the suspension of the law that required government permission for the establishment of joint stock companies. "Not until the suspension of the law requiring permission was the door opened to lucrative large banking firms. It created the framework of liberal free trade in which the founding of new banks and industries could take place."[149]

The foundation of the North German Alliance and the victory over the French army in 1871 were spectacular political successes to match the earlier economic successes. Together they drew the southern states into the arms of Prussia. The reparations imposed on France amounted to billions of dollars and were pumped into the German economy. Böhme describes Germany's situation after the victory over France:[150]

The call for the emperor and the empire (Reich) finally drew the majority of the population, especially the liberal German nationalists, politically to Prussia's side. In the face of the enthusiasm over the reestablishment of the empire southern German independents and the democratic parliamentarian opposition became suddenly and surprisingly quiet. The population of the new empire accepted the tradition of Prussia as a German tradition. The national enthusiasm over the established unification joined the euphoria over the advantages of the economically successful politics of Delbrück. The war and the ensuing war inflation revived the economy. Freed from political risks, driven by the billions from the French reparations, the prosperity gave way to a boom of economic growth. In less than three years Germany joined the other Western European industrial producers.

The Kaisergalerie in the new capital of the Reich was built by one of the countless newly founded shareholding companies, the Aktien Bauverein Passage. Berlin's self-image as the new German commercial and political metropolis manifested itself in the construction of the arcade. The arcade introduced Berlin to the ranks of cosmopolitan cities. The Kaisergalerie, with its refined, polygonal ground plan (betraying the influence of the Schinkel school), with its continuous terra-cotta facade and massive show windows, was Berlin's first "modern" commercial building.[151] The arcade offered the awakening big city not only an alleviation of traffic on that narrow section of the Friedrichstrasse, but also a close conglomeration of amenities—a concert hall, conference rooms, club rooms, post office, cafés, restaurants, and a hotel. Its complex spatial program resembles that of the Galeries St. Hubert in Brussels rather than the simpler organization found in Milan. This first arcade in Berlin, the symbol of the rising modern city, was opened in 1873 and was frantically celebrated by the population. For the opening the emperor rode through the arcade with his entourage, surrounded by his jubilant subjects—hence the name "Kaisergalerie." Soon thereafter it was the stage for the first public system of electric illumination.[152]

The Kaisergalerie, which, like most German arcades, was destroyed in World War II, was praised and admired in illustrated journals and became a model for cities oriented toward Berlin. In the following decades a whole series of more modest Kaiser-Wilhelm arcades appeared in smaller German cities, for example, in Frankfurt and Karlsruhe. Just as the Milanese arcade attempted to give a tradition to the recently united Italian nation, the Kaisergalerie attempted to fortify the claim for leadership made by Prussia and its capital, Berlin.

The Movement toward Giganticism and Imitation: 1880–1900   This period is characterized by the transfer of the theater of war to countries outside Europe, by imperialist conquests, and by the division of the world among the great colonial powers. It introduced the "Belle Epoque" on the continent. The center was Paris. Society was divided by an unbreachable gulf. A small, undirected part began to enjoy the fruits of its mercilessly attained prosperity; the other, evergrowing part began to consolidate in order to make its demands heard. Architecture was transformed into an overflowing stylistic bazaar which outdid itself in its offers. The facade became an end in itself, so independent that it concealed where it should express. It became a stage set where it was no longer desirable to perceive real conditions. Its dimensions evaporated into the gigantic and the monstrous, becoming theatrical gestures. There is a tendency to think of the nineteenth century as a revival of the Roman Empire; yet the criteria are misconceived. The Palace of Justice in Brussels, the World Exhibition buildings in Paris, and the Reichstag in Berlin are examples of a hopeless gigantomania. The century attempted to present itself in these examples in order to pass on its unresolved oppositions to a new, more radical century.

Roger Shattuck[153] exposes the caricature of the period, already developed at that time. He writes in his fascinating book, *The Banquet Years*, of the Paris world exhibition:

After such a stunning success in 1889, Paris staged for the new century a still more fabulous and universal fair; it had been under construction for ten years. The nineteenth centenary of the birth of a certain well-known religious figure was not prominently featured. For more than a year after the April opening, the banks of the Seine for a mile on both sides of the Trocadero were transformed by exotic buildings—or at least exotic façades. Paris looked and acted like an overblown Venice.

Both expositions lay at the feet of the same gigantic monument . . . the Eiffel Tower. . . . This great anomaly of modern engineering expressed all the aspirations of a period which set out to surpass its heritage. And it remained: styleless, functionless, unhistoried, and soon as familiar as an *urinoir*. . . . The Eiffel Tower in its truculent stance is the first monument of modernism. [Quoted from Shattuck, *The Banquet Years*, pp. 17–18.]

Next to this tower, which is celebrated today as the ingenious product of engineering, the arcades no doubt take a modest second place. Yet in the arcades, too, one sees the movement toward giganticism. The imitations have already been mentioned: the mass of Victorian arcades, the majority of which belong in this period, and the many arcades derived from those of the great cities like Berlin, Brussels, and Milan.

If the Eiffel Tower was for a long time the tallest building on earth, the New Trade Halls in Moscow were the largest arcade complex built in the nineteenth century. In Moscow, in Red Square across from the Kremlin, this gigantic bazaar replaced an entire district of heterogeneous constructions with a single building. This building is traversed by three parallel arcade spaces extending nearly 250 meters, which are connected by spaces crossing at right angles. These three arcades are independent of the city's traffic pattern and provide access to more than one thousand units on three levels by means of continuous galleries, shortcuts over bridges, and opposed stairways. In these rooms, movement through the crisscrossing, penetrating, and overlapping levels becomes an event. In the structure of the New Trade Halls, the arcade broke away from the feature which had defined it for a century, namely that it must connect something. It became a total system of open space and accessibility, according to which one could organize an entire city. This structure suggests most clearly the future of the arcade.

Its counterpart is the gigantic, arena-like Cleveland Arcade in the United States. It spans two frontal structures which are early high-rise buildings. Its interior is made accessible on all five stories by galleries and stairs. The iron construction that bears the glass roof grows forth out of the galleries and becomes more independent as it rises. The Cleveland Arcade is, therefore, a colossal steel skeleton with an arcade space cut out of the center like a light well. It is the extension of an earlier American variation of the building type—the graduated gallery in Philadelphia and Providence—into the gigantic.

Decline of the Spatial Idea: After 1900   Around the turn of the century, there were changes which threatened existing arcades and prohibited the construction of new ones in many places. The city became suspect; its social, spatial, and hygienic conditions were subjected to criticism, and the garden city was proclaimed as the escape from this misery. Real estate reform was intended to counteract speculation, and the practice of constructing rows of adjoining buildings was given up. City planning became a separate discipline which learned to work with scientific methods. Baumeister, Sitte, and Unwin were names connected with this new discipline. In 1898 Howard wrote his *Garden Cities of To-Morrow,* the second edition of which, published in 1902, contained diagrammatic plans.[154] Among them was an arcade planned in the form of a ring closing off Central Park from the bordering residential area. Its name, "Crystal Palace," indicated the origin of the idea. Howard commented:

Running all around the Central Park (except where it is intersected by the boulevards) is a wide glass arcade called the 'Crystal Palace,' opening on the park. This building is in wet weather one of the favourite resorts of the people, whilst the knowledge that its bright shelter is ever close at hand tempts people into Central Park, even in the most doubtful of weathers. Here manufactured goods are exposed for sale, and here most of that class of shopping which requires the joy of deliberation and selection is done. The space enclosed by the Crystal Palace is, however, a good deal larger than is required for these purposes, and a considerable part of it is used as a Winter Garden—the whole forming a permanent exhibition of a most attractive character, whilst its circular form brings it nearer to every dweller in the town—the furthest removed inhabitants being within 600 yards.

And so, even at the end of the century, we find once again a vision of an arcade which rises above the thicket of the inner city. It is conceived as a promenade which should connect the pleasant with the useful. About 1900 the large cities already possessed a well-developed and centralized bureaucracy for handling technical matters—building authorities, surveying administrations, and bureaus of urban planning and underground construction. These offices controlled and advanced urban expansion and maintenance.[155] Zoning laws, prescribed street-frontage lines, limited development of certain sites, regulations by the building surveyors and fire departments, all this channeled speculation and guaranteed the maintenance of minimum hygienic standards. Advancing medical knowledge led to new conceptions of public health and the necessary amounts of air and light needed for a healthy life. As a result, the construction of buildings tightly closed in upon each other came to an end.

The type of this closed method of building as a form of public space was, of course, the arcade. Clearly, the end of the spatial idea of the arcade coincided with the task of shaping the urban spatial system as a whole. The city was to be punctuated with broad public spaces. The individual building became an independent entity and no longer played a subservient role. The city as a system of spaces was replaced by a system of separate entities. The distances between buildings were based on fundamentally different criteria from those used in the nineteenth century. The arcade had no place in this new spatial system, which still plagues us today.

The Friedrichstrassenpassage in Berlin, with its many imitations, can represent here the decline of the arcade building type. It was the first arcade constructed entirely of reinforced concrete, the material of the new century. It was also the last arcade in the classic form which was permitted by the building authorities.

The earliest arcade from the end of the eighteenth century was built completely of wood; the arcades of the nineteenth century were built of glass and iron, the materials which best conveyed the transitional character of the building. In the twentieth century, however, the new material was concrete, which is not appropriate for the problems of the arcade. Concrete is difficult to mask, since decoration is possible only through artificial techniques. It produces a heavy cover for the arcade space. It lacks the tight-knit rhythm of the iron profile, of the black ribbing and latticework which accent the contrasts of lighting and seem to remove the heaviness of the glass roof. The specific characteristics of concrete appropriate for spaces of transition were not exploited until it was used in the construction of subway tubes, ramps, highways, and bridges.

The Friedrichstrassenpassage in Berlin was built thanks only to the special permission of the building authorities, who stipulated that the arcade space be considered a part of a courtyard space. All other exposed interior steel structures had been forbidden in 1887.[156] The Friedrichstrassenpassage was the first great arcade with a flat roof. Light is admitted through a dust cover. Only in the massive rotunda is the structure visible.

After numerous changes in plan, the Friedrichstrassenpassage was conceived as a large retail store. The plan was to extend the traditional spatial program by building a department store which would be divided by an arcade into two awkwardly bridged halves. The financiers intended to compete with the department stores concentrated around Leipzig Strasse and to strengthen the specialty store vis-à-vis these department stores by means of modern organizational methods. Each dealer in the Friedrichstrassenpassage could preserve his independence, yet could enjoy the fruits of central maintenance and dispatch; he could lease floor space and use large central exhibition rooms. These points should in themselves indicate some of the flaws of this form of organization: the architectural structure stands in no relation to the use of the surface area; the arcade disturbs the inner concourse; and the arcade space is used only for shop windows. Just a few years after it was opened, this department store in spite of itself went bankrupt.

The end is symbolized in the senselessness of the massive, mislocated rotunda, in the awkward decoration with motifs from the world of trade, in the oversized cover for completely banal purposes. Or it could be expressed in the words of an article written for the opening of the building:[157] "Now the Friedrichstrassenpassage presents itself to the visitor as if it came from a mold! It is solidly built of indestructible materials so that it can represent to future generations the commercial and industrial aspirations which dominated the capital of the German Reich at the beginning of the twentieth century. It should bear witness to the enormous amount of private capital which was available to realize a new concept in public well-being!"

The witness to this refined deception still stands today—as a ruin, as one of the last great ruins of the former capital. The iron rods protrude from the concrete, the roofs have collapsed, some ribs in the dome have rusted through, and the last visitors, the pigeons, fly in and out of the empty window frames.

Wood, iron, and concrete form the material background against which the arcade building type proceeds through the nineteenth century, leaving the century in the stunted form of a subservient commercial thoroughfare lined with show windows. It is a building type associated with a society which celebrated its last great festival in the *belle époque*, only to be confronted with the reality of a new century on the fields of World War I.

The Arcade as Project and Utopia

It is necessary, even if it goes beyond the limits of the topic, to pursue the destiny of the arcade into the twentieth century. The architectural idea of the arcade is once again entering the consciousness of those who are discussing the future of the city as a form of life. They must seek out specific new forms under changed economic, technological, and social conditions.

Before World War I the arcade died an almost official death: no building authority would permit it in its nineteenth-century form (I have discovered this hard fact myself); no fire inspector, when faced with the prospect of such an arcade, could forget for a moment his laboriously developed categories, like fire containment, prevention of smoke accumulation and fireproof staircase; no real estate authority could permit such an exploitation of land. The only alternative left to the arcade was to go underground, to dissolve into its separate aspects, to mask itself, and to reappear in another form, another time, and another context, once again giving shape and space to an articulated need.

Its time came perhaps in the 1960s, a time both of intensified analysis of the nineteenth century and of unforeseen social restructuring and new approaches to architecture and city planning. The 1960s unmasked the bankruptcy of the garden-city ideology and the ideology of private property which drew further strength from it—theories espoused especially in the Federal Republic of Germany after World War II. Loose juxtaposition and similar treatment of buildings hide endless social isolation and immobility; they mask enduring social hierarchy by means of spatial separation. The arcade, understood as interiorized (and hence once again truly possible) public space, acquired an almost strategic importance. The arcade is a building with many entrances and exits. It has its own plane, which conquers and bridges everything. Its narrowness gives space to action and its closure echoes demands.

To open this historical analysis I would like to mention the short story published in 1904 by the Russian symbolist Valeriy Bressov. It is the gloomy vision of the "Republic of the Southern Cross." Bressov paints a picture of a republic at the South Pole that dominates 70 percent of world steel production and which houses its population exclusively in cities cut off from the rest of the world. The inhabitants live in a totally socialized world, regulated and controlled down to the minutest detail by the state—until one day the perplexing "mania contradicens," the epidemic of contradiction, breaks out and they destroy the republic in a frenzy and meet their end in one last frightful orgy.[158]

The capital of the republic, named Star City, was located on the pole. Precisely at that point which touches the earth's axis and where all meridians meet, stood the city hall, with the point of its flagpole raised to the zenith of the heavens. The city streets radiated from the city hall in the direction of the meridians, and were in turn intersected by those streets which followed the parallels. The heights and exteriors of all the buildings were identical. The walls had no windows because the interiors were illuminated by electricity. Electricity also provided the illumination for the streets. Because of the severe climate an opaque roof was constructed over the entire city, with massive ventilators to circulate fresh air. Those regions of the earth experience in the course of a year only one day six months long and one long night, likewise six months long; however the streets of Star City were constantly illuminated by the same bright light. In the same way the temperature of the streets was artificially maintained at the same level in all seasons. . . . As for the interior of the country, it remained unsettled. . . .

This is the vision of a Moscow poet in 1904, and one is tempted to assume that the Moscow Trade Halls (GUM), a world closed to nature and artificially illuminated and maintained, provided the basis of the story. The Star City is a utopia with ghostly features, a completely closed and temperature-controlled city, and an arcade city with roofs of more than glass because it is at the South Pole. Here is an extreme conception as early as the beginning of the twentieth century.

But in the meantime the arcade had to develop through its banal stages. After its last hollow demonstration in the Friedrichstrassenpassage in Berlin, it broke down into its parts. In the nineteenth century it was the unmistakable sign of a booming metropolis, the example of a complex architectural program, and building type for the then still unarticulated demands of the bourgeois public. In the first decades of the twentieth century it became dependent on other structures and barely recognizable in its reduced form:

1. As a light well or courtyard in office buildings, banking halls, factories, and public buildings
2. As *rue intérieure* in the large apartment and communal complexes
3. As a pedestrian level above or below vehicular traffic

4. As a dependent passage in commercial buildings or as an entranceway to cinemas and theaters

5. As a business street, shop street, or shopping center reserved for pedestrians and closed off to vehicular traffic.

In the first and second cases, the originally public arcade space has been made private. It serves a limited public, a situation that results in the decline of the interior facades and the reduction of the spatial proportions. In the third, fourth, and fifth cases, the opposite occurs; the public dominates and even owns the property. The arcade then loses its competitive role, its complexity and essential riskiness, a situation which results in the reduction of its appearance to a mere thoroughfare or vaulted passage.

These different cases can be demonstrated in many places. Not until the 1960s can one observe the reintroduction of the arcade as an architectural and spatial aspect of the urban environment. The arcade's future does not lie in its fashionable employment as a quotation in an unsuitable context, complete with coarse interior decoration. It can rise above the level of pure consumerism and become a crystallization point of urban life only if it is employed as a formulation of public space which answers pressing human needs; its construction must be based on changed architectural and financial interrelationships. The Town Center of Cumbernauld near Edinburgh, which is presently under construction, illustrates the process by which the arcade eliminates the individual building and becomes an entire system of open space and access, even if it is still only intermediary space and has the rough form of a multileveled interiorized street system (fig. 46).[159]

Let us pursue the five individual forms of the atomization of the arcade.

The Light Well or Courtyard The light well or courtyard, which we encountered already in its developed form in the French *magasins*, bazaars, and department stores, is an essential element of all public buildings well into the twentieth century. It makes the deeper recesses of the building accessible. The light well retains two possible functions: (1) entrance hall or orientation space, as in Poelzig's Rundfunkhaus in Berlin, or (2) production area, as in the Esder's tailoring establishment, built by Perret in Paris in 1919, or in Frank Lloyd Wright's Larkin Building of 1904. In the last case, the light well cuts through all the floors of the office building, forming a work area onto which the whole building opens and which can be supervised like a kind of exterior office. This early work of Wright's impressed Berlage during his journey to America[161] and inspired Louis Kahn to do a related design. It echoes still in a sketch by the Berlin architect Otto Kohtz for a high-rise office building on the Königsplatz:[162] the cruciform plan, with the stories rising above it like a pyramid, contains an interior cruciform arcade which cuts through the building and converts it into a public building. All stories have galleries overlooking this fantastically extended interior space, and they are connected at the ends of the long arms by bridges.

Following this development, the light well appeared again in a project by Colin St. John Wilson for the Liverpool Social and Civic Centre (fig. 47). The building was intended to unite twenty-two scattered activities of the local government into one large yet differentiated and easily extendable complex. The public reception hall is conceived as a massive light well. It aids circulation by means of

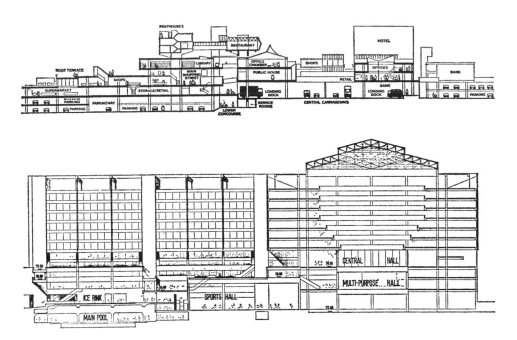

46
Cumbernauld, town
center, section

47
Liverpool, Social and
Civic Centre, design
by J. Wilson

48
Henri Sauvage, de-
sign for terraced
houses, 1920

49
Paris, apartment
building, Rue des
Amiraux, 1925,
cross section

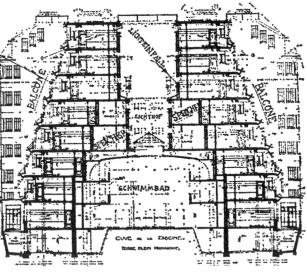

escalators and enables general orientation in the building, which extends away from it in all directions. "The form of the Public Reception Hall ensures that the visitor can easily find his way to it and within it since all of the enquiry counters and interview rooms of all Departments are grouped around the Galleries of one single Hall. This is both easy to understand and efficient. The Department required and the best means of access to it (by lift or escalator) can be easily judged: there will be no frustrating corridors to navigate."[163] This indicates a new understanding of public work which is served by architecture: the hall places the user of the building in the center, thereby giving him the feeling that the administration is at his disposal.

The *Rue Intérieure* Even before World War I one finds systems of access in socially oriented apartment house architecture which can be classified between the arcade and the simple corridor. Fourier and Godin were the forefathers of this development; Tony Garnier, Antonio Sant'Elia, and Henri Sauvage continued in the same tradition.

Garnier and Sant'Elia contributed ideas and sketches to the type of the arcaded house but their plans were never executed. Henri Sauvage, however, had the honor in 1924 of building a structure commissioned by the city of Paris. The building, for inexpensive apartments, was a terraced house with arcade-like means of access to the interior. It was located between the Rue des Amiraux and the Rue Herrman-Lachapelle.[164] The section makes it clear why the building is mentioned in this connection: the interior was completely cut through and illuminated from above. The apartments, all necessarily facing one direction, were accessible from continuous side galleries. The lower stories, wider as a result of the terracing, contained a swimming pool, also illuminated from above by natural lighting. The whole section produces the effect of a realized part of one of Fourier's phalansteries. Another design by Sauvage (1920) for a residential district with large, stepped-back buildings, which seem to be accessible from all directions, probably had a similar section (figs. 48, 49).[165]

The concept of a residential unit designed like a whole district providing for all immediate necessities—including recreational space, community institutions, and hotel-type services—was derived from Fourier's ideas. It was first applied by Le Corbusier in 1922 in his design for a tremendous apartment block.[166] The terraces, with more than one hundred villas, were to be accessible from arcaded walkways, and the roof was to be used for sports complexes and a social hall. The whole building is organized like an open arcade with entrances and stairways on parallel streets.

Designs similar to those of Le Corbusier can also be found in Germany where Adolf Rading published his plan for a communal apartment complex in 1928 (fig. 50)[167] and in the USSR, where the great October Revolution of 1917 and the shortage of apartments in the following years forced new and radical approaches. El Lissitzky wrote in 1929:[168]
The task in the West was the revitalization of architectural activity under changed economic and technological conditions after the war; we, on the other hand, have to solve a new social problem of fundamental cultural significance. All contrasts in dwellings, ranging from the basement hole of the urban worker to multi-storied apartment buildings or private villas, were removed. The Soviet architect faced the challenge of creating as a new standard of living a new type of housing unit which was not meant for unique individuals who stood in a state of conflict with one another, but for the masses. . . . Cooking should be transposed from the individual kitchen into the communal culinary labora-

tory, the main meal into public eating halls, the education of children into the kindergarten and schools. In this way the space which remains necessary for individual and intimate life is reduced, solving not only the present housing shortage, but also future problems. To make up for this reduction, the general and communal should become freer in measure and form. Architecture thereby becomes the expression of social conditions and an effective factor of social life. The goal today is to transform the housing unit from a collection of private apartments to a communal house.

The application of these considerations was undertaken by the state building committee of the economic advisory council of the RSFSR. It consisted of an association of progressive architects. Theoretical types were tested in experimental buildings. The illustration of one of these (fig. 51) reveals an interesting example of an interior system of access with skylighting: from the two stairways and two common floor areas to one side, one can reach three levels of one-room apartments.[169]

These developments in the USSR, with their many utopian approaches, were abruptly halted by the reactionary Stalinists. Today, however, they are awakening increasing interest among young architects. If one pursued the idea of the *rue intérieure* beyond the Unité d'Habitation, an experimental structure built by Le Corbusier after World War II in Marseilles with public funds; if one extended the *rue* from building to building (assuming, of course, that property lines were done away with); if one organized an entire complex around a system of interior streets with alternating heights and differentiated functions—then one would create a new architectural interrelationship and the possibility of communication.

The Smithsons, and many after them, developed such systems. The Fulham Study is based on this concept. Such a complex was actually constructed in 1961 for a tenement district in Sheffield, England. The Park Hill Development is particularly attractive because of its sloping site, which makes possible stairless entranceways to almost all levels of access.[170]

The Pedestrian Level Leonardo da Vinci proposed putting traffic underground. It was an idea that became a necessity with mass transportation. Almost in Leonardo's spirit, the idea reappears in a sketch by Le Corbusier dated 1915:[171] a city on stilts with pedestrian overpasses at roof level. Today the postulate of the separation of planes of traffic is the common property of all plans; however, it has only been realized in a few cases.

The arcade as an independent plane, as bridge, gallery, under- or overpass, develops in these projects in a way which could be summed up by Louis Kahn's statement: "A street wants to be a building." The emancipation of the pedestrian plane results from the necessities of traffic technology. As auto traffic increases and separates the sides of the street, the resulting burden becomes so unbearable that the traditional cross sections no longer can contain the problem; it must be solved by new architectonic methods. Systems and networks are constructed which follow their own laws and can be linked up at will. Yet what is solved by them? They still cannot control the increase in private automobile traffic.

The popular press in the late nineteenth century enjoyed describing the role of traffic in the city of the future. In 1914 these visions found their monumental culmination in the famous sketches of the "Città Nuova" of Sant'Elia. In 1910 Ed-

50
Adolf Rading, design
for a communal
dwelling, schematic
plan, entrance ar-
cade, center wing;
section; and glass
roof

Key to section:
1. Revolving door
2. Convenience
   store, post office,
   barbershop,
   drugstore
3. Gallery access
4. Stairs

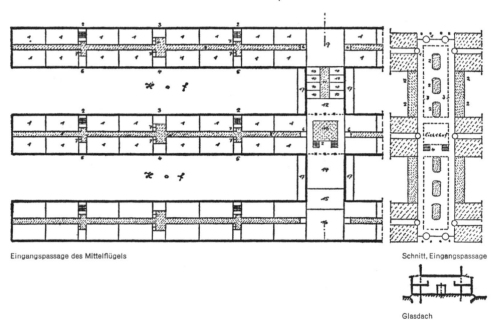

Eingangspassage des Mittelflügels

Schnitt, Eingangspassage

Glasdach

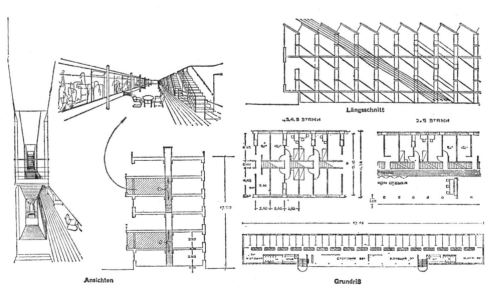

Ansichten

Längsschnitt

Grundriß

51
Building committee,
R.S.F.S.R., residen-
tial community,
"type E"

gar Chambless's project for "Roadtown" was published:[172] a two-storied Chinese wall winds through the countryside, on the ground floor a roadway, on the two upper stories apartments and occasional towers at the intersections, and on the roof an uninterrupted pedestrian promenade. This conception of an extended, nonlocalized city reappeared in Le Corbusier's projects for Rio de Janeiro (1929) and Algiers (1930–1934). In *Vers une Architecture* he displayed his enthusiasm for an auto test track on the roof of a Fiat factory.

The bridges built into these road buildings take on a new form. Once the superhighway is drawn as a building into the city center, it is filled underneath with commercial enterprises or parking lots; then the approach roads, buildings, and concourses link up with it; soon it is covered over with pedestrian levels while below it the plane of the local traffic network runs underground. This is the conception behind the Soho Study in London and the Harlem Study in New York (fig. 52).[173] In it we once again approach the complexity and the total utilization of a space that characterized the arcade.

The Dependent Passage   In the older or partially destroyed inner cities, reconstruction of the commercial districts has taken place by systematically reshaping blocks and opening their interiors for commercial purposes. In Prague, Munich, Brussels, Bern, and Hamburg—cities with historical significance and vital centers—one finds countless newly constructed pedestrian arcades. Even though they are dependent structures, they extend the surface area available for shop windows, create space for boutiques, and make the city accessible to the pedestrian and consumer. In these pedestrian arcades, the temporary and fluctuating retail trade in luxury items has the opportunity to remain in the city at reasonable rents. In this way they are parallel to the early stages of the arcade fashion.

Munich has already been systematically investigated in this connection by the geographer Walter Hantschk.[174] He distinguishes between the following arcade types on the basis of popularity, location, and number of stories (fig. 53):

Downtown arcades (considerable traffic during business hours; with boutiques; also for window shopping)
Cinema and theater arcades (rush hour in the evening)
Thoroughfare arcades (normal rush hour traffic)
Exhibition arcades (less populated)
Neighborhood arcades (local, short-term needs)

These distinctions and the classification according to the quality of the location are derived from a detailed analysis. This should indicate how many more precise studies of nineteenth-century arcades are still possible.

The Commercial Street   Once the old business streets are closed off to through traffic and made accessible to vehicles only for deliveries, their character changes. The sidewalks disappear, the displays spill into the street, benches and flower pots are set up, the street is transformed into a kind of arcade. It is a logical consequence, then, that proposals have already been made to cover the Hohe Strasse in Cologne and that closed-off business streets in Japan have already been completely covered with mats and glass roofs to protect the consumer from sun or inclement weather.

It is different, however, when so-called shopping centers with large pedestrian zones and arcade-like shop arrangements arise in suburban settlements, new

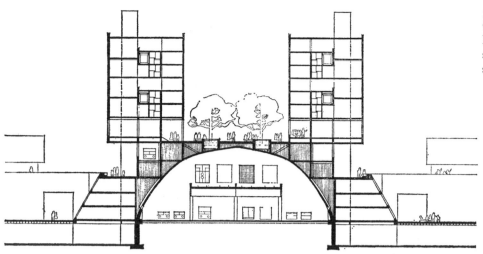

52
Columbia University,
Harlem Study, repre-
sentative cross
section

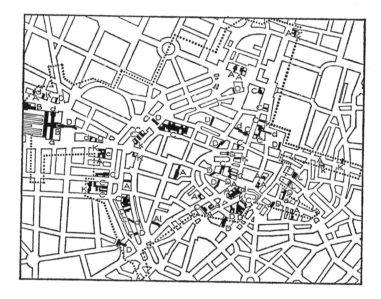

53
Munich, inner city
with existing retail
arcades

K Movie and thea-
ter arcade
C Downtown ar-
cade
D Thoroughfare ar-
cade
Al Neighborhood
arcade
B Train station ar-
cade
L Pedestrian shop-
ping street
A Exhibition arcade

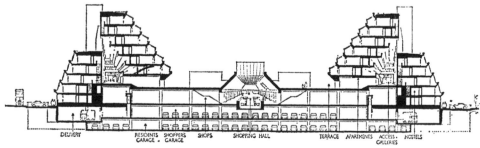

54
London, Blooms-
bury, Brunswick
Square Project,
section

neighborhoods, restored districts, or in newly established cities. This development can be traced from the Lijnbaan in Rotterdam (built in the 1950s), to the expansive American shopping centers or to the commercial districts of the new towns built in ever increasing numbers in Europe. However, not until the shopping area becomes an essential part of larger building complexes, including apartments, parks, traffic networks, and public establishments, does the arcade appear more clearly as the system of access.

The arcade serves this function, for example, in the Market East development in Philadelphia, designed by Mitchell Giurgola in 1964. This complex is located near the former site of the first American arcade, the Philadelphia Arcade.[175] Other examples are the design for the Redevelopment of Bloomsbury by Patrick Hodgkinson (begun 1967) (fig. 54), and Cumbernauld.[176]

The most recent attempt to revive the arcade in literal form is the proposal for the Piccadilly district in London. Under this plan, the Crescent and Regent Street would be completely reconstructed, and a multistoried vaulted glass arcade would be built over the entire width of Regent Street.

It is interesting to note here that the arcade has been proposed in recent competitions as the organizational system for other building types, for example, in universities, which, after all, have recently become the place where the public has gained back its original rights as the controlling factor.[177]
The history of the arcade has not ended but is still open. All the indicators suggest that the continuation of the arcade in its particular aspects and the ascertainable movement toward more complex formations of space will lead to the reappearance of the arcade as the protagonist of a new public space. The arcade of yesterday will be the street of tomorrow. Yet I doubt that that will be possible without social changes.

Meanwhile Herr Edelmann's great colorful snail will traverse the arcade of his fantasy[178] as once the idlers promenaded in it with their tortoises, taking from them their pace.[179]

Typological Listing

To give an impression of the variety, the ingenious use of space, and the architectonic fantasy which become evident in an investigation of the arcade building type, I have provided typological listings. Each list considers the arcade according to a series of criteria; together they convey a precise image of the forms which the building type has taken. The lists include only built arcades. Further possibilities consisting of combinations of these forms can be easily recognized. The lists do not take into consideration historical development, geographical proximity, or actual dimensions.

Each example is presented in cross section, longitudinal section, and plan, as well as in terms of its access pattern and glass roof construction. Typical elements are simplified for the sake of comparison. Misconstructed and unfinished structures, or buildings which otherwise deviate from the original plans, are schematized to approximate the recognizable intention or ideal form. The lists are classified with numbers and letters which enable complete definition of each arcade. Hence, even arcades that are not represented in the catalog by a photograph or drawing may be approximately reconstructed. The typological lists are headed: S (spatial types); B (building types); C (cross sections); L (longitudinal sections); D (subdivision); GR (forms of glass roof construction).

Spatial Types   The diagram of spatial types (fig. 55) demonstrates variations in arcade spaces, in their ideal forms, as they intersect the building block. The diagram is divided horizontally, according to the number of approaches and the figure described by the arcade space. It is divided vertically according to the following spatial elements: the street as directional space; the street and the central space as the basis for spaces that cross or meet at an angle; the central space alone—a rare case; and the arcade spaces that include an interior building block. This last case arises in a similar fashion in S 14a and in the arcades which occur in a series of two or three, connected merely by passageways. The Passage de l'Opéra in Paris and the large Moscow arcades exemplify this type.

The schematized presentations of spaces that narrow toward the front edge of the building blocks imply a passageway through a kind of antechamber. This antechamber is not always present and the arcade space may continue with a constant profile to the street. This possibility, however, has been neglected here. The constantly changing urban context of each example leads to manifold deviations from the simple, straightforward arcade type S 3a, which is the basis of the majority of examples. Number 12b is an example of the ideally pure form en route to the arcade as public building: the cruciform which encompasses an entire building block. This form appears for the first time in Trieste and later in its monumental form in Milan and Naples.

Building Types   The diagram of building types (fig. 56) depicts the relationship between the arcade as building and the surrounding building block: the part of

A Typology
of the Arcade

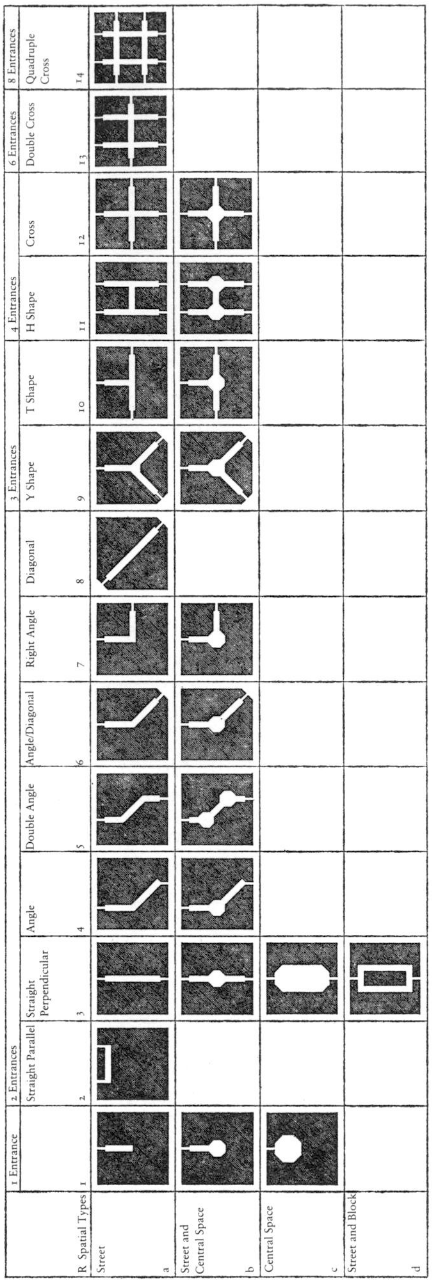

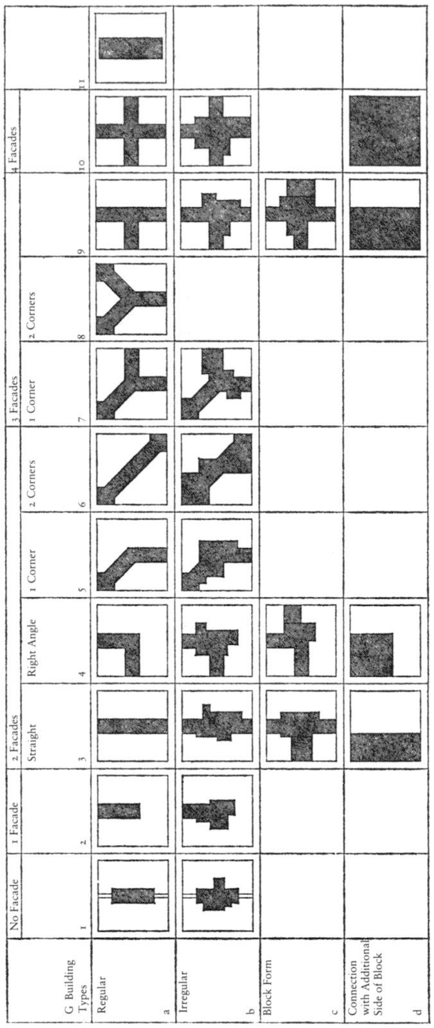

Spatial types (55)

R Spatial Types	1 Entrance	2 Entrances		4 Entrances					4 Entrances		6 Entrances	8 Entrances
		Straight Parallel	Straight Perpendicular	Angle	Double Angle	Angle/Diagonal	Right Angle	Diagonal	Y Shape	T Shape	H Shape	Cross	Double Cross	Quadruple Cross
	1	2	3	4	5	6	7	8	9	10	11	12	13	14
Street — a														
Street and Central Space — b														
Central Space — c														
Street and Block — d														

Building types (56)

G Building Types	No Facade	1 Facade	2 Facades		3 Facades			3 Facades	4 Facades		4 Facades
			Straight	Right Angle	1 Corner	2 Corners	1 Corner	2 Corners			
	1	2	3	4	5	6	7	8	9	10	11
Regular — a											
Irregular — b											
Block Form — c											
Connection with Additional Side of Block — d											

55
Spatial types

56
Building types

the block it occupies and its position within the larger unit. The arcade building is shaded in the diagram; the block itself is indicated by the square frame. A variety of possibilities can be established between the two extreme forms of the arcade. While one extreme does not have an antechamber and so does not constitute a building at the street ends (Bern, Von Werdt Arcade), the other occupies a whole block (Trieste, El Tergesteo). Horizontally, the diagram is arranged according to the number of street facades, analogous to that of the spatial types. Vertically, the criteria attempt to classify the plan of the building:

a. A regular, well-proportioned plan form

b. An irregular plan form dependent on the shape of the lot

c. A plan form providing contact with additional block sides by an adjoining or added building opening onto the arcade, like a cinema or theater

d. A plan form taking up an entire block. It is characteristic of these types that the arcade does not possess separate facades but occupies all or part of the block with the parts of the building which belong to it. Such is the case in the arcades in Trieste.

Cross Sections   The diagram of cross sections (fig. 57) shows arcade profiles. The shaded areas indicate building cross sections while the white areas depict the interior or exterior. The proportions of the profile of the arcade space are determined by the number of stories, the spatial enclosure overhead, and the contour of the facades of the structures bordering the arcade. These structures may be simply perpendicular, set back in a succession of steps, or interrupted by balconies. Furthermore, it is interesting to note whether the height of the arcade space is identical with that of the buildings, whether the buildings bordering the arcade are set back at the level of the glass roof to allow adequate lighting for additional stories, or whether the glass roof is inserted only into the arcade buildings.

Longitudinal Sections   The diagram of longitudinal sections (fig. 58) demonstrates the development of the depth of the arcade. The elements consist of the glass roof, the central space, the transverse space, the frontal building, the lateral building, and the passageway. They are combined to produce ever changing spatial sequences, which are also generally influenced by topographical factors. Differences in height are mediated by inclined planes or stairs which result in unique and ingenious spatial configurations, as in the Galleria Mazzini in Genoa (L 9d), or the Passage Pommeraye in Nantes (L 6d).

The diagram is arranged horizontally according to the number of glass roofs, and their combinations with central spaces, frontal buildings, and transverse buildings, which are depicted in the diagrams by shading. The diagram is divided vertically according to the number of stories.

Types of Subdivision and Means of Access   The diagram of subdivision types (fig. 59) shows the following elements: planes; ramps; steps; staircases (shown in black); the gallery as terrace, pergola, and bridge. The frontal buildings have been disregarded in this schema since as a rule they are independent structures which are dealt with prior to the arcade spaces and are accessible independently of them. The diagram therefore presents only parts of plans, with only as much of the length indicated as is necessary for an adequate understanding.

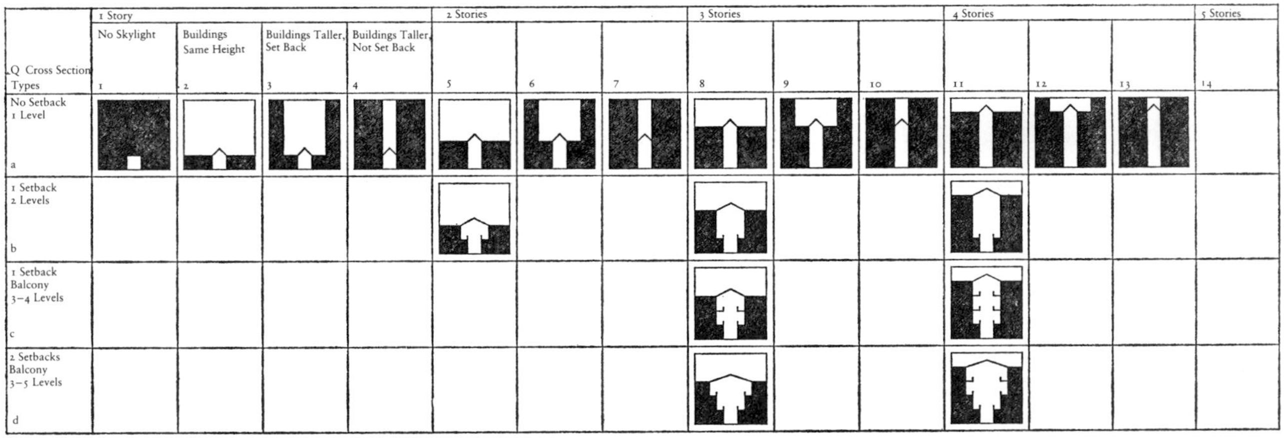

A Typology
of the Arcade

57
Cross section types

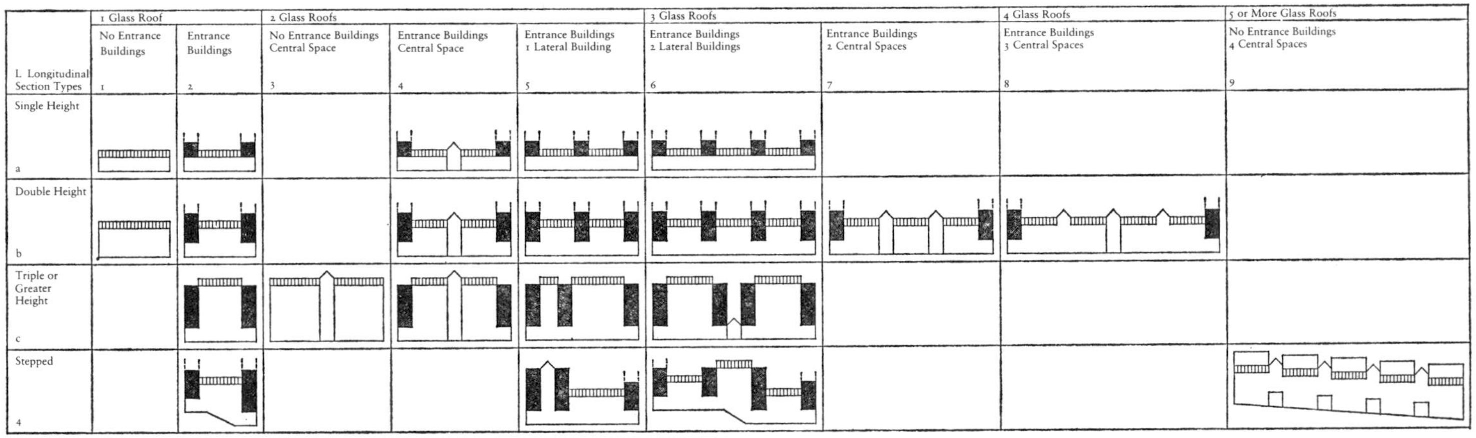

58
Longitudinal section
types

The diagram shows five columns which juxtapose functional elements and elements of the technique of subdivision. The subdivision of the arcades developed from the simple lining up of symmetrical arcades which lay opposite one another, creating complex systems of galleries, bridges, stairs, and layered levels. Each shop, and therefore each space, was accessible from a variety of points.

The subdivided space is also organized in relation to its use. The classic case is the arcade in which the stores on the ground level are accessible only through the arcade itself. Freestanding spiral staircases or enclosed stairs inside the shops make the upper stories accessible in cases where the same tenants occupy all stories of the building. The cellar, the shop itself, the entresol (used as a work area or office), and the residential spaces in the upper stories constitute an integral, organizational unit, a house which may be individually rented or purchased. This organizational form, which bespeaks the heritage of the building, is the basis of most of the Parisian arcades. The rentability of the arcades may be increased, however, if the shops and the upper stories can be rented separately, since not every shop proprietor will want to live in the arcade. Separate rentability necessarily entails separate accessibility. In this case the staircase is separated from the shop and is added as an independent shaft. Thus, it becomes accessible either from the back or from the arcade itself. The building then may be rented to a variety of tenants floor by floor or one tenant may occupy both the shop and the living quarters upstairs. This method of subdivision was adopted even in some of the Restoration arcades in Paris; it was, however, most fully developed in the Galeries St. Hubert in Brussels, where the upper stories were laid out in such a manner as to make possible their rental and utilization as club rooms, offices, or studios.

Where there is a problem of direct access to the staircase and to delivery entrances both from the arcade and the outside, the staircase is placed on the back side of the arcade buildings. It faces either yards or passageways which are accessible to neighboring streets by foot or vehicle. The great arcades in Milan and Naples, Sillem's Bazar in Hamburg, and the Lemonnier Arcade in Liège are divided and made accessible in this way; they thereby allow for use of the upper stories entirely independently of the arcade area.

The modes of subdivision and the resulting opening up of the arcade structure apply chiefly to arcades in continental Europe. In the Anglo-Saxon countries, another type of structure predominates, which is exclusively a commercial, not a residential, venture. In order to make the upper stories easily accessible to the public, they are set back; they thus make room for galleries or are made accessible by covered ways or pergolas. The galleries that run along the arcade area on both sides are connected at either end by pairs of staircases or by freestanding staircases located in the middle of the passage. Additional bridges may connect these galleries on the various levels so that a variety of promenades become possible. The rooms that adjoin these galleries may then be rented to businesses, small tradespeople, agencies, and so on.

The early arcade in Providence, Rhode Island; Lancaster Avenue in Manchester; and the massive Cleveland Arcade clearly illustrate this type. It is shown schematically in fig. 59, 4a–c. The Moscow examples may be found in the last column under fig. 59, 5a–c. Fig. 59, 5c shows a section of the division and access system in the Moscow Trade Halls. Systems D 2 and D 4 are combined in this triple arcade. Transverse and longitudinal connecting passages, which vary

A Typology
of the Arcade

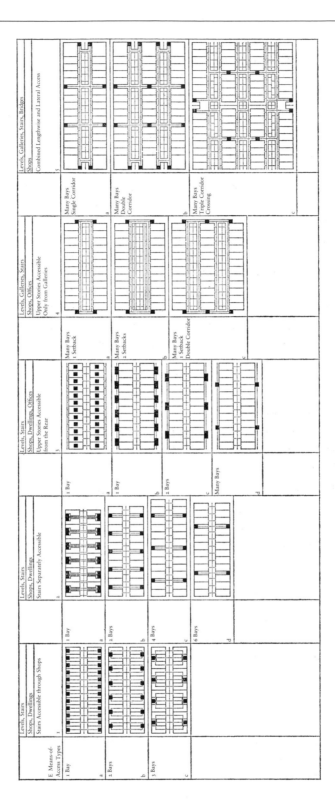

59
Means-of-access
types

and overlap one another in each of the three strictly commercial stories, make each room accessible from a variety of entrances. Here, then, at the end of the nineteenth century, we find the monumental solution to the arcade created in the middle of a cosmopolitan urban center. The arcade has become an entire quarter of the city with over a thousand rooms, with space to accommodate thousands of pedestrians, and with business and trade vast enough to create a commercial confusion almost Oriental in nature.

Types of Glass Roof Construction   This diagram (fig. 60) depicts the basic construction types of glass roofing in arcades. It does not include the various kinds of lantern structures designed for ventilation. The diagram is divided horizontally according to the way in which glazing is used in the roof of the arcade. This series is almost identical to the historical development of the arcade, since a full and continuous glass roof did not become a common feature until the 1820s. Only then did the technological know-how for such a structure exist and the costs become acceptable for building contractors. The profile of the glass roof serves as well as an additional horizontal divider. It may be pointed, semicircular, saddle, or vaulted.

The extent to which the two sides of the arcade connect, resulting in different interior effects, corresponds to the role played by the glass expanse in the enclosure of the arcade. The greater the area of glass, the more independent the opposite halves of the arcade structures are from one another. In turn, the glass roof itself becomes more a separate element, finally linked only by articulations or joints to the arcade buildings themselves. The arcade of the Galeries de Bois (Palais Royal, Paris), shown in the first column, is an integrally constructed unit with wooden girder construction and basilica-like cross section. In column two (Lowther Arcade, London), the skylights are located in the pendentive domes of the monumental structure. In column four, only transverse buttresses remain of the older, more integral connection; and in columns five, six, and seven, which represent the majority of examples, the arcade buildings consist of massive structures connected with one another only through the frontal or transverse buildings. The glass roof is here simply placed on the buildings without being architecturally related to their interior facades (Galeries St. Hubert, Brussels). Only later, with the emergence of an arcade structure supported entirely by a steel skeleton, did the arcade become once again a structurally integrated building with well-like recesses. The Deansgate Arcade in Manchester and the Cleveland Arcade are examples. At this point, the street character of the arcade disappeared completely.

The vertical columns of the diagram depict the typical support structures of the glass roof. The broader the arcade, the more complex the support structure must become to span the greater area. These spaces, however, usually range between 3 and 15 meters, a distance which does not pose any essential structural problems. Thus, we do not witness many original developments in glass roof constructions; they are, rather, reduced, ornamental, and derivative, taken over from building types with much greater ranges. As a rule the substructure is a relatively sparse construction designed to be as plain as possible in order not to hinder the entrance of light. In turn, it serves to remove any oppressive visual effect or impression of excessive strength from the roof itself. The glass roof should be light and ethereal like a kind of netting or skin so that unaesthetic intersections or overlappings of the girder structures above do not occur along the

A Typology
of the Arcade

K Glass Roof Construction Types	High Side Light	Round Skylights	Rectangular Skylights		Continuous Skylight		
	Saddle	Pendentives	Saddle	Saddle	Saddle	Barrel, Barrel Segment	Pointed Arch, Ogee Arch, etc.
	1	2	3	4	5	6	7
Roof Plans							
Self-Supporting a							
Beams b							
Parallel Trusses c							
Triangular Trusses d							
Buttressing e							
Cable f							

60
Glass-roof construction types

longitudinal axis of the arcade space. There are two distinct modes of construction: (1) those that bear their own weight, whereby the glass skin and supporting ribs lie in the same plane, and (2) those whose glass skin is supported by purlins which in turn may rest on various types of substructures.

The simplest kind of understructure is cast- or wrought-iron supports. The supports may be flat iron (Sillem's Bazar in Hamburg), I-beams, or may have a fillet above with ornamental piercing (Galleria Vittorio Emanuele in Milan). The support may also be a cast-iron framework, perforated and arched, a method often employed in Victorian arcades in England. If the height of the fillet is great enough, the support becomes a truss beam. Such a connection was employed as a substructure in the Galleria Umberto I in Naples because of the large span.

Under section d, a triangular substructure is shown, a form which occurs only with glass saddle roofs. The lower beam—which is not shown in the diagram—may be angled, straight, or curved. However, this substructure is uncommon because it is not necessary statically and conveys the sense of a market hall, thereby contradicting the spatial conception of the arcade.

Common to most glass roofs are the ribs which support the glass plates, exactly a human step apart. Two exceptions are the fish-scale roofs marketed by a Glasgow firm at the turn of the century and the concrete-glass roofs employed in isolated cases at the beginning of the twentieth century (Mädler Passage, Leipzig). The originally square glass plates, which grew wider over time, overlap one another in such a manner as to leave a small air space, thereby protecting the edges from dirtying and providing constant ventilation of the arcade.

The technical problem of sealing the glass roof occupied the engineers of the nineteenth century. Countless systems were invented to hinder deterioration of the ribbing and prevent leakage from weather. This explains as well why hardly any glass roofs may be found still in their original state. Once the iron ribbing, specially curved for drainage, was pressed and clamped around the glass plates, they provided protection from leakage with the help of a malleable, watertight substance. It is interesting, then, that this problem had not been solved by the mid-nineteenth century. A contemporary report, "Iron and Glass in Building Construction," in *The Builder* (May 10, 1856) states that the glass roof of the Crystal Palace in London was so leaky that large puddles developed on the floor of the exhibition hall during inclement periods.

Finally, a glass roof construction unique to the large Moscow arcade is shown in fig. 60, section f. It is the work of a famous engineer. The massive glass barrel vault extends 250 meters and is spanned transversely by a fan arrangement of barely visible cables, which give the glass roof the necessary transverse tension. Thin diagonal crosses, which line the building between the ribs at large intervals, provide the longitudinal tension. These technical strategies create an unparalleled glass archway of extraordinary lightness and net-like transparency.

Stages of Development

Figs. 61–63 present aspects of the arcade which cannot be classified by type: the development of its spatial dimensions, the interior and exterior facades, and the "furnishings" of the arcade space—its signs, posters, advertisements, and lighting fixtures. These relics of a former life mirror something which is now lost, which eludes description, and which can at best be retrieved through old photographs: the history of the building and its inhabitants.

A Typology
of the Arcade

61

Spatial development:
cross sections

1. Paris, Passage
   des Panoramas,
   1800
2. London, Royal
   Opera Arcade,
   1816
3. London, Burling-
   ton Arcade,
   1818
4. Paris, Galerie
   Vivienne, 1825
5. Paris, Passage du
   Grand Cerf,
   1825
6. Paris, Galerie
   Colbert, 1826
7. Paris, Galerie
   d'Orléans, 1829
8. London,
   Lowther Arcade,
   1831
9. Hamburg, Sil-
   lem's Bazar,
   1845
10. Brussels,
    Galeries St.
    Hubert, 1847

11. Milan, Galleria
    Vittorio
    Emanuele, 1867
12. Manchester, Bar-
    ton Arcade,
    1871
13. Berlin, Kaiser-
    galerie, 1873
14. The Hague, Pas-
    sage, 1885
15. Cleveland,
    Cleveland Ar-
    cade, 1890
16. Naples, Galleria
    Umberto I, 1891
17. Berlin, Friedrich-
    strassenpassage,
    1908

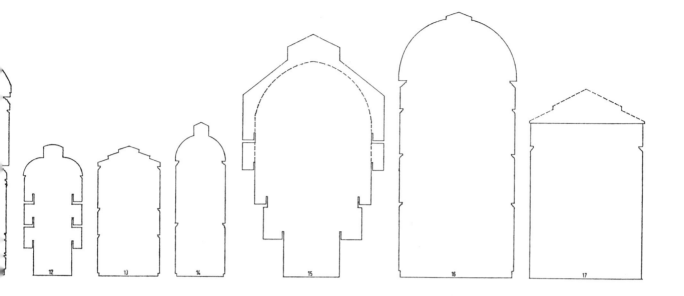

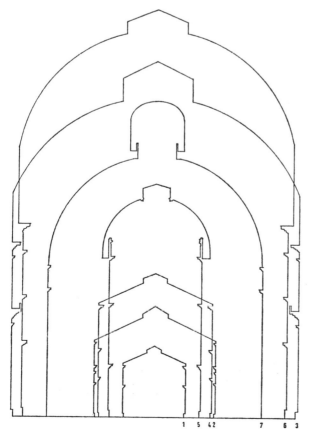

62
Spatial development:
dome sections
1. Paris, Galerie
   Vivienne, 1825
2. Paris, Galerie Col-
   bert, 1826
3. Milan, Galleria
   Vittorio
   Emanuele, 1867
4. Berlin, Kaiser-
   galerie, 1873
5. The Hague, Pas-
   sage, 1885
6. Naples, Galleria
   Umberto I, 1891
7. Berlin, Friedrich-
   strassenpassage,
   1908

63
Development of inte-
rior facades

1. London, Burling-
   ton Arcade,
   1819
2. Bristol, Lower
   Arcade, 1825
3. Paris, Galerie
   Véro-Dodat,
   1827
4. Paris, Passage du
   Saumon, 1828
5. Paris, Galerie
   Vivienne, 1825
6. Paris, Galerie
   Colbert, 1826

7. London, Royal
   Opera Arcade,
   1816
8. London,
   Lowther Arcade,
   1831
9. Newcastle,
   Royal Arcade,
   1832
10. Paris, Galerie
    d'Orléans, 1829

1

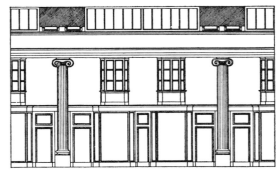

2

6

7

8

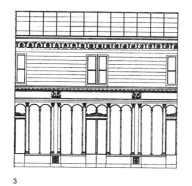

3

4

5

9

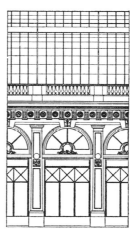

10

A Typology
of the Arcade

11. Milan, Galleria
de Cristoforis,
1832
12. Hamburg, Sil-
lem's Bazar,
1845
13. Brussels,
Galeries St.
Hubert, 1847
14. Milan, Galleria
Vittorio
Emanuele, 1867
15. Berlin, Kaiser-
galerie, 1873
16. Berlin, Friedrich-
strassenpassage,
1908

11

12

13

It was easy to piece together a picture of the development of spatial dimensions. However, it was more difficult to gain from existing plans an overview of the development of the interior facades. Moreover, the compilation of interior facades is not as complete as desired because it does not include facades of arcades with galleries running along the sides.

Spatial Development   The two series of spatial outlines (figs. 61 and 62) schematically present the development of the spatial profile of the longitudinal and central space of the arcade. They are drawn to the same scale as the plans in the catalog and numbered in chronological order. Only cross sections are shown, so the diagrams provide no information concerning the kind of construction and number of stories. Numbers 1–6 in fig. 61 are examples of arcades from the first decade of the nineteenth century; their profile is comparable to that of a narrow alley. In number 7 (Galerie d'Orléans, Paris), the width of the arcade is doubled as a result of its unique location. Examples 9 and 10 have the same width but twice the height. They are the first great arcades of the 1840s, in Hamburg and Brussels. In number 11 (Galleria Vittorio Emanuele, Milan) the spatial proportions of the earlier examples are maintained, but the dimensions are doubled. The following examples remain within these dimensions. Only numbers 12 and 15 (both Anglo-Saxon) present a completely different spatial cross section, as a result of their stepped structure.

From this series of developments, one can establish three stages which introduce new dimensions, each representing a doubling of the width and height. The years 1825, 1845, and 1865 mark these stages. The profile becomes more exaggerated as the arcade space expands: the glass roof becomes curved and the cornices and height of the arcade space are accented.

Number 17 (Friedrichstrasse Arcade, Berlin) depicts the decline of the architectural concept: through the introduction of a dust cover, the curved enclosure is transformed into a straight-edged, rectangular spatial cross section. Fig. 62 isolates the development of the central spaces around which the axes of the arcade are organized. Their increasing height results from the curvature necessary to span greater distances. One can see the clear transition from the tent roof to the dome and to ever steeper proportions imitating other massive structures.

Interior Facades   Despite its unfortunate incompleteness, the systematic presentation of the seventeen interior facades in fig. 63 is one of the most important products of this work. The facades are shown on a scale of 1 to 200 (larger than that of the other plans) in order to maintain detail. The illustration demonstrates that exterior architecture generally determines the form of the interior facades—although certain exceptions can be readily established. The interior facades reveal the following developments and general features:

1. Typically, the arcade motif in the continental arcades occurs as an alternation of columns or engaged columns and arches, as arches on columns, as the orders of columns derived from Italian palace facades, or finally as vertical divisions based on the model of cathedral interiors.

2. The glass roof is gradually emancipated from the facades and becomes an independent element whose only relationship to the order of the arcade columns can be seen in the interval between the beams.

3. The shop units and the glass fronts joining them to the interior of the arcade space develop from shop windows divided into square panes to entire store fronts consisting of one glass plate.

4. National differences are expressed in the variations between continental and British arcades. The latter are incompletely represented in my collection since no examples of continuous galleries are included. They would demonstrate a tendency to stress the interior facades by use of decoration.

5. Compared to the external facades, the relief of the cornices, walls, and sculptural decorations appears shallow. The absence of weather problems and the way the glass roof softens the shadows contribute to this effect.

A classification of arcade spaces according to spatial effect would differentiate between a bazaar type (Lowther Arcade, London), a gallery type (Weybosset Arcade, Providence), and a street type (Galeries St. Hubert, Brussels). The bazaar type is exemplified only in three British arcades. In each case the arcade space is domed, has round skylights, and recalls the spatial effect of the massive curved halls of the bazaar. The gallery type tends to emphasize the interior space because each story contains shops. It reminds one of a light well or courtyard. Most skeleton buildings are of this type. Finally, the street type places outer facades within its interior; these retain their independence and are linked only by the connecting glass roof.

These categories have their limitations. Stylistically, these facades have nothing unusual to offer, as they merely reflect the architectonics of the street facades and differ only in their endless arrangements and repetitions of the patterns. The Galeries St. Hubert in Brussels has a shallow relief facade in early Renaissance style; the Galleria Vittorio Emanuele in Milan has a variation of the Palladian city-palace facade; and the Kaisergalerie in Berlin has a somewhat bombastic, super-Italianate terra-cotta facade from the Renaissance. The gothic verticality of the other Berlin arcade resembles the department-store facades common at the turn of the century, thereby indicating the persistent influence of the development of commercial buildings on the arcade.

Exterior Facades   The development of exterior facades, that is, of the buildings surrounding arcade entrances, is considerably more difficult to depict, for here the particularities of the urban situation play a great role. Some of these facades can be found in the drawings in the catalog. Others, but by no means all, are reproduced in the photographs.

It is necessary to distinguish between arcades without entrance buildings and those with separate, generally taller entrance buildings. Most of the earlier arcades, which were built on previously undeveloped sites, have no entrance buildings serving independent functions. The entranceway into the arcade is thus accented and reflects the profile of the arcade interior. In these cases one could most properly speak of a facade development. In arcades with entrance buildings, however, the arcade interior ends with a building at right angles to the passageway. Entry is through a one-story hall in the form of a gateway arch or vestibule.

The development begins with a simple gateway arch opening up immediately to the arcade space (see, for example, the drawings of the Passage des Panoramas in Paris in the catalog). A sign with the name of the arcade is usually placed over the gateway arch. The arcade space of the Burlington Arcade in London is expanded to the full width of the entrance building at the opening to the street and possesses a massive facade. In the first version of this facade an entablature is borne by two columns and two jambs. In the second version, the one which was actually executed, the entrance is subdivided into three archways.

The simple gateway arch is enriched in the Parisian arcades of the Empire with sculptural and architectonic decorations. Some almost tend toward the motif of the triumphal arch (for example, the Galerie Vivienne). The arcades in Bristol, Philadelphia, and Providence, on the other hand, follow the model of the Burlington Arcade, eventually extending the three archways to form a kind of temple facade. Here we see, then, another contribution of the nineteenth century to the history of architecture: the temple as shopping center. The other point of departure, the central gateway, passes through numerous stages, finally becoming an imitation of the Roman triumphal arch. The southern entrance of the Galleria Vittorio Emanuele in Milan represents the epitome of this development. Here the arcade is a public festival hall, entered by way of the triumphal arch. The opposite form of the triumphal arch, its northern variation, is the medieval gateway which rises high above the street facade. This structure attains its most literal form in the Friedrichstrasse Arcade in Berlin.

Numerous entrance facades fall between these developments. They are assimilated into the existing street buildings and give little indication of the form of the arcade interior.

Advertisements and Attractions   A watercolor reprinted in the catalog depicts the interior of the Passage des Panoramas in Paris (the original is presently in the collections of the Musée Carnavalet). The picture dates from about 1810 and is the first and best representation of our topic. The large hanging oil lamp in the middle of the picture illuminates the arcade. It can be lowered by the rope for lighting and cleaning. Beneath the lamp hangs the sign of Monsieur Dehodenq, restaurant proprietor. Below that hangs a kind of treasure chest which would have been illuminated as well, for it advertises his specialities: "Coffee, ice cream, fork lunches." To the right and left one finds hanging signs which compete for the visitor's attention. Small objects—umbrellas, wreaths, and jugs—also announce the goods sold in the individual shops. The cornice above the shops is covered with the names of the entrepreneurs. Toward the front of the arcade the goods of the food market threaten to flow out of the entranceway. Precious cloth is displayed outside the shop across the arcade. A sign in the dark frame at the top of the picture points the way to the neighboring Théâtre des Variétés, which is accessible via a side entrance in the arcade. The narrow iron bridge in the background of the picture linked the main attractions of the arcade, the two panoramas.

The picture, made in the period before photography, captures the scene with almost photographic precision, and it accords with the contemporary descriptions which have been quoted in the catalog. Together they recreate a period in which the arcade was an active social and commercial center. The picture presents all those aspects which gave the arcade its life: the competition among the proprietors and their various attempts to capture the attention of the shoppers and casual strollers, as well as the owner's efforts to make the arcade itself an attraction.

The first experiments in public gas and electric illumination took place in the arcade. This method of lighting made advertisements and attractions possible even at night. Hence, from its beginnings, the arcade was superior to the poorly illuminated streets as a site for evening strolls and shopping. There were three basic methods of illumination.

1. A string of lanterns hanging on ropes or chains down the middle of the arcade. The lanterns could be attached to the saddle of the glass roof, iron brackets (Royal Opera Arcade, London), or a rope spanning the width of the passageway.

2. Massive chandeliers with numerous individual lights. Chandeliers were generally used in the large central spaces. Particularly impressive examples can be found in the Galleria Mazzini in Genoa and the Kaisergalerie in Berlin.

3. The wall bracket with one or two gas lights. This method was the most common since the lamps could be easily cleaned and refilled. Today it is used in only a few arcades (for example in the Galeries St. Hubert in Brussels) as it has been replaced by neon lights.

One can also differentiate between numerous advertising practices:

1. Actual objects, like pistols, gloves, umbrellas, and eyeglasses, that directly indicate the merchandise being offered.

2. Painted or written signs that either protrude into the arcade space from above the shop entrance or stand next to the doors on moveable stands.

3. Display boxes and glass cabinets set up in addition to the shop window and sometimes even placed outside along the sides of the arcade. They are therefore not bound to the location of the shops themselves.

4. Temporary exhibitions of merchandise set up in the arcade during business hours. The goods are hung in front of the store or spread out on tables.

5. Placards, announcements, and posters that can be attached to the shop walls, windowpanes, or cornice provided for that purpose. The writing takes the form of painted or partial-relief letters glued to the surface or sculptured words (as in contemporary neon advertising). The Galerie Véro-Dodat is particularly noteworthy for a uniform style of lettering and numbering which conforms to the general architecture of the arcade as well.

As shown in the photographs of the Parisian arcades from the last century, all of these advertising methods were usually employed simultaneously. They transformed the arcade into a jungle of exotic enticements through which the wanderer had literally to work his way. This almost tropical overgrowth of advertisements led in 1847[180] to an *ordonnance de police* concerning the private Parisian arcades. It set limitations and controls on the distances which the different advertisements could protrude into the arcade space. However, no one seems to have paid any attention to it.

The informative pictorial sign and the symbolic object remained the predominant mode of advertising well into the early nineteenth century, since a sizeable portion of the population was illiterate.[181] These signs also oriented the shopper, as the individual buildings did not have numbered addresses. The written word, the company sign as it still exists today, did not replace these symbolic representations until the nineteenth century. With this development an artistic element of the arcade was lost. The early nineteenth century saw a general trend toward larger systems of organization to meet the demands of the thriving businesses. Hence, where individual, often famous artists had once been commissioned to produce shop signs, specialized advertising agencies appeared, supplying the commercial world with a constant flow of new ideas. Advertisements were then liberated from the actual store site with the invention of lithography (1795) and the introduction of stencils, prefabricated adhesive letters, poster kiosks, roaming advertising wagons, and printed leaflets. One could follow in the development of the store front (which is yet to be systematically investigated) the gradual processes by which the whole facade is included as part of the advertising; commercial architecture thrives as it becomes an advertising factor. The domination of advertising over the interior of the arcade can still be seen in the Passage Pommeraye in Nantes. It is, however, the sole remaining example. Renovation and modernization have sterilized most arcades, robbing them of the extravagant advertisements which once had a determining influence on their character.

A variety of establishments offered entertainment and information to the arcade visitors. Each arcade had to include such attractions in its spatial plan to entice visitors and increase business. The individual entries in the catalog provide detailed descriptions. Besides the shops and apartments, the following attractions and establishments can be found in most arcades:

Cafés, restaurants, beer halls, taverns, bars, etc.

Brothels, gambling rooms, etc.

Hotels and pensions

Clubs, meeting rooms, etc.

Theaters, vaudeville halls, concert halls, cabarets, and, later, cinemas

Showrooms, for example, panoramas, dioramas, cosmoramas, picture galleries, panopticons, and bazaars

Reading rooms, where books and out-of-town newspapers could be read for a fee

Baths.

All these attractions appeared in the arcades in varying combinations. The Palais Royal, built at the turn of the century, provided the model. They belong to the general physiognomy of the arcade, making it a goal and place of relaxation for a city's inhabitants.

Conditions for the Existence of the Arcade
The arcade is an object of private speculation and does not belong under the jurisdiction of the city administration and maintenance. Nor is it an institution which would have been made indispensable by the development of urban civilization in the nineteenth century. Risk, the speculative element, is essential to it. Such risk can be reduced only by precise calculation and a suitable location. Many arcades listed in the catalog were unsuccessful speculations and led to the financial ruin of their owners. Since arcades were immobile they could not change with the fashion and mood of the society and thereby keep up with the changing business districts, at any given moment in vogue, throughout the city.

The nature of the visitors and the habits of the consumers are nowhere as intensely observed and feared as in the arcade. From a review of the construction histories of the arcades one would conclude that the success or failure of an arcade often depends on reasons other than the arcade itself. Changes in the environment, in the composition of the arcade's clientele, or in the public's sense of space can all have a great effect on the life of an arcade. Only such changes can explain, for example, why the Passage des Panoramas in Paris, formerly the promenade of high society and home of luxury shops, is deteriorating today. It is overdeveloped, too narrow for its purposes, and filled with low-quality shops, cheap restaurants, and run-down apartments. Such changes—or, as in this case, the absence of them—also explain why the newly renovated Burlington Arcade in London has kept its standing, even though it is almost as old and just as narrow as its Parisian counterpart. The arcade, in London's West End, has been the main attraction of Bond Street for over 150 years. It is the center of the traditional business district, where wealthy Londoners have always come to meet and to shop in established firms; this constancy of tradition does not exist on the boulevards of Paris.

Location   The arcade requires a specific location. It must be situated in the center of the city where people meet, shop, stroll, and relax. A prerequisite for a good location is a certain minimum of people, commercial activity, and traffic. It is extremely difficult to express this minimum quantitatively, but it must be high enough to guarantee a constant flow of visitors. It directly affects the financial success of businesses and must offset the intensive exploitation of the land and the high cost of construction. The arcade must be frequented day and night by shifting and overlapping sets of visitors: shoppers, tourists, strollers, and people seeking entertainment.

This first condition limits considerably the possible locations for an arcade. Indeed, many cities could not offer a viable site. Even in large cosmopolitan cities, the areas where an arcade would be feasible are generally no larger than one square kilometer. In Berlin the intersection of Friedrichstrasse and Unter den Linden was once the most obvious choice; in the Paris of the early nineteenth century, the area between the Palais Royal and the boulevards; in London, the blocks between Piccadilly, the Strand, and Oxford Street; in Brussels, a small section of the old city that could be traversed on foot in five minutes; in Milan, the large squares and their connecting streets; in Moscow, Red Square and the streets radiating from it into the center.

Hence, the arcade can thrive only when located in the heart of a city where public life is at its most intense. The more expansive it is, and the more it is traversed with equal intensity from all directions by commercial avenues, the more suited a city center is for an arcade. A linear commercial district is not well suited since here the arcade leads away from the main business areas. Sillem's Bazar in Hamburg, for example, met its downfall because of such a mislocation.

Position   Besides requiring sufficient flow of people the arcade must also function as a traffic artery. An arcade that possesses two or more entrances, offering a passageway, must necessarily provide a connection, shortcut, opening, or easement. It must make contact with a pre-existing or incomplete street system, ideally connecting two evenly frequented streets. If this last condition is not met the chances of the arcade's success are considerably reduced.

Fig. 64 represents the functional roles the arcade could play in the spatial systems of a nineteenth-century city. Each square depicts schematically the possible locations in relationship to streets, building blocks, and plazas. The arcades are shown from the perspective of the glass roof. Five basic locational schemes are possible:

1. The arcade connects a street with a building or another street. It thereby provides a shortcut and facilitates traffic between two points.
2. The arcade is the continuation of a street or the connection between two stretches of one street which had formerly been separated by a building.

S Location System	Access 1		Continuation 2		Connection 3		Competing System 4		Independent System 5
Street to Building a		1 Street a		Street to Square a		Linear a		2 Entrances a	
Street to Street b		2 Streets b		Square to Square b		Parallel b		4 Entrances b	
Street to Street c		3 Streets c				Intersecting c		8 Entrances c	
		4 Streets d							

64
Location types

3. The arcade connects a street and a public square, two squares, or even two squares and two streets, as in the Galleria Vittorio Emanuele in Milan.

4. The arcade is a part of a larger private unit which competes with the public street system. It makes the block accessible, draws the pedestrian traffic off the streets, and supplies a large number of businesses in a compact area. The arcades can be developed as a linear system, as in the two examples in Bristol; can run parallel to a main avenue, as in the Galleria Mazzini in Genoa; or can form a whole complex of passageways which intersect the block, as in the Passage des Panoramas, Passage Jouffroy, and Passage Verdeau in Paris.

5. The arcade can exist independently of the street system only, however, if it forms its own internal circuit with entrances from all directions and completely enclosed sections. The arcade then actually becomes a building similar to a covered market or department store. The Palais Royal and the Moscow Trade Halls best exemplify this type, and it is interesting that the latter have been converted into the GUM (State General Department Store).

Internal Organization In addition to the particular attractions of its environment, the arcade must provide its own unique attractions. The fulfillment of this condition influences the use of the building, the methods of access, and the architectonic approach to the arcade interior and facades. The architects must not only accommodate as many shops as possible within the space of the arcade but also make the traversal of the arcade as pleasant and entertaining as possible. The most essential attractive aspect of the arcade is clearly the continuous glass roof, which protects the interior from inclement weather, making it a preferred place for an undisturbed promenade.

A second aspect is the line of shops on both sides of the arcade space. The shops must be as narrow and deep as possible in order to achieve maximum diversity and a bazaar-like atmosphere. A third aspect is a systematic division of levels, which guarantees ongoing activity in the arcade parallel to street life. Culinary, cultural, and recreational establishments are necessary elements of the arcade to transform the casual pedestrian into an active participant. In this way the arcade can be indispensable to urban society. Ideally the arcade kaleidoscopically reflects in miniature the entirety of city life.

As a fourth attractive aspect, the arcade maintains the anonymity of the street. The arcade interior must create the illusion of a street with exterior facades. The visitor should never feel as if he has entered an interior space, for psychologically the entrance into a room is generally associated only with a particular goal and concrete intention. In this respect the glass roof construction is ideal, as it forms an unattached, ethereal net arched high above the ground. The glass roof must therefore by so transparent and light that it is hardly noticed. The combination of iron and industrially produced glass plate first satisfied this aesthetic criterion. The Galeries St. Hubert in Brussels, built shortly before the Crystal Palace, best approaches this ideal.

The Public The arcade attracts its own public. It is the product of a liberal economic system, a particular social class, and a public sphere, all of which grew out of the tumult of the French Revolution. The sense of space, the needs and desires of this society, constitute the life-giving element of the arcade. When they change—as they did in the beginning of the twentieth century—the spatial concept of the arcade declines, ending finally as nothing but an accompaniment to the shop windows, a mere thoroughfare for other businesses, a structure subordinated to the needs of surrounding buildings.

In the time of its conception the arcade was home to luxury and fashion. It offered to the bourgeois public in all its various guises—the *flâneur,* the bohemian, the *boulevardier*—the opportunity to display itself to the world. It presented the myriad products of a blossoming luxury industry for gazing, buying, flaunting, and consuming. The public served by the arcade felt at home in the artificial lighting of the theaters, cafés, restaurants, bars—and glass-covered arcades. It reveled in this illusionistic realm, this man-made jungle under glass, this urban reality which replaced nature.

This section gives an overview of the most important literature on the topic of the arcade—as far as I have been able to compile it. The list at the end is incomplete and has been pieced together from careful studies of individual examples, from quite unreliable and brief entries in encyclopedias, handbooks, and architectural histories, from articles dealing with individual arcades, and from literary works in which the arcade is the locus of the action or object of description.

Walter Benjamin, in his fragmentary and unfinished work, "Paris, Capital of the Nineteenth Century," was the first to recognize the arcade as a phenomenon of the century and to view it in context. Günther Bandmann treated the arcade from an art historian's perspective in his article on the Galleria Vittorio Emanuele in Milan. Three unpublished works in England deal with arcades. The first investigates the British arcades, the second analyzes the great Milan arcade, and the third, which at this writing is in preparation by Mr. Fenner of the Courtauld Institute in London, examines the Parisian arcades. A general description and compilation on the arcade building type, complete with drawings and photographs, has never been undertaken. A thorough investigation of the phenomenon of the arcade in the nineteenth century would have to be based first on such a general compilation of the existing materials. This work attempts to provide this basis. A systematic analysis of the arcade in its economic and social context remains a project for the future.

The building type of the arcade, of which I collected nearly 300 built and projected examples, was considered marginal among the wide variety of nineteenth-century building types. It was therefore mentioned only sporadically in the literature on the architectural history of the nineteenth and twentieth centuries. The first attempts at a systematic presentation are restricted to handbooks and construction manuals; the most impressive of these is the chapter in the great *Handbuch der Architektur* (1923). In the *Dictionary of Architecture* (1848–1892) and the classic texts by Planat, Bosc, Mothes, Joseph, Guadet, Stübben, Gurlitt, Hitchcock, and Giedion, one comes across entries or observations on arcades, but justice is never done to the topic. All of them name the same examples, use the same outdated descriptions; they differ only in the inclusion of chance discoveries.

A number of articles of varying quality in construction journals, magazines, and urban histories treat the history of the arcade in individual countries or cities. I will mention here some of the more useful treatments. Patrice Boussel wrote the entry "Passage" (arcade) in the recently published *Dictionnaire de Paris*; Carroll Meeks devoted an extended section of his *Italian Architecture, 1750–1914* to the great Italian arcades; MacGrath and Frost in England offered a detailed study of the London arcades and utopian projects of the 1850s in their voluminous book *Glass in Architecture*. I was naturally unable to compile all the rich material in archives and urban history collections which concerns the construction of individual arcades. The existence of the arcade is mirrored in contemporary newspapers, its opening hailed, its anniversary celebrated, and its demolition mourned. Only later, from about 1830 to 1840, does the arcade begin to appear in the new architectural magazines. A few arcades eventually became known through monographs published by the architects, some of which include plans and perspectives.

Most of the information comes from works on urban history, from travel reports and guides, especially from the small red Baedeker volumes with their precise descriptions. The first detailed publications on arcades appeared in architectural journals around 1850. In 1848 the plans of Sillem's Bazar in Hamburg were reprinted in the *Zeitschrift für praktische Baukunst*. In 1855 the Galerie Colbert in Paris was published in the *Zeitschrift für Bauwesen*. This arcade, with the neighboring Galerie Vivienne, had actually already been discussed in print at the time of its completion in Thiollet's collection of the latest Parisian architecture. In 1868 *The Builder* introduced its readers to the Galleria Vittorio Emanuele in Milan, which had been built by an English architectural firm with English capital. In the following years this journal often reported on the new arcades being constructed in industrial towns. After the World War II, with the increased interest in the nineteenth century, the arcade became a subject for researchers in architectural history. Robert Alexander studied the arcade in Providence and Mary-Peale Schofield examined the Cleveland Arcade. Their articles appeared in the *Journal of the Society of Architectural Historians* (U.S.A.). A British journal of the same name published pictures of the Royal Arcade in Newcastle when the building was threatened with demolition. More and more architectural magazines now provide photographic coverage of old arcades and designs for new downtown areas with arcade-like systems of access.

Three more recent works are concerned with the most famous of all the arcades, the Galleria Vittorio Emanuele in Milan. It is the only arcade whose history has been fully researched. These include an unpublished dissertation by P. J. V. Smyth, an article by Bandmann in the *Zeitschrift für Kunstgeschichte*, and an overly extravagant commemorative publication for the arcade's centennial produced by the city of Milan.

There are countless descriptions of the early Parisian and London arcades in nineteenth-century literature. Selections from travelogs, memoirs, and diaries are quoted in the catalog. Heine lived in an apartment in an arcade and enjoyed his promenades in them; Börne praised the new Galerie d'Orléans; Zola employed the arcades in his *Thérèse Raquin* and *Nana* as the gloomy setting of his tragic works of social criticism. Montigny provided the most precise description of an arcade, the Passage des Panoramas, in his *Le Provincial à Paris*. The most biting and comprehensive use of an arcade can be found in Balzac's *Illusions Perdues*. The picture he painted of the Galeries de Bois in the Palais Royal (the first arcade ever built) is exemplary. The last two texts are quoted in their entirety in the catalog.

In the twentieth century the phenomenon of the arcade becomes an independent literary theme, a metaphor. It is raised to a historical and philosophical level. Aragon revealed the arcade, in one of his early works, *Le Paysan de Paris* [published in English as *Nightwalker*], as material for the surrealists. The secure bourgeois world is unmasked and reality becomes illusion, delusion, absurdity.

Fantasy and dream join in an image of the world which transcends the world. Where else could one better demonstrate the truth of this surrealist theory than in an arcade? One chapter of *Le Paysan de Paris* bears the title, "Passage de l'Opéra." Blanqui, the leader of the 1871 revolution of the commune, lived there. Here too one found the Café Certa, where the circle around Breton held its meetings. Aragon describes the arcade in minutest detail as it appeared shortly before its demolition and the construction of the Boulevard Haussmann. He recalls the advertisements, the sayings on the signs, the inhabitants, the café, the hairdresser, the little brothel, and other aspects.

Walter Benjamin translated the description of the Café Certa into German and published it in the *Literarische Welt* in 1928. In the winter of 1925–1926 Benjamin had begun a joint translation of Proust with Franz Hessel. It was probably Hessel who interested Benjamin in the complex of Parisian arcades. This interest was to be the kernel of the project "Paris, Capital of the Nineteenth Century." The only fruits of his work, however, are an essay, two versions of sections on selected Parisian themes, and a collection of sketches, which has never been published. The essay has six sections: Fourier, or the Arcades; Daguerre, or the Panoramas; Grandville, or the World Exhibitions; Louis-Philippe, or the Interior; Baudelaire, or the Streets of Paris; Haussmann, or the Barricades.

I would like to quote here Benjamin's first sketch because it contains all the elements which I struggled to compile in this book.

Most of the Paris arcades are built in the decade and a half after 1822. The first condition for this new fashion is the boom in the textile trade. The *magasins de nouveauté,* the first establishments to keep large stocks of goods on their premises, begin to appear, precursors of the department stores. It is the time of which Balzac wrote, "The great poem of display chants its many-colored strophes from the Madeleine to the Porte-Saint-Denis." The arcades are a center of trade in luxury goods. In their fittings art is brought in to the service of commerce. Contemporaries never tire of admiring them. They long remain a center of attraction for foreigners. An *Illustrated Guide to Paris* said: "These arcades, a recent invention of industrial luxury, are glass-roofed, marble-walled passages cut through whole blocks of houses, whose owners have combined in this speculation. On either side of the passages, which draw their light from above, run the most elegant shops, so that an arcade of this kind is a city, indeed, a world in miniature." The arcades are the scene of the first gas lighting.

The second condition for the construction of the arcades is the advent of building in iron. The Empire saw in this technique an aid to a renewal of architecture in the ancient Greek manner. The architectural theorist Bötticher expresses a general conviction when he says, "with regard to the artistic form of the new system, the formal principle of the Hellenic style" should be introduced. *Empire* is the style of revolutionary heroism for which the state is an end in itself. Just as Napoleon failed to recognize the functional nature of the state as an instrument of domination by the bourgeois class, neither did the master builders of his time perceive the functional nature of iron, through which the constructive principle began its domination of architecture. These builders model their pillars on Pompeian columns, their factories on houses, as later the first railway stations are to resemble chalets. "Construction fills the role of the unconscious." Nevertheless, the idea of the engineer, originating in the revolutionary wars, begins to assert itself, and battle is joined between constructor and decorator, École Polytechnique and École des Beaux-Arts.

In iron, an artificial building material makes its appearance for the first time in the history of architecture. It undergoes a development that accelerates in the course of the century. The decisive breakthrough comes when it emerges that the locomotive, with which experiments had been made since the end of the twenties, could only be used on iron rails. The rail becomes the first prefabricated iron component, the forerunner of the girder. Iron is avoided in residential buildings and used in arcades, exhibition halls, stations—buildings serving transitory purposes. Simultaneously, the architectonic scope for the application of glass expands. The social conditions for its intensified use as a building material do not arrive, however, until a hundred years later. Even in Scheerbart's "Glass Architecture" (1914) it appears in utopian contexts. [Quoted from the version in Walter Benjamin, *Reflections*, trans. Edmund Jephcott (New York: Harcourt Brace Jovanovich, 1978), pp. 146–147.]

Benjamin says of Fourier a few lines later: "In the arcades, Fourier saw the architectonic canon of the phalanstery. His reactionary modification of them is characteristic: whereas they originally serve commercial purposes, he makes them into dwelling places. The phalanstery becomes a city of arcades. Fourier installs in the austere, formal world of the Empire the colorful idyll of Biedermeier. . . ." [*Reflections*, trans. Jephcott, pp. 148–149]

Benjamin's first notes on arcades date from 1927–1928. What followed was a continuation of one of these chapters,* the planned three-part book which was to bear the title *Charles Baudelaire: A Lyric Poet in the Era of High Capitalism.* Only the middle section of this book was begun. It consisted of three chapters: "The Bohemian," "The Flâneur," and "Modernism." The last two chapters were finally published in German in 1968.

In the chapter "The Flâneur," a human type is related to the building type of the arcade. Benjamin writes:

The arcades were a cross between a street and an *intérieur*. If one can speak of an artistic device of the physiologies, it is the proven device of the *feuilleton*, namely, to turn a boulevard into an *intérieur*. The street becomes a dwelling for the flâneur; he is as much at home among the façades of houses as a citizen is in his four walls. To him the shiny, enamelled signs of businesses are at least as good a wall ornament as an oil painting is to a bourgeois in his salon. The walls are the desk against which he presses his notebooks; news-stands are his libraries and the terraces of cafés are the balconies from which he looks down on his household after his work is done. . . . If the arcade is the classical form of the *intérieur,* which is how the *flâneur* sees the street, the department store is the form of the *intérieur*'s decay. The bazaar is the last hangout of the *flâneur*. If in the beginning the street had become an *intérieur* for him, now this *intérieur* turned into a street, and he roamed through the labyrinth of merchandise as he had once roamed through the labyrinth of the city. . . . [Quoted from the version in *Charles Baudelaire: A Lyric Poet in the Era of High Capitalism*, trans. Harry Zohn (London: NLB, 1973), pp. 37, 54.]

So much for a sampling of quotations directly related to arcades. Their content has been distilled out of an exact knowledge of the voluminous literature on Paris. They span disparate contexts, illuminating the century as had never been done previously. Following these sections of the first version, Benjamin reworked the "flâneur" chapter, calling the second version "On Some Motifs of Baudelaire."

* *Das Argument*, vol. 46, 1968, pp. 71f., afterword by Rolf Tiedmann for the first publication of the chapter "Die Moderne" (Modernism). ["Paris, Capital of the Nineteenth Century" is published in English in Walter Benjamin, *Reflections*, trans. Edmund Jephcott, New York, Harcourt Brace Jovanovich, 1978, and in *Charles Baudelaire: A Lyric Poet in the Era of High Capitalism*, trans. Harry Zohn, London, NLB, 1973. The second work also includes "The Flâneur" and "Modernism."]

The arcade complex, on which Benjamin worked until his death, was intended to become a historical and philosophical reconstruction of the nineteenth century. The word *arcade* remained, although it was only a piece of the picture. Benjamin left piles of notes and aphorisms behind. However, as a result of the deplorable secrecy surrounding his legacy, I have been unable to ascertain to what extent Benjamin was occupied with individual arcades in his research in Parisian libraries. Yet references in his letters suggest that the work on arcades would be a montage of startlingly juxtaposed quotations.*

From Balzac to Benjamin: This is the connection Benjamin proposes in an entry in his notebooks. He says: "Balzac anchored the mythic constitution of his world in a topographical substructure. Paris is the foundation of his mythology. Paris with its two or three great bankers, Nucingen, du Tillet; Paris with its great physician, Horace Bianchon; with its entrepreneur, César Birotteau; with its four or five great coquettes; with its moneylender, Goseck, its few great lawyers and military heroes. But above all it is always the same streets and alleys, lobbies and corners, which provide the arena for this circle of figures. What else could all this mean than that the topography is the framework of this—indeed any—mythological space. It is the key which unlocks the myth, just as it was for Pausanias' Greece. The history and situation of the Parisian arcades will become for this century the underworld into which Paris descended." With this, I end the discussion of Benjamin's work, which was fragmented by war and persecution.

Chapters on the Berlin Kaisergalerie by Hessel and Kracauer demonstrate their indebtedness to Aragon. They have been reprinted in the catalog. Second-generation surrealists like Mandiarges and Marcel Schneider were fascinated by the haunting Passage Pommeraye in Nantes. Scenes from Céline's novel, *Death on the Installment Plan*, take place in an arcade, I believe the Passage Choiseul in Paris. In one scene a child has an anxiety dream in which the typical saleswoman appears, a woman both desired and feared by the arcade's inhabitants. She grows larger and larger, eventually breaking out of the confines of the arcade. All the people wander after her up to the banks of the Seine where she, now a giant, disappears from sight.

I have included in this bibliography only those works dealing in general with the topic of the arcade. Literature concerning individual arcades is referred to in the footnotes of the catalog.

* On Benjamin's literary estate: "Walter Benjamin und das Paris Baudelaires," broadcast script by Rolf Tiedmann, 3rd Program of the SFB-Berlin, February 19, 1965. It states on p. 22: "Finally, and above all, the sketches and materials for the arcades work have been kept: thousands of pages of notes, aphorisms, reflections, supporting material, quotations. Adorno, whom Benjamin named as his executor, comments: 'The whole can hardly be reconstructed. It was Benjamin's intention to reject all obvious interpretations and to let the meaning proceed from the unexpected montage of materials. Philosophy was not only to overtake surrealism but itself to become surrealistic! The masterpiece consisting solely of quotations was to be the crowning achievement of his 'antisubjectivism.' " Also, *Alternative,* Benjamin volume, 56/57, 1967, and the reply by Tiedmann in *Das Argument,* vol. 46, 1968, pp. 74–93. The arcades papers will appear as the last volume of the Suhrkamp Verlag critical edition of Benjamin's complete works, originally announced for 1975.

Literature on the Arcade

Reference

Baukunst des Architekten, 2d ed., 1902, vol. 2, part 5, pp. 186–192, "Passagen."

Bosc, *Dictionnaire d'Architecture,* 1879, entry "Passage."

The Dictionary of Architecture, 1848–1892, entries "Arcade" and "Bazaar."

Dictionnaire de Paris, Larousse, 1965, entry "Passages."

C. Gurlitt, *Handbuch des Städtebaus,* 1920, part 2, p. 32.

Handbuch der Architektur, 3d ed., 1923, IV/2/2, pp. 110–120, "Passagen" and "Galerien"; 3d ed., 1924, IV/9, pp. 63–66, "Städtebau."

L. Klassen, *Grundriss-Vorbilder,* 1884, part 6, pp. 592f.

R. MacGrath and A. C. Frost, *Glass in Architecture and Decoration,* 1937, pp. 141–145, "Arcades."

O. Mothes, *Illustriertes Bau-Lexikon,* 4th ed., 1883, entry "Passagen."

P. Planat, *Encyclopédie de l'architecture,* Paris, 1888–1892, vol. 6, pp. 83–86, entry "Passages."

Works on Architectural History

S. Giedion, *Space, Time and Architecture,* 13th ed., pp. 177f.

J. Guadet, *Théorie de l'architecture,* 4th ed., 1912, vol. 4, pp. 83–87, "Passages."

L. Hautecoeur, *Histoire de l'architecture classique en France,* Paris, 1952–1957, vol. 6, pp. 67f., on Parisian arcades.

H.-R. Hitchcock, *Architecture: Nineteenth and Twentieth Centuries,* 1958, pp. 119f., 146, 157.

D. Joseph, *Geschichte der Baukunst des 19. Jahrhunderts,* n.d., 1st and 2nd half-volume, pp. 374, 405, 451, 723, 773, 786, European arcades.

D. Joseph, *Geschichte der Architektur Italiens* 1907, pp. 442–449, Italian arcades.

E. Lavagnino, *L'arte moderna dai neoclassici ai contemporanei,* 2 vol., 1956–1961, pp. 487f.

M. Major, *Geschichte der Architektur,* 1960, pp. 70f., 226, 228, 232.

C. L. V. Meeks, *Italian Architecture, 1750–1914,* 1966, pp. 290–292, Italian arcades.

Articles

Architecture in Australia, June 1963, articles "Arcades of Melbourne" and "Sydney's Arcades," pp. 80–90.

Günther Bandmann, "Die Galleria Vittorio Emanuele zu Mailand," *Zeitschrift für Kunstgeschichte,* vol. 29, no. 2, 1966 pp. 81–110. Includes general information on the arcade.

G. Bauer, "Passages de Paris," *Plaisir de France,* Nov. 1964, pp. 28–35.

Peter Blake, "Shopping Streets under Roofs of Glass," *Architectural Forum,* vol. 124, Jan.-Feb. 1966, pp. 69–75.

The Builder, vol. 108, 1915, "Some London Arcades," pp. 352f., and vol. 138, 1930, "The Revival of the Arcades."

Reginald Colby, "Shopping off the City Streets," *Country Life,* Nov. 1964.

Commission de Vieux Paris, 1916, pp. 270–273, "Les Passages Couverts," catalog of Parisian arcades.

Ramon Gomez de la Serma, "El Alma de las Galerias," *Revista di Architectura* (Buenos Aires), Jan. 1948, pp. 13–32.

Heikki Hoppania, "Sisakatu," *Arkkitehti Arkitekten,* vol. 5, 1968, pp. 30–33.

Dissertation

B. Fineberg, "The History and Design of Shopping Arcades," Regional College of Art Library, Manchester, England, 1953.

Catalog

Introduction

Although I have attempted to be as thorough as possible, this catalog of arcades is necessarily fragmentary. I was able to study European arcades by traveling to see them, but reliance on written sources was inevitable for examples from Russia, Australia, and the United States.

All arcades in the catalog can be considered independent structures by the criteria established in the typology. I have omitted borderline cases and dependent arcade structures, both simply absorbed into the interior of commercial establishments as mere thoroughfares without their own source of illumination.

Individual arcades are listed in the catalog under the name of the city in which they are located. Within the individual city listings, the arcades are arranged by date of construction.

Four types of illustrations are included in the catalog: street plan overviews, site plans, drawings of arcades as designed and built, and photographs. Street plans are provided for cities with numerous arcades. They help to clarify the context in which the arcades are located. All street plans have been uniformly redrawn and oriented to the north, and are reproduced at a scale of 1 to 4000. In these drawings the outline of the arcade structure is shaded; the arcade space itself has been left white. Covered passages without glass are indicated by diagonally crossed lines. The outlines of the arcade buildings may be inaccurate, since maps only occasionally show more than the outlines of the site itself.

Site plans of the most important European arcades are provided in cases where I could obtain the necessary documents from the planning authorities and archives of the various cities.

To show interesting planning stages or later additions, I have included additional site plans to illustrate the phases of a project.

Drawings of structures have been redrawn and reproduced at a scale of 1 to 500* to enable comparison and demonstrate the development of increasing dimensions. Redrawing was necessary because most of the documents could not be reproduced at a scale suitable for this work. All of the drawings have been redrawn to the same specifications, using a method of clean outlining without door markings or projections for lintels or archways. I cannot guarantee exactness of scale since both the conversion of scales and successive photographic enlargement and reduction of the originals may have produced certain inaccuracies. The location of the originals from which the drawings were made may be found in the notes.

Photographs were selected from a large collection of pictorial documentation. They are supplemented by contemporary engravings to illustrate the early arcades.

*Except as noted in captions.

Arcades Described in the Catalog

City	Country	Name	Built	Status
Aarhus	Denmark	Borgporten	?	Standing
Adelaide	Australia	Arcade	1885?	?
Amiens	France	Passage du Commerce	?	Destroyed
		Passage de la Renaissance	?	Destroyed
Amsterdam	The Netherlands	Passage	1884?	Demolished
		De Beurpassage	1894/1963	Standing
Antwerp	Belgium	Cité	1844	1860 Demolished
Ashton under Lyne	England	Clarence Arcade	?	Standing
Athens	Greece	Stoa Arsákiou	?	Standing
		Stoa Mela-Kostopoulos	1890	Standing
Atlanta, GA	USA	Peachtree Arcade	1916	1964 Demolished
Autun	France	Arcade	1848–1850	Standing
Auxerre	France	Passage Medefiori	ca.1850	Standing
Barcelona	Spain	Pasaje	?	Standing
Bath	England	The Corridor	1825	Standing
Berlin	Germany	Kaisergalerie	1871–1873	1944 Destroyed
		Arcade	1874	Project
		Lindengalerie	1891–1892	1944 Destroyed
		Friedrichstrasse Arcade	1908–1909	1944 Ruin
Bern	Switzerland	Von Werdt Arcade	?	Standing
Birmingham	England	Great Western Arcade	1875–1876	Modified
		Central Arcade	1881	Demolished
		Imperial Arcade	1884	Demolished
		North Western Arcade	1884–1885	Demolished
		Gothic Arcade	1884	Demolished
		City Arcades	1899–?	Demolished
		Piccadilly Arcade	1926–1927	Standing
Blackburn	England	Twaite's Arcade	1882	?
Bordeaux	France	Galerie Bordelaise	1831–1834	Modified
		Bazar Bordelais	1835	1872 Demolished
		Passage Sarget	1878	Modified
Bournemouth	England	Gervis Arcade	1866–1873	Standing
		Westbourne Arcade	1884–1885	Standing
		Boscombe Arcade	1891	Standing
Bradford	England	Swan Arcade	1877–1881	1962 Demolished
Braunschweig	West Germany	Sedan Bazar	1878	1944 Destroyed
Brighton	England	Royal Arcade	1868?	Project
Bristol	England	Upper Arcade	1824–1825	1943 Destroyed
		Lower Arcade	1824–1825	Restored
Brussels	Belgium	Passage de la Monnaie	1820	Modified
		Galeries St. Hubert	1846–1847	Restored
		Galerie Bortier	1847–1848	Modified
		Galerie du Commerce	1872?	Demolished
		Passage des Postes	1875	Demolished
		Galerie du Parlement	1880	Demolished
		Passage du Nord	1881–1882	Standing
Budapest	Hungary	Harisch Bazar	?	Demolished
		Röser Bazar	1883	Modified
		Königsbazar	1899–1900	?
		Pariser Hof	1910–1911	Standing
Buenos Aires	Argentina	Galeria Bon Marché	1890	Remodeled
		Galeria Güemes	1913–1915	Standing
		Passage Barolo	1923	Standing
Cardiff	Wales	Royal Arcade	1869	Standing
		Queen Street Arcade	1880?	Standing
		Wyndham Arcade	1887?	Standing
		High Street Arcade	1887?	Standing
		Castle Arcade	1889?	Standing
		Andrews Arcade	1896?	?
		Morgan Arcade	1897	Modified

City	Country	Name	Built	Status
Cardiff	Wales	Duke Street Arcade	1902?	Standing
		Celtic Corridor	1905?	?
		Dominions Arcade	?	?
Carpentras	France	Passage Boyer	ca.1860	Standing
Charleroi	Belgium	Passage de la Bourse	1891	Standing
Chemnitz (Karl-Marx-Stadt)	East Germany	Arcade	1884	1945 Destroyed
Chester	England	St. Michaels Arcade	?	Standing
Chicago, IL	USA	Pullman Arcade	1880	Standing
Cincinnati, OH	USA	Emery Arcade	?	?
Cleveland, OH	USA	Cleveland Arcade	1888–1890	Standing
		Colonial Arcade	1898	Standing
Cologne	West Germany	Königin Augusta Halle	1862	1944 Destroyed
		Passage Tietz	1902?	1944 Destroyed
		Stollwerk Halle	1906	1944 Destroyed
Copenhagen	Denmark	Jorcks Passage	?	Standing
Cremona	Italy	Passage	?	Standing
		Passage	?	Standing
Danzig	Poland	Passage	?	Destroyed
Derby	England	Strand Arcade	1882?	?
Dewsbury	England	Arcade	?	?
Dortmund	West Germany	Krügerpassage	1916?	Standing
Dresden	East Germany	Zentral Theater Passage	1898	1945 Destroyed
		König Albert Passage	1899	1945 Destroyed
Edinburgh	Scotland	Arcade	1829–1834	Project
		Princes Street Arcade	1876	Demolished
Exeter	England	Eastgate Arcade	1890	1943 Destroyed
Frankfurt/Main	West Germany	Kaiser Wilhelm Passage	1901	1944 Destroyed
Geneva	Switzerland	Passage des Lions	?	Standing
		Passage du Terraillet	?	Standing
		Passage Malbuisson	?	Standing
Genoa	Italy	Galleria Mazzini	1875	Standing
Ghent	Belgium	Van der Donckt Doorgang	1852/1886	Standing
Glasgow	Scotland	Argyle Arcade	1827	Standing
		Union Arcade	1846	Project
		Wellington Arcade	?	1930 Demolished
		Royal Arcade	?	1906 Demolished
		Queen Arcade	?	Demolished
		Milton Arcade	?	Demolished
		Millar's Arcade	?	Demolished
		Arcade	1874	Demolished
Görlitz	East Germany	Strassburg Passage	1908	Standing
Great Yarmouth	England	Central Arcade	?	Standing
Hague, The	The Netherlands	Arcade	1883–1885	Modified
Halifax	England	Arcade	?	?
Hamburg	West Germany	Sillem's Bazar	1842–1845	1881 Demolished
		Arkadenpassage	1847?	Standing
Hannover	West Germany	Georgspassage	1900	1944 Destroyed
Harrogate	England	Lowther Arcade	1896	Standing
		Prince's Colonnade	1898	1924 Demolished
		Royal Arcade	1898	1921 Modified
		King's Arcade	1899	1927 Demolished
		Beulah Arcade	1902	Standing
Helsinki	Finland	Vanha Kauppakuja	1888	Modified
Huddersfield	England	Byram Arcade	1880–1881	Standing
Hull	England	Paragon Arcade	1890	?
		Hepworth Arcade	1896	Standing
Indianapolis, IN	USA	Arcade	1895	?
Istanbul	Turkey	Aurupa Pasaji	?	Standing

The table continues on the next page.

City	Country	Name	Built	Status
Johannesburg	South Africa	The Arcade	?	?
Karlsruhe	West Germany	Kaiserpassage	1887	1944 Destroyed
Königsberg	USSR	Rossgärter Passage	?	?
		Traigheimer Passage	?	?
Lausanne	Switzerland	Galeries du Commerce	1909	Threatened
		Galerie St. François	?	Standing
Leeds	England	Thornton's Arcade	1878	Restored
		Market Street Arcade	1878	Demolished
		Queen's Arcade	1888	Standing
		Grand Arcade	1897	Standing
		Country Arcade	1898	Standing
		Cross Arcade	1898	Standing
		Victoria Arcade	1899	1959 Demolished
Leicester	England	Royal Arcade	1877	Standing
		Silver Arcade	?	Standing
		The Corridor	?	Standing
		Morley Arcade	?	?
		Angel Gateway	?	?
		Victoria Parade	?	?
Leipzig	East Germany	Speck's Hof Passage	1908–1909	Restored
		Mädler Passage	1912–1914	Standing
		Königshaus Passage	1915–1917	Modified
Leningrad	USSR	Passage des Grafen Steenbock	1848	Standing
Liège	Belgium	Passage Lemonnier	1837–1839	Modified
Lima	Peru	Arcade	1924	Standing
Liverpool	England	Lord Street Arcade	?	Restored
London	England	Royal Opera Arcade	1816–1818	Restored
		Burlington Arcade	1818–1819	Restored
		Bazaar	1826?	Project
		Lowther Arcade	1829–1831	1902 Demolished
		London City Arcade	1830?	Project
		Exeter Arcade	1842–1843	1863 Demolished
London	England	Gye's Arcade	1845	Project
		London Bridge Arcade	1850–1851	1863 Demolished
		Royal Arcade	1850?	Demolished
		Crystal Way	1855	Project
		Great Victorian Way	1855	Project
		Royal Arcade	1862	Project
		Royal Arcade	1879	Standing
		Liverpool Street Arcade	?	Standing
		Brompton Arcade	?	Standing
		Park Mansions Arcade	?	Standing
		Grand Arcade	?	Standing
		Piccadilly Arcade	1912	Standing
		Regent Street Arcade	?	Demolished
Luxembourg	Luxembourg	Passage de l'Hôtel de Ville	?	Standing
Lyon	France	Passage de l'Argue	1825–1828	Modified
		Passage de l'Hôtel-Dieu	1859	Demolished
		Passage des Terreaux	?	?
Malaga	Spain	Arcade	?	Standing
Manchester	England	Barton Arcade	1871	Standing
		Lancaster Avenue	1873?	Standing
		Exchange Arcade	1876	Demolished
		Victoria Arcade	1875–1885	Demolished
		Deansgate Arcade	1899	1956 Demolished
Marseille	France	Passage Saint Férreol	?	?
Melbourne	Australia	Queen's Arcade	1853	1868 Demolished
		Royal Arcade	1869	Restored
		Eastern Arcade	1873	1927 Remodeled
		Victoria Arcade	1875	1920 Remodeled
		Cole's Arcade	1878?	1927 Demolished

City	Country	Name	Built	Status
Melbourne	Australia	Queen's Walk	1889	Standing
		Block Arcade	1892–1894	Standing
		Metropole Arcade	1893	Modified
		Centreway	1912	Standing
Messina	Italy	Galleria Vittorio Emanuele III	?	?
Milan	Italy	Galleria de Cristoforis	1831–1832	Demolished
		Galleria Vittorio Emanuele II	1865–1877	Standing
		Arcade	?	Standing
		Arcade	?	Standing
		Galleria del Corso	1930?	Standing
Moscow	USSR	New Trade Halls (GUM)	1888–1893	Standing
		Petrovsky Arcade	?	Standing
		Alexander Arcade	?	?
		Golovteer Arcade	?	?
		Ssolodównikow Arcade	?	?
		Portnikov Arcade	?	?
		Dshamgarov Arcade	?	?
		Lubyansky Arcade	?	?
Mulhouse	France	Passage du Théâtre	?	Standing
Munich	West Germany	Schüsselbazar	1859	1944 Destroyed
Namur	Belgium	Passage de la Gare	?	Standing
		Galerie St. Joseph	?	Standing
Nantes	France	Passage d'Orléans	?	Standing
		Passage Pommeraye	1840–1843	Standing
Naples	Italy	Galleria Principe di Napoli	1876–1882	Standing
		Galleria Umberto I	1887–1891	Standing
Newcastle	England	Royal Arcade	1831–1832	1966 Demolished
New York	USA	Central Arcade	1906	Standing
		New York Arcade	1827	Demolished
		Times Square Arcade	?	?
		Windsor Arcade	ca.1890	Demolished
Niort	France	Passage du Commerce	?	Standing
Norwich	England	Royal Arcade	?	Standing
Odessa	USSR	Arcade	?	Standing
Oradea	Rumania	Arcade	?	Standing
Paris	France	Galeries de Bois	1786–1788	1828 Demolished
		Passage Feydeau	1791?	1824 Demolished
		Passage du Caire	1799	Standing
		Passage des Panoramas	1800	Modified
		Passage Delorme	1808	1896 Demolished
		Passage Montesquieu	1811	Demolished
		Passage de l'Opéra	1821–1823	1924 Demolished
		Passage du Pont-Neuf	1823–1824	1912 Demolished
		Passage Lafitte	1824	Demolished
		Passage du Grand Cerf	1824–1825	Standing
		Galerie Vivienne	1824–1826	Standing
		Galerie Colbert	1826	Partially demolished
		Galerie Véro-Dodat	1826	Standing
		Passage du Ponceau	1826	Shortened
		Passage Choiseul	1825–1827	Standing
		Passage Saucède	1825?	1857 Demolished
		Passage du Saumon	1827–1830	1899 Demolished
		Passage Vendôme	1825–1827	Shortened
		Passage Brady	1828	Modified
		Passage du Bourg l'Abbé	1828	Shortened
		Galerie d'Orléans	1828–1830	1935 Demolished
		Passage Prado	1830?	Modified

The table continues on the next page.

City	Country	Name	Built	Status
Paris	France	Galerie de Cherbourg	1838–1839	Demolished
		Passage du Havre	1845–1847	Standing
		Passage Jouffroy	1845–1847	Standing
		Passage Verdeau	1846	Standing
		Galerie de la Madeleine	1845	Standing
		Passage de la Sorbonne	1853–1854	Demolished
		Passage des Princes	1860	Standing
Périgueux	France	Passage Ste.-Cécile	?	Standing
Philadelphia	USA	Philadelphia Arcade	1825–1827	1863 Demolished
Pontypridd	Wales	Arcade	1888	?
Prague	Czechoslovakia	Koruna Arcade	1910–1913	Standing
		Lucerna Arcade	1912	Standing
		Alfa Arcade	1926–1928	Standing
		U Nováku Arcade	1928	Standing
Prague	Czechoslovakia	Cerná ruže Arcade	1932	Standing
		Zivnobanka Arcade	1938	Standing
		Sevastopol Arcade	1938	Standing
Preston	England	Miller Arcade	1896?	?
Providence, RI	USA	Providence Arcade	1827–1829	Standing
Quezaltenango	Guatemala	Passage	?	Standing
Rheims	France	Passage de Talleyrand	?	Standing
Rio de Janeiro	Brazil	Galleria Rio Branco	?	?
Rochester, NY	USA	Burlington Arcade (Kopie)	?	?
Rome	Italy	Galleria Colonna	1926?	Standing
		Galleria Sciarra	?	Standing
Rotterdam	The Netherlands	Arcade	1878–1879	1940 Destroyed
Ryde	England	Royal Victoria Arcade	1845–1846	Modified
Seville	Spain	Pasaje de Oriente	?	?
		Pasaje del Duque	?	?
Sheffield	England	Cambridge Arcade	1875?	?
		George Arcade	1900?	?
Singapore	Singapore	Clifford Arcade	1909	Standing
Southport	England	Cambridge Arcade	1876?	?
		Leyland Arcade	1898	?
Stonington, CT	USA	Arcade	1827	?
St. Paul, MN	USA	Endicott Arcade	?	?
Sunderland	England	New Arcade	1876?	?
Swansea	Wales	Alexandra Arcade	1890?	?
		Victoria Arcade	1893	?
Sydney	Australia	Sydney Arcade	1881	Demolished
		Royal Arcade	1882	Modified
		Victoria Arcade	1887–1888	Standing
		City Arcade	1890	Project
		Imperial Arcade	1891	Standing
		Strand Arcade	1892	Standing
		Her Majesty's Arcade	1928	Standing
Toulouse	France	Passage	?	Standing
Toronto	Canada	Yonge St. Arcade	?	?
Trieste	Italy	El Tergesteo	1840–1842	Modified
Turin	Italy	Galleria Natta	1858	Demolished
		Galleria delle Alpi	1864	Project
		Galleria Subalpina	1872–1874	Renovated
		Galleria Nazionale	1890?	Demolished
		Galleria Umberto I	1890?	Standing
		Galleria S. Federico	1930?	Standing
Valencia	Spain	Pasaje de Ripalda	?	?
Vichy	France	Passage Giboin	?	Standing
		Passage Clemenceau	?	Standing
Vienna	Austria	Arcade in Bank and Stock Exchange Building	1856–1860	Standing

City	Country	Name	Built	Status
Walsall	England	Arcade Buildings	1885	?
Winterthur	Switzerland	Town Hall Passageway	1872–1874	Standing
Wolverhampton	England	Central Arcade	1904	Standing
		Queen's Arcade	1909	1967 Demolished
Warthing	England	The Arcade	1925	?
Zagreb	Yugoslavia	Oktogon	1899	Standing
Zandvoort Resort	The Netherlands	Arcade	1882	Demolished

AARHUS
Borgporten
Lille Tor
This modest arcade was built about 1925
as part of a commercial structure. However, it has its own glass skylight.

ADELAIDE
Arcade
Rundle Street—Grenfell Street
An account of this arcade may be found in
an article published in a construction journal.[182] It was designed by the architects
Withall and Wells of Adelaide and opened
on December 1, 1885. I was unable to ascertain if the arcade is still standing.

AMIENS
Passage du Commerce
Rue des Trois Cailloux—Rue des Jacobins

Passage de la Renaissance
Rue des Trois Cailloux—Rue des Sergents
Both arcades are noted in Baedeker's
guide;[183] both were destroyed in World
War II and have been replaced by new
structures. The Passage du Commerce is
noted in the *Handbuch der Architektur*
(Architectural Handbook) for its special
feature of an arcade space 3 meters
wide.[184]

AMSTERDAM
De Beurspassage
Damrak 71–79
De Beurspassage is part of the General Life
Insurance complex which was built in
1894 by Hendrik Berlage and expanded in
1903–1905. It burned down in 1963. The
one-story arcade had a vaulted glass roof
in a honeycomb pattern, whose profile was
carried forward in the bowed sandstone
facades.[185]

Passage
Prins Hendrikkade—Nieuwen Dijk
This small arcade, no longer extant, stood
across from the Amsterdam main train station, which is built on a dike. The arcade is
noted in Baedeker's guide[186] along with a
Hotel du Passage, opened in 1884.

ANTWERP
Cité
Rue Oudaan—Théâtre de la Cité
This arcade was the first of many designed
and built by Cluysenaar, the architect of
the great Galeries St. Hubert in Brussels.[187]
It was built in 1844–1845 but torn down
as early as the 1860s because it was a commercial failure.

A detail of the 1846 cadastre plan reveals
that Cluysenaar's Cité was a very complex
structure. There were two exits onto the
Rue Oudaan, a narrow one onto the Rue
des Peignes, and another onto the Rue
Everdy, one of a series of streets leading to
the Place Verte. A large, glass-covered
block, apparently a market, was attached
to the main arcade, which filled the entire
interior of the block. On the opposite side,
there was a glass-covered gallery with
small shops, distinguishable by the variation in the size of the units.

A new guide comments: "As a result of
the construction of the new government
center (designed by Braem) the block of
buildings between Everdeijstraat and Oudaan was torn down. A Cité built in 1845
and used as a meat market also disappeared on this occasion."[188]

ASHTON UNDER LYNE
Clarence Arcade
Stanford Street
I discovered the Clarence Arcade by
chance on a drive to Manchester. It stands
on Stanford Street, which passes through
Ashton under Lyne on the way from Manchester in the direction of Huddersfield.

The arcade is a brick structure dating from
the late Victorian era. It runs parallel to
Stanford Street and has two entrances
from this street; it thus serves no apparent
function as a traffic artery. The arcade
space, approximately 10 meters wide and
60 meters long, has two stories. The upper
story is widened by a circular gallery accessible by means of two open staircases near
the entrances. On the ground floor there is
a variety of stores; offices are located off
the upper gallery. The passageway is tiled
in yellow; landings and stairwells are of
cast iron. The glass saddle roof is supported by girders in the form of a truss
frame. In spite of its location within the
central commercial district, Clarence Arcade is deserted today because of its unfa-
vorable location. The stores have been
closed and are now used only for storage.

ATHENS
There are said to be in Athens and Piraeus
an entire series of arcades which make up
one part of larger more modern building
units. Only one, built in the nineteenth
century, has a glass roof.[189]

Stoa Arsákiou
Stadion—Panepistimlou

This arcade, whose name comes from the private girls' school next to it, is built in a T-form. The shorter third wing runs in the direction of Arsákes Street. Baedeker describes how the Stoa Arsákiou continues beyond Stadion Street, ending next to the Orient Bank in Sophocles Street.[190] The arcade is said to have been built in the last quarter of the nineteenth century and to have been designed by the architect Kaftanzoglou.

Stoa Mela-Kostopoulos
Ermous Street—Perikeous Street

This small, approximately 43-meter-long glass-covered arcade is near the bazaar. It was built in 1890 and was called the Mela Stoa after the early owner until 1950, when the Greek Credit Bank purchased it. On both sides of the arcade are two-storied shops between Corinthian marble columns.

ATLANTA
Peachtree Arcade (fig. 65)
Peachtree Street—?

The architect Ten Eyck Brown designed and built the Peachtree Arcade in 1916 on the site of the old National Hotel. It was destroyed in 1964 against the protests of the city's population in order to make room for the construction of a modern high-rise office building.

The arcade, which Peter Blake describes as a "charming, popular downtown shopping center, complete with fountains and permanent good weather,"[191] was built in the tradition of the Cleveland Arcade and patterned on its every detail. It reveals a peculiarly American tradition, particularly in cross section. The arcade interior is divided into numerous levels; the lower level, set below street level, is reached by means of elegant iron staircases, and the wide glass roof spanning the hall-like interior is supported by a rather ponderous girder construction.

AUTUN
Arcade (figs. 66–67)
Rue aux Cordieres 26–28—Champ de Mars

Le Monde announced on October 2, 1974, that this richly organized arcade and several others would be listed as historic monuments. The arcade is not threatened although it needs careful restoration. For a brief while it was restored—or at least cosmetically restored—for use as a film set.

The Autun arcade shows Parisian elements in both ground plan and elevation, although it has to accommodate several meters of height differential over an expanse of 65 meters. It is an alternate, covered portion of the tourist route from the train station to the cathedral via the expansive market, the Champ de Mars. It stands on the southern edge of this market, whose name recalls the great Roman past which Autun can no longer live up to today. In the nineteenth century, the location still witnessed great cattle markets on its huge sloping space of cobbled pavement. The portal of the arcade establishes the market's early history; Market Hall, dedicated in 1746, "was not covered over and lined with shops until 1848–1850," according to a local guide.[192] It was thus modified from a market hall into a glass-covered arcade.

Approaching from the Champ de Mars, one sees shops on the ground floor level. There are stone stairs at the end of the glass-covered section. One senses intensive public use from the worn steps. The stairs connect in a clever way the upper arcade levels with the two pergolas of the second floor by means of a continuous semicircular flight of steps. To the side of these steps, spiral staircases lead through the arched gates to the central basement area under the arcade. The arcade space is approximately 3.6 meters wide. The pergolas and the three pairs of staircases provide access to the apartments. The third-floor apartments extend beyond the arcade's glass roof. Since the arcade does not illuminate the second- and third-floor apartments, its old structure of small panes of glass is preserved.

The patterned stone floor, the supports covered with mirrors, the stuccoed band of the pergola balustrade with its rich ornamentation, the simple wooden supports, hung with pots of flowers, connecting the finely carved wooden moulding to the glass roof—all produce an impression of space showing just how livable a nineteenth-century building could be if the site was properly utilized. Under what spatial conditions the inhabitants of the upper two floors have to live will immediately become obvious if one examines them with the eyes of a building inspector rather than with those of an admiring passerby.[193]

65
Atlanta, Peachtree
Arcade, 1916, de-
molished 1964

66
Autun, arcade

67
Autun, arcade,
entrance

AUXERRE
Passage Medefiori (?)
Rue Philibert Roux—Rue des Lombards
This short arcade, dating from about
1850, was modeled on the Passage Véro-
Dodat in Paris. It is located in the old center of Auxerre between the market and the
cathedral and ends in a staircase leading to
the street three stories below. As a one-
storied structure, the arcade probably
served originally as a large warehouse in
which the arcade form multiplied the show
window areas.

BARCELONA
Pasaje
Las Ramblas—Plaza Major

BATH
The Corridor (figs. 68–71)
*High Street 18–19—Union Passage 18–19,
8–9—Union Street 17–18*
Bath, of Roman origin, was in the eighteenth century the most fashionable spa in
the civilized world and the setting of many
contemporary novels. In the nineteenth
century, its prestige was challenged by
competing baths on the Continent; it became an area for retirees and pensioned
officers. Its architecture was made famous
by extensive development of the city, constructed in yellow Bath stone and designed
by John Wood, Robert Adam, and
Thomas Baldwin.

The baths themselves, surrounded by colonnades, lie in the middle of the city. Pul-
teney Bridge, constructed in 1771 and
designed by Adam, goes over the Avon
River; the symmetrical rows of shops prevent a view of the river. Across from the
Guild Hall lies the entrance to Bath's only
arcade, The Corridor. It is part of a network of open arcades giving interior access
to an entire block. But only The Corridor
is roofed over. There are symmetrical rows
of shops arrayed along the sides. The arcade is divided by the Union Arcade, accessible only to pedestrians, into a long
and short wing. The arcade entrances are
polygonal and each of them is emphasized
by two red granite columns. A cornice
above the shops, the majority of which
have been altered extensively, runs the
length of the arcade, joining the main
structure at those places where the interior
of the arcade becomes two-storied. A glass
roof covers the longer wing of the arcade
which consists of two one-story sections;
the roof forms a semicircular vault. The
ribs are self-supporting. The glass has been

replaced recently. A saddle roof allows illumination for the higher, central part,
which has two iron balustrades at the
ends, each flanked by two life-sized
Graces, today covered with a coat of shining lacquer. It is said that musicians once
sat in these balconies and played for the
promenading visitors to the baths. The interior arcade buildings, like the end buildings, are three stories high, and their
interior facades form one continuous line.
Internal staircases make them individually
accessible. At the level of the cornice are
hanging planters filled with flowers which
alternate with ugly neon tube lighting. The
shops now have been expanded almost to
the neighboring arcades, as is evident from
the plan. Many of them thus have two
entrances.

The Corridor is very animated during business hours, as it is located in the small but
intensely utilized commercial district of
Bath. The arcade has been restored with
great care and preserves its early character
as a covered promenade in a resort area.

The arcade was opened in 1825,[194] at approximately the same time as those in Bristol. Its continuous arching glass roof is one
of the first of its kind, assuming that it is as
old as the structure itself; I was unable to
verify this point. The local architect Edmund Goodridge (1797–1864) was both
the builder and the owner. The Corridor
remained in the family for over sixty years
and was then sold. Today the arcade is
owned by several shopowners, who share
responsibility for its maintenance. The last
constable,[195] who patrolled the arcade in
uniform to ensure propriety, quiet, and or-
derliness, retired in 1965. A famous resident is remembered by a tablet mounted
in the Union Arcade: "William Friese-
Greene, who had his studio at No. 9 The
Corridor nearby, the inventor of commercial Kinematography being the first man to
apply Celluloid Ribbon for this purpose."
Schinkel was among the prominent visitors
to the arcade; on July 29, 1826, after an
outing to Bath from Bristol with his friend
Beuth, he wrote in his diary: "After lunch,
we made a second tour of the city, during
which we noticed the terraces built high
along the walls on the rear side of the
buildings. These built up the street very
high on both sides. An old church with a
courtyard, which is set off from the street
by a Propylean hall, is rather abrupt in its
Corinthian style next to the architecture of
the Middle Ages; it is not, however, unin-

68
Bath, site of The
Corridor, 1886

69
Bath, The Corridor,
1824, entrance, High
Street

70
The Corridor, gallery

71
The Corridor, arcade

teresting. We noticed in addition several public buildings as well as galleries for shops similar to those in Paris. . . ."[196]

BERLIN

The first arcade in Berlin was built in 1869, although the idea had been current decades earlier. City plans, insofar as they are preserved in the archives, offered a whole series of studies on the topic. Schinkel was probably responsible for the idea. Notes in diaries and remarks in letters prove that he saw arcades in France and England during his trips there in 1804 and 1826. Several quotes will suffice to illustrate the point. On December 12, 1804 Schinkel wrote to Valentin Rose from Paris that he had taken part in Napoleon's coronation: ". . . it is a calm pleasure to come from the wild celebrations at the Palais-Royal, in the boulevards and theaters, the public gardens and in almost every street to the sacred halls of the excellent museum dedicated to art. . . ."[197] He wrote to his wife on April 29, 1826, shortly after his arrival: "On the way from the Humboldt Hotel we observed several of the glass roof arcades which are elegantly and comfortably appointed, the Palais-Royal as well. . . ."[198] He wrote in his Paris diary on May 16, 1826: "After even the airy and measured arcade on the Rue St. Denis and the assembly room have been taken into consideration. . . ."[199] These few citations in Schinkel's characteristic telegraphic style show that the Paris arcades had attracted his attention. As he met with Percier, Fontaine, and the architect Debret, who had built the Passage de l'Opéra, he was probably well informed about the arcade vogue in Paris. His initial impressions of Paris can be seen in his design for the extension of Neue Wilhelmstrasse across Unter den Linden. The only arcade elements missing from the symmetrical rows of shops behind the gateway building are the glass roof and the restriction of the street to pedestrians.[200] Even Friedrich Wilhelm IV,[201] with whom Schinkel had planned numerous projects, had in the 1830s occupied himself with sketches for a large, single-story hall. It would open onto two two-story colonnaded courtyards connecting with both the Werder Market and the Schlossplatz (palace square). The concept was clearly the eighteenth-century one of a large arcade situated between two squares. Businesses would be located in these halls. Friedrich Wilhelm IV's plan was inspired by both the Palais Royal in Paris and the Gostinny Dvor in Leningrad, both of which he visited.[202]

Schinkel's famous 1827 design for a department store where the National Library stands today was planned for the same situation. Interestingly, the plan (figs. 72, 73) is a direct reaction to the Paris impressions of the previous year. The department store, in the form of an *H,* consists of arcade-like rows of shops with apartments above them and then systematically doubled over them. The difficulties of lighting the two interior halls on the ground and third floors are solved in Schinkel's design by expanded glazed light wells through which the upper central hall leads over a bridge. The exterior, two-storied monumentality of the proposed structure betrays little of the interior. Although carefully planned, the interior retail shop complex would not have complemented or functioned well within Berlin's expansive spatial relationships.[203]

Of Schinkel's designs, only the so-called Red Palace (Roter Schloss) was built during 1866 and 1867; it had been planned as one part of a large, open arcade enclosure which was never built.[204] I found a small series of preliminary studies in addition to these plans. There was no direct need for arcades in Berlin, since public promenades already existed and streets were quite spacious. Also, parallel streets with the same intensity of commerce did not occur frequently. Nevertheless, one such study was discovered recently and purchased by the Kunstbibliothek. The rest of the studies are collected in folios of the *Monatskonkurrenzen* of the Berliner Architekten-Verein, which have been salvaged; they are located in the plan collection of the Technische Universität. Only one of the plans cannot be exactly identified; all of the rest refer to two locations in the Berlin of the 1830s, where the Friedrichstadt bordered on the old city and the municipal ditch (today filled in) prevented direct street connection: between Französische Strasse and Oberwallstrasse, and between Taubenstrasse and Hausvogteiplatz. The concept of the arcade always cropped up in situations where the city street system had somehow been disturbed.

I will deal with these studies collectively since they were never intended to be built. The earliest competition entry belongs to

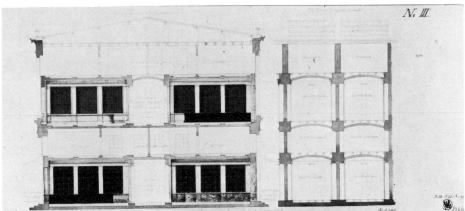

72
Berlin, department
store, design by Carl
Friedrich Schinkel

73
Berlin, department
store, design by
Schinkel

Dallmer; it is dated February 1832 and is shown in figs. 74 and 75.[205] This arcade connects Hausvogteiplatz with Taubenstrasse. The arcade space itself is angled, the change of direction mediated by a rotunda over the filled-in ditch that spans the corner. The entrance buildings on the square are only two stories tall. The glass roof is supported by a wooden structure. Both wings of the arcade are visually separated from the rotunda by crossways on the second story level. These passageways connect the two sides of the arcade. The austere skeleton-like system of arcades is fascinating; it is reminiscent of Schinkel's Feilnerhaus, built in Berlin in 1829. In this study the arcade building type is represented in perfect detail. The emergence of the hall-like rotunda can be traced to the Galerie Vivienne and the Galerie Colbert in Paris, already published at the time. Three further plans[206] (figs. 76, 77), of which two are reproduced here, date from about 1835 and were designed for the Platz am Operngraben facing Oberwallstrasse. They are traversed by intersecting arcade areas, which extend beyond the bridges to Französische Strasse. Tischbein's sketch shows a motif of skylights in pendentive cupolas, as in the eastern bazaars. The chronological difference makes possible a knowledge of three English arcades, located in London and Newcastle, which were illuminated in the same way. The spatial arrangement, which differs in all three sketches, was apparently left to the designers. It includes shops, restaurants, even concert halls and theaters, and is in this respect quite similar to the Kaisergalerie, built decades later. Interestingly, in 1840 Eduard Knoblauch, one of the founders of the Architekten-Verein, who participated in the competition, suggested an arcade connecting the Schlossplatz to Französische Strasse, for which he is supposed to have submitted several sketches.[207]

Another sketch, submitted by E. Vogel, was an examination project.[208] It consists of nine carefully drawn pages in color; the longitudinal section of the arcade and a plan of the ground floor are reproduced here (figs. 78, 79). The stylistic characteristics suggest that the date of the project was about 1865; its close theoretical relationship to the Rotes Rathaus (1859–1870) is evident. The siting is similar to that of Dallmer's project except that Vogel pays little attention to the municipal ditches. A single arcade cuts through the building on a slight diagonal; the plan of the building itself utilizes its depth in a clever fashion for a series of ballrooms and dining halls. The last project of this group, entitled "Wohnhaus mit Passage" (Residential Unit with an Arcade), has neither date nor site, but was a project for the state architectural examination by F. Zekeli. The longitudinal section and part of the interior facade are reproduced here; the arcade, shown in the drawing down to the last details of the glass roof, is one of the few designed in the Gothic style[209] (figs. 80, 81). Only three arcades were constructed in Berlin: the Kaisergalerie, the Linden Arcade as part of a theater complex, and the Friedrichstrasse Arcade. All three stood in connection with the intersection of the Friedrichstrasse and Unter den Linden. That there were not more arcades may be attributed to the layout of the commercial avenues of the city.

Kaisergalerie (figs. 82–90)
Unter den Linden 22–23—Behrenstrasse 50, 52, corner at Friedrichstrasse 164
The development of the commercial firm in Berlin must be explained for a better understanding of the construction of the Kaisergalerie in Berlin in the 1870s and of its significance.

As early as 1830 the first store fronts appeared near the palace as renovations of existing houses.[210] A majority of the shops and small stores were confined to the ground floors of residential buildings until the 1870s, as the public could not adapt to the notion of a commercial area on more than one story. Gerson's fashion shop, Am Werderschen Markt, and Israel's Haberdashery were for a long time the only exclusively commercial establishments. The Rotes Schloss (Red Palace) followed soon thereafter, so-called because of its proximity to the newly built city hall, the Rotes Rathaus. The first independent, so-called modern, purely commercial building, modeled after the Brussels and Milanese prototypes, was the Kaisergalerie. Its design made it suitable for many purposes. Begun during the Franco-Prussian War, it was considered the first expression of its successful outcome for Germany. The name was solemnly approved by the Kaiser, who celebrated its opening by riding through the arcade with his birthday guests.[211] Stylistically, this building signals the be-

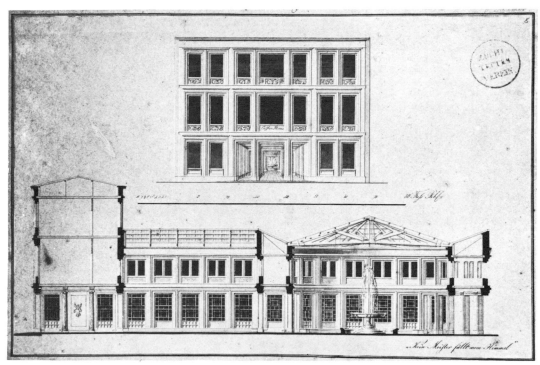

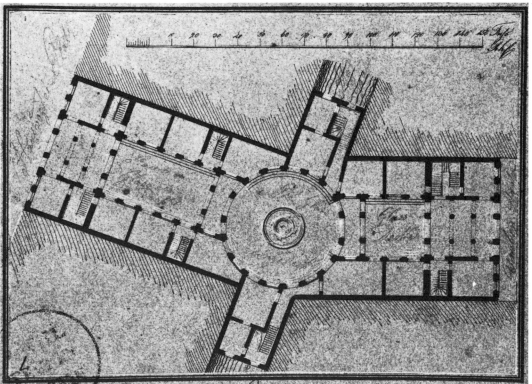

74
Berliner Architekten-
Verein (Dallmer), de-
sign for an arcade,
1832, facade and
longitudinal section

75
Berliner Architekten-
Verein (Dallmer), de-
sign for an arcade,
plan

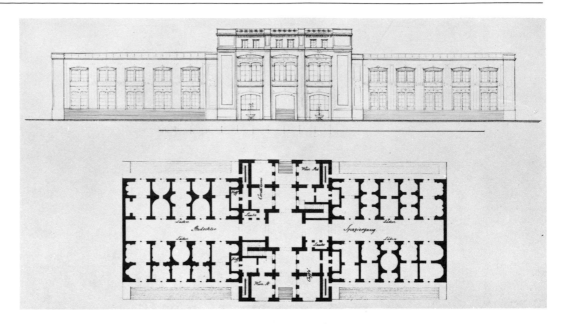

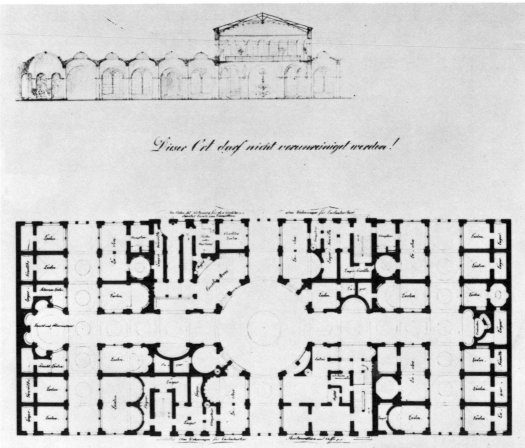

Dieser Ort darf nicht verunreinigt werden!

76
Berliner Architekten-
Verein (author un-
known), design for
an arcade, 1835

77
Berliner Architekten-
Verein (Tischbein),
design for an arcade

78
E. Vogel, design for
an arcade, examina-
tion design, undated
(ca. 1855), longitudi-
nal section

BERLIN

79
E. Vogel, design for
an arcade, plan

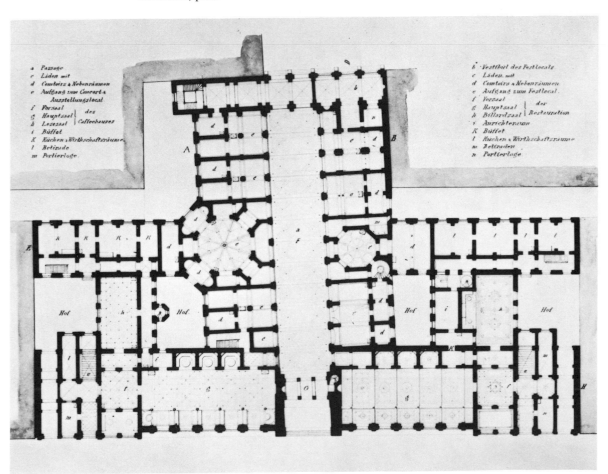

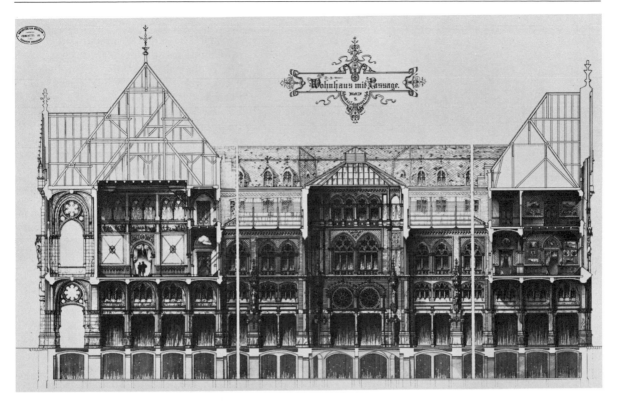

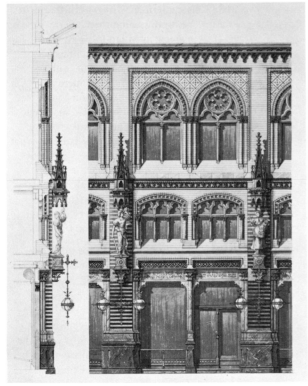

80
F. Zekeli, design for
a residential unit
with an arcade, state
architectural exami-
nation project, un-
dated, longitudinal
section

81
F. Zekeli, design for
a residential unit
with an arcade, inte-
rior facade, detail

BERLIN

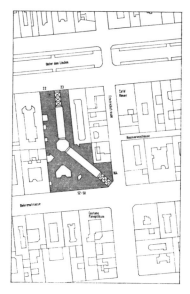

82
Berlin, site of the
Kaisergalerie, 1909

ginning of the turn to "Gründerzeit" architecture.* The infinitely variable corner towers that consistently reappear later, appear here for the first time.[212] This building, informed completely by the rich forms of the Renaissance, was the first to turn away from the spare and disciplined tradition of Schinkel. The interior was overloaded with decoration and detail. It distorted the nascent tradition of urban architecture in Berlin into a colossal form. The facade became an almost totally independent element, which served more as decoration of the street, of public space, than as an expression of the interior. It seemed even to ignore the site of the building entirely.

Tradition persisted, however, in the precision of detail and the elaboration of the plans, which in the case of the Kaisergalerie had to contend with the problem of many dovetailed lots. The Kaisergalerie was not only a technical necessity in terms of traffic patterns, but was fashionable as well. After the construction of huge arcades in Brussels and Milan, an arcade became an essential feature of a major city. The Kaisergalerie was thus built to glorify Berlin. Yet upon seeing the Galleria Vittorio Emanuele in Milan in 1875, two years after the opening of the Kaisergalerie, Fontane wrote: ". . . next to it [our arcade] . . . shrinks down into a mere alley. Oh what a city! Oh Berlin, how far away you are from a real capital of the German Reich! You became it overnight because of the political situation, and not because of what you are yourself. And from this point of view you will not become it for a long time. Perhaps it is the materials which are lacking, or certainly the disposition. . . ." There is a striking parallel between the fate of the Third Reich and the Kaisergalerie.

In the early planning stages of the Kaisergalerie, a location was sought where such a building would be possible and would promise financial success.[213] The intersection of the Friedrichstrasse and Unter den Linden was exceptionally busy even then but was inconvenient for pedestrians since the Friedrichstrasse narrowed considerably between the Behrenstrasse and Unter den Linden. The arcade was planned as an alleviation of this narrowing; it led from the corner of the Behrenstrasse and the Friedrichstrasse at a 45-degree angle into the center of the block, veered off under the

*Gründerzeit refers to a period in the late nineteenth century of economic expansion, German unification, and the founding of German banks and industry.

octagonal cupola, and intersected Unter den Linden at a 90-degree angle instead of a preferable second 45-degree angle. Lengthy real estate consolidations, overseen by A. H. Heymann and carried out through the arcade construction corporation, the Aktien Bauvereins Passage, which he had founded, preceded the construction of the arcade. August Orth was one of the first critics of the arcade and its function. He commented in his article "Toward an Architectural Reorganization of the City of Berlin" ("Zur baulichen Reorganisation der Stadt Berlin"):[214]

Traffic has increased to the point where a reorganization of the inner city is of utmost importance and necessity, and is perhaps in some cases already too late. . . . Some sins have been committed that, although they were mostly sins of neglect, would be very hard to rectify at this point. It is only through a thorough reorganization that the upper echelons of government can help. Those mistakes which were particularly detrimental for the city and its development and were difficult to rectify, should be specially cited; the narrowing of Friedrichstrasse between Behrenstrasse and Unter den Linden, for example, which under any circumstances should have been avoided, at least for the length of the new arcade building. But the arcade will not improve the situation in any significant way; certainly an expansion of Friedrichstrasse will still be necessary in the near future. But in that case a remedy would be possible only through fundamental harm to the arcade. The relief of traffic in Friedrichstrasse by the arcade is not so significant that the widening of the street should be held up for any lengthy period of time. The expansion of Friedrichstrasse will of course not be in the best interest of the arcade; in any case, there is no one who is ready to undertake the cost of the expansion.

The site of the Kaisergalerie covers 4,756 square meters. It runs from Behrenstrasse straight through to Unter den Linden, but is stepped back twice from Friedrichstrasse. The facade along Unter den Linden is 29 meters long; those on Friedrichstrasse and Behrenstrasse have a total length of 90 meters. The length of facade available for shops was increased to 360 meters by the arcade, permitting an extraordinary degree of utilization. Ninety percent of the area is multistoried construction; the remainder is used for one large and numerous smaller light wells. The entrance buildings are four-storied; the structures along the length of the arcade are three-storied. The arcade is divided into three parts, the long wing at a forty-five-degree angle to the cor-

ner of Friedrichstrasse and Behrenstrasse, the octagonal cupola, and the short wing at a ninety-degree angle to Unter den Linden. The openings reach to mezzanine height and are vaulted over with baskethandle arches. The corner exit is tripartite; the exit onto Unter den Linden is placed asymmetrically and is not incorporated into the facade. A similarly proportioned opening on the other side provides symmetry; together they form the ground floor of the center bay. The second opening, however, is a false one as it is glassed over and contains a shop. The arcade is 128.75 meters long[215] and has a continuous width of 7.85 meters; it is 13.50 meters high up to the upper edge of the moulding and 16 meters up to the crown of the glass roof. The projected wreath moulding forms a visual termination. The facades of the entrance buildings and of the arcade show the same only slightly modified exterior architecture in sandstone on the ground floor and terra cotta on the upper stories.

The facade develops in the following way: columns and entablature; low, round-corner arches above; and, on the third floor, semicircular arches. The increasing depth of the cornice and the narrowing surface area of the windows express increasing plasticity with every story. The shop area is broken up into large, rectangular window surfaces of single panes which in each bay are interrupted only by the cast-iron supports framing the shop entrances. The arcade was illuminated at night by a series of gas lamps, some freestanding and others wall-mounted. A huge, wrought-iron chandelier also hung in the cupola. The landings and railings were gilt; with the elaborate terra-cotta decorations produced by the March company, they must have impressed Berliners unaccustomed to such display.[216]

The levels were used in the most varied ways. The storage rooms in the cellar were linked by iron tracks to the exits on Behrenstrasse. Fifty-one shops of varying size and purpose occupied the ground floor; some even had additional rooms on the mezzanine. The octagon had a pastry shop with several rooms and a series of business offices grouped around the light well. On the upper floors, these offices extended as far as Behrenstrasse. A whole variety of curved staircases gave access to the upper stories. Some were accessible

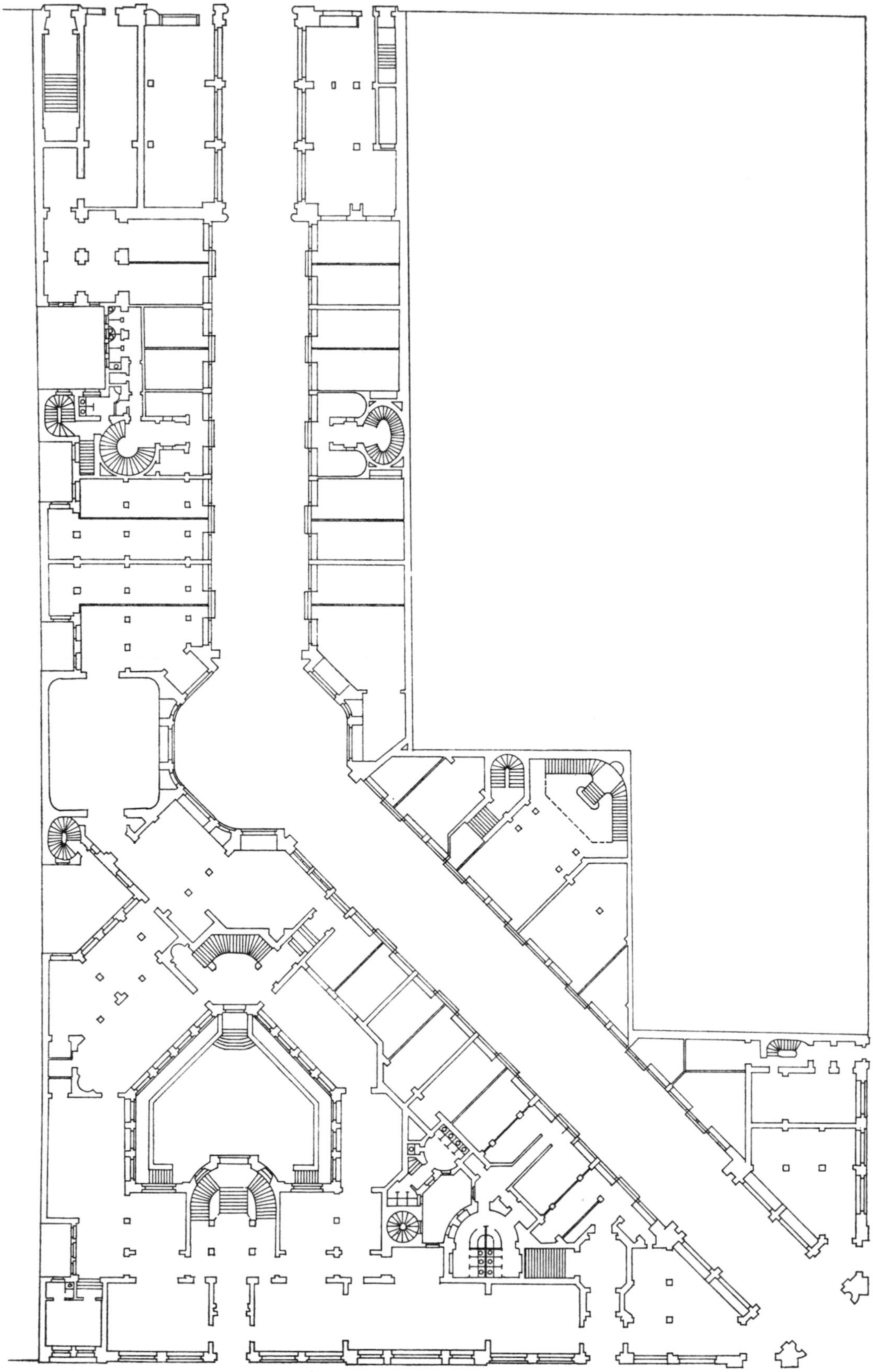

83
Berlin, Kaisergalerie,
1871–1873, destroyed
in 1944, ground plan

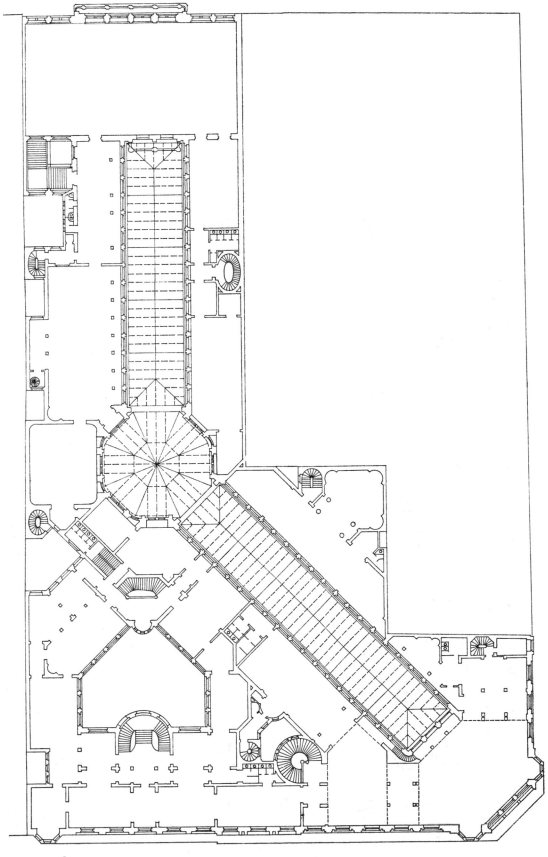

84
Kaisergalerie, second
floor plan

BERLIN

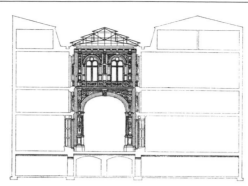

85
Kaisergalerie, cross
section

86
Kaisergalerie, interior

from the street; others could be reached from within the arcade via separate corridors.[217] A magnificent restaurant was located on the second floor in the corner space on Friedrichstrasse; it included sixteen rooms, a concert hall with stage, billiard rooms, and social rooms. The entire length of the frontal building on Unter den Linden was occupied by a two-story concert hall and a ballroom with measurements of 28.25 meters by 15.22 meters, along with two other rooms, checkrooms, and a longer hall for banquets. This series of halls was accessible from Unter den Linden by a separate staircase. The large concert hall, designed by Begas, Hildebrand, and Ewald, was decorated in yellow and gold and had windows with painted panes.[218] More offices were located in the middle section of the arcade; they housed writing rooms, some with their own post offices—an unheard-of novelty for Berlin at the time!

The glass roof was built up in articulated stages from the uppermost cornice. It was supported laterally by iron beams with a curved bottom boom; lengthwise it was braced by a lattice truss, which allowed continuous ventilation, as the glass panes were movable at that point. Ventilation of the arcade was also provided through the temperature regulation made possible by the positioning of the north and south entrances.

The Kaisergalerie was the work of the Berlin architectural firm of Kyllmann and Heyden. The building was approved by a Supreme Order on April 13, 1870, and begun in the spring of 1871.[219] It was dedicated on March 15, 1873, in the presence of Kaiser Wilhelm I and many royal guests who had traveled to Berlin for the Kaiser's birthday. The announcement celebrating the participation of the Kaiser was framed and later hung in the arcade Panoptikon. A concert festival was held under the direction of the royal music director Bilse, who was subsequently responsible for directing daily concerts in the arcade concert hall. Elegant shops moved into the many stores. The large, extravagantly appointed Vienna Cafe was located in the octagon; it has reading rooms, game rooms, and billiard parlors. Julius Faucher wrote in an article in the magazine *Vergleichende Culturbilder*:[220]

It was only at the Vienna World's Fair in 1873 that a large majority of the population of Berlin realized—by witnessing the comfort, luxury, and other charms of life in the Vienna cafes—that Berlin was at an apparent dead end in this area; a reversal had to be sought. The first attempt to build a cafe in the Viennese style came with the new and elegant Kaisergalerie, which led from Unter den Linden to Behrenstrasse. The attempt was as successful as could have been expected. The coffee was made in the Viennese way, but with the addition of so-called *Feigenkaffee*; it was served in glasses instead of in cups. The various combinations of coffee and cream—following the Viennese example—were given special names according to the color, such as *Mehr weiss, Melange*, and *Capuziner* although no one in Berlin knew at that point what a Capuchin monk looked like. The cafe arranged to serve *Kipfel* and other Viennese coffee cakes which an already considerable number of bakeries calling themselves Viennese had begun to produce; in a similar way, so-called English bakeries had appeared in Berlin some time before. All of the waiters were originally from Vienna; this gave the whole affair an air of authenticity. There were cashierwaiters, newspaper boys, etc. Although the clientele could not entirely understand the new phenomenon immediately, it soon began to acquire a taste for it.

Across from the café was a post office with writing rooms equipped with writing materials, envelopes, and stamps; reading and discussion were also possible. There was also a hotel, a *Kaiserpanorama*, an English bar, and a large luxury restaurant—all accessible from Behrenstrasse.[221] The bar located there was Berlin's first. One historian[222] writes the following about it: "As far as we can remember the first bar in Berlin was located in a small corner store in the arcade on Behrenstrasse. It was named the Buffet Français but was commonly called the Französische Bar (the French bar). The male clientele which frequented this bar—it was that remarkable golden age when our fashionable gentlemen were still men of means—was the most elegant imaginable. The bar swarmed with princes and dukes; the officers of our most elegant regiments arranged their meetings there. The ladies who frequented the bar alone, that is, without male escort, were carefully chosen and did not disturb the atmosphere even in the most boisterous moments. The majority of the men were accompanied by their female friends, mostly women of easy virtue, who were there at the most only for amusement, and not for 'business.' "

The first of the three phases of the arcade's life must have been lively, when it was the fashionable promenade of the aristocracy

BERLIN

87
Friedrichstrasse at
the turn of the
century

88
Kaisergalerie, en-
trance, corner of
Friedrichstrasse and
Behrenstrasse

89–90
Kaisergalerie, mod-
ernization, 1928

still living in the city.[223] In 1879 a first attempt at electrification came when the firm
of Siemens installed a system of centrally
controlled arc lamps which replaced the
gas illumination.[224] In 1886 a utilities center
for all electric illumination of the rooms
and shops was installed in the basement.
But the initial response of Berlin's population was by no means positive.[225] The
bright lights were harmful to the eyes; the
alternation of light and dark was too
abrupt; it made faces look washed out; it
was too expensive; and in any case it went
beyond the needs of the public.[226] Already
by 1888 large areas of the upper stories
had been vacated. The famous arcade
Panoptikon moved in and opened on December 7, 1888.[227] A society had been established for the founding; the sculptor
Richard Neumann was entrusted with the
artistic direction of the project. This display, which spread out into the various
stages of the arcade, was a hotch-potch of
dioramas, panoramas, facsimiles, molded
replicas of scenery, patriotic souvenirs, and
all kinds of cinematographic attractions and
apparatus. The catalog of the Panoptikon
has been preserved.[228] The titles of individual works give an impression of the
wonderful chaos which captured the imagination of the people of Berlin; recollec-
tions may still be heard today from those
who saw it with their own eyes. The texts
of Kisch, Kracauer, and Hessel give a feeling for the details of the attractions.

The second phase began at the end of the
century, when the aristocracy had moved
into the western section of the city. The
amusement or entertainment district had
established itself on Friedrichstrasse. Tourism and prostitution came soon thereafter.
The displays and makeup of the shops
changed; now they could sell postcards,
pictures, souvenirs, and enticing articles of
clothing—all unmistakable harbingers of
advancing disintegration. The Panoptikon
tried to retain its clientele with films, stereo-
scopes, and amusement-park rides. For
only twenty *pfennigs* you could take a
seat in a real express train compartment:
under your feet you could feel the rush
of the train, and pictures of the Riviera
passed by the windows. The third stage began after World War I; the invalid's condition became critical. Now there were only
wanderers through the arcade. The space
seemed darker and had a strange effect on
the pedestrians; the panes of glass had become dim, the facades dusty and gray.

Kraus, Kisch, Hessel, and Kracauer, whose texts are reproduced here, describe the corpse of the arcade.[229]

The first suggestion for restoring the arcade came from Alfred Grenander in the 1920s. He wanted to install a flat, paneled, lighted ceiling and to make the walls smooth.[230] The arcade was restored and modernized in 1928; the space was reduced to one story by a vaulted glass roof through which the outlines of the original arcade could still be made out. Bombs destroyed the arcade in 1944; after the war, the ruins were removed. Today Friedrichstrasse has been widened and there is no trace of the Kaisergalerie, Berlin's and Germany's most famous arcade.

Text 1: Karl Kraus, Beim Wort genommen

No grass grows in the arcade in Berlin. It looks like after the end of the world, even though there are still people moving around. All organic life is dried up and exhibited in this state. Kastan's Panoptikon. Oh, to be there on a Sunday in summer at six o'clock. An orchestrion plays for Napoleon III's lithotomy. An adult can see a nigger's chancre. The last Aztecs who cannot be brought back. Chromolithographs. Street cowboys with thick hands. Life goes on outside: a beer cabaret. The orchestrion plays: "Oh Emil, you are a plant." Here it is, a machine which produces God.

Text 2: Franz Hessel, Spazieren in Berlin

I just don't know how long the giant Nuremberg will be able to endure against the competition of the eternally streaming bands of neon advertisements which have conquered the facades of Berlin, making them flat and monotonous. Historically at any rate, it is just like its contemporary, the Kaisergalerie, which was modeled on the Paris arcades. I cannot enter it without a damp chill coming over me, without that fear that I might never find an exit. I am hardly past the shoe shiners and the newspaper stand under the lofty arches of the entrance, and I feel a mild confusion. A window promises me dancing daily and that Meyer without whom no party would be complete. But where is the entrance? Next to the ladies' hairdresser there is another display: stamps and those curiously named tools of the collector: adhesive pockets with guaranteed acid-free rubber, a perforation gauge made of celluloid. "Be sensible! Wear wool!" demands the next window of me, but the shop to which it belongs is in some other area far away. I turned around and in doing so, almost stumbled over the peep shows, where one poor schoolboy stands, his school bag under his arm, wretched, immersed in the "Scene in the Bedroom."

So many store fronts, display windows, and so few people. You can almost feel the beer-hall renaissance decay under these high vaults with their brown contours. The dust of the years darkens the glass of the arcade; it cannot be cleaned away. The displays are the same as they were twenty years ago. Knickknacks, travel souvenirs, purses, thermometers, rubber bands, postage stamps, rubber stamps. The only new addition is the Telefunken building with that most convincing legend: "One Switch —and Europe Plays for You."

At the optician you can see the entire process of producing a pair of glasses—as if you were watching a caterpillar turn into a butterfly on an instruction sheet. "Man's Development" calls to me from the anatomical museum. But that seems too horrible to me. I linger over "Mignon, the Delight of the World," a flashlight, whose light plays on a young couple trying their luck, over the Knipp-Knapp cufflinks, which are certainly the best, and over the Diana air rifles, certainly an honor to the goddess of the hunt. I shrink back before grinning skulls, the fierce liqueur glasses of a white bone cocktail set. The clowning face of a jockey, a handmade wooden nutcracker graces the end of the musical toilet paper holder. Baby bottles full of alcohol await the members of the "Former Toddlers' Club." And if they already should happen to smoke, there are the "health hypodermics" heaped up in confusing proximity to the rubber dolls, who tower next to hygienic knickers over the sign "Discreet and Uninhibited Service." I want to linger at the consolingly yellow amber cigarette holders of the "First and Oldest Amber Store in Germany" but the anatomical beauty of the museum keeps on casting furtive glances over at me. The skeleton shines through under her naked flesh like the corset of a martyr. Swimming in the emptiness inside are her painted organs, heart, liver, lungs. I turn away from her to the white-coated doctor who leans over the stomach cavity of an extraordinary sleeping blond. Quickly, move on, before I have to experience the replacement of the nose with skin from the arm. I'd rather go on to the book and stationery stores, with their pamphlets on sensuality and the soul, on women's sexual rights, the little salon magician and the complete card trickster, to learn about things which can make one popular on any occasion.

The arcade turns at a wide angle; the chairs, tables, and potted palms of a restaurant appear under a sign—"strictly kosher." The studio of the portrait painter appears to be "strictly treife" in contrast with its carpeted entrance. Inside you can see the man himself, the artist with a full beard, as he paints the President of the Republic. Hindenburg sits in the salon; at his feet lies his dog. Between him and the painter is a picture in which he is once again portrayed, although without the dog. The way he sits and the way the painter stands—they seem, it is confusing, only painted images themselves, nothing more than enlargements of the photographs all around. In fact, in this shop, you can have a picture made from any photograph at all!

Starting at a hundred marks, life size! Portraits of the dead are made from the most faded of photographs. No sittings to waste your time! Testimonies of important personalities! In a printed notice the court painter turns to us, to the passersby, and explains that he, unlike modern portrait painters, who champion no more than a confused taste, supports Goethe's (!) notion that "art and nature are one"; it is his guiding principle. A young girl and a woman from the country stand before his many beauties with dogs and winter gardens, his bemedaled soldiers, his bearded worthies. So as not to disturb their fascination, I turn to the competition, a few windows down, "Original Paintings by a Painter Schooled at the Academy; Prices Can't Be Beat." My eyes wander from original autumns and springs over Rothenburg's walls to the famous blind men in the cornfield and that favorite, the slave girl sold at market. But I have been watched. "You can get it from me straightaway," says a voice next to me; I look at the face of a little old man with a thinning beard. He blinks through the window glass next door, where original sketches show half naked girls, who busy themselves with their stockings and shoulder ribbons. I should have struck up a conversation with him to broaden my knowledge. But I'm scared by the false glitter of lights here— and the streaks of shadows. I let him slip over to the suspicious young rogues with the cute neckties for whom he does tricks with a pocket mirror. The whole center of the arcade is empty. I rush quickly to the exit; I feel ghostly, hidden crowds of people from days gone by, who hug the walls with lustful glances at the tawdry jewelry, the clothing, the pictures are tempting reading material of earlier bazaars. At the exit, at the windows of the great travel agency, I breathe more easily; the street, freedom, the present!

Text 3: Siegfried Kracauer, "Abschied von der Lindenpassage"
The Linden Arcade has ceased to exist. That is, it is still in form an arcade between Unter den Linden and Friedrichstrasse, but it isn't really an arcade anymore. When I was there a short time ago strolling as I used to do in my student days before the war, the demolition was almost complete. Cold, flat sheets of marble clothed the pillars between the shops, and a modern glass roof arched over them; there are some dozen of them. Only a few pieces of the old Renaissance architecture luckily still peeked through, that horribly

pretty stylistic imitation of our fathers and grandfathers. A hole in the new glass roof skeleton allowed a view onto the upper stories with their endless series of corbels under the main moulding, their connected series of round windows, their columns, the balustrades, and the medallions—all the wilted extravagance which now passersby will no longer enjoy. And one pillar, apparently destined to be saved until the last minute, carried its brick relief unabashedly for display, a composition of dolphins, tendrils, and a mask in the center cartouche. Now it all sinks into the cool mass grave of marble.

I can still remember the shudder that the word "passageway" brought on in my boyhood days. In the books that I raced through, the darkened passageway was usually the place of deathly attacks, to which a pool of blood testifies later, or at least that transient environment of questionable lives which existed there together and consulted one another on their gloomy plans. Even if my childhood fantasies were too outrageous, some of the significance with which they invested the passageways still clung firmly to the lonely Linden Arcade. But not only the Linden Arcade, but all real bourgeois arcades too. It makes sense that Thérèse Raquin takes place in the back of the Passage des Panoramas in Paris [author's error: the Passage du Pont Neuf], which too has been smothered since by the concrete burden of splendid new buildings. The era of the arcade has come to a end. Its special characteristic was to be a thoroughfare, a way through bourgeois life, which resided in front of its entrances and above them. Everything that had been forced to take leave of that world because it was not representative or because it ran against the official line, found its way into the arcade, which sheltered the rejected and the refugees, a collection of things which were not suitable for dressing up the facade. These transient objects attained here in the arcades a sort of resident status, like gypsies who were not allowed in the city, but could only camp on the country road. You could easily pass them by during the day between the streets. The Linden Arcade is still filled with shops, whose displays are such passages in the midst of the bourgeois arrangement of life. And in fact they satisfy physical needs, the desire for images, just as they appear in one's daydreams. Both things, extreme closeness and great distance, give way before the bourgeois public sphere which cannot tolerate them and retreat into the secluded twilight of the passageway, where they flourish as in a swamp. In fact, as an arcade, the thoroughfare is also the place where, as in no other, the journey, the departure from the near into the distant, can be portrayed; body and image become united. The Anatomical Museum occupies the place of honor in the Linden Arcade, with its exhibitions dedicated to corporeality, to the body itself. It is the queen of the arcade; she constitutes the kingdom that is her birthright among the medallions, the vines, and the dolphins. And since all of the objects, secreted behind the store front, must still sport bourgeois attire, the inscriptions which cajole the passersby are all sanctimonious.

One of them states: "The exhibition *Man* will improve your health." A picture in the display window betrays the kind of revelations the visitor will experience inside; a frock-coated doctor presides over an operation on the stomach of a naked female; there is quite an audience present, all dressed in as old-fashioned a manner as the doctor. The patient had been a woman in former times. But here it is a question of the stomach, of the internal organs, of all that is purely corporeal. The body's internal growths and monstrosities are shown in painful detail; for the adults, sexual diseases rage in a special display. They are the result of uninformed sensuality, stimulated by a nearby bookstore. Once during the inflation, a Communist bookstore installed itself in the arcade of a German city; it lasted only a short time, even though the arcade dated back to prewar days and was reminiscent of a dressed-up underpass with its wrought-iron sunflowers. But the store's merely tangential relationship to the arcade was in itself enough to drive the propaganda out. Illegality wants to be out in the open, while pornography is at home in the twilight. The bookstore in the Linden Arcade knows what it owes its environment. Brochures whose titles call up desire and whose contents will hardly still it sprout up in an apparently harmless jungle of paper vegetation. Sometimes the forbidden is seen in a curious relationship with the legitimate, as though the chief of police had written a booklet on some sexual perversion. Trivia flourishes close by this sensuality, those countless little objects which we carry around and surround ourselves with—partly because we need them, partly because they are so useless. They swarm in the bazaar of the arcade: nail pincers, scissors, powder boxes, cigarette lighters, little tops handmade in Hungary. Knick-knacks appear like vermin in hordes; it's frightening to think that they may always be with us. They would like to consume us, crawling around the worm-eaten buildings in which we live; and one day, when the balconies collapse, they will darken the sky. Even the street shops, which provide us with the higher necessities of life, have moved into the arcades to pay homage to the Anatomical Museum. Pipes of amber and meerschaum glow, shirts sparkle like a fashionable evening affair, hunting rifles point toward the sky, and at the far end of the corridor, a hairdresser sends out its fragrances and greetings. It divulges its

close relation to the cafe, which is located nearby in the rotunda. The visitors seem to wander, if only through the jungle of illustrated newspapers; they evaporate with the chatter; they follow the line of pictures which flutter beyond the cigarette smoke. The word cries "Onward!"

It was a clever coincidence that the entrance to the Linden Arcade was flanked by two travel offices. But the trips to which ship models and advertisements call you have nothing in common anymore with the trips one used to take in the arcade; the modern luggage store too belongs only partially to the thoroughfare. Since the astonishing shrinking of the earth, bourgeois existence has taken over travel for its own purposes just as it did the bohemian; it sustains itself by appropriating just such activities for its own needs, degrading them into amusements. How much more distant, but more known, was the foreign in the time of souvenirs! The arcade shops are full of them! "Souvenir of Berlin" is plastered on plates and jugs; the flute concert of Sanssouci is often brought home as a memento. This tangible aid to memory, these authentic reproductions of local originals are parts of the body of Berlin; they are doubtless better suited to reinvest the visitors with the strengths of the city they have devoured than photographs offered next door—personalized development included. The pictures invoke a return of the foreign lands once seen; the world panorama on the other side dangles that for which we long in front of us and quickly snatches away the familiar. It towers in the arcade like the anatomy. The distance to the tangible body from the ephemeral distance is just a tiny leap. Whenever I visited the world Panorama as a child—it was secreted there even then—I felt myself as if transported to a faraway place. It was just like looking at picture books; both are simply unreal. It could hardly be otherwise. Behind the peepholes, which are as close as one's own window frames, cities and mountains glide by. They look more like faces than travel highlights in the artificial brightness. Mexico and the Tyrol, which looks like a second Mexico in the Panorama.

These landscapes look almost like homeless pictures, illustrations of transient monuments, which shine here and there through the holes in the wooden fence which surrounds us. Such things must become visible through magic glasses; it's just astounding that the optician in the arcade doesn't offer any for sale. The glass foliage which climbs up the sides of the display window, hard and round, seems to set straight the things which belong in the arcade—in theory anyway. The stamp shop takes care of the required destruction of all the deceptive objects there; heads, buildings, emblazoned animals and exotic places are mounted next to each other with numbers and names. In this place the world is jogged and shaken until it falls into a form that is perfect for the consumption of the passersby. The visitor who wanders through can always try his luck in the lottery to see if Fortune, his companion, is well disposed toward him, or he can test her at cards. And if he wishes to confront in the flesh the glossy images of his dreams, he will find them realized in color, lots of them, in the picture postcard shop.

Flower arrangements greet him in ingenious language, little dogs run up to him full of trust, the student life struts by bright and tipsy, and the nakedness of warm female bodies steeps him in desire. On their own, the imitation necklaces nestle close to the neck and arms of the buxom beauties in the shop next door and an out-of-date hit from the music store urges the arcade stroller on in the middle of the illusions he has discovered.

It is the retreat from the bourgeois front which unites the objects of the Linden Arcade, which invests them with the same function. Desires, geographical excesses, and some kinds of images which arouse one out of a sound sleep, cannot be displayed in lofty places like cathedrals and universities, ceremonial speeches and parades. People tried to do away with them, and where they could not be totally destroyed, they were exiled into the deep, inner recesses, the Siberias of the arcade. But they had their revenge on the bourgeois idealism which had oppressed them in that they played off a shameful existence against a usurped one. Brought low and humiliated as they were, they nevertheless succeeded in banding together, and in the twilight of the thoroughfare, they contrived an effective protest against the facade culture. They exposed idealism and revealed its products to be kitsch. The arched windows, the wreath moulding, the balustrades—the extravagances of the Renaissance, which made themselves out to be so superior, were tried and discarded in the arcade. Now, as you are walking through the arcade, reproducing that movement to which we alone are suited, you can see through it already; its arrogance becomes unabashedly apparent in the arcade. The reputation of the persons of high and highest rank, whose portraits, guaranteed to be accurate, stood and hung behind the windows of Fischer, the court painter, suffered no less. The ladies of the Kaiser's court smiled so respectfully that their respect turned rancid like their oil portraits. And the lights, which illuminated the interior in the form of red and yellow roses, gave the lie to the much praised inwardness which carried on so monstrously behind the Renaissance facades. And thus the arcade criticized the bourgeois world through the bourgeois world, a critique which beset every pas-

serby. (The vagabond will somehow manage to unite himself with the man of the changed society.) The Linden Arcade disavowed a form of existence to which it still belongs—this is what gave it the power to testify to the past. It was both the product of a time and an intimation of its decline. What had just been brought into being cut itself off from the living sooner than anywhere else in the arcade simply because it was the arcade; it passed, still warm, into death (Castan's Panoptikon was located there for this reason). That which we inherited and still called our own—in the arcade it was displayed as if in an exhibition hall and revealed only a lifeless grimace. We re-encounter even ourselves as deceased in the arcade. But we take from it that which belongs to us now and will always belong to us, all that which is unknown and shimmers even though disfigured.

But now, under a new glass roof and decked out in marble, the former arcade reminds me of the vestibule of a department store. The shops still exist, but picture postcards are the standard fare; the world Panorama has been overtaken by the film and the Anatomical Museum has long ceased to be a famed attraction. All the objects are struck dumb. They shyly crowd behind the empty architecture, which maintains a completely neutral mien for the time being but which later might hatch—who can say—fascism, or perhaps nothing at all. What could become of an arcade in a society which is itself no more than an arcade?

Text 4: Egon Erwin Kisch, Das Geheimkabinett des anatomischen Museums

The most beautiful thing in Berlin is the Linden Arcade.

The most beautiful thing in the Linden Arcade is the Arcade Panoptikon.

The most beautiful thing in the Arcade Panoptikon is the Anatomical Museum.

The most beautiful thing in the Anatomical Museum is the Special Chamber.

The most beautiful thing in the Special Chamber is—pst!

To prove the correctness of the aforementioned four theses, let it first be mentioned that nowhere else in Berlin is there such a lack of hurriedness as there is in the arcade, such a detachment from materialism as in the subcutaneous connection between the utilitarian Friedrichstrasse and the representative Linden. The street may serve the traffic well; the arcade certainly does not. (At least it does not serve the traffic patterns in general.) It is in fact an evening promenade. Here one goes for a stroll, yes, a stroll in the atmosphere of fairground romance and passionate love; the book shops do not display books that explain how to read the stock exchange lists or tomes on the origins of war. Instead they display

The Sex Life of Homosexuals, When I Wore Men's Clothing, The Rebirth of Eros Uranos, Cruelty with Special Reference to Sexual Factors, The Rights of the Third Sex, Gynomastia, Feminism, and Hermaphroditism. There are not any Liebermann, Pechstein, or Brangwyn graphics on display in the art stores; we see instead boys swimming off the cliffs of the Blue Grotto and an innocent blonde girl, clothed only in pigtails. There is also a panorama there—that ancient middle step between daguerreotype and the movies—with a program that changes weekly, an automatic palm reader that cries out with a large sign, candy and sweets shops, special rubber products, errand boy agencies, two express photographers, automats for food; a scent shop keeps its door open for a long time.

The Panoptikon in the arcade is the only one left since the Castan's demise. There are magnificent genre groupings: *The Duel, A Chimneysweep in Love, Avenged!, A Spoiled Wedding Suit, The Beginning Is Always Hard* (especially at a parade! Very authentic!), *Barbarossa at Kyffhäuser, At the Gate of the Foundling Hospital, Berlin by Night, or Youth in Chambre Séparée,* the Prince's Hall, and the academy of famous personalities, the fairytale rooms, and the humorous distorting mirrors, very humorous, and the famous *Criminal History of the Incident at the Scaffold in Eight Groups,* of which number 105 (*Breaking into the Chamber of the Dead and Theft of the Body*) is especially fascinating. Of course—and this should be emphasized—none of this is at all instructive, but rather disconcerting—and this is commendable—just as the offerings of the automats in the vestibule, "Secrets of the Bedroom," "The Knothole in the Fence at the Ladies' Baths," "Trial Marriage" should not be considered very enlightening. My young friends, you who stand before the peepholes with enchanted fifty-*pfennig* pieces, believe me, an experienced old man, it is not true that five wretched and (luckily) clothed females from the 1880s are paralyzed in a can-can pose in a bedroom! The peep show "The Wedding Night" doesn't work, by the way, although it's not posted that it is broken. Beware, girls!

Come, immerse yourselves rather in observing the badly faded, but nevertheless real, true, and authentic photographs up on the wall on the right; there hangs framed and under glass the portrait gallery of those famous personalities whom our parents, and on Sundays most certainly their maids, used to make pilgrimages, the temple of fame of those monstrosities, who traveled all over the world with posters and loud cries to let themselves be stared at. There is nothing left of them anymore, except perhaps some preparation in a pathology laboratory somewhere, and this

gilt Valhalla in the vestibule of the arcade Panoptikon. Greet them with respect! Lionel, the lion man, darling of the ladies and of the virgins—that's what you look like—Hunyadi Sanos, the man with the bird head is there; Elizabeth Liska, the giant child of Russia, eleven years old, and six feet eleven; the Siamese twin sisters Bozena and Milada Blazek, joined at the spine, Miss Crassé the Tiger Girl; the huge Mariedl of Tirol with her favorite cow, Melken; the Giant Teenager Dora; La belle Annita; Princess Kolibri; the tattooed beauty; the smallest woman in the world; Pirjakoff, the largest man who ever lived; Machnow, the largest man who ever lived, Hassan ben Ali, the largest man who ever lived; Mr. Masso, the Chain-Breaker; Haarathlet Simson, Papus and Succi the Hunger Artists; Mr. Tabor, the Muscle Man with the Thrice Twisted Arm; hairy Miss Pastrana; Tall Joseph, the biggest soldier in the Prussian Army, with Toni Marti, the heaviest child in the world; the Willfried Sisters, the strongest children in the world, one and a half and two and a quarter years old, November 1902. Alas, no one looks at this pantheon of former greats anymore, whose life it was to travel around in the world to exhibit themselves in front of a tenpenny audience in the flat, early morning light of a carnival tent, a restaurant room, or in the all-too-harsh light of the evening circus. Exploited, they point to monstrous birth defects and explain them with unnatural, memorized text. Or were they somewhat proud of them? We don't know anything about them anymore except that they performed in the arcade Panoptikon in Berlin. Their picture is still here, but it becomes more faded every year.

The Anatomical Museum, on the other bank of the arcade in the mezzanine, is much more frequented. Here too the manikins down below already entice the dolls and the tarts and those too, who will become so. A waxen Virchow, lecturing in front of a skull, is the mute crier, in league with a girl who reveals her innermost secrets; even her stomach cavity is revealed. An advertisement board shows the effects of wearing a corset and calls: "Know yourself—protect yourself!" It costs twelve and one-half marks to know oneself, of which two paper bills go for the entertainment tax; the special room "For Adults Only" has no special entrance fee. A curtain separates the holy of holies of the arcade from the profane part of the Anatomical Museum and is forbidden to visitors under eighteen. A board, turned over every quarter hour, announces "Now Women Only" and "Now Men Only." The sex which is excluded at any moment must loiter around in the meantime in the public rooms and study the plastic representation of the digestion process, hemorrhoids, the effects of cholera, a tongue operation for cancer, the internal devastation caused by whiskey and the like, and a caesarian section in a picture automat. But then, then the adults—men and women in their turn are allowed to enter the inner sanctum (fourteen-year-olds are usually eighteen here), where colored plastic in life size shows all the things that one comprehended from dictionaries only with difficulty and learns about in life only by chance.

Everything is authentic or at least lifelike, real fetuses, man's development from fertilization through to normal, breech, or forceps delivery, perforation, or caesarian section. Organs and so on—everything exact down to the last detail and even more exact in the catalog. Under the heading "Female Venereal Disease" the hymen, or vaginal membrane, is correctly given as the first object, being easiest and most quickly cured of all diseases. But not too long; you are only allowed a quarter of an hour. Outside the other sex has already begun to gather.

The Linden Arcade has a regular public who will not be discouraged; no other street has so many friends and such a tight-knit circle of admirers. And among those who are the friends of the arcade, there are some who love the Panoptikon passionately and faithfully. Among these, there are some of fanatic attachment to the Anatomical Museum, and of these, some absolute slaves of the Secret Chamber, enchanted by one or the other display. It is according to them choicest of the choice—thus the greatest beauty of Berlin.

Arcade (project)
Schadowstrasse extension
There is a discussion in the journal *Deutsche Bauzeitung* of the project which the architects Fiebus and Lange presented at the architecture exhibition in Berlin in 1874:[231] "A sketch for an arcade in the extension of Schadowstrasse by Fiebus and Lange shows a quite satisfactory solution; there are shops at ground level, expansive function rooms and restaurant space in the upper stories. A rotunda-like central space, which in the Heyden and Kyllmann project [the Kaisergalerie] allows for the fact that the streets take different directions, appears here too, although its design is not well suited to the overall plan because the street is straight. The sandstone facade on Schadowstrasse displays a heavy Renaissance [style], massive in both form and proportions."

Lindengalerie (fig. 91)
Unter den Linden 17–18—Behrenstrasse 55–57
The Lindengalerie[232] was built a few buildings west of the Kaisergalerie in 1891–

1892 as part of a building complex composed of the Unter den Linden Theater (later the Metropol Theater), the Linden Hotel (later the Westminster Hotel), and the Lindengalerie as the connecting element and the western boundary of the site. In charge of construction of the complex, which was destroyed in bombing raids in 1944, was a shareholders' union, Aktien Bauverein Theater Unter den Linden; the architects were the Viennese theater building specialists, Fellner and Helmer. The arcade had only a few shops and served as a means of access to the hotel and the theater rather than having an independent commercial function. It was one story and had three skylights. The Linden Theater had been conceived as a multipurpose theater for plays, concerts, and ballets. In the 1890s the enterprise was threatened by bankruptcy. The subsequent Metropol Theater became famous as an artistic and musical center; it was rebuilt at the same location after World War II.

Friedrichstrasse Arcade (figs. 92–102)
Friedrichstrasse 110–112—Oranienburger Strasse 54–56a
In approximately 1908 appeared a monograph on the subject of the Friedrichstrasse Arcade.[233] Discussing one of the last great arcades ever built, the publication presents all of the plans of the building as well as information about the intentions of its builders. Since the Friedrichstrasse Arcade was constructed entirely of reinforced concrete and the cupola was the first of ribbed concrete construction, the event was analyzed in many trade journals.[234]

The Friedrichstrasse Arcade was the second most important arcade building in Berlin and was the last attempt to carry over this building type in a grand style into the new century. It was located at the northern end of Friedrichstrasse and turned from there to the Oranienburger Strasse. Its function was to relieve the traffic on Friedrichstrasse and to encourage business in an overcrowded area where many traffic arteries met. Bus and tram lines, the Friedrichstrasse central train station, the Stettiner train station, and the Exchange train station were all located side by side. The north-south subway had just been built, and the Oranienburg Gate station was situated in front of the entrance to the arcade and was accessible directly from the arcade itself, as is shown in fig. 92. Whoever walks through the ruins today—one of the last great ruins in Berlin—

and wanders through the surrounding area
feels confronted with something completely unreal and displaced. It is hard to
imagine the whirl of traffic, the commercial bustle which once filled this place. But
the actual lightening of the traffic crush by
the arcade was considerably less than the
planners had anticipated. It was possible to
take a shortcut through the arcade, but it
only led away from Friedrichstrasse into
less frequented streets. The purpose of this
arcade was rather a maximum opening up
of the interior of the site.

In 1906 the owner of Friedrichstrasse 111,
a Mr. Markiewicz, planned to add to his
holdings by purchasing numbers 110 and
112; he intended to build a large mixed-
use development of factories and retail
stores.[235] This kind of planning had been
the trend in the whole of Friedrichstrasse
in the period before World War I:[236] to
combine narrow lots and to build investment properties—businesses, department
stores, large hotels, and banks. The building consultant Franz Ahrens whom Markiewicz commissioned for the planning
was able to finance the project through his
connections with the building corporation,
Berliner Terrain und Bau Aktiengesellschaft. Ahrens suggested an additional
widening of the area as far as the Oranienburger Strasse in order to build an arcade
open to vehicles. This idea persuaded the
director of the corporation, Leopold Falk,
to support the undertaking. He took over
the arrangements for acquiring the lots on
Oranienburger Strasse 54–56a and for
completing the financing for a new corporation, the Berliner Passage Bau Aktiengesellschaft. The final project was licensed by
the Royal Police Praesidium on May 18,
1907. According to building regulations
for the utilization of lots in this district,
construction could cover only seven-tenths
of the site. But the project was financially
feasible only if the arcade itself and the
rotunda space could be considered as areas
free of construction and if the areas leading into the arcade could be licensed for
full-time pedestrian use. After long,
drawn-out discussions, this dispensation
was awarded and the district commission
recommended the original plans: "To give
Berlin an arcade which will be deemed
worthy of being considered with the rest of
the existing arcades in the world."

The arcade's architectural program and
use designation were modified after construction began; originally it had been

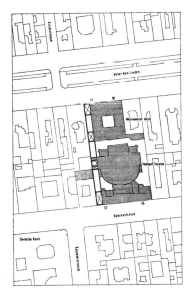

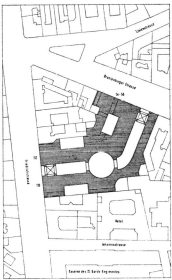

91
Berlin, site of the
Lindengalerie, 1909

92
Berlin, site of the
Friedrichstrassenpas-
sage, 1909

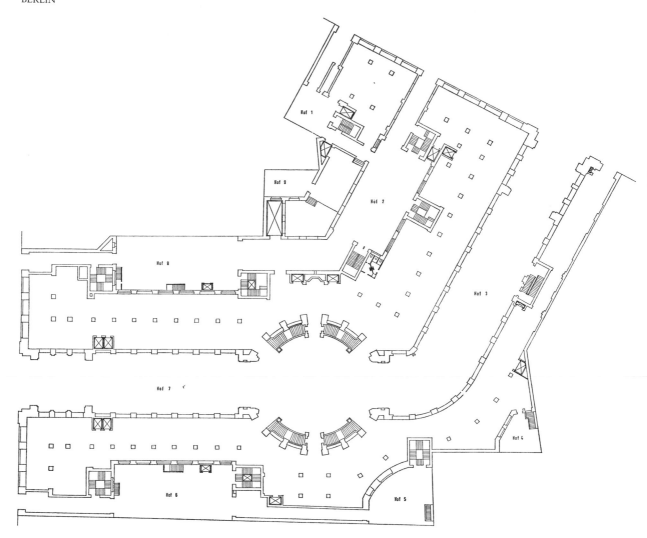

93
Friedrichstrassenpas-
sage, ground floor
plan
(Scale: 1 : 850)

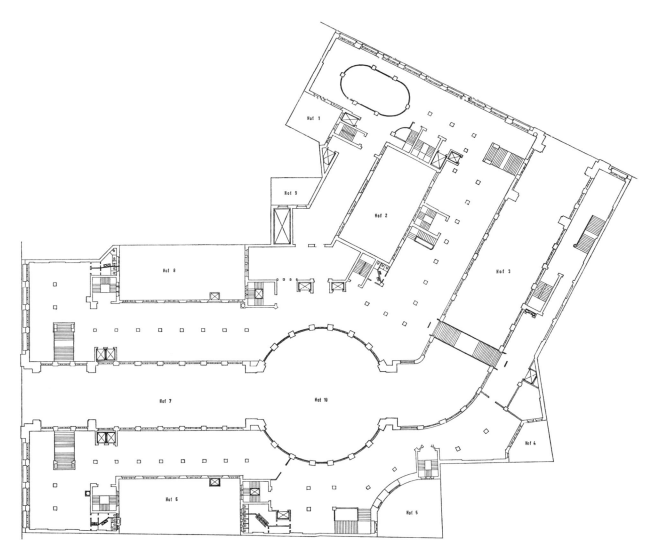

94
Friedrichstrassenpas-
sage, second floor
plan
(Scale: 1:850)

planned to include restaurants, cafés, and single shops on the ground floor with wholesale businesses, offices, and entertainment establishments on the upper four stories. The center building was to be a single large club. But these plans were altered. Markiewicz, the director of the construction corporation, wanted to build a department store in the arcade, in which approximately 100 smaller and larger specialty shops would consolidate in order to compete against the larger department stores. These businesses would maintain their own direction, but their costs would decrease through the use of centralized facilities such as elevators, shipping, staff rooms, restrooms, and storage rooms. Forty-nine large show windows were planned as well as rooms for special exhibits. Fourteen entrances would assure easy and quick access. In addition, there would be a luxury department store composed only of individual shops.

In the built version, staff rooms, shipping, and storerooms were in the basement; five stories of easily rearrangeable surface area were set aside for the shops; the large rooms for special exhibits as well as the bridges to the other side of the arcade were located above the arcade entrances in the entrance buildings; and the maintenance and service facilities were located around the courtyards along the edges of the site. The arcade department store was opened in the autumn of 1909 after a mere fifteen-month construction period. But the building seemed not to fulfill anyone's expectations. Before World War I it was sold at auction out of financial necessity.[237] The enormous construction costs (7 million marks) and the architectural display were extravagant given the amounts received in rent; also, small shops suffered from the new concept of the department store. The auctioning off of the department store was not the only occurrence of the kind; it was connected with the collapse of a whole series of building speculations in Berlin.[238]

After World War I, the complex came into the hands of the AEG, which opened its Haus der Technik in the arcade, using the building for displays, both informational and decorative, of all the products manufactured by the concern. But the Friedrichstrasse Arcade was left a partial ruin by the bombing raids of 1944. The arcade has collapsed, the mighty cupola is left only as a brickwork structure, and the concrete skeleton has been torn down. Some of the side wings are used as garages and offices, but the days until final demolition are numbered.

The Friedrichstrasse Arcade is almost twice as large as the Kaisergalerie; it covers 8,800 square meters. The site is 90 percent built over; in addition to the arcade, there are seven courtyards of varying sizes, only two of which are not open to vehicles. The arcade has one cellar extending the entire area of the site. The arcade buildings are all five-storied. The arcade space itself is divided into three parts. From Friedrichstrasse one enters through an entrance under a basket-handle arch. The straight arcade wing leads to the large rotunda. This wing is not involved in the change of direction to Oranienburger Strasse. The second wing, after a short, straight stretch, is angled. The Oranienburger Strasse entrance is of the same design as the one on Friedrichstrasse. Both are accentuated by monumental gatehouses with hipped roofs.

Three bridges carry traffic between parts of the department store separated by the arcade. Two are suspended underneath the entranceway arches; the third, two stories high, spans the arcade angle at the second and third floor levels. In addition to these bridges, others pass through the gatehouses and smaller passages in the arches separating the rotunda and the arcade spaces. The vertical traffic is accommodated by ten staircases along the external walls, nine interior staircases, eleven passenger elevators, ten freight elevators, and six spiral chutes—a special delivery system to carry purchases to the cellar for packing and shipping.[239] The largest freight elevator has an area of 30 square meters and transports automobiles and large exhibition items. The stairs leading directly to the Oranienburg Gate subway station come into the straight wing of the arcade; two sweeping open staircases set opposite each other in the rotunda lead to the second floor. The dimensions of the arcade are impressive; the total length of the passage is 153 meters, the wings are 14 meters wide and 19 meters high (up to the dust cover); the cupola has a diameter of 27.5 meters and is 34 meters high without the lantern.

A brief description of the traffic areas and facilities reveals that they are disproportionate to the usable space. Since the arcade is cut through by the department store ground plan, everything had to be planned for twice. The result is that the visitor cannot simply wander through the arcade with no apparent direction, but must constantly think about how to get where. This was one of the reasons for the commercial failure of the arcade department store.

If we consider the utilizable spaces floor by floor, in the basement we find a series of storerooms, cloakrooms, refreshment rooms, restrooms, public eating establishments, and the heating and plumbing facilities. The ground floor, the mezzanine, and the second through the fourth stories are all identical; together they form a grid capable of supporting surfaces which can be used for whatever purposes one wishes. Two vaulted, two-story sales rooms are located on the third floor above the gateway arches. Passage from one side of the arcade to the other is possible through these rooms. A supermarket was planned for the uppermost story. It would have been independently accessible by means of two narrow halls in the arches separating the rotunda from the wings of the arcade.

The Friedrichstrasse Arcade is one of the earliest examples of reinforced concrete construction in Berlin. In 1906 the same firm had already built a department store using the same technique in Kottbusser Damm. All of the foundations, interior columns and beams, the cupola, and the entire roof were of reinforced concrete. The construction of the cupola is particularly interesting. It is the first ribbed cupola of its kind—a kind of commercial Pantheon. The wide diameter measures 28.3 meters; it has a semicircular section and is supported by twenty ribs placed equidistant from one another and resting on sixteen columns. Four ribs sit on the two portals which span the arcade and disperse the concentration of weight. At the uppermost point the ribs press against the lantern ring, which braces them as a rigid frame. The base ring, which surrounds the ribs on the outside, is constructed of two hefty iron rods (60 millimeters formed into a twenty-sided polygon). The rods may be tightened by means of bolts. The ribbed construction was chosen here to give the cupola the spatial sense of an open hall; for glass plates could be placed between the ribs and the rings which reinforce them. Suspended concrete roofs spanned the two halls in the entryway buildings;

the hall arches were suspended in the fashion of Rabitz arches (i.e., with wire-mesh cores).

The problem of the decorative details of the rooms, the ceilings, and the pillars was solved by the architects in the following way: the ceilings and the pillars of reinforced concrete were not sculpted or decorated. Rather, immediately upon being removed from their forms, they were smoothed out by a special method. They were then painted, set with colored mosaic patterns, or clad with bronze ornament. Some were decorated by stonemasons. Thus, no embellishment of tamped concrete was used. The disadvantage of this procedure is that the concrete mold must be prepared even in its rough stage to accommodate the low-relief ornamentation.

Both the interior and exterior facades of the Friedrichstrasse Arcade have the same character although they differ in the details of their construction. The two street facades are of tufa and have a predominantly vertical organization similar to the facades of most of the department stores of this period. The entrance buildings project slightly and are flanked by jambs which rise to the roof. Two overlapping baskethandle arches span the pillars and to a certain extent outline the profile of the arcade. The street facades are stepped back. The ground floor and the mezzanine are aligned with the gateway buildings; they are organized by archways filled by large, plate-glass show windows. This socle finishes in a balustrade with copper lanterns mounted above the columns. The three stories above these recede. For each bay there is a triple window with marble balustrade; the uppermost story is decorated with lattice-like bronze ornament. The pillar profiles have the same width throughout, and they end in a cornice. On the fifth floor are forty-nine window bays; they are connected by rounded arches. In the cupola the pillars extend through a moulding into the ribs of the cupola itself, tapering off consistently up to the lantern with ever narrowing glass inserts. This design gives the space an impressive compactness. Statues by the sculptor Pritel, representing the expansion of commerce throughout the world, stand on the pedestal cornices of the third floor.

The facades of the lower arcade area are of freestone; in the upper stories they are clad in polished marble and porcelain. The bridges, doors, and frames are in bronze.

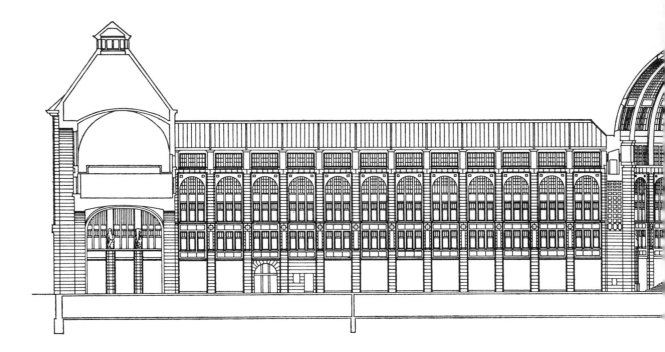

95
Friedrichstrassenpas-
sage, longitudinal
section

96
Friedrichstrassenpas-
sage, cross section

97
Friedrichstrassenpas-
sage, facade on
Friedrichstrasse

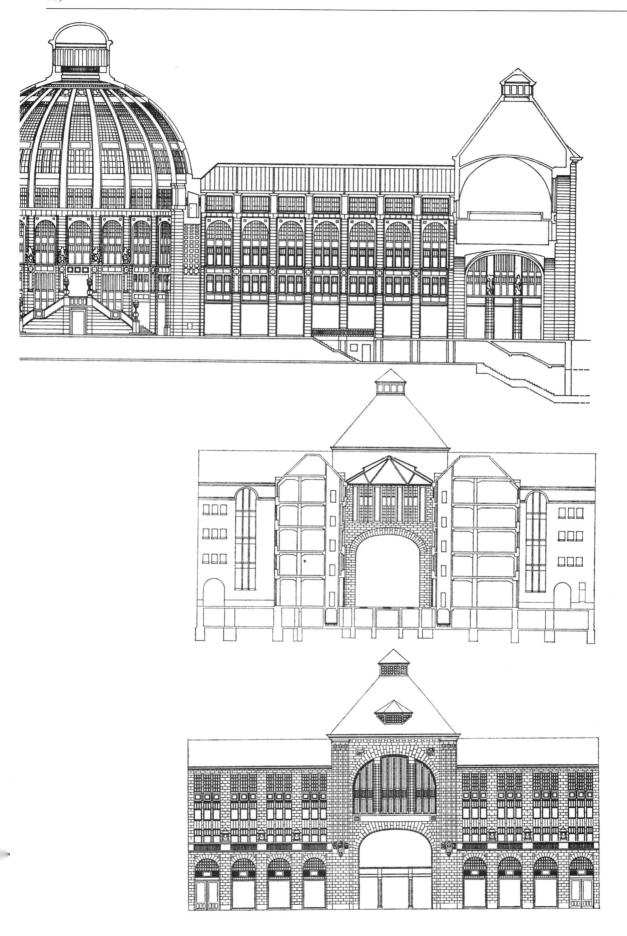

BERLIN

98
Friedrichstrassenpas-
sage from
Friedrichstrasse

99
Friedrichstrassenpas-
sage, two-level bridge

BERLIN

100
Friedrichstrassenpassage, concrete ribbed dome, 1967

101
Friedrichstrassenpassage, rotunda, 1967

102
Friedrichstrassenpas-
sage, entrance,
Oranienburger
Strasse, 1967

103
Berlin, plan for redevelopment of the inner city, by R. Ermisch

The floor of the arcade is covered with a glass mosaic. The glass saddle roof over the arcade wing possesses a horizontally suspended, box-like dust cover; it is ornamentally pierced for ventilation and suspended from the iron girders of the roof. The roof of the arcade wing seems to bear little relation to the facades or to the cupola. A glazed barrel vault of concrete arches would have been the corresponding form of enclosure.

The Friedrichstrasse Arcade is the great keystone in the development of the building type which began as a wooden structure in the eighteenth century. The particular aesthetic characteristic of this type was the use of iron as an organizing element of the roof. In the Friedrichstrasse, however, reinforced concrete was used for the first time. The building itself seems not quite right, although a certain grandness cannot be denied it: the arcade disturbs the function of the building as a department store; the boxy glass roof seems to be more appropriate for a bank; and the rotunda is overwhelmingly meaningless. Even the gothicizing facades, with all of their mosaic and bronze ornament, could not distract from the fantastic emptiness, the lifelessness of such a gigantic space. Milan was not to be repeated.

Arcade (project) (fig. 103)
Friedrichstrasse—Leipzigerstrasse
I must also mention the plan done by Richard Ermisch in 1945 for a huge cruciform arcade for a Berlin destroyed by World War II but still politically unified. To be located between Friedrichstrasse and Leipzigerstrasse, it was part of a redevelopment plan for the center of the city which bears the name of K. Bonatz—the architectural minister of the first elected city government.[240] This plan, which ignored the coming partition of the city, created a traffic network still regarded erroneously today in West Berlin as a highway plan. The proposed pedestrian cross beneath a huge square covering of glass seems like a toned-down version of Speer's megalomanic designs taken back in time to the absolutist city of Frederick the Great. If the one lacked the time, the other lacked the building materials. Hidden treasure waits here for researchers in the field of "continuity." But seen from today's point of view, Ermisch's dreams evoke a picture of a beneficent spatial arrangement appropriate for the resuscitation of the idea of the arcade on the indestructible Kurfürstendamm.

BERN
Von Werdt Arcade
Spitalgasse 36—Neuengasse 41—43
Bern's inner city was especially suited to
the planning and construction of arcades,
offering the ideal situation of several
streets with the same amount of commercial activity.

The medieval city center of Bern, almost
800 years old, is almost intact.[241] The original plans for the area as a court location
date from 1191. The block layout of the
center city has undergone constant change.
Today it can absorb functional and structural change as well as commercial traffic
without resorting to regulation and without injury to the appearance of streets and
facades. Bern's old city consists of a grid of
building blocks, each 300 meters long and
between 40 and 90 meters wide. Almost
all of the blocks have vaulted pedestrian
promenades all the way around; some are
situated slightly above or below the street
level. The arcades are common to all of the
buildings, but they were not planned uniformly. They were added on, individually
designed, and became public space independent of the street. Each building is connected to the street by a small set of steps;
in many cases there is an entrance to the
basement at the ground level. The extended blocks are subdivided into deep
sites, some of which reach as far as the opposite side of the street. Narrow alleys and
passageways accessible only to pedestrians
subdivide the blocks further and connect
the arcades to one another. The built block
proceeded through the following sequence:
Single buildings or houses
Row houses
Buildings that extend from one street to
another with small interior courtyards
Large commercial buildings with two entrances
Large commercial buildings with arcades.

The last development occurred when the
show window frontage became too limited
for the number of shops. Entrances that
penetrated the building block preceded the
construction of one-story arcades without
overhead illumination. Three kinds of
public space solely for pedestrian use may
be found in Bern today:
Arcades (total length of 6.7 kilometers)
Cross streets (total length of .7 kilometers)
Newly developed arcades (total length of
.5 kilometers).

The development of Bern's old city into a
strictly commercial and government center
has not yet been completed. New arcades
will be constructed. The interiors of the
twenty-two blocks will change completely.
But this change will not be apparent on the
exterior as the historical dress of the arcades' facades will hide it. As a result,
public space will be expanded.

The Von Werdt Arcade is the only arcade
in Bern which has the character of an independent building.[242] Located between
Neuengasse and Spitalgasse near the train
station, it is one story and is fully interior,
with no street facades. It is connected to
other arcades by passageways through
buildings. A low glass saddle roof lights
the arcade area, which is approximately 5
meters wide. On one side is a row of
shops; on the other, a number of entrances
to the splendid Palace Theater. The theater
is accessible only through the arcade and
was probably one of the reasons for its
construction.

BIRMINGHAM
The Birmingham Mail[243] reported on
March 8, 1882: "Birmingham seems to be
. . . quite an Arcadian town, not perhaps
in the sense of primitive innocence and
pastoral simplicity, but in the number and
magnificence of its arcades. . . . Windows
stocked with fancy goods, ladies' work,
knick-knacks, bijouterie, rare pottery,
curios, and 'objets d'art' seem well-be-
stowed in a thoroughfare whose construction invites a pleasant dawdle for those
who do not use it as a short cut from one
street to another."

The city of Birmingham, with its millions
in population, first took a great upturn
in the Victorian era; it grew powerful
through its steel industry, which provided
weapons for entire wars. Birmingham
demonstrates the classic development of
young Victorian industrial cities. Its relatively small, constantly overcrowded and
overdeveloped center is ringed by large
train stations. The great industrial plants,
including commercial buildings and multistoried rental establishments, are situated
on the periphery of this area. Then follow
row upon row as far as the eye can see of
workers' houses of dark brown brick. Birmingham's business district is undergoing
its second complete renewal. Whole sections of streets have been laid; the old,
melancholy office buildings, with their Renaissance terra-cotta facades, are coming
down; countless office high-rises are shoot-

ing up; and the city is strangled by a new elevated ring expressway system.

With the building of the Great Western Arcade in the late 1870s, downtown property, which had become valuable, began to be opened up in depth. The favorable proximity of the main commercial streets —New Street, Corporation Street, Dale End, and Colmore Row—made possible the construction of numerous arcades which promised to be commercially successful. The era of the arcade is now at an end in Birmingham. New arcades do appear, but only in the stunted, dependent form of a one-story thoroughfare without any independent source of illumination.

Great Western Arcade (figs. 104–107)
Colmore Row—Temple Row
The Great Western Arcade was the first and most beautiful arcade in Birmingham. Still standing, it is animated every day by streams of hurried passersby who rush from the train station to the business district. But it is only a torso. The glass roof, the dome and semidomes, the candelabra, and the Renaissance decoration were all lost in an air raid. A new, distinctly inelegant saddle roof covers the arcade now, giving it almost too much light and the utilitarian quality of a market hall. The candelabra have been replaced by neon lights distinctly lacking in taste.

The Great Western Arcade was built on a site created by the construction of the Great Western railway tunnel; it was built by the Great Western Arcade Company, formed especially for this purpose. It opened on August 28, 1876, after only a year's construction, and all of the shops were rented immediately.[244] British architectural journals carried many reports, articles, and analyses of the architecture of the arcade and the details of its construction. The Great Western Arcade is located directly across from the entrance gate of the Great Western Railway Station; it cuts across the block of buildings parallel to Bull Street and ends in Temple Row across from the Royal Hotel. It was further developed and extended into the North Western Arcade, creating a direct connection to Corporation Street. The street buildings, "built in the French-Italian style of architecture," are all four-storied. The staircases to the galleries on the second floor of the arcade are located in them. The arcade has one setback; the shops on the ground

floor project slightly. On the top floor is a series of galleries from which the offices are directly accessible. This division of space may be found in many Victorian arcades in England; its models are Georgian terraces and the "rows" of small towns.[245] In the middle the arcade is emphasized and widened by a domed space with two semidomes set perpendicularly to its axis. The galleries, however, run uninterrupted around it. Originally a barrel-vaulted glass roof with rectangular panes and self-supporting ribs covered the entire arcade. Its ribs were probably wooden. The pendentive cupola, whose four arches echoed the profiles of the barrel vault and the semidomes, was glazed in the same manner as the roof. The spandrels carried decoration.

Three large chandeliers, each with forty-two lamps, lit the arcade by night; there were in addition forty-four three-armed candelabra which stood on the balusters of the gallery. All the lighting was gas. There had been a competition for the lighting contract among the firms in Birmingham specializing in gas fittings; the contract was awarded to the firm of Best and Lloyd.

The rear access ways, approximately 1.5 meters wide, are a special feature of the Great Western Arcade. All 100 shops and offices in the arcade have them; they end on the rear side of the street buildings and are accessible from the arcade entrances.

Central Arcade
Corporation Street—Cannon Street
Opened in 1881, the Central Arcade was Birmingham's second arcade. W. H. Ward, the architect for the Great Western Arcade, also designed the Central Arcade. Alfred Humpage directed the construction. The arcade is no longer standing, but there is a detailed description of it in *The Architect*.[246]

The Central Arcade was only 35 meters long and had an incline of 1.5 meters; it connected Cannon Street with Corporation Street. There does not seem to have been any direct function for the arcade in terms of traffic patterns, given the street plan. The small size of the site permitted a space for only one row of shops. The neighboring shopowners, however, received permission to open up their stores onto the arcade side. The frontal buildings are four- and five-storied respectively; they are constructed of sandstone in a rather free Renaissance style. The arcade itself was

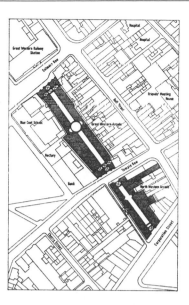

104
Birmingham, sites of
the Great Western
Arcade and the
North Western Ar-
cade, 1889

105
Birmingham, Great
Western Arcade,
1875–1876, en-
trance, Temple Row

106
Birmingham, Great
Western Arcade, ar-
cade space with
modified glass roof,
1966

only two-storied; a barrel-vaulted glass roof arched over it. The vault was ribbed by ornamental iron arches, at the interval of the shop bays which supported the roof. There were eight shops on the ground floor and two rows of offices with four rooms each on the top floor, which was accessible from stairs in the entrance buildings. A large room with its own skylight, called the Gallery, extended over the entire length of the arcade above the glass roof. The Central Restaurant with its Grill Room[247] was located in the two-storied basement, which was lighted through the leaded glass floor of the arcade. It was accessible from both ends of the arcade.

Imperial Arcade
Dale End
The Imperial Arcade belongs to the infrequent and nonfunctional type of arcade which possesses only a single entrance.[248] The site is on one of Birmingham's former busy commercial streets, Dale End. It extends approximately 40 meters into the block. The entrance leads through a tall archway—locked at night by a heavy iron gate—into an arcade with a single setback which ends in a rotunda 9.2 meters in diameter, covered with a glass cupola.[249] The architect Henry Naden designed the Imperial Arcade in 1884, using the Renaissance forms typical of the period.

North Western Arcade
Temple Row—Corporation Street
The North Western Arcade, located between Temple Row and Corporation Street, was built in 1884–1885 as the extension of the Great Western Arcade and designed by the architect W. Jenkins.[250] The southwest side borders on the narrow Bradford Arcade, to which it is connected by a passageway. The positioning of the North Western Arcade with relation to Bull Street is difficult to ascertain from the old plans of 1889.

The North Western Arcade is no longer standing. There is only a one-story arcade which cuts through a newly built department store to remind us of its existence.

Gothic Arcade
Snow Hill—Slaney Street
Like most of the arcades in Birmingham, the Gothic Arcade has been torn down. The arcade was located at the side entrance to the Great Western Railway Station diagonally across from Snow Hill, which was one of the largest main roads to

107
Great Western Arcade, rotunda, from
The Builder, 1876

108
Birmingham, City
Arcade, 1897–1899,
demolished

the north. The Gothic Arcade was designed "in early Gothic style" by the Birmingham architect J. Statham Davis in
1884.[251] The structure is described in an
article in *The Builder*:[252] "The frontage to
Snow Hill will consist of large shops four
stories high, divided by a bold Gothic
arched entrance. Into the elevation towards Snow Hill, buff glazed bricks, Min-
ton's tiles, particolored stone, ornamental
red brickwork and terracotta, ornamental
metal work, etc., will be introduced. A
large enriched centre gable, filled in with
panelling, tiles, etc., will emphasise this
front. The elevation to Slanery Street will
be of plain Gothic character. The shops in
the arcade will also be of somewhat plain
design, glazed with white brickfacings,
ganged brick arches, moulded brick cornices, bay-windows, etc. . . ."

City Arcades (fig. 108)

The City Arcades were the last great arcade project in Birmingham at the end of
the nineteenth century. It was an arcade
complex of three wings which ran together
in a windmill form, intersecting in a
triangle which enclosed a single store surrounded on all three sides by arcades. One
of the three wings was bisected by Union
Arcade and has its own name, the Midland Arcade. This short wing still stood in
1966, although it was already closed and
marked to be torn down.

A prospectus of City Arcades Birmingham
Limited gives us a good idea of the development and the commercial intention of
the builder.[253] Shares were sold to raise the
necessary capital; they must have been
subscribed to very quickly since the prospectus dates from 1897 and City Arcades
was opened in 1899. The prospectus includes site plans, sketches by the architects
Newton and Chatle, descriptions of the
guarantees offered and profit projections,
references to a report, and letters from
tenants who had already agreed to rent.
In addition, we learn that in 1897 the
Great Western Arcade and the North
Western Arcade were flourishing and fully
occupied.

The construction of City Arcades is described in the prospectus:

. . . The proposed Arcades will provide
shops in the centre of the City where there
is a great and ever increasing demand for
them, and where there are no shops void at
the present time, except those in Union
Passage kept vacant for the purpose of
these Arcades. . . . An idea of the immense

traffic passing through these Arcades may
be gathered from the evidence given by
Mr. Walter Ludlow, F. S. I., in connection
with the Birmingham City Tramways Bill,
before the Select Committee of the House
of Commons, on May 17th, 1897, in
which he stated that on Thursday, April
29th, between the hours of 12 noon and 6
p.m. 25,563 foot passengers passed and re-
passed, or about 4,260 per hour, which
may be regarded as a fair average.

It is difficult to increase the shop accom-
modations in the centre of the City except
as proposed by these new covered thoroughfares as the central area available for
shops is greatly restricted on account of (1)
the high level of the land and the steepness
of the approaches on two sides; (2) the
great space occupied by New Street Station
on the south and St. Philip's Churchyard
on the north-west; and (3) the ring of
manufacturers surrounding the central
area. The shopping area, including High
Street, New Street, Bull Street and Corporation Street, and the streets connecting
them, is quite inadequate to provide for
the expansion of retail trade of the city.
The result of the restriction in the area is
that the land produces abnormally large
prices and high ground rents. The total
ground rent payable by the Company on
its area of nearly one acre and a quarter
is less than £1 per yard, and compares
favourably with the ground rents of
other properties in the immediate
neighbourhood.

When these New Arcades have been carried out, it is improbable that in the future
there can be any material increase in the
number of the city, as there is no available
space.

When the North-Western Arcade was
opened in 1885, the population of the
Borough was 412,606. Since then Greater
Birmingham has been added; and together
with Handsworth, Aston, Moseley and the
adjacent suburbs, the population is now
about 683,305; while within a radius of
twelve miles of the city the population is
about 1,250,000. A large proportion of
this great population do their shopping in
the centre of the city.

The prospectus contains the following information concerning the architecture of
the arcade. The wings of the arcade were
three-storied; the corners and the pavilions
were distinguished by pediments and small
turrets.[254] The facades are described as
"one of the 'busy' terra-cotta facades now
so popular in Birmingham." Large, two-
story arched gateways formed the entranceways to the arcade wings, which met
the entrances at an angle. This feature
caused adverse comment. The interior construction of the arcade was the same in all
of the wings. It was stepped back once.

The side galleries on the second floor, however, were not accessible but were divided as individual balconies belonging to the upper stories of the shops. City Arcades had a total of seventy-six shop units, each with a tall-ceilinged ground story, an office on the upper floor, and a large storage room in the cellar accessible by means of separate entrances from the street.

The arcade was covered by a barrel-vaulted glass roof supported by its own so-called "Ellipse system of Messrs. Mellows and Co.," a method of construction which had been used since 1882 for all types of larger glass roofs. Half-ellipse T-beams were bolted to a semicircular, supporting I-beam. The ends of the T-beams held the purlins. In this way the actual glass roof seemed to be lifted off the framework. Two other curved T-pieces, which proceeded from the same joint, provided the longitudinal support. The center strip of the glass roof was elevated and allowed for ventilation. At the same time, the glass could be adjusted according to need. Beneath the center strip and resting on the beams were pieces of lead ornament from which lighting globes were suspended. The facades of the shops were of polychrome glazed terra-cotta tiles;[255] the pilasters framing the shop bays were topped by tempietti, which gave the arcade a rather bizarre air.[256]

The Builder commented on the construction of City Arcades in an article entitled "More Arcades for Birmingham":[257] "It appears that there is a desire to form a new shop arcade system in Birmingham, with entrances from New Street, High Street, and Union Street, the arcade consisting of three covered streets at different angles. There is no greater convenience and comfort in a town, in bad weather, than is afforded by such covered streets and shops, and it is surprising that this way of building shops has not been more largely made use of in large towns in this country, with its wet and uncertain climate."

Piccadilly Arcade
New Street—Stephenson Street
The Piccadilly Arcade is a modern arcade without a separate skylight built in 1926–1927.

BLACKBURN

Twaite's Arcade
Market Place—Lord Street—Church Street
The arcade was built in 1882 by the architect H. Thompson;[258] it is approximately 60 meters in length and three-storied, and has twenty-four shops.

BORDEAUX
Galerie Bordelaise (figs. 109–115)
Rue Ste. Cathérine 16, corner Rue St. Rémi 69—Rue des Piliers de Tutelle 7, corner Rue de la Maison Dorade 3
The Galerie Bordelaise in Bordeaux is one of the most beautiful, best preserved arcades in France. It still serves its original function, and is still full of activity, even though the elegance of the shops can no longer be compared to what it once was, according to the description of the opening.[259] The interior of the arcade has been beautifully renovated; even the glass roof was replaced by a milky, opaque roof which gives an artificial sense of space.

The Rue Ste. Cathérine is similar in commercial significance to Hohe Strasse in Cologne; it is Bordeaux's old main business district, cramped and always full of an undescribable tumult of traffic. It runs between the Place de la Victoire on the south and the Place de la Comédie in front of the Grand Théâtre in the north. The Galerie Bordelaise begins at the corner of the Rue Ste. Cathérine and the Rue St. Rémi and ends at the corner of Rue de la Maison Dorade and Rue des Piliers de Tutelle, which runs up alongside the Grand Théâtre. It crosses the block of buildings formed by these four streets on the diagonal. This is a unique situation within the typology of the arcade but is an exemplary case in terms of its function as a shortcut. The facades surround almost the entire block, including the buildings which do not belong to the arcade. They are three-storied, not counting the mezzanine. Constructed in sandstone, they display a rather ponderous classicism without any deep profiling. An arcade unites the ground floor and the mezzanine. The ground floor frieze is used for advertising and signs. The two upper stories are separated by a continuous balcony with iron railing supported by stone corbels. The two corners from which the arcade may be entered are rounded off. After passing through the entrance, composed of three identical archways, one comes upon an intervening vestibule, polygonal in shape. Passing under two Palladian vaults with marble columns and Corinthian capitals, one enters the arcade itself, which runs through to the Rue Ste. Cathérine, where it is divided by an overhead crossway which be-

109
Bordeaux, sites of the
Galerie Bordelaise
and the Bazar Bor-
delaise, 1872

110
Bordeaux, Galerie
Bordelaise,
1831–1834, rear
passageway

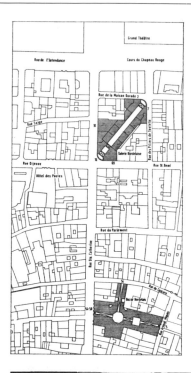

longs to an apartment on the second floor.
The rooms in the apartment thus formed a
kind of circle.[260] The arcade motif for the
shops on the ground floor is carried out in
the interior of the arcade, although the pillars are inlaid with mirrors, the entabla-
tures are decorated with gilded ornaments
and medallions, and the upper walls
and mouldings are varnished in yellow.
The model for the arcade was obviously
the Parisian arcades built several years
previously.

When constructing the building, special
care was taken about fire protection and
exits.[261] Fire walls of ashlar that extended
beyond the roof were erected on three
sides of each shop; special attention was
paid never to allow the wooden ceilings to
penetrate a stone wall. The glass roof was
built with metal scaffolding and had to
have good ventilation capacities. The
shops had individual cast-iron spiral staircases to the upper stories; and each had an
emergency exit through a back way to one
of the staircases in the corner buildings
which led directly to the outside. Today
offices and residential units occupy the upper stories.

The cornerstone to the Galerie Bordelaise
was laid in 1831, and the arcade was
opened on April 1, 1834. It was designed
by the architect Gabriel-Joseph Durand
(1792–1858), the official district architect
at the time. Durand was the official architect of the city of Bordeaux later, in
1840–1849.

The arcade was the speculative business
enterprise of four Mexican immigrants,
named de la Torre, de Irigoyen, Ginet, and
Caillavet, who had made their fortune as
businessmen in Bordeaux. The arcade is
still in foreign hands today. The Bordeaux paper *L'Indicateur* stated at the
opening:[262]

The new Galerie Bordelaise has been
opened to the public here. As one might
have expected, the crowds which it drew
during the day and during the evenings
were considerable. There was not enough
praise for the good taste and luxury employed in the building of this structure,
which fills a need in Bordeaux, and which,
as we have said, seems to be rivaled only
by the Orléans arcade in Paris. The happy
use of marble and mirrors is particularly
noteworthy and, as soon as all the occupied shops add their splendor to that of
the gas lamps which are suspended from
the vault, the effect will be truly magical.
Yesterday, this splendor of light was lost in
the empty shops and detracted from the to-

111
Galerie Bordelaise,
view from the con-
cièrge's apartment

112
Galerie Bordelaise,
vestibule, Rue Ste.
Cathérine

113
Galerie Bordelaise,
arcade space with
modernized glass
roof

114
Galerie Bordelaise,
detail of corner

115
Galerie Bordelaise,
lithograph made for
the opening, April 1,
1834

tal effect. Certainly this small distraction will be remedied in a few days.

Although the arcade was not yet completed, the owners did not want to disappoint public interest and curiosity. On the whole, the crowds were satisfied. . . . The arcade is certainly a tribute to the various craftsmen who worked together to erect it.

Bazar Bordelais

Rue Ste. Cathérine 54–58—Rue de Cancera 54—Rue Arnaud Miqueu 5
The Bazar Bordelais was also located on the Rue Ste. Cathérine.[263] However, it had two additional entrances. It was built in 1835 by the architect J. A. de Thiac (1800–1865) in the wake of the commercial success of the Galerie Bordelaise. He also designed the Palais de Justice and the prison in Bordeaux. The arcade space was two-storied and had only occasional skylights. The Bazar was replaced in 1872 by the construction of the Nouvelles Galeries.

Passage Sarget

Place du Chapelet—Cours de l'Intendence 19
The Passage Sarget was a small arcade[264] which was opened in 1878 by the businessman André Acquert. It is still used today and has been substantially modernized.

BOURNEMOUTH
Gervis Arcade

Old Christchurch Road—Gervis Place
Three small arcades are located in the small resort town of Bournemouth on the Channel coast; the oldest is the Gervis Arcade. It was built between 1866 and 1873 by the local builder Henry Joy between some country homes near the Bourne River.

Nikolaus Pevsner writes of the Gervis Arcade:[265] ". . . Henry Joy . . . managed to let the flanking, bow-shaped façades appear Regency in style, survival rather than revival. The arcade itself has a glass tunnel-vault. Much of the detailing alas now modernistic."

Westbourne Arcade

Poole Road
Henry Joy also built the Westbourne Arcade in 1884–1885.[266]

Boscombe Arcade

Christchurch Road—Boscombe
The Boscombe Arcade, constructed in brick, was built by the architects Lawson and Donkin in 1891.[267]

BRADFORD
Swan Arcade (figs. 116–118)

Brock Street—Charles Street—Market Street
The cramped downtown area of Bradford —center of worsted cloth spinning mills in the Victorian era—cuts through Market Street and connects the Town Hall with Midland Station. The Exchange and Exchange Station are located diagonally across from it. At the intersection formed by these public buildings lies Bradford's only arcade, the Swan Arcade, named after the White Swan Inn, a pub which was previously located there. The arcade was contracted by Angus Holden,[268] who had bought up individual lots between Market Street, Brook Street, and Charles Street. It was designed by the architects Milnes and France. Construction was begun in 1877; the opening was in 1881. The entire enterprise cost £150,000.

The Swan Arcade, torn down in 1962, was an almost square block of buildings which had facades facing three streets. Three arcades cut through the block on the east-west axis and two on the north-south axis. The overall length of the arcades was 180 meters. The two-storied building housed forty-four shops, forty-six offices, and sixty-five market and storage areas. The arcade was thus a multipurpose structure. The six exits could be locked at night with iron gates. "Central Avenue," the central concourse, had a glass saddle roof supported by graceful iron arches; the surrounding avenues had only lean-to roofs.

BRAUNSCHWEIG
Sedan Bazar

Breite Strasse—Gördelinger Strasse
The Sedan Bazar is located near the Altstadt Market; since 1928 it has been called the Handelsweg (commercial way). This small arcade, built in approximately 1878, had actually existed since 1700. It had been called the Neuer Hof (new courtyard) and had served as a meeting place.[269] Only vestiges of the arcade, which had no real buildings of its own on the street, are still standing today. The glass roof and parts of the arcade buildings were destroyed; fragments of the polygonal dome structure can still be seen. The interior facades were of yellow brick with Gothic motifs.

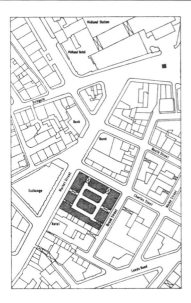

116
Bradford, Swan Ar-
cade, 1877–1881,
demolished 1962

117
Swan Arcade,
entrance

118
Swan Arcade, roof

119
Brighton, Royal Arcade, project, from
The Builder, 1868

BRIGHTON
Royal Arcade (project) (fig. 119)
West Street—Middle Street

In 1865 *The Builder* carried an illustrated article on the project for the Royal Arcade in the famous resort town of Brighton.[270] The article names John Ellis of London as the architect and dates the building from 1865. The arcade is an important one in the development of the arcade in England since it is the connecting link between the Greek Revival arcades of the 1820s through the 1840s and the many Victorian arcades built from approximately 1875 on. The design of Brighton's Royal Arcade shows no influence of the Galleria Vittorio Emanuele in Milan, which first became widely known in England in 1868 through publications in *The Builder*.

The Royal Arcade was designed to run parallel to the Esplanade, the large boardwalk promenade, and to connect the two busy streets of West Street and Middle Street. It would be 98 meters long and 7.6 meters wide with a total of thirty shops. The three-storied arcade would not have entrance buildings; a double-window facade order, widened by one window as a finishing motif at the street exit end, would form the enclosure. The shops would have their own kitchens, cellars, showrooms on the second floor, and two bedrooms on the third floor. The arcade as planned is described in the article just mentioned: ". . . Each front, as may be seen in our engraving, is included within an arch, and will be formed of bronze, granite, and serpentine. The decorations will be principally in Majolica ware, expressly designed for this building, and the whole will be covered with an ornamental iron roof, which will ventilate the entire arcade." If we consider the arcade as it is shown in fig. 119, it is striking that its spatial feeling is of a church rather than a street. If we examine the architectural details, we discover a kinship with the interior of Lincoln Cathedral.[271] The pointed arches have been rounded, and the piers support iron beams rather than a vault. The piers are meant, with their ornamental bombast, to give an impression of massiveness. In fact, they support only a ridgepole which carries the ribs of the glass roof.

BRISTOL

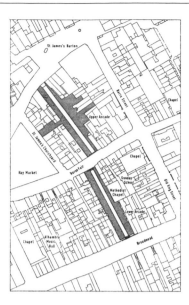

120
Bristol, sites of the
Upper Arcade and
the Lower Arcade,
1885

121
Bristol, Lower Ar-
cade, 1824–1825,
entrance, Horse Fair

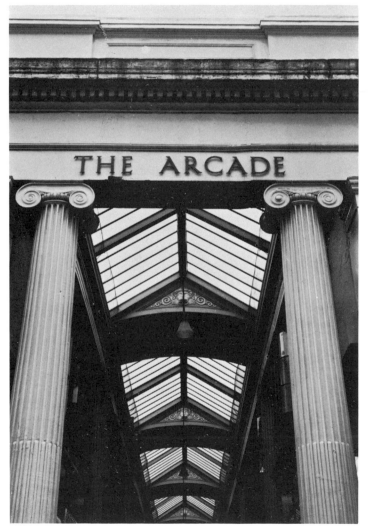

BRISTOL
Upper and Lower Arcades (figs. 120–127)
Broadmead—Horse Fair

The Upper and Lower Arcades in Bristol
may be treated together since they were designed by the same architects, were built at
the same time, and exhibit only minor differences. The facades are different because
of varying widths in the lots; the depths
differ as well. The slope of the site made
small steps necessary in the Lower Arcade.

The Upper and Lower Arcades were built
in 1824–1825 by the architects James and
Thomas Foster of Bristol.[272] The location
was a then newly developed commercial
district east of the old city. An article in
the *Western Daily Press* reported on the
cornerstone ceremony:[273] "In May, 1824,
the Foundation stone of the Upper Arcade,
which extended from St. James' Barton to
the Horse Fair, was laid with much enthusiasm and public ceremony. At the time
Bristol people generally looked upon this
scheme as almost the last word in public
enterprise, and there was more rejoicing,
when the building was opened in the following year. Much was hoped from this
venture, and a loquacious poet published,
at the time of the opening ceremony, a
long and fulsome ode to this 'lofty canopy'
of glass."

Walking today through the rebuilt commercial district of Bristol, it is a surprise
suddenly to find oneself before a classical
gate; one enters and wanders through an
ancient temple, hollowed out, endlessly extended. It is illuminated from above and
serves for the retailing of wares of all
kinds. Show windows in black enameled
frames with colorful displays push themselves between the towering Ionic columns
into the middle of the hall and confuse the
visitor so ready to be solemn: London's
Burlington Arcade is the obvious model.
But the spatial feeling created by the entablature is special. If we analyze the arcade, we find two competing elements: the
structural framework of opposing engaged
Ionic columns, which support the flat entablature, and the smooth walls of the
shops, which thrust themselves forward
with their bay windows and alcoves in the
upper story, make the colonnade into an
interior space, into a temple whose inner
sanctum is a shopping center.

The grand rhythm of the classical columns
(placed much too far apart from one another) competes with the small, neat, and
regular series of shop windows and shops

122
Lower Arcade, arcade space, view toward Horse Fair

BRISTOL

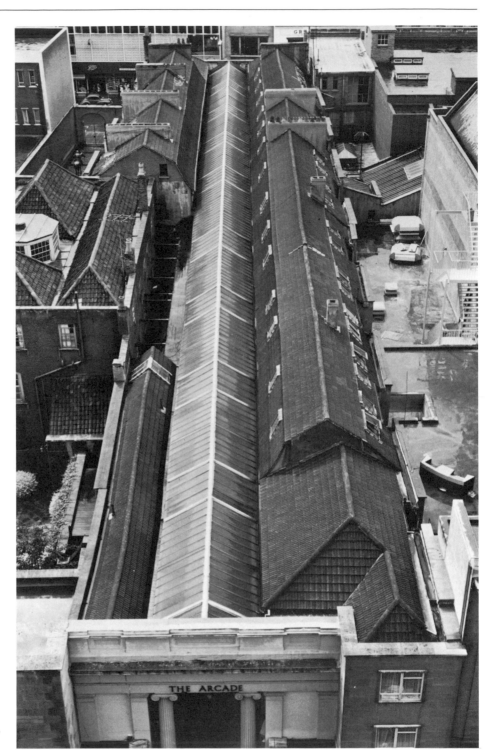

123
Lower Arcade, view
of the roof

124
Lower Arcade, longi-
tudinal section

125
Lower Arcade, en-
trance, Broadmead

126
Bristol, Upper Ar-
cade, 1824–1825,
destroyed 1943,
entrance

127
Upper Arcade after
bombing

which together form a projecting plane. The columns stand free of the wall only at the arcade entrances, which they frame. The street facades are set back slightly to allow room for side stairs to the cellar and the entrance stairs. Because there are no entrance buildings, the arcade may be perceived from its facades as a unit. It is one of the early attempts at a facade treatment adapted specifically to the arcade building type.

The interior organization of the Lower and Upper Arcades is as simple as can be imagined. The engaged columns stand in front of the shop partitions, which extend above the roof and which contain the chimney stacks. These walls, which also function as fire barriers, partition cellars, shops, offices on the upper floors, and additional rooms exposed to light above the glass roof. Each shop has its own stairs for all floors; deliveries are made through a middle passageway in the cellar underneath the gallery of the arcade. This passageway is accessible from stairs located to the side of the exterior facades. The arcade buildings are of brick, the columns and socles of sandstone, and the support structure for the glass roof of wood. The floor of the arcade is of heavy stone slabs resting on the cellar partition walls. The glass roof is continuous although interrupted by massive, slightly arched panels adorned with lions' heads which serve no apparent function.

I could find neither plans nor specific historical information on this early example of the building type in Bristol, so important for its further development. Only the Lower Arcade still stands today; the Upper Arcade was destroyed in World War II. The Lower Arcade was to be torn down as part of a clearing project to make room for the redevelopment of the entire area.[274] But the City Council was persuaded by popular protest to restore the building.

BRUSSELS

Brussels is divided into the lower Flemish and the upper French city, which grew up after the fire of 1731 and the peace of Aachen in 1748 and later became the kingdom's capital. The Park, the Palais de la Nation, the Rue Royale, and the ministry buildings, as well as the wide, gableless, multistory buildings are subject to a strict ordering principle which reveals an affinity with its Parisian model. The upper city is connected to the old lower city by outdoor balustraded stairs on the slopes of the

Koudenberg, which overlook the close rows of gabled roofs, the winding alleys, and the slim tower of the city hall on the Grand Place.

The first new construction on a grand scale in the lower city was the Place de Martyrs, in the eighteenth century.[275] It was developed further through the construction of the classical Théâtre Royal and the Place de la Monnaie, both built in 1817. The first small arcade was built in one of the new structures bordering the Place.

In the first half of the nineteenth century new public buildings were constructed in the growing city to meet specific needs. The warehouse, market hall, two train stations, the Botanical Gardens, and the grand arcade, the Galeries St. Hubert, appeared in the city center but failed to create any new spatial unity or context. Only in the 1860s did a third Brussels develop, the modern Brussels. It was a development paralleling Haussmann's thoroughgoing changes in Paris, and was brought about by two important mayors, Jules Anspach and Charles Buls.

Fritz Stahl describes this new stage in the development of the city:[276] "The idea is becoming ever more apparent that the city as an entity must be a work of art, an art-object, and that . . . the street is more important than the building. Its planning is more of an artistic act than the articulation or even the ornamentation of a facade. Of course, these undertakings are so complex, requiring so much economic insight and feeling for the totality of life to plan, so much energy to follow through, that they must be the work not of architects, but rather of rulers, of the community as a whole, as it always has been, and in a certain sense, always will be." The first step was to construct perimeter boulevards where city walls, torn down in the eighteenth century, had once stood. The boulevards were wide promenades which ringed and enclosed the old city; they improved communication within the city and made new sections accessible. Wide allées radiated from them, leading to the Stadtwald (city park), Laeken, and summer residences of the well-to-do.

The second step was accomplished under the direction of Mayor Anspach between 1867 and 1871; the interior boulevards were constructed. They were laid straight through the old city to rid the area of the stagnant Senne River and to connect the southern and northern train stations. These interior boulevards became the commercial competition for the Rue Royale and the Galeries St. Hubert. In their wake came the Passage du Nord, the Passage de Commerce, and the Passage des Postes, all of which connected the new commercial district to the old center at the Grand Palais and the Place de la Monnaie. A competition was opened for the development of the inner boulevards, the twenty best facade designs to be selected. The winner was Henri Bayaert, an architect who had concerned himself intensely with street planning in the old city.[277]

The high point of the design of the inner boulevards is the Place de Brouckère, a victim of the recent building fever in Brussels. The keystone of this third Brussels is Polaert's Palais de Justice, in which the megalomania of nineteenth-century architecture outdid itself.

In the twentieth century, parts of the old city have been destroyed by the building of the central train station. Empty, untended spaces now separate the lower from the upper city. The naming of Brussels as the headquarters of the European Economic Community has infected the city with building fever once more; the building commission and city development and planning commission have barely been able to control the rampant speculation. The Palais de Justice is beginning to receive some competition. Whole quarters of the old city have been turned into bazaar-like shopping centers. Individual shops are lined up along arcade-like ways and artificially illuminated courtyards. These allow unhampered shopping and maximum usage of the floor space. The Agora, the Galerie du Centre, the Galerie Louis, the Galerie Ravenstein, and the Galerie d'Étoile are all examples of the arcade, which, although perhaps in a somewhat stunted form, has been resurrected.

Passage de la Monnaie (figs. 128, 129)
Rue de l'Ecuyer—Place de la Monnaie
The classical design of Brussels also began in the lower city in 1817. The theater architect Louis-Emanuel-André Damesme from Paris built the Théâtre Royal on the Place de la Monnaie and surrounded it with arcades, the very first arcades in Brussels. The architect J. B. Vifquain wanted to design the arcades of the entire square on the Parisian model, but the project failed in the face of objections from individual interest groups. Unified but spare facades were built instead.

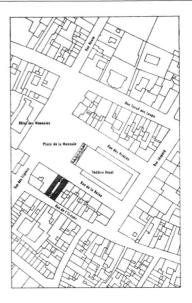

128
Brussels, site of the Passage de la Monnaie, 1866

129
Brussels, Passage de la Monnaie, detail of the facade

An arcade at number 3 on the south side of the Place de la Monnaie leads to the busy thoroughfare of Rue de l'Ecuyer. Built in 1820 on the site of the Saint Eloi chapel, it was the first glass-roofed arcade in Brussels and the first arcade on the continent outside of Paris. Its dimensions are modest; it measures 25 meters in length and only 2.5 meters in width. It exists only in part today since parts of the arcade on the square were included in the renovation of a cafe in 1882. We can enter the arcade from the Rue de l'Ecuyer and judge its dimensions, although the glass roof has been modified.[278] A sketch of the ground floor of the facade through to the Rue de l'Ecuyer from the city archives is reproduced in fig. 129.[279]

As Henri Hymans comments, the Passage de la Monnaie served as inspiration for Cluysenaar, the architect of the Galeries St. Hubert.[280]

Galeries St. Hubert (figs. 130–146)
Rue du Marché aux Herbes—Rue Montagne aux Herbes Potagères—Rue des Dominicains
The Galeries St. Hubert is the first example of a monumental arcade. It exemplifies the architectural concept of an arcade in idealized form: interior space becomes exterior space. Both its dimensions and its design are derived from the Palais Royal and the Galerie d'Orléans in Paris. Its siting is similar to that of the Passage Lemonnier in nearby Liège. Its cubic capacity was not surpassed even by later arcades. The Galeries St. Hubert was also the first arcade built with public support, official sanction, financial guarantees, and authorized expropriations. The arcade in this case is like a train station, market hall, slaughterhouse, or hospital in that it necessarily belonged to the architectural inventory of a nineteenth-century metropolitan center which wanted to become modern and civilized. The arcade thereby took on an official and institutional character. Appearing in the middle of the century between classicism and eclecticism, the Galeries St. Hubert is the connecting link between the countless arcades in Paris and London built by private speculation and those in the European cities where public interest and private speculation counterbalanced one another.

The architect of the building was Jean Pierre Cluysenaar.[281] His involvement with the Galeries St. Hubert project in 1837 coincided with the beginning of his career;

before the Galeries St. Hubert was completed, he had built another, small arcade in Antwerp in 1844–1845, which, however, was subsequently torn down.[282] In 1846–1847, he built another smaller arcade, the Marché de la Madeleine, connecting the Galeries St. Hubert to the Galerie Bortier. A competition project is reported to have been submitted in 1852 for arcades and a stock exchange building in Berlin, but I was unable to locate any plans. In Cluysenaar's announcement of the project for the Galeries St. Hubert,[283] we may learn in detail all the considerations which underlay his design, the weighing of advantages and disadvantages, and the results of his study of the arcades in Paris and Liège. We become acquainted with the conditions which, from the contemporary point of view, were necessary for safe construction of the arcade. For these reasons, I have decided to reproduce his report as Text 1.

Cluysenaar, who had built many buildings, must have been an excellent designer, engineer, and accountant. His works include market halls, train stations, palaces, and concert halls. But his greatest achievement was the Galeries St. Hubert. He fought for ten years to see it built. Mengoni, the architect of the great Galleria Vittorio Emanuele in Milan, visited him in the 1860s,[284] seeking encouragement and advice for his building.

Inspired by the small Passage de la Monnaie in Brussels, built in 1820,[285] Cluysenaar joined with W. Hauman, a businessman, and Jan De Mot, a banker, to propose the construction of a large arcade to the city. The location was to be north of the Grand-Place and the largest market, the commercial center of the city. At that time, this square was difficult to reach. The numerous alleys that led to it were too narrow to put down sidewalks; they were ordinarily crowded with carts and pedestrians. The Rue des Fripiers was the only suitably wide connecting artery to the north. Cluysenaar and his partners suggested widening the Rue St. Hubert, a narrow alley; such an expansion had been considered for some time. They suggested breaking through to the Montagne aux Herbes to create a new connection between the market and the well-to-do Rue du Marais quarter, extending to the new train station on the boulevard. The proposed arcade would serve several functions: it would relieve the traffic congestion, create new commercial areas where pedestrians could shop undisturbed by traffic or bad weather, and, with its widely diversified architectural program, attract numerous visitors to the city. It would represent pride and wealth, the economic upswing after the revolution of 1830; it would compete with the arcades in London and Paris, which the planners intended it would far outdo in size. The Galeries St. Hubert was to be the Palais Royal of Brussels.

The following chronology sketches the history of the project from 1837 to 1947.[286]

December 1837: Cluysenaar and his financial backers Hauman and De Mot along with others proposed the arcade to the Conseil de Régence of Brussels. They petitioned for the building to be classified as a "monument for public use" to facilitate the numerous expropriations necessary for the intended site. A construction permit was issued on December 4.

January 1838: The pamphlet "Projet de Communication entre le Marché aux Herbes et la Montagne aux Herbes Potagères appeared.[287] The pamphlet was intended to acquaint a broader public with the arcade project.

March 7, 1838: The following points were agreed upon after long debate in the Conseil Communal:
A connection between the Marché aux Herbes and the Montagne aux Herbes Potagères was necessary.
It would be advantageous to provide a type of connection similar to an arcade, accessible to both traffic and pedestrians.
In the case that this arcade should be accessible to pedestrians only, as the petitioners had suggested, that type of connection would also be useful.

March 15, 1838: The Permanent Deputy of the Provincial Council agreed.

April 11, 1838: The Minister of Justice agreed. The completion of the project was assured. The debates on June 6, June 15, and November 15, 1838, all concerned minor details.

April 30, 1838: Date of the first sketches attributable to the project:[288] facades, site plan, and longitudinal section.

February 6, 1839: Leopold I, who was very interested in the project, signed a royal decree stating that the construction of the building was in the public interest and authorizing the necessary expropriations. Appended to the decree was the Cahier des Charges, which included, among its seventeen articles, the official construction documents:[289] the plans for sewerage, specifications of the types of stone for the facades and floors, fire regulations, and the stipulation that the building must be completed within four years of the beginning of construction. In case of default on this article, the site would return to the possession of the city.

September 1, 1839: Date of the preliminary plans on a scale of 1 to 250.

1840: A second, extensive pamphlet by Cluysenaar on the project appeared. It included the first exact floor plan, an interior view, and a description of the projected premises. The pamphlet was entitled: "Plans et Description des Deux Galeries Couvertes à Construire à Bruxelles." The explanatory text, twelve pages in length, is reproduced here as Text 1.

1840–1845: During the following years the unpopular expropriations and the tearing down of often unstable buildings were carried out. There were many incidents, some quite strange. Some residents refused to vacate. Cluysenaar's project became suspect and fell into disrepute. These events persuaded the city authorities to reject further extension of the arcade through to the Rue Fossé aux Loups, Rue des Fripiers, Rue Léopold, and Rue de la Montagne to avoid further expropriations. The project also encountered financial difficulties during this period because of the unstable credit situation created when the Banque de Belgique suspended payment.

February 22, 1845: The Public Council accepted by a vote of nineteen to five the decision of the financial board, which guaranteed a minimum of three percent interest on the capital of two and a half million francs used for the construction of the arcade.

July 5, 1845: The Galeries St. Hubert and its branch societies were established. Capital was secured, stock was offered, and the administrative structure of the society announced: two directors (Cluysenaar and De Mot), three administrators, and a supervisory committee consisting of three members of the society and three representatives of the city of Brussels. Léopold I approved the statutes of the society immediately; several days later stock was offered to the public.

August 1, 1845: The society petitioned the Minister of Public Works and Count d'Hoffschmidt for permission to trade the stock on the stock exchange. Permission was granted on August 5.

May 6, 1846: The cornerstone was laid at a ceremony. The king, the mayor, and other notables from the city attended. Two arcades of the Galerie de la Reine were converted into royal boxes; stakes holding torches outlined the future form of the arcade, since construction of the building had not yet progressed beyond the cellar. A sample show window was exhibited. Fifty grenadiers from the Corps de Musique de la Société Royale de la Grande Harmonie provided music. The king buried a small chest filled with mementos; it was covered with the flags of the 1830 revolution and placed under the base of the left column of the entryway peristyle. Speeches were made; Cluysenaar was honored with the Order of Léopold. There was a huge banquet immediately following, with duck filets with truffles, venison, punch glacé, and Nesselrode pudding. Fine wines made the rounds. Over three hundred workers celebrated until late into the night with beer and cigars.

December 4, 1846: After a lively session, the society announced the names for the individual wings of the arcade. Since Cluysenaar and De Mot had declined, there was common agreement on the names Galerie du Roi, Galerie de la Reine, and Galerie des Princes. The slogan *Omnibus omnia* (everything for everyone), which would decorate the entrance to the arcade, was taken over from the business of a goldsmith whose shop was closed by expropriation.

June 20, 1847: The Galeries St. Hubert was christened almost a month sooner than anticipated. The rapidity of construction, astonishing even by today's standards, testifies to the talents of the architect. The king made an appearance for the occasion with his entire court. He was ceremoniously received by the members of the society and the mayor in the peristyle of the arcade. The king was said to have addressed Cluysenaar several times, expressing his amazement. The arcade was officially opened to the public at a grand ceremony in the Théâtre de la Galerie with music and speeches. After the king and his entourage had left the arcade, to the acclaim of the crowds, the people of the city

were allowed to enter. The Galeries St. Hubert was open for visitors from 8 A.M. to 8 P.M.; the entrance fee was 25 centimes on Sunday and Thursday, 10 centimes on all other days of the week. The arcade was an immediate success. In 1848 only eighteen apartments and fifteen shops in the Galerie des Princes were still available; by 1850 all had been occupied. The records of the society in subsequent years showed a steady profit:

1847–1848	89,724 francs
1863	184,575 francs
1876–1877	260,196 francs

The Galeries became a gathering place, the last stop of the daily promenade of the citizens of Brussels who walked from the Rue Royale through the Rue de la Madeleine to the arcade. The intelligentsia, clubs, editors of newpapers, the Association Libérale, and the Cercle Artistique et Littéraire all took up residence there. The arcade became the intellectual and artistic center of Brussels. After the coup d'etat French refugees made their way there,[290] held their talks and their political discussions, and lent an international flavor to the social life of the arcade. Victor Hugo, Edgar Quinet, Alexandre Dumas, Emile Deschanel, and Charles Baudelaire are among the best known.

November 15, 1851: The casino, accessible from the arcade, was opened on the site of the former Flower Market, which Cluysenaar had covered with a glass roof. Located next to the Théâtre de la Galerie, where the French Opéra Comique was usually on the bill, the casino was the second entertainment establishment in the arcade. It was a "café chantant" and was directed by the exiled French Count Juvigny. The audience enjoyed the show, drank beer, and ate baked potatoes. The Taverne de la Galerie became the meeting place for exiles and political refugees of all sorts. The arcade's social life reached its zenith from the 1850s to the 1870s. It was a society of extremes; in close spatial proximity coexisted all classes and types, from prostitutes to intellectuals to the nobility.

1864: Baudelaire, living in a hotel in the neighborhood of the arcade, worked on the sketches for his *Pauvre Belgique* and walked the entire length of the arcade eight times a day, 250 paces for each story.

July 10, 1873: At about 9 A.M. Paul Verlaine appeared in the arcade, drunk and desperate. He entered the shop of a

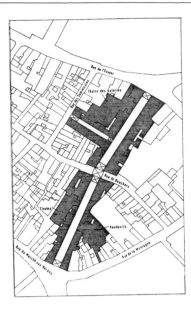

130
Brussels, site of the
Galeries St. Hubert,
1866

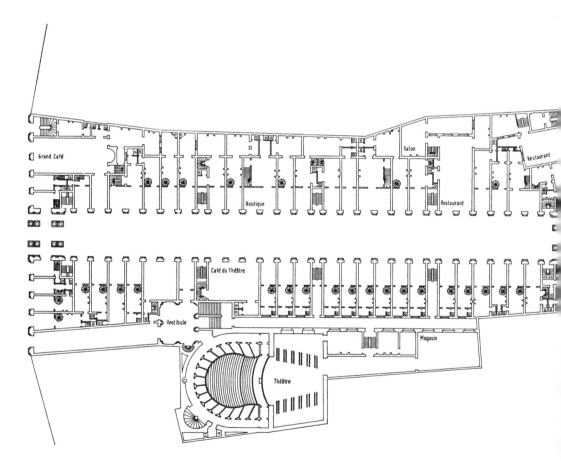

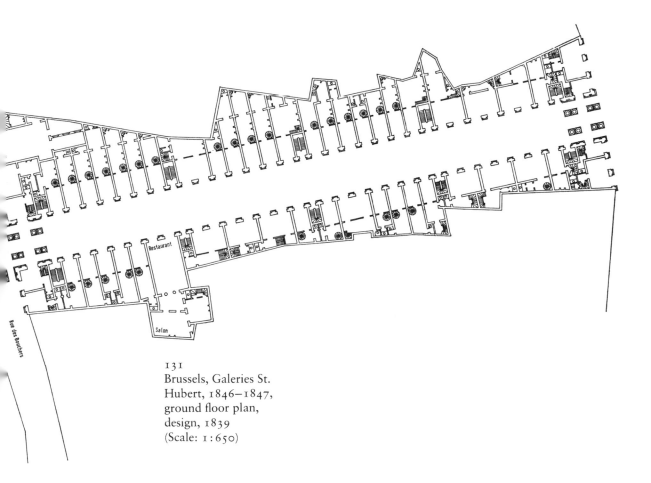

131
Brussels, Galeries St.
Hubert, 1846–1847,
ground floor plan,
design, 1839
(Scale: 1:650)

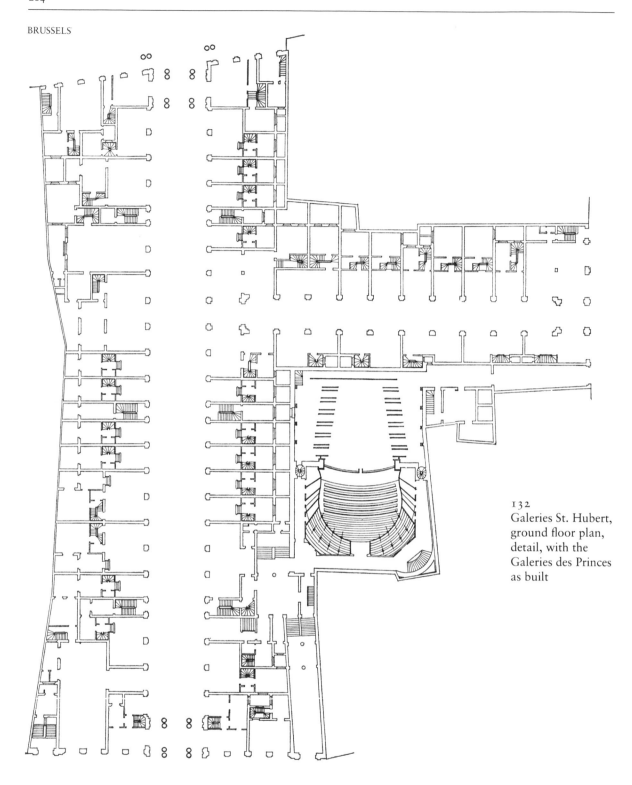

132
Galeries St. Hubert,
ground floor plan,
detail, with the
Galeries des Princes
as built

weapons dealer and bought a seven-millimeter revolver with six shots. "That is for you, Arthur Rimbaud, for me, for all of us!" A noisy argument after lunch in a room on the Rue des Brasseurs ended with a gunshot. The rest is well known. Verlaine was arrested and charged with "wounding with a gun shot the individual Mr. Rimbaud, Arthur. . . ."

These two spotlights, two stories stand for the many nameless others for whom this arcade served as a stage for their lives.

1875 on: The competition from the inner boulevards, from the Rue Neuve, had its effect on the Galeries St. Hubert. The character of the shops changed; the luxury businesses moved to the Rue Royale.

1887: A vaudeville show replaced the casino; the chanson yielded to the comic intermezzo.

March 1, 1896: The first performance of the Cinématographie Lumière in Brussels took place in number 7, Galerie de la Reine. Today a memorial plaque marks the occasion. The Cinéma de la Galerie opened in the Galerie de la Reine at the turn of the century.

June 10, 1947: The centenary anniversary of the Galeries St. Hubert was celebrated. A festschrift was published for the occasion and a memorial coin was minted. The arcade was to be restored.[291]

The arcade is still lively today. All of the shops are occupied; a jazz club, the Blue Note, has opened in the Galerie des Princes. There are residential units and a gambling club. The *gardiens du passage*, security officers, follow attentively the activities of the passersby. Theater goers stroll in the arcade during intermission in the evenings. Quiet finally sets in around midnight; the torrent of voices slows; the lamps that festively light the arcade are put out. But there is a bygone air about the scene; a century seems to fade away.

The Galeries St. Hubert has been preserved with all of its detail and retains its original architectural feeling. Part of this feeling results from the preservation of almost insignificant details which continue to astound and sadden us as we gaze at photographs of remodeled or destroyed arcades: the shops' placards, oddly shaped gas lanterns, small panes of glass which cover the windows like cellophane scales, the curtains, the advertisements, crowded with different kinds of lettering, the chandeliers,

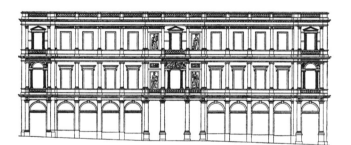

133
Galeries St. Hubert, facade, Marché aux Herbes

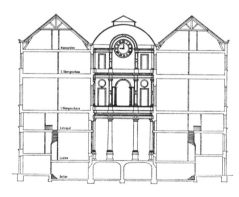

134
Galeries St. Hubert, cross section

135
Galeries St. Hubert,
longitudinal section,
design, 1839

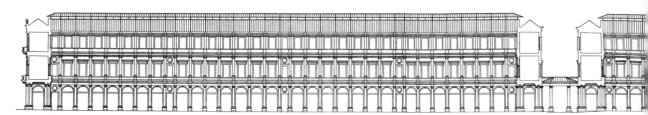

136
Galeries St. Hubert,
second floor plan, de-
sign, 1839
(Scale: 1:650)

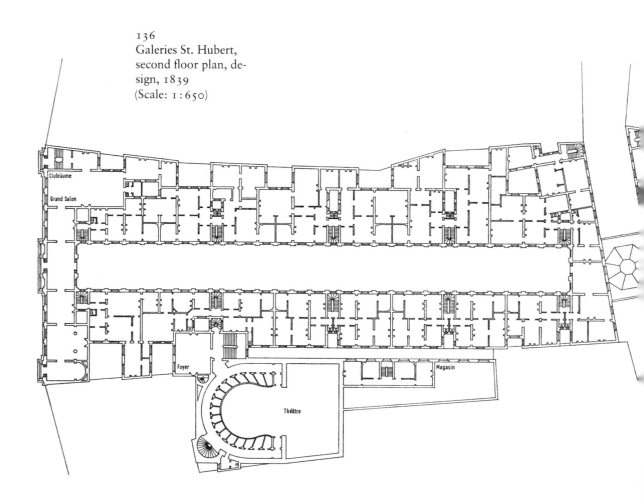

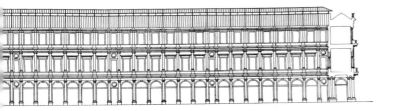

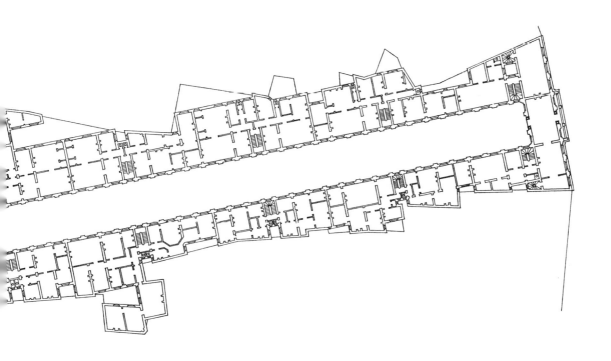

the ornaments, the colors, the gold and black, which give the objects a corporeality endowed with meaning.

It is hard to imagine without an examination of the plans the scale, depth, and difficulties with which an arcade architect must struggle. He cannot merely design facades or only give a regular form to the interior of the arcade. Rather, he must fill available sites, often irregular in shape and with a variety of depths, with a new plan every time. He must make it accessible, find new forms of illumination which at least appear adequate, and make the interior space comfortably accessible. Cluysenaar was equal to the task; construction was carried out according to the original plan with very few changes. The plans for the Galeries St. Hubert show the richness of his ideas. They also reveal that the Galeries St. Hubert was the most complex arcade construction of the century. The design is much richer than those of the great Italian arcades of the later period, which were schematic and emphasized only the impression of space.

The Galeries St. Hubert begins on the south side at the triangular Marché aux Herbes with a facade of nine bays; the Galerie de la Reine cuts through the block of buildings to the Rue des Bouchers and crosses it with a peristyle. The Galerie du Roi continues, branching off from the Galerie des Princes, and ends at the Montagne aux Herbes Potagères. Here the arcade displays a facade of thirteen bays with a central projection of three bays over the main entrance and two single-bay side projections above the entrance to the theater and the large clubrooms on the second floor. The arcade, which is a consistent height throughout, includes cellar, shop level, mezzanine, second floor (whose rooms have the highest ceilings), third floor, and mansards above the glass roof.

The interior and exterior facades are designed almost identically in a combination of three orders: Tuscan pilasters on the ground floor, which alternate with the arches of the show windows, Ionic pilasters on the second floor; and Corinthian pilasters on the third floor, with capitals only on the exterior facade. An attic balustrade tops the exterior front; the beginning of the glass vault finishes the interior facades. The glass roof bears no connection in its construction to the bays of the facade, thus giving the arcade a particularly exterior effect. The projections of the

street facades and the faces of the arcade rooms are more richly decorated with sculpted figures: fluted columns, loggias, balconies, figure groups in niches, and reliefs.[292] The connection of the glass vault to the end surfaces was left without a true resolution. The round clock faces fit the architectural context, but the glass roof simply sits on the unfinished wall without benefit of any attempt at mediation.

There are two large arcade spaces, approximately 80–90 meters long, 7.5 meters wide, and 15 meters high to the top moulding. They have the profile of the wider alleys of Brussels's old city. The arcade may be entered through peristyles, each with four pairs of columns and raised on steps. The arcade buildings are accessible only through the arcade. The stair enclosures are arranged to form a series of double staircases. In the original design there were staircases planned for every seven bays in the Galerie de la Reine and every six bays in the Galerie du Roi, with one after seven bays because the arcade is shorter. This system, however, was changed in the final design of 1845. Cluysenaar increased the width of the bays to approximately 3.5 meters. Thus, there is now a staircase located every six bays in the Galerie de la Reine; in the Galerie du Roi the first staircases are located four bays from the ends and are seven bays apart to allow for the entrance of the Galerie des Princes exactly in the middle. The narrower staircase bays display oval niches decorated with statues instead of round arches above the doors; statues also stand in the window frames of the upper stories.[293] Another rounded window on the second floor, shown in the first design, was replaced in the final design by a rectangular relief.

The staircases provide access to the vaulted cellar rooms under the arcade; the shops and mezzanine have their own interior connections with the cellar. The staircases lead as well to rooms of the upper stories that are rented as apartments, clubs, studios, and offices. The arcade spaces are on the average 10 meters deep; side buildings forming courtyards and light wells fill the space up to the irregular boundaries of the site. Each room receives natural light and has its own chimney. The sanitary facilities are located on the landings of the staircases. We have, then, a completely regular system of plans which varies only in depth, thereby creating a variety of spatial arrangements. The arcade buildings are constructed in a row 10 meters deep. Behind them are other establishments, built in a superimposed manner, such as the theater, with private boxes, backstage, and storage area, a cinema, and a vaudeville theater. Only here do the size of the sites permit such buildings as well as allow for an emergency exit via courtyards and alleys.

Approximately seventy shops display a basic plan: entrance to the shop and show windows in the archways, a floor area of approximately one to three bays, stairs, facilities (only in the final design), a rear room or office, some further rooms in the case of larger lots, a storage area in the basement, and an apartment or work area on the mezzanine. Since Cluysenaar wanted to make possible a large variety of widths in the shops and in the apartment layouts, he chose a design which called for a bearing wall, supported by intersecting cross walls, only every second or third bay, thus every 7 meters as a rule. This system allows for a maximum of variety in spatial arrangements, without sacrificing the regularity or symmetry of the facades.

The glass roof in the initial design had a supporting structure that was related visually to the pilasters of the facades; but this arrangement resulted in structural irregularities, as with the staircases. In the built version, the glass roof is semicircular in section and is supported by a series of closely spaced arches made of approximately 6-centimeter-high flat iron beams, which iron rods brace and hold apart at an interval the width of a glass plate. The individual glass plates are almost square and lie on angle irons screwed on the side; they overlap one another with a slight airspace to prevent dampness from condensing and the unavoidable dirt resulting from direct contact between two plates of glass. They also allow consistent ventilation. At that point at which the slope of the curve becomes critical for the penetration of rainwater, the glass saddle roof of the ventilation layer begins, spanned by the iron arches. The construction is a simple, aesthetic one; it avoids unnecessary construction expense, and the glass vault is poised ethereally or like a taut lattice over the arcade. During the day you see only an endless series of ribs outlined in black. Evenings, when the light changes, they curve up, white against the black sky. And when you wander at midnight through the arcade, lit now only by a few shop windows and clocks, you are no longer aware of the glass roof and believe you are on the street.

The shop level and the breadth of the arcade were doubtless inspired by the Galerie d'Orléans in Paris. And yet the facades and dimensions are without precedent. Only the streetlike spaces of the Uffizi in Florence come to mind as an inspiration from architectural history. Some details show an affinity with the courtly facades of Lescot's Louvre. But such analogies are idle, since the interior facades cannot be viewed head on. They are more effective in their flow, through the profile of their mouldings, the sequence of pilaster and window surface and the archways, which are constantly alive with new and changing perspectives.

This arcade has been called the "Parapluie de Bruxelles" (the Umbrella of Brussels). It has outlived the decline of the building type and the demolition of Brussels's old city. It is the most beautiful example of the mercantile phase of the arcade, which could sublimate social demands and which organized commerce spatially before the advent of the department store.

Text 1:

It was in December 1837 that the project for a connection between the Marché aux Herbes and the Montagne aux Herbes Potagères was submitted to the Public Council of Brussels. There was a petition to the government for authorization to construct it as a building in the public interest and for public use.

The request gave rise to a lengthy investigation. It was necessary to demonstrate not only the usefulness, but also the necessity of a new avenue of communication, in order to defeat the government's natural disinclination to make use of extraordinary powers which, used irresponsibly, could lead to abuse and actions that are a challenge to the sacred right of private property.

After an investigation as thorough as it ought to have been, and upon unanimous recommendation by the appropriate authorities, the requested authorization was granted by royal decree on February 6, 1839.

At approximately this time, political events of the sort which could jeopardize public prosperity put suspicion into everyone's minds; the closing of the Banque de Belgique had complicated the situation by throwing the country into a financial crisis from which business and industry proceeded to suffer a great deal. Numerous

137
Galeries St. Hubert,
facade, Marché aux
Herbes, lithograph

138
Galeries St. Hubert,
Galerie de la Reine,
lithograph

BRUSSELS

139
Galeries St. Hubert,
Galerie de la Reine

140
Galeries St. Hubert,
detail of corner,
Galerie du Roi

fortunes were compromised by speculations in which the chances for stability and
success had not been sufficiently investigated; all business enterprises, without
further examination, took the brunt of the
general disapproval.

The authors of the project with which we
are concerned here were too firmly convinced of the good that the city of Brussels
would derive from its execution to expose
it to the incertitudes of a moment of panic.
To delay would assure success. They
waited. The memory of disaster was too
recent; perhaps prudence would demand
waiting even longer. But individual considerations and the interests of the owners to
be expropriated necessitated that the public administration insist that all delay be
avoided from now on.

When one casts one's eye on the map of
Brussels, and sees the admirable position
of the Grand-Place and of the markets of
which it is the center, when one sees that
it is equidistant from all of the furthest
points ringing the city, it is obvious that re-
locating the markets could never be seriously considered. Only one idea presents
itself naturally, that is, to create several
secondary markets to fulfill the daily needs
of the more removed quarters. But it is certain that the location necessitated by the
plan of the capital for the principal markets (or rather, of the central market destined to supply all of the others) is that
location which the markets occupy today.

Once this necessity is recognized and admitted, what the public interest demands is
easy access to the principal market. If one
studies access to the Grand-Place today, if
one examines the streets which connect
with it, and at the same time, the importance of the areas that the Grand-Place is
intended to serve, one would be strangely
surprised by the scantiness of connections
to the entire northern part of the city,
where big business, the bank, the theater,
and the Stock Exchange are located.

Thus, on the northern side as well as in the
direction of the Place de la Monnaie, the
Rue Fossés-aux-Loups, the Rue Neuve,
and the Rue du Marais, the Rue des
Fripiers is the only regular connecting artery. The Rue de la Fourche and the Rue
de la Courte des Bouchers are too narrow,
irregular, and constantly obstructed to be
considered. The Rue des Fripiers is itself
too narrow for the construction of sidewalks and is completely inadequate for an
ever-growing vehicular and pedestrian
traffic. Pedestrians are constantly in danger
of their lives in this street, through which
more vehicles pass than in any other section of the city; to assure the pedestrians of
any security, it has been necessary to re-
strict buses moving through the area almost to a walking pace, an action without
precedent. What will happen when a train

station at Bogards is opened or a new station at the end of the Rue Neuve, a long
street? The number of vehicles will double,
triple, perhaps even quintuple in the Rue
des Fripiers, which is the inevitable transit
route between the three stations. The
opening of a new connection, already so
necessary, already so desirable, would then
be indispensable.

This primary, to some extent concrete,
utility having been established, let us cast a
glance at the plan of the city of Brussels. A
new means of connection, a single line, at
once the longest and straightest which the
capital would have to show, would immediately connect the Rue du Marais with
the Grand-Place. Apart from a slight detour for the Rue des Eperonnies, the length
of the city would be divided exactly in two
from the northern boulevards to Porte de
Hal.

What is the means of access for pedestrians
today, if we leave aside the Rue des
Fripiers (the inadequacy of which for vehicles is acknowledged) and the Rue de la
Fourche and the Rue de la Courte des
Bouchers, both streets unworthy of a
capital city? The only way is a lane hardly
three meters wide, which, located at the
bottom of Rue de la Montagne where it
runs into the Marché aux Herbes opposite
the Rue de la Colline, communicates with
the Rue de l'Ecuyer by means of the
lengthy Rue des Bouchers and the tiny Rue
des Dominicains. It is with this alley, in
which a ray of sunlight has never been
seen, that the pedestrians must be content
in spite of its drawbacks and in spite of the
detours which it makes necessary. The
straightening and enlarging of the little
Rue Saint-Hubert are the first steps to be
taken in the interest of the capital and its
population. But whatever the larger purpose of this undertaking, it will attain a
very different importance by continuing
through buildings a line connecting the
Rue des Bouchers, a long street, with the
Rue de l'Ecuyer, running into the latter opposite the Montagne aux Herbes Potagères
and the Rue d'Or and the Rue du Marais.
Such is the project to which the communal
authority and the higher authorities have
given their consent. There is only one other
point to make among these general considerations, which is the advantage that execution of the project will give to the city
of Brussels which, as a capital city, must
make itself attractive and agreeable in all
ways both to Belgians and to foreigners, so
that from both inside and outside our borders they will come eagerly and stay with
pleasure. Much has already been done to
this end. The boulevards are a magnificent
piece of work which in the center of Brussels promise to rival in part the boulevards
of Paris. They were undertaken, carried
out, and finished in the midst of financial
difficulties of all sorts which still hobble
the conduct of public administration. The
gates of the city, dirty and hideous enclo-

141
Galeries St. Hubert
after midnight

BRUSSELS

142
Galeries St. Hubert,
Confiserie Neuhaus,
Galerie de la Reine
no. 25

sures, have been replaced by grilles and elegant kiosks. The suburbs of Laeken, Schaerbeék, Saint-Josse-ten-Noode, and Ixelles are readying themselves for their aggregation with the capital day by day through the buildings which cover them and which constantly stimulate growth in their population.

Another, much more powerful attraction joins this one; it is the railroad, which makes possible rapid communication among all points in the country. By completing this grand undertaking, already accepted as a model in Europe, by its necessary extension through France and Germany, Brussels is called upon to serve as a stopover point for a flow of travelers greater than one could ever have imagined. With improvements, the only thing that Brussels will lack to be one of the most attractive capitals will be an interior worthy of its exterior. All that has been done up to now—the boulevards, new quarters, train stations—concerned not what we will call the exterior of the city (since we admit without hesitation the inclusion of the suburbs as an inevitable fact), but rather the most "eccentric" parts of the city. Inside, there is nothing; in the center of the city, nothing. Brussels, in distinction to many other capital cities, is deficient at the center. Brussels is a capital in the area around the park and the Rue Royale, in the outlying areas. Within, it is a third-rate provincial town, and this at a time when all the major cities of Belgium, Liège, Ghent, and Antwerp, are constructing spacious and comfortable connecting arteries and filling themselves with elegant structures.

Although nothing has been done, let it not be said that we are finding fault with the municipal administration; at no time has it lacked zeal. The conditions to which we are now calling attention have been the focus of its attention for a long time; it was with sorrow that the administration saw itself deprived by lack of resources, by the enormity of the expenses which weighed upon it, from realizing all of the improvements which had been planned. It went to begin work on the land which had been cleared and was forced to withdraw by the costs of expropriation resulting necessarily from improvements in the inner city.

But in spite of the fact that the administration was unable to make the improvements itself, it was happy to see the enterprise undertaken by the association; it accepted with understandable eagerness the assistance of private industry. It appreciated from the first moment the project submitted for consideration, and with its acceptance came the acceptance of the majority of the city's citizens. It saw in the project not only its material utility, but also its monumental importance for the city.

The new connection will not in fact be an ordinary one; it will be a monument of which the city can be proud, a monument which in its opulence will equal anything similar in Paris or London. Picture a rich facade occupying the major part of the square at the Fontaine de Marché-aux-Herbes from which there will be a view of the first gallery, 30 feet wide, 380 feet long, which then will lead to a second, where a slight deviation from the straight line in the layout of ornate shops of marble, glass, and copper would add a unique beauty to the whole.

One last general consideration: the embellishment of cities contributes more than one might perhaps think to their material well being. It is not enough to attract tourists by a favorable geographic location. We must keep them as long as possible by the attraction of public and private buildings, by the enticement of everything that a happy variety of amusements can offer; in short, delay their departure by filling their days and long leisure evening hours with new and different sources of enticement.

Everyone has had the opportunity to view the plans of the project for the gallery, which we have named in advance the Palais Royal de Bruxelles. Will these brilliantly lit galleries not become a daily promenade? Won't there be everything there that can please and seduce? They will offer, in the center of the city, places for rendezvous, theaters, clubs, restaurants, cafés, and evening promenades such as can be found only in the greatest capital cities, among whom Brussels should certainly find her place. Even in the summer, with their transparent coverings designed to bring in a constant supply of fresh air, they will be a valuable refuge against the inclemency which is so frequent in what we call, probably in remembrance, "la belle saison." Look at the clever placement of the covering, which without stopping the air circulation mitigates nevertheless the influence of humidity and fog, allows the shops and stores to glitter both inside and out, a decorative luxury which the weather prevents in ordinary streets. The well-established reputation and the fine work of the architect who prepared the plans and who is in charge of their execution are a sure guarantee that nothing will be lacking to make this new gallery one of the major monuments of the capital city, an abode as pleasant as it will be convenient. In addition, the opinion of the project held by public authorities is generally too positive for us to have any trouble in establishing it. The overall advantages which will result are clear; their evidence is palpable. The specific advantages which will result from the completion of the project for two sectors specially called to support its success are easy enough to demonstrate. This last observation addresses itself to the large and small businessmen. Above all, an ini-

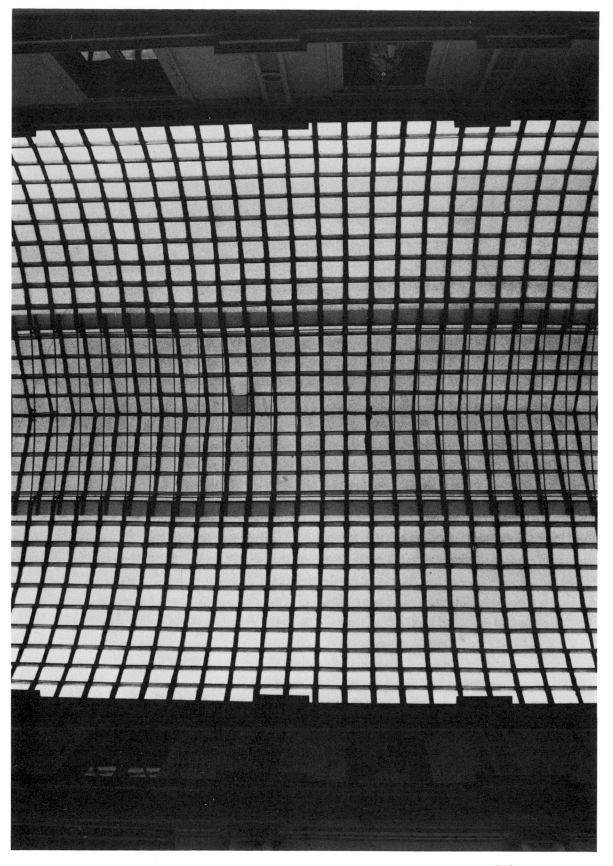

143
Galeries St. Hubert,
glass roof, interior

144
Galeries St. Hubert,
base of glass roof

tial objection must be overcome. It is said rather generally that numerous arcades built in various cities have not all had the same success. People cite several, even in Paris, whose execution has caused the financial failure of the entrepreneurs. In order to weigh the implications of this objection, the authors of the project have had all the requisite information gathered, right on the site, concerning all the major known arcades, with respect both to location and layout.

Paris, after many other fevers, succumbed to construction fever. Between 1820 and 1825, people built simply to build without reflecting at all on the possibility of using what had been built. Before, Paris had had only two arcades, the Passage des Panoramas and the Passage Delorme. These two arcades had acquired an enormous importance. Nothing more was necessary to make the entrepreneurs enthusiastic, and arcades followed everywhere. But, apart from the competition they necessarily became for one another, not all of them were situated so as to become equally successful immediately. Many of the arcades created a new connecting artery to one which already existed, but did not create a connection where there had not been one, did not shorten the path from one place to another. Let us take at random one of these arcades, the one called Passage du Saumon, which leads from the Rue Montmartre to the Rue Montorgueil. This narrow arcade, for a long time denied an entrance on the Rue Montmartre as a result of arguments with former owners, had only a very gradual success. The reason for this is simple; it offered only one of the advantages which is demanded of the arcade—it sheltered, but did not shorten. In order to enter it optimally, it is necessary for pedestrians to find themselves in a rather limited section of either the Rue Montmartre or the Rue Montorgueil. Otherwise they would naturally tend to take one or the other of two streets parallel to the arcade. To choose the arcade means to make a detour and thus to take the longer way.

We could say the same of many other arcades. We could pick arcades which had to compete not only with streets, but with very beautiful squares; others which led nowhere, or led to places frequented only at a particular time of the day. All the same, the advantages of these connecting arteries are such that it was not success which eluded the entrepreneurs, but rather the patience to wait for it. For success did come; it came more slowly than if the new creations had offered a more complete package of advantages, but it came.

There has been enough talk of the Lemonnier Arcade in Liège; it will certainly be successful some day, but that day is slow to arrive. The arcade is beautiful; it is a connecting artery of great convenience. But

BRUSSELS

145
Galeries St. Hubert,
glass roof, detail

146
Galeries St. Hubert

its function is not indispensable; it may be preferred by some to others, but it is not necessarily taken. People will get used to it, but when it is a question of habit, one must allow time.

The projected gallery destined to replace the wretched alley Saint Hubert in Brussels does not fit any of these descriptions.

It does not compete with any serious alternative.

It leads to one of the most well-to-do and most populous sections of the city.

It shortens the distance by almost half.

It is not one connecting artery added to another connecting artery; it is a connecting artery created where there was none. It is a necessary route and so indispensable that from the very day of its opening, everyone who must pass through this section of town will be obliged to utilize it. These are not habits which must be formed by force, but habits that are born naturally out of the course of things. All the conditions for immediate success have thus been united.

But still, it will be said, the arcade is an innovation, and among us innovations are always difficult. We are used to having our own homes, to living alone; we don't like having neighbors too close by. This is true, but it is true history of all cities, especially cities which for a long time have had a low level of commercial activity. But Brussels has become an important commercial center and has seen her populations, both settled and transient, grow to an inordinate degree. It is expanding outward, but the outlying areas are not the commercial center. And everything that business is destined to become in either the near or the distant future contradicts those habits of ease and comfort which disappeared long ago from all the great European business centers. It is true that everywhere people desire fresh air, isolation, and ease; but if you go to London, certainly the quintessential commercial city, you will see that the businessmen there think little, if at all anymore, of such habits of leisure.

Business goes where it can sell; it goes there even if it has to crowd itself in. It is only the idle class which seeks constantly to avoid population growth by moving out. As for business, it stays at the center; it retrenches and forgets its former habits. And was there any sign of leisure before in the houses of the Marché-aux-Herbes, the Rue de la Fourche, the Rue Courtes des Bouchers, and the others? So, we are not afraid of confirming it; the plans for the new arcade are there to prove it, the galleries, with their light and airy designs, will add a great deal to it, with all their advantages of cleanliness, convenience, and comfort over the gloomy houses in the streets which it is destined to replace, even those in the Rue des Fripiers and on the Madeleine side. So we see that the objections are not serious; they collapse by themselves under close scrutiny. With the objections destroyed and the prospects for success completely established, what remains to be said to the capitalists whose support we are soliciting?

No operation has ever been more straightforward. For some shareholders, it may be speculation, but it is above all the most solid of investments, an investment in real estate. Expenses have been estimated high; return has been estimated low. Anyone who examines the estimates will be convinced of this.

Subtracting outlay from return yields a net return which is higher than that from most ordinary real estate investments and which could increase still more. This possible, probable, and necessary increase is the part of speculation. A certain, known return, guaranteed by the capital itself, is the reward of the businessman who does not speculate in his investments.

The natural shareholders in the enterprise will be the expropriated owners. They had an investment; an investment will be offered to them. Another group will be the property owners whose buildings will have the advantage of bordering on the new arcade and thus of an increase in value. Their future interests are bound to the future of the enterprise. Of course financial investments are not easy at this point; the fever of industrialism, having abated a little, no longer offers numerous chances to try one's luck and either double one's fortune or (more likely) to lose it entirely. Serious business is desired these days, the kind of business in which each development can be followed exactly. No operation has ever offered these possibilities to such an extent as the one which we present. Everything will and must be done out in the open. The shareholders are less shareholders in the ordinary sense of the word than owners united by a common interest to make the most of a common property in everyone's interest.

Capital from knowing foreign investors would not be lacking for such an enterprise. But the authors of the project have had to remember that here it is a national enterprise, a municipal enterprise, and that it is fitting to summon first of all those who ought to gain from it and those who are the most intimately interested in that success, and in the broadest manner. The deed of the society has been drafted in such a way as to give the most solid of guarantees. Once again, it is a speculation of the sort which has the possibility of increased return. Here the opportunity is clear cut. But it is above all a real estate investment with all the advantages and security of such an investment and a higher interest than ordinary real estate investments.

There is only one more aspect of the problem for us to examine. We have already been able to assess the advantages of the project for Brussels as a city and as a capital city. We have seen that there is no exaggeration in our rendering of the importance of a new connecting route. Furthermore, our readers have in front of them the plans for both the new arcade and the city of Brussels. Finally, we have seen that the prospects for success which the enterprise presents are such that to deny them would be to shut one's eyes to the evidence. It only remains to establish the immense interest which business will have in making use of such an arcade.

The busiest commercial districts in Brussels today are the following: the Rue Montagne de la Cour, the Rue de la Madeleine, the Marché-aux-Herbes, and the Rue des Fripiers. Why are these streets and squares busier than others? It is clearly because the movement of traffic is more regular and more continuous; one does not usually go to search out a particular shop; it is necessary that it be on the way. If we may establish that the new arcade will itself alone be busier than all of the other streets together which we have just named, we will have established by the same token that it will be the very center of retail trade of all kinds. It is for this reason that Rue des Fripiers is essentially commercial, because it is today practically the only connecting artery between the populous quarter of the Grand-Place and the well-to-do Quartier de la Monnaie. We have demonstrated the inconvenience of this street, which is constantly full of traffic and which is a hazard to pedestrians. Clearly, when it is possible to use a covered arcade between the Grand-Place and Place de la Monnaie, it will be preferable to the unsafe Rue des Fripiers. The street will be for carriages, buses, and hackney cabs, but the real consumer, the pedestrian who is attracted by shop displays, will come to the arcade because it will be an economical use of time; it will be convenient and a safe place to walk.

The galleries will not be merely an arcade; by their favorable location, they promise to become a promenade night and day, summer and winter. In Paris, the most commercial areas (wholesale business and fancy goods) are the Palais-Royal, the boulevards, the arcades, and the streets which are necessary connecting routes. But both the boulevards and the Palais-Royal are still preferred by business, because these are the promenades, and pedestrians and strollers are the natural clients of retail and wholesale shops. So, we repeat, the galleries are not only a necessary traffic artery, but an almost perpetual promenade as well.

Our galleries will be visited for other reasons; there will be a theater, a concert hall, restaurants, and cafes. A theater brings with it twenty businesses which must be located nearby. All such shops are a constant attraction for pedestrian traffic, and as we have established, plentiful pedestrian traffic is the very life blood of retail trade.

It is thus a fact, the evidence for which it would be impossible to deny. The projected galleries will cause a large increase in traffic. Consequently they will certainly share the kind of commercial monopoly which the Rue de la Madeleine, the Marché-aux-Herbes, and the Rue des Fripiers enjoy now. It is clear to everyone that the Théâtre du Parc is much too far away from the center of town; it is clear that a second large theater, conceived on a totally different basis than the Théâtre de la Monnaie, would have good prospects for success. Thus, the authors of the project have already received proposals for the location of a hall whose design is hard to make out in the overall plans. It is somewhat the same with theaters as with retail merchants; a trip to the theater is not always planned or deliberately decided upon. You go because you find yourself in front of the theater doors on your way, or because you are tired from your walk, because on finishing a meal or leaving a cafe you search for a way to spend your evening. This is the accidental factor in theaters, an accidental factor which determines the traffic just as in the case of retail commerce. Which is the most successful theater in Paris? The theater in the Palais-Royal, to be sure. And to what does it own its fortune? Is its theater better decorated than the others? No; to the contrary, in fact. Are the actors there better? No; there are two or three good actors, and many bad ones; it is that way everywhere. But the theater is located in the Palais-Royal; the Palais-Royal is an important connecting artery, a commercial center, an arcade, and a promenade. There are restaurants, cafes; many of their doors open into or lead to the theater. The theater that will open in our new galleries, with all due allowances made, will have the same chances for success as the theater in the Palais-Royal. And, like everything in such a system, it will furnish a new contingent of visitors itself; it will do its part certainly toward the commercial success of the galleries.

All of this is completely understandable. Right now, not a finger has been lifted, all the houses destined to come down in the future are still standing, and already a third of the proposed stores have been reserved.

This anticipated result is the most convincing of reasons for the construction of the project. It is with the most convincing that we will finish our presentation.

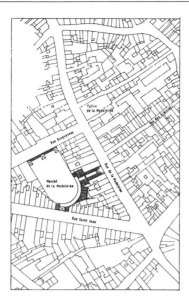

147
Brussels, site of the
Galerie Bortier, 1866

148
Brussels, Galerie Bor-
tier, 1847–1848

Galerie Bortier (figs. 147–149)
Rue St. Jean—Marché de la
Madeleine—Rue de la Madeleine
The demolition of the former Hôpital St.
Jean east of the Grand-Place, between the
Rue de la Madeleine and the Place St. Jean,
made available a wide building site.[294] It
was purchased by a Monsieur Bortier, who
owned a house on the Rue de la Madeleine, formerly the Hôtel des Messageries,
built in 1763, where the postal carriages to
Paris began their trip.[295] Bortier appeared
before the Municipal Council on January
9, 1847, with the plan to build the first
covered market in Brussels. This would relieve the traffic on the squares which were
already congested by the markets held
there. Bortier estimated the yearly income
of such a market hall at 62,000 francs; he
wanted to loan the city 100,000 of his own
and to petition the city for acquisition of
the entire site. The city accepted Bortier's
proposals and acquired the lot on April 2.
The Bureau of Public Works prepared provisional plans which, however, proved un-
acceptable because of the sharply inclining
site. The members of the Council thought
of the architect Cluysenaar, who had built
the grand Galeries St. Hubert in just fourteen months. They retained him for the
plans.

Cluysenaar divided the inaccessible, oversized block with new streets, the Rue St.
Jean and the Rue Duquesnoy. He located
the market hall in the block which was
now formed by the Rue de la Madeleine,
the Rue St. Jean, and the Rue Duquesnoy.
It is two stories and semicircular at one
end and has a long facade on the Rue Duquesnoy. There is an open loggia modeled
on the Loggia dei Lanci in Florence but
with only nine bays. A narrow arcade, the
Galerie Bortier, is located in the semicircle
on the upper story; it provides entrances to
the market hall both from the Rue de la
Madeleine through the aforementioned
house which M. Bortier owned and from
the Rue St. Jean. The arcade has a total
length of 65 meters, and twelve shops,
squeezed into the remaining corners of the
site, and its width varies. The Marché was
opened in September 1848 with a great
ball and exhibition of paintings; directly
afterward the flower, vegetable, and poul-
try dealers paraded around the Marché de
la Madeleine, constructed entirely of iron,
and the antique dealers around the Galerie
Bortier.

149
Galerie Bortier,
ground plan, as built

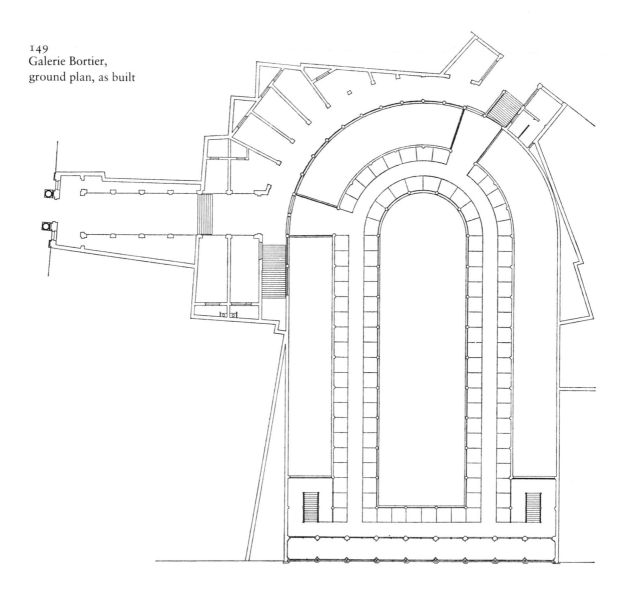

The entire complex is still standing today, although the Marché was renovated and converted into a municipal hall in 1957 by the firm of Mignon Frères.[296] Booksellers are still located in the rest of the arcade today, which still has the old glass roof with its small glass plates. The arcade was located formerly on the section of the street which led from the Galeries St. Hubert through the Rue de la Madeleine to the Place Royale; it was the promenade, the daily meeting place of fashionable Brussels.

A plan of the arcade may be found in the files of the Municipal Archives.[297] A figurative plan of the new St. Jean quartier may also be found there. It is signed by Cluysenaar and dated June 20, 1843.[298] This site plan reveals that Cluysenaar had already considered building on the location a few years earlier. It is subdivided by regular sections of street; there is a square with a theater in the middle. Across from the theater an arcade through to Rue de la Madeleine is projected. This is a forerunner of the Galerie Bortier.

Galerie du Commerce (figs. 150–151)
Rue Neuve—Rue d'Argent—Place des Martyrs
The Galerie du Commerce was one of the three arcades built in connection with the opening of the interior boulevard in the new commercial district around the Rue de Brouckère. It still stands today as a one-story passageway leading to a new structure, a large department store belonging to the firm of S. A. Sarma.

The Galerie du Commerce[299] has a fragmentary character which is clear from the old plans of the city. Originally it was to have been cruciform in plan and to have connected the Rue Neuve with the Rue d'Argent and the Place des Martyrs with the Rue du Fossé aux Loups. The longer arm, however, was never extended far enough to make the latter connection. The short wings of the arcade cross are displaced with respect to one another and form two rotundas. The arcade was three-storied and had a vaulted glass roof with a ventilation strip. Access to units from the interior area, 5.5 meters wide, was made possible by narrow staircases located between every two broad shop bays.

The construction history of this arcade cannot be unraveled in spite of the records in the Municipal Archives and the firm of Sarma. They are full of an endless paper war between the city and the owners of the many lots. Countless fragments of plans indicate new changes and partial views, so that the actual building is difficult to imagine. The arcade must have been built in the early 1870s. The architects named are Edmond Le Graive and Stasseyns.[300] The sculptor Von den Kerckhove executed the row of caryatids at third-floor level, a motif that we will find again in the nearby Passage du Nord. I have reproduced a fragmentary section here to give an approximate impression of the interior architecture.

Passage des Postes
Boulevard Anspach—Place de la Monnaie
The small, insignificant Passage des Postes was built about 1875 by the architect Louis de Courte; today it is used as the entrance to a movie theater. Originally it connected the Boulevard Anspach with the Place de la Monnaie. However, as early as the late 1880s, it was truncated by the construction of a new Bureau Central des Postes et Télégraphes (Central Post Office and Telegraph Bureau) on the Place de la Monnaie; this new construction succeeded in robbing the arcade of its function.

Galerie du Parlement (fig. 152)
Rue de l'Enseignement—Rue de la Croix
The Galerie du Parlement[301] was located in the upper part of the city in the vicinity of the Rue Royale and the Palais de la Nation, as the name reveals. It led from the Rue de l'Enseignement to the Rue de la Croix de Fer. The Bain Royal and the Théâtre Eden lay across from the entrances to the arcade. The two angled wings of the arcade intersect in a large rotunda which serves on the one hand as a market hall with open stands in the middle and on the other as the entrance to the neighboring Cirque Royal. The dome was entirely of iron and had a gallery which circled the entire second floor and which could be reached by stairs. There was a fountain in the center of the area.

The arcade served less as a traffic artery than to relieve the congestion of the main entrance to the Cirque Royal. Thus one could get on line to buy entrance tickets while sheltered from the rain or one could go strolling during the intermission. The arcade was built around 1880 by the engineer Emilie Thoas; it was torn down in the 1960s.

Passage du Nord (figs. 153–160)
Rue Neuve 40—Boulevard Adolphe Max
The Passage du Nord is the second most

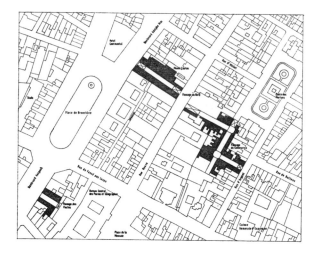

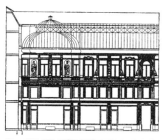

150
Brussels, sites of the
Galerie du Com-
merce, the Passage
du Nord, and the
Passage des Postes,
1894

151
Brussels, Galerie du
Commerce, interior
facade, elevation

152
Brussels, site of the
Galerie du Parle-
ment, 1894

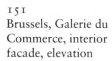

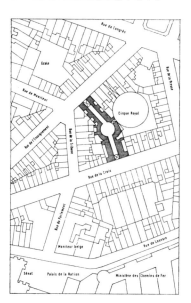

153
Brussels, Passage du
Nord, 1881–1882,
facade, Boulevard
Adolphe Max

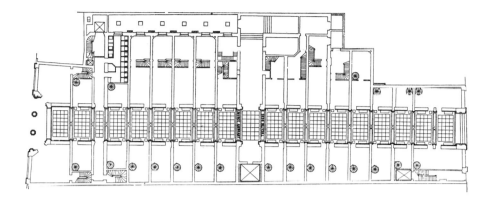

154
Passage du Nord,
ground plan
(Scale: 1:600)

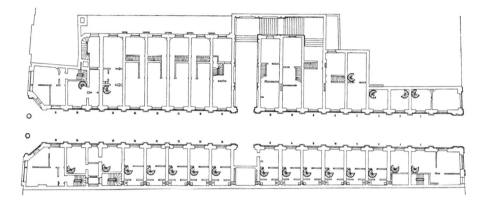

155
Passage du Nord,
mezzanine plan
(Scale: 1:600)

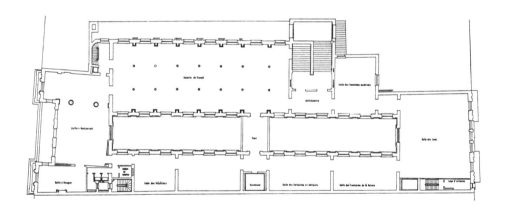

156
Passage du Nord,
second floor plan
(Scale: 1:600)

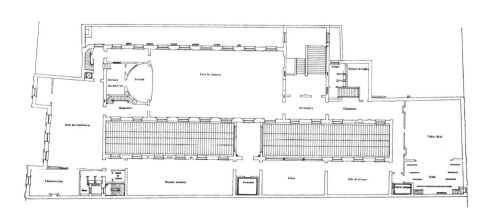

157
Passage du Nord,
third floor plan
(Scale: 1:600)

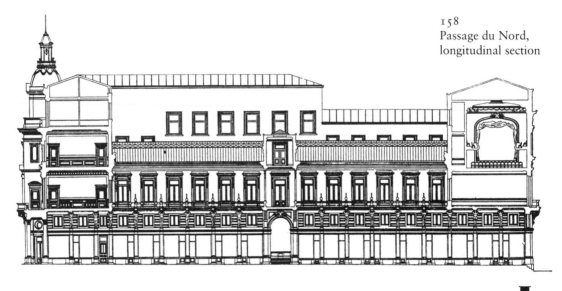

158
Passage du Nord,
longitudinal section

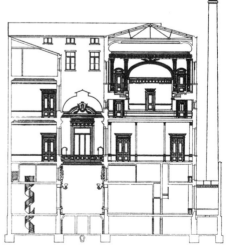

159
Passage du Nord,
cross section

160
Passage du Nord,
bridge

noteworthy arcade in Brussels after the Galeries St. Hubert in terms of architectural history. It is still standing in its original form, still in use, although the upper stories are used today for purposes totally different from those originally planned. The structure is especially important for its architectural program, which can be documented from complete plans, sections, and elevations. The complete working drawings may be consulted in the Municipal Archives of Brussels.[302] The impressive use of site and space reveal the precision and technical skill of the planners.

The arcade was designed in 1881–1882 by the architect H. Rieck and was built by 1885. It was one of the new structures that gave the inner boulevard its appearance. It connects the Rue Neuve with the Boulevard Adolphe Max, two equally busy streets and commercial arteries. It occupies the former site of the Banque de Belgique. The two entrance buildings display richly decorated facades with symmetrical, almost Baroque formal elements which compete with their neighbors. These facades are far more effective in conveying the ceremonial impression the newly built street was meant to give than they are in representing the building and its function. The central part of the frontal building on the boulevard is set back to extend the area for a terrace for the restaurant on the upper floor. The arcade itself is two-storied and is divided in the middle by a raised passageway beneath which is the entrance to the upper stories. There is a total of thirty-two shops on the ground floor and the mezzanine, each with its own cellar accessible by means of spiral staircases. The facades of the arcade are divided into three zones: the shop area, occupied by large panes of plate glass, the mezzanine, embellished with thirty-two caryatids and rusticated walls, and the high windows of the upper story, which are inserted in the flat wall. A self-supporting glass vault with a ventilation strip arches over the entire arcade space.

The thirty-two caryatids, designed and sculpted by Joseph Bertheux,[303] represent those disciplines whose emblems the figures carry in their hands: architecture (compass), decorative art (flowers), metallurgy (anvil and hammer), sculpture (bust), painting (palette), commerce (caduceus), astronomy (globe), naval arts (rudder), etc. But it is difficult to distinguish them anymore because of the frequent coats of paint.

The two upper stories, accessible either by a wide, comfortable staircase or by elevators, are occupied today by a large hotel. They contain an astonishing series of rooms, each of a different orientation and dimension. Earlier they were used as either the Musée Castan or the Musée du Nord; the early room designations reveal their purposes. They served as a kind of public reception hall. Concerts, smaller theatrical productions, and exhibitions took place here. There were writing materials and newspapers; one could read one's mail, eat, have gatherings, and hold conferences. The whole atmosphere was part of a sophisticated plan to guarantee the arcade a life of its own and total utilization.

On the second floor, we find the Salle des Jeux along the Rue Neuve. The Salle des Inventions Modernes, the Salle des Curiosités et Antiques, and the Salle des Fantaisies de la Nature are alongside the arcade. Along the boulevard are the large restaurant, the Galerie du Travail (the Hall of Work), the Salle des Dépêches, the sanitary facilities, and service stairs. Various pedestrian routes were possible via the bridge which divided the arcade.

The small Théâtre Bébé is on the third floor along the Rue Neuve. On the side above the Galerie du Travail, there is a large concert hall, also two-storied, with a semicircular dais. The lecture halls, administration (a single, modest room), and smaller reading rooms are located along the boulevard. The elaborate decoration of these rooms can be seen clearly in the sections. The glass roof of the arcade could be seen from the second story.

The program, then, was one of mixed use which could draw a widely varied public into the arcade. This spatial planning, already realized on a larger and more elaborate scale in the Galeries St. Hubert, is the idea of the Parisian Palais Royal in its most concentrated formulation: all of the essential cultural and civilized necessities offered to the individual under one roof, an idea which continues to exist in the shopping center of our own times even though now it has been virtually severed from the urban context.

BUDAPEST

I was unable to obtain the design and construction histories of a series of arcades in Budapest. The majority were built between the turn of the century and World War I;

161
Budapest, Harisch
Bazar, demolished

BUDAPEST

162
Budapest, Pariser
Hof, 1910–1911,
view showing both
entrances (far left
and far right)

SARAH SCHULTZ

DIRECTOR. EDUCATION AND COMMUNITY PROGRAMS

sarah.schultz@walkerart.org

TEL 612.375.7621   FAX 612.375.5802

163
Pariser Hof, arcade
space

164
Pariser Hof, dome

their design shows the influence of Viennese architecture. There are glassed-over rows of rear courtyards, and used for commercial purposes and extending from street to street. They are borderline cases of the arcade, much closer to the tradition of the walk through house.

Harisch Bazar (fig. 161)
Now the Harisch Köz

A Viennese construction journal names Adolf Feszty as the architect.[304] The arcade is no longer standing, but in an old photograph we may discern the passageway leading to a large rotunda with entrances to two transverse arcade wings and a fountain in the center. From the depth of the passageway, we may assume that the arcade was built into existing courtyards.

Röser Bazar
Karl Ring 22

The partly glassed-over Röser Bazar[305] was built in 1883 by the architect Joseph Kauser. It was converted in 1904 and has an entirely changed appearance.

Königsbazar
Franzen Square

This courtyard arcade was published in the journal *Die Architektur des 20. Jahrhunderts*[306] with the following description: "The Königsbazar in Budapest is one of the most striking, but also one of the most clearly consistent works of the Wagner school. The architects Aladar Kármán and Julius von Ullmann completed the building between December 5, 1899, and November 1, 1900, at a cost of 1,110,000 marks; the structure, well executed in all its parts, is of brick covered with plaster, with granite columns and vaulted roofs between riveted supports. Both plan and structure demonstrate a remarkably successful solution in the exterior linking of the two corner buildings with one lying between them, the result being one large magnificent building penetrated by an arcade. And this was achieved without compromising the independence of the individual buildings."

Pariser Hof (figs. 162–164)
District 5, Petöfi Street 2

The Bavarian architect Heinrich Schmal (1849–1913)[307] designed this building block with a small arcade for a savings bank, the Innenstädtische Sparkasse. His plans were accepted in 1909, and the building was constructed in 1910–1911. Figs. 162–164 give an impression of the seven-storied building corner and the interior of the arcade. The roofs are of stained glass and in part constructed as Moorish honeycomb vaults—a unique design among arcades. The Pariser Hof is the only arcade in Budapest still in use today.

An old photograph in the 1974 edition of the *Historische Enzyklopädie von Budapest* suggests that the arcade had a modest precursor after the style of the Parisian arcades.[308]

BUENOS AIRES
Galeria Güemès
Florida—San Martin

Built 1913–1915 by the architect Gianotti, this arcade is 116 meters long and in the Neo-Baroque style.[309] Julio Cortazar, who describes the arcades in Paris as his "patrie sécrète" (secret homeland), remarks: "During the 1930s, the Güemès arcade was a cave of treasures where the vision of sin and the smell of menthol candies mingle, where they shout out the evening news with crimes on all the pages, where the lights flicker from the rooms downstairs with their forbidden films. . . ."[310]

Pasaje Barolo
Avenida de Mago—Calle Hipolito Yrigoyen

This arcade was built in 1923 by the architect Mario Palanti as part of a high-rise block.[311]

Galeria Bon Marché

The Galeria Bon Marché was planned in 1890 after the Parisian model as a large department store made accessible by an arcade but was never used for this purpose. Aslan and Ezcurra are given as the architects.[312]

CARDIFF

The crowded commercial district in Cardiff is covered by a network of arcades which are built in a very irregular fashion but render accessible sites set back a considerable distance from the street. These arcades date, almost without exception, from the last quarter of the nineteenth century. The city, however, will look completely different in the future; the well-known British planner Colin Buchanan has been commissioned to renovate the central area of the city. Some of the arcades will be preserved and integrated into a complex commercial district with continuous pedestrian areas. Arcade-like passageways will supplement the system.

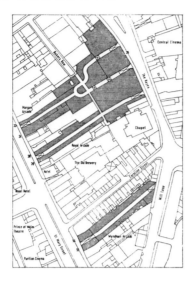

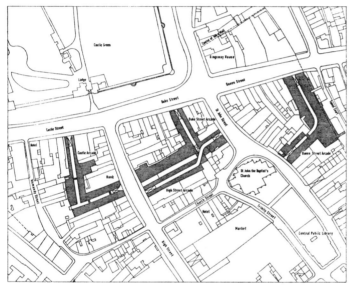

165
Cardiff, sites of the
Morgan Arcade, the
Wyndham Arcade,
and the Royal Ar-
cade, 1955

166
Cardiff, sites of the
Castle Arcade, the
High Street Arcade,
and the Queen Street
Arcade, 1955

Royal Arcade (fig. 165)
St. Mary Street 38–39—The Hayes 34–36
The Royal Arcade is said to be the earliest
Cardiff arcade and to have been built in
1869.[313] It is still standing today.

Queen Street Arcade (fig. 166)
Working Street 6–8—Queen Street 24–26
1880?

Wyndham Arcade (fig. 165)
St. Mary Street 54–55—Mill Lane 12
1887?

High Street Arcade (fig. 166)
High Street 12–13—St. John Street
1887?

Castle Arcade
High Street 24–25—Castle Street 5–7
1889?

Andrews Arcade
1889?

Morgan Arcade
*St. Mary Street 33–34—The Hayes 10
and 32 (cross connection to the Royal
Arcade)*
Morgan Arcade was built in 1897 by the
architect Edwin Seward for David Morgan;[314] it was altered by the later addition
of department store buildings on The
Hayes.

Duke Street Arcade
Duke Street 22–23—High Street Arcade
1902?

Celtic Corridor
1905?

Dominions Arcade
Queen Street 33–37—Greyfriars Place

CARPENTRAS
Passage Boyer
Rue des Halles—Place de l'Ange
This deep, four-storied arcade with a
vaulted glass roof is reminiscent of the
Galeries St. Hubert in Brussels. There are
shops on the ground floor, apartments on
the upper floors. Built about 1860, the arcade today is open to vehicles. Earlier, as
may be seen from old postcards, this was
not the case.

CHARLEROI
Passage de la Bourse
Rue du College—Rue Léopold
The Passage de la Bourse is a large, three-
storied arcade built in 1891. It connects
the train station with the sloping old city.
The entrance building toward the train sta-

tion has been replaced by a high-rise, and the glass roof has been redone. The Brussels model is unmistakable in the spatial proportions and in the style of the pairs of columns inserted at the entrances. The exterior facades are Dutch-brick Renaissance. The facades of the interior, which incorporates a slight bend, are classical and today are painted a cream color. Lively shops, a movie theater, and a comfortable café are located in an addition to the nearby classical church.

CHEMNITZ (Karl-Marx-Stadt, East Germany)
Arcade
Rathaus Market—Lange Strasse
The arcade was built in 1884 by C. J. Richter and was destroyed in 1945.[315]

CHESTER
St. Michaels Arcade
Bridge Street—St. Michaels Street
Chester, a small town of Roman origin, has lost the importance it once possessed as a harbor because of the silting up of the Dee River; but the slightly dislocated intersection of main roadways still exists today, along with the famous Chester Rows, dating from the Renaissance. There are pergolas at the second floor level accessible by stairs from the street level, where most of the shops are located; they are ideal strolling areas even in the worst of weather. The Rows may be considered to have been the models for the Victorian arcades with their galleries.

St. Michaels Arcade was built about 1910 as a pedestrian throughway between one of the Rows and St. Michaels Street, which is a dead end. The arcade is two-storied, lined with bright, glazed terra-cotta, and covered with a simple glass saddle roof. Today it is included in an entire network of arcades which have their own parking garage, department store, and a restaurant.

CHICAGO
Pullman Arcade (fig. 167)
In 1880 the industrialist George Pullman built a workers' model town south of Chicago, next to the lake and to his factory. It housed 2,500 families in small brick multifamily dwellings. In the center was a shopping center with an arcade building, which was freestanding and housed all necessary shops in two stories: bank, theater, and library. Solon Spencer Beman was the architect.[316]

CINCINNATI
Emery Arcade
Vine Street—Race Street
This arcade is listed in the 1904 edition of Baedeker's guide to the United States.

CLEVELAND
Cleveland Arcade (figs. 168–171)
Euclid Avenue—Superior Avenue
The Cleveland Arcade has already been treated in great detail in various American journals.[317] I will base my discussion on their findings.

The Cleveland Arcade is the work of John Eisenmann and George H. Smith, two little-known architects who built nothing else of comparable quality in their subsequent careers. It was built in 1888–1890 under contract with the Cleveland Arcade Corporation[318] (today called the Arcade Company). Nothing is known of the reasons for planning the arcade. It was built at approximately the same time as the gigantic Moscow commercial complex and is comparable only to it in its huge dimensions. It is the largest arcade in the Anglo-American countries and displays all the unique characteristics of the non-continental arcade in a monumental exaggeration that was never to be outdone. All levels are used exclusively for commercial establishments; all rooms are accessible from the arcade space by means of galleries. The tendency toward interior space that distinguishes the Anglo-American from the European arcades is exemplified clearly here. It lacks interior facades, showing only a steel skeleton. The spatial effect is more that of a light well, or better still, of a wide, sloping sports arena whose breadth makes a wide-span roof construction necessary. The comparison with an arena is suggested by the semicircular spatial enclosures, which are unusual for arcade structures and which make understandable the association with a velodrome. Since one can no longer look inside the galleries from the street, the transitional character of the space is eliminated and is replaced by a turning, involuted movement. A photograph from the article I cited earlier[319] shows the arcade transformed into a celebration hall, decorated with banners and garlands, for the 1895 National Convention of Republican Clubs, attended by 2,000 delegates.

167
Chicato, Pullman
Arcade

Today the Cleveland Arcade is a complex of buildings between the busiest commercial streets in downtown Cleveland, Euclid Avenue and Superior Avenue. The division of the complex into three parts is clear from the plans. Nine-story office buildings are located on each of the two streets, which run at an angle with respect to each other; the buildings are of dark brick and red Pennsylvania sandstone in the Byzantine Romanesque style so popular for office buildings at the time. The lengths of the entrance buildings are 40 and 55 meters; the building lot is 115 meters deep. Each entrance building has a towerlike central projection above a mighty archway which describes a semicircle, the arcade entrance. H. H. Richardson's influence is obvious here. The staircases and elevators, which are located at both entrances, lead to both the office levels and the arcade galleries. The five-story connecting link of the arcade is inserted between the two office buildings, which are set at an angle to each other in conformity with the course of the streets they front on. The rounded end areas of the arcade penetrate the office buildings in such a supple manner that the skewing of the axes is not apparent within the arcade. In addition to this measure, another difficulty had to be overcome for successful construction of the arcade. The ground sloped rather drastically (a difference of 4 meters) away from Superior Avenue. An adjustment by means of an outside staircase was necessary. The architects of the Passage Pommeraye in far-away Nantes had already dealt with this problem by moving the open staircase into the middle of the arcade, thereby enhancing the spatial effect. The architects of the Cleveland Arcade used the gradient to penetrate both levels, making the arcade accessible in the same way as contemporaneous Moscow arcades. The arcade thus becomes a total theater with numerous tiers, and the to-and-fro of the pedestrians becomes the play.

The five-storied arcade expands through three setbacks to attain a width of 18.5 meters; with the steep glass saddle roof, it reaches an overall height of 30.5 meters. In the two lower stories there is room for a total of 100 shops, all with polygonal, projecting show windows. Small offices occupy the three upper stories; some of them may also be used as shops. The Superior Avenue concourse begins with a semicircular vestibule, in which a slightly modified open staircase stands today. This concourse cuts through the length of the arcade, ending in a wide open staircase that leads directly to the exit onto Euclid Avenue. The Euclid Avenue concourse branches off in two directions but is connected in the middle by a bridge, built later, which runs as a pergola around the semicircular opening near Superior Street. The third concourse can be reached only via the built-in staircases; it is, however, symmetrical while the walkways of the fourth and fifth floors cross over one another.

The support system of the steel skeleton is visible in the two uppermost stories.[320] Forty-four griffin heads mark the base of the roof construction, which consists of a network of girders supported from beneath by pointed arches which are reinforced at either side by diagonally crossed braces. This difficult glass-roof support structure, without precedent, had to be designed by a bridge construction firm in Detroit, since no one could be found in Cleveland to undertake the project. To relieve the bareness that the iron seemed to give the arcade space, the galleries were decorated with wrought-iron railings with spiral motifs; candelabra were placed on the jambs, and sections of iron still visible were painted.

The Cleveland Arcade still serves its original function today. Only details have been altered—the open staircases, the lighting fixtures, and the entrance archways on Euclid Avenue. The arcade itself—even though it is a bit extreme—was one of the most fascinating architectural discoveries from the end of the nineteenth century that I made in working on this book. The horizontal thrust of its layered levels, the gradually disappearing vertical structure of the supporting skeleton, the finely jointed latticework, the glass walls in their framing, and the sculpted, projecting show windows—all create a unique space which allows each element its independence and corporeality and also reveals its function, while at the same time assuming a unity in spatial ordering and the overlapping of perspective. The arcade is free of the overbearing flamboyance and theatricality so characteristic of the time. We can orient ourselves once again within controlled fantasy made visible in the architecture of this structure.

CLEVELAND

168
Cleveland, Cleveland
Arcade, 1888–1890,
arcade space with
original lighting
fixtures

169
Cleveland Arcade,
arcade space after
modifications, show-
ing bridge and new
lighting fixtures

CLEVELAND

170
Cleveland Arcade,
original staircase, en-
trance, Superior
Avenue

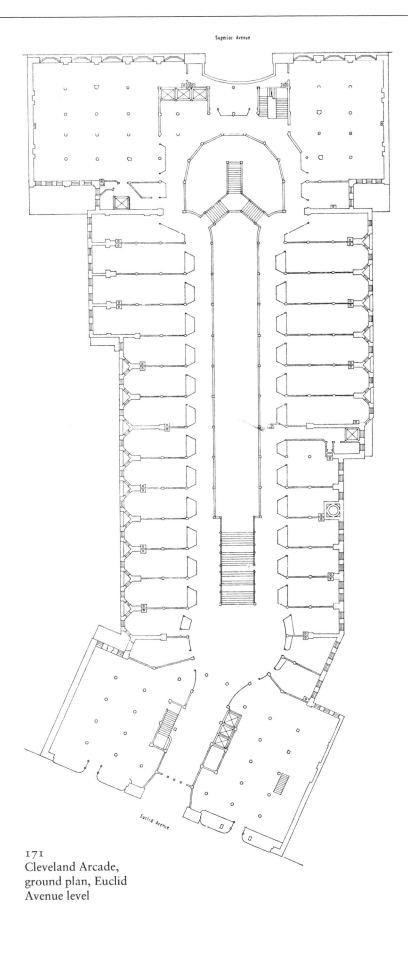

171
Cleveland Arcade,
ground plan, Euclid
Avenue level

Colonial Arcade
Euclid Avenue—Prospect Avenue

A second, smaller arcade is located not far from the Cleveland Arcade. It was built in 1898, ten years later than the first arcade, by George H. Smith, one of the two architects of the Cleveland Arcade. Mary Peale-Shofield remarks:[321] "The Colonial Arcade, still standing across Euclid Avenue and a bit east of the Cleveland Arcade, runs through to the Colonial Hotel, also by Smith, on Prospect Avenue. It is a more conventional two-storied passage with shops on the ground floor and one balcony. The skylight is a simple gable of glass supported by riveted girders. Despite the unfortunate remodelling of the shop fronts and changes of the balcony, the upper story and the skylight show that it must originally have had considerable charm."

COLOGNE

Königin Augusta Halle (figs. 172–177)
*Hohe Strasse—Brücke Strasse—
Ludwigstrasse*

All three of the Cologne arcades, which were destroyed in bombing raids of 1944, were located on Hohe Strasse. Today the entire length of the street is closed to vehicular traffic.

The Königin Augusta Halle, occasionally called the Hohen-Strassen-Passage, was the oldest. After Sillem's Bazar in Hamburg, it is the second most significant arcade in Germany and had as its model the arcades of Restoration Paris. The construction history of the Königin Augusta Halle is a complicated one. Plans were prepared in 1845–1846 by Johann Peter Weyer,[322] who had stepped down from his position as Cologne's municipal contractor in 1844. It was nevertheless built as late as 1862–1863. The reasons for this delay of over a decade recall the early history of the Galeries St. Hubert in Brussels.

Karl Josef Bollenbeck, an engineer from Cologne, has treated the history of the arcade in depth. It is interesting that the architect and the contractor traveled to Paris, Brussels, and Liège in 1845 and studied a total of eleven models. Bollenbeck writes: "At that time in Brussels he may have seen the plans and at best the site of the Galeries St. Hubert, where work would have just begun, since the cornerstone had been laid on May 6, 1846. The subsequent years of crisis prevented him for the time being from realizing his plan for the construction of the arcade in Cologne. The

project was revived only in 1859. In August of 1861, exactly 15 years after the completion of the building plans, construction began, underwritten by the Schaafhausen Bankverein. The opening took place on December 15, 1863, just in time to make good use of the Christmas business. Shortly thereafter the queen visited the city and gave a great deal of attention to the building. She permitted the shopping concourse to be named after her—Königin Augusta Halle."[323]

Weyer was a willful but imaginative designer. He had studied at the École des Beaux-Arts in Paris and had certainly seen arcades there. He became an assistant to the Cologne municipal contractor in 1816 and later took over this position. He resigned in 1844 when Cologne was entering into a construction boom which lasted through the 1860s, and invested his money in building speculation and in opening up tracts of land for construction. He lost everything in the process. During this time the arcade was being built, just such an object of speculation. It has been said:[324] "Municipal Contractor Weyer worked with the Schaffenhausen Bank for a large-scale remodeling of the city and its network of streets. In fact he brought entirely new residential areas to the old outer districts to replace old monasteries and courtyards. The building of an arcade was the final project, characterized by Weyer's well-thought-out facade technique, never lacking in grand line. Modeled on London and Paris predecessors, it created one of the most noteworthy commercial streets of the time."

We know about the architecture of the arcade from a few surviving sketches and photographs.[325] Fig. 177 is an interior photograph of the arcade from Hohe Strasse. The only dated documents, two photographs of the exterior facades and a ground plan, together with a section belonging to the ground plan, are reproduced here in the form of tracings. The ground plan is dated August 1846, but Weyer's signature does not appear. This ground plan, from the design phase, is quite similar to the built version when compared with the site plan. Only the extension of a third short arcade to Ludwigstrasse is missing.

The arcade is part of a narrow street network in Cologne's old city. It consists of three arcade wings of varying lengths at an

172
Cologne, site of the
Königin Augusta
Halle, 1910

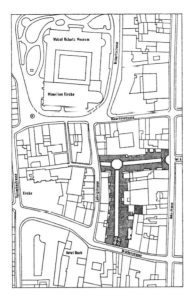

173
Cologne, Königin
Augusta Halle,
1862–1863, de-
stroyed 1944, cross
section

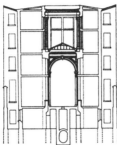

174
Königin Augusta
Halle, facade, Hohe
Strasse

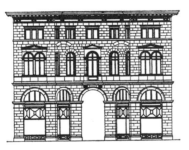

175
Königin Augusta
Halle, facade,
Bruckestrasse

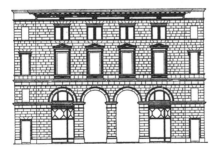

angle of almost 90 degrees, which meet in a polygonal central area. Two of these wings correspond to and meet alleys which end directly across from them. The facade of the arcade's entrance building is set back as a semicircle allowing a small plaza in the narrow street.

The numerous arcade buildings, which varied considerably in depth, were all four-storied and formed a sharply rising arcade space about 4 meters wide. The glass saddle roof was supported by pairs of ornamented beams with arched undergirding. It covered the wing of the arcade on Hohe Strasse above the fifth floor level and the wing on Brückenstrasse above the third floor level.

The number of shops is given as fifty-six in the 1846 planning sketches; there must have been more when the arcade was built. All of them follow the same system of accessibility—independent access to each shop from the arcade. Thus, the arcade is formed by a series of individual buildings, each separated from the others by a fire wall and accessible only from the arcade. The rows are terminated by the entrance buildings, which alone have larger spaces on the upper floors. Generally, each arcade building has a single, unsubdivided shop area on the ground level and a spiral staircase which leads to a kitchen in the cellar as well as to an enclosed courtyard and a narrow storage area, which is accessible from a service hall running directly under the arcade. Above the shop level are the mezzanine and the second and third floors, which may have served as apartments. As the depth of the lots increases, the spiral staircases become more practical two-way stairs. As additional secondary rooms are added, the courtyard space increases. Thus, the simplest access system has been chosen here, similar to those of the early arcades in Paris and to the Galerie Bordelaise in Bordeaux.

The interior facade treatment covered, oddly enough, only two stories, although there were four stories. At ground level was the familiar arcade motif, famous from the Paris arcades, the Galerie Vivienne and the Galerie Colbert. Above that there was a continuous moulding, on which rested a tall upper story, an alternating combination of overscaled residential windows and Corinthian pilasters, which created the illusion of collapsing the two residential levels into one level. The beams of the glass roof (raised for ventilation) rested on the upper story.

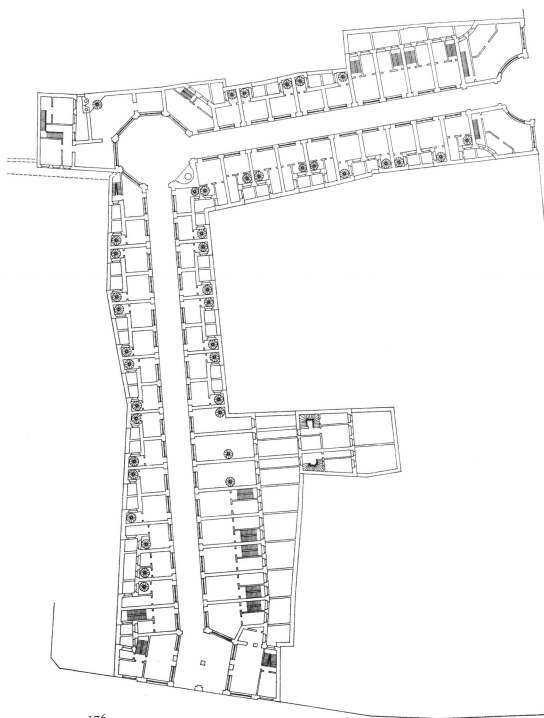

176
Königin Augusta
Halle, plan, design,
1845
(Scale: 1 : 600)

177
Königin Augusta
Halle

The Königin Augusta Halle was a colorful place. The 1969 Christmas supplement of the *Kölner Rundschau* contains an article entitled "De Passach": "Let us remember, for example, Fischer's famous restaurant in the arcade or the progressive bookstore which always exhibited contemporary artists after World War I. The arcade was very popular at the time. But before World War II—the economic crisis—it became rather off the beaten track." The "progressive bookstore" was Der Neue Buchladen, Arcade number 53, which carried literature, art, and politics, and arranged the Friday evening gatherings of the artists' aid society. Both the inside and outside of the store were painted in 1924–1925 by Seiwert and Hoerle, who belonged to the Cologne Progressive Artists' Group.[326]

Despite these enticements, the arcade was never a commercial success. Success went rather to Hohe Strasse, constructed on the same location after World War II, which was a pedestrian zone as early as in 1947. From its fate we may study the results of real estate ownership without the least social obligation.

Passage Tietz (fig. 178)
Hohe Strasse—An St. Agatha
The Tietz Arcade also lay in the Hohe Strasse,[327] Cologne's main business street, just a few streets farther to the south. It was a part of the second extension of the Tietz department store. One story high and possessing only display windows and entrances to the store, it was not really an independent structure. It was built about 1902 to a design by the architect F. Fritz. The arcade was torn down in 1912–1914 when W. Kreis replaced the whole complex with one large store.

The old photograph reproduced in fig. 178 provides a view of the arcade's entrance and of the building's architecture, with its mixture of late Gothic and *Jugendstil* elements.

Stollwerk Halle
Hohe Strasse—Am Hof
The Stollwerk Halle, no longer standing, was located near Cologne Cathedral on Wallraf Platz. It was built by the Cologne architect Carl Mortiz in 1906–1907.[328] The short arcade was part of a commercial building and took the place of a narrow old alley. It served as the light well for a commercial building whose ground floor was divided up into shops. The upper floors were occupied by wholesale merchants.

178
Cologne, Passage
Tietz, 1902, demol-
ished 1912

COPENHAGEN
Jorcks Passage
Skindergade—Vimmelskaftet
Jorcks Passage was built toward the end of
the nineteenth century. It has only one
flaw: there is no glass roof.

CREMONA
Passage
Corso Campi—Piazza Rama

Passage
Corso Mazzini—Corso Campi

DANZIG
Passage
Kohlen Market—Dominikswall

DERBY
Strand Arcade
Strand—Warwick?

DEWSBURY
Arcade
Market Place—Corporation Street

DORTMUND
Krüger Passage
Osten Hellweg—Westen Hellweg
The Krüger Passage was built around
1916; it is part of a commercial building
and connects Dortmund's two main business arteries, which run parallel to one
another. It was built by the architects
Steinbach and Luther and is still in use today, since Westen Hellweg is closed to
traffic and has become the place for the
Sunday promenades of the people of Dortmund. The bakery in the arcade is a favorite meeting place.

The Krüger Passage belongs to the group
of arcades built after the turn of the century. Like the Mädler Passage in Leipzig
and the Koruna Passage in Prague, it has a
concrete and glass roof and is not really an
independent arcade structure.

DRESDEN
Zentral Theater Passage
*Prager Strasse—Waisenstrasse—
Trompeterstrasse*
This three-wing arcade served only to
make the interior of a triangular block accessible.[329] It did not have any shops of its
own but rather provided show windows
for neighboring stores. It was built by Los-
sow and Vichweger in 1898 and was destroyed in 1945.

179
Edinburgh, arcade,
project, plan

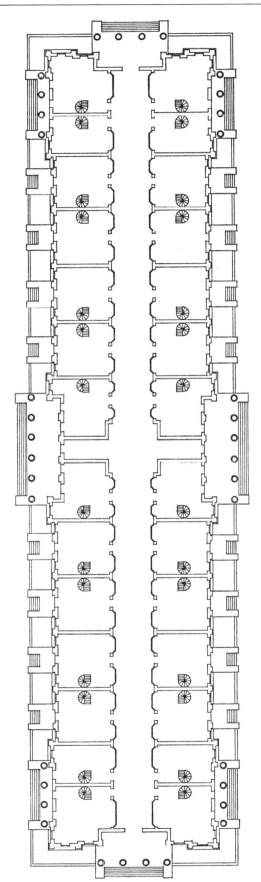

König Albert Passage
Grosse Brübergasse—Wilsdruffer Strasse
This arcade is part of a commercial building complex between Grosse Brübergasse
and Wilsdruffer Strasse. It was built by the
architect Kirsten in 1899 for the firm of
Sendig and Ulbricht.

It is not clear from an article in the *Baugewerks-Zeitung*[330] whether the arcade had a
glass roof. The König Albert Passage is no
longer standing.

EDINBURGH
Arcade (project) (fig. 179)
The Mound
The central point of interest in Edinburgh
is the castle on the cliffs high over the city,
the legendary seat of Scottish kings. Below
this ridge on the east side lies the old city,
irregular and built on many levels, with
buildings that reach to twelve stories because of the uneven terrain. The new town,
across from the old on the north, has regular quarters, wide streets, and sidewalks,
going back to a design of 1767 by James
Craig.[331] The area across from it is conspicuous because of a deep ravine which,
according to Craig's plan, was to be a
canal but as late as 1800 was still a barren,
stony pasture.[332] Only later was this ravine
turned into the Princes Street Gardens, so
called after the southernmost street of the
new town, built up only on one side. This
park was divided in half by James Skene in
1817 by means of a landfill, concisely
called "The Mound,"[333] meant to serve as
a direct connection between the old city
and the rapidly expanding New Town. Before this, access had been possible via a
series of bridges on the eastern side of the
city. The New Town, which had been developed strictly as a residential area, began
to change after 1800. The wealthy inhabitants moved, and Princes Street became a
commercial area. A whole series of public
facilities became necessary, requiring suitable sites within the city.

The Bank of Scotland had been built on
the southern edge of the ravine in 1806.[334]
William Henry Playfair's Royal Academy
followed it on The Mound across from the
intersection of Hanover Street with Princes
Street. Further development of The Mound
was discussed in the course of many improvements.[335] Everyone agreed that the
ravine would be kept free of any construction and that only independent buildings
would be constructed on The Mound so
that the view in all directions would remain unobstructed. Alexander Trotter's

"Plan of Communication between the New and the Old Town of Edinburgh" (1829) was among the many suggestions submitted.[336] Trotter suggested leveling The Mound, which ascended to the south, and erecting a palatial building in line with the Royal Institution which would contain two rows of two-storied shops. The shops would be accessible from both the outside and the inside through an interior arcade. He characterized his concept as a "Rue des Marchands in the interior of a splendid Edifice." Archibald Elliot[337] designed this freestanding arcade structure. He was the son of the London architect of the same name, who had been in charge of much construction in Edinburgh. The ground plan reproduced in fig. 179 is a tracing taken from the second draft of the project (1834) by Alexander Trotter.[338] Trotter presented his argument for the building in the following statement:[339] "The high prices given for shops in the finest situations of the New Town were destroying the residential character of the principal streets and squares, and . . . this character could be preserved by providing a dignified, central shopping area. . . . The Mound is a situation peculiarly adapted to this purpose. . . ."

The plan for a luxury retail establishment was never realized; the National Gallery was built in 1845 on the site intended for the arcade. Its architect, William Playfair, had already built the Royal Academy and had expanded it in 1836. The dimensions of the National Gallery give an idea of how the freestanding arcade would have looked. Many years later, the train line took over the ravine, laid track, and built a tunnel through The Mound exactly underneath the central section of the gallery. Edinburgh's center city, which the Romantics called the "Athens of the North," acquired a very noisy element.

Elliot's plan for a freestanding arcade was without precedent. It is at most comparable to the Galerie d'Orléans in Paris's Palais Royal, built at approximately the same time, whose shops are accessible from both sides. But the expression "Rue des Marchands," which Trotter used, refers to the Galerie des Marchands, which stood until the eighteenth century in a hall of the old palace of the French kings.

Princes Street Arcade
Princes Street—Rose Street
Only in 1876 was an arcade built in Edinburgh. Referred to in Baedeker, it is no longer standing today. *The Building News* reports on it in a short article:[340] "A new arcade has just been completed in Princes Street, Edinburgh, on the site of the old Clarendon Hotel, from designs by Mr. W. Beattie, architect, of that city. The frontage is Italian in style, and is built of freestone. The roof is of glass, supported on perforated girders of lacework pattern, and picked out in gold and colors. The floor is of Austrian marble, laid in alternate squares of black and white. On the ground floor there are seven shops on each side. . . . Access is obtained to galleries by means of a grand central staircase at the south-west corner. . . ."

EXETER
Eastgate Arcade
High Street—Southernhay Green
Eastgate Arcade, listed in Baedeker, must have been built before 1890.[341] It adjoins the city wall and connects the main commercial street, High Street, with a wide promenade, which circles the old city on the east. The arcade is 75 meters long and is level. According to Pevsner,[342] everything on High Street was destroyed in the bombings of World War II.

FRANKFURT/MAIN
Kaiser Wilhelm Passage (fig. 180)
Kaiserstrasse 10–10a—Grosse Gallusstrasse 5
Johann Valentin Albert, the planner and cofounder of a Frankfurt society for furthering the practical arts and their auxiliary sciences (Frankfurter Gesellschaft zur Beförderung der nützlichen Künste und ihrer Hilfswissenschaften) designed an arcade on Paris models as early as the 1840s. It remained, however, only a plan.[343]

The only arcade to be built in Frankfurt was the Kaiser Wilhelm Arcade, of about 1901, which cut across the corner formed by Kaiserstrasse and Grosse Gallusstrasse. It was built after the Berlin model by the versatile Frankfurt businessman Gottfried Leonhard Daube.[344] It did not, however, fulfill the commercial expectations it created. The following list of shop owners, taken from the 1908 Frankfurt telephone book, gives an idea of the kind of shops which were located in this kind of building.

The 1908 Frankfurt telephone book listed the following shop proprieters in the arcade:

Left side:

1. M. Meyer, Fancy Goods
3. M. Meyer, Fancy Goods
5. C. Stanitz, Ladies Hair Salon
7–9. Cocoa House; Th. Reinhardt's Cocoa Company
11. Lypstadt and Co., Cigarettes
13. A. Dirsch, Porcelain
15–17. Müller-Herbold, Postcards
19–21. Schlesiky-Ströhlein, Industrial Photography
23–25. W. Qeimar, Mechanical Optical Toys
27–29. E. Michaels, Coal Company
31. Darmstadt Furniture Factory

Right side:

2. M. Meyer, Fancy Goods
4. M. Meyer, Fancy Goods
6. A. Welmer, Bookstore
8. Th. Reinhardt Cocoa Company
10. H. Brandes, Dolls
12–14. H. Brandes, Hairdresser
16–18. (Empty)
20–22. A. Dirsch, Porcelain
24–30. Darmstadt Furniture Factory

Daube had acquired the lots, Grosse Gallusstrasse 5 and Kaiserstrasse 10–10a, in 1889. A new structure already stood on Kaiserstrasse,[345] built in 1886 by Wallot for the International Construction and Railway Company. Entrance to the arcade was obstructed by this office building. The passage turned off while still on the Kaiserstrasse lot; the change of direction was absorbed architecturally by a small glass cupola over a pentagonal rotunda.[346] The frontal building on Grosse Gallusstrasse gave way to a new building whose facade was entirely glass set in a wrought iron frame. The entrance to the arcade was covered over by a large glass niche. The arcade itself was two-storied, had thirty-one shops, and was illuminated by simple glass saddle roofs.

The Frankfurt Gas Company acquired the real estate from the Kaiser Wilhelm Arcade Corporation in 1925[347] in order to build a new administrative building there and to use the arcade for advertisement. New frontal buildings, constructed in 1926–1927, became the headquarters of the Frankfurt Gas Company, and the arcade, now essentially a completely interior space, hosted a permanent exhibition of gas appliances, model kitchens and so forth.

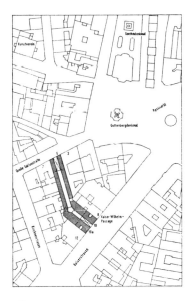

180
Frankfurt am Main, site of the Kaiser Wilhelm Passage, ca. 1910

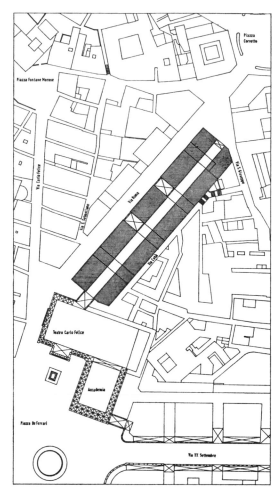

181
Genoa, site of the
Galleria Mazzini, ca.
1930

Everything was destroyed in 1944. But in 1962 the new building was ready for occupation and serves the same function today as it did in 1927. Even now the spatial characteristics are reminiscent of the former situation of the arcade.

GENEVA
Passage des Lions
Rue de la Confédération 5—Rue du Rhône 6
The Passage des Lions connects Geneva's two main commercial arteries. It belongs to a block of buildings whose lower stories are used for retail purposes. The arcade consists of a covered rotunda with a tapering glass roof and two wings which extend in opposite directions. The arcade, built around the turn of the century,[348] belongs to an insurance company. Its entrances are emphasized by sculpted pairs of lions. It is still standing. The glass saddle roof of the two-storied arcade is supported by ornamental girders with an undergirding of semicircular arches. The glass roof was replaced in 1966.

Passage du Terraillet
Rue du Marché 18—Rue de la Rôtisserie
The Passage du Terraillet is a short arcade which overcomes the considerable difference in level between the two streets by a series of steps and at the same time gives access to buildings. A small skylight qualifies the arcade, which was built in the twentieth century, for inclusion in this catalog.

Passage Malbuisson
Rue du Rhône 38—Rue du Marché 5
This arcade was built only after World War II. It runs parallel to the Passage des Lions on the eastern side. It has its own skylight in the form of a suspended, coffered, illuminated ceiling.

GENOA
Galleria Mazzini (figs. 181–186)
Via Roma—Via Ceba—Via S. Giuseppe
The Galleria Mazzini, which can be seen in figs. 182–186 as it appears today, is one of the monumental arcades built subsequent to and in competition with the Galleria Vittorio Emanuele in Milan. It is named after the Genoese revolutionary and companion of Garibaldi who fought for the unification of Italy.

The Galleria Mazzini is unique of its type. It runs parallel to a street, onto which it has exits at intervals, and continues

182
Genoa, Galleria
Mazzini, 1875, ar-
cade space

183
Galleria Mazzini,
glass wall and dome,
view from the Via
Roma

184
Galleria Mazzini,
view of roof

185
Galleria Mazzini,
view of dome

186
Galleria Mazzini,
ventilation hood on
the dome

lengthwise into the open, arcaded galleries of the Teatro Communale dell'Opere Carlo Felice, the Academy, and into Via XX. Septembre, which has open arcades on both sides. The arcade is thus part of a continually covered way one kilometer long which is today still the preferred daily promenade of Genoa's citizenry. This group of buildings between Piazza Corvetto and Piazza de Ferrari is located near the inconceivably cramped old city of Genoa, which it confronts with the generous spatial proportions of the nineteenth century.

I could learn little about the construction history of the Galleria Mazzini[349] except that it is said to have been designed by the engineer Giovanni Argenti. It is almost 190 meters long and is one of the most monumental arcades, with a width of 9.5 meters. The land slopes upward in the direction of Piazza Corvetto, and the incline is apparent inside the arcade, as it does not have interior steps. Because of the slope, it was necessary to group the arcade buildings into ten blocks to facilitate stepping the facades. At the same time it allowed room for four lateral wings with additional entrances from parallel streets. These additional wings are only one story and form terraces between the blocks of buildings; they have an unobstructed view of the arcade, since its glass roof is at the level of the terraces. The crossings are elevated and are covered by glass roofs in the form of octagonal pyramids. These interrupt the main vaulted glass roof of the arcade, thereby allowing it to step down. This design also facilitates ventilation of the arcade space. The intersection points are emphasized in the interior of the arcade by heavy iron chandeliers which, with the wall brackets, illuminate the arcade (which is open all night). The arcade space is four-storied; the buildings, however, are six to seven stories and extend beyond the glass roof. The construction of the glass roof is similar to that of the arcade in Milan. It may be assumed that the arcade was built by an English construction firm. The arched supports of perforated sheet metal were used for the first time in 1850 for the covering of Paddington Station.[350] Only the ventilation strip is missing. Ventilation is provided through narrow, ornamentally perforated latticework inserted in the areas where the glass roof steps down, as may be seen in photographs from the turn of the century. The interior of the arcade gives the impression of a street; this feeling is emphasized by the disposition of the buildings, the stepping of the moulding, and the variety of the facades, which suggests a row of houses.

GHENT

Van der Donckt Doorgang (fig. 187)
Rue de Flandre—Rue Digue de Brabant
This two-part arcade, divided by an alley between two streets which run into one another, is located in the train station quarter, that is, in the southeastern section of the old city in the direction of Brussels. The quarter has been expanding out of the city since the nineteenth century. As early as 1846 a wing was planned along the line of the alley in the direction of the Rue de la Station. The section of the arcade toward the Rue Digue de Brabant was built in 1852 by the contractor Donckt. The second section was added in 1886, connecting the arcade across the alley with the Rue de Flandre.[351]

GLASGOW

I found a total of eight arcades in Glasgow, the large industrial city on the Clyde.[352] Only a single arcade, both the largest and the most important, still stands today: the Argyle Arcade. The rest have been destroyed. They were modest in their dimensions and will only be listed here. Almost all of the Glasgow arcades were built in the first part of the nineteenth century, as far as I could ascertain from an 1858 city map.[353] They were distributed throughout the grid sheet layout of the city at the main focal points of public and commercial life.

Argyle Arcade (figs. 188, 189)
Argyle Street—Buchanan Street
The Argyle Arcade may be understood as an enterprise competing with the Burlington Arcade in London. It is Glasgow's oldest arcade and was built in 1827 by the architect John Baird, Sr. He had also built the famous iron Jamaica Street Warehouse.[354] The arcade runs from Glasgow's main commercial street, Argyle Street, and turns a right angle to Buchanan Street, forming an equilateral V. The entrance buildings have been modified today, but the arcade itself has been preserved. The arcade is 145 meters long and is two-storied; the glass roof is suspended from a beautiful wooden construction leaving room on the sides for latticework through which the arcade is ventilated. The stark

187
Ghent, van der
Donckt Doorgang

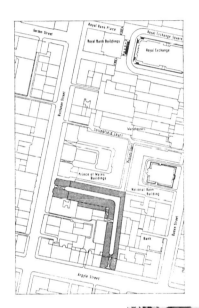

188
Glasgow, site of the
Argyle Arcade, 1859

189
Glasgow, Argyle Arcade, 1827

190
Glasgow, Queen Arcade, demolished

interior design of the facades has been preserved only in the upper story; the shop area has been replaced by new buildings.

Union Arcade (project)
Argyle Street—Great Clyde Street
An article[355] mentions "the Union Arcade, for the construction of which an act was obtained in 1846. It was to run between Argyle Street and Great Clyde Street, coming out near the Suspension Bridge across to South Portland Street. This Arcade, however, was never constructed, and in 1852 a further act was passed authorising the dissolution of the Glasgow Union Arcade Company, and the abandonment of the undertaking. . . ."

Wellington Arcade
Sauchichall Street—Renfrew Street, northern extension of Wellington Street
The Wellington Arcade, said to have had Doric entrance ways, was built by John Baird. As far as I could tell, it was built before 1858 and torn down in 1930 to make room for a new building belonging to the Woolworth Union Concern. The arcade is said to have reached its zenith around the turn of the century. At that time, there were a theater and a series of small cafés on Renfrew Street.

Royal Arcade
Hope Street—Cowcaddens Street
The Royal Arcade, said not to have had a glass roof, was located next door to the Theatre Royal. It was torn down before 1906, when Hope Street was expanded to meet Cowcaddens Street. It was built before 1858.

Queen Arcade (fig. 190)
Renfrew Street—Russell Street, extension of Findlay Street
Queen Arcade is the continuation of the Wellington Arcade after it crosses Renfrew Street. This arcade was also built before 1858; not even its remains can be found today.

Milton Arcade
William Street—Steward Street—Garshube Road
Milton Arcade is also shown on the 1858 city map. It had entrances on three streets. It was replaced toward the end of the nineteenth century by the Grand Theatre Picture House.

Millar's Arcade
Salt Market—King Street
This arcade is no longer standing.

Campbell Arcade
Trongate
The Campbell Arcade is no longer
standing.

Arcade
*Hope Street—Bothwell Street—Waterloo
Street*
The arcade was 40 meters long and 2.9
meters wide. Reputedly, it was part of a
hotel.[356] It was built in 1874 by the Edinburgh architects Peddie and Kinear, but it
is no longer standing.

GÖRLITZ
Strassburg Passage
Berlinerstrasse 6–9—Jacobstrasse
The Strassburg Passage, called the HO-
Passage today, is one of the very few ar-
cades still standing in either part of
Germany. It was part of the specialties
store of Otto Strassburg for textiles and
fashions and was built around 1908.

The arcade has two stories; it is divided by
two passageways into three areas.[357] Several entrances flanked by show windows
lead to the individual departments of the
store. The glass roof has the profile of a
Tudor arch; it is a form of the glass roof
unique to the Strassburg Passage.

GREAT YARMOUTH
Central Arcade
King Street
This long, one-storied, slightly sloping ar-
cade ends on King Street in a two-storied
shop building with a modern facade.

THE HAGUE
Arcade (figs. 191–199)
*Buitenhof, corner Kettingstraat—
Spuistratt 26–28*
(Third wing added later, Hofweg 5–7)
Near the Binnenhof, on the corner of
Buitenhof and Kettingstraat, is the entrance to the only arcade in The Hague.
This large arcade crosses the Achterom
and has one wing leading to the commercial street of Spuistraat and another ending
in Hofweg. A vaulted rotunda absorbs all
of the different directions. The wing leading to the Hofweg, while an integral part
of the original plan, was built as late as
1929. The cupola was replaced apparently
in the wake of this expansion; the facades
of the arcade were also robbed of their
decorative richness at this time. The arcade
is preserved as a unit today, and is lively
and busy, but the spatial impression is
somehow very false.

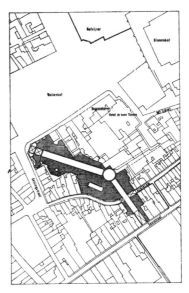

191
The Hague, site of
arcade, before 1900

192
The Hague, arcade,
1966

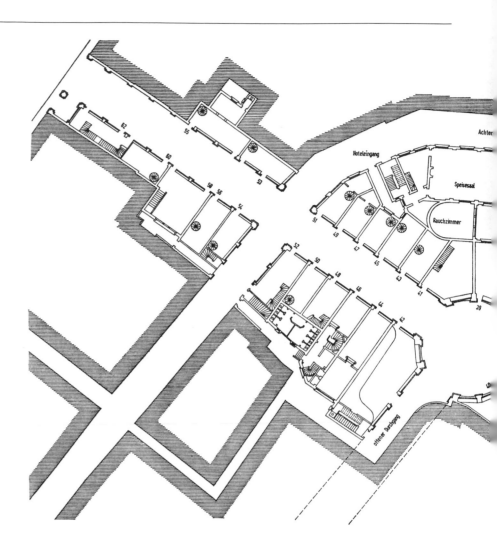

193
The Hague, arcade,
ground plan, design
by van Wijk

194
The Hague, arcade,
longitudinal section,
design by van Wijk

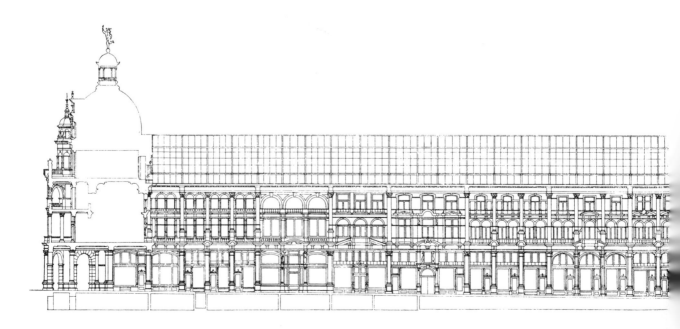

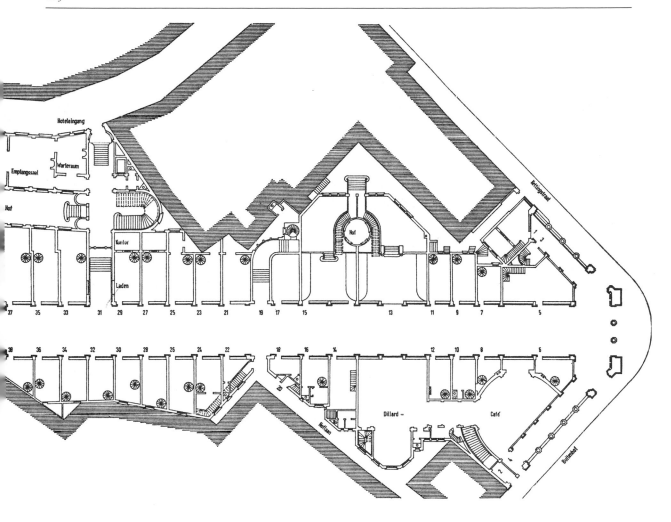

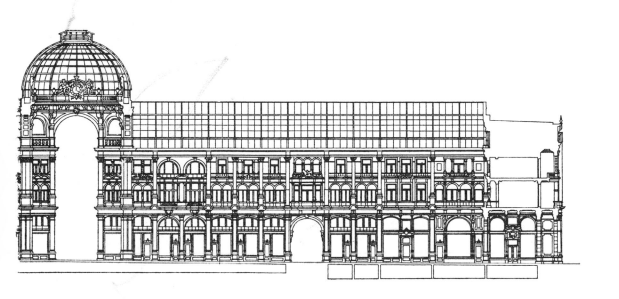

195
The Hague, arcade,
1883–1885, en-
trance, Buitenhof,
corner of Kettigstraat

196
The Hague, arcade,
arcade space after
modernization

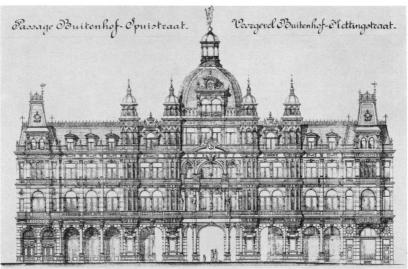

198
The Hague, arcade,
dome as originally
built

199
The Hague, arcade,
facade design by van
Wijk, modified in
construction

197
The Hague, arcade,
dome with new roof
at time of construc-
tion of third arcade
space, 1929

The modernization of The Hague began on July 4, 1858, with the establishment of a commission to investigate the possibilities of expanding and improving the city's street system.[358] The first problem attacked was the important connection between Buitenhof and Groen Market. To place an arcade in the oldest commercial quarter with its busy streets, Achterom and Spuistraat, would serve to improve the network of essential traffic patterns. The idea was suggested in 1882 and realized between 1883 and 1885.

The opening of the southern parts of the Binnenhof and the cutting through of the Hofweg followed this construction around 1900, the second street thereby connecting Spui and Buitenhof, which had before been linked only by narrow, crooked alleyways. The arcade took this new traffic pattern into account with a third wing which offered an additional possibility for shortening the route.

The construction of the arcade has a rather infamous history of which we know much from a comprehensive account by the architects van Wijk and Wesstra (van Wijk had already built an arcade in Rotterdam) in the March 21, 1885, issue of the *Bouwkundig Weekblad*.[359] The article was conceived as a justification of the original project; thus, the plans of the original and not of the modified buildings were included in it.

In the spring of 1882, it was agreed to found a joint-stock company, the 'sGravenhagschen Passage-Maatschappij for the construction of an arcade in The Hague. P. J. De Sonnaville was elected as the chairman. It took only five months to buy up, clear out, and tear down the existing structures occupying the proposed site. The ground was excavated on October 1, 1883, to a depth of 2.5 meters, which was the distance to sand. On October 18, plans were announced for the foundation, cellar, and drainage of the site; this work was completed by April 1, 1884. By this time, the architects had prepared all of the drawings, details, and specifications for the construction of the arcade. Cost estimates were obtained from three contractors, and a figure of approximately 1,500,000 gulden was arrived at. But the company did not have enough capital. It had sold only 600,000 gulden worth of stocks and needed 700,000 gulden for the first mortgage and 300,000 gulden for the second.

Since the financial situation in Holland was quite strained, the company turned to foreign investors, specifically to the Caisse-Hypothécaire, a Brussels bank. It agreed to carry the first mortgage at high interest rates on the condition that the construction be awarded to a famous contractor from Brussels.

The articles of the contract, drawn up in the absence of the architects, specified that all of the detail drawings (done by the contractor) would be delivered to the arcade company and approved within eight days. No member of the company and none of the architects could direct construction. As a result, the architects gave notice on April 26, 1884, and had nothing more to do with the building which, however, was constructed to a large extent according to their plans,[360] except for particular modifications that proved highly economical. The entrance building on Buitenhof was simplified; towers, cupolas, and terraces were eliminated. The decoration of the interior facades was reduced, and the cupola was lowered by one story. In spite of all these measures, the total costs for the building exceeded the lowest estimates of the Dutch contractors by 62,000 gulden. It is not hard to imagine what intrigues went on behind the scenes.

The architects assert their justifications at the end of the article: "We urgently call upon every unprejudiced expert to compare the execution of this work with our designs. They should consider that the building was to be constructed 'according to the attached plans and specifications' (namely those designed by us). We are prepared to present all available information to enquirers and to procure the specifications of the present building for inspection. We hope as well that the work of our fellow architects will never be mishandled as was ours—it was a work to which we devoted our energies for more than one year."

The arcade was built entirely by Belgian labor,[361] whose careful work received much praise. The Belgian architects Mortiaux and Rieck were invited to the dedication ceremony, held May 1, 1885, approximately one year after construction had begun.

The description of the building that the architects give in their article applies equally well to the structure today, although much has changed in terms of its utilization. The arcade has been expanded through to Hofweg by an additional wing, which had been foreseen in the original design. The two original wings of the arcade have a total length of 157.5 meters. The wing leading to Buitenhof is 7 meters wide; the wing to Spuistraat is 6 meters wide.[362] A planned third wing would have been 44 meters wide, containing a theater in addition to the regular shops. The diameter of the rotunda is 14 meters. The arcade space is four-storied: shops, mezzanine, and two floors of apartments. Thus, the arcade was made up of:

49 shops with apartments
4 shops without apartments
5 apartments with private entrances
1 hotel with access from Achterom and the arcade with 60 rooms, dining room, elevator, smoking room, waiting room, and private courtyard
1 cafe on Buitenhof with 2 rooms on the ground floor and 3 rooms on the upper floor.

A gas-powered elevator was planned for the shop at number 1 to take visitors to a viewing platform in the cupola approximately 29 meters high. Shop number 20[363] was planned as a *salon au gourmet* (a gourmet meeting place) with special luxuriously appointed rooms on the second floor. The public sanitary facilities were located behind it and were accessible from the outside as well. In the shops at numbers 47 and 48 there was a beer garden under the loft area illuminated by its own light well, notable for "special lighting effects." Both the hotel and the café had costly inlaid wood and marble floors. Almost all of the shops had their own cellars, some even beneath the arcade itself. Cast-iron stairways connected all the floors. The floor of the arcade was of brick glazed in various colors and arranged in a variety of patterns. Glass bricks provided lighting for the rooms in the cellar. The 1.65-meter slope within the arcade was compensated for in the shops, although the main moulding ran at a consistent height. The authorities gave permission to build over the Achterom, which allowed the arcade to be lengthened as far as Spuistraat.

The glass roofs of the cupola and the arcade wings were to have been made out of cast-iron ribs, supporting wooden frames and glass panes (.66 millimeter thick) made watertight by lead strips. In the summer, sea water was to be pumped in through the drainage pipes in order to spray the glass roof and thus cool it. However, the glass roofs were finally constructed of vaulted T-beams into which the panes of glass were inserted directly, recalling the construction of the roof of the Galeries St. Hubert in Brussels.

The architects had planned a richly ornamented facade facing Buitenhof; it was to be of *waalsteen* (a type of brick), with columns and pilasters of Swedish granite and white sandstone with many decorative allegorical figures. Grand loggias, four corner towers, a cupola, and a slate roof with leaded ornaments were to attract passersby to the arcade. However, a less sculptural, more austere facade was built. The decorative figures were limited to Neptune, Mercury, and two female figures in cast iron representing agriculture and industry.

HALIFAX
Arcade
King Edward Street
A notice in *The Builder*[364] announces: "An Arcade and billiard Saloon is to be built in King Edward-Street. The plans for the proposed work have been drawn up by Messrs. W. C. Williams a. Son, architects, and have received the sanction of the corporation." I was not able to ascertain whether the arcade was ever built.

HAMBURG
Sillem's Bazar (figs. 200–211)
Jungfernstieg 15–17—Königastrasse 47–48
This is a building which enjoys the approval of the layman. Public opinion has made it into a "Hamburg lion." Anyone who has left the city without having seen the Bazaar is about as badly off as one who has been in Rome without having seen the Pope. Of course public praise for works of architecture is in most cases fairly unreliable. But where it is given, we can assume at least two characteristics: grand dimensions and luxurious decoration. In fact both of these characteristics occur in the present building to an outstanding extent. In all of the major modern European capitals, there is nowhere to be found an arcade which can boast of such an imposing overall effect as the Bazaar in Hamburg. It is in fact shorter than most of the arcades in London and Paris, but exceeds them considerably in the proportions of its profile and in the beauty of its illumination. And as for the richness of the decoration, it is not surpassed by any building which we know. . . .[365]

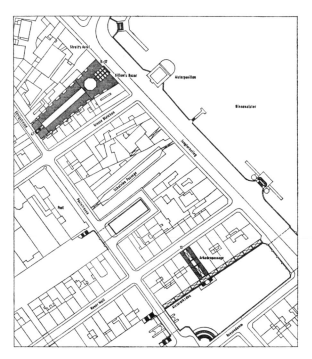

200
Hamburg, sites of
Sillem's Bazar and
the Arkadenpassage,
1866

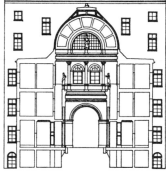

201
Sillem's Bazar,
1842–1845, demol-
ished 1881, cross
section

202
Sillem's Bazar, longi-
tudinal section
(Scale: 1 : 650)

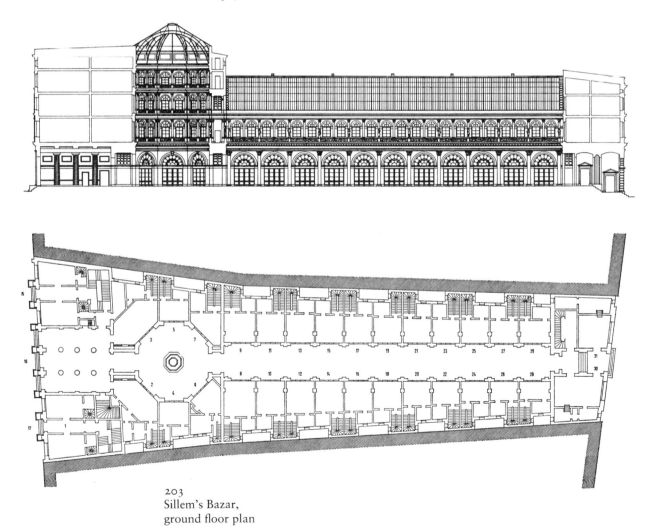

203
Sillem's Bazar,
ground floor plan
(Scale: 1 : 650)

Thus begins the article in the 1848 *Försters Allgemeine Bauzeitung.* I am indebted to this article for an exact description and architectural evaluation of this first great arcade. It is illustrated with plans and details of the glass roof construction.

Sillem's Bazar, so named after the builder, W. Sillem, was one of the first large buildings constructed in Hamburg after the devastating fire of May 5–8, 1842, destroyed a large part of the center of the city. Consultations and discussions about the planning and rebuilding of the street network went on for years. They coincided with the decline of austere classicism; Gothic and Renaissance stylistic elements were mixed, and unplastered brick was exposed. There was a hard battle over the design for a more spacious city center, over the location of the new city hall, and over its situation in relation to the Binnenalster. The fire had in fact brought about the first real city planning: the passing of a building code, the building of a sewerage system, and the establishment of straight streets to make Hamburg's medieval, winding streets, which were laced with waterways, adequate for new traffic. Gottfried Semper, Alexis de Châteauneuf, and the English engineer William Lindley were the outstanding designers of this renovation. There is extensive literature on its various phases.[366]

The site of the bazaar lay on the edge of the area destroyed by fire and explosions. It belongs to the block formed by Jungfernstieg, Grosse Bleichen, Königstrasse, and Gänsemarkt. Both Jungfernstieg and Grosse Bleichen were graded and widened with a larger building setback. The lot ran through from Jungfernstieg to Königstrasse, tapering slightly from an end frontage of 35 to one of 22 meters. It was 100 meters deep down the center. The owner engaged the young builder Eduard Averdieck[367] (1810–1882) who had traveled a great deal. He had studied with Fersenfeldt in Hamburg, Gärtner in Munich, and Stier in Berlin. I was unfortunately unable to ascertain whether he had been in Paris. He had settled in his hometown of Hamburg in 1832, and had already made a name for himself with his highly individual buildings on nearby Büschstrasse am Gänsemarkt (1841–1842).

Averdieck designed the bazaar. He directed construction in 1842–1845 and created an object of public amazement within the context of the renovation of the center city (an operation thwarted by many private interests) which the public followed with great interest.

The reservations that accompanied the general admiration of the building's grandeur from the very start were of a functional nature. These were doubts about its commercial success, since it led from a very busy street to one that was relatively unknown at the time. The aimless wanderer would probably be discouraged by the upper levels of the arcade, accessible only by steps. No consideration had been taken of these characteristics of the *flâneur,* a new kind of individual born along with the metropolitan city. Sillem's Bazar is the classic case of a badly located arcade with no real traffic function.

The building was divided into two entrance buildings of varying depth, separated from the wings that formed the arcade by fire walls. The entrance building on Jungfernstieg was five-storied and had nine bays. The ground floor and the mezzanine projected in the form of an arcade motif with pilasters and a wide entablature from which the upper levels were recessed. The three central archways were left open and led via four steps to a peristyle. A narrow passageway led from there to the large five-story octagon covered by a pyramidal glass roof. The arcade shops, three on each side, began in the octagon. Their floor plans were varied and awkwardly angular. In the upper stories the octagon served to light the rooms of the Hôtel de Russie, which occupied all of the upper floors of the frontal building, originally planned as a rental building. The central space, here a means of utilizing the depth, opened onto the actual arcade by double, tiered arches. The arcade was visible from a passageway-cum-balcony at the second-floor level.

The frontal building on Königstrasse displayed an entirely different construction. It was not very deep; all of the rooms faced the street. The facade was three-storied: a rusticated ground floor with three large round arches and two upper stories of seven bays, with Corinthian pilasters and Romanesque windows. The facade projected slightly; the doors to the cellar access halls were located in the narrow, windowless wings which were set back. The two shops at street level were accessible from the arcade entrance, which was raised nine steps above ground level.

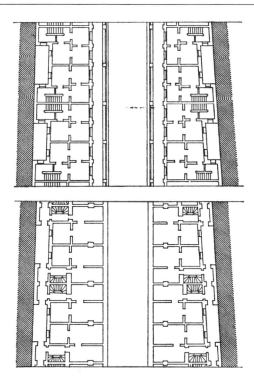

204
Sillem's Bazar, plan
of upper story, detail

205
Sillem's Bazar, plan
of basement, detail

The interior of the arcade was the unique illusionistic architectural fantasy of the architect Averdieck, as can be seen from the sections and the interior photographs. The lofty facades of the shops, crowned by an elaborate moulding with rows of statues on the balustrades, stood out into the arcade space, which, with its cover of vaulted glass, actually dropped back behind them. If one stood in the center of the concourse, the receding facades of the upper stories disappeared, and the glass roof seemed to float over the arcade space. This expansion of the space made better lighting possible and rid the arcade of a sense of narrowness and closure, benefiting especially the apartments on the upper levels.

The innovation of a graduated arcade space, expanding as it ascends, is one which often appeared later in England. In Sillem's Bazar it was achieved with completely illusionistic techniques which become clear only by studying building sections. The semicircular windows of the mezzanine were false; behind them was a narrow, unusable hall. The moulding and attic of the shop facades were freestanding and cast a shadow on the windows of the next story, which was slightly set back. There were eleven shops on each side of the arcade, all equally wide and decreasing in depth as the site became narrower. A small cashier's room and a two-directional stair were set aside from the overall space. Paired stairways, projecting to the boundary of the lot, formed narrow light shafts for the access hallway in the cellar. Each shop had a kitchen, furnace room, and sanitary facilities in the cellar, with apartments on the mezzanine and upper story. The staircases were connected to the two exits onto Königstrasse via the cellar hallway. Thus, the shops and the apartments could be rented separately; deliveries could be made independently of the arcade.

The interior facades of the arcade were dominated by the motif of window archways with Corinthian pilasters, a design also used in the Galerie d'Orléans and the Galerie Colbert. The interval between the pilasters was the shop bay, corresponding to the interval between the ribs of the glass vault. The upper stories of both the octagon and the arcade displayed the same motif, only foreshortened and with half the distance between pilasters. All of the balustrades had cast-iron railings decorated with a swan motif. The rows of life-sized allegorical figures opposite one

HAMBURG

206
Hamburg,
Jungfernstieg

207
Sillem's Bazar, en-
trance on
Jungfernstieg

208
Sillem's Bazar,
Königstrasse facade

another on the pedestals on the second floor formed an imaginary gathering, their gestures suggesting a constant conversation, and stood in for—we could add ironically—the absent audience. They were the work of the sculptor Schüler. The wall areas of the archways between the shops were covered with mirror-finished marble. The doors, mouldings, and glass frames were lacquered white and fitted with bronze decoration and French mirror glass. Gas wall brackets and three bronze ceiling fixtures provided nighttime illumination.

The glass roof, vaulted in an exact semicircle, is especially interesting because the details of its exclusively cast-iron construction are known. Its spatial and aesthetic effect was similar to that of the roof of the somewhat later Galeries St. Hubert although the latter is of wrought-iron construction. The former is an exemplary demonstration of how rationally and satisfactorily the static problems of ventilation, illumination, and drainage of the glass roof may be solved. At the same time, it provides an example of the precision of nineteenth-century detail and the confidence with which the functional as well as the spatial effect of each part was handled.

The support structure of the glass roof consisted of forty-five cast-iron quadrants which were jointed at the center of each arch. The ribs were 1.32 meters apart and rested on a cast-iron plate running the length of the vault, to which they were attached. This plate, shaped to prevent water from entering, was bolted to a wooden sill which formed the top of the masonry wall. The vault had a span of 8.75 meters and rested on the walls without any additional transverse bracing. The wooden sill was buttressed by small braces from the ceiling beams of the building wings in the direction of the thrust, to receive the transverse thrust of the ribs. Milled purlins, serving as fixed end supports for the glass frames, were wedged into the ribs at an interval of 1.13 meters. They provided longitudinal support as well. Every 33 centimeters—that is, about the length of a step—they were crossed by frames in whose grooves overlapping glass panes were firmly fastened with putty. The center section of the glass skin was inset at an angle of 45 degrees to the ribs, which parted in order to give the glass the necessary incline and to allow for constant ventilation. A sheet-metal strip covered the peak of the roof,

with chimney-like flues for ventilation. This system, however, was clearly inadequate, as large windows were installed on both sides at the foot of the vault. They could be opened or closed by chains at any time by the tenants of the arcade. The octagon had a low-pitched pyramidal tent roof whose glass covering was supported by spanning wrought-iron lattice arches. I could discover no further details about this somewhat awkward construction.

The construction of the bazaar by the architect Averdieck under contract to W. Sillem cost the equivalent of 1.5 million reichsmarks and was carried out between October 1842 and March 1845. The building took its place in the row of classicizing and Romanizing facades of the newly created Jungfernstieg. To the right stood the house (built by Forsemann) of the banker Salomon Heine, uncle of Heinrich Heine; next to this was Streit's Hotel. The arcade was welcomed enthusiastically, but its location was criticized from the very beginning.[368] An excerpt from an 1845 issue of *Der Freischütz* may serve as an example of this criticism: ". . . of course its practical utilization and possibility of profit is another question. The exit onto Königstrasse is uninteresting and not important enough to attract significant traffic. The arcade will be used mostly for promenading; is it possible to think, for example, of a more splendid umbrella during bad weather? But strollers seldom consume. There will be many hours of the day when the arcade will be a sparkling desert, and the tenants will necessarily feel a sort of isolation. It would clearly be advantageous for the entire area if several already popular and highly frequented shops would open up there so that their customers would benefit all of the bazaar's tenants. Up until now only a few shops have opened, and these do not seem of outstanding significance to *Der Freischütz*. The more imposing have yet to come. . . ." In March 1845 the Hôtel de Russie, with its own restaurant, was opened in the entrance building on Jungfernstieg by Messrs. Röhn and Lamarche.[369] A rumor was reported in *Der Freischütz*[370] on July 19, 1845, that the bazaar would be the object of a lottery to recover the construction costs as quickly as possible. Although Sillem energetically denied this rumor in the next issue, there was probably a plan to this effect. Perhaps even then there were

209
Sillem's Bazar, ar-
cade space shortly
before demolition

210
Sillem's Bazar,
rotunda

211
Sillem's Bazar, ar-
cade space, view to-
ward Jungfernstieg

intimations of a bad investment; as soon as spring of 1859 the bazaar was put up for sale.[371] The first offer, of the equivalent of 840,000 reichsmarks, found no buyer; only upon the second offer of 516,000 reichsmarks was a buyer found on December 10, 1850. The building had depreciated 65 percent in only five years. The bazaar continued a twilight existence for another thirty years, without a function, and with an architecture whose display, without the resonance and confusion of the passing crowd, seemed unreal and ghostly.

The arcade was bright and animated only around Christmas, at the time of the Hamburg Christmas fair. The arcade was decorated for the holiday, and there was music by a small orchestra hidden away in the upper rooms.[372] Visitors strolled through for a small entrance fee credited to any purchase made in one of the shops. The arcade changed ownership once again in 1880, becoming the property of a construction company, the Hanseatische Baugesellschaft, which had it torn down in 1881 with the buildings at numbers 16, 18, and 20 on Grosse Bleichen. The same year saw the beginning of construction of an ostentatious new building of red sandstone, the Hamburger Hof, a "first class hotel."[373] If Sillem's Bazar had survived, it would today stand between Poststrasse and Jungfernstieg, in the middle of the hectic commercial life of Hamburg's inner city. It would probably be, with the Alster Arcade, the center of luxury retail trade.

Königstrasse was expanded through to Gänsemarkt only in 1883, thereby acquiring the importance it has today.

Arkadenpassage
Alsterarkaden 11–13—Neuer Wall 11–13
The Arkadenpassage is a small, insignificant lateral access way from Alster Arcade to Neuer Wall. Across from its exit to the arcade, steps lead down to a landing to the Kleine Binnenalster. Even today the layout of the Alster Arcade, in conjunction with the space formed by Rathaus Square and the Kleine Binnenalster, which is squared off on the Venetian model, is the greatest example of inner-city planning and the most successful part of Hamburg's rebuilding after the fire.[374] The site of the Alster Arcade was one of the first strictly pedestrian zones in the city[375] and was occupied earlier by the Borsenarkade.

The architect of the Alster Arcade was Alexis de Châteauneuf,[376] one of the most important and versatile contractors of the mid-nineteenth century in Hamburg. His work was comparable to that of Cluysenaar in Brussels. I was unable to ascertain whether he also built the Arkadenpassage himself or simply selected its location. Two versions of the sketches of the arcade have survived.[377] They differ from each other only in story heights and in some details. In contrast to the Hansestadt Senate, which was to have identical facades, Châteauneuf's arcade had a series of facades which would be similar in character but individual in details. Only the open arcades were obligatory for building owners, and they had to be constructed according to Châteauneuf's designs.

Only one letter from Châteauneuf's papers survived the war; in it, he characterizes the architecture and the site of the arcade:[378] "This square, defined partly by the waters of the Kleine Alster, partly by the land, would be magnificent; everything depends on the size of the opening from the Binnenalster into the city. If one were to liken the view into the city to a group, with the Rathaus the central figure, then it is better if I can survey ¾ of it than [if I could see] through a slit the tip of its nose entirely symmetrically. The fact that the Rathaus is set back from the Alster Basin in this way, and not in the manner of Semper's frontal embankment, offers an extraordinary advantage, the framing of the arcades' two wings; what could be better?"

HANNOVER
Georgspassage (figs. 212–214)
Georgstrasse 8–10—Limburgstrasse 7, corner of Heiligerstrasse 16
The Georgspassage is part of a large commercial complex built in 1900 and designed by the Hannover architects Schädtler and Hantelmann. Its construction was fully documented in the *Baugewerks-Zeitung* of 1904.[379] Located at the corner of Goethestrasse on Georgstrasse, Hannover's main commercial artery, the arcade formed a shortcut for pedestrians coming from the northern suburbs to the old city. The corner building is late Gothic on its left side and early Renaissance on its right. Its facade, executed in sandstone and topped by an ornate tower, displays a canopy over the entrance with the figure of St. George slaying the dragon. This part of the building, with the beginning of the ar-

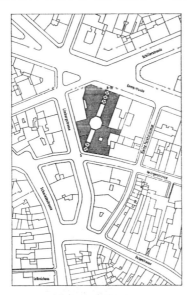

212
Hannover, site of the
Georgspassage, 1938

214
Georgspassage,
Georgstrasse facade

213
Hannover, Georgs-
passage, 1900,
destroyed 1944,
rotunda

cade, survives today; the rest was destroyed by bombs in World War II.

The arcade was 72 meters long and 5 meters wide. The center was distinguished by an octagonal rotunda with a vaulted, round cupola of shining green glass. The six larger archways of the octagon were decorated with wall paintings dedicated to large firms in Hannover such as the bakery of H. Bahlsen and Günther Wagner, whose production was represented allegorically. Also in the octagon was the entrance to Hannover's first automat restaurant. This institution made the arcade the topic of the day on its opening on May 15, 1901.[380] An article mentions Berlin's Kaisergalerie as a model for the design of the arcade.[381]

HARROGATE

There were a total of five arcades in Harrogate in Yorkshire, a town similar to the other British spa towns of Bath and Bournemouth. Only two of them are still standing.[382]

Lowther Arcade
Cambridge Street
Built about 1896, the Lowther Arcade is still standing.

Prince's Colonnade
Prince's Street
This arcade was built about 1898 and torn down in 1924.

Royal Arcade
Parliament Street
Built about 1898, the Royal Arcade was remodeled into a furniture store (1921).

King's Arcade
Jane's Street
King's Arcade was built about 1899 and torn down in 1927. Fineburg gives 1876 as the construction date.

Beulah Arcade
Beulah Street
The Beulah Arcade, also called Central Arcade, was built in 1902 and is still standing.

HELSINKI
Vanha Kauppakuja
The dimensions of this large arcade recall those of the arcade in Milan. It was built in 1888 to the designs of the architect Wrede. A glass-roof covering was planned for the four-story space but was never completed. Today the arcade serves more as a delivery area for neighboring buildings. The facades are symmetrical. There

are three stories above a high, rusticated, arcaded ground floor. The space terminates in a polygonal form and is reminiscent of the north side of the Galleria Vittorio Emanuele.[383]

HUDDERSFIELD
Byram Arcade
Westgate
The Byram Arcade, which is described as having "a very surprising interior—tall and galleried," is still standing. It is probably identical to the "new one" in Huddersfield, one of the most famous in England, mentioned in an English architectural dictionary of the time.[384] It was built in 1880–1881 as an extension of the Byram Building by the London architect W. H. Crossland for the landlord of Huddersfield, Sir John William Ramsden.[385]

HULL
Paragon Arcade
Paragon Street—Carr Lane
This arcade was built about 1890; I am unsure if it is still standing.

Hepworth Arcade
Silverstreet—Market Place
This arcade was built about 1896; I am unsure if it is still standing.

INDIANAPOLIS
Arcade
Washington Street—Virginia Avenue
Toward the end of 1895 in Indianapolis a work of architecture was completed from the designs of the architects Vonnegut and Bohn and dedicated to a function similar in many respects to that of Berlin's arcade by Kyllmann and Heyden which connects Behrenstrasse with Unter den Linden. At the very center of the busy capital of Indiana, in direct proximity to the War Memorial in Circle Park, designed by Bruno Schmitz, the arcade connects the city's most prominent commercial artery, Washington Street, with Virginia Avenue, one of the main diagonal streets which cut through the grid city of Indianapolis from northeast to southwest and northwest to southeast, intersecting at Circle Park with the aforementioned memorial.

Indianapolis is a busy commercial city; the number of larger commercial buildings is not small, and there are numerous office buildings. But there is a dearth of small, well-situated, and well-stocked shops. The firm of Dickson and Talbott wanted to remedy this situation by the construction of the arcade in question. . . .

Thus begins a report[386] which somehow found its way into the *Deutsche Bau-*

zeitung, of an arcade which, although designed for practicality, was nevertheless quite conspicuous in its huge advertisement arches, which were located as a kind of facade in front of the entrance and which towered over the two-story arcade buildings. The arcade shortened the streets, which intersect one another at sharp angles. Its central axis was bent. The twenty-eight almost identical shops each had a room on the upper floor and space in the cellar. Deliveries were made through a cellar corridor underneath the arcade, which was connected to the sidewalks of the neighboring street by elevators. The arcade, which was entirely of cast iron with fireproof ceilings, had a barrel vault of pressed glass squares set in cast-iron frames. The upper story of the arcade was set back to allow the shops additional light from the glass floor of the gallery.

The interior of the arcade was visible in a profile from the street; there were no frontal buildings. The report comments on the arches:

Both facades, including the arches, are of reddish-brown terra-cotta. It is suspended from the iron construction behind it. The arches and the lanterns crowning them are covered in chased copper. The cupola of the lanterns and the ornamentation of the arches are gilt. Red slate covers the roofs, insofar as they are visually part of the facades. The element of color plays a major role in the arcade and serves the function of advertisement in an artistic way. The style consists of a free mixture of forms from the Italian Renaissance with Moorish elements.

I am unable to say if the arcade is still standing.

ISTANBUL

Aurupa Pasaji

Hamal Basi Caddesi (?)

The Aurupa Pasaji, located in the wealthy eastern suburb of Taksim, is two-storied and is approximately 60 meters long. It is occupied today exclusively by small shops serving neighborhood needs. The interior facades with double arcades on the upper story are in Renaissance forms; the space is covered by a simple glass saddle roof.

JOHANNESBURG

The Arcade (fig. 215)

The Arcade has a vaulted, fishscale glass roof,[387] the technical specialty of the Glasgow iron construction company of Walter Macfarlane and Co.,[388] which displays this arcade as an example in their trade catalog. It was built about 1900. The Alex-

215
Johannesburg, The
Arcade, ca. 1900

andra Arcade in Swansea was the only other arcade to use this type of glass roof construction.

KARLSRUHE
Kaiserpassage (figs. 216, 217)
Akademiestrasse 33—Waldstrasse 34, corner of Kaiserstrasse
A connection between Kaiserstrasse, the main east-west commercial artery in Karlsruhe, and Akademiestrasse was considered as early as 1870[389] but realized only in 1887. The opening of the Kaiserpassage took place on November 24, 1887. Gustav Ziegler was the architect and Gustav Binz his sculptor. O. Betz was the contractor. The Kaiserpassage is in the tradition of the Berlin Kaisergalerie. It has the considerable length of 150 meters but only very modest transverse dimensions. The arcade is quite irregular and its width varies from 3 to 5 meters. It has two stories and a simple glass saddle roof. It was broken up by an irregular alternation of polygonal central spaces and passageways.

The arcade suffered as a result of being composed of a string of sites which were fitted together rather badly; it is a model of poor location of an arcade. It led away from a busy main street to an unimportant secondary street without through traffic. It did not provide a shortcut. The commercial performance of the arcade was correspondingly bad, as we can see from the surviving construction documents,[390] which are full of requests for modifications and petitions for alterations and installation of advertisement billboards, all with the goal of lending the arcade a new appeal. In 1929, for example, there was a plan to remodel the arcade. There was to be a department store on Kaiserstrasse, a bank on Waldstrasse, and a cinema inside the arcade, which was to be made wider by 8 meters.

The areas of the arcade were occupied as follows around 1930:
bicycles, sewing machines
artists' supplies
hair stylist
plumber-electrician
Japanese and Chinese imports
hospital and medical supplies
office and household supplies
Lions Club

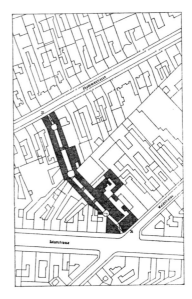

216
Karlsruhe, site of the Kaiserpassage, 1930

217
Karlsruhe, Kaiserpas-
sage, 1887, destroyed
1944, entrance, cor-
ner of Kaiserstrasse
and Waldstrasse

photographer's studio
goldsmith
stationery store
cigarettes and smoking supplies
Löwenrachen restaurant with a wine club,
"Zur Eule," the Cockatoo Bar, café, and
dance hall

It is clear from this partial listing that the majority of the occupants were businesses which were not dependent on casual customers.

The arcade was destroyed in September 1944 by a bombing raid. The Kaiserstrasse section was rebuilt after the war. The ruins of the sections on Akademiestrasse could still be seen in 1966.

KÖNIGSBERG
Rossgärter Passage
Königstrasse—Vorderrossgarten
The 1932 city map mentions a café, a picture theater, and a vaudeville in the arcade.

Tragheimer Passage
Mitteltragheim—Krugstrasse
This angled arcade, located across from the university library, is still standing.

LAUSANNE
Galeries du Commerce
Rue Edward Gibbon—Rue de la Grotte
In the May 1978 issue of *Bauwelt* there was an article which, like an earlier, more extensive piece in the review *Habitation*, called for the preservation of Lausanne's second arcade, the Galeries du Commerce, threatened with demolition. The article reports:

The site was rented in 1908 by the owner, the Postal Ministry of the Swiss Confederation (PTT), to a corporation for the construction of a building for offices and shops, with an option to buy in accord with growth in its own needs. In 1969 the PTT (with 325 million francs profit for 1977) decided to tear down the structure and to replace it with a building of three times the capacity, above an underground parking garage, to accommodate the technical facilities for a central telephone exchange.

. . . Located on a sharp incline beneath Place Saint-François, which since 1896 has become the retail and commercial center of the city, the three-storied Galeries du Commerce supplement the public space with a covered arcade on the top level and with a pair of roof terraces which are accessible from two pedestrian bridges. An elevator and a monumental, multidirectional staircase provide good vertical connections with the lower city.[391]

The typological description is somewhat confusing at first. In fact, this is an unconventional arcade, perhaps comparable, as a completely freestanding building, at least to the old arcade in Edinburgh or to the department store design by Schinkel for Berlin. Its unique roof access can be understood only in terms of the topography of Lausanne, which developed on a steep slope.

The linear building was built in 1908–1909 by the architects Paul Rosset and Otto Schmid and shows the Viennese influence of Wagner. There is a real, glass-vaulted arcade with shops only on the top level; the three floors below it are office spaces, illuminated by glass blocks, which can be flexibly arranged because of the reinforced concrete construction. In the open central space, with its round skylight and colorfully ornamented dust cover, an open staircase connects the levels with one another gracefully. While the exterior facades recall the department stores that were so fashionable at the time, the interior of the arcade belongs to those unique transitional forms in which we can see future possibilities for combining indoor public access to residential units with other uses, just as Fourier, Sauvage, Le Corbusier, and others thought of it in its social implications.

According to the report quoted earlier, "The Department of Architecture at the ETH Lausanne has publicly announced its interest in a study on restoring the Galeries du Commerce of the PTT; the Art History Department at the university has, through an exhibition and guidebook, brought the significance of the building for the architectural history of the turn of the century in Lausanne to the attention of a wider public. A petition with 2,500 signatures has been submitted to the municipal authorities, but there has been no response. For this reason it is necessary to call it to the attention of the international community. . . ."

I hope that the preliminary plans for demolition of the PTT can be stopped. The management of a public facility must be distinguished from that of a private undertaking. Or has this notion long since become a fiction?

Galerie St. François (fig. 218)
Rue de Bourg—Boulevard Benjamin Constant
The Galerie St. François, named after the

218
Lausanne, Galerie St.
François

nearby church of St. François, is located in the center of Lausanne. Built after the turn of the century, it has been restored and is owned by a foreign concern. Four interior staircases overcome the total of 6 meters difference in height between the two streets. The arcade has a five-story entrance building on the boulevard but is itself two-storied. It has an undulating illuminated ceiling which is hung from the exterior glass roof.

LEEDS

Leeds, the center of British fabric manufacturing, had by 1900 a population of a half-million. In the short time between 1878 and 1900, eight arcades and many extensions were built.[392] Additional arcades were planned but never executed. They all have entrances on the major commercial street, Briggate, which cuts through the relatively cramped center of Leeds on a north-south axis. The center of the city is located slightly west of it around Town Hall and the cathedral; southeast of it are the markets, stock exchanges, and large factories along the Aire River. On the southwest, train stations hem in the city. The commercial section, where the cinemas and theaters are also located, is defined by the three parallel streets— Lands Lane, Briggate, and Vicar Lane— and by the cross streets of The Headrow (where the department stores are centered today), Commercial Street, Kirkgate, and Boar Lane. The deep and narrow lots of the blocks formed by these streets were originally accessible through courts or yards, with parallel rows of small residential buildings. They were entirely suitable for the construction of arcades.

Five of these arcades are still standing today. They form entire complexes and are situated either parallel to or across from one another. It is quite an experience to wander through them in the middle of a constant stream of pedestrians and to see them restored and preserved in every detail. They are a piece of late Victorian architectural mastery, without monumental ambitions and full of spatial and decorative innovation. It is to be hoped that they will survive the wave of demolition that has swept over the commercial areas of British cities since the beginning of the sixties and to which so many arcades have already fallen victim.

Thornton's Arcade (figs. 219–221)
Briggate 78–80—Lands Lane 36–38
Both the earliest and the most original of Leeds's arcades is Thornton's Arcade, which connects Briggate with Lands Lane. It is 74 meters long and has recently been repainted. It is named after its founder, a Mr. Thornton, who owned the music hall in Leeds.

The entrance buildings and the arcade are three stories. The entrance bay is emphasized by a tower-like addition, against which the glass pointed vault rests. The window walls and arches of the facade are of sandstone and the walls are brick. The facade on Briggate is now whitewashed and the shop level has been miserably modernized. The narrow, high arcade is only 4.5 meters wide. Its aesthetic effect is produced by the succession of three materials. On the ground floor are slightly projecting show windows of dark wood. Gothic arched windows line the upper floors and above them, the iron structure, painted light blue, which supports the roof. The arcade slopes upward about 2 meters in the direction of Lands Lane. Cast-iron arches, ornamentally pierced and resting on narrow supports, mediate the change of level of the facades and make possible constant ventilation of the arcade by overlapping layers of the glass roof. On the front of the arcade, on Lands Lane, one discovers, in an archway over the passageway, a strange group of figures, part of a mechanical clock, which represents Richard Tuck and Richard the Lionhearted taking turns striking the hour. These figures were made by a sculptor from Leeds, a Mr. Appleyard; the clock itself comes from the famous firm of Potts and Sons, Leeds.

Thornton's Arcade and the Gothic Arcade in Birmingham are the only arcades in the Gothic style, even though Gothic proportions suit the arcade space.

Market Street Arcade
Briggate—Central Road
Market Street Arcade was built in 1878, according to Fineburg. It was torn down in the 1960s and replaced by a new building in which another, attached arcade is located.

Queen's Arcade (figs. 219, 222)
Briggate 72–75—Lands Lane 28–30
Queen's Arcade, built in 1889, runs directly alongside Thornton's Arcade. It was constructed on the site of the former Rose-

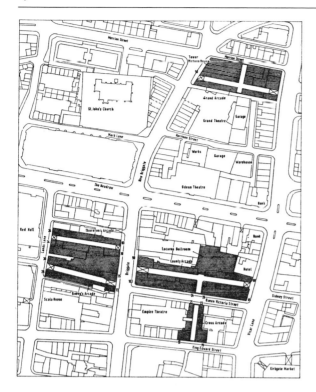

219
Leeds, sites of Thorn-
ton's Arcade,
Queen's Arcade,
Grand Arcade,
County Arcade, and
Cross Arcade, 1961

and-Crown Yard which connected Brig-gate with Lands Lane.[393] The site plans show that Queen's Arcade occupies the ideal location for an arcade. Its entrances are situated across from the intersections with King Charles's Croft and Queen Victoria Street, which was built later.

The entrance buildings of the arcade are uninteresting, as they seem not to stand in any architectural relation to the arcade itself and are partly renovated rebuilt older buildings. The arcade, on the other hand, is magnificent. The motif is set by the floor, which slopes approximately 2 meters. It is echoed at the level of the galleries and in the decorative arches of the glass roof. The lack of any ornamental flamboyance and the contrasting colors of white, red, brown, and black produce the aesthetic effect.

The arcade has one setback. The galleries are accessible via staircases at the end and lead to the shops and small offices of the upper stories. The galleries ascend in stages; they have a cast-iron balustrade which extends into the arcade and which corresponds to the wrought-iron beams of the low-pitched saddle roof. The facades, which step up approximately every four meters, are emphasized by pilasters of black marble with white Corinthian capitals. They support a stepped-up, freely designed moulding upon which the ribs rest. The completely undecorated expanses of wall are covered with white glazed tiles. The colors, the materials of iron, glass, and glazed tiles, the shop signs, the hanging lamps, the rounded corners of the shop entries, and the rows of springing, bounding architectural members all produce an authentic and typical example of the precision and spatiality of Victorian commercial architecture.

Grand Arcade (figs. 219, 223)
New Briggate 48–50—Vicar Lane 122—Merrion Street
The Grand Arcade is the northernmost of the arcades in Leeds. It was opened in 1897[394] and covers the entire block formed by New Briggate, Merrion Street, Vicar Lane, and a small alley north of the Grand Theatre.

Two parallel arcade wings, North and South Avenues, run through the building complex on a west-east axis; they are intersected by a lateral wing with an exit onto Merrion Street. The length of the

220
Leeds, Thornton's
Arcade, 1878, arcade
space, view toward
Lands Lane

222
Leeds, Queen's Arcade, 1889

wings totals 80–86 meters; the length of the lateral wing is 32 meters. Originally there was a total of 56 shops, the majority of which had entrances from two sides. Today the northern wing is no longer used. The western section was rebuilt after World War I through to Tower Picture House. The eastern section of the arcade has been preserved, but is used only as a furniture storage area.

The entrance buildings on New Briggate and Vicar Lane are three-storied; the two entrances of the arcade wings are located between three Renaissance gables of sandstone and red terra cotta. The proportions of the wings are evident in the large semicircular arches which connect the gables.

The arcade spaces are two-storied. The concourses are clearly stepped at every shop bay. A steep glass saddle roof, supported by an inelegant wooden beam construction, weakens the architectural effect and creates ugly overlap. The shops are projected over a distance of about 50 centimeters. The upper story is illuminated by a series of wretched bay windows.

We find a clock by Potts and Sons of Leeds on the eastern facade on South Avenue. The figures of a "Guardsman, Scotsman, Irishman, Canadian, and others" stand in a circle on a small, revolving platform. When they disappear, a rooster crows on a balcony above the face of the clock and strikes the hour with his metal wings. Once a line from Macbeth ran underneath the clock: "Come what may, time and the hour runs through the roughest day." Today we may read: "Time and tide wait for no man."

County Arcade (figs. 219, 224–226)
Briggate 98–103—Vicar Lane 65–69—Queen Victoria Street 24–25
The County Arcade is the longest and largest arcade in Leeds. It has been preserved in its entirety. It is very busy and occupies the southern part of the block formed by the streets of Briggate, The Headrow, Vicar Lane, and Queen Victoria Street, which was built in conjunction with the erection of the County Arcade. The entrance on Briggate lies across from Queen's and Thornton's arcades. There is a lateral wing approximately at the middle of the 120-meter-long arcade. This wing continues across Queen Victoria Street into the Cross Arcade which ends in King Edward Street. It was built at the same time as the County Arcade. At the short end of this lateral wing—perhaps it was thought

to extend it to a cross—is the entrance to the popular Locarno Ballroom. A secondary exit of the Empire Theatre leads toward the Cross Arcade.

The street facades, which are symmetrical on Queen Victoria Street, display Renaissance details. They are three-storied and constructed of red (now blackened) sandstone, terra cotta, and brick. Great arcade arches mark the entrances; ornamental latticework fills in the arches and displays the arcade's name. As we walk through these arches, we find ourselves in a steep, two-storied arcade, with one setback, that seems to fade out in the distance. Several features give the arcade a sense of frenzied movement, an atmosphere that yearns for crowds of people but which never appears grotesque when deserted—the rows of columns supporting the galleries, the wrought iron, Baroque latticework, the stone spheres resting on the jambs of the balusters, the triple motif of the round windows, and the pilasters, weighed down by small pediments which conceal the supports of the heavy cast-iron vaults.

The spatial effect of this arcade is dominated by the semicircular, decoratively pierced cast-iron frames, which have a cross section measuring 50 by 50 centimeters. The I-beam purlins rest directly on top of them, carrying the rafters in their upper and lower flanges. The glass barrel is interrupted and accentuated by a cupola above the lateral wing. Its pendentives are decorated with mosaics symbolizing freedom, labor, trade, and art. Approximately in the middle of the two parts of the glass barrel, we find two attenuated cupolas whose pendentives are also inlaid with mosaics. The glass roof is clearly modeled after that of the Galleria Vittorio Emanuele.

The most pleasing view may be had from the lateral wing of the County Arcade across Queen Victoria Street to the Cross Arcade—an exemplary urban design solution, by which pedestrians and vehicle traffic have their own intersecting spaces; only different levels for each are missing.

The County Arcade was built in 1898–1900 by the architect Frank Matcham for the Leeds Estate Company, Ltd. The firm, which was founded in 1897, still owns the arcade today.[395] Derek Linstrum writes of the architect: ". . . [he] had been responsible for over 100 theaters and music halls, including the London Coliseum and Palladium, and the development included the gaudy Empire Music Hall and the King Edward Restaurant which was richly furnished with a Mexican onyx and marble staircase, mosaic floors, polished marble walls and columns in the 'handsomest Grill Room in the United Kingdom'; statues of the Venus de' Medici and the Venus de Milo and paintings by eminent Royal Academicians showed that culture was not forgotten in the riot of richness. . . ."[396]

Cross Arcade (figs. 219, 227–228)
King Edward Street 13–19—Queen Victoria Street 21–23
This arcade is part of the County Arcade and was built at the same time.

Victoria Arcade (fig. 229)
Lands Lane 17–21—The Headrow 75–79
Victoria Arcade was a continuation of Thornton's Arcade across Lands Lane; it then turned off at a 90-degree angle in the direction of The Headrow. It was built in 1898 by the firm of Thomas Ambler and Son for the owner of the lot, a Mr. Dawson. It was opened in 1900 "in celebration of Queen Victoria's Diamond Jubilee."[397] The arcade had twenty-six shops. It was expanded in 1949, torn down in 1959, then replaced by a new department store, Schofield's Ltd. The 1951 photograph shows a view of the large entrance arch; its curvature is identical to that of the interior beams which support the steep glass saddle roof.

LEICESTER

I could only establish the existence of three arcades in Leicester, although Fineberg mentions five, presumably modest examples.[398]

Royal Arcade
Silver Street—Hinckley Road
The construction date of 1877 may be found on a plaque over the entrance.

Silver Arcade
Silver Street—Cank Street—North Market
This arcade has two parts with side galleries on the upper floors.

The Corridor
Market Place South—Market Place North
This narrow arcade does not have a glass roof.

Morley Arcade (?)

Angel Gateway (?)

Victoria Parade (?)

223
Leeds, Grand Arcade, 1897

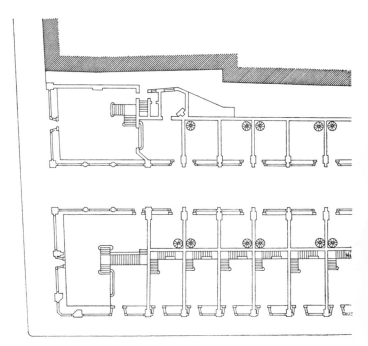

224
Leeds, County Arcade, 1898–1900, ground floor plan

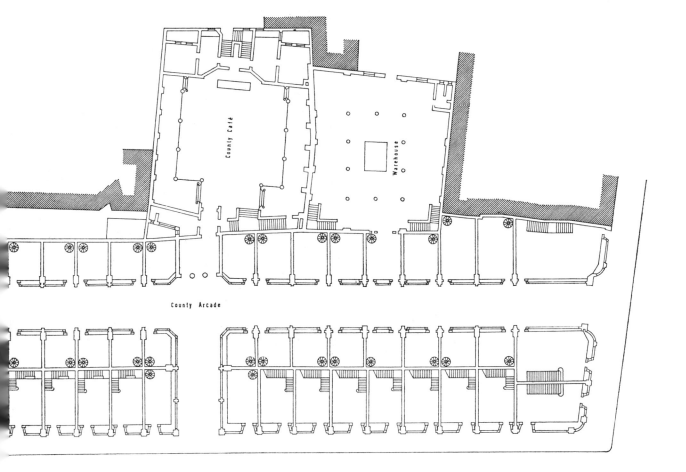

County Café

Warehouse

County Arcade

225a
County Arcade,
dome

225b
County Arcade, cor-
ner shop in rotunda

226
County Arcade,
wing, view toward
Vicar Lane

227
Leeds, Cross Arcade,
extension of County
Arcade across Queen
Victoria Street,
1898–1900, view
through to County
Arcade

228
Cross Arcade, entrance, Queen Victoria Street

229
Leeds, Victoria Arcade, 1899–1900, demolished 1959, entrance, The Headrow

LEIPZIG

Leipzig became an important location very early in its history because it was the crossroads of old trade and military routes. It was an important market and later became an international convention city. The characteristics of its city plan led to the development of an early form of the arcade building type. We find references to a Leipzig fair as early as the fourteenth century; the university was founded in 1409. Both assured the city of a distinctive cultural life and of its own architectural tradition developed over centuries.

Three phases may be distinguished among the buildings which served the *Messe*, or fair.[399] Originally, the fairs took place on the marketplace under the arcades of the city hall and in numerous temporary buildings and stalls surrounding the city hall; beginning in 1500 an additional fair began to develop in the courtyards of the merchants' houses. Auerbachs Hof, built in 1530, a "little Leipzig" with its 100 fair booths, is the famous example of this phenomenon. In order to develop this form of commerce undisturbed and apart from the overcrowded streets of the old city, deep blocks (60 by 200 meters) were made accessible by means of so-called walk-through houses. Buildings across from one another were connected by side courtyards and were made accessible by gates. The vaulted areas on the ground level of the buildings were rented for retail trade; there were smaller apartments on the upper floors and storage lofts in the attic. The walk-through houses thus served the fair.

Uniformly designed walk-through houses began to be built around the beginning of the eighteenth century. Koch's Hof is the most beautiful example; its courtyard facades are as elaborate as those on the streets. Its houses are four-storied on all sides. Koch's Hof, like many other walk-through buildings, was a victim of the World War II bombing raids.

In the nineteenth century, some of these structures were glassed over; the Paris arcades were certainly the model for this procedure. Several new buildings of this type carry the name *arcade*, for example, Steckner Arcade and Plauensche Arcade. Nevertheless they have neither continuous glass roofs nor symmetrical interior space.

At the beginning of the twentieth century, when the fair came to be used for display rather than for retail, the structures which served it underwent a third transformation, assuming the form of the fair hall (*Messehaus* or *Messepalast*), which today is part of Leipzig's inner cityscape. The fair halls are department-store-type complexes, the majority of which are five-storied. They are almost completely covered, and all of the floor space is used for fair booths. On the ground floor, there are usually arcades with shops to prevent the buildings from being completely empty between fairs. Several fair buildings among these complexes have regular systems of arcades with glass skylights. These are included in the catalog: the Mädler Passage, the Königspassage, and Speck's Passage. Others, such as the Theaterpassage, built by Bestelmeyer in 1927–1928; the Peterstrassenpassage; and the Messehofpassage will be mentioned; but they are not independent arcade buildings. The walk-through houses, including Bartels Hof on Hainstrasse, one of Leipzig's oldest commercial buildings, have all been destroyed. The fair halls have been preserved, rebuilt, or restored and give an idea of how the cramped inner city of Leipzig was once interlaced with a system of competing arcades, courtyards, and passageways restricted to pedestrians.

Speck's Hof Passage
Reichsstrasse—Nikolaistrasse, passage through to Hansahof
The arcade is part of a large fair building[400] built by the architect Franz Hänsel in 1908–1909. It has shops on the ground floor and exhibition space on the upper floors for temporary use. This space can accommodate 200 stalls and 800 open stands. The arcade is illuminated from above by three courtyard-like, glassed-over openings. Parts of the building were destroyed in the war but rebuilt in 1947.

Mädler Passage (figs. 230, 231)
Grimmaische Strasse—Neumarkt
In 1530 Dr. Heinrich Stromer von Auerbach built Auerbachs Hof.[401] The building, on Grimmaische Strasse, had three gables and a courtyard which turned the corner to Neumarkt. There was room for 100 fair stands; there were a separate guard room, stables for carthorses, and a wine cellar—the famous Auerbachs Keller immortalized in Goethe's *Faust*.

Ulrich Gross wrote about this "Hof," an early form of the later walk-through buildings, in 1587: "A beautiful building! It is

230
Leipzig, Mädler Passage, 1912–1914, concrete ribbed dome

231
Mädler Passage, entrance to Auerbach's Keller

built with majestic vaults, rooms, and halls. Italians, Dutch, and merchants from Nuremberg, all wealthy men, occupy it, and display such a rich assortment of beautiful wares and goods that it could easily be compared with an especially magnificent market." Luxury articles, jewels, ceramics, fabric, and specialties from abroad were traded at Auerbachs Hof, which was favorably located at the intersection of the great highways of the Reich. At the same time, the Hof was the promenade of polite society and a place for entertainment. Augustus the Strong played his coarse jokes here; Peter the Great was given a tour. In 1779 it is reported: "Auerbachs Hof is the place where polite society, the landed nobility, and anyone who would be seen, assembled in full dress, preferably during the middle of the day between 11 and 12 o'clock." It was the Palais Royal of Leipzig.

The walk-through buildings and Auerbachs Hof lost their importance in the nineteenth century as the retail fairs became strictly for the display of goods. The Hof became quiet, offering only picturesque angles for photographers, although the cellar was still loud and full of life. The leather goods manufacturer Mädler acquired the building complex in 1911 and authorized a competition among five Leipzig architects for the design of a new fair building. The winner was a member of the board of works, who suggested replacing the Hof with a corner arcade with a central rotunda. As the construction plans became known, a storm of protest began over the fate of the historic Keller, a favorite place in Leipzig. But the cellar had been included in the planning. Two bronze groups, which portray the bawdy crew and Mephistopheles and Faust, flank the steps which lead downstairs from the arcade. In February of 1913, the bar was reopened. The Goethekeller, the Lutherkeller, and the Fasskeller on the lower level were freed of disfiguring additions, and a new transverse hall was added. Criticism was silenced; the Leipzig citizenry was placated and a local patriot composed a poem:

We praised the patron with thanks, till our
    moist lips began to babble:
God bless all your coffers; the cellar is
    saved!

The arcade and the fair building were made public in 1914. They were built in the typical commercial architectural style of the pre–World War I era. The arcade here is covered with a flat vault with concrete ribs; the sections between them are filled with glass building blocks.

There was a plan to create a direct connection (which exists today) between the rotunda and Peterstrasse via a parallel structure, the Königspassage. The plan failed at the time because of the impossible demands of the building owners.

Königshaus Passage
Grimmaische Strasse—Petersstrasse
The Königshaus Passage, today altered, ran parallel to the Mädler Passage; it was also called the Königspassage for short.[402] Built by the architect Gustaf Pflaume in 1915–1916 as part of a fair building, it was opened in the spring of 1917. Mr. Starke[403] wrote me concerning its earlier condition: "It had a glass roof, but not in the smaller section which formed the connection with Grimmaische Strasse inside the Königshaus. The glass roof extended only the width of the walkway area, and thus did not cover the secondary galleries on either side."

Although the Königshaus Passage and other arcades in fair halls have been destroyed, newspapers in 1970 stated that the tradition will be revitalized in Leipzig.

LENINGRAD
Passage des Grafen Steenbock
This great arcade was built as early as 1848, shortly after the Galeries St. Hubert in Brussels. Gassner's Anatomical Museum had previously occupied the site. The arcade was renovated in 1900. Today it is used as a department store like the GUM buildings in Moscow. There is also a large theater hall in the arcade; the Leningrad State Theater gives its performances there.[404]

Arcade (fig. 232)
Newvsky Prospect 48—Italyanskaya
This arcade, on Leningrad's main commercial street, is today occupied by the Department Store for Women.[405] It is three-storied, has steps at either end, and a very high-peaked glass roof, obviously of a more recent date. The uppermost story is set back approximately one meter on both sides.

Erich Mendelsohn, in his book *Russland-Europa-Amerika*, illustrates the interior of a Leningrad arcade and declares:[406] "Let us build multi-level tunnel structures as cosmopolitan retail galleries! Let us technologize the East! A bazaar without dream-light."

232
Leningrad, arcade

LIÈGE
Passage Lemonnier (figs. 233–235)
*Rue Vinave de l'Ile—Rue de l'Université;
crosses Rue Lulay des Fèvres*

The Passage Lemonnier in Liège, the first large arcade in Belgium, was opened ten years before the Galeries St. Hubert in Brussels and was obviously influenced by Parisian models.[407] The dried-up tributaries of the Meuse, along which the boulevards run today, were drained completely in the early decades of the nineteenth century, and the Rue de la Régence and the Rue de l'Université were opened.

In the mid-1830s several well-to-do citizens suggested building an arcade between the Rue de l'Université and the Rue Vinave de l'Ile in the vicinity of the new Théâtre Royal built at the beginning of the century.[408] They consolidated and formed a *société anonyme* (limited liability company) on July 28, 1836, and submitted a project to the city on September 7, 1836. Their goal was to acquire the nine necessary lots, to have the buildings on them torn down, and to build the arcade, making a profit from the sale and rental of space. They established 1.6 million Belgian francs as common capital, which was distributed as 1,600 shares at 1,000 Belgian francs per share. The prime mover was the architect Louis Désiré Lemonnier,[409] for whom the arcade was later named.

An arcade 160 meters long with forty-eight shops was planned. The Conseil Communal gave its approval of the project on April 8, 1837. Work began soon thereafter, on May 22. The projected completion date (June 24, 1839) was in fact beaten; the arcade was opened to the public on January 25, 1839. Théodore Gobert reports that Lemonnier worked with Beaulieu, the Liège city architect, on the project, and that the problem of naming the arcade was solved between the two of them, "the name of Beaulieu remaining in the urn of the Fates, and the gallery being baptized Passage Lemonnier."

The arcade is still standing today, but the architecture has been ruined by modernization, probably done in the 1920s, which destroyed the street-like effect of the arcade space. The glass rotunda was replaced by a massive vault; the glass roof was changed to a milky sunscreen. Some consolation can be had from a visit to the Restaurant de la Renaissance, off the rotunda,

233
Liège, Passage Le-
monnier, 1837–
1839, octagon over
the Rue Lulay des
Fèvres

234
Passage Lemonnier,
entrance, Rue Vinave
de l'Ile

235
Passage Lemonnier,
arcade space as orig-
inally built

whose interior is entirely authentic. Among magnificent chandeliers, potted palms, marble tables, and bronze ornament, one can sample Luxembourg specialties and watch the passersby through half-drawn curtains. The arcade is lively, the shops all occupied, since it is located in what is still today the commercial and entertainment quarter of Liège between the Place du Théâtre and the boulevards.

The entrance buildings display a spare, restrained classicism. The building on the Rue de l'Université is five-storied and has seven bays, the middle bay emphasized by a gable. The entrance building on the Rue Vinave de l'Ile has only three stories but its facade arrangement is the same. Both the store level and the mezzanine have been altered. A wide black metal band arches over each entrance, carrying the name of the arcade in large letters. The arcade wings are two-storied.

Old photographs show the original appearance of the arcade. The shop level was unified by a wide moulding which rested on marble pilasters. The shops were all equally wide, and each had a show window on either side of the entrance. The upper story displayed a large window down to the floor over each shop entrance and a latticed balcony. The arcade was covered by a self-supporting glass hip roof with small, overlapping panes of glass, a feature typical of the early arcades. The arcade wings are at a slight angle to one another. This design was intended by the architect, says Gobert, to diversify the spatial sequence of the arcade. (A similar solution may be found in the later Galeries St. Hubert in Brussels.) The wings are connected by an octagonal rotunda, which is situated on the small street of Rue Lulay des Fèvres, where it crosses the arcade. The rotunda opens onto the street through two archways. It was originally covered by a pyramidal glass tent roof, and had an entrance on each of its four enclosed sides. Interior access to the arcade buildings is provided by narrow corridors, accessible from the street, along the edges of the site, which also give access to the staircases. This system of access, which corresponds to that of Sillem's Bazar in Hamburg, guarantees maintenance and supply of the shops and apartments independent of the arcade.

LIMA
Arcade

According to a travel account, the arcade in Lima crosses a block diagonally in the center of the city; the building has a central area with a cupola roof. Although the structural framework is there, it is unglazed, as the dry climate makes glass unnecessary. The shops and offices on the two levels, accessible by galleries, are now occupied by the post office and serve as windows. The year of construction is given as 1924; Perreira was the architect.

LIVERPOOL
Lord Street Arcade
Lord Street—Button Street
This arcade is no longer standing.

LONDON

At the end of the eighteenth century, London was the opposite pole to Paris and the point of departure for the spread of arcades in the Anglo-Saxon nations. The city pushes the student of arcades to the limits of his ability to distinguish differences among them. A casual glance out of a car window reveals arcade-like forms even in the suburbs, which, however, are only market halls, extended subway entrances, or train station vestibules.[410]

The number of arcades built in London is comparatively small given the size of the city. There are only three early ones, the Royal Opera Arcade, the Burlington Arcade, and the Lowther Arcade. They are the first arcades in England and the models for all arcades in the Regency style and Greek Revival style in England and America. This group of early arcades dating from the 1820s and 1830s were constructed in the fashionable commercial and residential areas in west London around Piccadilly and Regent Street. These neighborhoods competed with the old City in the eastern section. The arcades were built in connection with the large urban planning projects which John Nash, as with an architect's magic wand, created between Regent's Park and the Strand. They profited from the public which was drawn by the first metropolitan improvements. In the early Victorian period, only the Exeter Arcade on the Strand and the Royal Arcade on New Oxford Street were built, both bad examples of the genre and badly located as well.

The enthusiasm over the gigantic glass palace for the Great Exhibition in Hyde

Park in 1851 revived the idea of a larger arcade. At the same time, there was a plethora of utopian plans for solving London's traffic problems and for urban renewal. A palm conservatory, an exhibition hall, and separate railroad passages such as tunnels and viaducts merged with the idea of an arcade to create solutions for London's traffic problems and the hopelessly congested inner city. William Moseley, Joseph Paxton, Frederick Gye, and others suggested multilevel arcades extending for several kilometers which would accommodate train, subway, and pedestrian traffic. If one studied systematically the archives, acts of Parliament, and hearings of the Metropolitan Board of Works (established in 1855 to facilitate city planning in London on a large scale), more utopian improvement plans would probably be discovered. However, all were destined to fail because London was split between irreconcilable factions representing tradition and private interests which any student of Hausmann would have known to avoid.

London was a metropolis and an incomprehensible jungle of ever new layers, "a province covered with houses; its diameter from north to south and from east to west is so great that persons living in the furthest extremities have few interests in common; its area is so large that each inhabitant is in general only acquainted with his own quarter and has no minute knowledge of other parts of the town. Hence the first two conditions for municipal government, minute local knowledge and community of interest, would be wanting if the whole of London were, by an extension of the present boundaries of the city, placed under a single municipal corporation. The enormous numbers of the population, and the vast magnitude of the interests which would be under the care of the municipal body, would likewise render its administration a work of great difficulty."[411] This contemporary description shows London as the great exception, as a city without a central administration until 1888, when the London County Council was established. It is obvious that the utopian arcade projects included here were not to be realized without considerable participation by the public sector.

From the late Victorian era only the small but extraordinarily appointed Royal Arcade on Bond Street deserves to be mentioned. There was an arcade revival[412] in the twentieth century, primarily in conjunction with the new building on Regent Street and in Piccadilly. But the structures are mostly dependent arcades inside the great commercial buildings.

Royal Opera Arcade (figs. 236–244)
Charles II Street 24—Pall Mall 56
If one strolls through the elegant London district of St. James ("Club Land") and through Pall Mall, one meets at the eastern end the block dominated by the New Zealand House skyscraper. Next to the skyscraper is the entrance to an arcade of almost toy-like dimensions; this is the Royal Opera Arcade, which crosses the block in the direction of Charles Street. The building's name denotes its historical significance. The Royal Opera Arcade, or Colonnade, as it is also called, was the first arcade built in England. The block formed today by Charles Street, Haymarket, Waterloo Place, and Pall Mall has a history which goes back 265 years and which is interesting enough to recount here.[413]

In 1703–1704 John Vanbrugh built the first theater, the Queen's Theatre, on land in the Haymarket which belonged to the crown. It was located at the Haymarket and Pall Mall, and was bordered on the west by Market Lane, a small alley which led to Charles Street, then not yet connected to the Haymarket. Market Lane lay approximately where the Royal Opera Arcade connects the two streets today. The first Italian opera performed in England was produced in this theater in 1708; Handel's operas were staged here beginning in 1710.

The Opera House, subsequently called the King's Opera House, burned to the ground in 1789. The new building, designed by Adam and Lewis, was built by Michael Novosielsky who gave the theater itself the form of a horseshoe. It was the first building of this type in England and also the largest theater. It was parallel to and accessible via the Haymarket. The facades were not completed.

In the first decade of the new century, this building was included in the domain of the great Metropolitan Improvements, engineered by the architect John Nash beginning in 1806 for the Prince of Wales.[414] This comprehensive urban plan created a monumental connection between Carlton House and Regent's Park, including the areas of Waterloo Place, Regent Street, the Circus, the Quadrant, Portland Place, Park Crescent, and the terraces which framed

LONDON

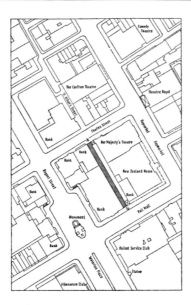

236
London, site of the
Royal Opera Arcade,
1966

Regent's Park. Since Nash had also built Suffolk Street and the Theatre Royal on the Haymarket, a facade suitable for the elegant surroundings, a continuous front, had to be considered for the King's Opera House. Thomas Leverton[415]—one of the many architects who participated in the individual projects of the Improvements—had already suggested a new design for the Opera, which provided for a corridor in place of Market Lane "for the accommodation of visitors in sedan chairs." John Nash and his partner at the time, George Repton, took up this suggestion in the final plans for the architectural refinement of this area.[416]

Repton's plans for the renovation and expansion of the block have been preserved. They show the following:[417] Charles Street is extended through to the Haymarket, forming an enclosed block. The lots around the theater are filled with shops and apartments out to the new lines of the bordering streets. A Doric colonnade adorns the entire front, its corners marked by pavilion-like arcades—a motif which Nash had also used in Park Crescent and in the Quadrant. The main facade on the Haymarket is articulated by towerlike, corner projections, by the alternation of arches and columns in the colonnade, and by two-story pavilions which accentuate the entrances to the theater.

In order to make the building visible from all sides and independent of its immediate surroundings, the colonnade is also extended through the block. The natural illumination is replaced here by round skylights in the bays of the vault. A row of shops forms the side of the building. An arcade is the result, a byproduct; although not an independent structure, it fulfills all of the necessary criteria for the building type. It has modest dimensions with only one row of shops and an additional entrance to the theater. But it is the prototype of a particular English variant of the arcade building type which is more closely related to the vaulted bazaars of the Orient than to other examples.[418] The Royal Opera Arcade was built in 1816–1818, somewhat earlier than the Burlington Arcade, located nearby. As the arcade has no real function in the traffic pattern, the shops were difficult to rent. In 1854 the arcade was described as infrequently visited. The same writer characterized the shops:[419] ". . . Several hairdressers and other shops where opera glasses and books

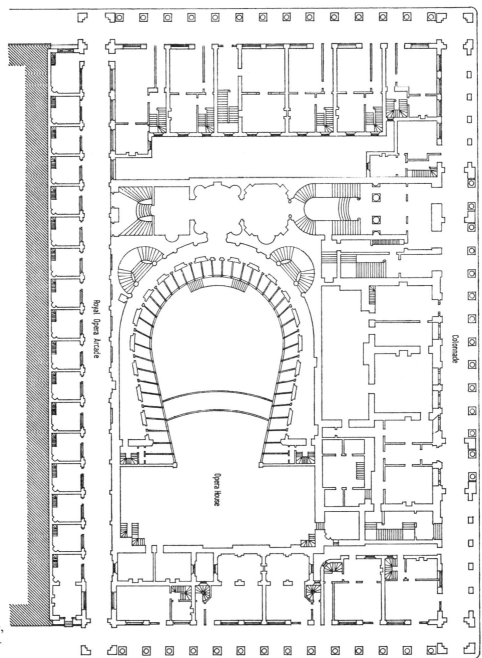

237
Royal Opera Arcade,
1816–1818, plan in-
cluding the Opera

238
Royal Opera Arcade,
cross section

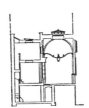

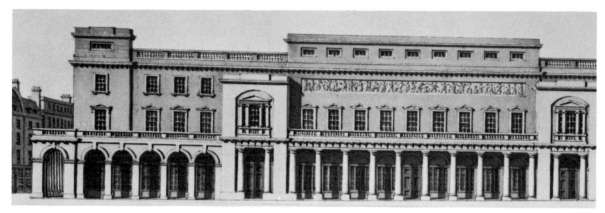

239
Royal Opera, Pall
Mall facade, drawing
by Repton

240
Royal Opera, Hay-
market facade, draw-
ing by Repton

241
Royal Opera Arcade,
entrance, Pall Mall,
1966

242
Royal Opera Arcade,
view of the roof,
1948

243
Royal Opera Arcade,
arcade space, 1948

244
Royal Opera Arcade,
arcade space after
renovation, 1966

of the opera can be hired and great-coats, bonnets etc., left during the opera performances."

In the Victorian era, Pall Mall, Lower Regent Street, and Waterloo Place were taken over by many clubs; the shopkeepers of the arcade began to serve customers from the literary and political world. Here one could have his hair cut and beard waxed, as well as purchase shoes, shirts, gloves, and ties; in short, everything that was indispensable at the time for a well-turned-out appearance. Thus the arcade came to be called "Fops' Walk." Only two of the shops from that period still exist: Burgess, the barber, and English, the shop where Gladstone used to purchase his ties. At the same time, the theater was rechristened Her Majesty's Theatre in honor of the queen. This building also burned down in 1867 but was rebuilt to the same dimensions and with more adequate fire safeguards. The entire complex on the Haymarket, including the colonnade, was torn down in 1892 and was replaced by a new theater, with its back on the corner of Charles Street and the Haymarket and its front perpendicular to the Haymarket. The Carlton Hotel was opened next door. The arcade was spared once again but lost its two entrance buildings, which had connected it with the surrounding arcade.

With the end of the Victorian era, the arcade lost its public, since the new theater had no exit into the arcade. It was increasingly neglected. Its existence was threatened one final time in the 1960s by the demolition of the Carlton Hotel, which was followed by the construction of the New Zealand buildings. The skyscraper of this new group stands directly next to the modest arcade, which has been carefully restored. It is listed today as an "ancient monument." It is a memorial to Georgian London and, for anyone who strolls through the area, a discovery.

Today, without the additional areas in the colonnade, the Royal Opera Arcade measures 80 meters in length.[420] It has eighteen groin-vaulted bays, in which round openings have been cut. These are filled with glass that admits a filtered light. The transverse dimensions are modest—a width of 7 meters and a height of almost 6. Each bay holds a shop with its entrance; each shop has a slightly projecting bowed show window with a fanlight which opens up the space of the upper story to the arcade. These facades, less independent because of

the vaulting, display in their small panes of glass and in their wooden mouldings and sills the typical storefronts of the period. The arches of the vault rest on Tuscan pilasters between which elegant lanterns, which light the arcade by night, are suspended.

The eighteen shops all have a similar design. The area is square with a chimney in the corner and a narrow stair which connects the mezzanine, the shop, and the cellar. The cellar is lit by a shaft from the floor of the arcade. The mezzanine has its own skylight. The other side of the arcade is blind, with a few shop windows belonging to neighboring shops at the entrances. Since it slopes up slightly in the direction of Charles Street, each succeeding bay is slightly offset. The Royal Opera Arcade was built in Bath stone, now painted.

Burlington Arcade (figs. 245–255)
Piccadilly 51—Burlington Gardens
"The Burlington Arcade is a sublimate of superfluities . . . paintings and lithographs for gilded boudoirs, collars for puppy dogs, and silver-mounted whips for spaniels, pocket handkerchiefs in which an islet of cambric is surrounded by an ocean of lace, embroidered garters and braces, filigree flounces, fireworklooking bonnets, scent bottles, sword-knots, brocaded sashes, worked dressing-gowns, inlaid snuff-boxes, and falbalas of all descriptions; these form the stock-in-trade of the merchants who have here their tiny boutiques."[421] This was George Augustus Sala's description of the Burlington Arcade in 1859. It was the first important arcade in England with wide-reaching influence on the development of the building type in both England and America. It has an excellent location in the center of Mayfair, which was at the time the fashionable west section of London and today is the center of luxury trade. This location never detracted from the popularity and commercial success of the arcade, as happened in Paris. It became famous for its elegant architecture, and through the revenues it brought to its builder and owner, Lord Cavendish, the arcade became the embodiment of fashionable, snobbish London.

In August 1815 Lord George Cavendish purchased Burlington House and garden between Piccadilly and Vigo Lane from his nephew, the sixth Duke of Devonshire.[422] He had since the beginning of the year owned enough of the mortgage to begin occupying himself with the plans for remodeling. Thus, as early as April 3, 1815, the following announcement could appear in the *Times*:[423]

Covered Passage, Burlington House, Shopkeepers and Persons in Trade.

. . . being in contemplation to make a communication from Piccadilly in a parallel line with Old Bond Street, through Burlington Gardens to Cork Street and New Bond Street, by means of a covered passage with shops on each side, attention will be paid to persons of respectability desirous of renting such shops. . . . It is intended that the passage should have a uniform and handsome appearance, and that the shops should be constructed on an elegant and commodious plan.

Address, post paid, to Mr. Ware, architect, 5, John Street, Adelphi.

Samuel Ware[424] (1781–1860) was the architect whom Lord Cavendish had engaged for the planning of his "covered passage." He submitted on May 5, 1815, a plan and cost estimate with the following preliminary remarks on the nature of his project: "Report of the Cost and advantages arising from the erection of two Entrance Facades and a double row of shops with a skylight roof between them; forming under it a covered walk extending from Piccadilly through Burlington Gardens to Vigo Lane opposite to Cork Street, intended as a Passage to New Bond Street and as a Piazza for all hardware, wearing apparel, and articles not offensive in appearances nor smell—. The Piazza to consist of two entrances and four double ranges of shops, separated from three open spaces in which the walking way is proposed to be wider than in other parts. The open spaces are called 'Intershops' and the places for selling goods in them and in the two Entrances are called 'Stands.' They will be after the principle of those in Exeter Change. . . ."[425]

Two points are interesting in this text: mention of the Exeter Change and the various designations for the building type, which was new to England, among which the one later used in English-speaking countries, "arcade," seems to be missing. "Covered passage" suggests but does not establish Parisian influence. *Walk, piazza,* and *row* are attempts to create a new concept.

The question of models may be answered partly in the following way. Lord Cavendish had been in Paris and had seen the Passage des Panoramas—clearly related in siting, in proportions, and in the form of the glass roof—had told his architect about it, and had grasped the extent of the commercial success to which the construction of an arcade could lead. He commissioned a design for an arcade from his architect. Ware, for his part, investigated possible models and had in front of him the Exeter Change, still standing at that time, with its interior double row of open stands. He attempted to create something new out of the two, the local model and the model described to him. There were three design stages: 1815, 1817, and 1818. Ware took more and more to the idea of a continuous arcade, an indication of probable conversations with Lord Cavendish. But these are only guesses. I was unable to find any documentation of the early history of the Burlington Arcade, a structure so important for spreading the arcade building type throughout the world. The Burlington Arcade was only one part of Lord Cavendish's remodeling projects and of his overall goal of remodeling the house and screening off the garden from the rear buildings on Old Bond Street.

Ware worked until 1817 on the remodeling of the old palace, which the third earl of Burlington had built for himself at the beginning of the eighteenth century. In July 1817 he submitted a new plan in which his basic idea from 1815—four double rows of shops divided by three open intervening spaces—was contained. Small steps, to change the sloping floor into level sections, were the only addition. The undated plans[426] now in the Royal Academy Library seem to belong to this stage. The ground plans reproduced here are from these drawings. They show that the number of shops had risen from the 1815 figure of thirty-eight to fifty-four and the number of open stands from twenty to twenty-two. In addition, each shop now had its own open steps which led to an upper story and a mansard level above the glass roof. The financing was planned in such a way[427] that Lord Cavendish would assume the costs only for the rough brickwork and the facades; the finishing of the shops would be imposed on the tenants, who would be responsible for holding to the architect's plans. These were sophisticated techniques for holding down the amount of personal investment and decreasing risk.

The construction project was announced a second time in September 1817 in *The*

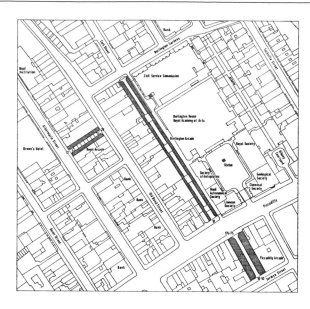

245
London, sites of
Burlington Arcade,
Royal Arcade, and
Piccadilly Arcade,
1966

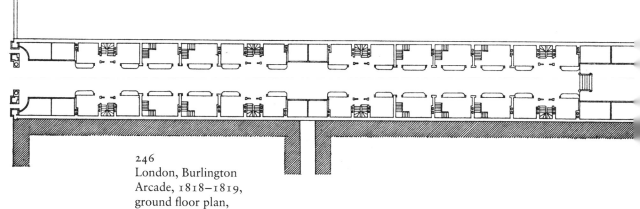

246
London, Burlington
Arcade, 1818–1819,
ground floor plan,
design, 1815

247
Burlington Arcade,
plan of upper story,
detail, 1954

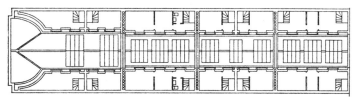

248
Burlington Arcade,
ground floor plan,
detail

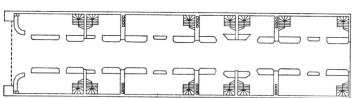

249
Burlington Arcade,
cross section

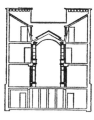

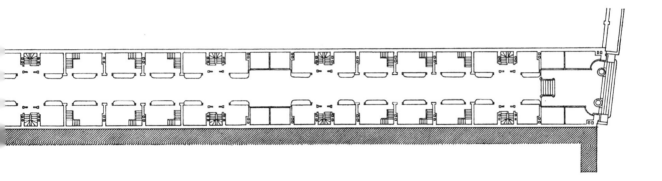

250
Burlington Arcade,
entrance, design,
1815

251
Burlington Arcade,
entrance as built

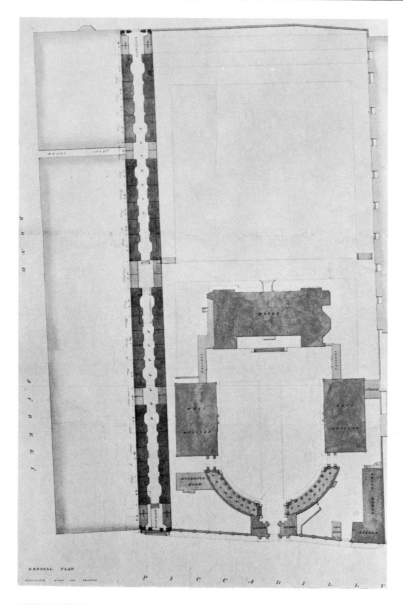

252
Burlington Arcade,
site plan, first ver-
sion, Samuel Ware,
1815

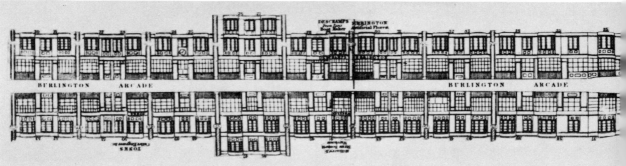

253
Burlington Arcade,
shops, from *Tallis'
Street Views*

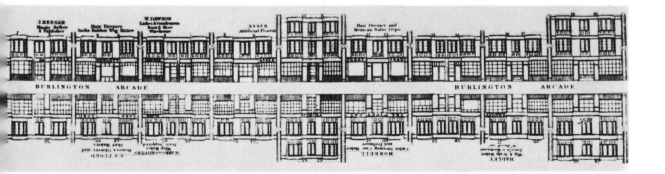

254
Burlington Arcade,
arcade space, view
toward Burlington
Gardens

Gentleman's Magazine,[428] in an article that gave a specific justification for the building concept: "What first gave birth to the idea was the great annoyance to which the garden is subject from the inhabitants of a neighboring street throwing oyster-shells etc. over the walls. . . ." Ware's cost estimate was accepted in February 1818 and construction began. The arcade was opened on March 2, 1819, and within the same month all of the shops were occupied. In the end there were no "intershops"; what would have been their location was perceptible only as a slight widening of the arcade space. The arcade now had only closed shops of varying sizes. The seventy-two shops were divided into twenty-one double shops and thirty single shops.

The Burlington Arcade was a success from the very beginning. In the nineteenth century it was an outstanding luxury and fashion center, an elegant promenade; today, it is more an astonishing selection of jewelry, ties, tobacco, and souvenirs. Robson's *London Commercial Directory*[429] enumerates the following tenants for 1828: "8 milliners, 8 hosiers or glovers, 5 linen shops, 4 shoemakers, 3 hairdressers, 3 jewellers or watchmakers, 2 lacemen, 2 hatters, 2 umbrella or stick sellers, 2 tobacconists, 2 florists, 1 shawlseller, 1 ivory turner, 1 goldsmith, 1 glass manufacturer, 1 optician, 1 wine merchant, 1 pastrycook, 1 bookseller, 1 stationer, 1 music seller, 1 engraver."

The list has a surprising similarity in its composition to those of the Paris arcades. It reveals little, however, about the use of the upper stories, which probably served as residential units. But in Henry Mayhew's book we find a comment which illuminates the occasional use of these rooms:[430] "A friendly bonnet shop for purposes of prostitution: men of position who wished to avoid publicity in their amours dreaded being seen in the vicinity of the arcade at certain hours." These few words indicate the multipurpose character of the arcade and the as yet unexhausted adaptability of this building type. The Burlington Arcade had in addition to the two street entrances a third entrance from Bond Street through the Western Exchange, a generously sized bazaar. A fire from this bazaar spread through a door which was left open into the arcade and destroyed a number of shops on March 26, 1836. This entrance was closed subsequently and is no longer recognizable.

255
Burlington Arcade,
roof

The arcade remained the property of Lord Cavendish's family until 1926, and was then sold. It changed hands after three months once again for the amount of £330,000. In 1931 it was owned by the London Freehold and Leasehold Property Company, Ltd. The company had torn down the entrance facade on Piccadilly (to which a story had been added in 1911) and replaced it with a single wide archway. The architect for the remodeling of the facades was Beresford Pite, whom the *Architectural Review*[431] praised as having "a Michelangelesque provincial manner that gives full scope to the mahogany shop-fitting expert. . . ."

The other entrance facade was replaced in 1937 by a new, modernistic one. Air raids destroyed the four north sections of the arcade in 1940. They were, however, restored to their original condition by the architect W. G. Sinning.[432] The reopening took place on September 16, 1954. Today the Prudential Assurance Company owns the Burlington Arcade.

The Burlington Arcade occupies an elongated rectangle measuring 180 by 11 meters. The boundaries of the site are entirely uninterrupted. The arcade borders to the west on the rear of buildings on Old Bond Street but is still unattached along its entire east side. The body of the building is divided into seventeen sections by fire walls reaching from exterior wall to exterior wall with an archway across the arcade space.[433] The depth of these sections varies by approximately one meter; within each section, the shops vary both architecturally and functionally. The glass roof is also divided by each of the fire walls, thereby making it possible to go up one more story in the three intervals where there was to have been open space and which now differ from the shop sections only in their greater width and a third floor which projects slightly into the arcade. In this way Ware avoided giving the entire length of the arcade a uniform, and, given its length of 180 meters, certainly boring appearance. The differing widths of the shops, the variations of height and width of the arcade space, the different treatment of the arches (with and without archivolts) and the widths of the skylights, which change with the width of the shops—all this transformed the arcade, prevented any monotony, and made it a series of contrasting architectural intervals.

The building is made up of the following components:[434]

a. Double shops with two doors, two large and one small show window which project like bay windows
b. Two narrow shops with a party wall which form a unit, each having an entrance and two show windows
c. Shops set back slightly with a third floor in the arcade
d. End areas with one small and one large shop.

These components are combined in the following way:

d | aba | c | aba | c | aba | c | aba | d

d | aba | c | aba | c | aba | c | aba | d

Each shop in the 3.7-meter-wide arcade has its own spiral staircase,[435] which leads to the cellar rooms; to the upper story, which has projecting windows with bowed corners overlooking the arcade space; and to the mansard, which is outside the arcade space and is lighted by small windows. This composition of units which are both grouped and independently accessible corresponds fully to the early Parisian arcades.

The interior facades of the Burlington Arcade are full of contrast, with their sculptured projecting show windows and the colorfulness of their wood, brick, and glass. The facade grouping of each succeeding section is slightly stepped up to compensate for the gradual slope in the direction of Burlington Gardens.

The ground floor facade, with its alternating show windows and doors, is painted the color of mahogany. The show windows, which were originally divided into small square panes, are of more recent origin. One can see ventilation latticework for the cellar rooms below the sills. The numbers and shop names are uniformly displayed on the wooden moulding strip which crowns the ground floor. The upper story alternates windows, which still have the old small panes, with narrow wall areas of thin, unplastered brick. A wooden moulding at the tops of the window bays finishes the interior facade. The low-pitched wooden saddle roof rests directly on the moulding. The support structure is invisible, as all the surfaces are paneled with wood. Skylights of varying breadth are cut into the compartments of the roof. The ridgepole, with two iron rods on each side, provides lateral support for the glass plates. The long plates of glass are set in an iron framework which is clearly new because old engravings show smaller panes.[436] The lighting technique used in the Burlington Arcade is similar to the one used in the Passage des Panoramas in Paris, as fig. 379 demonstrates.

The two entrance facades necessarily underwent changes as well during the major remodelings. They are the first instance of independent exterior facades in an arcade having no entrance buildings. They are the beginning of an independent Anglo-Saxon development, with examples in Bristol, Philadelphia, and Providence, in which a temple peristyle emerges in place of the modest arcade motif. We can distinguish three phases in the development of the facades for the Burlington Arcade:

1815 (design): The two facades were designed differently.[437] On Piccadilly there is a straight entablature, supported by two Ionic columns with two pilasters in front of the fire wall. Steps lead to the arcade concourse; an iron gate between the columns allows the arcade to be locked. On Vigo Lane, today Burlington Gardens, the entablature is supported by two pairs of close-set columns on either side of an arch on smaller columns.

1818 (construction): In the built version, the two entrances are identical.[438] Three arches on three-quarter Ionic capitals, on square shafts inside and out, support a balustrade with three divisions. The capitals, the archivolts, the abutment moulding, and the coping stones are identical to those on the arches inside the arcade. The archway openings were originally meant to have double doors, but in the end only an iron gate was installed.

Remodelings, 1911, 1931, 1937: In 1911 Pite added another full upper story to the south facade as well as a stylistically related "loggia" on the lower level. He placed the coat of arms of the Chesham family, the last owners of the arcade, in the center of the upper balustrade.[439] The three arches were removed by the same architect in 1931 and replaced by a shallow segmental arch over the entire expanse, projecting to the line of the street. The decorative additions to the arches, somewhat bombastic in style, stand in crass opposition to the arcade's restrained Regency style. The north entrance was replaced in 1937 by a large opening with a projecting, overhanging roof. It might as well have been the entrance to a large parking garage.

In spite of these changes, the Burlington Arcade, with the Galeries St. Hubert and the Galleria Vittorio Emanuele in Milan, is one of the best-preserved arcades built in the nineteenth century.

Bazaar (project)
The Strand—Exeter Street
Dating from 1826[440] and attributed to John Nash[441] is a plan belonging to a proposal entitled "Proposed for Widening the Strand in the Vicinity of Exeter Change."

The Strand, the only direct connection between the City and the West End, varied in width, a situation which constantly caused traffic jams. The outstanding success of the Regent Street improvements induced the Commissioners of His Majesty's Woods, Forests, and Land Revenue once more to commission John Nash to rebuild the areas between Whitehall, Pall Mall, and the Strand to relieve the traffic between the City and London's new commercial areas.[442] The plans that Nash submitted envisioned the creation of a large square, bordered by the National Gallery on the north—in 1830 named Trafalgar Square—and the straightening of the West Strand between St. Martin's Lane and Bedford Street, along which new and uniform blocks would be constructed. It also suggested the demolition of the Exeter Change and the widening of the Strand on its north side between Southampton Street and Catherine Street.

The proposal was for a "glass roofed bazaar" with two rows of shops to be located at the point where the Exeter Change projected into the Strand and obstructed the way. This bazaar would have connected Exeter Street with the Strand and would apparently have been a freestanding building, to leave access to the rows of houses situated behind it, in the manner of the Albany. These intentions, however, are not immediately recognizable in the plan itself. Exeter Hall, a meeting hall, was built in place of the bazaar, and serves religious and political gatherings.

The West Strand Improvements were completed not by Nash but by others—architects who had worked under his direction.[443] They were built in 1829–1831 in a uniform style. The buildings were all four-storied, had stucco facades, and uninterrupted storefronts on the ground level. The shop owners and businessmen of the city hoped to stem the migration of their customers to the new, fashionable commercial districts of the West End.[444] In conjunction with the Improvements, two further arcades were built in London, the Lowther Arcade and the Exeter Arcade, neither of which had much commercial success and neither of which is still standing.

Lowther Arcade (figs. 256–267)
Strand—Adelaide Street

The Lowther Arcade was the third large arcade built in London. It was part of the West Strand Improvements of John Nash. Lowther Arcade crosses a triangular block formed by the West Strand, Adelaide Street, and William Street. Only ruins of the original construction on this block still exist today. The entire ground plan, however, has been preserved in an 1830 etching by William Herbert.[445] The only record of the architecture of the arcade is an architect's building survey done in 1902 when the structure was torn down. The most important leaves have been redrawn for reproduction here.[446] It is one of the few arcades for which plans of all of the stories are available.

In terms of typological development, the Lowther Arcade follows the Royal Opera Arcade; its assumes its spatial system but doubles the proportions. It has in turn only one direct successor, the Royal Arcade in Newcastle. With the turn to Renaissance forms in the Victorian era, this variant of the building type, indebted to the Roman vault, took a further step: The arcade was roofed with an iron framework, with less expenditure of time and money. Lowther Arcade fulfilled a real traffic function by connecting the north side of Trafalgar Square to the West Strand through St. Martin's Courtyard.

Between 1829 and 1831 the north side of the West Strand was developed according to Nash's ideas and to Decimus Burton's more exact plans. New blocks were built between Charing Cross, St. Martin's Lane, and Agar Street; various architects participated. Robert Smirke is said to have built the double turrets, which were called "pepper pots" locally. Witherden Young and William Herbert[447] are considered the builders of the Lowther Arcade. I was unable to find documentation for any attribution.[448]

The Lowther Arcade was named after Lord Lowther, the former Chief Commissioner of Woods and Forests. It housed twenty-five shops inside and six additional ones on the street. The Adelaide Gallery,

an elongated hall with rounded skylights used for exhibitions and display of inventions, adjoined it on the north. In this place "Mr. Jacob Perkins exhibited his Steam Gun. A living electrical eel was shown here from August 1838 to March 1848, when it died; and in 1832 was formed here a Society for the Exhibition of Models of Inventions. The rooms were subsequently let for concerts, dancing and exhibitions."[449]

The Lowther Arcade has gone down in the history of London's commercial life as the toymakers' arcade. French, German, and Swiss toy merchants established themselves there and made the arcade a specialized marketplace, the object of every child's dreams. Throughout the Victorian era, children crowded the arcade with their governesses.[450] The high point was Christmas time. The arcade was lit up for the occasion and transformed into a bazaar by additional open stands. It was called "an Aladdin fairy palace crowded with all the glories and wonders a child's fancy can conceive."[451] Further details of its story may be culled from an article in *Country Life*:[452] "Long after it was demolished in 1902 older people would recollect with nostalgia the Lowther Arcade's particular smell—a mixture of lavender and sawdust, and the gay din of toy trumpets, musical tops and the shouts of glee from the hundreds of excited children. Sherlock Holmes knew the Lowther Arcade and in 'The Final Problem,' Dr. Watson, on Holmes's instructions, used the double entrance of the arcade to try to outwit Moriarty, by driving in a hansom to the Strand entrance and dashing to the top end, where a brougham was waiting to rattle him off to Victoria Station. . . ." In spite of all these lively reports, the Lowther Arcade was not a commercial success. It was not located in London's main commercial district and had to content itself with the chance customer. Thus, serving a genuine traffic function is not alone a guarantee of financial success.

The Lowther Arcade was put up for auction in 1898 but, with a price tag of £30,000, could not find a buyer.[453] It was purchased only in 1901 by Coutt's Bank. Previously the bank had been located on the site of the former New Exchange. The building survey was made in the process of remodeling the arcade into a bank.

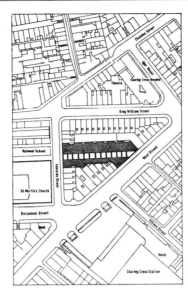

256
London, site of
Lowther Arcade,
1875

The Lowther Arcade was an incomparable piece of architecture. Its spatial dimensions were imposing—75 meters long, 6.1 meters wide, and 10.5 meters high. Here there occurred, at the same time as in the Galerie d'Orléans in Paris, a leap in proportions. The use of pendentive cupolas is comparable only to the Eastern bazaars (Constantinople, Isfahan). Yet it is doubtful that these domed bazaars were known and therefore chosen as models.

The Lowther Arcade stood on a site parallel to William Street. It ran straight through on the northern side but dovetailed on the southern side and ran diagonal to the Strand. The structure is made up of twelve square bays of identical plan partitioned by fire walls. With this system a diagonal section, necessary on the Strand, was impossible, so the architect resorted to some bold tricks, as is clear from the plan and sections. The facades on Adelaide Street and on the Strand were one story higher than the arcade buildings. They served as the center projections for the blocks, which were flanked by turrets. They had a colossal order of pilasters reaching to the third story and stood in no direct relation to the arcade behind them, which was accessible only through an opening with two Doric columns on the ground floor. These incongruities become clear when the plans are compared to the old photographs of the Strand approach.

The entire block to which the Lowther Arcade belonged consisted of buildings of a single type. On the ground floor there was a shop (the depths varied) with an independently accessible staircase and a light well. The staircase served the shop as well as the upper stories, which had a separate function. This design also characterized the arcade buildings.

Let us look at the individual floors in more detail. The cellar offered enormous storage areas, since it extended under the entire arcade space. It was accessible via paired stairways, one for every two arcade units. The light shaft reached to the height of the landing. The stairs also provided access to the sanitary facilities. In line with the steps there were usually four cellar rooms which could also be used by the tenants on the upper stories. The two rooms underneath the arcade itself were illuminated through the floor above. Vaulted cellar rooms extended far under the street.

Twenty-five shops occupied the ground floor. They ran the length of the arcade, al-

257
London, Lowther
Arcade, 1829–1831,
demolished 1902,
basement plan

258
Lowther Arcade,
ground floor plan

259
Lowther Arcade, sec-
ond floor plan

260
Lowther Arcade,
third floor plan

261
Lowther Arcade,
fourth floor plan

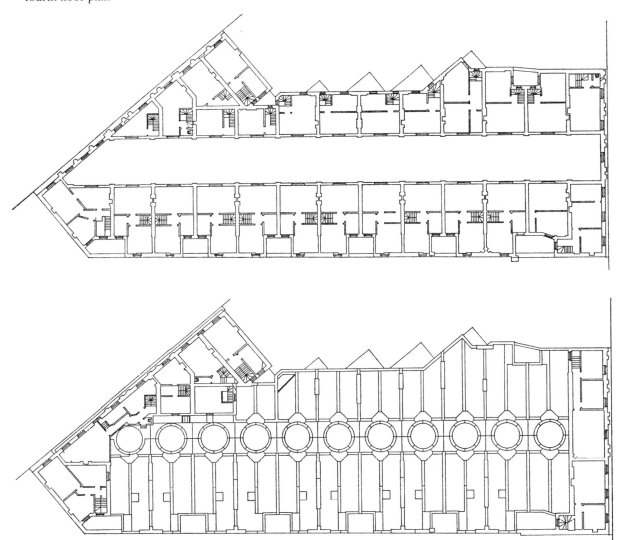

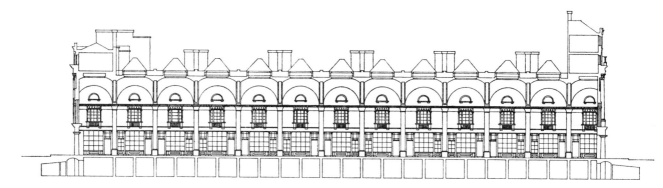

262
Lowther Arcade,
longitudinal section

263
Lowther Arcade,
cross section through
middle of bay

264
Lowther Arcade,
cross section through
division between
bays

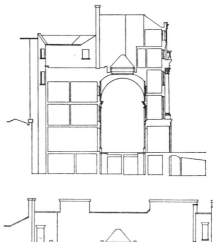

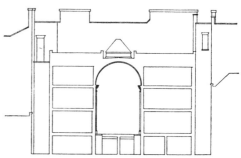

265
Lowther Arcade, ar-
cade space

266
Lowther Arcade,
West Strand facade

267
Lowther Arcade, in-
terior facades, from
Tallis' Street Views

ternating with Corinthian pilasters which extended two stories and were joined to the support arches of the vaults. The shop facades had three vertical divisions created by a central show window with square panes and doors on either side of it. A glass door led into the shop, a solid one into a narrow hallway which led to the steps. The steps were combined in pairs and had a common light well, which by this arrangement could be as large as necessary to light both the stairs and the rear area of the shop. The fireplaces were all on the walls without steps. The ground floor plan from the 1902 survey provides only an incomplete notion of the original design, since in over seventy years of use both the shops and the staircases were individually altered.

The second floor gave onto the arcade space only through triple windows, of which the middle section opened. Within was a stairway that made a complete turn. The depth of the space was divided by a lateral stairwell into a larger room facing the arcade and a smaller one illuminated by the light well. The turn in the stairs made possible the subdivision of the space on the third floor into three rooms, of which the smallest may have been the kitchen or bathroom. The room that opened onto the arcade had only a small lunette and was on a level with the pendentives. The second and third floors could thus be rented as separate apartments or as apartments for the store. The modifications on the ground floor reveal that the apartments were rented in the majority of cases by the store owners themselves.

The arcade was roofed by twelve pendentive cupolas on a square base; openings with a diameter of 3 meters were set into the vault. The arches, the baselines of the cupolas, and the web of the vault were covered with stucco ornament. If we can trust the etching reproduced in fig. 266, the cupolas were originally glass hemispheres which were constructed of concentric rings of specially cut glass panes with an opening at the center. The building survey, however, shows conical cupolas constructed of triangular panes of glass, similar to those of the Royal Arcade in Newcastle.

The fourth floor had rooms only in the two entrance buildings; they allowed a view of the arcade's roof structure. The ridge was sheathed with lead, which also edged the round skylights and saddled the roof areas over the fire walls. The roof was drained by gutters over the light wells. The chimneys extended above the roof as blocks in the coping. The stairwells on the uppermost story were lit by a dormer window.

The longitudinal section reveals the carefully balanced proportions of the interior facades: window and door openings which decreased in size with the height of the structure and a balance between horizontal thrust and vertical line. The alternating fall of light and shadow and the mighty rhythm of the spanning arches in contrast with the small divisions of the facade in continuous line must have created a spatial experience comparable only to that of the nave of a church. The full longitudinal section, reproduced in fig. 267, is taken from Tallis, who writes:[454] "Lowther Arcade is short but for beauty will vie with any similar building in the Kingdom; its architecture is chaste and pleasing; its shops well supplied, tastefully decorated, and brilliantly illuminated at night. It forms a pleasant lounge either in the sultry heat of summer or the biting cold of winter. . . ."

City Arcade (project) (fig. 268)
Bank of England—London Wall
I was able to find only a site plan of this project, which introduced a series of monumental arcade projects during the 1840s and 1850s.[455] The proposed arcade was to cut through the old City where arcades had never been built before. The project, the work of Jeffrey, was submitted about 1830. Although later arcade projects appeared primarily in conjunction with an express conveyance system, only a pedestrian zone was planned here. There was to be a large rotunda in the middle.

Exeter Arcade (fig. 269)
Catherine Street—Wellington Street
One can hardly pick out the location of the Exeter Arcade (also called the New Exeter Change) on a modern city map. It lay between Wellington Street, which had been extended in the 1840s through to Bow Street, and Catherine Street.[456] It was built by Sydney Smirke, Sr., in 1842–1843, but had been torn down by 1863 because of a total lack of success. The demolition made way for the Strand Music Hall.[457] The construction of the Aldwych and the widening of Waterloo Street changed the entire area dramatically. Exeter Arcade was the first arcade in London to be inserted into a city block already completely occupied by

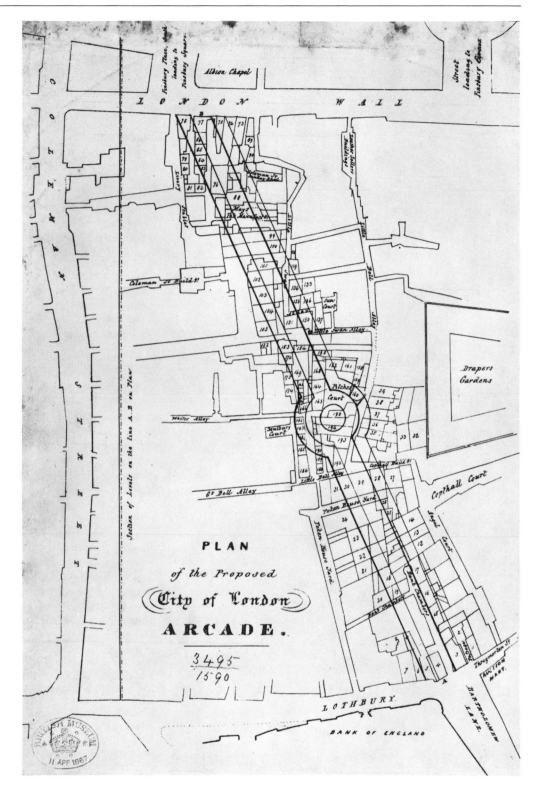

268
London, City of Lon-
don Arcade, project,
ca. 1839

LONDON

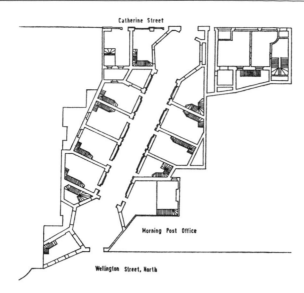

Catherine Street

Morning Post Office

Wellington Street, North

269
London, Exeter Arcade, ground floor plan

buildings. The site was so angular and irregular that only an arcade which cut through the block on a diagonal was possible.

This aesthetic flaw was concealed by two hexagonal spaces which were vaulted but had no glazing; they accommodated the oblique entrances. The interior "avenue" had a continuous glass roof[458]—London's first. There were nine shops along the "avenue," each with its own upper story. The dimensions were very modest; the length of the arcade was 32 meters, the width 3.2 meters, and the height 6.1 meters. The interior of the arcade is said to have been painted with Pompeian-style murals.

Coming after ten years during which not one arcade was built in England, the Exeter Arcade, together with the tiny arcade on the Isle of Wight, is one of the first of the Victorian era.

Gye's Arcade (project)
Bank of England—Fleet Street—Strand—Trafalgar Square
In 1855 the House of Commons considered proposals by Joseph Paxton and William Moseley for "metropolitan communications" for London, which threatened to suffocate in its own traffic. As a result of the debates, an article[459] appeared in *The Builder* in December 1855, announcing plans for a "glass street," which the author, Mr. Gye, Director of the Royal Italian Opera, Covent Garden, had already submitted in 1845 to Sir Charles Barry and Mr. Manby, secretary to the Society of Civil Engineers. Excerpts from the article are quoted here, because they convey a city planning vision which was totally new but which was immanent in the architectural concept of the arcade. According to Gye's report:

The Arcade will extend from a point near the Bank of England to another at Trafalgar Square, taking the line north of Cheapside, Fleet Street, and the Strand. It will be constructed entirely on arches of sufficient height to pass the numerous streets, without presenting any obstacle to the ordinary traffic entrances being made at the principal cross streets. The width of the arcade itself, besides the space occupied by the shops, will be nearly that of King William Street, City, from house to house. The roof of glass will be 70 feet in height. The structure will not be in one straight line, but will present a series of direct arcades, crescents, and rotundas, forming one uninterrupted covered promenade, accommodating itself to the various churches and public buildings by which it will have to pass. To these buildings it will serve as a most convenient approach, and will have branch avenues to many of the most important, such as the proposed railway stations, the theatres, etc.

As in some parts of the line, property of comparatively inconsiderable value will be passed through, the dimensions of the structure will in places be greatly increased; the arcade, on its way, expanding into several magnificent galleries, or halls.

Portions of the arcade will be appropriated to reading-rooms, exhibition-rooms, concert-rooms, large apartments for public meetings, baths, cafés on the Paris plans, etc., as well as to shops of every variety of trade, except such as might from their nature be unfitting to the place. An extensive flower market, constructed entirely of glass, will occupy one portion of the line. [Barry had built the Opera Flower Market near the opera during this period.] In fact, it is intended that the whole shall form a splendid avenue, combining the grand desideratum of a covered communication with a spacious and luxurious promenade. . . . With the exception of the brick walls, iron and glass will be the chief materials throughout. . . .

The article reports a little further on that Mr. Gye also planned a pneumatic postal service using iron tubes; it would be driven by compressed air created by a propellor. "The objects of the projector are not confined to this one line, east to west, his proposal being to carry out a system of arcades throughout the metropolis."

It is fantastic that as early as 1845 there should have emerged from the realm of private enterprise a proposal for such a system, a suprastructure laid over the city that would solve countless problems in one stroke. What London tourist does not have this vision today as he crawls along the hopelessly congested streets at a snail's pace, always in first gear, and daydreams away? Here, in 1845, one year before the building of the more than block-long Galeries St. Hubert in Brussels and five years before the construction of the Crystal Palace, we find them imagined in perfect form. Perhaps Gye had thought of the many arcades of Paris and envisioned them as an independent and cohesive system. We will never know. But it is certain that knowledge of the great new train stations, with their long glass halls, which had collected on the periphery of the inner city, influenced this vision.

London Bridge Arcade

Tooley Street—London Bridge Station

London Bridge Arcade, or Railway Arcade,[460] was built in 1850–1851 by the South-Eastern Railway Company. From descriptions, it was similar to the Lowther Arcade and was a kind of vestibule to the train station. It proved, however, to be a bad risk, and gave way to the viaducts of the new train line to Charing Cross in 1863.[461]

The arcade is said to have been approximately 45 meters long and 18 meters high, as it was two-storied. The ground floor was level with Tooley Street and the upper floor with the train platforms. According to descriptions, there was a large refreshment area in the center; the decoration was elegant and in the Renaissance style. In type, this arcade would have been the equivalent of the large lateral halls of arcade character in the major train stations, such as Hamburg.

Royal Arcade

New Oxford Street—West Block, North Side

In 1847 the direct communication between Oxford Street and High Holborn, called New Oxford Street, was opened to traffic, thus initiating the development of Oxford Street into one of London's main commercial arteries. The new street led directly through one of the most infamous sections in London: St. Giles's Rookery. The street was lined with commercial buildings, as *Old and New London* describes: "Many of the houses, especially on the north side, have a pleasing appearance, built as they are of red brick and stone dressings, in the domestic Tudor and Louis XIV style of architecture, whilst some of the housefronts are of Ionic and Corinthian character. In about the centre is what is called the Royal Arcade, a glass-roofed arcade of shops extending along the rear of four or five of the houses, and having an entrance from the street at each end. The shops here are mostly confined to the sale of drapery and haberdashery. This arcade was opened about 1852 with great expectations, but it never took with the public, and is almost unknown. . . ."[462]

Old city maps suggest that the arcade lay parallel to New Oxford Street on a site occupied today by new department store buildings. Merrick and Pennethorne have been named as architects and the date of construction placed at various points between 1845 and 1852. The arcade could not have been much of a success since its only advantage was that it served as a detour.

Crystal Way (project) (figs. 270–271)
Cheapside—Chancery Lane—Drury Lane—Seven Dials—Regent Circus and Piccadilly Circus
On May 10, 1855, William Moseley, the London architect, was invited (one month before Paxton) to appear before the Select Committee on Metropolitan Improvements to answer questions on his project for a Crystal Way.[463]

We can envision the scale of Moseley's project from the details of a report included with the plans.[464] It is somewhat similar to Gye's proposal of ten years earlier. Like Gye, he suggested a new communication between the City and the West End which would relieve congestion on Oxford Street and the Strand. Yet his arcade structures looked different in section, were designed to serve several means of conveyance, and were multilevel. The system, somewhat clearer if one looks at a section, may be described in the following way. The arcade is a continuous building which contains two levels of arcade space. The lower level is illuminated from the side and serves trains, or rather, subways. The upper level has a continuous glass skylight and serves the pedestrian. The streets cross and run as open bridges through the half-buried lower arcade space. Both floors are accessible by staircases at these intersections. Both arcade spaces are lined with buildings which house shops, apartments, offices, hotels, and public facilities. Their depth is determined by the possibilities of the location. It is clear from the minutes how accurately Moseley calculated the business that would be generated and the anticipated costs and profits.

I quote here Moseley's rationale for the project:[465]
The object of the railway which I propose, is to relieve the great lines of traffic of Holborn on the one side, and the Strand on the other . . . [by taking] an intermediate course, commencing on the east at the end of Cheapside . . . [Thus,] having two terminations, it forms a fork at the western end; one end terminating at the Circus, in Oxford Street, and the other at the bottom of the Quadrant, in Piccadilly; the object being to take the great stream of traffic coming down Oxford Street on the one, and that which comes down Piccadilly on the other, and bring them over and under all the existing thoroughfares to the end of Cheapside. I propose that it shall specially apply itself to those who would walk otherwise, or who would ride in omnibuses or cabs, and who would therefore wish to get in the safest or at the quickest rate from one point to the other; and though it has no communication with any other line of railroad, I think it would offer sufficient public advantage to be complete in itself. A question has been put, whether it should be connected with any other line of railroad; But I am myself of opinion that it is of itself complete, and I think the calculations which have been made as to the traffic will show, that it is complete in itself as a paying undertaking, and will sufficiently relieve the population of London passing by the Strand or Holborn. Some streets have been proposed partly in this very line; but I believe that if a street were constructed, instead of the railway and superway which I intend, it would not give the relief required, because, as it would be shorter by a furlong to the end of Oxford Street, it would have the effect of diverting at once both streams of traffic into one line. But I believe I avoid that entirely, by selecting from the streets the class which I have before named, and by taking them independently of the thoroughfares and streets. Those who walk I conceive require a safe and dry mode of transit; those who ride require a quick mode of transit; as it is, by an omnibus 20 minutes would be consumed going from one point to the other, and by railroad five minutes only would be consumed. I generally believe that I offer a mass of people such facilities for which they would be willing to pay that a sufficient sum will be realised to pay for the whole undertaking.

On closer study it becomes clear that a total of ten stations were projected. They were to be located at points where the line intersected important cross streets. The Crystal Way would cross over these streets as described. The overpass at Farrington Street would be the only exception. It was cut in so deeply that even the train line had to cross it by means of a viaduct—the function that the Holborn viaduct serves today. Stations were proposed for the following points: Oxford Street, Wardour Street, Green Street, Great St. Andrew's Street (where the other arm branched off to the Quadrant), Drury Lane (south of Lincoln's Inn Fields), Chancery Lane, Farringdon Street, and Cheapside. The dimensions of the arcade were such as to accommodate 25,000 visitors daily on each level. Each train could accommodate 139 passengers and run at intervals of five minutes. The entrance fee for Crystal Way would be one penny.

The overall length of the structure would be approximately 3.8 kilometers. Approximately 5.3 kilometers of storefront would

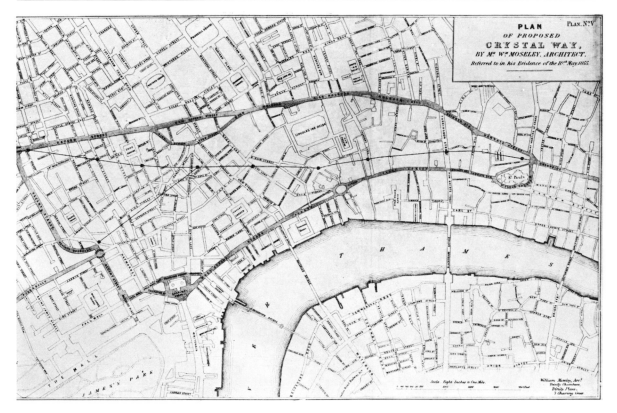

270
London, Crystal
Way, project, 1855,
site plan

271
Crystal Way, cross
section

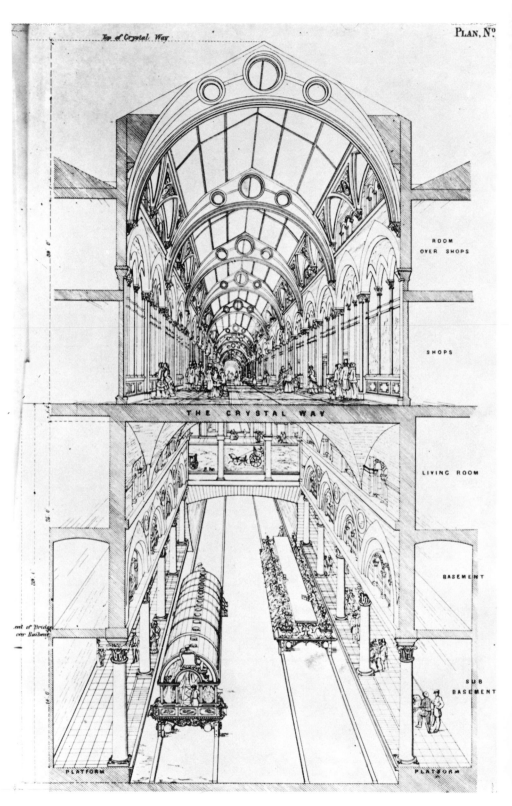

PLAN, Nº.

Top of Crystal Way

ROOM
OVER SHOPS

SHOPS

THE CRYSTAL WAY

LIVING ROOM

BASEMENT

SUB
BASEMENT

PLATFORM

PLATFORM

be provided. To make way for the building, 427 structures, most privately owned and many in considerable need of repair, would be torn down. Two million pounds was the estimated cost.

Given such huge figures, it is small wonder that the Crystal Way remained a project. It failed, like so many other improvements proposed throughout the century, because of the inertia of countless large and small property owners, businessmen, and merchants who still today prevent any all-inclusive solution for the problems of London's inner city.

Great Victorian Way (project) (fig. 272)
Ring arcade, which connected all of London's train stations and turned into the center in the direction of Piccadilly Circus
On June 7, 1855, Sir Joseph Paxton,[466] landscape architect and creator of the huge, prefabricated glass house for the first world's fair in 1851 in London, was examined by the Select Committee on Metropolitan Improvements.[467]

The old Crystal Palace, which stood in Hyde Park, had inspired his proposal to solve all of London's traffic problems at once in a decidedly new way. He saw in its transept of the palace one part of a huge arcade which would enclose central London as a ring boulevard. It would connect all of the train stations and would contain pedestrian zones and unimpeded rapid transit on several levels.

Paxton had begun with the conservatory, which sheltered stationary objects, plants. From it had developed the exhibition building, which could contain and shelter moveable objects. Its character as a space of transition and movement led directly to the idea of an arcade. It would serve the mobile individual above all and would protect him from inclement weather. Paxton had represented his idea to the committee as a traffic space transformed into an endless compound. Unfortunately, the report includes only a city map with the directional lines drawn in; the sections and details for the Thames crossing no longer exist.[468] We are thus forced to construct a picture for ourselves out of his answers.

The Great Victorian Way was designed to be 16 kilometers long; it would connect station to station with wide arcs and would cross the most important traffic arteries, and, with a branch from south of the river, thrust directly into the new city center, Piccadilly Circus, thus crossing the Thames three times. It would have the same section throughout. Paxton's idea of the arcade bridges was inspired by the houses on old London Bridge. He refers to it expressly. The floor of the arcade space, 22 meters wide and 33 meters high, would be at street level. A total of eight train lines would run above this level in closed side galleries. There would be four express train lines and four local train lines. The buildings supporting the glass vault would serve various functions. There would be shops and offices between the City and Regent Street, apartments in Brompton, and wherever sites allowed it, hotels, entertainment establishments, pensions, and other facilities would be built along the back of the arcade. The arcade would be interrupted at Kensington Gardens, and the railway line would go underground at this point. Special fixtures would guarantee ventilation of the space, control the thick smoke of the trains, and heat some parts of the arcade. Vehicle traffic would be permitted in the arcade at night in order to make deliveries to all of the projected establishments.

It was a logical but gigantic and unrealizable project. It would cost £34 million and would be built in individual stages. The project was publicly discussed and was praised; even the Queen and Prince Albert requested a private presentation and were warmly enthusiastic.[469] Everyone's imagination was on fire, but no one was able to offer an idea of how to set the colossal plan in motion.

Paxton's project for the Great Victorian Way is the last of a series from the early Victorian period. All used the arcade concept to solve public problems with private capital. Anyone who is familiar with London today and has experienced its unsolvable traffic problems will appreciate the undiminished relevance of this proposal for a master system of traffic control, overcoming all local problems, of such architectural quality. But the Great Victorian Way, or the Paxton Arcade, as it was also called,[470] remains a utopian vision.

Royal Arcade (project)
Regent Street—New Bond Street
In approximately 1862 there appeared a sketch for a long arcade which would connect Regent Street to New Bond Street south of Conduit Street.[471] C. B. Richards was named as the architect. The design was shown in April 1864 in an "Architec-

LONDON

272
London, Great Victo-
rian Way, project,
1855, site plan

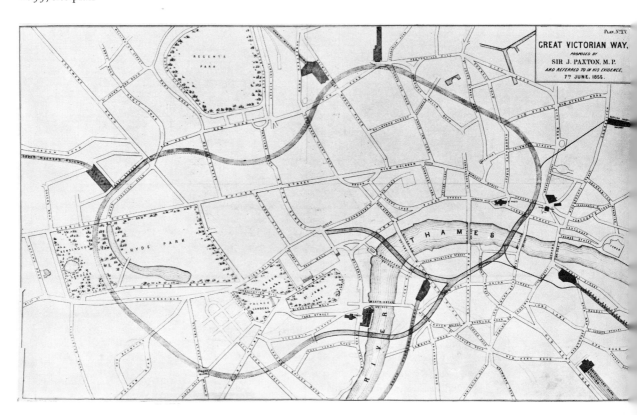

tural Exhibition of Conduit Street" and was discussed during the same year in many city committee meetings. The proposal, however, was rejected.[472] There was doubt as to the need for such an arcade, and fear that it would provide new hiding places for prostitution, as had the Burlington Arcade.[473]

A 9-meter-wide, three-story-high building was planned for the arcade. Art galleries were to have occupied the upper floors. The width of the space suggests that the upper stories were reached by galleries.

Royal Arcade (figs. 273–275)
Old Bond Street—Albemarle Street 12
One of the most beautiful Victorian arcades lies between Old Bond and Albemarle Streets in the midst of some of London's most exclusive shops and galleries. Liveried figures jump to open doors, Rolls Royces move slowly, and impeccably dressed nobility from all over the world visit and shop here. This is the Royal Arcade, ennobled by Queen Victoria's purchases of riding habits from H. W. Brettel's and of knitting wool.[474] Built in 1879, the Royal Arcade was originally called simply The Arcade. It was renamed in 1882 to honor the numerous customers of royal descent. It has a single traffic function; it connects Brown's Hotel, formerly one of the city's most famous hotels, directly to Bond Street. It facilitates moving from shop to shop; both street and direction may be changed via the arcade.

The architecture of this arcade is extravagant in the high Victorian style, but the decoration and the individual architectonic elements counterbalance one another. The architecture is ideally functional; it advertises and tempts. The spatial relation to the bazaar is apparent.

The Royal Arcade was partially destroyed in the war but has been fully restored. The structure fits flush into a continuous block of buildings. It has three stories. Each has nine facing shops from which the upper stories are individually accessible. The architectural division of the arcade space corresponds to the shop unit. It is subdivided into square bays which in their overall arrangement are reminiscent of the Lowther Arcade, except that they do not support cupolas but are open. The glass saddle roof is continuous. The ridgepole rests on arched sections with round perforations in the manner of early cast-iron beams. They produce a cross between two

roofing systems which leads to a considerable reduction of perspective, thereby giving the space, in spite of its short 40 meters, a fascinating liveliness. The architecture exploits the contrast of light and shadow. This play is facilitated by the use of color on the facades, which are lighter on the upper stories. The typical large, projecting show windows are done in black and gold, as are the columns. The upper stories were originally pink but are now white and yellow. The profile of the arcade space is also expressed by the street facades, except that a bridge is suspended in each of the end sections. The bridges are glassed in on both sides and have balconies toward both the street and the arcade. The street facades are reminiscent of the nearby Burlington Arcade; they were originally tripartite with a high, pedimented center, flanked and crowned by statues. The four giant columns were crowned with urns; today they are gone, and the columns have been replaced on the ground floor by a continuous lintel which destroys the structure of the facade.[475]

Liverpool Street Station Arcade
Old Broad Street—Liverpool Street
This is one of the many smaller arcades which were built in conjunction with Underground stations in London. It connects Liverpool Street Station to the entrance of the Underground.

Brompton Arcade
Brompton Road—Dasie Street
This small arcade was built around the turn of the century.

Park Mansions Arcade
This small, angled arcade has a beautiful glass cupola over the center. It is located diagonally across from the Brompton Arcade.

Grand Arcade
Northumberland Avenue—Charing Cross, corner of Strand
This arcade was part of the Grand Buildings on Charing Cross, designed by the architects M. E. and D. H. Collins.[476] The small, wide arcade space originally had a vaulted glass roof which, however, has been altered. The arcade, although prominently located, is completely neglected.

Piccadilly Arcade (figs. 276, 277)
Piccadilly 174–175—Jermyn Street 52–53
In the extension of the Burlington Arcade, south of Piccadilly, the Piccadilly Arcade, built almost 100 years later, connects Pic-

273
London, Royal Arcade, 1879, arcade space

274
Royal Arcade, Albemarle Street facade

275
Royal Arcade, corner

276
London, Piccadilly
Arcade, 1909–1910

277
Piccadilly Arcade,
ground floor plan

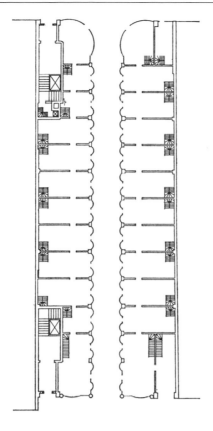

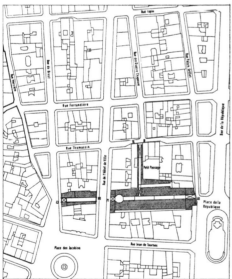

278
Lyon, site of the Passage de l'Argue,
1966

cadilly to Jermyn Street. It is the most recent arcade in London of any architectural importance.[477] It belongs to a whole series of smaller arcade structures in the center of the city and in the neighboring sections. The building of the market halls and of the entrances to the Underground led to the construction of these arcades.

Piccadilly Arcade already demonstrates a certain atrophy of architectural thinking. It is a dependent structure and becomes simply a passageway with shops. It is barely illuminated by a few round skylights. The arcade descends toward Jermyn Street. The facades step down correspondingly. With their close-set, bowed show windows, they give the arcade a certain charm which stays in one's memory.

The ground plan of the arcade[478] reveals a supporting skeleton into which fit a total of twenty-six shops, each with its own stairs to the low-ceilinged mezzanine levels, visible from the arcade because of the small balconies squeezed underneath the roof. The two staircases to an additional four upper stories are accessible only from the street. The arcade was built in 1909–1910 after a design by Thrale Jell.[479]

Regent Arcade
Regent Street—Argyll Street
Regent Arcade was a small arcade with twenty shops which crossed one of Regent Street's largest commercial blocks.[480] Today it is no longer standing. It was illuminated by a low central cupola and two rectangular skylights. It was praised for its interior metal facade. Gordon Jeeves was the architect.

LUXEMBOURG
Passage de l'Hôtel de Ville
Rue des Curés—Place Guillaume
This tiny arcade with a few shops is little more than an expanded corridor.

LYON
Passage de l'Argue (fig. 278)
Rue de Brest 43—Rue de l'Hôtel de Ville 71–80—Place de la République 40—Rue Thomassin
Passage de l'Argue is the earliest of the three great French arcades outside Paris.[481] It was built in 1825–1828,[482] Vincent Farges of Lyon was the architect.[483] The center of Lyon is located on the small peninsula between the Saône and the Rhône across from the old city. Its main axis is the Rue de la République, which

connects the Hôtel de Ville and the Place de la République. Before construction of the arcade, a small, dirty street ran along the area which the architect used for the new arcade construction. The name de l'Argue refers to a gold and silver refinery which had formerly been located in the alleyway. The arcade connects the Place de la République to the Rue de Brest, the second most important north-south street at the time, running from the Place de Terreaux to the Place des Jacobins. This location between two lively commercial streets was favorable; and it seems that the arcade was in its early days the center of luxury trade in Lyons and the preferred locale for *flâneurs* of Lyon.

The arcade's 142-meter length is accentuated by an octagon which divides it not quite in half. It has a secondary wing toward the Rue Thomassin, called the Petit Passage, and forms a continuation of the Rue des Quatre Chapeaux. In 1856 the Rue Président Herriot was constructed as the third north-south axis, dividing the Passage de l'Argue into two parts. This is the layout of the arcade as it stands today. The entryways, glass roof, and some of the shops were remodeled about 1850 in the style of the time. The entry on the Place de la République, however, is still in its original form. The architecture of the arcade space has been distorted by shop renovations and remodeling. Some of the shop facades have been preserved and display show windows divided by close-spaced rows of arches reminiscent of the Galerie Véro-Dodat in Paris. The buildings in the interior of the arcade are two-storied and are set back about 2 meters above the glass roof, where there are two additional stories with apartments. The staircases are accessible through the arcade.

We can learn something about the history and the continually changing uses of the Passage de l'Argue from Louis Maynard, *Dictionnaire de Lyonnaiseries*.[484] In chronological order:

March 2, 1828: Opening of the Théâtre Café by Monsieur Seguin, celebrated by pantomimes and dancing.

April 9, 1834: Rebelling workers barricaded themselves in the arcade during the unrest in Lyon and shot at soldiers, who could think of no solution but to bring in two cannons and fire on the arcade.

1836: A fashionable restaurant was opened in the arcade by Monsieur Caillot.

1860: The Théâtre des Bouffes Lyonnaises (comic opera) opened on the south side of the arcade. The cinema which stands on the site today has kept the same name.

The Théâtre de Guignol stood for a long time in the Petit Passage, the narrow wing of the arcade toward the Rue Thomassin, where the tradition of the famous Lyon Punch and Judy shows was preserved. Later, there was a cabaret at the same location.

Passage de l'Hôtel-Dieu
Quai Courmont—Place de la République
The passage de l'Hôtel-Dieu was opened in 1895 by Dubusson de Christot on the site of the former Boucherie de l'Hôptial,[485] which had been torn down in 1840. The arcade is no longer standing but is said to have been the center of the jewelry and goldsmith trades.

Passage des Terreaux
Mentioned in a book on the streets of Lyon as a "passage couvert," this structure is no longer standing.[486]

MALAGA
Arcade
Plaza de la Constitution—Calle de Santa Maria

MANCHESTER
In Manchester, the great industrial and commercial city, conditions for the building of arcades were different from those in Leeds. There were no parallel commercial streets of equal activity, but only streets at angles to one another which connected the stations to: Deansgate, Market Street, Piccadilly, and Oldham Road. As a result, the five arcades of Manchester did not flourish. Deansgate Arcade, Barton Arcade, and Exchange Arcade had entrances on Deansgate. Victoria Arcade was part of a block between Deansgate, St. Mary's Gate, and Victoria Street. The fifth arcade, Lancaster Avenue, connected the Corn Exchange to Victoria Station.[487] All five were part of a commercial block rather than independent, established buildings, and they had arcade spaces furnished with galleries and set back toward the top.

These commercial buildings equipped with arcades were products of the changing city center of Manchester during the boom years 1870–1900. They transformed Manchester into a modern commercial city whose character was expressed in the Town Hall, the Royal Exchange, and the

Corn Exchange. Today, the center city of Manchester, partially destroyed by bombs in World War II, has suffered the same fate as that of Birmingham, although the extent of the demolition has been less. The noble commercial city of the Victorian era with its then red office buildings and warehouses (now blackened by soot and factory smoke), which lent the city a mournful monumentality, has given way to one of sober and unimaginative new buildings, which destroy the integrity of the Victorian streetscape and turn Manchester into a characterless city which could be anywhere. Perhaps the re-evaluation of nineteenth-century architecture will lead to the preservation of some buildings. The Corn Exchange and Lancaster Avenue are threatened with demolition. Lancaster Avenue particularly merits preservation. It is the best example of a spatial innovation of the nineteenth century—arcade space equipped with galleries, widening as it ascends.

Barton Arcade (figs. 279–285)
Deansgate—Bank Square—Red Lion Street
Barton Arcade is the earliest of the five arcades built in Manchester between 1870 and 1900. Its facade composition was doubtless influenced by the Galleria Vittorio Emanuele in Milan, which the journal *The Builder* had covered extensively in 1868.[488]

Barton Arcade occupies an area between Deansgate and a totally insignificant alley, which leads to St. Ann's Square; the site is wider than it is deep. Deansgate had recently been widened by the Corporation of Manchester from 6 to 18 meters because of the heavy traffic, and Barton Arcade, 55 meters long, was the first building constructed on this new frontage.[489] Barton Arcade, an exclusively commercial building, is four-storied throughout. The two lower stories of the facade on Deansgate are entirely glass, united by ironwork arches. The two arcade entrances are two-storied and accentuated by arched filigree latticework and by one-story tower-like additions.

The plan reveals on the street level thirteen shops of varying dimensions with elegantly bowed entrances and two staircases to the upper stories. The site is completely developed except for a narrow strip of a courtyard on the north boundary. The arcade space expands above the shops. The three upper stories are accessible from continuous galleries which connect with the ends of the arcade wings in a semicircle. Small offices and showrooms are located on these levels, which may be rented just like the shops. These galleries, embellished with iron gates, are public and may be reached via the staircase in the south wing of the arcade. The aesthetic effect of the arcade space, which may be experienced from many perspectives and intersections, is determined by the iron railings of the gallery and by the vaulted glass roof with two additional cupolas at the points of intersection of the arcade wings. The plan of the cupola is octagonal, the pendentives are glazed, and the beams and girders are refined by the addition of iron ornament. The beauty of this glass vault lies in the use of a conventional element—the glass pane —to create new architectural forms. The narrowness and height of the space, the absence of any sort of facade, and the relatively short arcade wings turn the interior of Barton Arcade almost into a light well as we know it from nineteenth-century banks and department stores.

Barton Arcade is still standing in its original state. Only the uppermost interior moulding has been removed, making the transition between the uppermost story and the beginning of the glass roof too abrupt.

Lancaster Avenue (figs. 286–287)
Todd Street—Fennel Street
Lancaster Avenue, located between Todd and Fennel Streets, connects Victoria Station and the Corn Exchange. The Corn Exchange is no longer in use and is threatened with demolition along with Lancaster Avenue, where today a few shops, smaller businesses, and offices are left to waste away.

The arcade, insignificant and with badly built street facades, has an arcade space which is set back twice with walkways on three levels; they are accessible by staircases and open stairs on the facade side. There is a slight bend at about the midpoint. The floors, store fronts, and roof construction are entirely of wood; only the railings are of iron and are reminiscent of ships' railings. The facades of the shops and offices are the same on all three floors: they are without ornamentation, divided by five wooden mullions and by a rail at the height of the balcony railings.

The glass roof is a low-pitched saddle with a span of approximately 7 meters. The

MANCHESTER

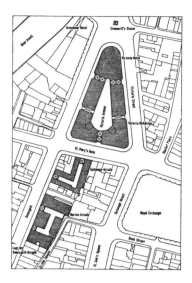

279
Manchester, sites of
Barton Arcade, Ex-
change Arcade, and
Victoria Arcade,
1889

280
Manchester, Barton
Arcade, 1871, en-
trance, St. Ann's
Square

281
Barton Arcade, lateral wing

282
Barton Arcade,
galleries

283
Barton Arcade, roof

284
Barton Arcade,
facade, Deansgate,
from *The Builder*,
1871

285
Barton Arcade,
ground floor plan

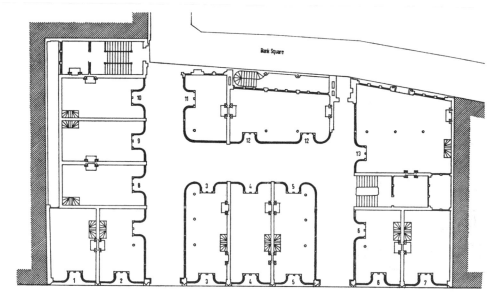

286
Manchester, Lancas-
ter Avenue, ca. 1873,
arcade space

shafts that carry the glass roof are free-standing on the top story. On them rests the wooden beam construction, whose arches are braced lengthwise by heavy wooden beams with the look of moulding. The glass roof continues over the uppermost walkway at a lesser incline so that the arcade space below is adequately illuminated. Nearby Chester Rows would have served as an excellent model. The wooden architecture is reminiscent of British half-timbered construction. It is said to have been built around 1873.

Exchange Arcade (fig. 279)
Deansgate—St. Mary's Gate
At the intersection of the two main commercial arteries in Manchester, Deansgate and St. Mary's Gate, a block of commercial buildings was built in 1876 by the architects Mangnall and Littlewoods "in the free type of Italian style known as Renaissance." It was named the New Exchange Arcade since it was located next to the Royal Exchange.[490] The arcade connected the two streets by forming a right angle. Nothing stands at this location today. The block was entirely destroyed in World War II by air raids.

The building had four stories. The ground floor stood entirely on cast-iron supports to give the twenty-five shops as much space and transparency as possible. The upper stories were used as offices. There were forty-six on the first floor and forty-one each on the upper floors. The arcade space had ornamentally pierced balustrades around ornate galleries and was covered by a semicircular glass vault.

Victoria Arcade (figs. 279, 288)
Deansgate—St. Mary's Gate—Victoria Street
The Victoria Buildings occupied an entire triangular block which was formed by the streets of Deansgate, St. Mary's Gate, and Victoria Street. They were also the victim of bombing in World War II. The site was originally occupied by a series of insignificant commercial and residential buildings. The old Smithy Door Market was located on the side toward Victoria Street. The Victoria Buildings were at the time the largest private construction project ever undertaken in Manchester, carried out as part of the expansion and rebuilding of Deansgate.

In 1874 the Corporation Property Company Ltd. was established;[491] it purchased the land, which belonged to the city, and engaged the Manchester architect William

Dawes to design a unified building complex. The building came to a standstill because of financial difficulties; only the south sections of the arcade were built by 1878. The north apex, which the Great Victoria Hotel would occupy, was finished only in 1885. The city had taken over the building by then and had finished the construction under its own direction.

The block, reminiscent in its dimensions of the large Paris department stores, was difficult to handle, requiring the architect to accommodate a highly varied program in a predetermined form. The Victoria Buildings had several components (plans and views were published in the trade journal *The Architect*).[492] A five-storied facade, the ground floor entirely glass and supports, went around the entire block. The three corners were rounded and emphasized by round towers. Five entranceways, accentuated by towers of a modest height, led from the three streets into the arcade space. The arcade's ground plan was teardrop-shaped and a huge glass dome was designed to cover the center. I was unable to ascertain if the project was actually carried out in this way. Around the three upper stories ran galleries from which the offices were accessible by staircases placed diagonally in the two south corners.

The apex was occupied by the Victoria Hotel, whose rooms were grouped around a rectangular light well. The entire sixth floor and parts of the fifth floor were given up to the 140 private rooms of the hotel, which also had numerous luxuriously appointed public rooms and a huge billiard room in the cellar with sixteen tables. There were twenty-eight shops and eighty-eight offices of varying sizes in the Victoria Buildings and 475 meters of galleries in the arcade. I was unfortunately unable to find any visual documentation of the arcade's architecture.

In 1927, the *Manchester City News* commented:[493] ". . . the arcade . . . was intended to rank with its neighbour, the Barton Arcade, an idea which has never fructified."

Deansgate Arcade (figs. 289–293)
Deansgate—St. Mary's Gardens—College Land
Deansgate Arcade was the last arcade constructed in Manchester and was opened only in 1900.[494] It connected Deansgate

288
Manchester, Victoria
Buildings, 1875–
1885, from *The
Architect,* 1875

289
Manchester, Deans-
gate Arcade, 1900,
demolished 1956,
ground floor plan

290
Deansgate Arcade,
upper story plan

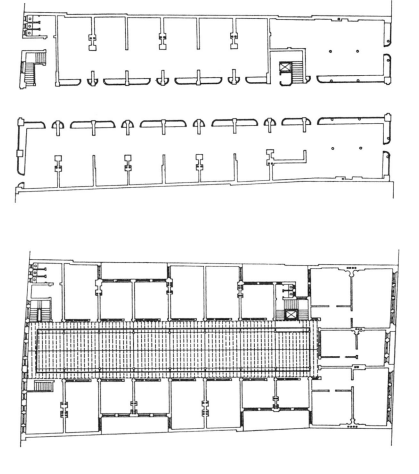

291
Deansgate Arcade,
cross section

292
Deansgate Arcade
during demolition

293
Deansgate Arcade,
bare roof structure

with College Lane, an insignificant second-ary street. Its traffic function was to pro-vide a more direct way between Salford Station (beyond the Irwell River) and the Royal Exchange, which was accessible only via the Burton Arcade diagonally across from Deansgate Arcade—in theory a promising path, if one looks at the site plan. The plans for Deansgate Arcade, drawn by the architect John Burke in 1897, have been preserved.[495] The facade of the entrance building on Deansgate was five-storied; the architecture displayed Spanish motifs. The central bay was em-phasized by a three-story arch.

The structural organization of the arcade space is interesting, being faintly reminis-cent of the Crystal Palace. The space was three-storied and set back once. Slim, cast-iron columns rose from the first gallery, resting on the structural divisions between bays, that is, on the piers which divided the shops on the ground floor. These col-umns supported the lattice girders of the glass saddle roof. The contour of the col-umns and the semicircular undersupport of the beams suggested the actual arcade space, whose walls and galleries were be-hind this contour, thus producing varying zones of shadow. The glass roof construc-tion, freestanding for two stories, was braced longitudinally and laterally by lat-tice trusses placed where the roof began; we have already seen this design in a sim-pler form in Lancaster Avenue. The slen-der pillars were prevented from bending by the gallery attached to them on the third floor, which was set back slightly from the second floor gallery. Both galleries circled the arcade.

We can experience the spatial effect of this arcade in a series of photographs made in 1956 at the time of its demolition.[496]

MARSEILLE
Passage Saint Férreol?
Planat refers to this arcade, but I was unable to ascertain whether it in fact existed.

MELBOURNE
Arcades have been built for a long time in Melbourne, appearing earlier here than in Sydney.[497] Since 1859 the city has been the capital of Victoria. Melbourne's rise to the status of Australia's major trade and finan-cial center and its development from a small settlement to a metropolis are without par-allel among the cities of the nineteenth cen-

294
Melbourne, city plan, detail

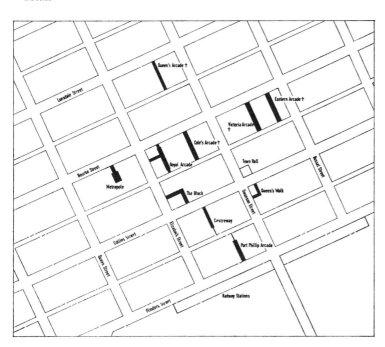

tury. Its growth took place within fifty years. In 1835 the first white settlers established themselves in a basin-shaped valley between Batman's Hill and the hill where the Parliament House stands today.[498] In 1837 were sold the first lots of land, designated on a city plan drawn up in Sydney that was as simple as possible and free of all hierarchical urban planning concepts. With no reference whatever to the topography of the area, three main streets 30 meters wide were laid out east-west and seven north-south, dividing the valley into rectangles of equal size, which were subsequently subdivided by longitudinal "little streets" 10 meters wide. Neither squares nor public buildings were planned, since Melbourne was conceived of as a "village."

In 1850 Melbourne had a total of 23,000 inhabitants. Between 1851 and 1861 this number tripled as gold fever drew adventurers and businessmen by the thousands to the area. By the end of the century, Melbourne had almost a half-million residents. It had become a district consisting of a conglomeration of independent suburbs which had their common center exactly in the center of the area designated in 1837. The gold rush, which would from time to time nearly depopulate the city, lasted until 1870, creating a booming industrial and agricultural community and attracting British development capital to the area through high interest rates. A sure sign of the role that Melbourne began to play on the Australian continent was the 1880–1881 World's Fair, which put Melbourne on the map.

Melbourne was overwhelmed in the 1880s by the establishment of firms. A speculative mentality began to develop among the vital and colorful mixture of personalities who were thrown together there, bringing Melbourne a reputation as a cross between Chicago and Paris. This development of reckless expansion and the carefree life reached its peak in 1888. Asa Briggs writes:[499] "By then the city had been provided with its first electric light, with telephones, with new suburban railways, with cable trams, with lavish new shops, complete with hydraulic lifts, with busy highly decorated arcades, with new theaters, hotels and restaurants, and with dozens of opulent new mansions in the suburbs." The arcades, which all ran parallel to the north-south streets, did not have to deal with height differentials as in Sydney. The product of the Melbourne boom from

1850 to 1890, they were the unmistakable sign of speculative building.

The first financial troubles began to make themselves felt as early as 1888. The drop in the price of wool on international markets unleashed an avalanche of bankruptcies within an overheated and irreversible cycle which led to the flight of capital and ended with the closing of the Federal Bank. No arcades were built beyond this point, except for a few built in the twentieth century to help improve pedestrian access to the train stations.

Queen's Arcade
Little Bourke Street—Lonsdale Street
Queen's Arcade, the first arcade in Melbourne, was built in 1853. It stood, however, for only fifteen years. It represented an attempt to make Lonsdale Street, almost a country lane, into a commercial artery. The competition afforded by Bourke Street, however, doomed it to failure.

Royal Arcade
Bourke Street—Elizabeth Street—Little Collins Street
Royal Arcade was built in 1869 after the design of the architect Charles Webb who had won the competition for the arcade announced by the owner of the property, John Fawkner. The press commented on the event: "Slowly but surely the old landmarks of Melbourne are being swept away, and the antiquated and dilapidated buildings which have long been eyesores in our principal thoroughfares are gradually being replaced by buildings of a totally different description."

Directly after the opening, the arcade was a tremendous success. One year later, all twenty-nine shops were occupied. In 1903 it was expanded to include a lateral wing toward Elizabeth Street. Until 1958 the arcade was in the possession of the Spensley family of England, descendants of the first construction supervisor. After World War II, however, they allowed it to deteriorate. In 1958 it was put up for sale. The thirty-five tenants of the arcade consolidated and formed a corporation which auctioned the Royal Arcade for the terrific sum of £541,000—the largest ever obtained in Melbourne at an auction. The arcade was carefully restored by its new owners and is classified today by the National Trust of Victoria as "highly significant, worthy of preservation."

The arcade has three stories and a glass saddle roof whose central ventilation strip is unglazed, dividing the glass into two areas. The roof is supported by beautiful, ornamental beams with a semicircular arched undersupport which rests on pilasters on the third floor. The glass roof was originally meant to be cooled by a sprinkler system on hot days.

Eastern Arcade

Bourke Street—Little Collins Street
The Eastern Arcade was built in 1873 on the site of the Haymarket Theatre, which had been destroyed by fire. It had sixty-eight shops and a surrounding gallery on the upper story. In spite of initial popularity, more and more of the shops were vacated in the following decades. The reasons for this development may be found in the extension of Melbourne's commercial district from north to south between the university and the train station, so that the Eastern Arcade was soon located on the edge of Chinatown, where "ladies of sensibility" could not let themselves be seen. It was remodeled in 1927.

Victoria Arcade

Bourke Street—Little Collins Street
The Victoria Arcade was built parallel to and slightly to the west of the Eastern Arcade. It was constructed in 1876 by the architect Joseph Reed under contract with Joseph Aarons. It belonged to Melbourne's main entertainment district—a block consisting of four theaters, six music halls, an opera, and a wax museum. Its commercial success, however, was limited. Between 1887 and 1920 the arcade served primarily as the vestibule for the Gaiety and Bijou theatres. In 1920 the Bourke Street entrance was closed, and the arcade was turned into a café.

Cole's Arcade

Bourke Street—Little Collins Street
Cole was a book dealer. After several attempts to set up a store, he finally opened "Cole's Cheap Book Arcade" at the end of the 1870s in a popular section of Bourke Street, an undertaking which he described as "Cole's New Book Arcade, first of its kind opened anywhere . . . 200 ft. deep, 40 ft. wide . . . walks a third of a mile long. . . . The galleries are supported on 140 brass pillars. . . . The sign of the establishment is the rainbow. Forty-six of these beautiful objects decorate the building, and one, of enormous dimensions, the Bourke Street front. . . . Goods to beautify the interior of houses, as books beautify the interior of the mind. . . . Intellectual, well behaved people collect, and friends meet and feel happy in this palace of intellect." The arcade enjoyed great popularity and flourished during the entire time that Cole managed it. He died in 1918. The arcade was sold in 1927 and replaced by a large fashion department store.

The architecture of the arcade was described in the following way: "The Arcade comprised a ground floor and two balconies, and the entire roof was supported on heavy curved iron beams combined with decorative tie rods and struts in approximately the form of a queen post truss. Curved glass panels flanking the central iron roofing sheets suggest a considerable technological development from the earlier gable roofs."

Queen's Walk

Swanston Street—Collins Street
Queen's Walk is a small corner arcade built in 1889. There are glass cupolas over the entrances; in the interior, everything is of glass and steel. There were plans in 1963 for it to be torn down.

Block Arcade

Collins Street—Elizabeth Street
Block Arcade, like Queen's Walk, is a corner arcade. It is, however, larger and more elaborately decorated, and is today Melbourne's most elegant arcade. It was built in 1892–1894 (the years of the great bank crash and the economic recession) by the firm of Twentyman and Askew.

Its architecture is described in the following way: "Built at the height of the Italianate period, the four-storey building and basement are of load bearing wall construction, while the Arcade itself with its mosaic tile floor is divided into a series of bays at minor changes of direction by plastered brick arches with triangular infil panels, and further sub-divided by heavy cast iron trusses. Over the change in direction four large trusses intersect to support an octagonal, conical 'dome,' which additionally provides ventilation."

Metropole Arcade

Bourke Street
Metropole Arcade was part of the Metropole Hotel, built in 1893. It had only one entrance and is said to have served as a coach yard. The arcade was taken over by a department store in 1960.

Centreway
Collins Street

Centreway was built in 1912 as a continuation of the Block Arcade in the direction of the train station. It was "always busy, and at peak times thronged with jostling people, yet its design is thoroughly utilitarian. Steel beams support a pitched ochre painted glass roof spanning a very narrow thoroughfare with scarcely a hint of the glamour of the previous half century." The Centreway is supplemented by the Port Phillip Arcade today, which was built in 1962 and which leads directly to the train station. This modern arcade has two stories and a flat roof with a narrow strip of skylights.

MESSINA
Galleria Vittorio Emanuele III
Piazza Antonella—Corso Cavour—Via Consolata

Like all of the Italian arcades, the Galleria Vittorio Emanuele III covers an entire city block. It has three wings which meet in a hexagonal rotunda. The cupola was destroyed in World War II. As the arcade is dedicated to Vittorio Emanuele III, it must have been built after 1900.

MILAN
Galleria de Cristoforis (figs. 295–299)
Corso Vittorio Emanuele—Contrada del Monte—Contrada S. Pietro all'Orto

The first arcade in Italy was the Galleria de Cristoforis in Milan. It is no longer standing today since it had to make way in the 1930s for the new construction of Piazza Babila. However, the architect, Andrea Pizzala, did publish a series of engravings of the building,[500] which gives us an idea of what the arcade was like. Pizzala accompanied the engravings with a foreword explaining the reasons for the construction of an arcade.[501] Milan was the first city in Italy to construct wide, clean streets and a large theater, but it lacked a place where a certain public could spend inclement days and long winter evenings. To remedy this situation, Giovanni Battista, Vitaliano, and Luigi de Cristoforis suggested the construction of a glass-covered gallery after the Paris and London models on the site of the Palazzo Serbelloni. Pizzala reports that he had made extensive trips to France, England, and Scotland with Luigi de Cristoforis. He must then have seen all of the most important arcades.

Construction was begun at the end of September 1831. The arcade was opened a

year later, on September 29, 1832. This accelerated construction schedule, short even by today's standards, may be explained by the fact that up to 450 workers at a time took part in the project.[502]

The Galleria de Cristoforis was located at the end of the Corsia de Servi, today the Corso Vittorio Emanuele, once the promenade of the most elegant Milanese. It led to the Contrada del Monte at an angle of about 95 degrees; a third small side exit ends in the Contrada S. Pietro all'Orto. This location was criticized as early as 1844 by Luigi Tatti,[503] who said it would have been better to build the Galleria adjacent to the cathedral so that one could reach S. Margherita via one wing and S. Fedele via the other. He was describing the site of the later Galleria Vittorio Emanuele.

The Galleria de Cristoforis had only one entrance building, of five stories, facing Corsia de Servi. The entrances to both the arcade and the courtyards were combined with the entresol in a finely carved rusticated basement; the upper stories were embellished by balconies but had no setback. The central section, with triple arches, projects forward like a pavilion but only slightly. Through these arches the pedestrian entered a large vestibule, off which were stairways. The vestibule was decorated with four statues of famous Italians, carved by the sculptor Alessandro Puttinati and representing Columbus, Vespucci, Marco Polo, and Flavio Giola. A passageway two bays in length and a two-story arcade followed. The latter was covered by a glass saddle roof with no undersupport. This long wing (110 meters) ended in a kind of central space above which the glass roofs simply intersected. It was the first attempt anywhere at a cruciform plan, a spatial concept which several decades later reached perfection 100 meters farther west. A large cafe with a wine shop and a music emporium lay across from this long wing.[504] The end wall was covered entirely with mirrors and gave the illusion that the arcade space extended beyond the point of intersection. The short wing was approximately 35 meters long and led to the Contrada del Monte.

The Galleria de Cristoforis included seventy shops, some interconnecting, and rooms belonging to them on the mezzanine. Thirty rental apartments of varying sizes were located above the shops; they were accessible from the back by their own

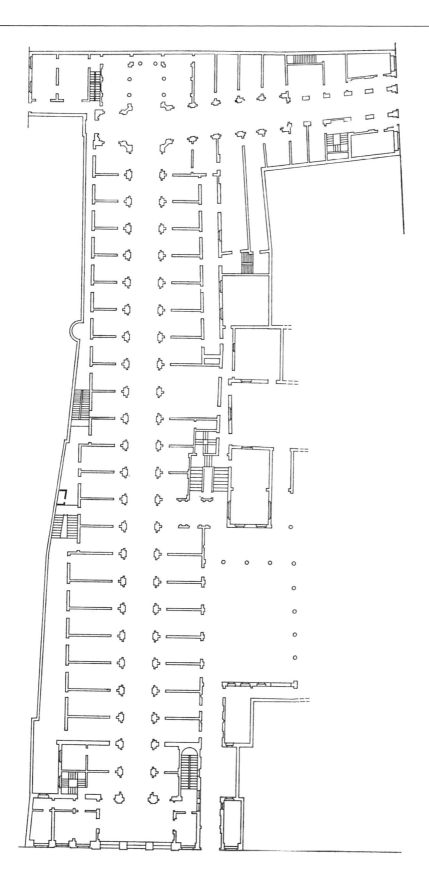

295
Milan, Galleria de
Cristoforis, 1831–
1832, demolished,
ground floor plan

297
Galleria de Cris-
toforis, entrance
facade

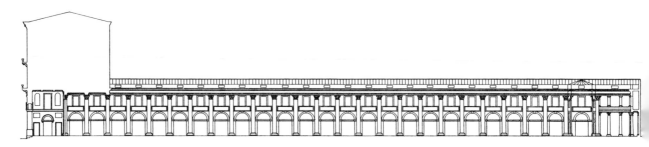

296
Galleria de Cris-
toforis, longitudinal
section
(Scale: 1 : 650)

298
Galleria de Cristoforis, ball in the arcade, February 10, 1834

299
Galleria de Cris-
toforis, view from
vestibule into wing

steps. In addition to the café already mentioned, there are said to have been a mechanical theater, a hotel, and a trattoria in the arcade. The east section of the arcade shows a certain confusion in the ground plan which may be explained by the inclusion of existing buildings and courtyards into the structure.

The plans and details that Pizzala published reveal a very careful handling of decoration. The precision of detail and the frugality of its use mark the building as a neoclassical work. The facades, with the grand rhythm of their pilasters, bespeak a close study of the Palais Royal, of its garden facades, and of the Galerie d'Orléans. The basic schema of the interior facades is repeated in the Galleria Vittorio Emanuele, except that there we find two additional stories. Each pair of pilasters frames an arch of the wall arcade with a show window, an entrance with a space above it for advertisement, and an apartment window. An ornate moulding delineates the upper edge of the arcade space. Ventilation is provided through open areas in a band above it which supports the glass roof but is not visible from below.

Text 1: Andrea Pizzala, architect, 1832

... The floor of the entrance hall, of the Galleria itself, and of the cafe are of Carrara marble which is white and rough-textured. All of the walls are of polished plaster and the glass roof is supported by grooves of iron fastened with brass screws. The capitals of the Galleria are of composite order; and with such liberty it is possible to characterize the purpose of the place by combining into one the head of Mercury with the Caduceus symbol and that of Ceres, the emblems respectively of commerce and agriculture. In the building connected with the interior of the Galleria, there are 30 apartments both big and small, a mechanical theater, a hotel, and a small restaurant. I have made four etchings of this grand building, which I believe will be of service to the public; they represent (1) the facade toward Corsia de Servi; (2) the perspective view; (3) the geometrical plan and elevation; and (4) details. I would fail in a particular duty, a duty which is too dear to me not to fulfill, if I did not give credit here to Luigi de Cristoforis, one of the owners of the Galleria, the credit due him for having directed all of the work connected with mechanics. His talents in this science are well known among us; and, having accompanied him on his journeys throughout almost all of Europe, I am able to attest to the esteem in which he is held by the most distinguished foreign mechanics, as I was a witness to his refusal of several honorific and advantageous offers

made him in England and Scotland to become director of several of these important establishments. If my meager work should find acceptance among the public, this would satisfy the sole aim to which I aspire.

Degen's monograph on the Galleria de Cristoforis must also be included as a bibliographical reference.[505]

Galleria Vittorio Emanuele II (figs. 300–324)

Piazza del Duomo—Piazza della Scala—Via Silvio Pellico—Via Ugo Foscolo

The Galleria Vittorio Emanuele II in Milan marks the zenith of the development of the arcade building type. The process that began with the Paris arcades and had an intermediate stage in the Galeries St. Hubert in Brussels finds its end here. From an anonymous object of private speculation, the arcade has become a public building built by competition and financed by foreign capital, as well as a part of monumental redesign of the city center.

Here the arcade has become a national political symbol. In conscious references to St. Peter's in Rome, Roman imperial architectural forms, the cross in the coat of arms of the family which brought about Italian unification, the arcade legitimatizes the new nation by calling on a widespread background of tradition. With the Galleria Vittorio Emanuele, the arcade building type enters the gallery of the great representative buildings of the nineteenth century. In these buildings—the theaters, the palaces of justice, city halls, stock exchanges, parliamentary buildings—bourgeois society becomes manifest.

The idea of building an arcade in conjunction with the extension of the Piazza del Duomo and its insertion into a functioning network of streets dated from the Austrian occupation.[506] Already after the construction of the Galleria de Cristoforis—the first Italian arcade after the French model, intended to fill Milan's need for a covered promenade—the notion developed of building an arcade near the cathedral[507] to connect cathedral square to S. Margherita and S. Fedele. The idea thus initially belonged to the plans to set the cathedral off from other buildings as a monument and to give Milan an impressive public space.

The wide cathedral facade was finally finished in 1806 and required a structure to balance it visually. The Palazzo Reale,[508]

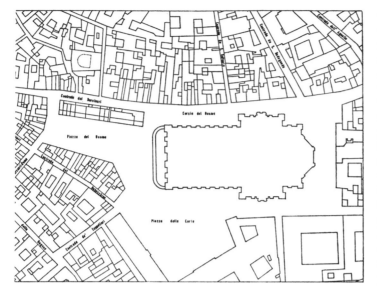

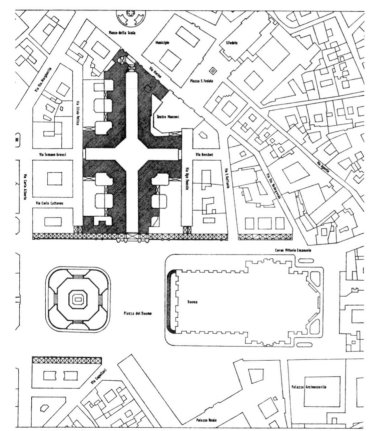

300
Milan, Piazza del
Duomo before 1850

301
Milan, Piazza del
Duomo and Galleria
Vittorio Emanuele II,
1900

which met with the Piazza del Duomo on the diagonal, seemed an impossible site for a regular piazza in axial relationship to the cathedral. In none of the many projects was its existence ever questioned. Between 1838 and 1863 many proposals for the Piazza del Duomo were submitted by architects and non-architects alike; these proposals will be analyzed here in relation to the idea of an arcade. The idea of connecting the Piazza del Duomo to the Piazza della Scala or to the Piazza S. Fedele with a street or an arcade was taken up time after time and finally became part of the official program. Several projects are known from before the era of the political developments which led to Italy's unification and accelerated Piazza del Duomo project. I will describe them briefly here.

The architect Carlo Amati envisioned a cathedral square expanded to the west, north, and south which would be bordered by arcaded walkways surrounding the square in a semicircle on the west side. A through street was planned only for the cathedral axis.[509]

Beccaria proposed a wider square, arcaded, *U*-shaped, and strictly related to the cathedral. It would continue in two sections on the north side and echo the transept facade of the cathedral.[510]

Caimi submitted two proposals.[511] The first was similar to Beccaria's; the other envisioned a polygonal enclosure of the square on the west and one running straight across on the north. A path designated as a bazaar is included, however, approximately at the present entrance to the arcade, connecting the Piazza del Duomo to the Piazza S. Fedele. An octagonal space was planned for the center of the arcade; this widening corresponds almost exactly to Mengoni's proposal of 1863 even though Mengoni's arcade led to the Piazza della Scala. Mengoni was clearly influenced by Caimi's suggestion.

The planning for the cathedral square moved into the stage of concrete proposals and estimates with the political events of 1859, which were decisive in ushering in the unification movement in Italy. After the victory at Magenta on June 4, Napoleon III (who had commanded the French troops) and Vittorio Emanuele entered the city of Milan side by side. On June 10 Count Luigi Belgioioso was named the commander of liberated Milan.[512] He saw his most important task as following through with the Piazza del Duomo project. On June 28 he met with the king in Turin to suggest that both squares, the Piazza della Scala and Piazza del Duomo, be connected by either a street or a bazaar bearing the king's name. On December 4 a royal decree authorized a lottery of two million lire, the profits from which would go exclusively to benefit the project.[513] On February 9 it was announced. The engineer Ponti submitted a plan, dated May 31, 1860, for the Nuova Strada Vittorio Emanuele including a perspective.[514] It shows a wide commercial avenue with symmetrical facades and colonnades on both sides. The Piazza del Duomo, widened by tearing down Coperto dei Figini and Isola del Rebecchino, is connected to the Piazza della Scala, straightened and widened on the north side. In this proposal the colonnaded street takes precedence over the buildings on the Piazza del Duomo, thereby contradicting the notion that the arcade was only a chance byproduct. The situation of the projected street corresponds exactly to that of the later arcade.

In February 1860 Antonio Beretta was elected as mayor of Milan.[515] He had models made of the Piazza del Duomo and its surroundings on a scale of 1 to 100 for the use of all those interested in the competition. They were available beginning in April 1860. According to reports, in the following years the project for the Piazza del Duomo and Via Vittorio Emanuele was on the agenda of every session of the Consiglio Comunale. By June 8, 1860, 220 projects had been submitted and were put on exhibit in the Brera.[516] Only 142 were designed by architects. They ranged (since precise restrictions had not been set) from serious urban planning studies to the irreverent suggestion of simply enlarging the Piazza del Duomo by shortening the cathedral and using the stone, a costly material, for the new structure.

I must interject here that I found a short text in the Milan archives by the engineers Daverio and Tarantola, dated March 12, 1860,[517] containing a proposal which looks very much like the city commission proposal of November 15, 1860: arcaded walks along the sides of the cathedral, a freestanding structure on its axis, and a narrow arcade leading to the Piazza della Scala. It utilizes the widened Contrada del due Muri up to the point where it turns off to the west. Beginning there, it is glassed in and ends in a semicircle on the piazza,

which accommodates the oblique entrance. This motif reappears, but on a larger scale, in Mengoni's 1863 proposal. Clearly, Mengoni carefully studied all previous proposals and selected all the useful elements.

A city commission met on July 27, 1860, and judged the projects submitted without coming to any conclusion. Eleven members of the commission formed a committee under the leadership of the architect Luigi Tatti to formulate a proposal,[518] which was submitted on November 10, 1860. It incorporates all of the essential elements of Mengoni's later proposal, which was approved for construction. The cathedral is set off in an oblong square, the west side of which is arcaded. It is divided into three building groups. On the north, the Nuova Galleria Vittorio Emanuele is presented as a street with promenades on both sides and a glass covering down the middle. In the south is the pendant to the arcade entrance, the Loggia Reale; across from the cathedral is the Palazzo del Fondo, a freestanding structure with surrounding arcaded walkways and connecting passages to the neighboring sections of the building. Since the Piazza del Duomo would be closed to vehicles, a new street network around the square was proposed which would allow an up-to-date traffic solution. The suggestion by the eleven members became the basic plan for the subsequent limited competition.

The lottery closed in 1861.[519] It had an unexpectedly unhappy outcome: instead of the expected five million lire, only one million lire were netted. The demolition and construction costs were estimated at 15 million lire. Credit and other financing possibilities were sought.

Finally, in February 1862 an initial competition was announced among eighteen invited participants; there would be three major prizes and six prizes to cover costs.[520] The announcement included as its basic scheme the proposal of the Tatti study group, which the participants were free to modify. They could choose between a "Via Cielo coperto porticata" (Heavenly Way covered with a portico) and a "via coperta a vetri" (glass-covered way). The jury met in June but could not agree on the first prize. However, the "Dante proposal," by the architect Giuseppe Mengoni of Bologna,[521] which followed the guidelines closely, was under consideration. Those in the city who did not understand

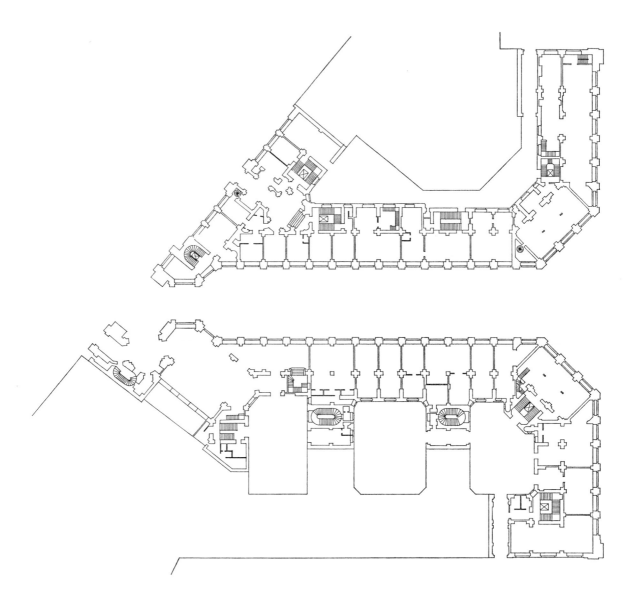

302
Milan, Galleria Vit-
torio Emanuele II,
1865–1867; trium-
phal arch, 1877;
ground floor plan
(Scale: 1 : 800)

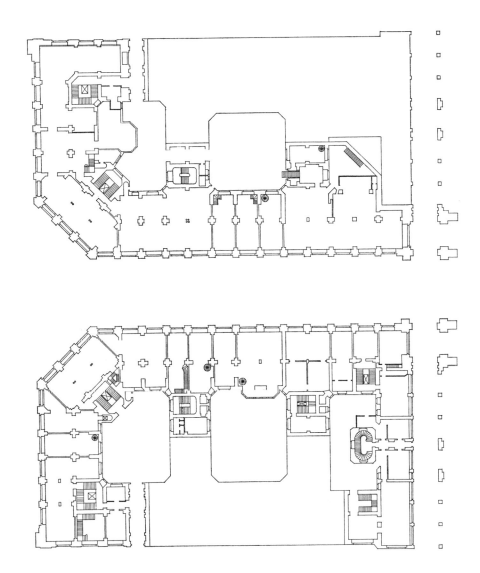

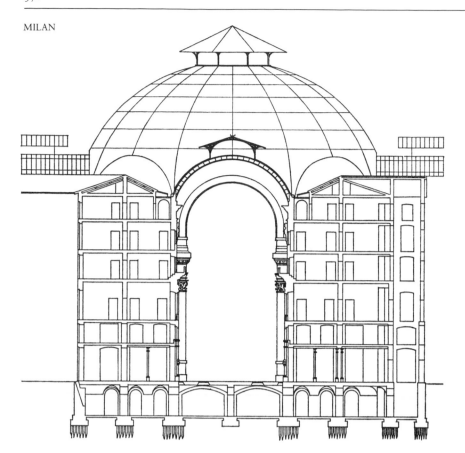

303
Galleria Vittorio
Emanuele II, cross
section

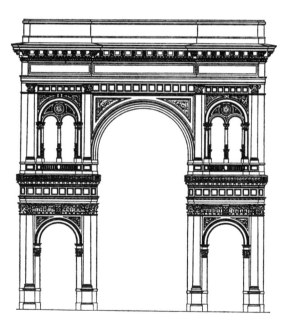

304
Galleria Vittorio
Emanuele II, trium-
phal arch on the
Piazza del Duomo

305
Galleria Vittorio
Emanuele II, first de-
sign, Mengoni, 1863

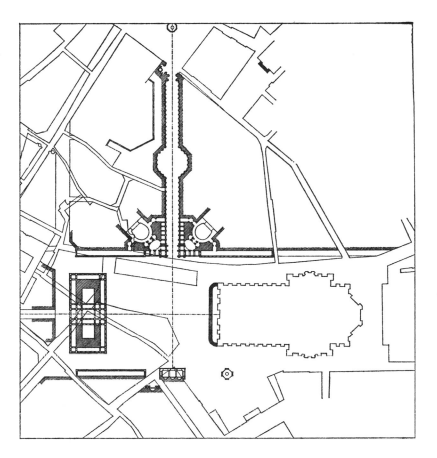

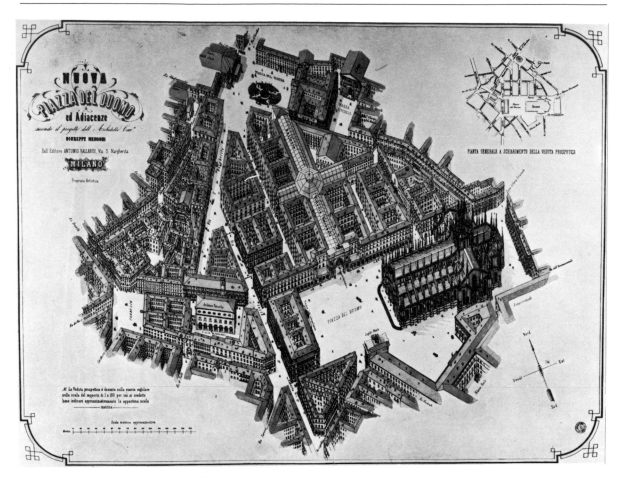

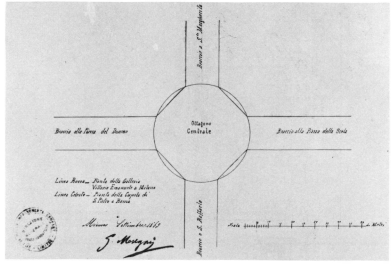

306
Galleria Vittorio
Emanuele II,
isometric drawing,
projected develop-
ment of the Piazza
del Duomo

307
Galleria Vittorio
Emanuele II, com-
parison of the dome
with the dome of St.
Peter's, sketch by
Mengoni

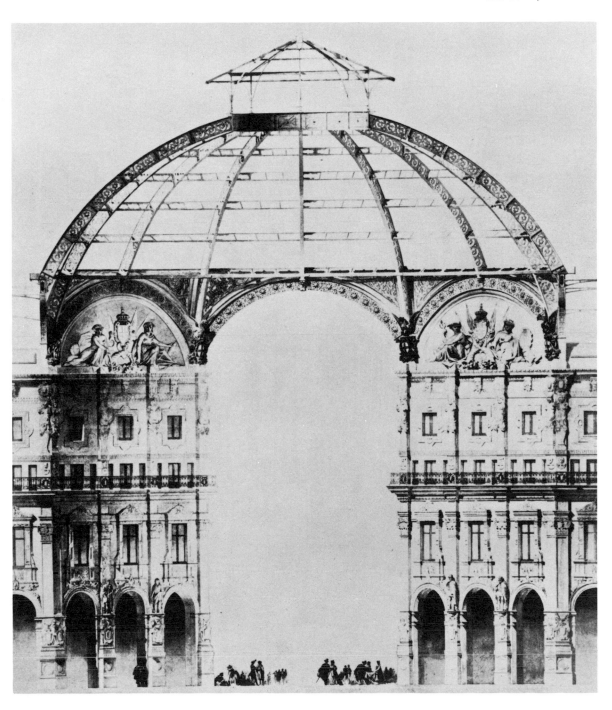

MILAN

309
Galleria Vittorio
Emanuele II, arcade
under construction

310
Galleria Vittorio
Emanuele II, dome
under construction

311
Galleria Vittorio
Emanuele II, "Il Rat-
tin," the machine
used to light the gas
lights in the dome

312
Galleria Vittorio
Emanuele II, con-
struction of roof

the protracted procedure began to make themselves heard; the protests against the intended clearing of old Milan around the cathedral increased as well. The debate was fueled by the newspaper *Pungolo*, whose main offices were in one of the buildings destined to be torn down.

In August the Consiglio Comunale accepted Mengoni's proposal but only the part which dealt with the arcade; it contracted with three architects to develop a final plan for the Piazza del Duomo. It was left to Mengoni, Pestagalli, and Matas, director of the cathedral construction, either to cooperate or to develop individual proposals.[522] Matas withdrew, as he was under contract to work on church facades in Florence; Pestagalli and Mengoni worked separately. Their concepts differed only with respect to nuances, to stylistics. Pestagalli wanted to balance the cathedral with three independent structures which would define the square, thus giving up the uniformity of a continuous arcaded walk. Mengoni planned a triumphal gate in front of the arcade, balancing the Loggia Reale; each would carry a quadriga.

Much time was spent on working out the new proposals, until finally, on September 15, 1860, the Consiglio Comunale met again. During three sessions, on the 15th, 16th, and 17th, they struggled to agree on Mengoni's proposal, submitted as a short memorandum.[523] Thus, it took almost three years to find a plan and a man who would carry it out. Two additional years passed before the cornerstone was laid.

It is worthwhile to analyze Mengoni's plan, included in the memorandum (reproduced here in a tracing), in terms of his concept of the arcade. The arcade that would connect the Piazza della Scala and the Piazza del Duomo is presented—astonishingly enough—only as space and not yet as a building. He planned two small theaters only, at the entrance, diagonally oriented toward the proposed triumphal arch: a Teatro dell'Opera Comica and a Teatro della Commedia. They are the two theaters now located on parts of the site destined to be cleared. But this is all there is in the way of concrete presentations. Only one double line in the plan, northwest of the arcade space, refers to the eventual possibility of a building. An octagon is planned for the center of the arcade; it already corresponds in size to the built version, but the transverse wing is missing. The diagonal exit onto Piazza della Scala is

accommodated by an apse which corresponds partially in form to its construction. On the Piazza, on the line of the axis, the Monumento a Leonardo da Vinci is already noted, although it was not made until 1872. There is no indication on the drawing that the arcade would also be glassed over. Mengoni, awarded the commission to build the arcade, translated his ideas into working drawings in 1864. Smyth notes that the cruciform plan appeared for the first time in a drawing dated April 28, 1864.[524]

Bandmann pursued the question of the origin of this motif, which was not part of the street layout, in more comprehensive investigations.[525] I can only add that the cruciform had appeared as a developed form in the Galleria de Cristoforis and more clearly in an arcade in nearby Trieste. In addition, Mengoni, in his drawing dated September 1865 (fig. 307), sketched in red, within the contour of the octagon, the circumference of St. Peter's in Rome,[526] which coincides with the circumference of the arcade's glass dome. This was an astonishing discovery and clear proof of Mengoni's ambition, of which Joseph wrote:[527] "I would call Mengoni self-assured, or proud, since he demonstrably possessed the ambition to be placed next to Raphael and Michelangelo in the history books."

In the face of so many literal interpretations, it is almost tempting to believe a third point of view. The Latin cross in the coat of arms of the house of Savoy, which embellishes the central floor mosaic in the octagon, suggested the form of the arcade. At any rate, Mengoni began to understand the arcade as the embodiment of Italian unification, which was brought about in spite of the territorial interests of the Church. Triumphal arch, baths, dome, cross, and apse were references to a traditional context. But the cruciform had another effect. It made the arcade into a central place of public activity independent of the cathedral square and granted it structural autonomy. Bandmann comments:[528] "Next to the cathedral, the building erected by the religious community, and the city palace of the sovereign, appears a structure which serves the citizen of the metropolis in a special way, in that beyond its basic function—that is, commerce and trade—it invites the citizen to tarry and provides the superstructure for his communal urban existence. It is here that the Galleria distinguishes itself from the other bourgeois construction projects which began with the eighteenth century, and which, like train stations and exhibition halls, baths, stock exchanges, museums, theaters, markets, concert halls, etc., fulfill only partial functions of the urban community."

The next important date was July 21, 1864.[529] On this day, the city of Milan signed an agreement with the City of Milan Improvement Company, Ltd., an English firm which had been persuaded to finance the ambitious project. The firm agreed to build the arcade within two years and to complete construction of the Piazza del Duomo within six years. The company acquired the 27,734 square meters of the site. One of the restrictions was that the covered but publicly accessible areas must remain common, but that the cellar underneath would be reserved for the use of the company—a new regulation for the arcade building type. The city guaranteed a profit of 5 percent on the company's capital of 16 million lire.

The Galleria Vittorio Emanuele became a project which attracted international participation. The English architect Digby Wyatt[530] was a director of the company; Sir Charles Barry was asked to be a judge. The dome was designed by a Frenchman named Joret.[531]

Mengoni traveled at the beginning of 1865 to London for business;[532] he was also in Paris and is said to have visited Cluysenaar and to have seen the Galeries St. Hubert, the only arcade whose dimensions were comparable to the Milan project. He was in Milan again on March 7, 1865, in time to participate in the cornerstone-laying ceremonies. The ceremony, portrayed in a large painting,[533] took place in the presence of the king and a number of guests of honor in the center of the future rotunda, which was marked at the time by wooden platforms.

Construction took two and one-half years. An average of 1,000 workers were employed on the structure at any one time; 700,000 working days of labor were expended. All phases of construction are documented in an album by the photographer E. Heyland, from construction of the roof to the floor mosaics.[534] Several of these beautiful old photographs are reproduced in figs. 309–314. They show the almost primitive bare brickwork of the arcade with tile roofing on the adjoining buildings and the construction of the glass

roof. To build the dome, scaffolding was erected to its lower edge; in the center a wooden tower supported the lantern ring. Turnable scaffolding made it possible to work on each part of the structure. First, the perforated arched beams were placed on their supports, then the circumferential supports were installed, and then the ribbing, which held the overlapping panes of glass. The interior facades were put up along with the roof. Finally, the floor mosaic was brought in, and the space facing the Piazza del Duomo was temporarily closed off.

On September 15, 1867, everything was finished and ready for the Galleria Vittorio Emanuele to open. Mayor Beretta and the artisans, "who seem[ed] to have become quite nervous," hoped that they would be cleared of all reproaches and suspicions after the dedication. The streets and squares were filled with people. The king, announced by a royal fanfare and accompanied by his ministers, was greeted by the mayor and by Mengoni and representatives of the British building society. The mayor addressed the king: "Sire, the city of Milan is confident that this great building, the result of the happy marriage of Italian artisanry with foreign capital, and an opportunity of great benefit to the working class, to whose well-being our thoughts constantly turn as if they were our own cares, will owe its success to Your Majesty." The king examined it all carefully and even visited the cellar. In Milan the saying became current: "They say there are no longer any miracles, but here is one!"

The response in the newspapers and trade journals was the greatest ever provoked by an arcade. The arcade was also of great significance in German-speaking countries, even during its construction; we see evidence of this interest in the *Leipziger Illustrierte Zeitung*.[535] Milan made the arcade its own. Its citizens strolled there at night and enjoyed the light provided by 600 gas jets. (The number was increased for festive occasions to as many as 2,000.[536]) The greatest attraction was the small machine which ran on a track and which used flints to light the gas jets on the lowest ring of the dome as evening set in; it was christened "il rattin." This unique product of the search for entertainment may be seen today in the Museuo di Milano.

On September 25 *Pungolo* reported[537] that a man had walked up and down the arcade

313
Galleria Vittorio
Emanuele II, interior
facade under
construction

314
Galleria Vittorio
Emanuele II, arcade
space after the
opening

315
Galleria Vittorio
Emanuele II, view
from dome into
arcade

316
Galleria Vittorio
Emanuele II, dome

with an open umbrella although the sun was shining brightly; he was compelled to close it because of the loud protests and threatening gestures of the rest of the arcade's public. This was the single attempt at persiflage and already ten days had passed since the opening. A few days later, political activities entered the arcade. Demonstrators, who wanted to protest Garibaldi's arrest, removed his picture from the Cafe Biffi and carried it through the arcade; they encountered the police in the rotunda. On June 13, 1874, a hailstorm of unparalleled violence destroyed almost all of the glass roof, and turned the floor of the arcade into a sea of glass shards. On March 5, 1876, appeared the first of the *Corriere della Sera,* a paper which had rented office space in the arcade.

Mengoni, who had become highly respected, fell to his death from the scaffolding of the as yet unveiled triumphal arch on December 30—ten days before the death of King Vittorio Emanuele II.[538] The erection of the arch was postponed for years because of financial difficulties. The Galleria Vittorio Emanuele was finally completed on February 24, 1878, and the triumphal arch was unveiled. But the cathedral square construction came to a standstill; neither the Palazzo dell'Independenzia nor the Loggia Reale was built. In 1880 the Cafe Gnocchi in the arcade became Milan's first building to be illuminated by electricity. At this time, the arcade was sold to the city of Milan for the sum of 7.3 million lire.

On May 1, 1890, the arcade was strategically occupied, as workers' unrest and demonstrations were feared. French soldiers marched through it in World War I, and it was heavily damaged in 1943 by air raids. The discussions on restoration versus modernization extended over a number of years; it was reopened in 1955. The centennial of the arcade was celebrated on September 15, 1967, and a publication issued in its honor, from which this loose chronicle of events and anecdotes was taken.

The arcade has been "il cuore della città" (the heart of the city) for 100 years in Milan, a city which always fancied itself the "capitale morale" of Italy. For 100 years it has been the backdrop for favorite stories, the mirror of daily life in Milan; political events can be felt there as at a stock exchange. No one is better suited to describe the events of the day in the arcade than the retired police officer Italo Piadeni whose beat included the arcade for years. His account is taken from *Architectural Review*[539] (Text 1).

Bernard Rudofsky mentions the great Galleria in Milan as a place made for the walking man; he names Ernest Hemingway and Mark Twain as two who were fond of strolling there. Hemingway refers to the arcade in *A Farewell to Arms.* Mark Twain wrote in *A Tramp Abroad*: "Blocks of new buildings of the most sumptuous sort, rich with decoration and graced with statues, the streets between these blocks roofed over with glass at a great height, the pavements all of smooth and variegated marble, arranged in tasteful patterns —little tables all over these marble streets, people sitting at them, eating, drinking, or smoking—crowds of other people strolling by—such is the Arcade. I should like to live in it all my life."[540]

The plan of the Galleria Vittorio Emanuele describes a Latin cross whose center has been expanded into an octagon. It connects two squares and two smaller secondary streets to one another. It is included in the regular construction of a block and led to this section's restoration. A statue showing the king mounted on his horse, riding from the Palazzo Reale toward the arcade, was meant to stand in the arcade's main axis at the intersection with the axis of the cathedral. The triumphal arch on the Piazza del Duomo bears the inscription: "To Vittorio Emanuele II from the Milanese people." The triple triumphal arch,[541] which according to Mengoni's sketch was to be crowned with a quadriga, is the monumental introduction to the arcade.

The Galleria Vittorio Emanuele is the arcade on the Continent most strongly influenced by Roman imperial models. The Galleria Umberto I in Naples and the Galleria Nazionale in Turin imitate it; however, their architectural contexts did not allow their entrances to be set off as in Milan. The Milan triumphal arch is part of a continuous colonnade which borders the Piazza del Duomo on the north. Only the middle arch, with a height almost equivalent to that of the glass roof, leads into the arcade. It corresponds exactly to the spatial profile of the arcade itself. The arch is set off by lower, recessed sections of facade on either side, creating the illusion of a freestanding triumphal arch. The exit onto the Piazza della Scala is also a triumphal

317
Galleria Vittorio
Emanuele II, view
into wing of the ar-
cade from the venti-
lation structure

arch, which, however, is set off from the facades only by glyphs. The archway is an opening in an apse with two smaller gates less than 45 degrees. Only one opens onto the arcade. Above it is a passage with windows on both sides which connects the arcade buildings. This semicircular termination of the arcade space on the north is singular.

The four-part building to which these archways lead is regular in plan only with respect to the arcade itself; on the back it dovetails with neighboring buildings and courtyards. The upper stories of the arcade are accessible from these almost square courtyards which, except on the Via Marino, where the space is occupied by the Teatro Manzoni, lie along the back side of the arcade buildings in a line. Four through streets facilitate access for approximately nine courtyards from the rear streets.

The ground plan of the arcade, which, including the cellar, has seven floors in every part, is constructed according to a simple scheme. A network of concealed intersecting supports, like those in the later Moscow Trade Halls, allows a fairly flexible use of space on all floors. Staircases and sanitary facilities are located on the rear side of the arcade buildings and are accessible through the courtyards so as not to disturb the (visual) unity of the facades of the arcade. The staircases are located as a rule on the through streets in the lateral wings between the courtyards. Their situation allows a rear delivery system and separate rental of the upper stories.

The seven floors of the arcade contain a total of 1,260 rooms. Both the ground floor and the mezzanine are occupied by shops of varying size, showrooms of large firms, cafes, and restaurants which number among the finest in the city. The third floor, with its greater height, is occupied by rented clubrooms, offices, and studios; the four upper stories, the uppermost of which is above the arcade space, are residential.

The arcade space has street dimensions. The principal measurements include:

longitudinal wing	196.62 meters
lateral wing	105.1 meters
area of arcade space	4,195 square meters
area of rotunda	1,148 square meters
diameter of rotunda	36.6 meters
concourse width	14.5 meters
height to wreath moulding	25.07 meters
height to first ring of dome	30.15 meters
height of vault	29.28 meters
height to apex of dome	41.83 meters
height to top of lantern	47.08 meters

These measurements were only exceeded individually by later arcades; the heights were exceeded by those of the Galleria Umberto I in Naples, the width by the Cleveland Arcade, and the length by the Moscow Trade Halls.

The interior facades are not identical to the exterior facades. Their only common element is the arcade motif. The narrow bays of the four-story facades are accentuated by two-storied Ionic pilasters on double pedestals, with ornament reminiscent of the early Renaissance. The pilasters support a broadly projecting moulding which serves as a balcony. There is a fourth story behind it almost hidden from view. On the fifth floor, the pilasters become caryatids, which alternate with square, richly framed windows. The supports for the iron beams of the glass vault above the wreath moulding correspond exactly with the lines of pilasters on the interior facades. Joseph writes: "Only the transition between wall and roof is unorganic." Happily so, I would say, for it allows each of the three zones its own independence.

One observes in the design of the facades a certain sculpted quality which seems to correspond to the filtering of light through glass and which differs from the solidity of the exterior facades. Many layers of influence become apparent in the facade composition and in the way in which it is tied to the areas above the balcony. I consider three to be essential:

1. The use of the same colossal order for the two lower stories that is employed in the Galleria Cristoforis in Milan

2. The reference to Palladio's urban facades, perhaps to the facade of the Palazzo del Capitano, in the attic level with the balcony running in front

3. The influence of the facade of the Palazzo Bianchi in Bologna,[542] the city from which Mengoni came. This colonnaded facade was designed by Vignola but altered in the execution. Moreover, the purpose served by the palazzo was very closely related to that served by the arcade.

318
Galleria Vittorio
Emanuele II, exterior
of dome

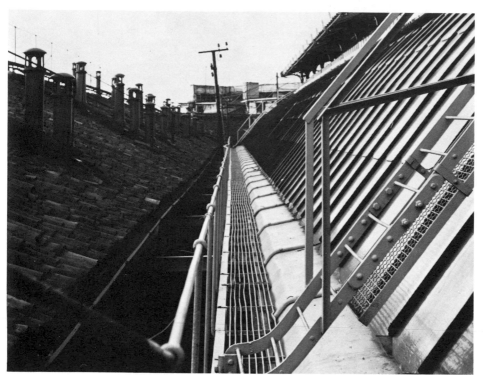

319
Galleria Vittorio
Emanuele II, base of
roof

320
Galleria Vittorio
Emanuele II, interior
of roof

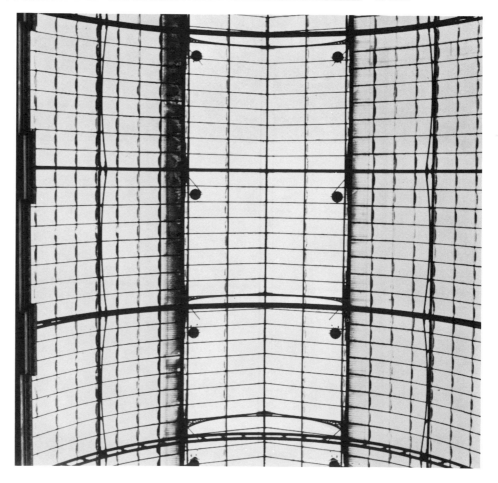

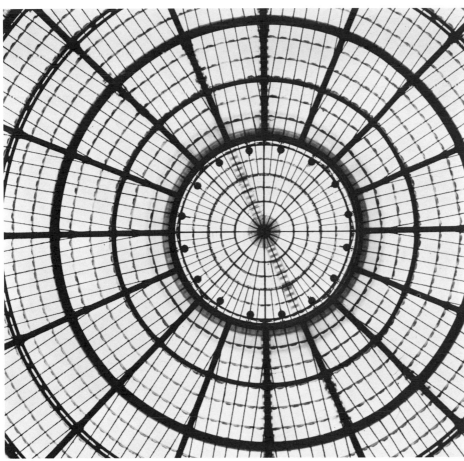

321
Galleria Vittorio
Emanuele II, interior
of dome

322
Galleria Vittorio
Emanuele II, ventila-
tion structure

323
Galleria Vittorio
Emanuele II, facade,
fifth floor

This facade composition is carried out in the rotunda except that the pilasters have pedestals which carry life-size figures, part of the iconographic program for the entire arcade. It is worth examining the program more closely, since it contains everything that could be observed in rudimentary form in earlier arcades. "The iconographic program, which is centered on the midpoint of the cruciform arcade," writes Bandmann,[543] "is penetrated by a main axis which is emphasized by its length, the introduction through the triumphal arch with the dedication to the king, and the focus on the Leonardo memorial."

The sculpture originally included:

1. Twenty-four statues the height of the arcade,[544] sixteen in the rotunda and two each inside the four entrances representing a pantheon of famous Italian artists, scientists, and politicians. They are still in their original locations today.

2. Alternating caryatids and atlantes and busts on the fifth floor, whose curious stares down into the arcade seem to be more important than their functional tasks. The "Omenoni," the giants on the ground floor of the house of the Milanese sculptor Lioni,[545] may have suggested these sculptures to Mengoni.

3. Eight iron eagles with extended wings which are perched on the coat of arms of the house of Savoy, thereby concealing the supports of the arches upon which the first ring of the dome rests. The coat of arms is repeated on a smaller scale in the iron railings of the surrounding balcony.

Paintings include:

1. The four great arches of the rotunda, depicting allegories of the four parts of the earth—Europe, America, Africa, and Asia—each painted by a different artist (see Text 2)

2. Half-sections over the entrance arches of the lateral wing representing the geniuses of art, agriculture, science, and industry, the motifs which appear most frequently in arcades

3. On the inner faces of the entrance arches of the lateral wing, the coats of arms of the eight cities of Florence, Monza, Venice, Treviso, Fiori, Padua, Bergamo, and Milan.

The floor of the arcade is also included in the iconographic program. Marble mosaics are set in a geometric pattern. The royal coat of arms lies in the center of the cross surrounded by a wreath of emblems of other Italian provinces, among which the Lombardy bull enjoys special popularity. It is the custom to tread inconspicuously on the realistically represented sexual organs of the bull.

From this enumeration it becomes clear that the arcade space is embedded in a many-layered network of references no longer meaningful to today's visitor. Historical and regional allusions, references to the purpose of the building to serve industry and trade, and the dedication to Italy's unifier, King Vittorio Emanuele II, make the arcade a memorial to the era, a secular counterpart of the cathedral, which celebrates the moment of rebirth of national self-consciousness. That such notions should be embodied in an arcade must appear to us today a fine piece of irony.

Text 1: From Architectural Review *(1966)*
Every Milanese feels compelled to take his stroll in the Galleria at least once a week so as to treat himself to a Campari or a rabarbaro at the "Camparino" or to window shop, to buy things and generally enjoy his own living-room. . . .

Now let me give a short timetable of the characters who gravitate round the Galleria. The Milan establishment goes to bed around one in the morning and then the taximen are left as masters of the area. The taximen have an intimate knowledge of all the nocturnal characters and are often in their confidence. Everything is quiet until three in the morning when the first dustbin men arrive on the heels of the refuse gatherers, and there is a real competition at speedy cleaning.

Soon after that the night establishments empty out, and you see night-club ballerinas, flower girls, cloakroom attendants, waiters, prostitutes making their last round of the night, pimps who pocket the cash, provincial types strutting along under the illusion that they have made a "conquest" —or else disappointed. Anyway they have all been skinned. Amongst them the so-called 'Voci Bianchi' insinuate themselves with their mincing little steps, waddling and trying to pick up the crumbs. This causes violent arguments with the professionals of the streets who are upright by comparison and furiously defend their status and beat.

Towards seven in the morning the mass of people on their way to work cross through the centre. After nine the most heterogeneous types make their appearance in this living room of Milan: first the tourists on their way to the agencies for a tour round the town; then the early news-vendors appear, followed by the traders or hawkers. With the arrival of the latter begins the traffic in diamonds (in front of the Biffi),

324
Galleria Vittorio
Emanuele II

watches, gold and jewellery (in the stretch between the Biffi and Piazza del Duomo), most of it contraband. In front of the Stipel building there gather middlemen, commercial travellers doing business with import and export firms, and finally illicit bookies for the races. Singers, artists, orchestra players and theatre agents occupy the octagon, and on Mondays the hairdressers meet in front of the Motta windows to discuss Trade Union matters, the distribution of labour and new hair styles, settings and make-up. Around eleven in the morning, amongst those who take advantage of being nearby to sip an aperitif you see a group of retired policemen and carabinieri gathered by the Camparino, talking about pensions or reminiscing about their old jobs.

All this means nothing to the mass of people who go to make purchases or stroll or visit the government offices in the centre. From eleven o'clock until one you have to look out for the pickpockets, then Milan eats. The coming and going of the morning begins once more about 4 p.m., but in a more imposing way with the addition of rows of prostitutes accosting passers-by whom they think have money and are not too busy—twisting their mouths, convinced they are not being noticed, offering their services and whispering the price; and now and again there waddles a male tart making languid glances and smiling at the tough males. From five until eight, near the big shops or inside them, it is "pick-pocket time" again. From eight onwards people are on their way home or on their way to the various evening shows.

Hidden among these masses, and playing hide and seek with the police and the night watchmen, are the tramps, amongst them the famous Domingo, Horrible Mary, and the Blind Man with the Dog, who with weeping and wailing try to wrest from your compassion a hundred lire to put together the wretched sum needed for buying . . . a new flat. And now a new species comes to life, the agitators, who hold their meetings in the square to talk about politics and boil themselves up in speeches to an audience which, for the most part, listens to them only with amusement and now and again asks awkward questions that the speakers try to answer to the diversion of the crowd. From time to time there is a stampede and the arrival of the shock police—this can happen till one in the morning on days of political calm— otherwise up till dawn.

At ten at night the "ballerinas" appear again, with the cloakroom attendants, the provincial types—in fact all the people we will find the following morning tired out after a long night, usually spent badly.

Text 2: Theodor Fontane's diary, July 10, 1875
The four frescoes [of the rotunda]:

1. Europe is enthroned as queen, the representative of monarchies all over the world, with crown and scepter. Six or seven other crowns lie on the ground next to her, like jewels, an ambiguous image meaning either "I have many of them" or "I am now beginning to rid myself of them." The genius of art and science stands before her, a flame rising from its head, holding the laurel crown over the attributes of the arts and sciences: globe, palette, capitals of a column, lyre.

2. America (a female figure, as are all four) is first characterized by a Mexican chief who stands next to her. This is a weak symbol. Bales which are being unloaded symbolize trade. Also weak. Next to America is a shield or a double medallion bearing the names of Columbus and Washington. Also pretty poor. More interesting—if I am interpreting it correctly—is the picture of a dark red evening cloud formation on the one side, and the first rays of dawn on the other. It must mean: the sun of an old day is setting; a new day approaches.

3. Asia is also not very happy. She wears a garland of flowers in her hair and sits half dreaming, half musing. This is acceptable. There is a Chinese—representative of the Mongol race—who does homage and bears gifts. Not terribly interesting.

4. Africa. Perhaps the most beautiful. Pyramids, obelisks; Cleopatra, I think, or some other Egyptian princess, sits enthroned. A Nubian (a Negro) has gathered golden sheaves of grain in thick bundles and presents them to her. The entire scene is quite picturesque. The Egyptian queen, the black Negro, and the golden grain complement each other perfectly.

The entire Galleria Vittorio Emanuele is very beautiful. It is more interesting than not. Even though the detail is very rich, the Galleria is nevertheless in good taste; all extravagances have been avoided. In addition, it is wide, airy, roomy, noble throughout. If the Leonardo statue outside on the Piazza della Scalla were better placed, it would be even more beautiful. And even though the building is a work of great talent, I still find the south [?] side of the cathedral square more beautiful, where (as on the Piazza San Marco) a palatial Renaissance building has now been added, which is a private residence and is quite restrained among the arcaded walkways and market halls. I consider this a brilliant piece of work.[546]

Arcade ?

Via Giuseppe Mazzini—Via M. Gonzaga
This single-story arcade with elegant shops, approximately 50 meters long, was constructed about 1900.

Arcade ?

Via Meravigli—Via Gaetano Negri
Part of a commercial building, this arcade

functioned as an entrance to a theater in the interior of the block.

Galleria del Corso
Corso Vittorio Emanuele—Piazza Beccaria—Via Passerella
This arcade was built about 1930, but was planned as early as 1918. It has three wings which meet in a central space. It is an example of an arcade in which nineteenth-century patterns of behavior were simply repeated. At night it and its big sister on the Piazza are the beat of the ladies of the Corso.

MOSCOW
In Moscow today, only the Upper Trade Halls and a double arcade near the Bolshoi Theater still exist, if the reports of friends who have been there are correct. Both have been taken over by the State and turned into department stores. The Russian Baedeker of 1912, however, indicates other arcades as well, but I have not been able to ascertain anything further about them. Nevertheless, I have listed them below.

New Trade Halls (GUM) (figs. 325–331)
Red Square—Vetoshchiny Proyezd—Ilinskaya—Nikolskaya
Red Square, showplace of the nation, the place where the decrees of the czars were read, at first a space for markets and parades, then for revolutions and demonstrations, was given its general outline at the end of the nineteenth century. The Kremlin and the New Trade Halls face each other; the Historical Museum and St. Basil's cathedral define the short sides of the rectangle. The Lenin museum with its stepped cubes, is located across from the main entrance to the New Trade Halls, now called GUM, and is the contribution of the twentieth century to this historic urban area.

Until the end of the eighteenth century, the quarter across from the Kremlin, called Kitaigorod, was Moscow's main commercial area, extending to the Moskva River. It was covered with a chaotic jumble of booths, decrepit granaries, and courtyards haphazardly organized into alleys. The first renewal measure was the expansive market hall (*gostinny dvor*) with colonnades on all sides, designed by Quavenghi and built in the 1780s.[547] In 1786 began the construction of a row of shops directly on Red Square, consisting of arcaded galleries along the Kremlin wall and across from it.

In 1815, after the great Moscow fire and as part of the reorganization of the Mos-

cow city plan, the architect Bové replaced the gallery with the New Trade Hall building. He had a moat in front of the Kremlin wall filled in and the shop buildings removed so that Red Square extended to the Kremlin wall.[548] Bové's building extended the length of the site which GUM covers today; it was elongated, had projecting wings, and a central temple portico, which, however, only concealed the shop alleyways behind it.

In 1869 the neglected condition of the buildings motivated the governor general of Moscow to request of the city government a comprehensive reorganization of the market section;[549] customers had already begun to do their shopping elsewhere. But the particulars of ownership were so confused that nothing could be done for a long time. Only twenty years later did the city succeed in organizing all of the shopowners into a corporation with municipal participation, thus preparing the way for a new building in the grand style. The capital of the corporation amounted to nine and one-half million rubles and consisted of taxable property belonging to the corporation.

A competition among Russian architects was announced on November 15, 1888, for the Upper Trade Halls, which in addition to practical, public-health considerations, also was directed toward completing Red Square on a grand city planning scale. The three prizes obligated the winners to submit to the construction society within two months of the decision a detailed design study, engineering calculations, and a cost estimate. The prizes would be paid only after this work was completed, thus necessitating a rational, replicable system.

Twenty-three architects registered for the competition. The winner of the 6,000-ruble first prize was the "academic of architects," Aleksandr Pomerantsev of St. Petersburg.[550] The other prizes went to R. I. Klein of Moscow and an entrant named Weber from Vienna. In the following years, a gigantic structure went up according to Pomerantsev's plans, a huge arcade complex with a logical system of longitudinal and lateral concourses, galleries, and bridges which made every space of the three levels easily accessible. The building block was a city of booths multiplied into the monumental, using an alleyway system as its organizational scheme.

The dedication of the new Upper Trade Halls took place in 1893 "in the presence of the most royal company." The ceremony honored a three-story shopping center, constructed through the city's initiative and using an arcade system of access. It cost five million rubles, was fireproof (of stone, iron, glass), and required such high rental fees (to pay for the interest on construction costs) that several early tenants chose to delay their occupancy.

R. I. Klein, the second-prize winner, was hired several years later to build the Middle Trade Halls, which would serve wholesale trade; the organization would be similar, but the interior streets would be larger and there would be no glass roof.

Over 200 private firms maintained retail stores in the Upper Trade Halls until the Russian Revolution. There were over 1,000 rooms at their disposal, whose sizes could be easily changed, as they could be rearranged within a support system and had light, mobile walls. Deliveries were made to the cellar, through which vehicles could be driven.

After the 1917 Russian Revolution, the Upper Trade Halls were converted into GUM, the State Universal Department Store.[551] In the 1930s Stalin closed it, and it served as a military hospital during World War II. It returned to its status as a department store only after Stalin's death. Today it is the place where everyone in the country wants to go, the house of the superlative. There are two and one-half kilometers of counters over an area of 47,000 square meters; behind them, 7,000 retail merchants served a billion customers in the period 1956–1966, selling wares of all kinds. One hundred thousand light bulbs are needed to illuminate all the passageways and 1,500 suppliers are engaged to keep goods in stock. There are no elevators of any sort, thus making this largest and most lively of department stores simultaneously one of the most impractical in the whole world. If it had been in private hands, it probably would have been torn down long ago. The journal of the Soviet Trade Ministry, *Sovetskaya Torgoviya*, announced in 1966 that GUM was to be renovated and modernized. A computer would direct the flow of goods; neon lights would replace the many light bulbs. We can only hope that the details of the architecture will be spared.

GUM has the outline of a parallelogram, 90 meters at the ends and 250 meters down the middle. It is bordered by Red Square, Ilinskaya, Vetoshchiny Proyezd, and Nikolskaya, which leads north to the Vladimir gate. There are three entrances on each of the four sides, each leading to three longitudinal arcade spaces and to the three lateral concourses, which are only two stories high. These interior streets divide the entire block into sixteen units which are all connected to one another on all three levels by steps, galleries, and bridges. Each unit is broken up by longitudinal and lateral walls, which have openings so wide that only intersecting concealed supports remain, between which thin mobile walls allow for flexible partitioning. Contra-rotating staircases, running from one longitudinal corridor to another, function as stable centers, connecting the retail levels to the cellar where deliveries are made. The two middle blocks each have two square, enclosed interior courts which were planned for removal of the masses of snow from the glass roofs. Deeper areas formed by the supports may be seen on the exterior longitudinal sides of the complex, allowing larger retail halls. The two large staircases in the center lateral corridor lead directly to these halls. The entire area has cellar space below, some with even two stories. Illumination and ventilation are provided by grates in the arcade floor or by vents disguised by showcases in the center of the space. Deliveries were made by ramps on Vetoshchiny Proyezd which led to an interior unloading court; I am unable to say if it is still done this way today.

The sections of the three arcade spaces vary. The arcades do not serve any traffic function within the city plan, but are rather a network of internal access, orientation, and circulation. The setback at the second-floor level is common to all three corridors, except that they differ in width. The central corridor is wider at the street level than the two side corridors. Only the two side corridors have galleries on the third floor, which project over and are supported by iron corbels. All three arcade spaces are equally wide on the third-floor level and are covered by continuous quarter-circle glass vaults interrupted only by the cupola halfway down the central corridor. The vaults terminate perpendicularly at the end facades. Their imaginative designer was named Shochov. These vaults are supported only by barely visible cables in a fantail formation. No further support is necessary in spite of the breadth of the span.[552]

Wetoschny Projesd

Nikolskaja

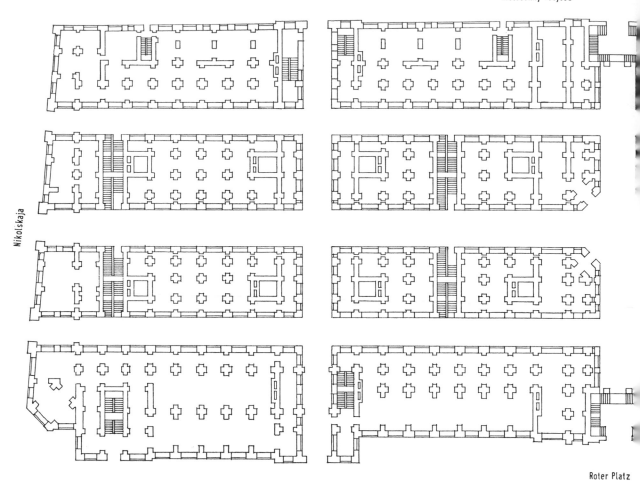

Roter Platz

325
Moscow, New Trade
Halls (GUM), 1888–
1893, ground floor
plan
(Scale: 1 : 800)

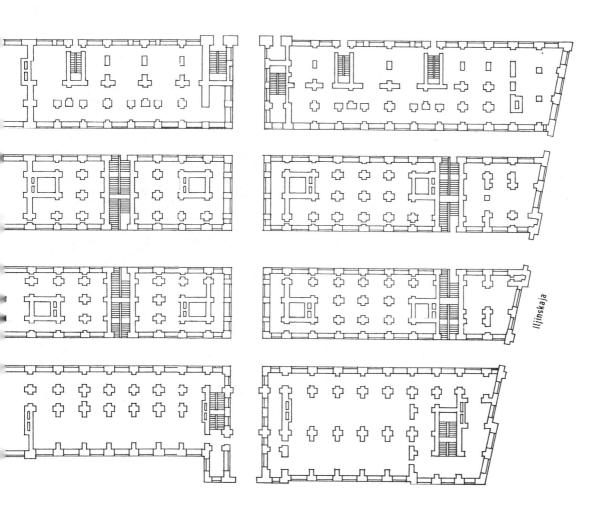

Moskau, Neue Handelsreif.

Iljinskaja

326
GUM, view onto Red
Square, the Lenin
mausoleum, and the
Kremlin wall

327
GUM, view from the
rotunda into the cen-
ter corridor of the
arcade

328
GUM, center cor-
ridor of the arcade

329
GUM, side corridor
of arcade

329
GUM, side corridor
of arcade

330
GUM, center cor-
ridor, upper story

331
GUM, bridges

332
Moscow, Petrovsky
Arcade (now a de-
partment store),
cable suspension roof

333
Petrovsky Arcade,
arcade space

The polygonal opening in the center of the intersecting corridors is reminiscent of the arcade in Milan, although the lateral wing does not reach the roof level of the longitudinal wings. The glass pendentive dome and the grand fountains are more orientation points within the network, more resting or pausing areas, than necessities of the design. The decisive feature of this building is the total accessibility of the rooms, the multiple access to the individual shops, and the penetration of the levels by competing walkways. Just as the Palais Royal was the prototype of the arcade, the Upper Trade Halls were the model at the end of the century for multileveled public systems of access. Bridges, staircases, galleries as balconies or terraces are used here in a more sophisticated manner than in the Victorian arcades. The multiple spaces provoke surprising perspectives, unintentional meetings, and interpenetrating streams of movement. Here we find a city within a city.

The interior and exterior facades differ stylistically, using a mix of Renaissance and Russian architectural elements, the latter as they were known from monasteries and basilicas of the Middle Ages. The facade on Red Square, which attempts to do justice to its function through the use of projections, towers, and mouldings, is the only one which combines marble, granite and sandstone; all other facades are white plaster. The interior facades use arch motifs that become finer and more delicate with height, alternating with pilasters which, with the moulding, frame each bay so that the facades vibrate in a curious way in the depth of the space. The pierced cast-iron balconies, the projecting iron corbels, the narrow, slightly arched bridges, the gold and black signs to label goods, the rows of Chinese hanging lamps, the awnings, the open stands with overflowing displays, and above it all the most delicate glass vault which has no relation to the interior architecture and seems to disappear in the distance—all give space to a life of Oriental or Asian multifacetedness which must be understood as the counterpart to the closed, anti-public collective authority less than 100 meters away: the arcade, the high-spiked wall, and in between the empty, slightly curving square paved with stones one could almost grasp in one's hand.

Petrovsky Arcade (figs. 332, 333)
Petrovka 10—Neglinny Proyezd
The Petrovsky Arcade, located east of the Bolshoi Theater, is Moscow's second arcade. Its two parallel arcade spaces are connected by passageways on each of the three shop levels, which are accessible via galleries and bridges. Its glass roof construction, its section, and its system of access correspond to those of GUM and suggest that Pomerantsev and Shochov collaborated here for a second time several years later. The details of the interior facade, from which the arcade motif has disappeared, suggest a construction date about the turn of the century. It is not clear whether Petrovsky Arcade is one of the two arcades Baedeker noted at this location.

Alexander Arcade
Petrovka—Neglinny Proyezd

Golovteev Arcade
Petrovka—Neglinny Proyezd
Baedeker remarks that there were special Asian textiles of all kinds here, especially silk and wool.

Solodovnikov Arcade
Petrovka—Neglinny Proyezd

Portnikov Arcade
Tverskaya

Dshamgarov Arcade

Lubyansky Arcade

MULHOUSE
Passage du Théâtre
Rue du Sauvage
This structure is not a real arcade. Although it has a continuous, slightly arched glass roof, there are no entrance buildings. The neighboring buildings have instead set up shops and roofed over the resulting alleys.

MUNICH
Schüsselpassage
Kaufinger Strasse 9—Fürstenfelderstrasse
Pre–World War II Munich had a single glass-covered arcade,[553] the Schüsselpassage (or Schüsselbazar) between Kaufingerstrasse and Fürstenfelderstrasse not far from the Frauenkirche.[554] It was built in 1859 by a businessman, M. Schüssel, and was Munich's first large department store. The arcade served more to provide access to courtyards and to the numerous entrances to the department

store than to fulfill a public traffic function. Its two courtyards were glassed over at the second-floor level. I could tell from the construction records, insofar as they have been preserved,[555] that the department store was constantly being remodeled. The facades were made to conform to the taste of the time, the show windows were enlarged, and the interior organization was improved. The glass roofs were raised to the roof level of the lateral buildings to open up the upper stories to the courtyards as arcades. The Schüsselpassage belongs to the building type found in the east, in Prague and Budapest. It was influenced by the walk-through buildings of the fair cities and is merely a marginal phenomenon, as the arcade space has no independent character.

NAMUR
Passage de la Gare
The arcade connects the square in front of the train station to the commercial district of Namur. It has seven square skylights. Built after 1900, it was apparently inserted at some later date into existing construction.

Galerie St. Joseph
Rue de Fer
The Galerie St. Joseph leads from the main commercial artery into a small, parallel side street. It has all of the characteristics of an arcade. The arcade space, which expands in the center into a polygonal shape, has a suspended roof of colored glass typical of the period after 1900. Twelve shops and six house entrances are included in the five-storied buildings, and there is a café in the bombastic, multipurpose turn-of-the-century building located across from one of the exits.

NANTES
Passage d'Orléans
Rue d'Orléans—Place Félix-Fournier
A small, insignificant arcade still connects the Rue d'Orléans to the Place Félix-Fournier and to St. Nicolas church. It was probably built before the Passage Pommeraye as part of a development scheme for the Rue d'Orléans. Here four-storied apartment houses have shops on the ground level in the arcade. The Rue d'Orléans belongs to the network of streets which runs through Nantes parallel to the Loire River between the cathedral and the Place Graslin and beyond. It is the most popular promenade area for the citizens of Nantes.

Passage Pommeraye (figs. 334–341)
Rue de la Fosse 20–22—Rue Santeuil—Rue Crébillon—Rue de Régnier
Anyone who visits Nantes, near the mouth of the Loire, and wanders from the semicircular Place Royale up the Rue Crébillon, hurried along by the constant throng, will cross a pedestrian flow at the top of the Rue Santeuil. It issues from a small archway at the corner of a block which does not quite project into the facade line of the Rue Crébillon. "Passage Pommeraye," read the letters, certainly once gilt but now tarnished, that hang in the archway. Inside, one would expect a discovery to equal the fantasies of Jules Verne, who was born in Nantes in 1828 and was fifteen years old when the arcade was opened. Nantes, the conservative commercial city, owns one of the greatest wonders of the century. This arcade, like no other, remains so unchanged and untouched that its entrances must have concealed it rather than invited passersby; they betray nothing of the spaces to which it provides access.

This arcade was built far away from Paris, in the provinces. It was the desire of Nantes's citizens to build the largest and most beautiful arcade in France. The Passage Pommeraye today is a museum of the ambience of a bygone century. The furnishings, advertisements, lighting, concourses, and shop signs have been preserved in their entirety. They mesmerize the passerby and make him believe that time is standing still. It is for this reason that the Passage Pommeraye is the subject of and inspiration for many surrealist stories.[556] It also appears, as a reminder of other days and of lost love, in the films of Jaques Demy.[557]

Nantes and France should realize that this is a living, inhabited museum. No stone, frame, or plaque should be changed; no neon lights, shop renovation, or clumsy restoration should falsify the picture or destroy the atmosphere created by so many details. I spent an entire day in the arcade. It was raining, and a gray, shadowless light made both the arcade and the vestibule seem like a festive underworld; shops, their owners, and displays seemed like living creatures who had simply forgotten death and progress. There are labyrinthine shops with high shelves full of books which should have been sold long ago, show windows with old guns, clothes, artificial limbs, bandages, and corsets which no one

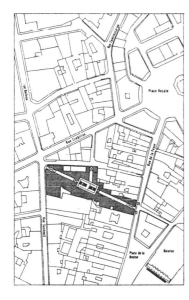

334
Nantes, site of the
Passage Pommeraye,
1966

335
Nantes, Passage
Pommeraye,
1840–1843,
cast-iron staircase

336
Passage Pommeraye,
arcade space, litho-
graph by Benoist

337
Passage Pommeraye,
upper level

338
Passage Pommeraye,
arcade space, view of
the middle and lower
levels

339
Passage Pommeraye,
upper level, balustrade

340
Passage Pommeraye,
upper level, Rue
Crébillon

341
Passage Pommeraye,
upper level, interior
facade, detail with
base of roof

wears anymore. Many articles here can only be found today in the twilight of the arcade.

Pierre de Mandiargues describes one of these shops, the "Hidalgo de Paris," in his book *Le Musée Noir* (The Dark Museum) (Text 1).[558]

Columns in the arcade support galleries upon which allegorical figures stand, holding glass torches that illuminate the arcade. Cast-iron steps compensate for the slope of the site, old vending machines stand on the landings. Passages, balconies, and balustrades confuse the pedestrian, make him turn and stare, tempting him to linger. The architectural repertoire includes strange Persian columns, Rococo garlands, cast-iron balconies with organic motifs, mannerist ornament, and the heavier forms of the French Empire style. A wild confusion—a tropical greenhouse of stone—an imitation of life; carnivorous plants lie in ambush for passersby. An old photographer has his studio over the arcade, with a view out over the wide glass roof. He makes photographs whose like can be found only in antique stores today. Portraits in soft focus with artistic retouchings look down out of gold frames onto the visitor who has made his way up here and sits down on the gilt sofa in accord with the old man's ceremonies. He gave me a photograph which he had made on the occasion of the centennial celebration of the arcade, showing the inhabitants of the building, dressed in historical costumes, on the steps under garlands, banners, and balloons.

The arcade is special in the excellent architectural solution it employs for its particular location: 9.4 meters of height differential had to be accommodated. The architects made a virtue of necessity by widening the arcade space three and one-half times to accommodate a staircase with continuous galleries and shops on all three landings. The unexpected spatial experience psychologically compensates for the difficulty of climbing the stairs.

The architect Jean Baptiste Buron surveyed the site of the arcade at the end of the 1830s. He was under contract to build a restaurant on the site, and suggested building an arcade there on the Parisian model.[559] He consulted the young architect Hippolyte Durand-Gosselin, and the two approached the rich Louis Pommeraye, a notary from Nantes, and interested him in the plan. Pommeraye found further interested parties who were willing to invest their money, and a society was formed. On June 15, 1840, they petitioned the city for permission to build a covered arcade which would occupy the following area: corner of the Rue de Santeuil, the Rue du Poits d'Argent through to the Rue de la Fosse, across from the Rue de la Bourse. This opening would connect the Stock Exchange directly to the center of the city and open to commerce a quarter which had hitherto been composed of unhealthy yards and barely inhabitable houses, by construction of a bazaar with sixty-six shops. On July 31, 1840, permission for construction was granted by the mayor, who had previously consulted the city architect, Denelon fils, and his supervisor of roadways, Driollet. But the project was nevertheless quite problematic. A total of ten buildings would have to be purchased and torn down; there would be protests to overcome, as residents would not want to move. Not all of the buildings could be acquired by the society. The consequence was a site too narrow for the construction of an arcade.

Demolition alone cost 36,000 francs—the equivalent of several million today. Only then did the slope of 9.4 meters become apparent. This situation made the construction of an arcade completely impossible. The architects overcame these difficulties by designing an additional staircase. The new landings almost tripled the number of shops that were directly accessible. The building was completed in 1843 and opened to the public in July of the same year. The arcade, which bears the name of its builder, was greeted enthusiastically. The rainy city of Nantes at last had a social gathering point, a promenade.

During construction, disagreements arose between Pommeraye and Driollet. Driollet refused to allow the stairs to be constructed in wood and required iron steps with iron landings to ensure fire safety. He also opposed covering the galleries with a wooden structure. But on July 4, 1843, the mayor authorized the opening of the arcade against the reservations of Driollet,[560] who wrote in his final report: "The principal arcade (called Galerie la Poste [aux Lettres]) and the middle arcades have not been built of iron nor vaulted—contrary to your orders—but in ordinary carpentry boards, with the exception of the entrance on the Rue de la Poste, which is vaulted.

My opinion has not changed on the subject ... I do not think that the staircase, which I find remarkable for its sturdiness, would, in spite of its perfect construction, provide the necessary stability in case of an emergency or the development of a crowd on the upper landings. It would have been better if the columns of the last bay, in order to prevent any shaking, had been connected to the large columns by cross-bars. Art would have lost something, it is true, but solidity would have gained. The light and very delicate ramps did not seem to me any more resistant to a violent shock, which could occur if a crowd stampeded. This is my opinion, perhaps a little severe, but set down in order to safeguard your responsibility. . . ." It is not clear whether the glass roofs and the main stairs were replaced with iron structures at this time or later.

The notary Pommeraye, however, did not enjoy the building for very long since he lost everything a few years later in extravagant and foolish speculation. The arcade fell to the liquidators. The Tribunal Civile (municipal tribunal) decided on August 23, 1849, to sell the arcade in three parts. Pommeraye died in 1851; his penniless widow was forced to ask the mayor for a small pension.

Baron Baillardel, who had bought the whole arcade, suggested on September 24, 1851, an additional connection to the Rue Régnier, which would open onto the middle staircase level. This proposal was carried out several years later. There is nothing further to report on the subsequent history of the arcade through the century, except that Planat praised it for the restaurants which made it a Mecca for gourmets. That is all gone today.[561] The Passage Pommeraye has lost its social function; it only helps those who work in the city to get quickly to their buses on the Place du Commerce. The shops seem to slumber peacefully.

The German bombings of Nantes in September 1943 and June 1944 left their mark. The glass roofs are damaged and the mouldings are broken. The damage has not been repaired, but the arcade does not seem threatened in any way.

The Passage Pommeraye has a completely irregular outline. It has street facades on three sides, two of regular building width, the third (on the Rue Crébillon) occupying the entire corner of the block, with its entrance placed diagonally on the corner.

The arcade is divided into four sections. The central staircase, 11 meters wide, is located in the middle. The arcade wings, 3 meters wide, are connected to each of the staircases' three levels. I assume that the architects divided the work among themselves. The upper arcade wing on the Rue Crébillon clearly shows its derivation from the Galerie Vivienne in Paris;[562] the facades have been copied but are sculpturally richer and more deeply profiled. The arcade is entirely of freestone. Its sculptor was Louis Grootaers of Nantes, who did the portraits of the French poets in the arch spandrels and the busts on the keystone corbels of the facades.[563]

The glass roof of this upper gallery is divided by stone arches into four identical sections. Parts of the original glass covering with square panes still exist. Through a passage with a coffered barrel vault one enters the wide middle space and comes to the steps which lead into the depth of the arcade. This space is four-storied; its balconies overlook the lower gallery. The space above the glass roof of the lower gallery opens up, following the profile of the arcade through an arched opening in which two iron figures, "Day" and "Night," stand on a pedestal; they lean against the arcade clock. Today this opening is partly boarded up; it is not clear whether it was ever actually open.

The sixteen columns which support the gallery on two levels are faintly reminiscent of the Hall of the Hundred Columns in Darius's palace, even though here it is brackets rather than bulls' heads that support the entablature. The columns are topped with smaller-than-life-size figures by the Nantes sculptor Jean de Bay, which face the interior space and look down into the stairwell. Their attributes reveal what they are intended to represent: navigation (anchor and line), agriculture (sheaf of grain), trade (sack and chest), fine arts (torso of Aphrodite), industry (hammer), viniculture (bottle), science, and others. Several figures are repeated. Behind each figure a cast-iron stem holds a light fixture. Curiously, the four figures in the corners of the staircase balance light fixtures as torches in their mouths. The two sets of cast-iron stairs are suspended from floor to floor; each has an intermediate landing.[564] The main staircase landings run around the galleries. Underneath the stairs are the entrances to the cellar rooms for the upper gallery. The architecture of this center space is amateurish and weak in its details, spare in profile and full of unresolved connections; but this impression disappears in the face of the fantastic spatial effect. The two dark, narrow levels in the shadows, the bright upper areas emphasized by advertisements, the expanse of the space, the ring of allegorical figures, and the passages which penetrate into the depths of the arcade wings—all make an unforgettable and incomparable picture.

The lower arcade, ending in the Rue de la Fosse, has three stories and a continuous glass roof similar in construction to that of the middle area and is sparsely ornamented. Access to the buildings is above the arcade. The third wing, the Galerie Régnier, ends diagonally on the middle landing of the staircase and is the continuation of the Rue de Régnier, which branches off from the Rue Crébillon.

The glass roof over the middle section was replaced after the bombing attacks on Nantes. An older support structure may be discerned beneath the simple glass saddle roof from its slightly arched cast-iron ribs, which are supported by iron rods at regular intervals. It is identical to the one represented in the old etching. The ridgepole was apparently carried by these arches through the use of two diagonal bars, as can still be seen today.

Text 1: A. Pieyre Mandiargues, Le Passage Pommeraye, *1946*
Slowly, I went up the Rue Crébillon, surprised to find it almost deserted at the hour when it is usually crowded with strollers and the fashionable ladies of Nantes. The emptiness made me notice something that had escaped me before: on the left, and a little back from the Rue Crébillon, there was a tiny square with the entrance to an arcade, above which was this inscription in gold letters on a black background: "Visit the Passage Pommeraye"; while a metal sign, looming up from within, presented the further instructions: "Tourists! Do not visit Nantes without seeing the display by Hidalgo of Paris, on your right, at the top of the stairs, in the statue gallery." How could I not obey this mysterious double injunction, which a large red hand, seemingly alone, the index finger raised in the darkness of the vault, made all the more compelling? The hand was the sign of a glove maker whose business was rather curiously called "Au Puits" (By the Well), perhaps because of the aquatic atmosphere evoked by all of these glassed arcades, or

perhaps because of the particular construction of the Passage Pommeraye, which occupies two levels connected by a deep-welled and very steep stair.

When you enter from the outside, from daylight, you must give your eyes some time to adjust to the half-darkness of this covered space; then you can discern that the upper part of the arcade has beautiful stucco decoration in the late Louis-Philippe style; busts, which the damp has given a green patina, stand out from a background of lunettes. All of this is decayed, crumbling in places. The decay seems invaded by denticulated algae, or by ferns, or by moss (which?), carpeted with a blue dust like a very delicate down. The contours of the arches, which are hazy, this marshy vegetation, the humidity, the opal and sea-green shades locate the Passage Pommeraye among the landscapes of the ocean depths of *Twenty Thousand Leagues under the Sea*, where the divers, guided by Captain Nemo, chase tortoises and sharks among the colonnades of a submerged Atlantis. . . .

Then I saw this curious gallery of statues whose name evoked a shadowy necropolis inhabited by still, white figures. Below a glass roof, through which slanted at this late hour the full light of day, there is a large rectangular balcony which surrounds and overlooks a large, steep staircase which is seen to submerge itself in the still more shadowy depths of the next level down. As for the statues, they are morose figures of adolescents of both sexes, placed at short intervals; they adorn the balustrade while turning their backs to the shop windows.

A naked child, who balances a torch on his chin, and whose pose, with distended cheeks and a stupidly passive expression on his tilted-back face, is rather obviously obscene, guards the threshold of the stair. Three rows of allegories embellish the two long balustrades; the smallest at the end of the gallery, where one can discern another lamp-child, the pendant of the first.

It is like a game of riddles. Seated next to an anchor on a coil of rope, Navigation contemplates the distance with a blank face which loses itself in infinity. Agriculture rests on a sheaf of corn, Trade on a pile of sacks and boxes. The slightly plump young girl, pensive and melancholy, leaning on the broken torso of Aphrodite, could just as well represent the Fine Arts in general as the individual arts of sculpture or archeology. Surely the young man brandishing a smith's hammer is Industry, and probably the maiden, with her long braids, is Science, who, a shell in the hollow of her hand, seems to have been abandoned by a fickle god between a globe of the earth and a printing press. Others, more imaginative in the choice of attributes, do not betray their identity. Some figures repeat themselves, although it is not clear why they are singled out.

Shabby figures, a little smaller than life size, pale, without smiles, plastered with a dirty, greenish yellow, you exude a sadness so great that you might be a seraglio of old children, sick children, poor and suffering children. At the same time, you are disturbing, under the veils which only half cover your wretched nudity, because of the effect of this curious atmosphere of melancholy, of resignation, and of repentance in which you bathe like a troop of gloomy beauties flung in costumes into the steam of a Turkish bath for a Mardi Gras orgy. Here and there on a cheek, a breast, a leg, touches of damp catch your eye like suspicious erosions of the flesh, symptoms of a hidden sickness. I wandered for a long time among the sad figures of this misty carnival, leaving the direction of my steps to chance. Incessantly, several words buzz in my head: *Le fardeur du destin*, the beginning of a vague sentence, a rhetorical figure, or what? And destiny, the sphinx in the cold and imposing desert of existence, what is it doing in the statue gallery of the Passage Pommeraye, where I find myself at this very moment facing the "modern dental clinic of Hidalgo of Paris"? A shop as bizarre as it is unique. Through quantities of posters gaudy with hot colors, yellow, red, orange, it resounds everywhere, this sonorous name which seems to jeer at geography: "Chez Hidalgo de Paris" and then again "C'est ici HIDALGO de Paris," in characters placed vertically one under the other as in Chinese signs. The shop front is a capricious bazaar where perfumes and instruments of dental surgery mingle with the most varied objects that you have ever seen gathered together in the service of publicity. A small glass case holds in tidy array on a shining, mawkish pad of pink satin wax casts of human teeth eroded by all the diseases to which they fall prey. I noticed as well with due admiration an ingenious advertising plaque for "Special Hidalgo Antiseptic Shampooing—from a base of organic capillary cells," which calls to the attention of the bald "several cases of alopecia photographed on our clients."

And if this were not enough, four plate-glass windows situated against the balustrade of the arcade contain many more things which one would expect even less to find in a dental clinic, however modern it might be. I came and leaned up against them and never in my life did I study a richer collection of dribbling glasses, fake turds, of firecrackers and detonators heaped up there together with everything one could imagine in the way of practical jokes and tricks. Amazing marvels, even their nomenclature is a fair of images too suggestive for one to be able to hold oneself back for very long from plunging into them and strolling lazily among the disorderly crowd, squealing and boisterous, of words set free: infernal machine to cause sneezing, devil's plate-lifter, lover's tape measure, Satan's fluid, assassin's soap, serpent hat, colic cushion, climbing mice, astounding sweets, trick cards, cigars and jugs with honeymoon wishes, water-pistol cigarettes, mysterious picture, flying cigar, endless string, rubber biscuits, surprise bombs, exploding grain of silver, invisible glue, devil's nails, joker's corkscrew, joker's hose nozzle. . . .

I walked several steps behind her; we descended the steps of the staircase together; we passed in front of the entrance of the Galerie Régnier; we covered the lower gallery of the Passage Pommeraye. Nothing of the distracting decor which we passed escaped me. I noticed and I remembered, with a sort of frenetic avidity, as painful as that intensified vision which often accompanies facial neuralgia, all of the objects, all the posters, all the signs in all the windows of all the shops. Bookstores come back to me forcefully with the titles of more than twenty books; the dance class and carriage of "Mlle. Robin, licensed professor," and portraits of her prettiest pupils. Elsewhere, art furniture, an abundance of Grand Prix terra cotta, melancholy representations of fleeing nymphs, lovebirds, and a poor scrawny lion. Further down, there was a bandage supplier, as there is in almost every arcade, which overwhelmed me with orthopedic corsets, surgical supports, apparatus for hernias, Galien cancers, guards for nose wounds, breast bands, gauntlet splints, cotton wool, suspenders, and support stockings. Finally, just before the exit onto the Rue de la Fosse, I saw the storefront of a gunsmith whose name I had to read on the window above the cut-off automatic pistols, the oiled and shining rifles. The gunsmith—the last bubble to make its fragile escape from the Passage Pommeraye—was named Brichet.

NAPLES

Galleria Principe di Napoli (figs. 342–344)
Piazza Museo Nazionale—Via Enrico Pessina—Via Broggia
The Galleria Principe di Napoli was the first large arcade in Naples and belongs to a series of arcades which were built in many cities in Italy on the model of the gigantic Galleria in Milan. An older "passagio coperto" leads through the Palazzo dei Ministri but has no shops.[565]

The building complex was erected, partly on the site of the former Convent of S. Maria di Constantinopoli, between 1876 and 1883 by the architects Breglia and de Novelli.[566] The arcade is at an excellent location in terms of traffic; it lies where the

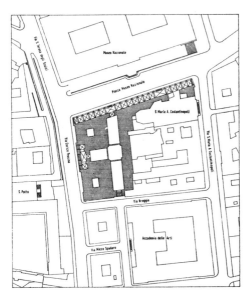

342
Naples, site of the
Galleria Principe di
Napoli, 1960

343
Naples, Galleria
Principe di Napoli,
1876–1883, en-
trance, Piazza Museo
Nazionale

344
Galleria Principe di
Napoli, arcade space

main commercial street of Naples, the lengthened Via Roma, branches off and forms a right angle to the wide arterial street, the Strada Foria. Across from the building complex lies the famous Museo Nazionale with its great archeological collection. Across from the museum is a large arcaded walk which runs alongside and is attached to the church of S. Maria di Constantinopoli. The arcade is *T*-shaped. The major wing is an extension of Via Bellini in the direction of the Piazza; the short wing ends in a three-part, arcaded staircase which forms the entrance from Via Enrico Pessina. The central space at the intersection of the wings is square. It is covered with a pyramidal glass roof resting on low arches and rising a story above the wings.

The Galleria Principe di Napoli is deserted today. Parts of the north facade have collapsed to reveal the interior of a hall in gilt and white plaster. While the traffic roars just around the block, it is quiet in the arcade. The floor is unkempt; the shops serve now only as storage areas. The only customers are a few tramps who have made themselves comfortable on the stone benches of the rotunda. The architecture is colossal in its dimensions—an essential characteristic of Neopolitan palaces. But the details are faded, lifeless, and seemingly dead today because of a yellowish gray patina.

Galleria Umberto I (figs. 345–353)
Via Roma (formerly Via Toledo)—Via S. Brigida—Via Giuseppe Verdi—Via Vittorio Emanuele III

The second of Naples's arcades is the Galleria Umberto I. It occupies almost the entire block formed by the Via Roma, the Via S. Brigida, the Via Giuseppe Verdi, and the Via Vittorio Emanuele III. It is located in the center of the city between the Piazza del Plebiscito, the Piazza Trieste e Trento, and the Piazza Municipio near the harbor. Across from the arcade are the Teatro S. Carlo and the Palazzo Reale. This location guarantees the almost equal use of all four entrances, and provides the ideal justification for the cross form of the arcade, which is crowned by a huge dome. It is superior to the Milan arcade in that, while the latter was originally planned as a connection between the cathedral square and the Piazza della Scala, it employed the cross form through the ambition of its architect, Mengoni, rather than to accommodate a traffic pattern.

The building of the Galleria Umberto I was motivated by the pride of the Neopolitan people.[567] They wanted to make Naples Italy's leading city, an aspiration of almost every large Italian city after unification. In order to come closer to this goal, it was necessary to lay out a city quarter where the Stock Exchange, the Chamber of Commerce, the great banks, and the Mediterranean shorefront could be accommodated in close relationship to each other. The construction of the Galleria was also the beginning of a thoroughgoing urban renewal project to improve public health. It was the devastating cholera epidemic of 1884 that brought about the clearance and rebuilding—that is, the opening up—of the inner city. It also led in 1885 to the construction of sewers and a piped drinking water system. This renewal program still exists today. But all of one's enthusiasm for Naples cannot hide the indescribable social and sanitary conditions that prevail in close proximity to the arcade. This situation justifies some strengthening of this program, which is now over eighty years old.

The construction of the Galleria Umberto I has a lengthy early history. It was preceded by an entire series of projects, which I will mention briefly here.

The chosen site posed two problems: the inclusion of the two churches already standing, S. Fernando and S. Brigida, and an architectural response to the wide front of the Teatro San Carlo, built in 1737 by Medrano and Carasale and still one of Europe's greatest stages.

The first proposal to include an arcade[568] was the work of the engineer A. Cottrau. He designed it at the end of 1881 and submitted it to the city government on June 15, 1882. Cottrau envisioned a bold subdivision of the block by short streets and a Y-plan arcade with three wings of equal length, one of which would be axially related to the S. Carlo facade. Colonnades would border the block along Via Roma and Via S. Carlo. His plan to tear down S. Fernando to create a direct line of street access to Piazza S. Fernando (today Piazza Trieste e Trento) brought about the end of his project; the church had considerable significance for the city, especially in its role in the 1656 cholera epidemic.

Subsequent proposals were submitted by Savino, Pisanti-Cossitto, and Emanuele Rocco. In 1885 a municipal commission was formed, which considered the pro-

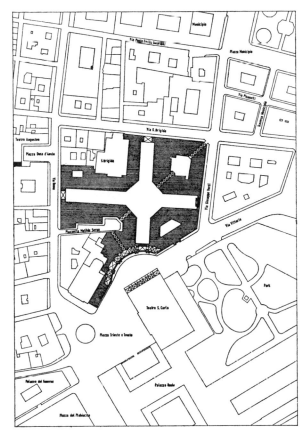

345
Naples, site of the
Galleria Umberto I,
1960

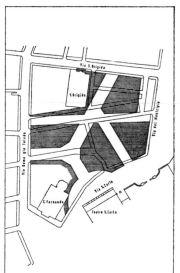

346
Galleria Umberto I,
first project by Rocco

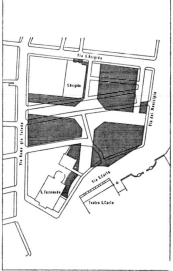

347
Galleria Umberto I,
second project

posals and decided on Emanuele Rocco's submission. He received the contract to develop the quarter.[569] Two phases of Rocco's design for the project are shown in figs. 346 and 347.[570] The first, clearly influenced by Cottrau, contains the Y arcade but has fewer streets. S. Fernando is preserved, forming a counterpoint to the facade of the Teatro S. Carlo with a semicircle whose origin is located in the theater facade.

The second project Rocco submitted to the city envisions a galleria with a cruciform plan and an octagonal rotunda in the center. The galleria occupies the entire block yet the wide entrance to the Teatro S. Carlo is preserved. The arcade wing runs diagonally toward the facade and a pendant to it is wedged in. S. Fernando, Palazzo Cirella, S. Brigida, and Palazzo Barbaia are preserved. The traffic patterns between the two squares are no longer so straightforwardly resolved, but the building gains independence.

It probably had something to do with the acceptance of Emanuele Rocco's proposal that he not only created a design that could compete with the Milan Galleria, but also traveled all over Europe to study other arcades in order to make the city of Naples a financial offer.[571] He combined with the Societa dell'Esquilino di Roma, which was prepared to offer a bond of 400,000 lire. In 1885, Rocco was awarded the contract for the construction of the Galleria Umberto I. Construction went on during the period 1887–1890 and the dedication took place on November 10, 1892. For the opening there was an exhibition in the arcade of handicrafts and artistically ambitious industrial products.

The Galleria Umberto I still stands today in its original form and is the largest public space in the entire city. It is gigantic in its dimensions, is protected from both rain and sun, and is cooled by the sea wind which blows through it. The center, the rotunda area, is full each noon with the noise of arguing, gesturing groups: the bourse of Neopolitan singers and cabaret artists. Sundays, the arcade is full to bursting. Naples discusses the state of its soccer team. At night the arcade is illuminated by a ghostly light; an army of street cleaners turns the marble floor into a sea. It is scrubbed to make it shine the next day. Some figures loiter at the bar by the Via Roma entrance, which closes at three.

348
Naples, Galleria Um-
berto I, 1887–1891,
entrance opposite the
Teatro San Carlo

Only the newspaper offices and the printers still have their lights on.

The lower level is also open to the public. Directly under the octagon is a round hall, today used as a cinema. One can walk around it; iron catwalks lead to the balcony. Night clubs, bars, billiard rooms, printing presses, and banks form the twilight underworld of the arcade. One can see the shadows of passersby through the round skylights of glass bricks which are set in the floor of the arcade. On the roof lives the caretaker. His is the realm of light, the rooftop made into large terraces. He can look down through the lunette window at the end of the arcade wings into the cavernous depths, into the swirl of humanity. From his small house, he looks over the bay of Naples.

An episode from the history of the Galleria Umberto I belongs to this description, since it has entered into literature.[572] Naples was taken by the Allies in October 1943. The earlier bombings had destroyed the glass roof of the Galleria. In the following period, the arcade became the center of an indescribable mixture of people: American, British, and French soldiers, Neopolitans, returning emigrants—all came here to stroll. In the novel *The Gallery*, by the American John Horne Burns, the Galleria Umberto I is the geographical center of the action. I have included some selections in Text 1.

The Galleria Umberto I occupies almost the entire block it crosses; it backs up onto S. Brigida and forms three separate interior courtyards with entrances on the diagonal. The portals of the four arcade entrances reach high to form coffered barrel vaults. The wall above rests on the transparent support of a loggia—a motif borrowed from the facade of the Teatro S. Carlo. At attic height is a wide frieze with the name of the arcade, and above it a group of figures as a terminating form. Across from the Teatro S. Carlo, the facade of the Galleria is arcaded with paired Tuscan columns. Two exits meet the square at a 45-degree angle to each other. One leads into the arcade; the other is merely decorative, included for symmetry, and leads nowhere. The exterior and interior facades of the arcade are equal in height and have the same design. On the interior, however, the pillars are sheathed with marble, and the upper wall areas are richly decorated and painted. A section of the arcade reveals three almost independent areas:

1. The lower level, which is almost 5 meters high in order to accommodate the height differential within the site. It is accessible to the public via separate stairs at the entrances. The facilities located there have already been described.

2. The pedestrian concourses, with their inlaid marble floor, countless shops, bars, cafes, and restaurants on the ground floor; four gate-like entrances on the diagonals of the octagon, which lead to staircases; and the three upper stories, where space is rented to private schools, papers, publishing houses, and studios.

3. The glass vault with a 56-meter-high dome whose pendentives frame iron angels blowing trumpets. The openings of the arches are glassed in. The zone formed by the glassed-over area has the effect of being an independent body. Almost free of decorative additions, it derives its beauty from technical skill and reveals all the more clearly the street character of the arcade space. The wings of the arcade are roofed with glass barrel vaults borne by arched lattice trusses which are supported by purlins whose undersupports are also arched. The understructure carries the fine net of ribs. Hinged panes of glass at the base of the vault and a ventilation strip allow for constant circulation.

The facades of the arcade space are divided into four zones, each of which is separated from the others by a moulding. On the ground level, wide pilasters separate the shops; the mezzanine level is marked by a balcony, used for advertisements. The second floor uses a Palladian motif; the third displays double-arched windows and the uppermost story presents pairs of almost square windows with apartments behind them. This facade division has been criticized, first by Joseph, who writes in his history of Italian architecture:[573] "The architecture leaves much to be desired in comparison to Mengoni's; it displays neither the refinement nor the originality of his detail. Also, the grandeur of the interior facade design of the Milan arcade is missing in Naples, since the Palladian motif on the main story and the closely spaced windows on the second story create, in their almost endless repetition, a trivial effect. An artistic transition between walls and roof is also missing here, where one would have at least expected an attempt at improvement." Hitchcock writes:

350
Galleria Umberto I,
caretaker's office,
roof level

349
Galleria Umberto I,
arcade space

351
Galleria Umberto I,
arcade space and
roof

352
Galleria Umberto I,
entrance, Via
Giuseppe Verdi

353
Galleria Umberto I,
exterior of roof

"The Galleria Umberto I in Naples is a late and rather inferior imitation [of the Galleria Vittorio Emanuele], whose ornate entrance most ungenerously overpowers Niccolini's S. Carlo Theatre across the street."[574]

The Naples arcade outdid its competitors in the north in section and in breadth, but failed to equal them in length or in conspicuousness of location. The cruciform plan and the design of the glass roof are similar, but the spatial effect is different. The facades of the arcade in Naples are layered; the window sequence is more closely spaced and more harmonious with the narrow (50-centimeter) interval between ribs of the glass roof.

The chief difference between Milan and Naples is that in Naples, there is no removed vantage point from which one can view the arcade and the space it covers. The entrances are perpendicular to the line of the street. One strolls unsuspectingly along Via Roma. A chance glance to the left, and the eye is overcome by the sudden revelation of the existence of this huge, hidden space. The passerby does not have to be of a special religion or have a ticket to enter. The arcade belongs to everyone. It is the monumental expression of this most characteristic achievement of the nineteenth century, the public sphere, in which everyone may participate.

Text 1: John Horne Burns, The Gallery
The Galleria Umberto I in Naples is a large arcade, a cross between the hall of a train station and the nave of a church. It feels as if you are in a museum until you notice the bars and the stores. The gallery had a vaulted glass roof in earlier days. The bombing attacks on Naples reduced the skylight cupola to ruins. The glass fell with a crash onto the flagstone; it was a horrible sort of downpour. But life in the Galleria continued. In August of 1944 it constituted the heart of Naples without being formally acknowledged as such; it was a living, breathing cell which continually divided and subdivided, forming itself, flooded by the Allied soldiers, the Italian people, and the smell of liquor.

Everyone in Naples went to the Galleria Umberto. The banners and the columns, the archangels which blew their trumpets from the mouldings, and the metal ribs which once supported the glass roof—all heard more at night than they saw during the day—the grating sound of American army boots on a pillaging foray, the sliding of Neapolitan sandals, the clicking of British boot nails, all accompanied rhythmically by the scent of liquor. The cries and the conversation, the pinching and the

staggering, kisses pressed hastily on lips, the sizzling on the flagstones of urine. Shadows chase one another by moonlight, single and in pairs, from one end of the gallery to another.

You could make a pilgrimage through the Galleria Umberto, as from portrait to portrait, wandering through deep in your thoughts. . . .

She loved the arcade from the very first day; she wished the entire glass enclosure had been bombed away. It was secretive here; it seemed like being inside a Baroque Underground station. With passion she meditated in front of the shops, lost in the sight of horribly spotted cushions and sofa covers, in which someone had embroidered "Mother," sometimes correctly, sometimes not. Tasteless tablecloths sported the red head of a bull, insignia of the 34th Division, or the mosque of the Fifth Army. But all this didn't spur her on to buy—nor did the fragrant oil, Vesuvius brand, and the pieces of jewelry (the GIs paid twenty times the correct price for their girls in Montana)—none brought her to buy. . . .

The form of this arcade is symbolic as well—a prostrate mighty cross, from which the corpse has been removed. . . .

It was appropriate to compare the arcade in 1944 with a commune, whose population shifted daily. The people who came here to drink and to consume, to gaze and to loiter and to pose any question at all— they were different from the rest of humanity at the time. You couldn't place them in any generic ordering—not mother, nor wife, not even by religion. The Galleria Umberto looked like that city which rose up out of the sea every hundred years to dry out under the powerful rays of the sun.

NEWCASTLE-UPON-TYNE
Royal Arcade (figs. 354–358)
Pilgrim Street—Manor Street
The counterpart to the Lowther Arcade in London, and following directly upon it chronologically, is the Royal Arcade in Newcastle-upon-Tyne. It was built with more costly materials and with greater precision in regard to detail. Its proportions are wider and its space is more differentiated. Like the Lowther Arcade, it is part of an improvement program, an urban planning project of wide scope.

Local pride expresses itself in the following way:[575] "The Royal Arcade is acknowledged to be superior to the Lowther Arcade, the finest in London, which only 212 feet in length, is not so well lighted and the front of which, above all, is formed of brick and stuccoed, while this is of polished stone. We do not believe that, as an Arcade this of Newcastle has its equal in Europe or in the universe."

NEWCASTLE

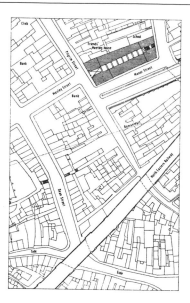

354
Newcastle, site of the
Royal Arcade, 1886

355
Newcastle, Royal
Arcade, 1831–1832,
demolished 1966;
longitudinal section

356
Royal Arcade, ar-
cade space

The architect was John Dobson;[576] at least the design originated with him, even though his authorship is not certain.[577] It has been suggested that Thomas Oliver was the architect, since he was designing plans for a new Newcastle at the same time Dobson was engaged in a similar enterprise. In any case, it is certain that Richard Grainger was the "speculative builder"; his initiative brought about Newcastle's new center.

Newcastle grew up out of a series of smaller towns. It is located on the banks of the Tyne, which cuts deep into the surrounding impoverished countryside.[578] It became rich from coal mining, and at the beginning of the nineteenth century was the largest British export port for coal, which was being used in increasing quantities since the invention of the steam engine. Iron and weapons industries developed there; Stevenson built his first locomotive there in 1814. The city's economic expansion demanded space for distribution and supply facilities. Medieval Newcastle, located on a river, could not expand and was connected to Upper Newcastle only by steep paths. In 1815 the first plans began to be made for a new center city on top of the old one.

Dobson was one of the first architects who settled in Newcastle. He had wanted to go to London, but opened his own firm in Newcastle. He began working on plans for the city in 1814, submitting them in various stages to the Newcastle Corporation. But he was unsuccessful because he lacked diplomatic skill and was poor with numbers. The man who had both these talents was Richard Grainger, a businessman and builder. They formed a partnership and Dobson designed for Grainger. Before they undertook the Central Development Scheme in 1834, they worked together on three preliminary projects:[579] development of Eldon Square and Blackett Street, Leazes Terrace and Leazes Crescent, and Royal Arcade on Pilgrim Street in the extension of Mosley Street, built in 1788. The model for these buildings may be found in Bath; it shows uniform facades and large-scale spaces.

In 1834 Grainger built an office to share with the municipal authorities, in the interest of better coordination. They began with the rebuilding of a large area which in all of England can only be compared to Nash's Regent Street in London. The first project was built in 1834, a city block whose interior was penetrated by a network of arcade-like retail streets with a total of 153 shops, the largest market of its time. In quick succession followed the development of Grey Street, Market Street, Nelson Street, Nun Street, Grainger Street, Hood Street. The Exchange, Royal Theater, Green Market, and the Grey Column mixed business and residential buildings with public institutions. In 1850 the immense Doric train station, Central Station, Dobson's last work, was added to the south of the new city, thus rounding it off and bringing long-distance traffic directly into the center of the city. A viaduct spanned the valley. A giant, two-level bridge, the High Level Bridge, connected Newcastle to the opposite bank without hindering water traffic.

In less than two decades, a new city center grew up with model public facilities and generous spaces that are almost unaltered today. The demands of traffic have brought about the first changes. The first victim was the Royal Arcade, which had always been badly located. It had to give way to a huge traffic complex, the Pilgrim Street Scheme, which opened up a north-south traffic route via the New Tyne Bridge. As early as one hundred years before, the demolition of the Royal Arcade had been considered to make way for the construction of the City Road.

Grainger had intended the site of the Royal Arcade for the Corn Exchange, which was built years later on Market Street. After the old development had been torn down, the cornerstone for the arcade was laid in June 1831. Three hundred workmen were employed at the site, and by May 1832 the building was finished and opened to the public. The cost was 40,000. An article in the *Newcastle Journal* marked the opening (Text 1).[580]

According to accounts, Dobson and Grainger could not agree on the location of the Royal Arcade. Two difficult factors had to be considered: that the sharply inclining site could be accommodated only by a long set of steps onto Manor Street, and that the arcade led out of the city and thus had no goal; it was effectively a dead end.

These disadvantages had drawn comment as early as 1840 in the *Penny Magazine*:[581] "[Grainger] desired to concentrate as many public offices as possible on this spot, and to make the remaining part a sort of inn of court, a collection of all the Lawyer's offices in the town. In this he has partially succeeded, but only partially, from the ar-

357
Royal Arcade,
facade, Pilgrim Street

358
Royal Arcade,
demolition

cade not being a necessary thoroughfare, [the] one and only opening into a busy part of the town."

The Royal Arcade was the first British arcade to be planned for the most complex program possible. The story of its tenants shows that this advantage could not compensate for the faulty location. Grainger had conceived of the Royal Arcade as both a shopping center and commercial center. In the entrance building on Pilgrim Street there was a stately sequence of spaces. The north side was occupied by the North of England Joint Stock Bank, the south by the Savings Bank. Inside the arcade were eight shops on each side, above them two floors of offices rented by architects, engineers, and lawyers. The post office and newspaper reading rooms drew additional customers. In the entrance building on Manor Street were established various city offices. Above them were an auction house and showrooms, and on the top a conservatory and steam baths. The vaulted cellar was partly at ground floor level because Manor Street sloped sharply. Wine merchants had their storerooms there, and, of course, there was a pub as well. In all, "a great variety of useful and ornamental attractions, calculated to render it a favourite promenade, and a place of general resort."

In the early days one could at least take a shortcut through the arcade to the police station and the Town Court; but as early as 1840 the space was occupied by new tenants: the Bankruptcy Court and the Newcastle and Gateshead Gas Company. After the construction of Central Station, the arcade was increasingly pushed to the outer limits of the commercial district; one tenant after another moved to the west. In 1876 alone the gas company, savings bank, bankruptcy court, and post office gave notice. The arcade was taken over by secondhand furniture dealers, the unmistakable harbingers of a battle lost.

Fineberg[582] describes the condition of the arcade in 1953, ten years before its demolition: "Today the Royal Arcade is a melancholy sight, black with grime, shabby and frowsy, the elegant glazing to the domes replaced by utility glazing and the shops with painted windows harbouring offices and small manufactures of little significance. The premises above now contain a School of Dancing, an 'Employers' Recreational Club and Canteen,' a Socialist Society, Spiritualist Church and 'Tara Cielidhe' Club."

I visited Newcastle in 1965 and could not find the Royal Arcade until I realized that an ugly, barren torso of a building which stood solitary in the middle of a traffic circle was all that remained. I found my way in through an opening which was not nailed shut and stood in the dark arcade. The glass was broken, the plaster falling, and the floors were torn up; and yet, no one had dared to tear down this Greek Revival fragment completely. In 1963 the ponderous facade on Pilgrim Street had been numbered stone by stone and removed. It is waiting for reuse. The protests of the Royal Fine Arts Club, the Victorian Society, private citizens, and local authorities were successful. The arcade is being rebuilt and included in an office complex designed to incorporate not only the arcade but the traffic circle as well.[583]

The Royal Arcade was the southernmost part of a block formed by Pilgrim Street and by Manor Street as it turns north. It was divided into three sections on different levels, each independently accessible.

1. The entrance building on Pilgrim Street, a huge, four-storied structure placed on the axis formed by Mosley Street
2. The middle section, which had a vaulted arcade area, eight shop bays, and three-storied arcade buildings
3. The entrance building on Manor Street, which lay on a lower level with steps to accommodate the 6-meter height differential. The ground floor was accessible from a stair landing.

The building was constructed in brick. The facade on Pilgrim Street and parts of the arcade space were of yellow sandstone which gradually blackened from air pollution. The facade had a high ground story and an entrance to the arcade supported by two Doric columns. Over that was a row of Corinthian columns two stories high between small corner projections. The facade also incorporated a frieze in a vine motif, a moulding which projected considerably, a fifth floor hidden in the attic, and finally a balustrade with several statues.

The arcade space was divided into eight domed bays. The domes were pendentive cupolas with drums cut so low that only the four pendentives remained. Light entered through the glass pyramids which covered the drums. The weight of the domes was carried on Corinthian pilasters in front of the lateral walls of the arcade buildings. The facade units, framed by arches, were divided into three levels by glazing: on the ground floor, show windows with doors; on the second, triple windows; and on the third, windows following the curve of the arch. Differences in use created a facade quite different from that of the Lowther Arcade, one which, however, produced structural problems that were not entirely mastered. A heavy, cast-iron brace anchored on top of the moulding of the ground floor had to support the thrust of the two center pillars.

Photographs of the arcade reveal a monumental enclosure, an affinity with sacred spaces, vaulted bazaars, and the interior facades of the basilica of Maxientius or the baths of Caracalla. The Royal Arcade was the last and most pronounced example of a particularly British version of the arcade building type which was inspired by the Royal Opera Arcade in London.

Text 1: Newcastle Journal, May 19, 1832
This magnificent building, now the scaffolding in front is removed, and the various works approach to a completion, has excited the liveliest emotions of pleasure in the minds of the inhabitants of Newcastle, and the admiration of every stranger. From its situation, the magnitude, the splendour of its front, the beauty of the interior—with the long row of conical windows in the roof throwing a rich stream of light upon the chequered marble pavements beneath—and the excellence of its arrangement throughout, the Royal Arcade cannot fail to become a prominent ornament to the town and an object of attraction to every intelligent visitor. Were we to omit all record of so spirited an undertaking we should neglect a portion of our duty, and we have therefore been at some pains to collect the particulars, which we have pleasure in laying before our readers: The front adjoining Pilgrim Street and facing Mosley Street is of elegant polished stone, 94 feet wide by 75 feet high. The architecture of the basement storey is of the Doric Order, with an enriched entablature surmounted with six fluted Corinthian columns. On the attic is a beautiful turned balustrade also of stone, in front of which, in the centre of the building, is to be placed a group of five figures, "Britannica" being the most prominent. The rooms on the north side of the entrance will, we learn, be occupied as the banking home of Messrs. Backhouse and Co., and those on the south side as the Savings Bank; over which will be three large public rooms. The interior of the Arcade is 250 feet long, 20 feet wide; 35 feet high, having conical ornamental skylights, raised upon an arched groined ceiling, richly furnished with pure Grecian ornament. On each side of the Arcade are 8 large and elegant shops, the first and second stories [the second and third, respectively, in American usage] having been arranged with every convenience for offices. At the east end of the Arcade are a suite of large and splendid apartments comprising a News Room, Auction Mart, a room for public purposes 72 feet by 32 feet with ante-rooms adjoining. Above there is to be a conservatory, with Medicated Vapour, and warm and cold baths adjoining. Underneath the whole of this splendid line of buildings are large arched vaults, with offices, the entrances to which are by Manor Chare. Some idea may be formed of the great skill, assiduity, and judgement by which the various operators have been directed by Mr. Grainger, when we state that, although all the apartments, offices, shops, and public rooms are expected to be fully occupied in the course of a few weeks, it is not yet twelve months since the first stone was laid. The munificent spirit by which so great a public ornament has been directed, and so much public accommodation provided, will not go unappreciated.

Central Arcade (fig. 359)
Grainger Street—Market Street—Grey Street
There is another arcade in Newcastle, the Central Arcade. It leads through a triangular block in direct proximity to the market, a place occupied previously by the Central Exchange. Grainger, Market, and Grey Streets are the bordering streets.

The Central Arcade was completed in 1904 and was designed by J. Oswald and Son.[584] It has a wide arcade space with one setback which is covered by a barrel vault, like the City Arcades in Birmingham. The facades and end walls are covered with yellowish-brown glazed terra-cotta architectural motifs, resulting in a stylized mishmash, a sort of sculptured wallpaper. The glass vault is carried by lattice beams to which the purlins are fastened at equal intervals.

NEW YORK
New York Arcade
The New York Arcade is one of four early American Greek Revival arcades built on the east coast about 1827. The two earliest were the work of John Haviland, the inventor of a prison design based on the arcade system. The first arcade, in Philadelphia, showed traces of the Burlington Arcade prototype. The second, in New York, is said to have been similar to the arcade in Providence. Robert Alexander[585] writes: "The New York Arcade had a simpler plan, close to that of the Providence building in size and proportions, and had a single vestibule. Most important, Havi-

359
Newcastle, Central
Arcade, 1906

land's buildings were lighted by long continuous skylights over the avenues and had balconies at the upper levels. In all probability the Providence Arcade depended for plan and section, as well as glazing, on the New York building."

The construction date is given as 1826–1827. I was unable to ascertain how long the building stood.

Arcade
Times Square
I can cite only literary evidence of the existence of this arcade.[586]

Windsor Arcade
Fifth Avenue, between 46th and 47th · Streets
In *Lost New York* is a photograph of this block of two-storied shops, the interior of which is accessible through a glass-covered arcade. The block was torn down in 1912 or 1920. Judging from the heavy, colossal facades, it was probably built about 1890.[587]

NIORT
Passage du Commerce
This large arcade connects two squares in the old center city of Niort, cutting across the block on the diagonal. There are shops on the ground floor and apartments on the upper two. The main body of the building is continuous with the two entrance buildings for the full height of the structure. The steep roof, which has no undersupport, is old and has ventilating panels set into it. The simple classicism of the facades and the entrance arches recalls the arcade in Bordeaux, so the date of construction was probably 1830–1840.

NORWICH
Royal Arcade (fig. 360)
Market Place—Castle Meadrow
The Royal Arcade was built about 1900; it is still standing.

ODESSA
Arcade ? (fig. 361)
Deribassovkaya—Preobrashenskaya
In Odessa there is a corner arcade[588] whose decorative elaboration can be glimpsed in fig. 361. It is three-storied and was built into a block of taller buildings. Baedeker's guide mentions a Hotel Passage.

ORADEA
Arcade
This large complex has a cruciform arcade with a cupola over the crossing and wings which vary in height. Sections of the wings have setbacks and curves, and many of the architectural details are imitative of Oriental bazaars.

PARIS
The arcade building type was invented in Paris. The Parisian arcades emerged in the period between 1786 and 1830. In order to understand more fully the relationship of the arcades to the development of urban architecture in Paris, it will be necessary first to sketch the history of the city's construction. In the Middle Ages[589] Paris was a confusing conglomeration of narrow, intertwining alleys, tall buildings, and overdeveloped courtyards. The cityscape abounded with churches and cloisters. There were no squares or open spaces to grant a broader perspective of the city's dimensions. The Seine, today the great public space of the city, was ill-kept; the bridges were built up with houses and shops blocking the view of the river, and the banks were scarcely stabilized.

Henry IV, who converted to Catholicism to gain control over Paris, was the first to introduce building regulation and urban planning.[590] The architects Ducerceau and Perret supplied theoretical concepts and idealized city plans. Under Henry IV began the construction of the Place Dauphine, along with the Pont Neuf, and the Place Royale. The squares, which provided the first open spaces in the city as well as beautiful, airy urban residences off the main traffic arteries, can be considered the precursors of the Palais Royal.

Later, under the rule of Louis XIV, the Place des Victories by Mansart and the Place Vendôme were built. Under his government the city walls were torn down and replaced by tree-lined boulevards which formed a green belt around the city and allowed for further expansion to the west.

The Place de la Concorde was built under Louis XV. Competition drawings for the square as well as other projects for the city were published by Patte in 1765, compiled as a master plan: forums, squares, and sequences of squares, almost all related to the Seine and almost all forming parts of larger street axes.[591] Although this plan was not based on an understanding of

360
Norwich, Royal
Arcade

361
Odessa, arcade, 1967

traffic or urban renewal, it does represent a kind of conceptual attempt to transform Paris into a model European city—proof that political motives are often manifested architecturally.

The Place de l'Odéon was built under Louis XVI. The shop-lined promenades along the sides of the theater deserve special mention here. On April 10, 1783, the "Royal declaration concerning the direction and width of streets" was published. It related the height of buildings to the width of streets and introduced a classification of streets and their potential for development. It thereby initiated a process which would continue through Haussmann and create the much admired uniformity of the Parisian street network. While this ordinance would undergo numerous modifications, it provided a general framework without hindering individuality and variation.

In 1785 Paris turned an architectural face to the world: the customs wall was built as a second concentric ring around the city. Its fifty-six watchtowers, the Propylées, none identical, were designed by Ledoux. All construction outside of this belt was prohibited. Only the eastern section was not heavily settled,[592] while the northwestern and southwestern portions consisted of a loosely organized series of gardens and city palaces. The city had to develop inward. The large plots of land in the inner city were made accessible and converted into leasable dwellings. Private residential streets arose in the form of the *cités, cours,* culs-de-sac, and arcades. They were not only places of dwelling but also of trade and manufacture. These forms of access could only have developed in the unique situation of Paris in the nineteenth century. They created new architectural traditions and prepared the way for the glass-covered arcade.

Between 1624 and 1639 Cardinal Richelieu had his town palace built across from the Louvre, the residence of the kings. It would become the Palais Royal. Between 1781 and 1786 the expansive Jardin du Palais Royal received its geometrical architectonic form: a large "U" of buildings with an arcaded promenade and shops facing the interior on the ground floor. The architect was Victor Louis.[593] The apartments, shops, cafés, and restaurants were rented as an additional source of income for the financially insecure royal family,

the inheritors of the Palais. This courtyard, which was completely closed off from traffic, was later the site of political speeches calling for the storming of the Bastille. It was also the site of the first covered arcade lined with shops on both sides and illuminated by means of high side windows. It was located at the end of the continuous promenades and separated the Jardin from the Cour d'Honneur of the Palais. Later, with the construction of the Théâtre Français and the Galerie d'Orléans, the Palais and the built-up garden became a totally enclosed formation.[594]

The Palais Royal became the prototypical arcade. The building complex was functionally and architecturally independent, containing all of the necessary facilities. For decades it was the focus of public life; the public life, that is, that was introduced by the bourgeoisie emancipated by the revolution. The Palais Royal became the mecca of the leisure class. Urban planning, which had been introduced in the eighteenth century, was conceived after the revolution as a task involving the entire city. In 1793 the "Provisional Commission of Artists," commissioned by the Constitutional Assembly, convened for the first time. The result was a city plan that showed areas of renewal, beautification, and division of expropriated property, represented by corresponding colors of blue, yellow, or red. Five classes of streets were established, ranging from *grandes routes* to *petites communications.* The development of each class was strictly regulated. Countless connecting routes between streets were proposed—made possible, in part, by the disbanding of the monasteries. One project proposed an east-west axis to connect the Place de l'Etoile, the Louvre, and the Place de la Bastille, which was to be the site of a monument to the revolution.

Even though this idea remained only a plan, it influenced both Napoleon I and Haussmann. Moreover, it provided the foundation for a functional network of streets and opened up the city space to expansive perspectives, two results which were necessary for a city whose population was rapidly growing toward one million.

The new century and the reign of Napoleon I brought the movement toward imperial and monumental design: the Louvre, Tuileries, Place de la Concorde, the Champs-Elysées, and the Place de l'Etoile with its massive Arc de Triomphe were all expanded into great public spaces. Like a stone honor guard, the Rue de Rivoli[595] shields this space from the city. These mechanically ordered facades masked the chaos behind their walls. The Madeleine temple, the Vendôme column, and the Rue de Castiglione served a function for this space by giving it a cross-perspective. The Louvre was expanded. The overdeveloped sections were cleared away. Nôtre Dame was opened to view. The Palais du Luxembourg was connected to the river and the Louvre by means of the Rue de Seine. This was one side of the Napoleonic reforms. The other involved hygienic and organizational tasks: reform of the water supply, removal of gutters from the middle of the streets, construction of sidewalks, numbering of buildings, new bridges and fountains, expanding the quais along the Seine, the closing of the old graveyards within the city and construction of the Père Lachaise cemetery outside the city. These were the first steps beyond mere beautification toward the humanization of intolerable living conditions.

Following the reign of Napoleon I came the period of the Restoration, characterized by its frugality in the area of public works. Nothing significant was built. Works that had been begun were completed; yet no new buildings arose even though the city was expanding, industrialization was beginning, and the population doubled in forty years.[596] The arcades built in this period were contributions of the private sector to the expansion of public space. The boulevards and the Chaussée d'Antin became the new centers of "le tout Paris." The arcades facilitated movement in the city. They provided the places where the products of the blossoming industries, novelties, fashion merchandise, and the luxurious decorative items could be presented to consumers in a compact situation resembling a department store. They created an undisturbed space for promenading, showing off, and leisure. With few exceptions most of the arcades were located in the triangle described by the boulevards, the Rue St. Honoré, and the Rue St. Martin. They all had the element of speculation in common. The arcades were built in order to create the maximum capital out of real estate and social customs. The arcade building type offered a possibility for the development of real estate which far exceeded previous methods. The fantastic commercial success of a few

well-located arcades led to rash imitations, many of which went bankrupt because the site was badly chosen or because the public on which the success of the arcade was so dependent, migrated to new, fashionable neighborhoods. The stock exchange, the new system of credit which developed after the British model, and the real estate market were necessary conditions for the extensive construction activity, the products of which can be seen in the arcades and the many categories of rentable buildings.

The arcades were built by rich, noble property owners[597] who wanted to exploit their gardens and inner courtyards in the inner city near the boulevards. In this way they improved their income by leasing the shops and apartments; they required considerable sums, more than the steady revenues from their estates, to keep up with the lifestyle of the time. Arcades were also built by bankers and businessmen who had become wealthy through stock speculation and trade.[598]

The arcades opened up the land in the inner city which had become available as a result of the disbanding of the monasteries. By purchasing and tearing down old houses, the builders could create large plots of land connecting the streets. They were then developed from one end to the other, subdivided, and resold or leased. If an individual could not amass the necessary capital, companies were formed which then built new arcades with the profits gained from former ones.[599] Although undreamed-of fortunes could be made from an arcade, success was always uncertain, since one had to depend on incalculable elements: the habits of pedestrians, changes in fashion, and the movement of traffic. The arcades expanded in concentric circles around the Palais Royal. Those in the western corner of the triangle were luxury buildings and social attractions, and were usually connected to theaters, panoramas, and other such establishments.[600] Those in the eastern section had a more local importance. They housed artisans' shops and the workshops of painters, bookbinders, and small merchants, such as those that can still be found today on the Rue St. Denis.[601]

The first arcades appeared in 1799, 1800, 1808, and 1811, still in the Napoleonic era. However, the major portion of the twenty Parisian arcades were built under

362
Paris, street plan, de-
tail of Right Bank

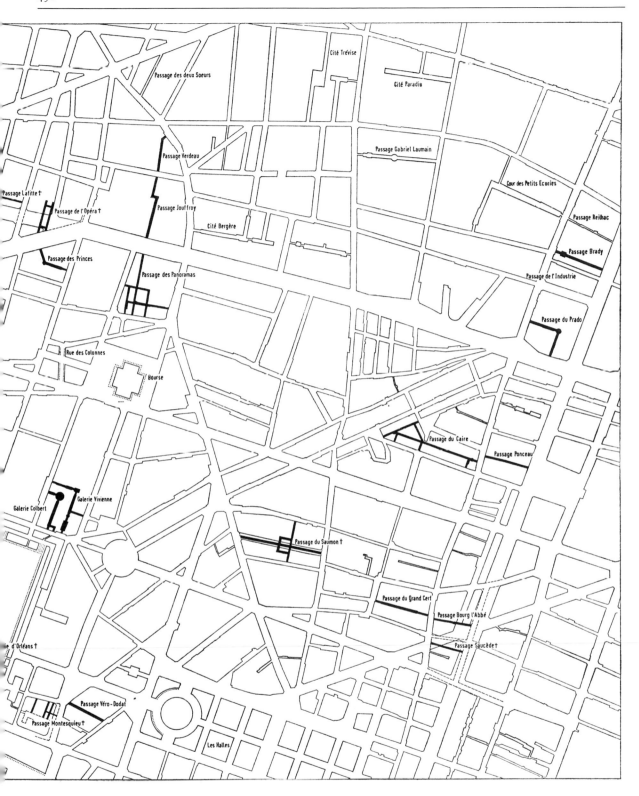

Cité Trévise

Passage des deux Soeurs

Cité Paradis

Passage Gabriel Laumain

Passage Verdeau

Cour des Petits Ecuries

Passage Lafitte †

Passage Reilhac

Passage de l'Opéra †

Passage Jouffroy

Passage Brady

Cité Bergère

Passage de l'Industrie

Passage des Princes

Passage des Panoramas

Passage du Prado

Rue des Colonnes

Bourse

Passage du Caire

Passage Ponceau

Galerie Vivienne

Galerie Colbert

Passage du Saumon †

Passage du Grand Cerf

Passage Bourg l'Abbé

ie d'Orléans †

Passage Saucède †

Passage Véro-Dodat

Passage Montesquieu †

Les Halles

Louis XVIII and Charles X. A few were built under Louis Philippe. The last dates from 1860, but it is insignificant.

Haussmann began his systematic and radical restructuring of the inner city under Napoleon III. The centers of luxury and high society shifted westward out of the city. The idea of the arcade came to an end and speculative interests were totally absorbed by the new development of straight streets which were interrupted only by the old city.

As early as the end of the 1802s the bazaar building type arose parallel to that of the arcade.[602] It consisted of a series of glass-covered courtyards with a large display of merchandise spread out over numerous stories connected by freestanding stairways. The bazaar was the immediate predecessor of the department store,[603] which began to sweep across Paris in 1852, replacing the arcade as the marketing technique most appropriate to the state of production. The light wells of the department store carried on the tradition of the arcade until the police and fire authorities prohibited them.

Finally, Parisian arcades have become fashionable again since the early 1970s. The shops that stood empty are occupied by young people who are setting trends. They deal in numerous kinds of exotic goods, have repair shops, and manage second-hand stores. They have learned to love the arcades. An entire series of essays has appeared in newspapers and journals; studies have been done at art schools. All of these publications have directed the attention of the city to these exotic objects nestled within its own walls.[604]

Galeries de Bois (figs. 363–370)
Palais Royal
The Palais Royal, as it stands today, conveys a sense of stillness and peace. It is an oasis in the center of Paris, a garden with children at play, landscaped hedges, splashing fountains. The arcade is inhabited by men sleeping on iron benches or hawking merchandise in the galleries. The shops hardly seem to sell anything anymore. The magnificent apartments have boarded fronts. It is all enclosed by a great row of pillars of yellow stone and a fence with gilded spearheads. This is the Palais Royal today, as it gazes back over its three-hundred-year history and the time when it was the center of European social life.

In 1629–1636 Cardinal Richelieu built his luxurious city residence with its own theater. It was located opposite the Louvre.[605] A broad, geometrically designed garden was placed behind the palace. Richelieu bequeathed his Palais Cardinal to the crown. After the death of Louis XIII Queen Anne of Austria moved into it with the young Louis XIV, and the name was changed to the Palais Royal. A covered passage led through the garden to the Palais Mazarin, the residence of the queen's beloved. Louis XIV presented the palace to his brother, the Duke d'Orléans. It remained in the possession of his family until the revolution. In 1780 the architect Victor Louis,[606] who had become famous with his theater in Bordeaux, was engaged by the Duc de Chartres,[607] who later became Philippe-Egalité. Louis was commissioned to completely redesign the palace, which had already been altered by the city architect Moreau. The goal of the Duke was to create a structure around the Jardin du Palais Royal, thereby increasing the size of the property. In that way he could lease the newly created apartments and shops to improve his financial situation, which had suffered from unlucky speculation and gambling debts.

Victor Louis had to endure the ever-changing moods and whims of the duke. In 1781 he presented his first plan:[608] a long *U* would enclose the gardens, closing them off from the surrounding buildings; galleries with shops—180 arches in all—faced the garden; the shops had apartments on the third floor which were independently accessible from the street. At the end of the garden was a tall cross-wing with a continuous colonnade which totally separated the garden from the Cour Royale and the Cour Intérieure planned for the Rue Richelieu. The palace on the Rue St. Honoré was entirely incorporated in the plan on one side.

In 1781 the Salle de l'Opéra on the east side of the palace burned down. This incident caused a comprehensive change in the Duc de Chartres's plans. In 1784 Louis presented his new plan:[609] the Théâtre Français replaced the Cour Intérieure and the Rue de Valois was extended through to the Rue St. Honoré. The process of exposing the Palais Royal on all sides began. In 1786 the galleries were completed and the foundations for the colonnades bordering

363
Paris, Palais Royal,
galleries, shown in a
watercolor, *La Sortie
du Numéro 113*,
1815

364
Palais Royal, gal-
leries, first design by
Louis, 1781

365
Palais Royal, gal-
leries, second design
by Louis, 1784

366
Palais Royal, Galerie
d'Orléans, design by
Fontaine, 1829

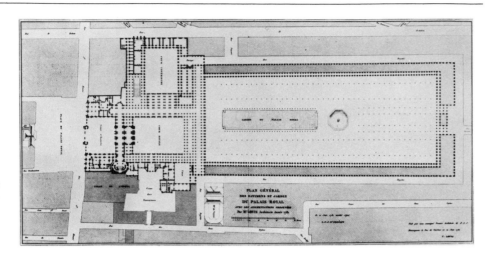

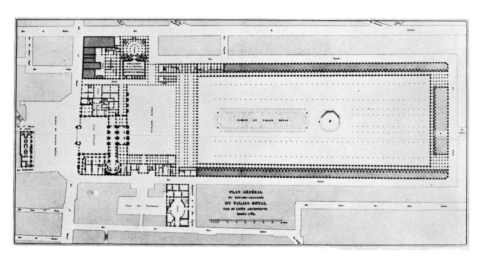

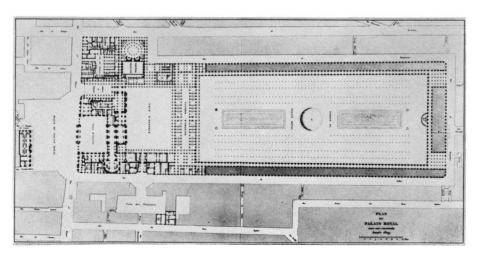

367
Palais Royal,
Galeries de Bois,
1786–1788, demol-
ished 1828, arcade
spaces

368
Palais Royal,
Galeries de Bois,
bird's-eye view, 1828

PARIS

369
Palais Royal,
Galeries de Bois, plan

370
Palais Royal,
Galeries de Bois,
cross section and
overhead view of
roof

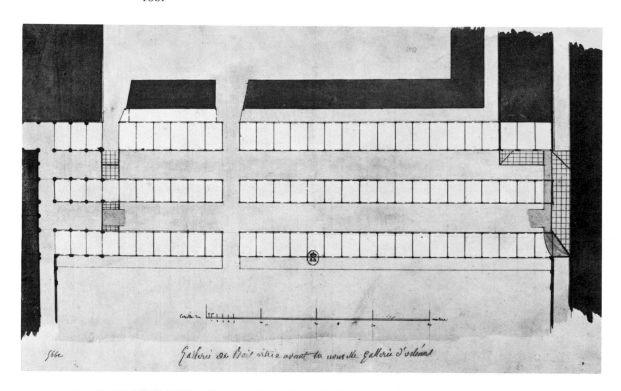

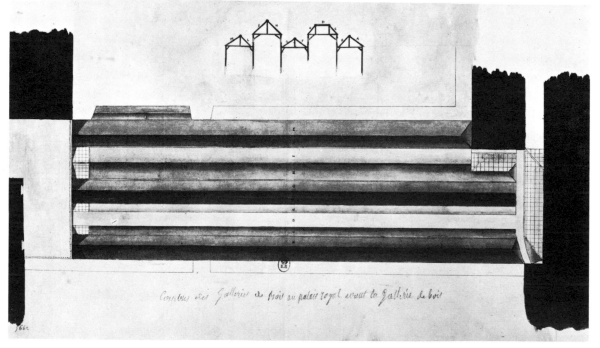

the south side of the garden were laid. Then the money ran out. The rest had to be improvised. The connection between the galleries and the palace remained unfinished. The Théâtre Français was not built until 1789–1790. The passages of the gallery were provisionally enclosed by wooden barracks, the Galeries de Bois, which were built on the plan of the intended colonnade of the cross-wing.[610] These Galeries de Bois—three rows of shops, which contained two taller passages with high side lights—formed the first arcade ever built. They already possessed the two required elements: shops on both sides and their own source of illumination. They were probably constructed in this way because the wooden beams of the support structure were built on the foundations of the originally planned six-rowed colonnade.

Hence, the history of the arcade began with a provisional structure, a building without an architectonic plan, without any direct model. It was built thanks to the greed and speculation of a wasteful prince. This ugly provisional structure was to last many years, establishing the political and social golden age of the Palais Royal. It was demolished in 1828.

After the palace had been taken over again by the Orléans family,[611] Fontaine altered and finished Louis's original plans. He joined the stone galleries to the palace by means of a peristyle and built a broad and elegant arcade, the Galerie d'Orléans, to separate the spaces. Mirrors and marble replaced the wood and plaster; a low-vaulted glass roof replaced the simple boarded roof frames. The rooms were festive, yet already life was receding from the Palais Royal. The merchants, concerned with upholding their reputation, had the police evict the prostitutes. The hour of the boulevards had arrived.

After 1877, thanks to the diagonal cut-through of the Avenue de l'Opéra and the construction of the Place du Palais Royal, the Palais Royal received its final, independent contours, free of the bordering private residences.

Since it was destroyed before the invention of photography, the Galeries de Bois is the only arcade of which no photographs exist. We therefore can never know the details of the arcade. Instead we are dependent on the etchings, lithographs, and two plans which can be found in the Bibliothèque Nationale.[612]

The Galeries de Bois consisted of a simple, unfinished wooden structure: six rows of supports held the beams, strengthened in each direction by struts, upon which rested the roof frames. The undersides of these roof frames had horizontal planking and were covered with plaster. The roofs of the inner buildings were sloped to permit illumination from above. The elevation of the two arcade spaces was divided as follows: skylights were placed in the spaces between the supports under the roof. These windows contained small square frames corresponding to the sizes of panes which could be manufactured at that time. Beneath these were the horizontal supports for additional strength. They were covered and hence offered a surface for advertisements, announcements, and shop signs of all kinds. Beneath the covered supports were the large shop windows, subdivided like the skylights; they rested on a small protrusion which commonly held open chests and displays. Some businesses—if we are to trust the depictions—were completely open to the arcade and were boarded up at night. The height of the arcade (4 to 5 meters) allowed ample space for a variety of structures. The middle row of shops had the advantage of access from both sides. The shops at the end of the rows even had show windows on three sides. The Galeries were rented as a whole, and the individual shops were then sublet at terrific prices. One of the first tenants had the task of connecting the theater to the galleries by a *galerie vitrée* (glass-covered gallery). Built in 1792, it had the form of a wooden arcade with varying heights. The roof was partially a lean-to and partially a saddle roof; but the whole roof was of glass, hence the first glass roof ever built. Of course, like all early glass-roof constructions, it was said to have afforded little protection from the rain.

Thus, the history of the arcade began in the eighteenth century with a wooden building. In the nineteenth century, iron was employed for the roof structure, and in the twentieth century, reinforced concrete was the main building material—until the architectural idea was totally lost.

The Galeries de Bois became a model for the many arcades which arose around it, not so much for its architecture but for its tremendous commercial success. There were many reasons for its success: its location, its supply of publicly accessible, undisturbed space, and its close proximity to institutions of entertainment, art, business, and knowledge. This multipurpose building, this city quarter, this city within a city became possible only with the revolution, the emancipation of the bourgeoisie, and the physical intermingling of all social strata: The nobility, bourgeoisie, capitalists, *flâneurs*, foreigners, the demi-monde, the fashionable set, the underworld—all played out their roles here in the human comedy, as Balzac portrayed them in his monumental work. We owe Balzac the great depiction of the Galeries de Bois—more significant than any photograph, for it penetrates the surface and gives a truer image (see Text 1).

Balzac's description explains the influence of the Palais Royal on Paris and all of Europe. There was no traveler who was not attracted to this place where vice was so visible, politics so lively, and information and the newest books were so available. It was a bazaar, not a marketplace of one branch of trade but an all-encompassing bazaar where everything could be bought, from the rarest luxuries to the commonest junk. It was a bazaar which, in the preindustrial age, still upheld the concept of unity. When carried into the new century, this unity was shattered into numerous forms—the fair, world exhibitions, department stores, and arcades. The Palais Royal contained reading rooms, bookstores, small food markets for the cosmopolitan palate. It contained shops that one could enter unwashed and in rags, and leave as a man of fashion. It contained furniture stores, jewelry and fashion shops, souvenir shops, pottery, tobacco, perfume, and antiques. It had restaurants of all categories, cafés,[613] gambling rooms, a stock exchange, a real estate agency, betting offices, brothels for all inclinations, and countless apartments and attic rooms for rent. It also contained theaters, picture galleries, and other exhibitions. And it had an inhabitant, a man named Lassagnole,[614] who supposedly never left the Palais. After the construction of the galleries of the Palais Royal, the people were outraged that a royal prince should have found it necessary to rent shops to supplement his income. Shortly thereafter, the people made their money in the same way.

This direct connection between business, consumerism, entertainment, politics, and information within a space protected from the traffic and the weather, that is, this direct unification of such heterogeneous functions, explains the significant role played by the Palais Royal not only in the Revolution of 1789 but also in the public life of the following decades. The revolution made possible for the first time the intermingling of social strata, the spatial proximity of previously separated classes. It made possible that emancipation of the public which became a dangerous and fearsome force. The instruments of this force were the journalist, backed by a world view, class, and association of interests; the newspaper, backed by capital and powerful opinions; and the critic. The Galeries de Bois was part of the Palais Royal. The crowds flowed without interruption through the stone galleries, the wooden galleries; they relaxed in the cafés and on the stone benches of the garden. It was also dangerous in the Galeries de Bois, which was therefore nicknamed, after the greed of its inhabitants, the "Champ des Tartares"[615] (see Text 2).

Text 1: Honoré de Balzac, Illusions Perdues *[quoted from* Lost Illusions, A Great Man of the Provinces in Paris, *trans. Katharine Prescott Wormeley (Boston, 1893), pp. 143–150]*

The new friends now entered the Galeries de Bois, where Dauriat's great publishing concern, called "The Novelty," reigned supreme. At the period of which we speak the Galeries de Bois of the Palais-Royal were among the most noted of the sights of Paris. It is by no means useless to draw a picture of that ignoble bazaar, which for thirty-six years played so great a role in Parisian life that there are few men of forty to whom the following description, incredible to younger men, will not be of interest.

In place of the present cold, lofty, and broad Galerie d'Orléans, a sort of greenhouse without flowers, there stood in those days a line of wooden barracks, or, to be more exact, plank huts, small, poorly roofed and ill-lighted from the court and garden and also from the roof by small sashes, called casements, which were more like the dirty openings of the dance-halls beyond the barriers than actual windows. A triple line of booths made two galleries about twelve feet high; those down the centre faced to each side, and the fetid air which rose from the crowded passageways had little chance to escape through the roof, which admitted only a dim light through its dirty casements. These centre booths or cells were thought so valuable, because of the crowds who passed them, that in spite of their narrow space (some being scarcely six feet wide and eight or ten feet long) they brought enormous prices,—some as much as three thousand francs. The side booths, which were lighted from the court and from the garden, were protected by small, green trellises, possibly to prevent the crowd ouside from demolishing by pressure the lath and plaster walls which formed the sides of the sheds. Here, therefore, was a space of some two or three feet in width where the most amazing products of a botany unknown to science vegetated, mingled with the cast-off scraps of industries that were not less flourishing. Rose-trees and wastepaper, flowers of rhetoric and flowers of nature, ribbons of all colors, remnants of the fashions, in short the refuse of the interior commerce was there collected. . . . On both sides a nauseous and disgusting approach seemed to warn delicate persons from entering these galleries; and yet delicate and refined persons were no more kept away by these horrible things than princes in fairy-tales recoil from dragons and other obstacles interposed by evil genii between them and the princesses.

These galleries were, as the Galerie d'Orléans is to-day, divided by passageways, from which they were entered by the present porticos, which were begun before the Revolution and left unfinished for want of money. The handsome stone gallery which now leads to the Théâtre-Français was in those days a narrow passageway of excessive height and so ill-covered that the rain wet it. It was called the Galerie Vitrée, to distinguish it from the Galeries de Bois. The roofs of all these miserable sheds were in such a bad state that the House of Orléans had a lawsuit with a famous shopkeeper who found his cashmeres and other goods injured during a single night to a large amount of money. The man won his case. A double thickness of tarred cloth served for a covering in some places. The floor of the Galerie Vitrée (where Chevet's fortune began), also that of the Galeries de Bois was the soil of Paris, with other soil added as the boots and shoes of a myriad of pedestrians had imported there. In all weather the feet were forced to stumble among mountains and valleys of hardened mud, constantly swept by the shopkeepers, but, even so, requiring all new-comers to learn a method of management in order to walk with safety. . . .

For twenty years the Bourse was directly opposite, on the ground-floor of the palace. Rendezvous were given before and after the opening of the exchange in these galleries. Consequently, public opinion and reputation were made and unmade here, and political and financial affairs incessantly discussed. The Paris world of bankers and merchants congregated in the square of the Palais-Royal, and swarmed into the galleries when it rained. The construction of these wooden buildings, which

had sprung up heaven knows how, made them singularly resonant. Bursts of laughter echoed through them; not a quarrel could take place at one end that the other end did not know what it was about. The place was occupied solely by the shops of booksellers and publishers (poetry, politics, and prose) and by those of milliners. At night the women of the town appeared there. Novels and books of all kinds, new and old reputations, political plots and counterplots, the lies of publishers and booksellers all flourished there. There, too, novelties were sold to a public that persisted in not buying them elsewhere. In the course of a single evening thousands of copies have been sold of a pamphlet by Paul-Louis Courier or the "Adventures of the Daughter of a King," which, by the by, was the first shot fired by the House of Orléans at the Charter of Louis XVIII. . . .

The shops of the milliners were full of wonderful bonnets, which seemed to be there less for sale than for show, hanging by hundreds on iron trees and enlivening the galleries with a thousand colors. For twenty years the loungers in the galleries had wondered on what heads those dusty bonnets would end their days. Saleswomen, for the most part ugly, but brisk, hooked the female sex adroitly in the style and language of marketwomen. One grisette, whose tongue was as free as her eyes were active, stood on a stool and attacked the passers: "Buy a pretty bonnet, madame!" "Let me sell you something, monsieur." Their rich and picturesque vocabulary was varied by inflections of the voice, and interspersed with knowing looks and criticisms on those who passed them. . . .

The appointments which the Parisian population gave themselves did not begin till about three o'clock, the hour for the Bourse. As soon as the crowd poured in, the gratuitous readings at the booksellers' counters by penniless young men hungry for literature began. The shopmen whose business it was to watch the books thus exposed for sale charitably allowed these poor fellows to turn the leaves. If the book happened to be a 12mo of two hundred pages, like "Smarra," "Peter Schlemil," "Jean Sbogar," "Jocko," two visits would enable the reader to devour it. In those days circulating-libraries did not exist; it was necessary to buy a book in order to read it; and this was why novels were sold in numbers that now seem fabulous. There was something indescribably French in these mental alms bestowed on youthful, eager, poverty-striken intellects.

The tragic aspect of this terrible bazaar began to show itself towards evening. Through all the adjacent streets women poured in, who were allowed to walk there unmolested; from every section of Paris came prostitutes to "do the Palais." The stone galleries belonged to privileged establishments, who paid for the right to expose their creatures, dressed like princesses, between such and such an arch with a corresponding right to the same distance in the garden; but the Galeries de Bois were the common ground of women of the town, "the Palais," par excellence, a word which signified in those days the temple of prostitution. Any woman might come there and go away, accompanied by her prey, wheresoever it pleased her. They drew such crowds to the Galeries de Bois that every one was compelled to walk at a snail's pace as they do in the procession at a masked ball. But this slowness, which annoyed no one, enabled persons to examine each other. The women were all dressed in a style and manner that no longer exists; their gowns were made low to the very middle of their backs, and also very low in front; their heads were dressed fantastically to attract notice; some were Norman in style, others Spanish; the hair of the one was curled like a poodle, that of another in smooth, straight bands; their legs, covered with white stockings, were shown, it would be difficult to say how, but always à propos. All this picturesque infamy is now done away with. The license of solicitation and answer, that public cynicism so in keeping with the place itself, is no longer to be seen, either there or at masked balls, nor in the celebrated public balls which are given in the present day. The scene was horrible and gay. The white flesh of the shoulders and throats shone and sparkled against the clothing of the men which was usually dark, producing magnificent contrasts.

Text 2: F. M. Marchant, Le Conducteur de l'Etranger à Paris *(Paris, 1815), p. 153*

A wretched wooden arcade has hidden the entrance to the garden on the side of the palace for forty years. It was the first fruit of the commercial speculations of a prince who, to increase his already immense revenues and to accommodate his disorderly expenses, remodeled all of the approaches to his palace with magnificent bazaars, but hardly fitting the majesty of a prince. On this double row of galleries, one could see crowding into the narrow shops booksellers and merchants. The portfolio and novelty merchants were located next to the studios of artistic decorators. The bookshop alone has the same prices as in the rest of Paris. The other merchants overcharge by at least two times; their rapaciousness has earned the locale the name of the "Champ des Tartares." The glassed arcade which leads along the Rue de Richelieu extends through to the Champ des Tartares. You must pay attention to your pockets in this narrow arcade, which is often congested with crowds. Robbers often ply their harmful trade there. On both sides there are cafes of a bad kind and billiard rooms which the light never penetrates fully; dark shops of furniture and clothing dealers, where the gloomy light which manages to reach them hardly allows one to notice the defects in the merchandise. Down below are the grottos and the small public houses where the little shows and the music invite the imprudent each evening to come to be duped by elegant women and swindlers who make their residence in these dark nooks.

Passage Feydeau (fig. 371)
Rue Feydeau—Rue des Filles St. Thomas
The Passage Feydeau seems to be the connecting link between the Galeries de Bois (1786–1788) and the first genuine, turn-of-the-century arcades. This arcade is nowhere documented in more recent compendiums. It was demolished, probably before 1824. I came upon two versions of the arcade in a series of plans for the reconstruction of the Palais du Grand Conseil on the Rue des Filles St. Thomas. The plans are held in the topographical collections of the Bibliothèque Nationale.[616] The first version is a large, undated plan which depicts the whole construction site through to the Rue Feydeau; this depiction is similar to that of the Plan Turgot. An arcade is sketched in for the entire length of the site. It extends from the eastern section of the courtyard, crosses the garden, continues in a newly planned section with a restaurant and café, and borders finally an undefined open space. Two continuous rows of shops line the eastern side of the arcade. The upper stories are accessible by way of stairways. Colonnades and shop windows join the arcade to the open area. The arcade, then, could be categorized between the colonnade and the covered arcade.

This plan must have been drawn before 1790, for in 1791 the architects Legrand and Molinos built the Théâtre de l'Opéra-Comique, also called the Théâtre de Monsieur, on the northern section of the site.[617] This building would have led to a shortening of the arcade as the second version, which is complete with all plans, sections, and elevations, reveals. One Madame Longlois is mentioned as the owner of the property. The ground floor plan has been reproduced in fig. 371. Written by hand above the plan is "constructed in 1790–91 under the orders of Monsieur Hubert Thibierge, architect." The arcade was moved into the interior of the old hotel. It crosses through the garden with shops on both sides, ending in front of the rear wall of the theater in a narrow passageway.

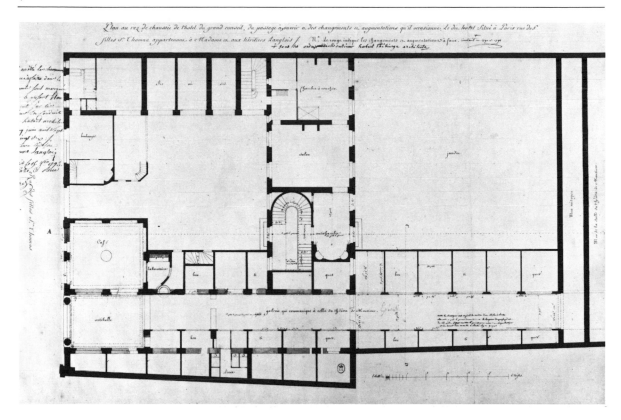

371
Paris, Passage Fey-
deau, 1791, plan

Written in the space of the arcade is the instruction: "Galerie which connects to the hall of the Théâtre de Monsieur."

It can be demonstrated that the arcade actually existed, for it is drawn in on the 1813 Nouveau Plan Routier de Paris.[618] There one can see clearly that the arcade extended, probably as an open passage, past the side of the Théâtre de Monsieur. One can also see that it then served a function as a traffic artery which it could not serve now. It extended the Rue Vivienne which formerly ended at the Rue des Filles St. Thomas, north of the boulevards. Ten years later, thanks to the construction of the Passage des Panoramas, one could therefore walk from the Palais Royal to the most active section of the boulevards along a direct, partially covered passage. This urban ensemble explains the importance of the Passage des Panoramas as a continuation of the Passage Feydeau beyond the Rue Feydeau. The Passage Feydeau was mentioned by Merchant in 1815,[619] along with the Passages des Panoramas, Montesquieu, Delorme, and du Caire. Pigeory called it a "somber passageway."[620]

The first covered arcade that was more than a corridor through a building, like the small arcades around the Palais Royal, did not stand for long. In 1798 the Rue des Colonnes, running parallel to the arcade, was opened, and in 1824, after the removal of the Thomasine convent and the construction of the stock exchange, the Rue de la Bourse was extended through to the Rue Richelieu. The Rue de la Bourse and the extended Rue Vivienne reduced the size of the site on which the Passage Feydeau once stood.

Passage du Caire (fig. 372)
*Rue St. Denis 234–9—Rue du Caire 44
—Place du Caire—Rue d'Alexandrie 33*
One of the results of the Revolution of 1789 was the disbanding of the monasteries inside the city. Large areas became free and were used for new development as the growth of industrialization drew more people into the city. The Passage du Caire, the first glass-covered arcade outside the Palais Royal, was built in 1798–1799 in one of these new open spaces which had formerly been the site of the convent of the Filles-Dieu.[621] While the cross section of this arcade is modest in size, its length is the greatest of all the Parisian arcades: its three wings and six entrances amount to a total length of 370 meters.

372
Paris, sites of the Passage du Caire and the Passage du Ponceau, 1952

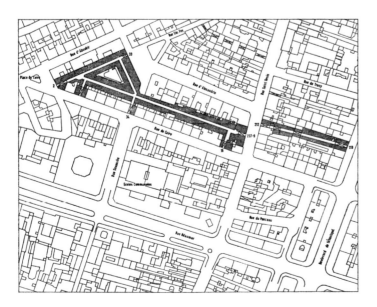

Kolloff[622] described the arcade in 1849: "The Passage du Caire between the Place du Caire and the Rue St. Denis is not, as the name might imply, a splendrous trading hall shimmering with marble, pearls, and rubies, and dotted with splashing fountains filled with rose-water. It is merely a narrow double passage, yawning like an abyss, filled with unpleasant odors and old greasy second-hand shops. . . .," The name Passage du Caire refers to a historical event: on July 1, 1798, Napoleon, who intended to destroy British trade in the Mediterranean, reached Alexandria; on July 25 he occupied Cairo. As a result, Egyptian objects and styles appeared throughout France: obelisks and pyramids as monuments, columns and ornaments on the facades of private homes and in interiors designed by Percier and Fontaine.[623] The craze for the exotic, the fashion of exoticism, began here and was to last through an entire century. In its search for expression and magnificence, the nineteenth century explored thousands of years of architectural history. The arcade has its place in this process.[624]

The Passage du Caire still stands on the Rue St. Denis in the crowded and developed eastern section of the second arrondissement. Here were housed the poor, artisans, and small tradespeople. This was the birthplace of industrialization. The courtyards were filled with small workshops. The deep lots were invariably made accessible and usable by passages, cours, and rear buildings. In as early a document as the Plan des Artistes de la Révolution (1793) we see that the site of the Passage du Caire was integrated into a street system of two parallel streets which crossed the Rue St. Denis and the Rue St. Martin at right angles. Therefore the arcade was not interrupted by an existing block of buildings but was a new structure built with the Place du Caire and the Rue du Caire. It was interconnected with the street network. This explains the orientation of the arcade's wings. They relate to the network, running parallel to the bordering streets. The main wing begins at the Rue St. Denis, accompanies the Rue du Caire, has three exits to it, and finally opens up in a semicircular extension to the wing which veers off at a 45-degree angle parallel to the Rue d'Aboukir and connects the Place du Caire to the Rue d'Alexandrie. These wings are connected by a third, making a block that forms an equilateral triangle. The original relationship of the arcade to its environs has changed: the Rue Réaumur and the Rue Dussoubs did not exist at that time, and the Rue d'Alexandrie has been widened.

The arcade is only 2.7 meters wide at its middle. It is a conglomeration of small, uniform three-storied buildings. In all there are 151 odd and 104 even address numbers; it has more numbers than buildings since each shop wanted its own number and address. Each building has a cellar. The ground floor houses one or more shops with a formerly continuous wooden casement which is today covered with advertisements, signs, and individual modifications. Above each shop are a small window and the indication of pilasters framing the shop bay. The pilasters bear a cornice strip and a brick attic with openings at intervals for ventilation. Above the attic lies the continuous glass saddle roof. The building is slightly recessed back from the roof and has a small mansard story over the arcade space. The glass roof was certainly built later.[625] Unfortunately, I have not been able to ascertain the original state of the roof. I assume that like the roof of the Passage des Panoramas, it was a wooden structure with skylights. The Passage du Caire is today surrounded by taller buildings. The one at 2 Place du Caire has three stone Egyptian heads, demonstrating the aforementioned historical connection. It is said to be the work of the architect Bertier.

The Passage du Caire is not one of the arcades which handles luxury items; rather, it houses trades and crafts. This orientation explains the lack of publicity about it. It is, of course, mentioned in guides and travelogues but is rarely described or starred. One can find on the title page of many a nineteenth-century book the address of a printer or lithographer given as "Passage du Caire" because it was predominantly the residence of printers, lithographers, and small publishing houses. Today the arcade is still a kind of museum of shops. Behind the glass panes men cut stamps, print, glue, and engrave visiting cards, carve pipes, dress up manikins. Doors slam, shop bells chime, disappearing steps echo on the arcade floor, which is said to have once been paved with the tombstones of the disbanded convent. One can see oneself reflected 2.7 meters across the arcade and entertain oneself by going from one dwelling to the next. Life and work are here under one roof.

Passage des Panoramas (figs. 373–381)
*Rue St. Martin 10–Boulevard Montmartre
11*

In 1800 the Passage des Panoramas, the
first truly significant arcade, was built. It
served luxury trade and the fashion industry. Its name explains the reason for its
construction: the panorama which had already been built in 1799 on the Boulevard
Montmartre. The arcade was added to exploit the property and create a direct path
from the Palais Royal, via the Rue Vivienne, the Passage Feydeau (1791), the Rue
Feydeau, and the Rue Neuve de Montmorency to the second center of public life,
the boulevards.

During the Empire the broad, tree-lined
boulevards were built up to become street
spaces and to compete with the Palais
Royal. Theaters, ballrooms, cafés, baths,
bazaars, and hotels sprouted up. Gardens
were divided and walls torn down. A reckless and unregulated development filled
this new area. The *flâneur* was offered all
he needed to overcome his boredom, spend
his money, and satisfy his desires. The ma-
chinery of luxury entered the public eye
here. It left the exclusivity of the court and
of patrician families and was offered to everyone: whoever could afford it could help
himself. The luxury industry no longer
produced under commission but for anonymous consumers who had to be reached
through advertising and packaging. The
place where as many purchases as possible
could be made was the city, the street—
and, in the most concentrated form, the
arcade.

Between 1790 and 1830 the neighborhood
between the Palais Royal and the boulevards changed fundamentally as a result of
the growth of the shop and the accompanying development of the shop window.
The rapidly increasing traffic required new
channels to permit meandering, strolling,
and direct connections to all points. Streets
were straightened and extended; gardens
were broken up and developed; the leased
building with shops on the ground floor
defined the contours of the streets. Development became more concentrated than
ever before. New institutions arose in the
area. The stock exchange became a new
focus, attracting the wealth and creating
habits which set the pace for industry.

To understand the position of the Passage
des Panoramas in the architectural development of the city, one must first investi-

gate spatial and structural changes in the
surrounding district. Older plans, especially the isometric Plan Turgot, provide
this information. The Turgot plan dates
from 1739 and gives an impression of the
second arrondissement in the mid-eigh-
teenth century, the period before the construction of the arcades. It shows broad,
tree-lined boulevards still lined with garden walls. Individual building aggregates
existed only on the side streets. Between
the Rue Montmartre and the Rue Richelieu one sees a rectangle built up on three
sides and open to the boulevard. Near the
middle one finds the Hotel Montmorency-
Luxembourg (1704) with a geometrically
designed garden and a small grove of trees.
The Passage des Panoramas was later built
on this site. The Rue Vivienne ended here
before the gate to the convent of the Filles
St. Thomas, which was later disbanded to
make room for the stock exchange.

The Plan des Artistes de la Révolution
from 1793 shows the proposed extension
of the Rue Vivienne through to the boulevard. However, this extension was not
undertaken until 1824, when it pre-empted
the traffic function of the arcade. In the
1813 Nouveau Plan Routier de Paris, the
Passage des Panoramas is included with
the two circular structures of the actual
panoramas on the boulevard. The remaining space between the Passage des Panoramas and the developments on the east side
of the boulevard is still blank. This is the
area in which Cellerier built the Théâtre
des Variétés (1807) for a company which
wanted to move from the Palais Royal to
the boulevard.

The same situation can be seen in the first
complete survey plan of Paris (scale, 1 to
1000), which Vasserot and Bélanger published in 1833. On this plan, a detail of
which is shown in fig. 362, we still see the
Hotel de Montmorency and next to it the
arcade. Two panoramas flank the entrance
on the boulevard and a third has been built
in the garden. The contours of the arcade
are irregular because individual shop owners made their own additions and extensions. The garden gate serves as the
entrance on the south side. It is unclear
whether or not the side wall of the Palais
bordering the arcade included shops. The
Théâtre des Variétés fills in the aforementioned space on the boulevard. There is a
rear entrance to the theater from the arcade. This almost totally enclosed group of
buildings borders the back side of the gar-

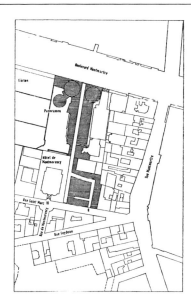

373
Paris, site of the Passage des Panoramas, 1833

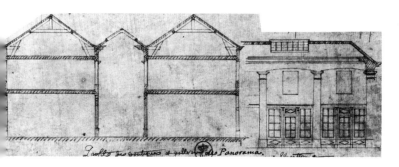

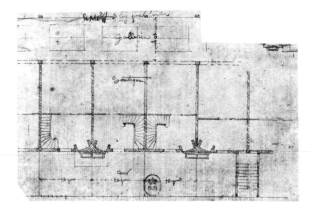

374
Paris, Passage des Panoramas, 1800, modified and expanded 1834, longitudinal and cross sections

375
Passage des Panoramas, plan showing skylights

dens of the Palais on the Rue Richelieu to the west.

This situation did not last long after 1824. In the Petit Atlas Pittoresque de la Ville de Paris en 1834, published by Perrot, we can see the changes: the Rue Neuve Vivienne has been extended in a straight line and the Hotel de Montmorency has been torn down. Furthermore, the panoramas were torn down in 1831 and replaced by new tall entrance buildings. The Passage des Panoramas was intersected by the new buildings on the Rue Neuve Vivienne. They incorporated in part the old shops and also provided new entrances and deep shops which extended through to the street. In the course of these alterations, the new wings of the arcade arose: the Galerie des Variétés, which connected the theater to the Rue Vivienne; the Galerie Feydeau, which runs parallel to the old wing; the Galerie Montmartre, which makes the arcade accessible from the Rue Montmartre through the existing buildings; and the Galerie St. Marc, named after the street which is joined by this wing to the end of the Galerie des Variétés. The arcade expanded, then, taking up more and more space in the block. It made up for its lost function as a traffic artery with added accessibility from all sides. The greater number of entrances were designed to attract more passersby. The essentials of the building remained unchanged throughout the nineteenth century with the exception of the renovation of the glass roof and the addition of some new buildings around the edges.

The arcade vogue died down after Haussmann's renewal measures were carried out. Their spaces were too narrow and dark, so the arcades were abandoned. The Passage des Panoramas, however, was able to enjoy great popularity for a long time thanks to its favorable location and integration with the consistently popular establishments in the neighborhood. In the twentieth century the entire south side was torn down, and a modern apartment building was constructed in its place. Parts of the arcade were replaced and the character changed. Hence, the structure labeled on present-day city plans as the Passage des Panoramas is but a shadow of its former self, engulfed by domineering buildings. It still undergoes constant alteration and parts are completely without activity. Fortunately, some shops, like the engravers'

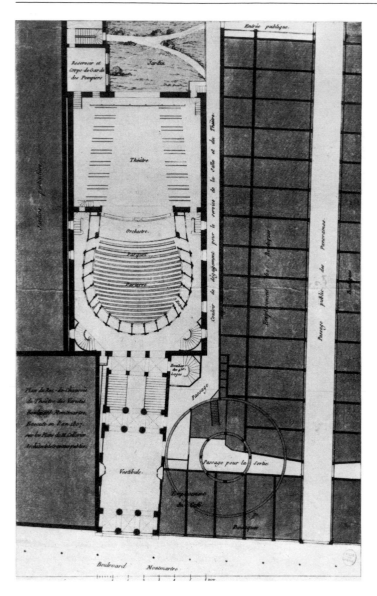

376
Passage des Panoramas, Théâtre des Variétés and part of the arcade, plan

and the Eastern restaurant La Caravane, still manage to recall the grandeur of the past. A countless number of signs, advertisements, and neon lights still attempt to attract the attention, at least for a moment, of the crowds hurrying past. But they cannot hide the fact that the arcade leads a quiet and retired existence.

Let us examine the original structure in more detail. After the revolution, the Hotel de Montmorency-Luxembourg was expropriated as the property of emigrés. Later, however, it was returned to the children of the Duc de Montmorency who then sold it to Mr. and Mrs. James Thayer. They divided up the gardens and built the panoramas and the arcade.[626]

The panorama was invented by the Scotsman Robert Barker in 1787.[627] He exhibited the first panorama in 1794 in a circular building in London. It depicted the battle at Spithead. In 1799 the inventor Robert Fulton received a patent in France to introduce panoramas to the country. However, because of his poor financial situation, he sold his rights to Thayer, who in 1799 built the two rotundas which flanked the entrance to the arcade. The one panorama portrayed a view of Paris from the main tower of the Palace of the Tuileries; the other depicted the withdrawal of the British from Toulon. Since the panoramas received widespread public acclaim, Thayer constructed a third panorama in the garden, connected to the others by a passage. It depicted the sea battle of Navarin. Thayer had formed an association with the painter Pierre Prévost, who specialized in panorama painting. He and his assistants executed eighteen panoramas in twenty years, each with a different topical subject. Napoleon himself visited the panoramas after he returned from his Egyptian campaign. He marveled at a depiction of the pyramids.

The panorama buildings were cylindrical, with cone-shaped roofs; they measured 14 meters in diameter and had a central platform with a diameter of 6 meters.[628] They surpassed the height of the two-storied front of the arcade on the boulevard. The corresponding subject was printed around the cylinder in large letters. One could enter the panorama through narrow hallways which branched off of the arcade. These hallways brought the visitor into a room behind the shops which contained a stairway leading into the inner, round platform. The panoramas were illuminated with natural lighting by a continuous crown of skylights. The panoramas, then, were an ingredient of the arcade; indeed, they were its main attraction.

We are fortunate that a small painting in the Musée Carnavalet depicts the original state of the interior of the arcade.[629] The painter is unknown. It is dated 1810 and shows the arcade before the first alterations. The most important information this painting offers is on the nature of the original arcade roof. It is a wooden, smooth-surfaced saddle roof with glass panels. A similar roof still exists today in the Burlington Arcade, which was built fifteen years after the Passage des Panoramas.[630] The similarity between the two roofs is so striking that I suggest direct influence—a distinct possibility considering the close relationship between the cities of London and Paris at the time.

The interior of the arcade is depicted approximately from the point where the side exit from the Théâtre des Variétés opens up into the arcade. This perspective is indicated by the inscription on the upper edge. The viewer is looking in the direction of the boulevard and can see the arched gate of the exit and even a part of the new development on the other side of the street. Shortly before the exits on the second floor, a decorative bridge spans the two-storied arcade. It probably formed a direct link between the two panoramas. The figures in this landscape—the painted signs, the displays flowing out of the shops, the pedestrians—give a realistic picture from the age before photography.

The architecture of the arcade space is documented by small anonymous fragmentary plans in the topographical collections of the Bibliothèque Nationale.[631] Sections, plans, and elevations of the arcade space clarify its construction and organization. Two series of narrow buildings line the arcade symmetrically, separated by about 3 meters. Shops with small back rooms occupy the ground floor. Each one contains its own stairway to the upper story. The sketch of the glass-roof construction corresponds to the painting except that its glass panels are deeper. The order of pilasters indicated in the upper stories does not seem to have been constructed.

The facade formation of the arcade space begins with the Passage des Panoramas. The interior facade is not yet differentiated from shops as they appear outside on the streets of commercial districts. The ground floor is punctuated by large shop windows divided into small square panes. Columns stand in front of the walls separating the shops. They bear a wide wooden cornice which covers the supports. The cornice is continuous and serves as an advertising space to which the shop signs are attached. The upper story is an undivided wall with small windows. A shallow groove forms the connection to the wooden saddle roof. This original front can still be found today on a small stretch of the arcade between the boulevard and the lateral wing. All the other sections have been removed or covered by later alterations.

The significance and fame of this arcade did not result therefore from its architectonic quality but from the life which thrived within its space. More interesting than the architecture is the society which for generations used this space as a rendezvous, the shops which served this society and its demand for refinement and luxury, and the atmosphere which attracted the public. The boulevard and the arcade supplemented each other, forming an uninterrupted area for the pedestrian to move within, free of hindrance and danger. The boulevard was open and tree-lined, the arcade covered and protected from inclement weather. Although the buildings on this section of the boulevard were not so systematically arranged and regulated as those of the Palais Royal, they offered a total and more flexible spatial program. This dynamic explains the fascination the boulevard held for the whole world at the time and the constant construction it attracted.

The Passage des Panoramas was extended to the north beyond the boulevard by the Jouffroy and Verdeau arcades, which formed a covered promenade nearly 400 meters long. The Musée Grévin, a wax-figure museum, was established next to the Passage Jouffroy. Hotels were built. Cafés, restaurants, theaters, baths, and ballrooms lined the boulevard. The Passage des Panoramas was located in the center of all this activity. Thus, it could sustain itself, longer than any other arcade, through the entire second Empire. Kolloff[632] wrote in 1849 that it was the most splendid and lively of all the Parisian arcades.

A wide variety of material about the inhabitants and businesses of this arcade appears in the travelogues, literature on the

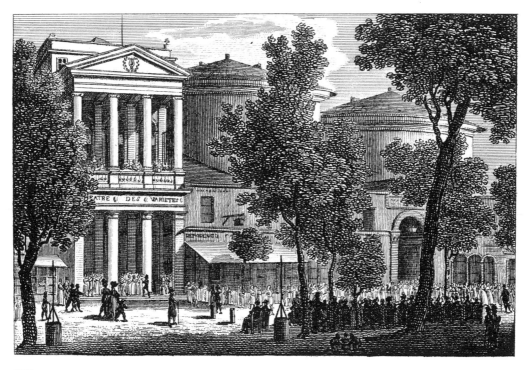

377
Paris, Boulevard
Montmartre

378
Paris, street scene in
front of the Passage
des Panoramas,
lithograph by Opitz,
1814

379
Passage des
Panoramas, view to-
ward the boulevard,
watercolor by an un-
known artist, ca.
1810

boulevard, and novels of the period. I have selected two texts. The first is a report by an enthusiastic *flâneur* (circa 1820). The other uses the arcade as the background for a novel on a social theme. The first text is by Montigny from his book *Le Provincial à Paris;* the second is from *Nana* by Zola.[633]

Individual shops—like the pastry shop of Noël and the confectionery of Millelot—were so famous and architecturally refined that they were written about during their time.[634] The most famous shop was certainly that of Susse, of which Wittkop wrote:[635] "Alexander Dumas cannot give enough praise to Susse's stationery shop, which has established itself here. 'What a businessman!' he exclaims. In Susse's shop one finds everything: not only any kind of paper, pens, lamp-shades, but also porcelain, fine woodwork, bronze figures, articles for oil-painting and water-colors, small frames for miniatures, and even sketches or paintings which in some cases can even be rented. Dumas acquired a Delacroix here for 600 francs. He later sold it for 15,000 francs to Khalil Bey, the Turkish lover of the 'Dame aux violettes' at the time of her blossoming sinfulness. Susse was also Gavarni's publisher. He handled the caricatures of the sculptor Dantan, many of which can also be seen in the Musée Carnavalet."

A portrayal of the Passage des Panoramas would be incomplete without a mention of its most renowned German admirer, Heinrich Heine. August Lewald wrote of him:[636] "His favorite promenade was the Passage des Panoramas, a place one avoided in the evening if one had a lady on one's arm. . . . Heine strolled up and down the arcade, his hands in his pockets, his head hanging low, his glasses on. Here he observed Parisian life. All around him were the enticing Zoës, Aglas, Desirées, Clarissas, Amelias, etc. They promenaded here constantly and he dedicated some wonderful songs to them, which he published in the first part of the 'Salon.' In the beginning he found French women too small. 'If one is accustomed to the long German members,' he said, 'it is difficult to become acclimated here.'"

Text 1: Montigny on the Passage des Panoramas (circa 1820)

Of all the arcades that clever speculations have opened, the most popular at the moment is the Passage des Panoramas. A successful exhibition and fashion motivated

its success; time helped it along. Today this beautiful arcade seems to stand under the special protection of the god of trade.

We do not want to deny ourselves the pleasure of visiting the arcade. Let us enter this gleaming bazaar from Boulevard Montmartre. We will begin our tour on the left side.

Right on the corner of the Boulevard is the Café Veron; the decoration and fittings are for sophisticated tastes. There are always happy customers leaving this establishment. Both before and after the Stock Exchange hours the tables are full, occupied by the Exchange employees, brokers, speculators on booms and slumps. These gentlemen eat heartily. Right next door is the Duchesse de Courlande confectionery shop where delicacies of all sorts are on display. The most beautiful fruits enchant the eye at all times of the year, but especially during the cold seasons. Astonished, one looks under the glass bells and sees red currants, peaches, cherries, and grapes. Sugar takes all forms here; it is Protean. Even prettier are all the truly natural colors. I should say to the customers who would make all of their "sweet" purchases here that the sales-ladies are especially attractive, and it is the custom to tell them so.

A little further on steel gleams so brightly that even the gold seems to tarnish. Here are sweet nothings, charming trifles. Mostly the ladies pause here. Let us hurry then past the shoe store and past the glove shops to stop at Susse, the fashionable stationery store in the arcade. Here are the most astonishing things. Are you looking for mechanical picture frames, pretty souvenirs? Would you like decorative boxes, desk accessories, or do you need a reading desk with secret compartments, or a case for visiting cards? You have only to chose, Madame. Should your husband accompany you, take care that he is not drawn to the charming portfolios of red, green, and black leather, because they are for you, Madame.

Let us cast a glance at Madame Lapostoli's charming straw hats and a longer glance at the equally charming persons who sell them.

There is nothing special at the shop of Monsieur Basin, goldsmith, so we hurry along to Mère de Famille, to Madame Mineur, and then to the glove maker, and then the famous Chaumière Allemande, where you can buy fashion clothing and perfumes at the same time. Afterwards, you get to the gloomy passageway that leads to the Théâtre des Variétés, and brush past the modest shop of a lorgnette dealer on the corner. Now we stand before Marquis's magnificent shop, where chocolate runs the gamut of possible transformations. We pause for a moment and inhale

380
Passage des
Panoramas, entrance,
Boulevard
Montmartre

381
Passage des
Panoramas, arcade
space, view toward
the boulevard

the tasty fragrances of coffee and truffles that stream out of the interesting delicacy shop on the corner of the Panorama.

There is a tailor after Marquis's, then a draper's shop and a carpet merchant. At the latter we may admire the loveliest of fireplace screens, on which historical themes or the deeds of war of our brave cavaliers are displayed. (Since peace and the discovery of lithography, the Parisians dream only of victory and laurels. They console themselves with fictions for the losses of reality.)

Let us cast a glance now at the branch store selling Morize's coffee machines. A wonderful invention, thanks to which we can prepare the delicious coffee mocha without losing its aroma. We will leave the public house to the smokers and stop briefly at Frère music publishers. Are you looking for fire, desire, paramours, troubadours? Here you may find them in numbers. Now we have come to Monsieur Comte's Petit Théâtre. Who are these noisy young scamps running around? Be quiet! These are the artists. The "père noble" is just biting into an apple, that small girl there is the "grande coquette," and the dignified financial magnate is just giving her a piece of cake.

Here is a tobacco shop and next to it a money-changer. Just look at the covetous gaze of the passers-by as they look on the wooden bowls filled with gold pieces. We move on quickly so that we may avoid the tortures of Tantalus; the real treasure is next door anyway in Nepveu's bookstore.

The arcade ends on this side with a shoe maker, a hairdresser, and a tailor. After visiting these three shops, you will emerge feeling reborn—provided you have the money to do so!

We heve covered the entire left side of this picturesque arcade, and we turn around now to visit the right side, for it seems worth our while.

We allow ourselves a glance at the shop of Mr. Fabry, goldsmith, a store which until recently was totally out of date, but which is today one of the most elegant in the arcade. We're sorry that the right side of the arcade must take the back seat here as in some other places. The other side is much preferred since the new means of illumination is already in use there. Even in the evening the show windows glow for the customers, while here they still use the dim oil lamps of our fathers' days. And here is even a shop for rent! But then there are two shops which respond to the needs of the times, one for gloves and a store for suspenders. You can only say the best of them. An artists' union, Aux Artistes réunis, was still missing here, but I am standing directly in front of their establishment. They sell brushes, English shoe wax,

and the daily paper. We proceed to the sweets shop, which is really not very interesting. The woman at the register is polite, and that means something anyway. But now we want to hurry on to visit the orange vendor; we barely glance at the glove maker, the fancy cabinet-maker, and the hatter. But why the hurry, the interested reader will query? The orange seller is just a nice little vending machine, which, however, deserves some of the compliments paid to it daily. If you could only succeed in bringing it to life and giving some of its character a little expression! After the orange and lemon shop, over which the gaslight pours out floods of light at the advent of darkness, we come to a toy store. Next to it, there is another glove maker, and next to him another toy store. There are so many children of all ages in Paris! But how is it that the old Argand lamps have not yielded their place here to the new, beautifully gleaming gas candelabra? Now the aroma of Marquis's cocoa laboratories reaches our noses. And we can admire the charming parasols of his neighbor, which are nevertheless a trifle expensive. Next door is a jewelry store which holds our attention for a moment. And next to it, a draper's shop lighted with oil. But the displays of the alabaster dealer are more interesting. And then Felix's pastry shop, where we will pause briefly.

After we have pushed aside the Englishmen and broken through the thick phalanx of Englishwomen who have apparently made themselves at home here, we come to the small salon of the famous pastry maker, Félix. We try his cakes and his wine, and then pay, discovering that for the same price we could have consumed a whole meal in most of our city's restaurants. And still Master Félix lights his store with oil! Shouldn't his bakery be more up to date?

Let us not tarry and hesitate to make our purchases at the confectionery with the somewhat odd name of Zum Wappen Werthers (Werther Arms). In my opinion, it is the best of its kind in the arcade.

We also want to mention the workshop where one can have all kinds of things silverplated. Now we stand before the Magic Lamp. In fact only gloves are sold here. But the sales ladies seem to be real fairies. To make our thoughts take a turn for the serious, let us pause for a moment before M. Fleschelle's shop. Here he sells bronzes and gilded objects. Let the crafts be honored which have found their haven in the arcade! The tailor is housed next to the most spacious of shops. The glamour of the fabric is seductive as it waits here for a customer. Will it all last? Fashion does not even permit the buyer the time to carry it home!

After a modest bonnet shop we reach the panorama from which the arcade took its name.

After a glance at one last toy shop, we reach the Grand Magasin de Nouveautés de l'Eclipse. Here our promenade comes to an end.

Text 2: Zola, Nana

It was a very mild evening. A shower had just driven a crowd of people into the Passage. There was quite a mob, and it was a slow and difficult task to pass along between the shops on either side. Beneath the glass roof, brightened by the reflection, there was a most fierce illumination, consisting of an endless string of lights—white globes, red and blue lamps, rows of flaring gas-jets, and monstrous watches and fans formed of flames of fire—burning without any protection whatsoever; and the medley of colours in the various shop windows— the gold of the jewellers, the crystal vases of the confectioners, the pale silks of the milliners—blazed behind the spotless plate-glass, in the strong light cast by the reflectors; whilst among the chaos of gaudily painted signs, an enormous red glove in the distance looked like a bleeding hand, cut off and fixed to a yellow cuff. . . . A damp and warm air filled the narrow thoroughfare with a kind of luminous vapour. Along the flagstones, wet from the drippings of umbrellas, footsteps reverberated continuously, without the sound of a single voice.

Passage Delorme (fig. 382)

Rue de Rivoli—Rue St. Honoré 177

The Passage Delorme never exposed its secrets—no photograph or description throws light on its history. It was built in 1808, was a great commercial success, was perfectly located between the Rue de Rivoli and the Rue St. Honoré, and was replaced in 1896 by the construction of a new hotel. The Rue de Rivoli had been proposed in 1793 by the Artistes de la Révolution. Napoleon expanded it into a showplace of a straightness unusual for Paris streets. By 1808 it had grown as far as the Passage Delorme. The Rue des Pyramides was still only a proposal; behind it to the east lay the irregular districts which separated the wings of the Louvre and the Tuileries. The Rue de Rivoli was designed to ease the load on the old Rue St. Honoré and to separate the overdeveloped and dangerous medieval city from the seat of the government. Forty streets and 500 buildings were sacrificed to this enterprise, which was finally completed under Haussmann.

382
Paris, site of the Passage Delorme, 1833

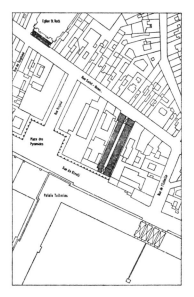

On the aforementioned plan by Vasserot and Bélanger, the Passage Delorme is drawn in as a ground plan. One can see that it had entrance buildings with their own stairways on both sides. In between came equally wide and deep shops on both sides of the approximately 3-meter-wide arcade. Around the borders of the regular site narrow strips were left open; they were accessible from the entrance buildings and provided a service entrance to the back of the shops. This is the first instance of a double system of access.

The Passage Delorme is named after its owner, who is considered the inventor of the arcade. I would qualify this claim, however. He was actually the inventor of the arcade with a continuous glass roof. Kolloff wrote:[637] "It was a question of building an arcade as bright as an open space which would be warm in winter, cool in summer, always dry, and never dusty or dirty. Delorme solved this problem. His masterpiece, the Passage Delorme, extends from the Rue St. Honoré to the Rue de Rivoli. Delorme has the honor, then, of being the inventor of the covered arcade. Since then the number of arcades has increased considerably. They are covered with plate glass and have shops on both sides, which contain apartments for the shopkeepers on the upper stories. . . ." Thus, eight years after the construction of the Passage des Panoramas, the inventor of the arcade appears, which can only mean, of the arcade with a glass roof. Unfortunately, we know nothing about the specific form of this roof.

One finds at least this one illustrative detail in Pessard:[638] in 1870 all of Paris marveled at the Devinck chocolate machine in the Passage Delorme. One machine ground the cacao beans, boiled them, kneaded the paste, and pressed it into bars—all this before the eyes of an astounded public. Lanzac de Laborie[639] called the arcade "an elegant and convenient connection." A long poem by Emanuel de Montcorin[640] bears the title "Passage Delorme" but contains no detailed references. In the list of *passages couvertes* compiled by the Commission de Vieux Paris of 1916 the name does not even appear.[641]

Passage Montesquieu (fig. 383)
Rue Montesquieu—Cloître St. Honoré
The Passage Montesquieu is the only covered arcade of the early Parisian arcades which was located in the immediate neighborhood of the Palais Royal.[642] It was built in 1811 and disappeared near the end of the century. One of the countless exits of the Palais Royal led on the east from the Cour d'Honneur—as the site plan of the Galerie d'Orléans reveals—to the Rue de Valois and continued as the open Cour des Fontaines. One reached the Rue des Bonnes Enfants through a large gate or through the narrow Passage Henri IV. Continuing along this connection one came upon the short Rue Montesquieu, which gave the arcade its name. The street was opened in 1802 on the site of the former Cloître de la Collégiale St. Honoré, which was disbanded in 1790 and sold in 1796.[643] The Rue Montesquieu had the function of linking the Palais Royal to the numerous shipping offices and markets. The arcade profited from the public it attracted. The Galerie Véro-Dodat, constructed fifteen years later, extended the Rue Montesquieu and opened into one of the entrances of the important post station.

The floor plans of all the stories of the Passage Montesquieu, located in the topographical collections of the Bibliothèque Nationale,[644] show three parallel wings between the Rue Montesquieu and the former monastery. A lateral wing led through two of the wings to the Rue Croix des Petits Champs. The ground plan reprinted in fig. 383 shows these wings. They were built out from the remains of old buildings which were expanded into short, narrow arcades. The motif of the double arcade was derived from the model of the Galeries de Bois.

The only event to confer historical importance on the arcade was the attempt by the widow of Philippe Lebon to introduce there the thermolamp invented by her husband as the first form of public gas lighting. This attempt was abandoned, however, because of the intolerable odor produced by the lamp.[645]

Passage de l'Opéra (figs. 384–390)
Boulevard des Italiens, side exits to the Rue le Pelletier, Rue Pinon and Rue Grange Batelière
The Passage de l'Opéra is no longer standing. It was sacrificed to the extension of the Boulevard Haussmann which, though planned decades earlier, was finally constructed in 1925. Louis Aragon memorialized the arcade in one of his first surrealist works, *Le Paysan de Paris*.[646]

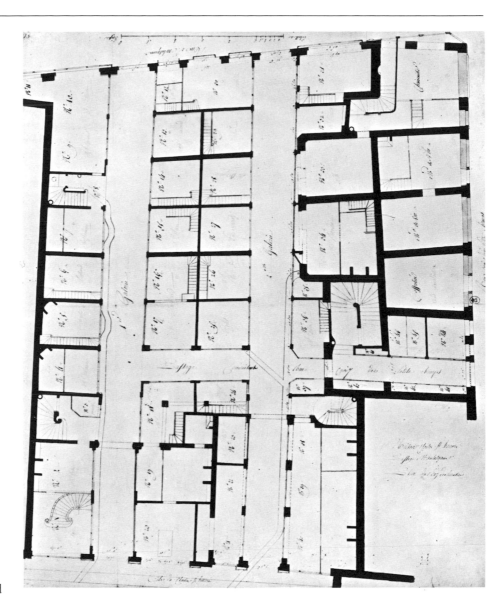

383
Paris, Passage Montesquieu, demolished
1811, plan

384
Paris, sites of the Passage de l'Opéra and the Passage Lafitte, 1833

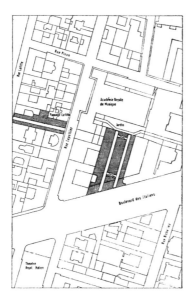

After a ten-year pause following on the collapse of the Napoleonic Empire, the Passage de l'Opéra resurrected the arcade fashion in the era of the Restoration. Its success encouraged other such enterprises.

The Passage de l'Opéra belongs to the type of the double arcade,[647] parallel arcade spaces connected by crossing passages. This arrangement enables an interior circuit and creates a certain independence from the demands of traffic. This form was important in the case of the Passage de l'Opéra, which served as an additional entrance and exit for the opera and had only narrow passageways without shops to the other streets which formed the building block.

The Passage de l'Opéra was built as part of the new Académie Royale de Musique.[648] Since the academy was located on a side street, the arcade made it directly accessible from the Boulevard des Italiens. The Académie Royale de Musique, the temporary Paris opera house, was dedicated on August 19, 1821. The architect Debret built it of wood and plaster on the site of the Hôtel de Choiseul. It was the twelfth home in the history of the Paris opera, a history marked by fires, temporary quarters, and moves from one neighborhood to another.

Before the revolution, the opera performed in the Salle de la Porte St. Martin. After the revolution it moved to the Rue de Richelieu. In 1820 the Duc de Berry was assassinated at its entrance. The bishop who administered the last rites had the condemned site demolished and replaced by a chapel. After a few temporary homes in other halls, the opera moved to the large building on the Rue Le Peletier, where it experienced its great era, although the building was in an obvious state of disrepair. There was a fire in 1873, and in 1878 the opera moved into the gigantic new theater by Garnier. Its tremendous dimensions still meet the demands of modern productions.

The architect of the opera, François Debret,[649] was also the architect of the arcade. He built it in 1822–1825 for the Viscount Morel Vindé, Pair de France, in a part of his garden.[650] Its opening was authorized by royal decrees on July 21, 1822, and April 16, 1823.[651] These decrees required that the arcade remain open between seven in the morning and midnight.

It seems from the two dates that the west arcade, called the Passage de l'Horloge, was opened first and that its great success led ten months later to the opening of the Passage Baromètre. This assumption seems to be confirmed by the text of a leasing prospectus (probably from 1822) which I discovered in the shop of a Paris print dealer. It says: "The first of these arcades will be finished next July. . . ." This beautiful article reprints a floor plan of the arcade and the great facade facing the Boulevard des Italiens. It describes the leasable property and gives the addresses which interested parties should contact.

The large entrance building stands three stories higher than the arcade and has sixteen apartments, a continuous shop front, and two tall archways. It follows the contour of the boulevard while the arcades run parallel to the borders of the site. Hence, the arcades and the frontal building intersect at a 60-degree angle. Both arcade spaces are connected by one-storied crossing corridors. They open up into a garden which runs perpendicular to the passages along the side of the opera house. The garden contains a pergola leading to the three arcades which wind their way to the surrounding streets. To the west is the Rue Le Peletier; the arcade continues on the other side of this street in the Passage Lafitte, constructed in 1824. To the north is the newly opened Rue Chauchat; pedestrians can proceed directly from it through the arcade to the boulevard. And to the east is the Rue Grange Batelière which is linked to the arcade.

The prospectus speaks of seventy shops, each with a rear room, a drying-loft, a kitchen, a small cellar, and a room with a stove on the second floor. The Galerie de l'Horloge was provided with public restrooms, a large hall in the cellar, and a total of twenty-five apartments and rooms above the arcade's shops. These rooms were accessible by separate staircases. This information is confirmed by the ground plan. In the old photograph shown in fig. 386 one can see that the arcade was barely 3 meters wide, although it had three stories and a total length of 170 meters. An older photograph not reproduced here[652] shows that the structure of the shop facades was continuous on the interior and that a simple glass saddle roof covered the arcade.

385
Announcement, Pas-
sage de l'Opéra,
1822

PASSAGES DE L'OPERA.

Façade sur le Boulevard des Italiens

Cet passages établis, sur le boulevard des Italiens, débouché par les rues Lepelletier Grange-batelière et Pinon vis à vis la nouvelle rue Chauchat Ils renfermeront au mois d'Octobre prochain 70 boutiques tant dans l'intérieur que sur le boulevard, un grand couvert de 650 pieds de longueur sur 48 pieds de largeur et 17 pieds sous voute propre a un grand Établissement. des lieux d'aisances publics. Le premier de ces passages sera terminé au mois de Juillet prochain. Chaque boutique a pour dépendances une arrière boutique, soupente au dessus, cuisine, petite cave et une Chambre à feu au 1er Etage.

Il y aura en outre dépendant de ces deux passages, 16 appartemens complets donnant sur le boulevard avec entrée indépendante des passages, 25 autres, tant sur la cour de l'Opéra que dans les passages et plusieurs appartemens de garçons.

S'adresser pour les locations de midi à 3 heures sur les lieux même à Mr Fuzelier ou avant 9h du matin chez lui rue du F.B. Montmartre No 43.

PLAN GÉNÉRAL DES PASSAGES ET DE LEURS DÉBOUCHÉS.

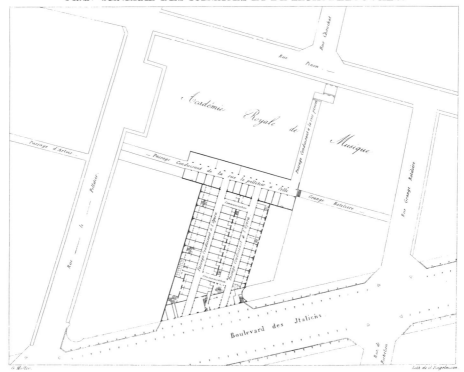

Gas lights, protected from drafts by glass shades, illuminated the interior from wall brackets.

The Passage de l'Opéra was perfectly located in the neighborhood betweeen the boulevard and the Chaussée d'Antin, an area which grew fashionable in the 1820s. The arcade became the "Eldorado of the aimless, the oasis of the lovers of the Chaussée d'Antin."[653] In 1826 the tenants issued a "Shopper's Guide or Almanac for the Passages de l'Opéra,"[654] which affords us a greater insight into the use of the space (Text 1). It provides evidence of an extensive and highly specialized selection of merchandise. One could purchase luxury items of all kinds, order elegant interior decorations, outfit oneself with clothes, and stuff oneself with delicacies from all over the world. It was possible to eat, drink, sip coffee, dance in the Bal d'Italie in the cellar, view all kinds of astounding pictures and wax figures in the Europorama. And in the apartments, not mentioned in the list, customers could find live entertainment and attractions. The Passage de l'Opéra was in fashion for the entire era of the Restoration. It furthermore acquired an international reputation as a kind of secret stock exchange for speculators. This "exchange" was closed down by the police in 1852.

Kolloff[655] gave the following description of the arcade in 1849: "The twin arcade of the Barometer and the Opera on the Boulevard des Italiens belongs exclusively to fashion. Since fashion sleeps till the sun is high in the sky one finds few people there before noon. Then the activity of the two galleries appears to come to life. The shops are set up and the pedestrians gradually stream in. Soon it is bubbling and humming incessantly."

On October 23, 1873, the opera house burned down. The arcade was left as a fragment of a no longer existing architectural ensemble. It lost its power of attraction. In 1880 Auguste Blanqui, the great anarchist leader,[656] leased space in the arcade for the publication of his journal *Ni Dieu ni Maître*. Yet the owner had him evicted (according to Wittkop)[657] because he did not agree with the movement. The result was "that the followers of the old revolutionary came in droves to demonstrate under the glass roof."

The existence of the Passage de l'Opéra had already been threatened in the 1860s by the planned Boulevard Haussmann. Its continuation, however, had been halted at the Rue Taitbout and the project became the joke of Paris. In 1898 the Rue Chauchat was supposed to be extended, the necessary area having become free after the fire in the opera house. That project was carried out, but only as far as the north entrance of the arcade. The arcade thus once again played a role in the regulation of traffic. This situation lasted until 1925, when the planned connection between the Boulevard Haussmann and the inner boulevard ring was accomplished.

With the arcade disappeared the Bar Certa, meeting place of the Dadaists and Surrealists. With it disappeared as well the weapons dealers, tailors, and the boutique of the hairdresser Gelis, patronized by famous personalities from Balzac to Breton.[658]

I would like to quote at least a few passages from Aragon's description.[659]

Now I have reached the threshold of the Certa, a noted café about which I have much left to tell. Welcoming me into it is a motto on the door, above a shield supporting a cluster of flags:

Amon Nos Autes

Toward the end of 1919, André Breton and I decided that henceforth our group would congregate here, out of repugnance for Montparnasse and Montmartre but equally out of liking for the promiscuity of the passage, seduced as we found ourselves by an unfamiliar decor which was not long in becoming our headquarters. Here the Dada movement assembled, either to plot one of those derisive, legendary demonstrations to which it owed alike its grandeur and fall, or else to loiter in the grip of boredom, lassitude and unemployment, or, again, to argue in the heat of some violent crisis which convulsed it from time to time, when the charge of moderatism was preferred against one of its members. I cannot speak of it except in a tone of wavering sentimentality. . . .

A delightful place withal, in which soft light, calm, and peace prevail behind the large windows extending down to the floor, and yellow curtains either revealing the passage or screening it from view, depending on which way the hand, by now out of patience from waiting, draws their pleated silk. . . .

And nurtured by this enviable peace, daydreams blossom untended. Here surrealism comes into its own. With the glass inkwell and the champagne cork they provide, you're launched. Images, rain down like confetti. Images, images everywhere: on

389
Passage de l'Opéra,
the arcade as secret
stock exchange

LA BOURSE AU PASSAGE DE L'OPÉRA

1ᵉʳ BOURSIER — J'ai quatre cents chemins !....
2ᵐᵉ BOURSIER — Quel chemin ?...
INTERRUPTEUR — Celui de la préfecture de police ......,où vous allez me suivre.......

387
Passage de l'Opéra,
flight from the arcade
during the Opéra
fire, 1873

388
Passage de l'Opéra,
ball in the arcade,
wood engraving by
Gustave Dore

386
Paris, Passage de
l'Opéra, 1822–1823,
demolished 1924, ar-
cade space

the ceiling, in the straw of armchairs, in the straws of drinks, in the sign above the public telephone, in the sparkling air, in the iron lanterns which illuminate the room. Start snowing, images; it's Christmas time. Snow down on the barrels and on the credulous hearts; snow on people's hair and hands. But, beset as I am by faint twinges of anxiety, waiting for someone who is supposed to meet me, I've combed my hair three times thinking about it—as soon as I lift the curtains, the passage recaptures my attention, with its hubbub and its passersby. A strange *chassé-croisé* of thoughts I cannot figure out but manifest in all this commotion. What is it they are after, these people retracing their steps? Their brows are both knit and smooth. There are as many ways of walking as there are clouds in the sky. One thing worries me, however: what do the pantomimes of these middle-aged gentlemen denote? They turn about, disappear, then bob up again. My suspicions are aroused, and suddenly I direct my gaze at the handkerchief boutique.

Text 1: Le Guide des Acheteurs ou Almanach des Passages de l'Opéra, *Names and professions of the merchants referred to in the Guide*

On the boulevard (by shop number):

1. M. Daubancour, watchmaker
2. M. Cartier, fils, successor to Mme. Beuve-Cartier, florist
3. Lottery office
4. M. Douix, soda fountain–restaurant
5. Didier Brothers, drapers and tailors
6. Simon Garveau et Cie, music and instruments
7. M. Devaut, ladies' bootmaker and clog seller
8. M. Cartulat, wallpaper
9. M. Manceau fils, millinery and hats from France and Italy, etc., stairway L, no. 2, on the mezzanine

Offices of the *Petit Courier des Dames,* fashion newspaper, stairway *L,* no. 2, on the first [second] floor

Galerie de l'Horloge—Bal d'Italie

3–5. Mme. Leube, silks and fancy goods
4. Messrs. Sazerac and Duval, gallery for paintings of the modern school, sketches, lithographs, etc.
6. M. Laprugne, boot- and shoemaker
7. Messrs. Legrand and Meloche, glovers, breeches makers
8. M. Letouze, hot-water jugs
9. Mme. Tugg, sweets, preserves, and syrups
10–12. Messrs. Barchand and Cerf Weil, pottery and porcelain, workshop and store
11. M. Deschamps, workshop and store for necessities, hardware, etc.

13. Mme. Simon, millinery
14. M. Havoue, tailor
15. M. J. F. Veyrat, goldsmith and plated gold, workshop and store
16–18. M. Pichenot, fils, ivories, mother of pearl, inlaid wares, bronzes
17. Mme. Metot, lingerie and novelties
20. M. Bourguignon, imitation gold and precious stones, workshop and store
19–21. M. Bourguignon, pearls and pearl jewelry, workshop and store
22–24. Mme. Detourbet, children's toys, workshop and store
23. M. Guerin, wax and brushes, workshop and store
26. Mme. Oury, haberdashery and sundries

Galerie du Baromètre

1 bis. Children's toys, clogs
3. Concièrge, rental office
5. M. Potdevin, pastries
6. M. Pichenot, fils, owner of Aux Petits-Gobelins, wholesale haberdashery, painted canvases and wool for tapestry-making
7. Mme. Thuringer, perfumes
9–11. Coqueret, hardware merchant (iron wares)
12. Reading room and bookstore
13. M. Rigaut, silks and fancy goods
15–17. M. Tissot, engraver and crystal merchant
16. Mme. Draux, corset-maker
18. M. Deschamps' table d'hôte
19. Mme. Scharles, millinery
20. Mme. A. Decouture, lingerie and sundries
21. M. Vallon, fils, certified barber
22. M. Gaillard, porcelain merchant
23. M. Vallon, cutlery
24–26. Messrs. Saterac and Duval, engravings and prints
25. M. Villain, fils, bronzes and clocks, workshop and store
27–29. M. Roche, stationery and fancy goods
28. Tobacco, wine, liquors, and groceries
30–31–33–35. M. Dezon, furniture and tapestries

Apartments—Stairways

C. M. Etienne, restaurant; 2 francs per person
G. M. Casaty, workshop, ornaments, vases in *pâte de serail*
H. Europorama, or scenes of Europe's main cities; exhibition of the plan of Jerusalem
   M. Beneck, M.D. and obstetrician
   M. Audoyer, writing professor (American method)
K. M. Remondon, tailor
   M. Jung, tailor

Passage du Pont Neuf

*Rue Mazarine 44—Rue de Seine 45,
extension of the Rue Guénégaud*

The Passage du Pont Neuf is almost the only arcade built on the left bank. There was no fashion industry and there were few fine shops in that area. The streets were old, narrow, and unsuitable for strolling.

The Passage du Pont Neuf is no longer standing, having been replaced in 1913 by the Rue Jacques Callot. Its name indicates its location and its function as a traffic artery. It linked the Rue Guénégaud, which led to the Pont Neuf, and the Rue de l'Echaudé, crossing the block between the Rue Mazarine and the Rue de Seine. The arcade, built in 1823,[660] was one-storied, narrow, and 65 meters long, and was interrupted shortly before the Rue de Seine by an open courtyard.

Zola made it famous as the setting of his novel *Thérèse Raquin*.[661] Its gloom and narrowness, the life under the artificial lighting, and the oppressive closeness made it the ideal backdrop for the drama. Zola was the first to characterize this aspect of the arcade.

Text 1: Émile Zola, Thérèse Raquin

At the end of the rue Guénégaud, as you come up from the river, you find the Passage du Pont-Neuf, a sort of narrow, dark corridor connecting rue Mazarine and rue de Seine. This passage is thirty yards long and two in width at the most; it is paved with yellowish flagstones, worn and loose, which always exude a damp, pungent smell, and it is covered with a flat, glazed roofing black with grime.

On fine summer days, when the streets are baking in the oppressive heat, a whitish light does fall through the dingy glass roofing and hang dismally about this arcade, but on nasty winter ones, on foggy mornings, the panes send down nothing but gloom on to the greasy pavement below, and dirty, evil gloom at that.

To the left open out dark, low, shallow shops from which come whiffs of cold, vault-like air. Here there are booksellers, vendors of toys, cardboard dealers, whose window displays are grey with dust and slumber dimly in the shadows; the small window-panes cast strange greenish mottlings on the goods for sale. The murky shops behind are just so many black holes in which weird shapes move and have their being. To the right a wall runs the whole length of the passage and on it the shopkeepers opposite have hung narrow cupboards, where on flimsy shelves painted a horrible brown colour are displayed a lot of nondescript odds and ends that have been mouldering for the last twenty years. A vendor of artificial jewellery has set out her stock in one of these cupboards, and here fifteen-sou rings are for sale, daintily perched on blue velvet cushions in mahogany boxes.

Above the glass roof rises the black, rough-plastered wall, looking as though it were covered with a leprous rash and slashed with scars.

The Passage du Pont-Neuf is no place to go for a nice stroll. You use it as a short cut and time-saver. Its frequenters are busy people whose one idea is to go straight on quickly: aproned apprentices, seamstresses delivering their work, men and women carrying parcels. But there are also old people picking their slow way through the dismal gloom shed by the glass roofing, and troops of little children just out of school who come running through here to make as much clatter as they can with their sabots on the flagstones. All day long the quick, irregular tap-tap of footsteps on the pavement gets on your nerves; nobody says a word, nobody stands still, everybody gets on with the job, head down, walking rapidly, with never a glance at the shops. When by a miracle passers-by do stop in front of their windows, the shopkeepers eye them anxiously.

At night the arcade is lit by three gas jets in heavy square lanterns. These gas jets hang from the glass roof, on to which they cast up patches of lurid light, while they send down palely luminous circles that dance fitfully and now and again seem to disappear altogether. Then the arcade takes on the sinister look of a real cut-throat alley; great shadows creep along the paving-stones and damp draughts blow in from the street until it seems like an underground gallery dimly lit by three funeral lamps. By way of lighting the shopkeepers make do with the feeble beams that these lanterns send through their windows, and inside the shop they merely light a shaded lamp and stand it on a corner of the counter, and then passers-by can make out what there is inside these burrows where in daytime there is nothing but darkness. The windows of a dealer in cardboard make a blaze of light against the row of dismal shop-fronts, for two shale-oil lamps pierce the gloom with their yellow flames. On the opposite side a candle in a lamp-glass fills the case of artificial jewellery with starry lights. The proprietress sits dozing in her cupboard with her hands under her shawl.

Some years ago, opposite this woman's pitch, was a shop whose bottle-green woodwork exuded damp from every crack. A long, narrow plank which served as a sign bore the word HABERDASHERY in black letters, and across one of the panes in the door a woman's name, THÉRÈSE RAQUIN, was written in red.

Passage Lafitte (fig. 384)
Rue Le Pelletier—Rue Lafitte
The Passage Lafitte is often called the Passage d'Artois on older plans. It was built in 1824 as the extension of a side exit from the Passage de l'Opéra. It was financed by the banker Lafitte, who also played a role in the Revolution of 1830.[662] Kolloff described the arcade as "superbly and elegantly decorated." It was used in 1870 by Paul Durand-Ruel as a picture gallery.[663]

Passage du Grand Cerf (figs. 391–392)
Rue St. Denis 145—Rue Dussoubs 10
The Hôtellerie du Grand Cerf was once located between the Rue St. Denis and the Rue des deux Portes (the latter has been widened along part of its length and its name has been changed to the Rue Dussoubs). The building, with exits to both streets,[664] was the point of departure for numerous mail carriage lines. The whole complex was sold in 1815; in 1824 or 1825 Monsieur Devaux had the Passage du Grand Cerf constructed. The name (Arcade of the Great Stag) seems like a piece of the past.[665] The arcade is located a few streets south of the Passage du Caire in the middle of the old industrial district. It forms an extension of the Rue Marie Stuart. The arcade itself was extended a few years later by the Passage Bourg l'Abbé, from which one could reach the Rue St. Martin by way of the open Passage de l'Ancre. The Boulevard Sebastopol has made this connection unrecognizable.

The Passage du Grand Cerf is interesting for the development of the arcade building type, since it exemplifies a new system of access and since the arcade space is the height of a normal urban building. The arcade is 120 meters long; the arcade space is 4 meters wide and three-storied. A fourth story is located outside of the arcade roof, set back about 1 meter from the edge of the roof to leave room for a walkway along the glass roof, which sits on top of a 1-meter-high brick rampart.

The four stories are accessible by stairways which are inserted on all four levels as narrow bays. The stairways on opposite sides are joined by small bridges which cut

391
Paris, sites of the Passage du Grand Cerf and the Passage Bourg l'Abbé, 1932

through the glass roof. The resulting openings in the roof ventilate the space and offer a surprising view into the depth of the arcade space. This system of access is repeated four times. It is interconnected in the direction of the arcade by the arcade space and by the invisible open walkways which run alongside the glass roof. The system enables a variety of spatial combinations: one shop alone, shops with apartments, multiple shop aggregates with an apartment, one apartment alone, and numerous apartments grouped together. The elevation of the arcade interior shows groupings of shops with large glazed areas, not only on the ground floor but also on the second story. Not until the third story does one see smaller apartment windows. This arrangement demonstrates that the arcade served production and handicraft more than luxury and merchandising. Today one can still find studios, delivery services, and shops of craftspeople who give the arcade its individuality.

Many features of the arcade space fascinate the onlooker. Colorful shop signs hanging at different heights offer varying perspectives. The four overlapping rows of black ironwork are equally eyecatching. The first story has decorated supports whose function is no longer obvious; the third story has four areas divided by bridges above which twenty arches, each at the top of a division between bays, hold the ridgepole of the glass roof. It is uncanny to look up through the glass roof and to see the black shadow of a person crossing one of the bridges. One understands why Louis Malle selected the Passage du Grand Cerf for the stage of the chase scene in his film *Zazie dans le Métro*.

Galerie Vivienne (figs. 393–398)
Rue Vivienne 6—Rue des Petits Champs 4—Rue de Banque 5–7
"The two arcades, Vivienne and Colbert, are indeed siblings, but two hostile siblings, and peace will not be negotiated between them for a long time. The public, the natural judge in this conflict, has already passed a positive judgment on the Passage Vivienne, which is now pompously thriving at the expense of its competitor." This was Kolloff's characterization of the situation.[666] It was grotesque and unique in the history of the arcade: two arcades

appeared almost simultaneously next to each other vying for public favor.

Both arcades have a 90-degree bend; both have interposed central spaces, and thereby differentiated spatial sequences—three new phenomena for the arcade building type. The Galerie Vivienne is one of the few Parisian arcades whose ground plan, sections, elevations, and details were published a few years after its opening.[667] It, together with the Galerie Colbert and the Galerie d'Orléans, made the architectural concept of the arcade well known throughout Europe. Its architecture is indeed impressive. It expresses the precision and skill with decoration of F. J. Delannoy, an architect who received his training under the Empire,[668] and the ambition of a contractor who took an active role in the project. The Galerie Vivienne made a virtue of necessity; it incorporated three existing buildings into one overall structure. As a result, independent structures were included in the open spaces, creating a chain of spaces with completely different proportions and spatial effects. This architectural concept found a more significant response in the construction of bazaars, the forerunners of the department store, than in the development of the arcade, which was dominated by the motif of the street.

The Galerie Vivienne is directly connected to the galleries of the Palais Royal by the small Passage des Deux Pavillons, which cuts diagonally through the narrow block between the Rue de Beaujolais and the Rue des Petits Champs. The site upon which the Galerie Vivienne was constructed had formerly held the stables of the Duc d'Orléans. It consisted of three parcels:

a site, approximately 23 meters wide and 105 meters deep, at 4 Rue des Petits Champs

a shorter, perpendicularly attached site at 6 Rue Vivienne, across from the Palais Mazarin

a short but wide site at the Passage des Petits Pères, today 5–7 Rue de Banque.

All three sites had buildings on the street, which were rebuilt and included in the arcade. This explains the irregularity of the ground plan. In the book that the architect M. A. Delannoy devoted to his father's work, site plans before and after construction are shown. They make quite clear how ingeniously Delannoy handled the problem.[669]

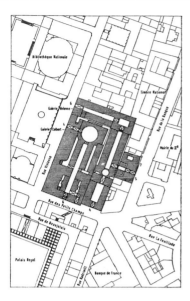

393
Paris, site of the
Galerie Vivienne and
the Galerie Colbert,
1966

The Galerie Vivienne was originally called the Galerie Marchoux,[670] after its first owner, the notary Marchoux. His daughter, Hermance Marchoux, later Comtesse de Caen, was a painter and sculptress. In 1844 she created the four caryatids which bore the balcony over the entrance to the arcade on the Rue des Petits Champs. The countess died in 1870, bequeathing a large portion of her fortune to the Institut de France and leaving money for artists studying in Rome with the stipulation that they produce a work for the founding of a museum. The Institut still houses this Musée de Caen and is also the proprietor of the Galerie Vivienne. The Institut now intends to raise money to restore the arcade.

In all the literature on the city's history, 1823 is given as the date of construction of the Galerie Vivienne.[671] However, Delannoy's commentary on its ground plan suggests another date:[672] "One (Monsieur Marchoux) began in 1824 the execution of the plan represented in plate 18 of Monsieur Delannoy's plans. Work was terminated in 1826." I consider these dates more credible.

The arcade was active into the Second Empire, at which time it fell into neglect. Besides the approximately seventy shops of various sizes, it also contained the cosmorama, invented in 1832 by the Abbé Gazzara. It reproduced landscapes in relief with the aid of magnifying mirrors. After 1888 the arcade experienced a renaissance thanks to the great popularity of the marionette theater of Signoret and Bouchor. Today one can observe at certain times of the day a trickle of passersby who use the arcade as a shortcut. The displays of Monsieur Petit-Siroux's bookstore on the bend of the arcade contain souvenirs and old items on the arcade which recall its past.

The Galerie Vivienne has three entrances, which used to be the carriage ways of the entrance buildings, to which a new decorative facade has simply been added. One can begin a tour of the main wing on the Rue des Petits Champs, crossing the courtyard of the old hotel. The width of the courtyard was reduced by 8 meters and covered by a glass roof. On the left one can still see the former open stairway. One then crosses the old garden wing of the hotel. Delannoy constructed a restaurant

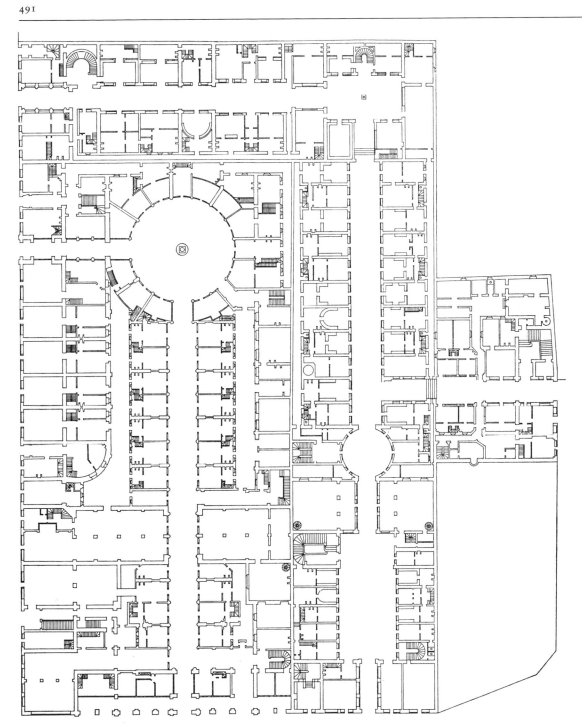

394
Galerie Colbert and
Galerie Vivienne,
ground floor plan
(Scale: 1 : 600)

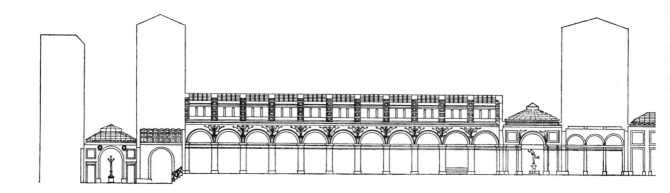

395
Paris, Galerie
Vivienne, 1824–
1826, longitudinal
section

396
Galerie Vivienne, en-
trance, Rue des Petits
Champs

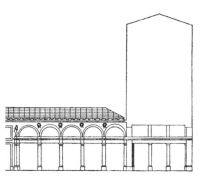

397
Galerie Vivienne, ar
cade space, view to-
ward the rotunda

398
Galerie Vivienne,
buttressing

on the ground floor, but it serves today as a storage room. One then enters the small rotunda with a diameter of 7.5 meters and a hemispherical glass dome which begins at mezzanine level. Originally a statue of Mercury stood in the center on a pedestal. There follows the 42-meter-long main room of the arcade which is taller by one story. The additional story is used for dwellings. Its spatial effect is dominated by the row of transverse buttresses which span the space,[673] connect the facades, and divide the glazing into broad bands. This space reminds one above all of the vaulted bazaars of the Orient. It is one of the few arcade spaces in which the original glass roof is still intact: small, overlapping glass plates give the glass roof more a net-like structure than a strip structure. Ventilation is achieved here in a unique way: the glazed panel between two ribs can be lifted as a whole on a hinge attached to the ridgepole and held in place by a pole.

Immediately to the right, the narrower Passage des Petits Pères opens into the main room of the arcade, thereby making the Galerie accessible to the Rue de Banque. Further along one reaches by way of a barrel-vaulted passageway and some steps a glassed-over courtyard enclosed on all sides by tall apartment houses. By making a 90-degree turn one can then exit from the arcade into the Rue Vivienne.

The shorter wing leading into the Rue Vivienne has an irregular width and a poorly joined glass roof. It is the least successful section of the arcade. Its architecture was criticized by a contemporary:[674] "This building lacks breadth; furthermore, the roof is too close to the ground, which considerably reduces the perspective. Moreover, it is neglected and poorly maintained. It is like a rich philistine who goes to the stock exchange with a fur cap on his head."

All the buildings of the arcade are accessible from the arcade interior. The newly built sections, however, are set back a few meters from the border of the site so that there is a space for a narrow corridor permitting a rear entrance to the stairways. These corridors open up in one or two places to the arcade interior. Interior access to the arcade buildings was provided in an innovative manner: every three bays have a common stairway on the rear wall

of the center bay. A common restroom is located next to this staircase. The upper stories, then, can be reached only through the shops or the rear stairways.

The architecture of the arcade spaces contains stylistic elements from the work of the Empire architects Percier and Fontaine: addition, stratification, composition of independent members such as pilasters, arches, mouldings, and framing; proportioning and profiling by means of soberly applied decorative elements such as a palmette frieze, coffering, and laurel wreaths, emblems such as the Aesculapian staff, anchor, palm branch, cornucopia, and lance, all symmetrically arranged in bas-relief in the arch spandrels. Plain wall areas with simple mouldings stand against the glazed openings, which are subdivided into small squares.

It is a soldierly architecture, propagated by intensive instruction, capable of great uniformity and resolution, while its unit construction system allows for infinite variations. This style became widespread in Europe at the time. Its materials, its ornamental accoutrements, were inspired by the rediscovery of antiquity (thanks to archeological expeditions and scholarly publications) and by the discoveries and reports of the scientists and artists who had taken part in the Egyptian campaign. The facade of the Galerie Vivienne, reproduced by Thiollet and Roux,[675] illustrates these points.

Galerie Colbert (figs. 399–406)
Rue des Petits Champs 6—Rue Vivienne 4
The Galerie Colbert connects the Rue des Petits Champs to the Rue Vivienne and occupies the square surrounded by the Galerie Vivienne. It is the first arcade about which a monograph appeared immediately after it opened. The monograph was published in 1828 by the architect of the arcade, J. Billaud,[676] and consists of four leaves: a view of the block, two interior elevations, and a ground plan. Other publications followed:[677] one in 1829 in Thiollet's work (appearing with information on the Galerie Vivienne) and one in 1855 in the *Zeitschrift für Bauwesen*.[678] The latter article begins its description of the arcade with the sentence: "This Galerie, one of the many arcades of Paris, indeed with its simplicity of decoration one of the most beautiful arcades, is located in the district between the boulevards."

399
Paris, Galerie Colbert, 1826, rotunda demolished, longitudinal section

400
Galerie Colbert, cross section

The Galerie Vivienne was not without influence; the Galerie Colbert also employed existing buildings and fit into existing courtyards. But competition led to greater efforts. The rotunda appears once again at the bend in the arcade but its dimensions are larger. This rotunda, which was well documented and known throughout the world, helped make the pivotal central space in a nonlinear arcade a tradition. The nearby Place des Victoires and the Halle au Blé may have inspired the architect to this idea.

The former Hôtel de Colbert on the corner of the Rue Vivienne and Rue des Petits Champs was expropriated after the revolution and came into the possession of Adam et Cie. They had the Galerie Colbert built in 1826 in order to profit from the crowds which congregated in the nearby Palais Royal. Shops were built into the ground floor of the hotel; the courtyards, made accessible by passageways, were almost completely lined with arcade buildings.

The Galerie Colbert had numerous cafes and restaurants. However, it was in business, its rotunda a favorite meeting place, for only a few short decades. As early as 1859 it was practically empty. Today only a short stretch is accessible from the Rue des Petits Champs. The rest of the arcade serves as a storage area, and the rotunda has been converted into a garage. A few shops still exist on the Rue Vivienne, and the old restaurant that extends to the arcade is still open for business.

The site plan shows how old and new building parts are interrelated. The old palace with its enclosed courtyard is located on the corner. The two wings are attached along the edges of the site. All the sections have five stories. They were converted by Billaud and given new facades. He placed three-storied arcade buildings in the courtyards without regard to the lighting of the lower levels of the wings, which have merely a 2.5-meter-wide glyph in the front. The stairways are accessible only through these narrow halls. One section of the arcade buildings of the rotunda is three-storied; the other section, bordering the northern edge of the property, is six-storied. Hence, the arcade is crowned on all sides by five- or six-storied buildings which have their own courtyard on a

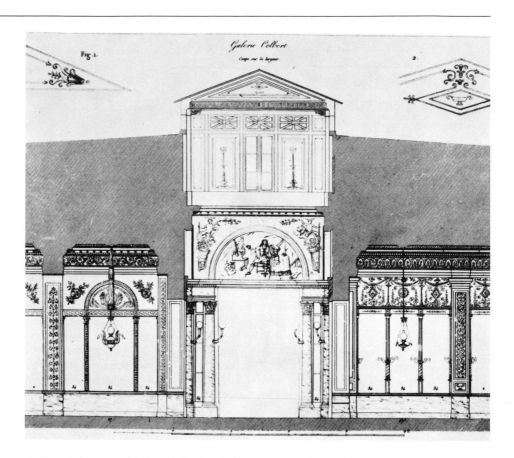

401
Galerie Colbert,
cross section

402
Galerie Vivienne and
Galerie Colbert,
doorway elevations

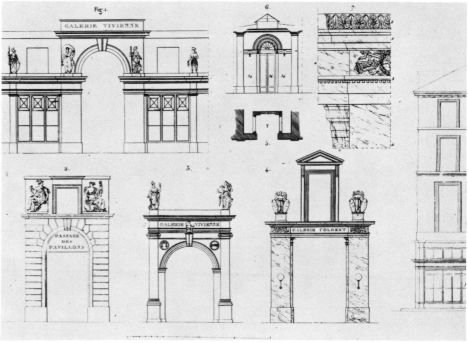

403
Galerie Colbert, en-
trance, Rue des Petits
Champs

404
Galerie Colbert, arcade space, view toward the rotunda, lithograph by Billaud, 1828

405
Galerie Colbert, rotunda, lithograph by Billaud, 1828

406
Galerie Colbert, view
toward the Rue des
Petits Champs

higher level above the glass roof. Such an exploitation of the site would no longer be possible today.

One used to enter the Galerie Colbert by a portico along the Rue des Petits Champs. Today it is fully enclosed. A passageway led to the 55-meter-long, 5-meter-wide, and 10-meter-tall main wing of the arcade which the architect depicted in a somewhat idealized perspective.[679] Astoundingly, this arcade space recalls not so much the Eastern bazaar as the early Christian basilica.[680] This effect was new in its day and had no successors. It was characterized by the following two factors:

1. The rows of Corinthian engaged columns with a corbeled entablature which united the arches. Since the glass between the columns was dark in perspective, a multinaved building was suggested.
2. The termination of the space by a stylized structure suggesting an open roof frame.

The lighting, however, was in fact completely reversed. The space was illuminated not by the clerestory but by the glazed areas between the wooden triangles of the roof structure. The windows of the top story were divided into three sections, the middle of which illuminated the living area behind it, while the other two were painted. The upper sections had latticework. They were located outside the roof and provided constant ventilation for the arcade space.

After leaving the main wing one entered the second independent spatial element of the arcade: the large rotunda, with its glass canopy. The space measured 17 meters in diameter and possessed the same continuous facade as the rest of the space. This rotunda functioned as the pivotal point in the bend of the arcade. It provided the arcade with a center which enticed the visitor to linger. The "Cocotier Lumineux" (the luminous palm), a bronze candelabrum with a wreath of globe lamps, occupied the midpoint.

The rotunda was covered by a low conical roof whose peak was raised to ventilate the space below. This iron structure was executed by the Douai cast-iron company. It was assembled on the following system:[681] the lantern rested on a thrust collar, which was borne by the main ribs, whose weight was borne by the wall ring and also by the outside wall buttresses. Between the main ribs, two thinner intermediate ribs held the glass plates. All the ribs were braced by concentric rings. The bottom area was not glazed but was strengthened by diagonally crossed braces. On the interior this bottom area was covered by a canvas-like panel and was decorated with laurel wreaths and curved fretwork to provide the illusion of an arch. The main ribs were decorated to look like tent poles. This tent motif was modeled after the decorative designs of Percier and Fontaine. It can be considered a recollection of the Napoleonic campaigns or an attempt to translate the classical canvas-roof structures for public buildings into a new material. A narrow passageway led from the rotunda to the Rue Vivienne.

Finally, the arcade interior was colorfully painted. Thiollet[682] describes the facades as follows: "The colors of the decoration are: red marble for the pedestals, yellow marble for the columns, veined grey marble for the frieze and background; the mouldings and cornices are white, the woodwork bronze; the medallions stand out in white against the purple background." If we consider the interior organization of the arcade buildings, we quickly discover another invention of the architect Billaud: while each shop had its own means of access to the upper stories, each pair of shops shared a staircase as well. The staircase took the form of two counterrotating stairways. This design is the most efficient use of space imaginable for the provision of access.[683]

Galerie Véro-Dodat (figs. 407–412)
Rue J. J. Rousseau 19—Rue du Bouloi 2
Formerly one of the most elegant arcades, the Galerie Véro-Dodat is still standing, although it has no public. It belongs to the group of arcades which arose in the neighborhood of the Palais Royal, taking from that model the name "Galerie"—a somewhat formal word for arcade. They are all architecturally more independent and elaborate than other arcades from the Restoration period.

The double name refers to the builders and owners of the arcade, the pork butchers Véro and Dodat, speculators and nouveaux riches who thus created a monument to themselves.[684] The Charcuterie Véro-Dodat existed throughout the century. It was located at 2, Rue du Faubourg St. Denis. It later changed its name to St. Antoine. The two gentlemen had pur-

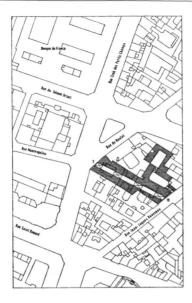

407
Paris, site of the
Galerie Véro-Dodat,
1955

408
Advertisement for
the *Charivari*

409
Paris, Galerie Véro-
Dodat, entrance, Rue
du Bouloi

chased the site of the former Hôtel de Poisson de Boervalais. In 1826 they had the arcade built with two bordering residential blocks accessible by their own gates. The arcade had at that time a superb function as a traffic avenue—one which can no longer be recognized from the present street network. The 1833 plan by Vasserot and Bélanger shows that the arcade created a direct connection to the Palais Royal from the Quartier des Halles. The entranceway to the Messageries Générales on the Rue de Grenelle St. Honoré was located opposite its east exit. One could proceed up this street, turn into the Rue Mercier, and thereby reach the Halle au Blé.

Today this connection has been replaced by the broad Rue du Colonel Driant, which runs from the Rue de Valois to the Halle au Blé. Entering the arcade today, one walks alone across the black and white checkered marble floor, gazes into the practically blind mirrors between the engaged columns, hears the echoes of one's footsteps—it is a ghostly emptiness under glass. A few businesses are still open: an antique shop, a hair salon, a real estate agency, a linen shop, two restaurants, and a printing shop. At the exit to the Rue du Bouloi one finds the once famous Café de l'Epoque—today one of the countless bistros where employees of the neighboring offices come for coffee breaks. The building on the corner once housed the shop of the publisher Aubert, who issued *Le Charivari*.

The arcade is approximately 80 meters long. The interior is 4.5 meters wide and two-storied. The entrance buildings, like the two lateral buildings which divide the glass roof into three equal parts, have five stories. The arcade space is rigorously subdivided by the following elements, which create an illusion of depth:

1. The uninterrupted diagonal pattern of the black and white marble paving stones in the arcade floor
2. The continuous shop fronts with their black and red wooden casements, their brass detailing, and their now vanished gas lamps
3. The low, brightly painted second story with small apartment windows and terminating palmette frieze which frames the subdivisions of the glass roof

4. The great rhythm of the three equally long sections of glass roof alternating with the dark undersides of the ceiling of the entrance and lateral hallways
5. The portal, which limits the depth of the space. It incorporates the name of the arcade, which hangs in the round arches on a semicircular sign with gilded iron letters.

The facade of the arcade belongs to the type of the Passage des Panoramas. It is not subdivided floor to ceiling vertically, but is layered. The shop facades are extraordinarily elegant and executed in expensive materials. One can read in Thiollet and Roux:[685]

Among the numerous commercial arcades and galleries which have been built in Paris over the past few years, the Passage Véro-Dodat takes first place for richness and uniformity of decoration. Without the aid of colors an artist could give only an imperfect idea of the beautiful effect produced by the double row of identical boutiques, with transparent shop windows united by yellow brass mouldings polished to imitate gold, with glass doors crowned by a beautiful arrangement of palmettes and gilded roundels, with the marble pavement. . . . One cannot overpraise these embellishments, the purity of their profile, the brilliant and picturesque effect produced by the globes providing gas illumination located between the capitals of the two pilasters framing each boutique, with decorative mirrors between them.—During the day the grilles in the base of the architectural order admit light to the kitchens and cellar rooms. —Nothing has been spared to make this arcade magnificent. The pavement consists of marble squares; the sections of the ceiling which do not have glass plates are painted, depicting landscapes and other subjects all around the gilded moulding.

Let us examine the facades of the thirty-eight identical shops in more detail. The main motif is the small panes of the shop windows, rounded off at the top,[686] which appear in pairs framed by brass mouldings in the form of slender columns. There are three of these pairs of windowpanes in each shop bay; a double door is inserted into the middle pair. Thin engaged columns with brass bases and Corinthian capitals stand in front of the door jambs. They rest on the sill and carry the wooden entablature, which masks the lintel. In front of the partition walls are pairs of engaged columns framing a mirror.[687] The white globes of the gas lamps hung down in front of the capitals, and the mirror reflected the light. The bays are emphasized in the sill and entablature by applied

410
Galerie Véro-Dodat,
shops

411
Galerie Véro-Dodat,
restaurant

412
Galerie Véro-Dodat,
arcade space, 1967

cast-iron reliefs which depict a lyre or a genius sitting atop a cornucopia. The entablature frieze is used as advertising space. The name of the shop is centered above the entrance in gilded letters, with the shop number to right and left. This uniform facade arrangement gave the arcade its monumental rigor. Today only fragments remain. Many shops have been converted over the years, windows have been removed, doors relocated, and signs replaced.

Passage de Ponceau (fig. 372)
Boulevard de Sebastopol 119—Rue St. Denis 212

The Passage de Ponceau also was constructed as an extension of an existing arcade, the Passage du Caire.[688] Since 1826 it has connected the Rue St. Denis to the Rue Ponceau (later renamed the Boulevard Sebastopol). It has been shortened over the years and received a new entrance building. The arcade space is only 2.5 meters wide. It is intersected by a lateral building, has three stories, and is the steepest arcade space I have ever seen. The site is fully developed. Fortunately, one can overcome the sensation of being deep in a tunnel in the earth by catching slices of street life through the exits. An eternal twilight falls through the glass roof, which was recently replaced by milky plastic plates. It is hard to believe that people still live and work here.

Passage Choiseul (figs. 413–417)
Rue des Petits Champs 44—Rue Saint Augustin 23

The westernmost arcade, and a larger one, is the Passage Choiseul. It belongs to the group which extends the arcades of the Palais Royal toward the boulevards, and is named after the Rue Choiseul (1779), which it extends to the south. It is still to be found today in the same condition as when it was built, in 1825–1827 by Tavernier[689]—except for the renovated glass roof and lighting system.

The Passage Choiseul embodies better than the other Parisian arcades the street character of the building type: two rows of buildings oppose each other, connected only by a visibly set-back glass roof. The 190-meter-long cavern also exemplifies the illusionary element of the arcade.

In 1825 the interior of the large block formed by the Rue St. Augustin, Rue des Petits Champs, Rue Ste. Anne, and Rue Gaillon was opened up.[690] Formerly, as can be seen on the Plan Turgot, it was developed only on the edges. Parts of it were expropriated after the revolution. The architect Huvé constructed the Théâtre Royal de l'Opéra Comique as a freestanding building in the center.[691] The site of the opera house was linked along the central axis to the street network by the Rue Monsigny and Rue Méhul. The rear wall of the Passage Choiseul functioned as the eastern border of the square. The arcade crossed the block as a parallel structure. To make way for the arcade, the Hôtel de Gèvres, built in 1655 by Le Pautre, was removed. But parts of this palace were included in the arcade; for example, the gate to the court became its north entrance. The remaining section of the construction site belonged to the Hôtel de Lyonne, built by Le Vau for the Count de Lyon, the foreign minister of Louis XIV. (The count never resided there, however.) The building changed hands, and in 1756 it was used as the main office of the financial administration. After this office was moved to the Rue de Rivoli, the banker Mallet purchased the building and had it torn down so that he could realize higher profits from this increasingly valuable real estate.

Mangot built the small Galerie de l'Opéra Comique; Tavernier built the Passage Choiseul and the Théâtre de Monsieur Comte on the Rue Monsigny with an exit to the arcade; Huvé built the theater with its beautiful facade and the boutiques bordering the square on the west. There arose (as we would say today) a small cultural center.

In the collections of the Bibliothèque Nationale one can find an undated page from a newspaper with the heading: "Terrains et Maisons à vendre et à louer, s'adresser à M. Guichard, au Passage Choiseul No. 28" (Property and buildings for sale and for rent; contact Monsieur Guichard at Passage Choiseul No. 28).[692] It shows the site with a projected version of the development and reveals something of the way in which such objects of speculation were offered for sale or for rent in advertisements and prospectuses. The architect builds with the money of a speculator, no longer identified with the building, for an anonymous tenant or buyer. We see the Passage Choiseul in the paper as a complete ground plan. The individual buildings are numbered (ninety-two in all). Two

511

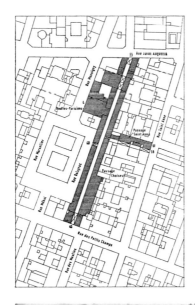

413*a*
Paris, site of the Passage Choiseul, 1966

413*b*
Paris, Passage
Choiseul,
1825–1827, plan,
from an announcement, lithograph

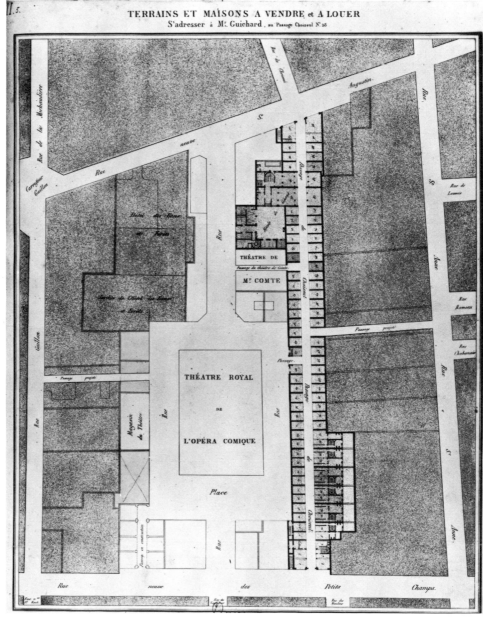

PARIS

414
Passage Choiseul

415
Passage Choiseul, arcade space, view toward the Rue St. Augustin

416
Passage Choiseul, ar-
cade space, view to-
ward the Rue St.
Augustin, 1967

417
Passage Choiseul,
view of the roof

other arcades are included as projects. They are intended to cross the block, making the interior accessible to the Rue Gaillon and the Rue Ste. Anne. The east arcade was actually built a few years later. It is the Passage Ste. Anne, constructed in 1829, which opens into the Passage Choiseul. It still stands but is totally derelict. The small Théâtre de Monsieur Comte was a children's theater. Comte, a magician and ventriloquist, directed it until 1855 and then sold it to Jacques Offenbach, who made it his winter headquarters, calling it the "Bouffes Parisiennes."

Siegfried Kracauer writes of it in his *Pariser Leben*:[693]

Like the wooden booth on the Champs-Elysées, so too the Théâtre des Jeunes Eleves was a site of high diversionary art—at least before it was transferred to Offenbach, who converted it into the winter residence of his Bouffes. The theater—which still exists—was located in the heart of the city, next to the Italian opera. Comte, its owner, performed magic shows here which he commonly introduced with the promise that he would make all the ladies disappear at the end. At the end, then, he reminded his esteemed audience of the promise and conjured up a magnificent bouquet of roses. "Are not all the ladies united in this bouquet?" he then asked. . . . Offenbach quickly had the neglected theater renovated, without regard to the cost. The little theater was hardly larger than his summer residence. . . .

The foyer—it was a modest indentation in the promenade which contained four worn benches, a piano and a stopped clock. The possibility for movement was all the less since the female ushers for the loges wore hoop skirts. Fortunately, though, the Passage Choiseul bordered directly on the theater and could serve as a promenade during the intermissions. It housed an overabundance of fruit dealers from whom the public loved to purchase its oranges. Their aroma was so strong in the auditorium that all other perfumes were superfluous. It was the purest orange grove. Soon the theater became a sight-seeing attraction which no foreigner of importance would pass by.

In the 1860s the operetta dominated the theater program; Offenbach was triumphant. He understood how to tap the sense of life of the time. Here, in the small theater, "Orpheus in the Underworld" was premiered; Hortense Schneider was the great star.

As for shops, there are ninety-three, whose tenants and owners have changed, whose displays have followed the fashions of the time. Their stories are countless. To choose one shop, number 33 was originally a store for religious writings, called Percepied. It was bought by an employee, A. Lemerre; he and his wife, a fashion designer from the shop across the way, transformed it into a small publishing house which became famous by publishing the Parnassian poets. Proudhomme, Coppée, Barbey d'Aurevilly, Leconte de Lisle, Heredia, and Theuriet all wandered in and out of the shop; Verlaine published his first poems here in 1864.[694]

The photograph reproduced in fig. 415 shows what a motley array filled the arcade: awnings behind which the sun never penetrated; oversized, symbolic shop signs in the form of pipes and gloves; bizarre placards at overlapping levels; and display cases which narrowed the arcade space. All contributed to the wild animation of the arcade—an animation created by the struggle for attention. One can appreciate here how these arcades inspired the surrealists. In the photograph of the Passage Choiseul a gigantic pipe hovers in the interior; high above the arcade is a loggia where no one is ever observed to enter, and above, a strange black clock; a model of a human hand hanging, as if broken off, on a thread; a jumble of poles, pots, odd containers, boxes, glasses, and mirrors.

In his novel *Death on the Installment Plan*, Céline used the Passage Choiseul as the abode of his main character.[695] He uncovered the macabre, the horrifying side of the arcade. He saw it as a human collective, a unique sociological formation in which spatial proximity makes the human inhabitants not only dependent on each other but also permanently at each other's mercy. The natural distance and the anonymity of the street is reduced to inescapable opposition, to undesired control, to necessary eavesdropping. It becomes a form of collective behavior which is disturbed only by the shopper, the passerby. The struggle for the customer converts mere competition into a merciless battle. A scene from the novel makes this point all too clear (see also Text 1).

I have to admit that the Passage was an unbelievable pesthole. It was made to kill you off, slowly but surely, what with the little mongrels' urine, the shit, the sputum, the leaky gas pipes. The stink was worse than the inside of a prison. Down under the glass roof the sun is so dim you can eclipse it with a candle. Everybody began to gasp for breath. The Passage took cognizance of its asphyxiating stench. . . . We talked of nothing but the country, hills and valleys, the wonders of nature. . . .

The Passage Choiseul is still intact, the only one in Paris, perhaps, of which that can be said. It still has its clientele, even if it is only the countless people who work in the surrounding offices. They find in this bazaar everything they need, which they can buy in off moments to take home. A new shop in art nouveau style selling fashionable dress patterns even seems to indicate a possible renaissance.[696]

The Passage Choiseul stands on a 15-by-190-meter site on which one could always build garages today. The continuous contour is broken once by the old Hôtel de Gèvres, which interrupts the arcade space where the hotel's gate became the northern entrance of the arcade. The basic pattern is uniform throughout: a double row of four-storied buildings with cellar, shop, mezzanine, *bel étage,* and mansard. Each building is independently accessible by a winding staircase. The facades unite these buildings into a row by means of arcades (which include the mezzanine), wall and windows, two narrow moulding strips, and a glass roof. The glass roof was originally self-supporting with small panes and triangular braces to strengthen the ribbing. It has been renovated, however, to make it structurally more stable: the latticed ridgepole is borne by lattice girders with arched undersupports, placed every two bays. The glass skin is set back from the cornice to allow constant ventilation.

Text 1: Louis Ferdinand Céline. Le Mort au crédit (Death on the Installment Plan)
Mademoiselle Méhon had the shop straight across from us. You can't imagine what a dog she was. She was always trying to pick a fight with us, she never stopped plotting, she was jealous. And yet she was doing all right with her corsets. She was an old woman and she still had her faithful clientele, handed down from mother to daughter for the last forty years. Women that wouldn't have let just anybody feel their bosoms.

Things came to a head over Tom, who'd got into the habit of pissing against the shopwindows. Still, he wasn't the only one. Every mutt in the neighborhood did worse. The Passage was their promenade.

The Méhon woman crossed the street for no other purpose than to provoke my mother, to make a scene. It was scandalous, she bellowed, the way our mangy cur befouled her window. . . . Her words resounded on both sides of the shop and up to the glass roof. The passersby took sides. It was a bitter brawl. Grandma, ordinarily so careful about her language, gave her a good tongue-lashing.

When Papa came home from the office and heard about it, he flew into such a temper you couldn't bear to look at him. He rolled his eyes so wildly in the direction of the old bag's shop window we were afraid he was going to strangle her. We did our best to stop him, we clung to his overcoat. . . . He had developed the strength of a legionnaire. He dragged us into the shop. . . . He bellowed loud enough to be heard on the fourth floor that he was going to make hash out of that damn corsetmaker. . . . "I shouldn't have told you about it," my mother wailed. The harm was done.

Passage Saucède
Rue St. Denis—Rue Bourg l'Abbé
This second arcade built by F. Mazois[697] was originally called the Passage de la Croix Blanche. It was built in 1825 and torn down in 1852 to make room for the Boulevard Sebastopol.

Passage du Saumon (figs. 418–420)
Rue Montmartre 80—Rue Mandar 8—Rue Montorgueil 67
"The Passage du Saumon (Arcade of the Salmon) near the fish market is not unlike a monstrous finned beast which flounders in the mire. The two streets, Montmartre and Montorgueil, the one holding its head, the other the tail, are full of filth and mud, thereby justifying the bold comparison."[698] Kolloff chose this metaphor in 1849 for an arcade which now no longer exists. It was demolished in 1899 and replaced by the Rue du Saumon, a private street which was renamed in 1900 the Rue Bachaumont. The original name was derived from that of a nearby inn, the Auberge des Deux Saumons, close by on the Rue Montorgueil, where the wagons unloaded their fish.

The reasons for its early demolition can be found in the arcade's poorly chosen location. Cluysenaar,[699] the architect of the Galeries St. Hubert in Brussels, studied the Parisian arcades and wrote in the 1830s:

Let us take at random one of these arcades, the one called "du Saumon," which runs from the Rue Montmartre to the Rue Montorgueil; this narrow arcade was deprived for a long time of an opening directly to the Rue Montmartre because of

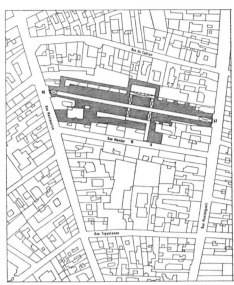

418
Paris, site of the Passage du Saumon, 1833

419
Paris, Passage du Saumon, 1827–1830, demolished 1899, entrance, Rue Montmartre, shortly before demolition

420
Passage du Saumon,
arcade space

disputes with former proprietors. It has had but little success. The reason for this is simple: it offers only one of the advantages which one has the right to demand of an arcade; it provides shelter, but not a short-cut. If they are to choose to walk through the arcade, pedestrians must be in a very restricted area on the Rue Montmartre or the Rue Montorgueil; otherwise they would naturally be led to take one of the two streets parallel to the arcade. To choose the arcade means to make a complete circuit and lengthen one's route.

At the date of the Plan Turgot, there was still, between the converging Rue Montmartre and Rue Montorgueil, and between the present Rue Cadran and Rue Tiquetonne, one of the large blocks with gardens typical of the old city of Paris.[700] By 1760 there was evidently a passageway, an open arcade, through the block. It was widened in 1780 by the Cour Charost. In 1790 the block was divided by the Rue Mandar, named after the architect who constructed and developed it. It was a private street with sidewalks and gates at both ends. In 1825 the architect Hubert Rohault de Fleury[701] began to rebuild the arcade for different owners. Construction was delayed since they disagreed on numerous issues. In 1827 the whole site was acquired by the Société Rohard, and the building was finished toward 1830.

In 1853 the arcade was purchased by the Tunisian General Ben-Aïad, who had come from Tunis to settle in Paris, bringing his fortune with him, and found in the arcade a reminder of the bazaars of his homeland.[702] The general thought the arcade too narrow, however. He therefore intended to purchase the entire block between the Rue Cadran and Rue Mandar to build a massive bazaar on the Eastern model. However, his idea remained a mere plan. In 1899 his heirs had the arcade torn down because it had become completely unprofitable.

A glance at the map shows that the arcade links nothing. Therefore, it could sustain itself solely by its own power of attraction and not from the business of chance passersby. Thanks to the numerous gilded shops, mostly leased by milliners, it survived for a few decades. It competed with the Rue de la Paix and the Chaussée d'Antin as the meeting place of fashionable Paris. The Passage du Saumon even created its own fashion. In 1827 the Jardin des Plantes received a giraffe as a gift from Mohammed Ali. Since the animal had till then been known only through pictures, it attracted many visitors. The fashion designers capitalized on this with a giraffe style, producing combs, hair styles, umbrellas, coats, and clothes "à la giraffe." One fashion designer in the arcade created a giraffe hat which was so successful that half of Paris ran to the arcade to marvel at the gigantic model.

Other establishments also entertained visitors: baths around a small converted garden; the ballroom, the Athenée Centrale, facing the Cour Charost; the Théâtre Molière, which was remodeled in 1838 for the students of Professor Saint Aulaire (among them the thirteen-year-old Elisa Felix, the later Rachel). The theater was later converted into a café, which closed in 1880.

Toward the end of the Second Empire, the importance of the Passage du Saumon seems to have steadily declined. It was, of course, still a rendezvous for lovers, but Pessard reported that besides fashion items one could also purchase musical instruments, accordions, hunting horns, and weapons. Furthermore, cloth-remnant dealers were doing a good business there—harbingers of the end.

The arcade was an extensive and branching building complex. The main wing, the Galerie du Salon, had the tremendous length of 175 meters. It was crossed approximately in the middle by a second wing, the Galerie Mandar, with an exit to the Rue Mandar, which was extended in the second half of the nineteenth century to the Rue Cadran and still exists as the Passage Ben Aïad. A third wing, the Galerie des Bains, formed an inner square with the Galerie Mandar. The square made the whole breadth of the building site accessible and opened in the form of a loggia onto a small garden on the north. The baths and the theater were located in this square. The Passage du Saumon afforded, then, a cut-through as well as an inner circuit.

The arcade space was 4 meters wide and 10 meters high. An elevation published by Thiollet and Roux provides information about the facade.[703] Some photographs taken shortly before the demolition of the arcade are in the topographical collection of the Musée Carnavalet. They show that the arcade was so long that one could hardly discern the opposite end. The arcade space was three-storied. An order of pilasters divided the arcade longitudinally. Brick arches rested on the pilasters, architectonically uniting the two sides of the arcade space as in the Galerie Vivienne.[704]

The glass roof spanned the space between these arches. The areas between the pilasters were each occupied by one shop and were broken up by windows on all three stories. Each zone had different fenestration. The highest cornice was carried on an arcade. This architecture contains some absurdities and was therefore criticized by Thiollet and Roux: "The Passage du Saumon presents a more original than tasteful decor. The mixture of the large and the small, of the noble and the shabby, the attic, whose decoration seems completely foreign to the taste of the rest—all these aspects give the structure a disconnected look. One has the feeling that two minds presided over its creation."

The photograph of the interior shows that the small-paned windows were replaced by large, continuous panes. One can also see in it the domineering pistol, the sign of the weapons dealer, which seems to be aimed at an imaginary person in the opposite building. Weapons dealers love the secrecy of arcades. A whole forest of signs grows in the arcade space, forcing itself out almost as far as the street facade, striving to call attention to something which lies back in the deeper recesses. Over the bar to the left of the entrance a notice is glued above the window: "Lease terminated, liquidation," and under the large board with the name of the arcade one can read the sign: "Large shops, boutiques and apartments to rent, immediate occupancy. . . ."

Passage Vendôme (figs. 421–422)
Place de la République 3—Rue Béranger 16–18
There is only one arcade, the Passage Vendôme, in the third arrondissement. It is located between the Boulevard du Temple and the Rue Vendôme, today the Rue Beranger.[705] It was built circa 1827 on parts of the site which had been occupied before the revolution by the convent of the Filles du St. Sauveur. The new owner was General Dariule. The arcade is approximately 60 meters long, 4 meters wide, is three-storied, and is divided in half by a lateral building into two glass-covered arcade spaces. It linked the boulevard to the Marché du Temple by crossing the Rue Dupuis. However, this function could not have been sufficient for its existence.

421
Paris, site of the Passage Vendôme, 1954

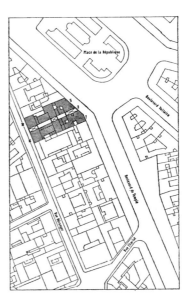

422
Paris, Passage du
Vendôme, 1827,
shortened 1869

Kolloff wrote of it as early as 1849:[706] "The Passage Vendôme on the Boulevard du Temple is, on the other hand, completely neglected. One finds it empty and hears no sound except the constant banging of the for-rent signs."

Under Haussmann the Boulevard du Temple was graded and the broad rectangle of the Place de la République was constructed. The arcade became involved when the end on the boulevard was shortened by four meters, cut off at an angle. In the old photograph in fig. 422,[707] one can see toward the front the first glass roof with pointed arches. I was unable to ascertain whether this roof was part of the original structure or was added with the staircase during the later construction of the Place de la République.

Passage Brady
Rue du Faubourg St. Martin 43—Rue du Faubourg St. Denis 46
The Passage Brady is the most northern of the arcades which open up narrow and deep sites in the blocks between the Rue St. Denis and Rue St. Martin. In 1854 these blocks were cut through by the broad Boulevard Sebastopol, which divided and shortened the Passage Brady and the Passage de l'Industrie. The latter was wider and uncovered, and its western half is the only part standing today.

The Passage Brady, originally 216 meters long, was named after its owner. It was opened on April 15, 1828,[708] extending the Rue d'Enghien to the east. The western section, the only one existing today, has a glass roof, evidently added more recently; the eastern section is an open passageway. The strictly symmetrical arrangement of the arcade buildings and the narrow distance between them (3.5 meters) suggest that the eastern section originally had a glass roof as well. The arcade space is introduced at both ends by a 10-by-10-meter-square space which in both cases is located behind the frontal buildings. Its function has not been ascertained.

Passage du Bourg l'Abbé (fig. 391)
Rue St. Denis 120—Rue de Palestro 3
The Passage du Bourg l'Abbé, built circa 1828, exists today only in abbreviated form.[709] It originally began on the Rue St. Denis opposite the entrance to the Passage du Grand Cerf and flowed into the Rue Bourg l'Abbé, from whence it received its name. It lost its eastern section with the extension of the Boulevard Sebastopol and

the construction of the parallel Rue de Palestro. The new exit was the work of the architect M. Blondel.[710] The arcade today is narrow and gloomy. The low-vaulted glass roof over the second story seems to have been added more recently.

Kolloff wrote of its life and of that of the nearby Passage Saucède (which disappeared with the construction of the Rue de Turbigo):[711] "The arcades Saucède and Bourg l'Abbé, like two firm bridges between the Rue St. Martin and the Rue St. Denis, will presumably collapse under the great weight of the pedestrians who constantly traverse them. Here one finds nothing of high society. The men, women, and children here are all common people. Idleness never strolls on these worn paving stones—instead the hammer strikes, the file grinds, and the anvil resounds with merry song."

Galerie d'Orléans (figs. 423–428)
Palais Royal, Peristyle de Valois—Peristyle de Montpensier
Starting in 1814 Pierre Fontaine[712] began the restoration of the Palais Royal. He worked under the auspices of the Duc d'Orléans, later King Louis Philippe. The building had never been completed and had also suffered some damage during the revolution. At this time were constructed the connecting sections among the theater, the old palace, and Victor Louis's galleries around the Jardin du Palais.

In 1828 the work had progressed far enough so that the old temporary wooden structures from before the revolution could be torn down, thereby making room for a new, elegant, and spacious structure, the Galerie d'Orléans, which opened up to two large peristyles.[713] In 1828 the Peristyle de Valois was finished, the Galeries de Bois torn down, and the Galerie d'Orléans begun. In 1829 the arcade was completed and attached to the system of palatial galleries by the Peristyle de Montpensier. This system varied from the original concept of Victor Louis, who had intended to build a tall lateral building on colonnades. The planners did not want to put the garden in shadow, however, and they wished to maintain the visual relationship between the garden and the old palace. Thus the roof of the arcade was designed as a continuous glass terrace, a garden on a higher level, accessible only to the Duke.

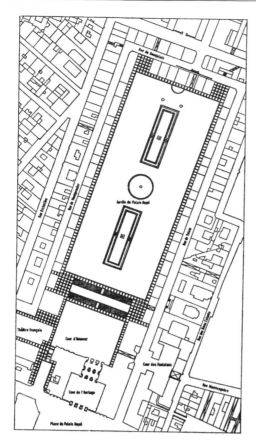

423
Paris, site of the
Galerie d'Orléans,
1833

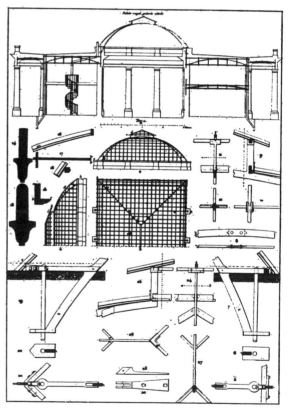

424
Galerie d'Orléans,
roof construction,
structural details

425
Paris, Galerie d'Or-
léans, 1828–
1830, demolished
1935, cross section

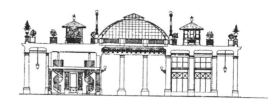

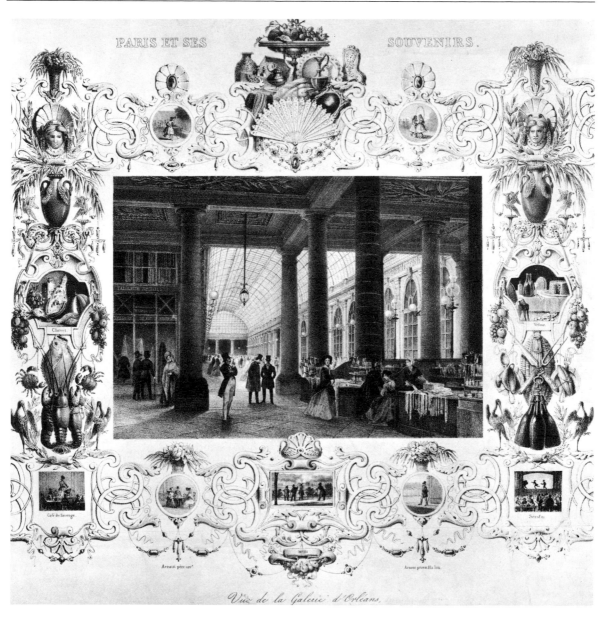

426
Galerie d'Orléans,
arcade space and
details

PARIS

427
Galerie d'Orléans,
under construction,
lithograph by David

428
Galerie d'Orléans,
arcade space

In 1830 the Palais Royal at last took on its final form: a complex conglomeration of buildings in which sections from different eras were incorporated into an asymmetrical yet uniform whole.

The Galerie d'Orléans was the large covered public space of the Palais Royal, measuring 65 by 8.5 meters. It was covered by a glass roof whose structure recalled the arbors of the great French palace gardens. Its dimensions far surpassed those of other existing Parisian arcades. Börne[714] described the Galerie enthusiastically in his *Pariser Briefer*: "The splendor and magnificence of the new Galerie d'Orléans in the Palais Royal cannot be described in words. I saw it yesterday evening for the first time with gas illumination like sunlight, and I was astonished as one rarely is. The glass alleys which we have seen in the past years, as much as they impressed us, are gloomy cellars or poor attic rooms compared to this. It is a large enchanted chamber, completely worthy of this enchanting people. . . ."

The ugly temporary structure was replaced, the space celebrated; yet the life began to disappear from this architecture with its aura of imperial coolness. The following facts were responsible:
Increasing competition of the more spacious boulevards
Prohibition of prostitutes in the Palais Royal by the police order of 1830
Closing of the gambling rooms in 1836
Absence of apartments (the arcade contained only shops) and hence the absence of a life of its own.

People regretted the glass sterility, the lost intimacy, and longed for the old wooden galleries.[715] By the end of the nineteenth century the Galerie d'Orléans was so neglected that the Musée Colonial was installed in it to use the space. The Galerie was torn down in 1935. Only the outer colonnades remained; the newly created open space was paved and the monotony relieved by fountains.

The Galerie d'Orléans is special among arcades because it is freestanding and placed to the side and, like an eighteenth-century palace gallery, connects two sections of a building.[716] Yet its significance for the development of the arcade building type is extraordinary. Pizzala, Cluysenaar, Mengoni, perhaps even Averdieck were all in Paris. One can tell from their arcades in Milan, Brussels, and Hamburg that they studied the Galerie d'Orléans in detail. The structure and contour of the glass vault, the interior facades based on Roman models, and the spatial expanse were all copied and developed further. Countless etchings, Fontaine's own publication on the history of the Palais Royal,[717] and Thiollet's detailed drawings of its architecture and of the structural details of the glass roof reproduced in his *Serrurerie et Font de Fer*— all made the building renowned throughout Europe.[718] A large model of the Galerie d'Orléans without the glass roof can be found in the Musée Carnavalet in Paris. It was a gift of Napoleon III to the English queen.

In contrast to the double Galeries de Bois, the Galerie d'Orléans had three spaces: two outer colonnades, which were attached to the colonnade of the Jardin and the Cour, thereby finally enabling a continuous circuit, and the wide central space, which opened into the peristyles and provided access to the bordering streets. The two rows of shops were accessible from both sides. Fourteen were one bay and ten were two bays wide, and there was a café which occupied six bays. Each shop had a mezzanine and a cellar which could be reached by narrow service corridors underneath the colonnades.[719] The three stories were linked by a cast-iron circular staircase around a flue which served as the chimney for the oven in the cellar. The flue was extended to the balustrade in the roof and drawn outside through the candelabras. In the café the heating pipes gave off additional heat through a freestanding burner.

The entire arcade, the interior and exterior, was illuminated by gaslight from wall brackets in front of mirror pilasters, which gave the space its fabulous brilliance. The interior facades had a monumental order of pilasters, extending full height, alternating with arches and bearing a Doric entablature terminating in a balustrade, behind which the glass vault began. The pilasters were sheathed in marble with mirror insets and the mouldings were gilded. The window and door frames were of brass, the rails and lamp brackets of cast iron, and the floor was marble. The wide span of the ceilings was reinforced by wedged lattice trusses of flat iron, like walls and columns of natural stone.[720] The prototypes for these interior facades can be found in Rome, a city which Fontaine had visited.

The design of the Galerie d'Orléans had an astounding resemblance to that of the Hippodrome,[721] which had the same order of columns and the continuous garden terraces which could be entered from the palace; it lacked only the glass roof. However, it is doubtful that Fontaine could have known the present state of the imperial palace since this section of the Domus Augustiana was not completely excavated until the end of the nineteenth century. The Theater of Marcellus, the Colosseum, the Basilica Julia, and even more literally the later (1455) Palazzo Venezia all have the same arrangement as the Galerie d'Orléans.

The glass vault covering the arcade space was the first of its kind and predated all known vaulted conservatories. It was hipped and described a segment of a circle. It was divided down the middle and employed a raised glass dome for ventilation. The glass skin was held by arches of flat iron, anchored to the pedestals of the balustrades. They described a smaller circle and held the glass vault slightly apart at two points, where poles were attached running lengthwise to hold the dome. Where the dome began the arches were braced lengthwise along the arcade. The ribs had a cast-iron groove to hold the inserted glass plates. The roof structure terminated diagonally at the ends. This was in essence the glass-roof construction used later in Brussels, The Hague, and Hamburg.

Passage Prado

Boulevard St. Denis 18—Rue Faubourg St. Denis

This corner arcade, with a rotunda at the bend, was originally named the Passage Bois de Boulogne.[722] The date of construction is 1830. The building probably did not have a roof. Today it has one story with a modern glass roof. It is now occupied by many small textile shops whose saleswomen call out to the passersby. The music piped into the hall through loudspeakers creates a unique atmosphere— perhaps it was not the women calling after all?

Galerie de Cherbourg

Rue de la Pépinière 8—Rue de Laborde 1
The Galerie de Cherbourg was a narrow, 60-meter-long arcade between the Rue de Laborde and the Rue de la Pépinière in the Quartier de l'Europe.[723] Constructed in 1839, it was the first in a series of arcades built under King Louis Philippe after a ten-year period without any major construction. It was originally called the Passage du Soleil d'Or (Arcade of the Golden Sun) after an old shop sign. It was one of the stations for the trains which departed from the nearby Gare de l'Ouest. Today the arcade has disappeared, replaced by the Rue Joseph Sansboeuf.

Passage du Havre

Rue Caumartin 69—Rue Saint Lazare 107
"Visit the Passage du Havre"—so reads the sign above the glass-covered archway leading into the commercial bustle of the arcade. It is located opposite the Gare St. Lazare, originally named the Gare du Havre. The arcade has one bend and connects the Rue Lazare to the Rue Caumartin. At the bend is a rotunda, covered with a new glass dome. Numerous property owners consolidated to build the arcade in 1845–1846. The opening of the arcade was authorized by an Ordonnance de Police on September 7, 1848.[724] It has a total length of 115 meters and the arcade space is two-storied throughout.

Passage Jouffroy (figs. 429–432)

Boulevard Montmartre 10—Rue Grange Batelière
The Passage Jouffroy extends the Passage des Panoramas to the north over the Boulevard Montmartre. A further continuation is formed by the Passage Verdeau. This succession of three interrelated arcades with a combined length of 350 meters runs parallel to the heavily frequented Rue Montmartre. It forms the beginning of an independent system of public spaces which are accessible only to pedestrians. In this respect it resembles the galleries of the Palais Royal with their bordering arcades.

The arcade aspires to a total system which completes, crosses, and overlaps the arrangement of the streets. If one imagines the arcades raised above street level and connected by bridges, thereby separating the pedestrians from the traffic and delivery vehicles on the ground, one arrives at the most recent architectural projects. In this way architects hope to give the city new life without breaking up its open spaces.

The Passage Jouffroy is the last of the Parisian arcades with architectural pretensions. It was built in 1845–1846 by the Société Jouffroy on a completely irregular site between the Boulevard Montmartre and the

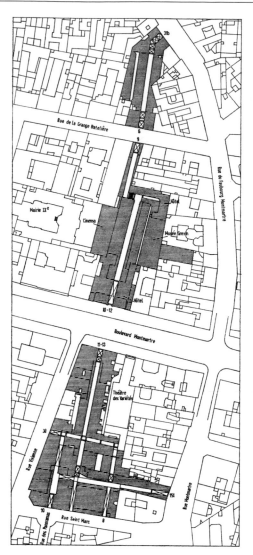

429
Paris, sites of the Pas-
sage des Panoramas,
Passage Jouffroy, and
Passage Verdeau,
1950

430
Paris, Passage Jouf-
froy, 1845–1847, ar-
cade space

Rue de la Grange Batelière.[725] The very small frontage on the Rue de la Grange Batelière necessitated a displacement of the arcade axis and a resulting reduction in the cross section of the shorter arm. The height differential was accommodated by stairs. The arcade was opened to the public by the ordinance of February 17, 1847. Hautecoeur names Hyppolyte Destailleur and his son-in-law Romain de Bourge as the architects.[726]

The frontal building of the arcade on the boulevard is the Hôtel Ronceray, which is set back a few meters from the street. Its side wings enclose a large terrace on the third floor. The social rooms of the hotel, the shops, and the entrance to the arcade lie beneath this terrace. The hotel, origi-nally called the Grand Hôtel de la Terrasse Jouffroy, can be reached from the arcade through two entrances in the side wings. The Bazar Européen was originally located on the western edge of the site; it housed the Théâtre Seraphim, formerly at the Palais Royal, in its cellar after 1858. There one could see phantasmagorias and mario-nette plays. In 1893 the bazaar was con-verted into a café-concert hall, the Petit Casino, the last of its kind in Paris. Today the space houses a cinema.

Wachenhusen[727] described a special attrac-tion of the arcade which I have found in no other arcade: "My favorite sojourn is the Passage Jouffroy, one of the largest ar-cades. The European Bazaar has an under-ground heating system. Therefore one can always find a crowd of people gathered around those spots where the floor is inset with iron rosettes, like grids. The crowds block the arcade but cannot be moved from the spot, because they are warming frozen limbs in the heat." And so, along with protection from the weather, artificial illumination, and a wide selection of mer-chandise, we find here a heating system for the arcade space. It was certainly the first publicly accessible heated space in Paris, existing long before the ventilation grills of the Métro attracted their own public.

On January 10, 1882, the artist Alfred Grévin opened his Musée Grévin on the property branching off from the arcade to the east. It was the great Parisian panop-ticon, the mecca of children, foreigners, and provincials and the counterpart to Madame Tussaud's wax museum in Lon-don.[728] It could be entered through the re-constructed east hotel entrance or through

431
Passage Jouffroy,
view of the roof
(Musée Grévin on
the left)

432
Paris, Passage Jouf-
froy, view into the
arcade from the
Hôtel des Familles

the arcade, on which it had display windows. The Musée Grévin is a multileveled labyrinthine aggregate of rooms in which the past is realistically and devilishly depicted in wax, as figures, as scenes, as frozen motion. The precision of the detail and the original accessories create a perfect illusion. Marat, for example, is portrayed in wax lying in the very same bathtub in which he was assassinated. This celebrated "art" of illusion astounded viewers. Now the daily public still streams through this remnant of the nineteenth century but is rarely deeply moved. In the long Hall of Columns one finds crucial scenes from French history and the revolution, and moments in the life of Jesus; upstairs is the enchanting theater with the magic tricks performed by an old man and his assistant. The high point is the Palais des Miracles, a round room which transports the visitor by mirrors, illumination, and changing sets into a Brahman temple, an enchanted forest, and a festival in the Alhambra. On the front side of the main wing one can enter the glass foyer of the Hôtel des Familles. It is squeezed into a corner of the arcade and its rooms are all located in the space above the arcade roof. The custodian lives in the mansard. The roof panorama reproduced in fig. 431 was photographed from his living room.

The Passage Jouffroy is the first arcade that owes its aesthetic impact entirely to the use of iron. The arcade space is made of glass, iron, and stone slabs; wood appears only in frames, bars, and mouldings.

The facades are reduced to flat sections, skeletons pieced together of supports, ceiling panels, sills, and glass. There is little ornamentation. The arcade space has two stories; the mezzanine has disappeared. On the ground floor is the following sequence: supports, display windows, doors with a ventilation flap, shop windows, supports. The upper story has five glass panels extending the entire vertical length. The one in the middle can be opened and therefore has a latticework railing. The strip of paneling above the ground floor is employed for advertising; over the second story it takes the form of a faintly projecting moulding. The edge of the roof lies flush with the supports, and on it rest the self-supporting pointed arches of the rib structure. The middle section of this glass roof is set back and serves for ventilation. The ribs above the supports are continuous; they brace the structure laterally while the T-bars which hold the ribs and the lantern strengthen it longitudinally. The square glass plates overlap without touching. This type of glass covering can also be found in the Galeries St. Hubert in Brussels, which was built at the same time. Its advantages are that it aids ventilation, prevents condensation, and thereby reduces the dirt that collects at the overlapping edges.

The ceilings and roof frames of the Passage Jouffroy, cast-iron structures, were discussed in the *Wiener allgemeine Bauzeitung* as among the first of their kind.[729] They were assembled according to Vaux's system of perpendicularly crossing flat iron girders by the metalwork and construction firm Leturc, Travers, and Roussel.

Hence in 1845 there existed in Paris an arcade whose architectural effect resulted solely from the requirements of construction, from the functional interrelationship of the parts. The movement toward interior space is recognizable. The arcade's relationship to the light well of later department stores and to their precursors, the bazaars, is also evident. One need merely imagine the walls of the arcade space without glass.

Passage Verdeau (figs. 429, 433)
Rue de la Grange Batelière 6—Rue du Faubourg Montmartre 31
The Passage Verdeau is the northern extension of the Passage Jouffroy, providing a necessary addition by connecting it to the lively Rue du Faubourg Montmartre. It was built in 1846 by the Société Jouffroy and the same architects who constructed the Passage Jouffroy.[730] It received its name from another presiding member of the society. The arcade is built into a block of tall rental buildings. The system of construction is the same as that of the Passage Jouffroy, with the exception that the glass roof is not hipped and has no lantern. The chance passerby will find the following businesses in the arcade: safes and vaults, sporting weapons, umbrellas, artificial flowers, funerary merchandise, cheap jewelry, plaster skulls, and copies of famous artworks. He can then recover from his impressions in a small bar at the entrance.

Galerie de la Madeleine (fig. 434)
Place de la Madeleine 9—Rue Boissy d'Anglas 30
The Galerie de la Madeleine is 53 meters long and 4 meters wide. It was built in 1845 as a subordinate part of a rental

433
Paris, Passage Ver-
deau, 1846, original
glass roof

434
Paris, site of the
Galerie de la
Madeleine, 1954

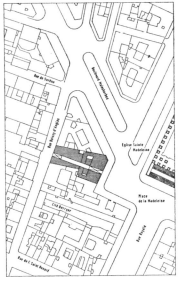

block on the Place de la Madeleine. The builders were probably once again the Société Jouffroy.[731] The arcade begins on the southwest corner of the Place de la Madeleine, ends on the Rue Boissy d'Anglas, and continues in the Cité du Retiro which bends toward the Rue du Faubourg St. Honoré.

The arcade is hardly used today. Worthy of mention, however, is the small-paned glass roof, which is buttressed in a manner similar to the Galerie Vivienne.

Passage de la Sorbonne
Rue de la Sorbonne 18—Rue Champollion 15
The Passage de la Sorbonne, built in 1853 and opened in 1854, was 82 meters long and 3.5 meters wide. It had a glass roof. In 1965 it was torn down and replaced by the Sorbonne laboratories.[732]

Passage des Princes
Boulevard des Italiens 5—Rue Richelieu 17
The Passage des Princes is the last covered arcade built in Paris. It was opened in 1860 under the name of its owner, the banker Mirés, as a part of a larger building complex.[733] It replaced the Hôtel des Princes, which later moved to the Rue Richelieu. It connects the Rue Richelieu to the Boulevard des Italiens, cutting across the sharp corner formed by the two streets. It formerly continued on the other side of the Boulevard in the Passage de l'Opéra. A police ordinance of September 3, 1860, permitted its opening to the public.[734]

Like the Passage du Havre, the Passage des Princes has a bend. The two arcade wings are mediated by a polygonal central space of the same height as the wings. The glass-roof construction of the 5-meter-wide arcade wing is interesting: the influence of the Galerie Vivienne is unmistakable, the only difference being that here the brick arches connecting the facades of the arcade space have been replaced by double cast-iron arched girders. They support the ridgepole, describe a full semicircle, and rest on the cornice above the shop level, thus allowing side as well as overhead lighting.

Among the shops that fill the arcade one cannot miss the ugly self-service restaurant. Across from it, occupying numbers eleven through fifteen of the Passage des Princes, is the pipe factory. Through the show windows one can look into the workshop where an old man with a white cap carves meerschaum pipes. Such great craftsmanship, generally exiled to dark back rooms, is used here as an advertisement for this shop, which has been here since 1855. In the shop next door one can admire and purchase countless varieties of pipes. Hillairet[735] reports that Théodore de Bainville, publisher of the *Revue Fantaisiste*, had his office in the Passage des Princes.

PÉRIGUEUX
Passage Sainte Cécile
Rue André Saigne—Place Bugeaud
This small, modest arcade has a frontal building only on the street.

PHILADELPHIA
Philadelphia Arcade (fig. 435)
Chestnut Street
The Philadelphia Arcade was the first arcade on American soil. It was designed and built by John Haviland, who built the New York Arcade almost at the same time. The Philadelphia, Providence, and Stonington arcades can be classified stylistically under the Greek Revival in America. The latter two, built by other architects, immediately followed Haviland's buildings in the period 1825–1830. They appeared at the same time as the majority of the arcades in Paris, London, Bristol, and Newcastle.

John Haviland[736] came from England. He was born in 1792 in Taunton, studied in 1811 under James Elmes, heard lectures by Soane, and traveled throughout the Continent. He emigrated in 1816—before the completion of the Burlington Arcade in London—settling as an architect in Philadelphia. It was a favorable time for him. Mills and Latrobe had left Philadelphia; Strickland was his only competitor. In 1818 he began publishing his three-volume work, *The Builder's Assistant*, the first architectural textbook in America to reproduce Greek buildings. He became prominent in 1818 after his first successful competition for the Second Bank of the United States, the building which introduced the imitative, archeological phase of the Greek Revival in America. The first commissions followed, among them the Eastern Penitentiary, the first prison on a radial system with arms whose cells were accessible according to the method of the arcade. This concept brought him further commissions for penitentiaries. In the years to follow, Philadelphia became a mecca for

435
Philadelphia, Phila-
delphia Arcade,
1825–1827, demol-
ished 1863, entrance,
Chestnut Street

foreign study commissions. Three years later, in 1825, he designed the Philadelphia Arcade and built it in 1826–1827, almost simultaneously with his second, the New York Arcade.

Information on this first American arcade is sparse. The etching reproduced in fig. 435 provides at least some indications of its form. The broad facade with its four large round arches recalls the front of the Burlington Arcade except that it is stricter in composition and more sparing in decoration. Was Haviland ever in Paris? He could not have seen the Burlington Arcade himself as it was not built until after his departure. Baigell refers to the model of the Adelphi Terraces.[737] There the motif of the round-arched colonnade at ground level served as a facade for commercial space.

One motif was completely new in the development of the arcade building type: both arcade spaces were set back once to make each shop on the upper story directly accessible by galleries. This innovation had a great influence on American architecture and became a characteristic feature of the later Victorian arcades in England and Australia. The phenomenon of the double arcade space, however, had already appeared in Paris in the Galeries de Bois and the Passage de l'Opéra. The most essential difference from the earlier European arcades was the strictly commercial function of the arcade as a shop, office, or display space. It lacked any real function as an avenue for traffic. There was no need to include apartments in the arcade since, in contrast to Paris, the city of Philadelphia had plenty of undeveloped land for dwellings.

The broad front of the Philadelphia Arcade comprised, then, three parallel building sections. The one in the middle seems to have ended—as far as one can ascertain from the etching—a few meters in front of the actual facade, thereby providing space for the open staircase and for a gallery which connected the two arcade spaces and continued across the arcaded front. This concept of an introductory stairway was perfected a few years later in Providence, where the facade became a temple front on two sides, the arcade a shopping center transformed into a temple. The Philadelphia Arcade was torn down in 1863.

A brief description of the Philadelphia Arcade appeared in 1832 in *Atkinson's Cas-*

ket.[738] I would like to quote it here since it offers a few additional details:

This beautiful building stands on the north side of Chestnut Street, west of Sixth Street; it is 100 feet front and 150 feet deep, extending to Carpenter Street, and is divided by two avenues 14 feet wide, upon which the stores open. These avenues are paved with flag stones, and are lighted by two sky lights, which contain together upwards of ten thousand lights; the rest of the roof is covered with zinc. On the first floor, which is supported by arches resting upon stone walls, are 34 rooms, 12 on each side and 10 in the centre.—The second storey is supported by arches on brick walls, and contains 36 rooms, 12 on each side, and 12 in the centre. The third storey is supported by arches and is divided into three large rooms and two saloons, all of which are occupied by Peale's museum. The cellars are divided into two spacious rooms, extending the whole length of the building, and have been handsomely fitted up, and are occupied by restauranteurs. Both fronts of the building are of Pennsylvania marble; . . . on Chestnut Street are two niches in which are to be placed two statues in iron bronzed, representing commerce and navigation. Over the niches are two basso relievo ornaments, one the state, and the other the city arms. The pilasters are ornamented with the head of Mercury. The lot upon which the Arcade stands cost 50,000 dollars, and the building itself 112,000 dollars. It is owned by an incorporated company, and the stock is divided into 1500 shares of 108 dollars each. Philadelphia is indebted to the enterprise of Peter A. Browne for this ornament, which was erected in 1826–27. John Haviland was the architect.

PONTYPRIDD
Arcade
St. Catherine Street—Market Square
This arcade was built in 1888 by the architects Taylor and Evans of Cardiff. It is straight, 73 meters long, and 3.7 meters wide. It contained twenty-eight shops. Its glass roof was "constructed with patent zinc glazing bars, supported by cast-iron principals."[739]

PRAGUE
A well-traveled person will immediately mention Prague as the city where, as in no other, arcades are still a vital ingredient of public life. None of Prague's numerous arcades, however, were built in the nineteenth century.[740] They are located in the new section of Prague—sloping Wenceslas Square and the river, which form the city's main commercial district. They make the

deeper portions of the blocks accessible, extend through courtyards and passageways, and provide access to newly built cinemas, theaters, hidden restaurants, and bars. They consist of an irregular conglomeration of partially glassed-in, partially open spatial elements of varying heights and architectural forms.

These arcades belong to the earlier tradition of walk-through houses in the old city, comparable to those in Leipzig and Vienna. One can proceed from one alley to the next through public inner courtyards whose upper stories are accessible by continuous galleries. The ground floors functioned as storage areas and temporary salesrooms. They created an entire market independent of the streets and were interconnected by the countless porticoes. In the original undisturbed, privately owned sections of Prague one can study today side by side the old and new systems which make the interior of the blocks accessible. One can walk through the maze of arcades which are extremely popular and heavily frequented. They exemplify the method of making pre-existing building units systematically accessible by arcades—a system which since World War II is being tried again in Munich and Brussels.

Koruna Arcade
Wenceslas Square 846–48—Na Prikope (On the Moat)
The Koruna Arcade, known to all visitors to Prague because of the automat on the ground floor, is a part of the commercial building on the corner of the Moat and Wenceslas Square. It has a bend with an octagonal central space which serves as a light well. Both wings of the arcade are irregular, have differing widths, and are sparsely illuminated by overhead lights. The architecture of the central space recalls the Friedrichstrasse Arcade in Berlin and the Mädlerpassage in Leipzig. It is covered by a concrete-rib dome with insets of yellow glass blocks. The dome is crowned by a lantern which provides ventilation. The architect was A. Pfeiffer; the arcade was built in 1910–1913.

Lucerna Arcade
Wenceslas Square 794—Vodicka Street 704—Stepanska Street 704
This completely irregular arcade with three wings provides access to the Lucerna cinema. It was built in 1912 by V. Havel. The wing to Wenceslas Square is in Secessionist style.

Alfa Arcade
Wenceslas Square 785—Cloister Garden —Vodicka Street 791
Also called the Styblo Arcade, this arcade was built in 1926–1928 by the architects L. Kysela and J. Jarolim. Only the section closest to Wenceslas Square has a glass roof.

U Nováku Arcade
Vodicka Street 699
This structure, built in 1928 by Osvald Polivka, forms a system of crossing arcades. Only the courtyard-like extensions have occasional skylights. The arcade is connected to the Lucerna Arcade.

Cerná ruže Arcade
Na Prikope 853—Lord Street
This broad arcade was built in 1932 by Oldrich Tyl. It has three stories, two continuous galleries, and a low-vaulted concrete and glass roof.[741]

Zivnobanka Arcade
Na Prikope 860—Havilcek Square
This arcade was built in 1938 by Fr. Roith.

Sevastopol Arcade
Na Prikope 988—Celetna Street
Providing access to the Sevastopol cinema, this wide arcade has rows of showcases down the middle and is illuminated by two concrete and glass skylights. It was built in 1938 by B. Kozak.

PRESTON
Miller Arcade
Fineberg gives 1896 as the date of construction.[742]

PROVIDENCE
Providence Arcade (figs. 436–438)
Weybosset Street—Westminster Street
The Providence Arcade is the only one of four early arcades in the United States which is still standing today. Located in the capital of Rhode Island on the main commercial street, Westminster Street, it crosses to Weybosset Street. However, its role as an artery for traffic is of secondary importance. The architect was Russell Warren (1783–1860), who was assisted by James Bucklin, to whom the facade on Weybosset Street is attributed.

Little is known about Warren. He worked his way up from carpenter-designer to an independent architect. The Providence Arcade, which introduced the Greek Revival to Rhode Island, is his first significant work. He was influenced by the architects Parris and Willard of nearby Boston and

436
Providence, Providence Arcade, 1827–1829, entrance, Weybosset Street

437
Providence Arcade,
entrance, Weybosset
Street

438
Providence Arcade,
arcade space

by Haviland, whose New York Arcade served as the immediate model. The financial backer was Cyrus Butler, who intended to compete with the leading Brown family with this building, constructed for purely commercial use.

The period of construction is generally considered to be 1827–1829, thus immediately following Haviland's arcades. The building was more successful aesthetically than commercially. Providence was proud of the structure. Contemporary journals reported that Butler was acquainted with the Paris and London prototypes. Yet while Butler gave Warren the idea of building an arcade, Haviland's arcades were the actual models.

Robert Alexander investigated the history of this building in an article published in the *Journal of the Society of Architectural Historians*.[743] The following is based largely on his findings.

The Providence Arcade is a broad building on a site measuring 68 by 23 meters. The facades are temple fronts whose pediments vary in design. It was originally planned with two stories, but the plans were altered in 1827 by reducing the heights of the stories and adding a third. Three, or, in one case, eight steps stretching across the full breadth of the fronts lead up to the arcade level and into the portico, the zone placed in front of the actual arcade space to accommodate the freestanding stairways to the galleries on the upper stories. The portico consists of six granite columns with smooth shafts and Ionic capitals, which are copies of the columns of the temple of Ilissos as published by Stuart and Revett.[744]

The interior facades are set back twice and can be seen from the portico. The two sides of the arcade space are connected to the frontal zone by galleries which extend across the entire width of the portico, dividing it behind the columns into two levels. The arcade space widens as it rises, thereby enabling a view of all concourses and direct illumination of all shops and offices, which decrease in depth on the upper levels as the arcade space widens.

The concourse on the ground floor is 4 meters wide and has thirteen shops on each side. The shop windows, like those of the Burlington Arcade in London, are slightly convex. On the second floor the arcade space widens by approximately 1.5 meters on each side. The resulting galleries have cast-iron railings and are connected by bridges in the middle and on the ends before the two fluted columns which frame a view of the street. Small white globe lamps on the posts of the railing are the only source of illumination for the arcade, which is open at night. The shops on the second floor have angularly projecting display areas which are not as deep as those on the ground floor. The third floor is also set back on each side by approximately 1.5 meters. However, its gallery continues all the way around the columns placed at the ends. The windows and doors on this floor, which probably housed small offices, all lie in the same plane and have the small, narrow panes common at the time. A continuous cornice terminates the interior facade. The outward-curving base of the wooden glass-roof structure begins above the cornice. The ridgepole rests symbolically at the ends of the arcade on a round arch with a recessed tympanum which bears the date 1828 and the name of the arcade. The glass roof is supported by rafters at even intervals. The spaces between are multipaned and have two divisions along the arcade axis. Ventilation devices are not visible.

All of the seventy-eight shops and offices have uniform signs with rounded corners which hang from triangular iron brackets. The large black Roman letters against a white background make it possible to read the names of the tenants of all the floors even from the lowest concourse. Thus, the purely commercial function of the arcade—the first building type in America to serve retail trade exclusively—is conveyed by simple devices which are precisely interrelated in their proportions and arrangement. The arcade building type exists here as a finished system, a shopping center in the guise of a Greek temple. Intensification and variation are still possible, and these occur with the construction of the Cleveland Arcade—the gigantic variation of the ground-plan system established in Providence.

QUEZALTENANGO
Arcade
This large, two-storied arcade has shops but no show windows.

RHEIMS
Passage de Talleyrand
Rue de Talleyrand—Rue Drouet d'Erlon
This two-storied, cruciform arcade in the center of the commercial district of Rheims

was constructed toward the end of the nineteenth century.

RIO DE JANEIRO
Galleria Rio Branco
Avenido Branco

ROCHESTER
There is said to be a copy of the Burlington Arcade in Rochester, New York.[745]

ROME
Galleria Colonna (figs. 439–448)
Piazza Colonna—Via Luigi Chigi—Via Sabini—Via S. Maria in Via
On May 14, 1881, a law was enacted in Italy to regulate financial assistance for the reconstruction and expansion of Rome.[746] In 1882 the city proposed a plan which, among other things, provided a considerable sum for the grading and widening of the Via del Corso. It also authorized the necessary expropriations. Not only would the Corso be widened, especially in the area of the Piazza Colonna, but the Via del Tritone would be extended to the Corso. The first step was to demolish the buildings between the Via San Claudio and the Vicolo Caccianove. In 1889 the old Palazzo Piombino opposite the Piazza Colonna was torn down as well. Further to the south more space was made available.[747] In this way a large construction site was created in the highly developed old section of Rome. It was flanked by the Corso and the Via del Tritone and stood opposite the Piazza Colonna. The architects were inspired by the possibilities of the site. Over thirty years, more than 100 projects were drafted, altered, and cast aside.

One of the first projects, proposed in 1884, recognized the possibility of constructing a large glass-covered arcade after the model in Milan. This concept can be found in many projects. The ground plans of the arcades varied greatly. Some of these plans are unique in the history of the arcade. Not until the 1920s, after decades of discussion, was the Galleria Piazza Colonna finally erected on the Piazza Colonna. However, it is not a major structure compared to the proposals which had been rejected.

The stages leading up to the construction of the Galleria Piazza Colonna are similar to those of the arcades in Milan, Genoa, and Naples: the arcade is part of an urban renewal program; it becomes a focus of

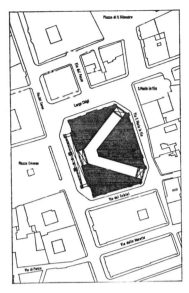

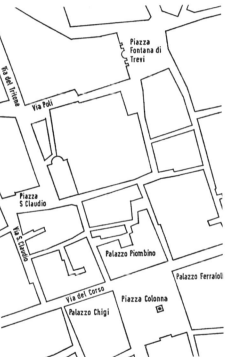

439
Rome, site of the Galleria Colonna, 1963

440
Rome, Piazza Colonna, before 1881

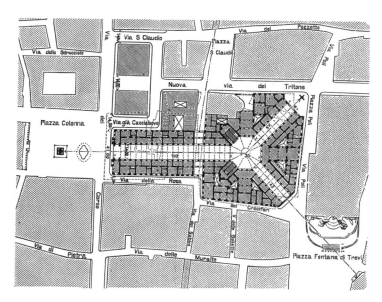

441
Rome, Galleria Co-
lonna, ca. 1925, plan

442
Galleria Colonna, en-
trance, project by
Mazzanti, 1884

443
Galleria Colonna,
facade, Piazza
Colonna

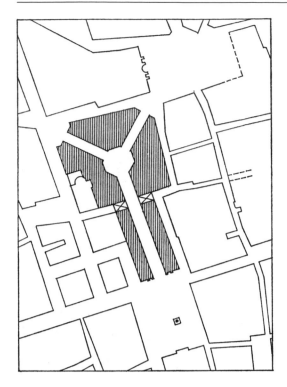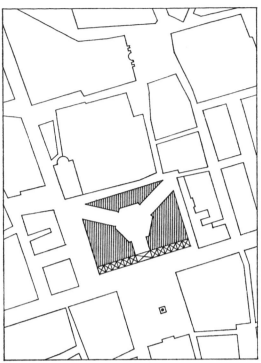

444
Rome, Galleria Co-
lonna, project by
Mazzanti

445
Piazza Colonna,
project by Deserti

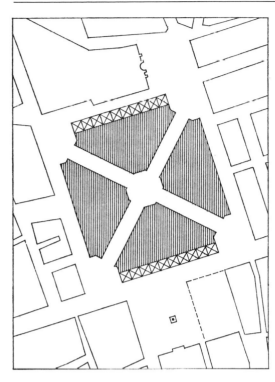

446
Piazza Colonna,
project by Coppede-
Carbone

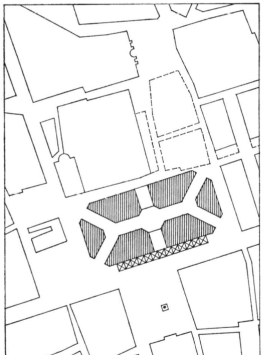

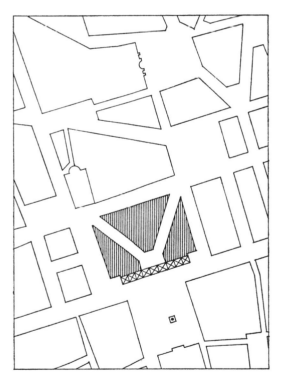

447
Piazza Colonna,
project by Penso-
Menozzi

448
Piazza Colonna,
project by Carbone

public interest and an object of competitions and of a general city planning debate; and it is expected to be a center of public life in the city.

The case in Rome was especially difficult. A large-scale planning solution could be realized only with difficulty, since the architectural-historical fabric of the surrounding area prevented major alterations. Furthermore, there was no specific justification for creating an arcade on this site since no new significant spatial relationship or line of communication could be established here as in Milan (where two squares were connected).

Following is a brief discussion of the most important projects which contained proposals for an arcade. They are arranged chronologically. Site plans show the course of development. All projects that I discovered were published in brochure form.[748]

In 1884 the architect Ferdinando Mazzanti,[749] in association with the Tiber Bank, proposed the first great glass-covered arcade across from the Piazza Colonna. It had a Y-shaped plan. The 110-meter-long and 14-meter-wide main wing opened up into an octagonal space with a 30-meter diameter. From there the other two wings (45 meters long and 10 meters wide) led to the Piazza Poli and the Piazza Fontana di Trevi. This plan extended far beyond the space intended for the structure. It attempted to place the arcade in an urban context that assumed that the arcade would be regularly frequented.

The publicly accessible covered space totaled 4,460 square meters and could accommodate 17,800 people. In the octagon, opposite the entrances to the diagonal wings, were two wide stairways to make the upper stories accessible to the public. The ground floor housed ninety-seven shops, some of which continued through to the bordering streets. The second story contained fifty additional shops. The remaining stories would be rented as clubs, offices, and apartments. Cafés and restaurants were planned in the octagon. It was thus an ideally varied spatial program which could be assured of a public throughout the day.

In his arguments for the project Mazzanti naturally referred to the model in Milan. But he also pointed to the concentration of public administrative offices, banks, embassies, and publishing houses in the immediate neighborhood. He made an additional appeal to history: the Roman custom of meeting and doing business in the basilicas, baths, and theater foyers. He pointed to the Italian traditions of the loggia, the arcaded street, and the basilica and demonstrated that, except for a few modest colonnades, nothing comparable existed in the Rome of his time. He knew that Rome had a long-felt need for a covered street, a magnificent arcade or gallery worthy of the city. It needed a place where high society, trade, and politics could come together, a place where business could be conducted, and where one could stroll, chat, and converse protected from the sun and rain.[750] The Y shape which he proposed, and which was based on the architectural context, appears in all subsequent projects, even if in altered form. It is even present in rudimentary form in the existing structure.[751]

The second project to be considered was by Deserti, Caffoni, and Petrignani.[752] It was proposed to the city in 1895 and was discussed in the press.[753] Following the basic form of the Mazzanti project, it also has a Y-shaped plan, but is reduced in size. The building is confined to the specified construction site. The massive rotunda, with a diameter of 40 meters, is a hexagon. Three wings of equal length radiate from it, one lying directly opposite the Marcus Aurelius column on the Piazza Colonna. The other wings lead to the Via Tritone and Via dei Crociferi. If in Mazzanti's project the facade of the arcade corresponds exactly to the fourth side of the Piazza Colonna, here it extends beyond the width of the square. The ground floor is arcaded along the Corso. The triumphal arch motif, which was employed in Milan and in the Mazzanti project, is retained here, although it is integrated into the facade. Sketches of the interior show that the Galleria Umberto I, built in Naples a few years earlier, influenced the design of the facades—for example, the Palladian motif on the second floor.

The project of Pietro Via[754] was proposed in 1900. Its precursor was an 1894 project by the engineer Boldi.[755] It still has two diagonal arcade spaces (which it names "galleria") with vaulted roofs. The arcades cut through the block across from the Piazza Colonna, opening up to the square in a semicircle which includes a continuous colonnade.

The Coppede-Carbone project,[756] proposed circa 1910, is interesting because of its ground plan, which takes a totally unique form: the square block, 150 meters on each side, is crossed diagonally by arcades which intersect in a great octagon. In the four indentations on the corners we find a theater facing the Piazza Colonna and bath-like sequences of spaces in the others, the use of which is unclear. This project is more forceful than Mazzanti's. It also extends to both the Piazza Poli and the Piazza Fontana di Trevi, but it does not take the existing architecture into account.

It can be considered perhaps the most monumental arcade project ever designed—"arcade" used almost in the sense of a public building. In its dimensions it is comparable to the Palace of Justice in Brussels or the designs for the Palace of Justice in Rome by Calderini or Rivas.[757] The block has four concave corners, each opening onto its own piazza. The architects also planned to remove the Palazzo Ferraioli, on the southern border of the Piazza Colonna, to make the square as wide as the arcade block.

The 1911 Penso-Menozzi project, of which only one site plan could be found, proposes a block running parallel to the Corso. It has no radial relationship to the Piazza Colonna.[758] The arcade ground plan can be described as a cross whose longer arms are split into Y's at the ends. Hence it is a conglomeration of earlier solutions with no recognizable advantages.

The two nearly identical projects submitted by the architect Dario Carbone[759] are dated 1910 and 1912. They represent the Galleria Piazza Colonna more or less as it exists today. The Galleria is in form one-half of the 1910 ideal project by Coppede-Carbone and is only one-fourth of the area. This scheme is all that remains of the decades of debates. Two diagonal wings meet in the semicircular vestige of a rotunda which borders the colonnade placed opposite the Piazza Colonna. This rotunda is, logically, entirely eliminated in the final version. Apart from minor variations on the plan, the two versions differ only in the radial arrangement vis-à-vis the Piazza Colonna. The 1910 project occupies the whole width of the square with its facade; in the 1912 project the central axis of the building points to the column. The present building has neither form. One sees in the Galleria Piazza Colonna as it was constructed in the mid-1920s a building which was debated and discussed to death.

The arcade wings cannot be recognized from the Piazza Colonna. They are gloomy because of the convex dust covers which give the arcade space the feeling of a bank. Even the wonderful ice cream and candy shops at the entrance and the music of the small band playing for the guests of a restaurant within cannot bring it to life.

Galleria Sciarra
Via M. Minghetti—Via Sciarra
This small arcade is located to the south of the Galleria Colonna. It consists only of a glass-covered courtyard and connects the Via di Sabini to the Via di S. Marcello.

ROTTERDAM
Arcade (figs. 449–451)
Coolvest—Korte Hoogstraat
The arcade in Rotterdam is the first of three arcades by Jan Christiaan van Wijk, the other two of which were built in The Hague and Zandvoort. Van Wijk was born in Gouda in 1844 and died in Rotterdam in 1891.[760] Before the construction of this arcade he had traveled to Paris, Cologne, Brussels, and Liège to study arcades in these cities.

The arcade, with all its architectural extravagance, was something completely new for Rotterdam, a city of merchants and sailors, people who tended to build frugally. The debates surrounding construction can be followed in the papers of the time.[761]

The arcade was opened by the Mayor of Rotterdam on October 15, 1879. People streamed into the building, which was located on the main commercial street, the Korte Hoogstraat.[762] The arcade had much to offer to the citizens of Rotterdam. It was 100 meters long, nearly 10 meters wide in its middle section, and three stories tall. A fountain splashed pleasantly in the center. Thirty shops with their own apartments offered clothes and assorted accoutrements, hats, shoes, walking sticks, umbrellas, children's toys, jewelry, tobacco, and much more. Sixty additional separate apartments were for rent. The Grand Hotel du Passage opened into the Korte Hoogstraat with the "Gourmet," a large restaurant with wood paneling in Dutch Renaissance style. It also offered a conversation salon off the loggia, a women's salon with a view of the arcade interior, and eighty luxuriously decorated rooms.

Two cafés were opened, which, according to an article in the local press, engaged in a

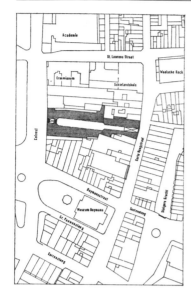

449
Rotterdam, site of
the arcade, before
1940

450
Rotterdam, arcade,
1878–1879, de-
stroyed 1940, arcade
space, view toward
Korte Hoogstraat

451
Rotterdam, arcade,
facade, Korte
Hoogstraat

Darwinian struggle for survival. The café located on the Korte Hoogstraat opposite the hotel entrance had a large hall in the cellar with a grotto garden, kitchen, and storage area. This cellar, called the Benedenpassage (underground arcade) was accessible from the Coolvest since the street lay approximately 2 meters lower than the level of the arcade. The actual arcade space could be reached only by stairs. This underground area also had a bathing facility with forty individual baths, a large booth-lined hall measuring 1,800 square meters for exhibitions and markets, a stalactite cave, and a beer hall with goldfish and corals in large bowls. The arcade was illuminated at night by countless gas lamps. All the establishments were leased quickly. The arcade became the place in Rotterdam where people met and promenaded.

It is reported that the shops were commercially successful. Many lasted for years.[763] Only the underground arcade did not enjoy the anticipated success. The space was put to a different use, and after a short time the cellar was only a storage area. In 1890 a bowling alley was introduced. The exhibition hall remained empty. In 1901 the bathing facility was equipped with Turkish, Russian, and Roman baths. In 1883, after many experiments, the gas lighting was replaced by Edison electric lamps. A steam engine in the cellar generated electricity.

The arcade was built with capital put up by the firm M. Hakkert & Co. After the demise of Martinus Hakkert the firm was transformed into an arcade corporation, which the architect van Wijk directed until 1891. The corporation amassed a capital of over 500,000 gulden. In the first years average dividends of five and one-half percent were paid; after 1892, however, they were lowered to two and three-quarters percent.

The arcade stood until that fateful day, May 14, 1940, when a German air raid reduced Rotterdam to ruins. The archive of the arcade corporation, also located in the arcade, was destroyed as well. Hence, no detailed information exists on the building. After the war the corporation proposed a new building for the same site. However, the project was not passed by the city council, since a completely different layout was planned for the inner city. A similar arcade was constructed after the war on Rotterdam's Lijnbaan.

The Gemeentearchief of Rotterdam possesses only three drawings: a longitudinal section and two facades. Unfortunately, these plans provide no significant information concerning the interior organization of the arcade. The first third of the arcade space was widened from approximately 6 to 10 meters since the greater depth of the ground plan allowed a widening of the arcade without altering the ground plans of the apartments. The facades of the arcade interior were not uniform. They had no rhythm because of the heterogeneous stylistic elements. The heights of the stories varied with the narrowing of the arcade space. Therefore the hotel rooms and apartments were at different levels. The shops were architecturally separated from the upper stories by a cornice which extended into the arcade entrances and was broken by paired cast-iron Corinthian columns. The entrances and display windows of the shops alternated. However, this alternation was also irregular since the entrances to the apartments on the upper stories were interspersed along the ground floor. The semicircular glass roof, rounded at the two ends, was divided by a series of identical ribs. Every fourth rib was a supporting arch which extended outside the roof.

RYDE, ISLE OF WIGHT
Royal Victoria Arcade
Union Street—Church Lane
The Royal Victoria Arcade is a small structure with fifteen two-storied shops. It has only one entrance on Union Street. Several steps lead up to the concave entranceway and into the arcade. The arcade ends in a rotunda. It was built in 1845–1846, probably by Westmacott. Today it has been converted into a supermarket. However, the interior shop facades still exist.[764]

The Royal Victoria Arcade was built at a time when almost no arcades were being built in England. It can be best compared to the Exeter Arcade in London.

SEVILLE
Pasaje de Oriente
Calle de las Sierpes—Sagasta
This corner arcade is on the main commercial street of Seville, the Calle de las Sierpes.[765]

Pasaje del Duque
Plaza Duque de la Victoria

SHEFFIELD
Cambridge Arcade
Fineberg gives 1875 as the date of construction.

George Arcade
Fineberg gives 1900 as the date of construction.

SINGAPORE
Clifford Arcade
Raffles Square—Collyer Quay
Travelers who arrive by ship in Singapore enter the city at the Clifford Pier. Opposite the harbor building, next to the Shell skyscraper, is the entrance to the Clifford Arcade. It connects the Collyer Quay to Raffles Place, the commercial center of the city.

In 1819 Singapore was still a fishing village. However, Thomas Raffles recognized its strategic significance, and in the nineteenth century it became the great center of trade in the Far East. The arcade was built in 1909, at the end of this era of almost unlimited expansion.

The arcade is over 100 meters long and four-storied, and is of the gallery type, similar to arcades in Australia. The arcade space, constructed of iron, widens on the second and third stories, which have continuous galleries. The fourth floor lacks a gallery. The space is illuminated by a simple glass saddle roof with the same width as the ground floor. The line of the facades is broken by a polygonal central space.

Papineau described the arcade in his guide to Singapore as "typically Moorish, its roof-line ornamented with minarets and its sides featuring unusual designs. . . ." Thus we see the Islamic architectural motifs that are so closely related to the concept of the arcade employed for the first time in the Far East. In the interior of the arcade these motifs are limited to ogee arches over the passageways and shop windows.

SOUTHPORT (England)
Cambridge Arcade
Municipal Gardens—Chapel Street, next to the Town Hall
Fineberg gives 1867 as the date of construction.

Leyland Arcade
West Street—Lord Street
Southport is a small bathing resort north of Liverpool. The Leyland Arcade was built in 1898 by the architect Bolshaw. A report in *Building News* describes it as follows:[766] "The arcade will comprise 45 lock-up shops and caretaker's house on the ground floor, together with numerous offices, ladies' clubs, sale room, and other conveniences on the first [second] floor, and assembly-room on the second [third] floor. . . . The whole will be covered in order to afford a sheltered promenade. Electric light is to be employed throughout. The whole of the premises are to be heated throughout by a circulation of hot-water so arranged that each tenant may regulate the temperature of his own premises. . . ."

The arcade is narrow where it begins on Lord Street and widens octagonally approximately in the center. It is wider from there to West Street, which is on the waterfront. It is one of the arcades located in bathing resorts which serve as extensions of the covered promenades.

STONINGTON
Arcade
This arcade was built in 1827[767] and is often mentioned in connection with the arcades in Providence and New York.

ST. PAUL
Endicott Arcade
Robert Street—East 4th Street
Discovered by Baedeker, this corner arcade was built before 1904.[768]

SUNDERLAND
New Arcade
Fineberg gives 1876 as the date of construction.

SWANSEA
Alexandra Arcade (fig. 452)
High Street—Alexandra Road
In 1890 *Building News*[769] published a wood engraving of the interior of the Alexandra Arcade in Swansea, an industrial city on the south coast of Wales. The print shows that to ensure fire protection the arcade is constructed completely of prefabricated cast-iron parts. The architect was Edward Bath of Swansea, and the iron-work was executed by the Glasgow firm of McFarlane, the same company which built the arcade in Johannesburg. It evidently had a patent for glass roofs with scale-shaped panes.

The Alexandra Arcade has two stories. The arcade space widens in the upper story and contains continuous arcaded, glass-covered galleries. The sides are linked by

452
Swansea, Alexander
Arcade, 1890, arcade
space, from *Building
News*

three bridges. The arcade, which has room
for sixty-six shops, is almost 5 meters
wide; the galleries on the upper level are 2
meters wide. The glass roof consists of two
glass vaults, each describing a quarter circle. A continuous ventilation strip connects the two halves. The glass roof is
borne on arched ribs which rest on purlins.
These purlins in turn rest on ornamented
intermediary supports which provide
strength laterally and longitudinally and
are inserted in the columns of the arcaded
galleries.

I have not been able to ascertain whether
the arcade was built as shown in fig. 452
and whether it is still standing.

Victoria Arcade
Waterloo Street—Coal Street
According to Fineberg, this arcade was
built in 1893 and destroyed in World
War II.

SYDNEY

The majority of the arcades in Sydney were
built in 1881–1892. This short period was
the end of the construction boom which
began in the 1870s as a result of the economic rise of New South Wales.[770] The
discovery of gold and increasing agricultural exportation attracted immigrants.
The population of Sydney quadrupled. A
wreath of suburbs grew around the city
center, which was confined between the
park and the harbor. This layout led to
almost insurmountable maintenance
problems.

Foreign investments aided the construction
of a street-car network and water system.
The two-storied development of the city
was replaced by three- to five-storied commercial buildings with great emphasis on
the installation of all the latest conveniences and on fire prevention. The arcades
offered a great opportunity as the city was
thus transformed by development: the
housing of a great number of shops and
offices in a small space, the expansion of
publicly accessible floor space, and the exploitation of the interior of city blocks.
More than six multileveled arcades were
built in a ten-year period. The construction
boom of the 1880s then ended abruptly
because an economic crisis resulted in the
drop of farm prices, the cut-off of investments, and the collapse of the banks. Arcades were not built again until the
twentieth century: one in the 1920s and
numerous others in the new construction
boom in the 1950s. As this boom con-

tinues Sydney is being transformed into a city of skyscrapers.

Sydney Arcade (fig. 453)
King Street—George Street
The Sydney Arcade was built in 1881 but is no longer standing. It was the work of Thomas Rowe, whose success with this project led to contracts for two more arcades.

Rowe had emigrated to Australia in 1848. After trying his luck in prospecting, he returned to Sydney and began working in an architecture office. In 1856 he opened his own studio and became one of Sydney's leading architects. The Sydney Arcade has a bend and contains two stories with shops on the ground floor and offices on the upper story. It has a "very delicate glass and iron roof."

Royal Arcade (fig. 453)
Pitt Street—George Street
The Royal Arcade was built in the next year, 1882, also by Thomas Rowe. Today it is completely altered: the glass roof has been removed and the number of stories increased to three. Where it has a slight bend, a two-level bridge has been introduced.

Victoria Arcade (fig. 453)
Elizabeth Street—Castlereagh Street
The Victoria Arcade was built in 1887–1888. It is unique among arcades because it consists of a single oval central space with two entrances. It was the first private commission of one of Rowe's young assistants, Hardling, who came to Sydney in 1876. The rotunda has four stories which are accessible by stairways in the entrances. Today the shops have moved into the arcade space, narrowing the arcade to the width of the entrances. The glass roof is enclosed in one central pointed oval. It is borne by cast-iron supports which extend down to braces at the third story level.

City Arcade (project)
Pitt Street—George Street
In 1890 a competition was held for the City Arcade. However, the arcade was never erected.

Imperial Arcade (fig. 453)
Pitt Street—Castlereagh Street
In 1891 Rowe and his assistant Campbell built the Imperial Arcade. It is 108 meters long and houses thirty-eight shops and twenty-nine offices. The entrance buildings contain the Arcadia Hotel.

453
Sydney, city plan, detail

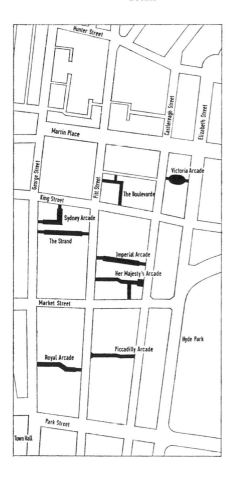

Its architecture has been described as follows: "The concourse has two levels of shops, one in a basement (now a single shop) reached by stairs at either end, and one level of offices with gallery access. The galleries are linked at the centre by a bridge and a single stair leads from the concourse to the middle of the bridge. The site slopes quite steeply, with a total change in level of more than ten feet, but no advantage is taken in the design, and the facades to the concourse and the roof-structure are simply stepped at five points with awkward packing pieces filling in the resulting gaps. . . ."

Strand Arcade (fig. 453)
Pitt Street—George Street
The Strand Arcade is Sydney's most beautiful arcade, with the most clearly developed interior. Opened in 1892, it was designed by John B. Spencer. Like Rowe, he had emigrated from England, first tried his luck at prospecting, and then returned to his original occupation. He opened an office with his partner, Backhouse.

The Strand Arcade, the longest in Sydney, is 112 meters long. It is set back once and has three stories. The top two stories are occupied by offices and have continuous galleries. They are connected in the middle by bridges. The glass saddle roof is supported by ornamentally perforated beams with a semicircular undergirding. The beams rest on brackets in front of the facades, and are arranged in a manner which leaves a space for ventilation between the highest cornice and the beginning of the glass roof. The ground-floor concourse has two rows of display windows above which neon signs and lamps hang from iron brackets. The arrangement of the arcade space recalls the Providence Arcade, except that it is more steeply proportioned.

Her Majesty's Arcade
Pitt Street—Castlereagh Street—Market Street
This arcade runs parallel to the Imperial Arcade. It was not built until 1928. Other one-storied open arcades, like the Piccadilly Arcade and the Boulevard, were built in the 1950s.

Her Majesty's Arcade is the work of the architectural firm Mould and Mould. It was extended in the 1930s to Market Street by another wing. Approximately 100 shops are distributed throughout the three levels, which can be reached by elevators.

TORONTO
Yonge Street Arcade
Yonge Street—Victoria Street
Baedeker's guide to Canada lists this arcade, which is no longer standing.

TOULOUSE
Arcade
Rue d'Austerlitz—Rue de Strasbourg

TRIESTE
El Tergesteo (figs. 454–459)
Piazza della Borsa—Via del Teatro—Via della Borsa—Piazza Giuseppe Verdi
Trieste, in the nineteenth century Austria's only seaport, and a free port since 1719, owed its economic prosperity to the construction of the Vienna-Trieste railway.

The old city of Trieste is located around the Castlello. The new city, planned in the eighteenth century, lies to the north. The center of the new city is the Canale Grande, which extends from the sea deep into the city, terminating marvelously at the facade of S. Antonio Nuovo. The Via del Corso forms the link between the old city and the new. It widens at the Piazza della Borsa, bends, and ends at the Piazza Grande. The great squares that are the center of public life in the city did not receive their final form until the nineteenth century. Between the stock exchange (Borsa), the Teatro Verdi, and the Cafe Specchi stands a massive gray, nearly square block, El Tergesteo. It is intersected by the first cross-shaped arcade in the world, which has two stories. Four narrow light wells and stairs to the five-storied frontal buildings are located in the four corners of the block. Here then we find the ideal type of the arcade: a cruciform interior space and a building that occupies an entire block. Although the glass-covered space of the arcade is identical in all four wings, the axis lying between the two squares is emphasized by triple entranceways and broad vestibules. The cross-axis contains only side entrances, which are now closed.

The interior of the arcade, which had been used for a time as the stock exchange, was modernized in 1957 in a frightful manner:[771] the glass roof was removed and replaced by a vaulted concrete roof with occasional round glass blocks which provide a kind of cellar illumination. The still recognizable architectural order was painted over in yellow, transforming the facades to a pasteboard trim. A curse on the architect Alessandro Psacaropulo, who is responsible for this renovation!

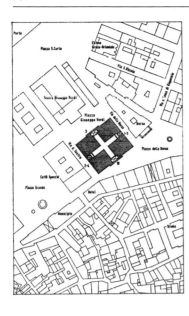

454
Trieste, site of El
Tergesteo, 1912

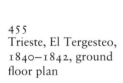

455
Trieste, El Tergesteo,
1840–1842, ground
floor plan

456
El Tergesteo, upper
floor plan

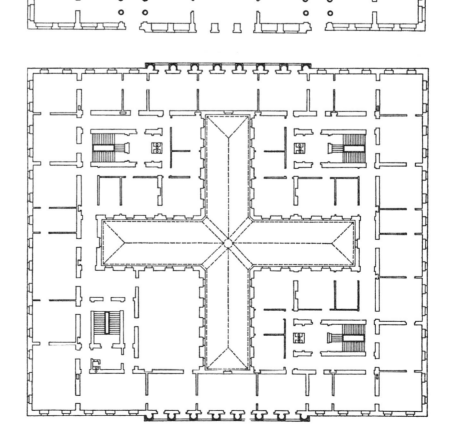

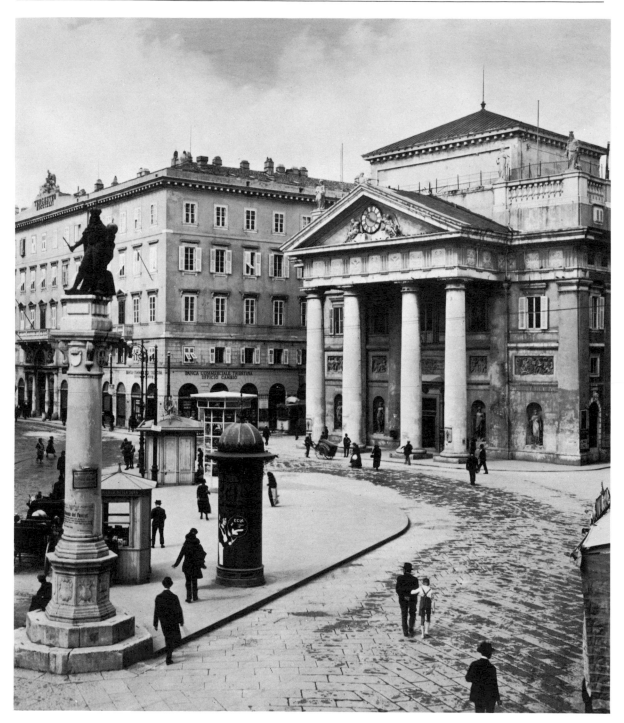

457
Trieste, Piazza della
Borsa, stock ex-
change, and El
Tergesteo

458
Buttazoni, design for
an arcade with a
vaulted glass roof

459
El Tergesteo, arcade
space, modified

Two plans exist for El Tergesteo.[772] The first is by the architect Antonio Buttazoni,[773] who began work on it in 1836 and presented it in 1840. In 1838 a corporation, the Società El Tergesteo, was formed[774] to build such a structure near the stock exchange to serve the needs of the business community. Buttazoni's project has come down to us in engravings and lithographs that he published himself. The architect F. Bruyn of Trieste actually built the arcade between 1840 and 1842 in slightly altered form. I have been unable to discover the reason for the change of architects.

Buttazoni's project shows clearly his dependence on Pizzala, the architect of the Galleria de Cristoforis in Milan. Numerous elements of the facades are similar: the rusticated base, the shape of the windows, the triple entrance on the main axis, and the arrangement of the balconies. The lithograph reproduced in fig. 458 points out the only differences: the greater width (6 instead of 4 meters), the Ionic engaged columns, the vaulted glass roof, and the richness of the sculptural wall decoration. The engraving by Bruyn in fig. 459 (which shows the structure as actually built) shows a low-pitched glass saddle roof and shallower, smaller-scaled subdivision of the facade. The upper story is separated from the shops by a cornice, and the wreath moulding is less developed. In neither version is the intersection of the spaces emphasized by widening or by a dome; instead the four corners are slightly sheared off.

The Galleria del Tergesteo is still popular today. One can drink coffee at tables in the arcade, where the discussions of stockbrokers and businessmen echo through the space. A small tablet on the facade facing the Piazza del Teatro tells something of the inhabitants of El Tergesteo:

There lived here as a boy and youth
  Ferruccio Busoni,
Nurtured from his first breath in the
  musical arts by a Triestan mother.
He is acclaimed here by the people of
  Trieste,
For the first time.

TURIN

Turin was the center of the struggle for the national unification of Italy. Between 1859 and 1865 it was the provisional capital. The city grew out of the regular street plan of a Roman colony. In the seventeenth cen-

tury it was systematically expanded by the princes of the house of Savoy. Its main streets, leading to the Castello, were furnished with uniform porticoes. This Italian tradition became the custom in Turin and today one can still walk for a kilometer along arcaded streets. Sections even have booths, so that they form true arcades with shops on both sides.

Arcades were first built here after 1858, appearing with Turin's assumption of its brief political role. They are based on the system of porticoes, extending it and creating additional cross-connections. They therefore cannot be considered independent structures. The one exception, perhaps, is the Galleria Nazionale, which strove to compete with the other great Italian arcades.

Galleria Natta
Via Roma—Via Santa Teressa
This arcade was built into the existing Palazzo Natta as a corner arcade.[775] The original proposal by the architect, Panizza, dates from 1856. It was constructed in 1858. The Galleria Natta was a modest arcade with a few shops and a restaurant, the Meridiana, which was fashionable for many years.[776] In the 1930s it was replaced by a spacious three-winged arcade, the Galleria S. Federico.

Galleria delle Alpi (project)
Piazza Castello—Piazza Carlo Felice
In the archives of the city of Turin one can find references to a whole series of projects from the period when Turin was the capital.[777] They are speculations on a future development which never took place. Yet it is interesting that people turned to the arcade building type as the means of creating space for growing public needs and the resulting private investments.

In 1864 the engineer Bruschetti presented a project for an arcade which would intersect numerous blocks. It would begin at the Piazza Castello and extend parallel to the Via Roma to the Piazza Carlo Felice. The streets would be bridged by porticoes—similar to the method employed in the Galeries St. Hubert in Brussels.

Galleria dell'Industria Subalpina
(figs. 460–462)
Piazza Castello—Via Cesare—Piazza Carlo Alberto
Even before the construction of the arcade a passageway existed through the Palazzo delle Finanze connecting the Piazza Cas-

460
Turin, sites of the
Galleria Subalpina
and the Galleria
S'Federico, 1966

461
Turin, Galleria
dell'Industria Sub-
alpina, 1872–1874

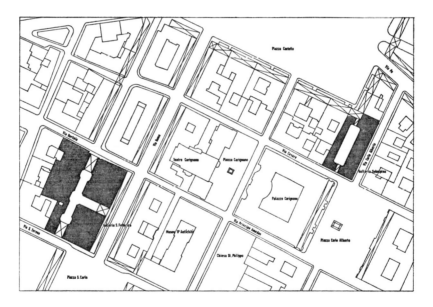

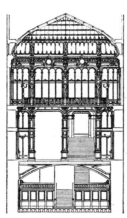

462
Galleria Subalpina,
cross section

tello to the Via delle Finanze, today the Via Cesare. The palace had a few shops and was heavily frequented because at that time the post offices were located in the Palazzo Carignano.[778] When the first parliament met as a result of the political events in the Palazzo Carignano, forcing the post office to move to a building south of the palace, the significance of the passageway grew.

In 1870 the mayor of Turin had the architect Gabetti[779] design a plan to convert the courtyard into an arcade. His design consisted of a two-storied arcade with a continuous gallery on the upper floor and a vaulted glass roof. The entrances were staggered to make each section of the attached galleries more easily accessible. When his design was published, other architects submitted proposals. In 1871 Ballati exhibited his project, which included a wide central space, in the Esposizione delle Belle Arti.

The engineer Pietro Carrera, who finally erected the arcade, presented a project resembling Gabetti's. He intended to tear down some of the sections of the old palace to allow the arcade to take a more regular shape. On August 15, 1872, after the purchase of the Palazzo delle Finanze, Carrera's design was selected; on July 13 construction began. The Banca Industriale Subalpina financed the project.

Carrera intended to exploit the site fully. He extended the arcade space to 45 by 14 meters and placed stairways opposite the staggered entrances. These stairways led to the continuous gallery on the upper floor and down to the large hall in the cellar beneath the floor of the arcade. The hall was originally used as a beer hall, but today it houses a cinema. The ground floor of the arcade contains shops, the upper floors storage areas and offices. The space terminates in a hipped glass roof whose supports are curved at the ends, becoming stylized braces which extend into the pillars of the facade. Thus the glass roof is integrated into the facades, allowed to develop out of the emphatically vertical structure, giving the space a more interior effect, resembling stock-exchange halls. The small stylized stone garden with the waterless fountains on the terrace floor seems like a parody of a winter garden. Since the arcade was restored in 1958, I am unable to say whether this stone garden was not perhaps the product of a more modern imagination.

I must mention the Caffe Baratti i Milano for the benefit of eventual visitors to this arcade. It occupies a space in the old palace by the entrance to the Piazza Castello. It has preserved its original decor and can compete with the Caffe Pettrocchi in Padua, the Caffe Greco in Rome, and the classistic Caffe S. Carlo in Turin. The business world of Turin meets here, at the "Piccola Borsa."

Galleria Nazionale (fig. 463)
Via Roma—Via dell'Arcivescovado—Via Venti Settembre
In its size and pretensions the Galleria Nazionale in Turin must be included among the monumental arcades of Italy.[780] It was built before 1890 and stood until the 1930s. The architects were Camillo Riccio and Constantino Gilodi. The great failing of this arcade was that it did not serve as a traffic artery.

The main entrance was on the Via Roma. One entered by a three-storied portal which terminated with a large statue above the attic. The main wing measured 100 meters long, 11.5 meters wide, and 17 meters tall (to the level of the wreath moulding). It ran parallel to the Via dell'Arcivescovado up to the Via Venti Settembre, a little-frequented street with a few businesses. In the center was a point of intersection from which a third, shorter wing extended as a passageway to the street. The wings therefore formed a *T*. This third wing ended in a one-storied covered hall which, perhaps with other such rooms, probably served as a market.

The arcade space had four stories. At the third floor level was a continuous balcony and wreath moulding which protruded out of the wall, blocking the view of the beginning of the glass roof. The glass saddle roof was born by riveted lattice beams with an arched undergirding. Over the point of intersection was a polygonal tent roof. The interior facades were a conglomeration of motifs from the Italian High Renaissance. One can recognize influences from the Palazzo Bevilacqua in Verona in the twisted engaged columns alternating with arches.

The Galleria Nazionale is said to have been most crowded on Thursdays, the day on which the grain dealers gathered.[781]

Galleria Umberto I
Via Basilica—Piazza della Repubblica—Via Milano
This is a two-storied, cross-shaped arcade near the marketplace on the Piazza della

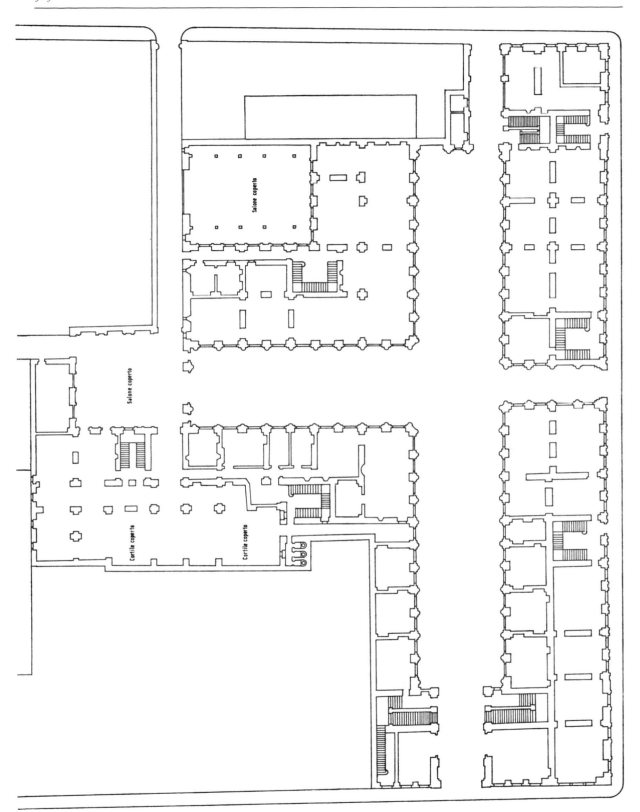

463
Turin, Galleria
Nazionale, ground
floor plan

Repubblica. The long wing extends from the Via Basilica to the piazza; the cross-wing ends in the porticos on the Via Milano. The 1888 "Correspondenza di Città di Torino" in the city archive mentions that the architect, Marsaglia, submitted a project for the Galleria Umberto I, which in 1889 received the "Dichiarazone di pubblica utilità." This 120-meter-long arcade must therefore have been built circa 1890.[782]

Galleria S. Federico
Via Santa Teressa—Via Roma—Via Bertola
This *T*-shaped arcade was built about 1930 by Eugenio Corti to replace the Galleria Natta.[783] It occupies the whole block and connects the Via Viotti to the colonnades of the Piazza S. Carlo. The arcade space is covered by arched concrete ribs, between which are small round concrete and glass skylights.

VALENCIA
Pasaje de Ripalda
Plaza Cajeros—Calle Moratin
This arcade is mentioned in Baedeker's 1912 guide to Spain and Portugal.

VICHY
Passage Giboin
Rue Clemenceau—Place St. Louis—Rue du Président Wilson
This small arcade connects the Place St. Louis to one of the main avenues of the spa park bordering the baths. Two parallel blocks push forward one-storied shops which are linked by a decorative glass roof open on the sides. A small railway station sells souvenirs.

Passage Clemenceau
Rue G. Clemenceau—Rue Ravy-Breton

VIENNA
Arcade in the Bank and Stock Exchange Building (fig. 464)
Freyung 2—Herrengasse 14
This arcade was built in 1856–1860 by Ferstel as a part of the Österreichisch-Ungarischen Bank. It houses shops on the ground floor, has varying heights, and serves in part as a light well. It is the only arcade in Vienna. However, some old walk-through buildings are still used as arcades.

WALSALL (England)
Arcade Buildings
Building News[784] published a report in 1885 on the plan for this arcade. It was to be part of a completely accessible triangular block of commercial buildings.

WINTERTHUR
Town Hall Passageway (fig. 465)
Marktgasse—Stadthausstrasse
In 1782–1784, following a competition, the Winterthur town hall was replaced by a new structure built by the Basel architect Johann Büchel. Büchel[785] belongs to the group which prepared the way for classicism in Switzerland. His talent is apparent in the Marktgasse facade,[786] which was incorporated into the conversion of the town hall to a public arcade. This conversion was made possible when the city administration moved to the freestanding city hall designed by Semper between 1865 and 1869. The Winterthur city architect Joseph Bösch,[787] a pupil of Semper, executed the actual reconstruction and made the building in the old city accessible for private use.

These phases of the development of the town hall must be viewed against the historical background. I quote:[788] "From this point on Winterthur remained subordinate to Zurich after the great upheaval which came in 1798 with the end of the old confederacy. The city was also severely limited economically by the capital. Not until the 'regeneration' of 1830 did Winterthur attain full equality. Once it did, however, it turned this equality into action. Politically, Winterthur was the center of the democratic movement which rebelled against the conservative politician and economist Alfred Escher in Zurich. In 1869 a new constitution was drafted for the canton. Economically, the now liberated textile, metal, and machine industries developed into enterprises which achieved some measure of world fame." The monumental new city hall outside the old city expressed Winterthur's new self-image.

Bösch converted the old town hall into an arcade, covered the courtyard with a glass roof, added new facades, and renovated the facade facing the Stadthausstrasse.[789] The reconstruction plans are located in the city archive. They still show open halls on the ground floor and not the thrice repeated Palladian motif which was employed later as a portal and spatial separation between the passageways and the three-storied courtyard. A driveway lined with curbstones was left through the middle of the arcade. Both stairways are accessible from the arcade space. The shops are occupied today by an antique dealer, a

464
Vienna, arcade in the
bank and stock ex-
change building,
1856–1860

465
Winterthur, City
Hall passageway,
1872–1874

small gallery, a women's salon, a drapery shop, a religious bookstore, and a fruit stand.

Fig. 465 provides an accurate depiction of the arcade. The Renaissance architecture is still fascinating although all life has left the arcade. The picture represents the destiny of many arcades: they will either be torn down or exist in the future as architectural monuments.

WOLVERHAMPTON (England)
Central Arcade
Dudle Street
The large Central Arcade has a bend and an octagonal dome over the central space. A third small passageway branches off from the middle to a side street.

It was built in 1904. Today it opens onto a new park and department store. Although it is still heavily frequented it is threatened with demolition. The level of the arcade is lower than Dudle Street, so every pair of shops is stepped, as are the balconies of the upper story, which project into the arcade space. The vaulted glass roof has two levels and is raised from one to the other by brick arches, which divide the glass roof in the middle.

Queen's Arcade
Queen's Square
The Queen's Arcade consists of a wide, glass-covered central space which is accessible from a street corner by two short arcade wings. When I visited it in 1966 the round central space, once occupied by one-storied shops with a balustrade, was already empty. The demolition of this 1909 arcade has certainly taken place by now. It is another sacrifice to the systematic urban renewal of English industrial cities.

WORTHING
The Arcade
Parade—South Street
This commercial building was erected in 1925 on the beachfront of a bathing resort by the architect Stonham for the Worthing Development Co. Ltd. Its interior is accessible by a two-storied arcade.[790]

ZAGREB
Oktogon
Ilica 5—Ulica Mirkabogovica, corner Trg. Bratstva Ijedinstva
This octagon arcade was built in 1889. It is located on the Ilica, the main commercial street of Zagreb.[791] It leads to an octagonal central space and bends, like the Kaisergalerie in Berlin, at a 45-degree angle, ending at the corner of the building facing the market square. The arcade has a polygonally concave entrance on the Ilica and a curved, projecting roof borne by two atlantes. It has two stories and is covered by a flat glass roof with square panes. The decorative details of the interior reflect the influence of the Viennese Secession.

ZANDVOORT-BAD
Arcade
Railway Station—Spa on Strandweg
An 1885 Baedeker says of this arcade:[792] "Zandvoort, until recently a modest seaside resort visited exclusively by the Dutch, has grown so much in the past few years that it is beginning to compete with Scheveningen. The railway ends immediately at the foot of the dunes. A wide stairway leads from the station up into a covered arcade with shops, cafes and wine- and beer-halls. It is bordered by the Hotel Kursaal, whose curved side wings surround a terrace with a music pavilion." The architect was J. C. van Wijk, the builder of the great arcades in The Hague and Rotterdam and the planner who laid out Zandvoort-Bad. Built in 1882, it is no longer standing.

Notes

1. Ernst Egli, *Geschichte des Städtebaus*, vol. 2, Zurich, 1962, pp. 254f.

2. Max Weber, *Wirtschaft und Gesellschaft*, vol. 2, Cologne, 1956, pp. 938–940.

3. Borrmann, *Die geschlossenen Platzanlagen im Altertum and in neuerer Zeit*, Berlin, 1912, p. 23.

4. Wasmuth, *Lexikon der Baukunst*, entry on Isfahan.

5. P. Coste and E. Flandin, *Voyage en Perse en 1840–41*, Paris, 1843–1854.

6. See (5).

7. Quoted from (3).

8. Charles Morazé, *Das Gesicht des 19. Jahrhunderts*, Cologne, 1959, p. 51.

9. Behcet Unsal, *Turkish and Islamic Architecture*, London, 1959, pp. 56–61.

10. C. Gurlitt, *Die Baukunst Konstantinopels*, Berlin, 1907–1912, pp. 49–52.

11. Lady Mary Montagu, *Briefe aus dem Orient* [translation of *Letters from the Orient*, 1784], 2d edition, Stuttgart, 1962, p. 192.

12. Roger Le Tourneau, *La Vie Quotidienne à Fes en 1900*, Paris, 1965.

13. See note 4: "In the aerial photograph one can recognize the long barrel vault of the bazaar, which crosses the city."

14. See note 1, pp. 302–305.

15. For further information on the Lübeck passageways: *Städtebauliche Übung über Lübeck*, 1963, Prof. Eggeling, Technological University, Berlin, Geist, Boye, Welter.

16. See John Summerson, *Georgian London*, 2d edition, Harmondsworth, 1962, pp. 142f; and *Survey of London*, vol. 31/32.

17. Eduard Kolloff, *Paris, ein Reisehandbuch*, 1849, pp. 114f.

18. See catalog, entry on Paris.

19. Paul Daechne, *1530–1930 Auerbachs Keller, Auerbachs Hof, Mädlerpassage*, Leipzig, n.d.

20. See catalog, entry on Leipzig.

21. Walter Dietrich, *Beiträge zur Entwicklung des bürgerlichen Wohnhauses in Sachsen im 17. und 18. Jahrhundert*, Leipzig, 1904, p. 75 and Figs. 126–127, Koch's Hof.

22. According to the Museum of the City of Vienna, Seitzer Hof was rebuilt in the described form circa 1837–1840 by the architect Stacke. It stood in this form until around 1910–1912. In an 1842 tourist guide of Vienna one can read, on p. 120: "The recently completed Seitzer Hof at Spenglergasse Nr. 427, a building in the most modern taste, with all the advantages of the newest architecture, in the interior provided with a bazaar, free-standing stairway, gas illumination, closed corridors to the flower exhibition, and the most elegant and tasteful decoration. . . ."

23. See note 37, p. 114.

24. Works on Palmyra: (a) Egli, *Geschichte des Städtebaus*, vol. 1, p. 242; (b) Wigand, *Palmyra, Ergebnisse der Expedition von 1902–17*, Berlin, 1932; (c) Albert Gabriel, *Syria, 1926*, plate 12, and site plan.

25. W. C. Behrendt, *Die einheitliche Blockfront als Raumelement im Städtebau*, Berlin, 1912, pp. 24f; and C. Gurlitt, *Handbuch des Städtebaus*, Berlin, 1920, pp. 23f.

26. See the ground plans of the Palais Royal in the catalog.

27. Leone Battista Alberti, *Zehn Bücher über die Baukunst* (Ten Books on Architecture), Leipzig, 1912, p. 436, table 12.

28. The earliest of these colonnaded bridges in Berlin is the Mühlendammbrücke, built in 1687 by Nehring. It had shops with apartments above. The later bridges, like the Spittelbrücke, the Mohrenbrücke, and the Königskolonnaden, had a more decorative character.

29. For a more detailed study of bridges with buildings, see Zucker, *Die Brücke, Typologie und Geschichte ihrer künstlerischen Gestaltung*, 1921, pp. 52–62.

30. Among the designs for the Pont Neuf is one with buildings by Jacques du Cerceau l'Ancien. Reproduced in Joseph Ponten, *Architektur, die nicht gebaut wurde*, 1925, plates, p. 34.

31. Larousse, *Dictionnaire de Paris*, 1965; entry on Pont Notre Dame.

32. Reprinted by Gurlitt in *Palladio*, plate 109.

33. T. Bolton, *The Works of Sir John Soane*, Sir John Soane's Museum publication, no. 8, undated, p. 2.

34. Grand Prix d'Architecture, *Projets couronnées par l'Académie Royale des Beaux-Arts de France*, various editions after 1829.

35. Illustration in *Domaines de la Couronne*, Fontaine, Palais Royal, plate 13, 1829.

36. V. Plagemann, *Das deutsche Kunstmuseum, 1790–1870*, Munich, 1967, p. 16.

37. On this relationship see Günther Bandmann, "Die Galleria Vittorio Emanuele II in Mailand," *Zeitschrift für Kunstgeschichte*, vol. 29, no. 2, 1966, pp. 90f.

38. *Baukunde des Architecten II*, Berlin, 1884, p. 627.

39. Literature referred to: (a) R. MacGrath and A. Frost, *Glass in Architecture and Decoration*, London, 1937; (b) Erich Schild, *Zwischen Glaspalast und Palais des Illusions*, Berlin, 1967, chapter on conservatories.

40. See note 39a, p. 108.

41. See note 39b, pp. 31–33.

42. See note 39b, p. 34.

43. For example, the Friedrichstrassenpassage in Berlin.

Notes

44. On the history of the prison building: (a) Graul, *Der Strafvollzugsbau einst und heute*, Düsseldorf, 1965; (b) *Handbuch der Architektur* IV/VII/I, Bauten für die Verwaltung und Rechtspflege, Stuttgart, 1900.

45. See note 44a, p. 52.

46. See note 44a, pp. 58–61.

47. See the ground plan variations in 44a, p. 47.

48. See note 44a, pp. 61–63, and (a) A. Gardner, "A Philadelphia Masterpiece: Haviland's Prison," *The Metropolitan Museum of Art Bulletin*, N.S. 14, 1955–1956, pp. 103–108; (b) G. B. Tatum, *Penn's Great Town*, Philadelphia, 1961, p. 179. On John Haviland: (a) Colvin, *Biography of English Architects*; (b) Matthew Baigell, Dissertation on Haviland, University of Pennsylvania, 1965; (c) Matthew Baigell, "John Haviland in Philadelphia, 1818–26," *Journal of the Society of Architectural Historians*, vol. 25, 1966, pp. 197–208.

49. See note 44a, p. 61.

50. Reproduced in 48a.

51. See note 44b, pp. 380f.

52. Sources on Charles Fourier (1772–1837) are (a) Victor Considérant, *Fouriers System der Sozialen Reform* (Fourier's System of Social Reform), Leipzig, 1906; (b) August Bebel, *Charles Fourier*, Dietz Verlag; (c) Dr. Käthe Morgenroth, *Fourier und der Sozialismus*, Berlin, 1920; (d) Charles Fourier, *Oeuvres complètes*, Paris, 1841–1845, reprint, 6 volumes; (e) Victor Considérant, *Destinée sociale*, 3 volumes, 1835–1844; (f) Elisabeth Lenk, introduction to *Theorie der vier Bewegungen* (German translation of *Théorie des quatre Mouvements*), Frankfurt, 1966.

53. See note 52f, p. 174.

54. See note 52c, p. 91, and *The Builder*, May 10, 1856, p. 55.

55. El Lissitzky, *Russland, Die Revolution der Architektur in der Sowjetunion*, Vienna, 1930, p. 15.

56. See note 52a, p. 79.

57. Appended in 52e; slightly different version in 52b. Considérant was the leader of the Fourierists, who had representatives in the National Convention after the revolution. A proposal to build an experimental phalanstery with state funds was rejected. Considérant emigrated in 1854 with 1200 followers to Texas to found a model phalanx as part of a colony named Réunion. However, the endeavor failed.

58. Quoted from Leonardo Benevolo, *History of Modern Architecture*, Cambridge, Mass., 1971, p. 152.

59. Heinrich Heine, *Lutezia*, appendix 1, "Kommunismus, Philosophie und Klerisei."

60. See note 52c, pp. 115–132, "Die Verwirklichung der Ideen Fouriers im Familistère de Guise." See also H. Honegger, *Godin und das Familistère von Guise*, Zurich, 1919.

61. Quoted from 52c, p. 119.

62. Quoted from 52f, p. 7.

63. Victor Baltard, *Les Halles Centrales*, Paris, 1863.

64. Reproduced in Lefrançois, *Paris à Travers les Siècles*, 1949, Saint-Eustache, fig. 7.

65. See note 37, p. 96.

66. Reproduced in Goulier, *Choix d'édifiés projetés et construits en France*, Paris, 1825–1850, vol. 3.

67. Richard Turley, "Early Victorian City Planning: Newcastle," *Architectural Review*, May 1946, pp. 141–146.

68. On the shop: Margot Aschenbrenner, *Buden und Läden, Werbegabe der Seidenweberei Schmitz & Co.*, Biberach/Riss, 1951.

69. See Otto Völckers, *Glas und Fenster*, Berlin, 1939. Also note 72b, p. 34.

70. See note 39a, pp. 136f. Also Paneth, *Entwicklung der Reklame*, Munich, 1926, pp. 149–154.

71. Thiollet and Roux, *Nouveau recueil de menuiserie et décorations intérieures et extérieures*; Paris, 1837. The book includes numerous illustrations of shops.

72. (a) Werner Sombart, *Der moderne Kapitalismus*, pp. 1902f; (b) Theodor Bohner, *Der offene Laden*, from *Chronik des Einzelhandels*, Frankfurt, undated; (c) Georg Steinhausen, *Der Kaufmann in der deutschen Vergangenheit*, Leipzig, 1899; (d) Réne Sédillot, *Vom Tauschhandel zum Supermarket*, Stuttgart, 1966.

73. See note 72a, section 2.1, p. 454.

74. See note 72a, section 2.1, p. 456.

75. See note 72a, section 2.1, p. 458.

76. See note 72a, section 2.1, pp. 460f.

77. Werner Sombart, *Liebe, Luxus und Kapitalismus*, DTV 458, 1967, p. 169f.

78. See note 77, p. 90.

79. See catalog, Paris arcades.

80. See note 72a, section 3.2, p. 861.

81. W. L. MacDonald, *The Architecture of the Roman Empire*, 1965, plates 74, 75, 89.

82. Rudolf Stein, *Das Rathaus und der grosse Ring zu Breslau*, Breslau, 1937.

83. K. H. Schreyl, "Zur Geschichte der Baugattung Börse," dissertation, Freie Universität Berlin, 1963.

84. See note 83, footnote 155.

85. For a description of the London exchanges see B. Fineberg, "The History and Design of Shopping Arcades," thesis, Regional College of Art, Manchester, 1953, pp. 17f.

86. Quoted from Alison Adburgham, *Shops and Shopping, 1800–1914*, London, 1964, p. 18.

87. See note 31, entry on Palais de Justice.

88. See (a) Pessard, *Nouveau Dictionnaire Historique*, Paris, 1904, entry on Foire St. Germain; (b) note 31, entry on Foire St. Germain.

89. See note 72, section 2.1, pp. 468–472.

90. An engraving is reproduced in 72d.

91. N. L. Durand, *Précis de Leçons d'Architecture*, Paris, 1805, vol. 2, p. 61 and plate 15.

92. Gottfried Semper, *Wissenschaft, Industrie und Kunst*, Neue Bauhausbücher, Mainz, 1966, p. 15.

93. See note 86, pp. 21–24.

94. Richard Knight, *Curiosities of London*, 1850(?), p. 40, entry on bazaars.

95. See note 86, pp. 18f.

96. For architectural details, see François Thiollet, *Serrurerie et Font de Fer*, Paris, 1832, figs. 26–27.

97. See note 71, fig. 59/60.

98. Paul Jarry, *Les Magasins de Nouveautés,* Paris, 1940, p. 46. Cross section in Hitchcock, *Architecture: Nineteenth and Twentieth Centuries,* Harmondsworth, 1958.

99. Paul Göhre, *Das Warenhaus,* vol. 12 of the series "Die Gesellschaft," Frankfurt, 1907.

100. See note 86, p. 137.

101. On the development of the department store: (a) note 98; (b) note 31, entries on *magasin de nouveautés* and *Grand magasin;* (c) Wussow, *Geschichte und Entwicklung der Warenhäuser,* 1906; (d) Schleissmann, *Geschichte der Warenhäuser,* Göschen, 1906; (e) A. Wiener, *Das Warenhaus,* Berlin, Wasmuth, 1911; (f) "Die ersten Warenhäuser," *Neue Züricher Zeitung,* December 19, 1964.

102. See note 101f.

103. In the words of Paul Sedille, the architect of Au Printemps, "Attract the crowd and hold its attention through decoration."

104. For the original form, before reconstruction by Percier and Fontaine, see note 36, fig. 8.

105. Plan in *Dehio,* Baden-Württemberg, 1964, p. 291.

106. For a more detailed account, see note 37, p. 90.

107. First formulation by Bandmann, the second by Walter Benjamin in his essay on the *flâneur.*

108. Hans Leiskow wrote on the situation in Germany, in *Speculation und öffentliche Meinung in der ersten Hälfte des 19. Jahrhunderts,* Jena, 1930, ch. 2.

109. Works on the train station: (a) Henry-Russell Hitchcock, *Early Victorian Architecture,* 2 volumes, New Haven, Conn., 1954; (b) H. Witteck, *Die Entwicklung des Stahlhochbaus,* Düsseldorf, 1964.

110. For example, City Arcade in Birmingham and the County Arcade in Leeds.

111. See note 109b, p. 52 and p. 5.

112. Brian Richards, *New Movement in Cities,* London, 1966, p. 51; this source also includes many of the turn-of-the-century projects mentioned here.

113. Paul Scheerbart, *Glasarchitektur,* Verlag der Sturm, 1914, XVIII, "Die Schönheit der Erde, wenn Glasarchitektur überall da ist."

114. See note 109b, p. 4: "Fire in a warehouse in Berlin (1887) caused the authorities in Germany to impose severe regulation on construction which prohibited exposed building material."

115. I have based the following on the German edition of A. Goodwin, *The French Revolution,* New York, 1962.

116. See note 115, pp. 38f.

117. Jürgen Habermas, *Strukturwandel der Öffentlichkeit,* 2d edition, Berlin, 1965, pp. 81f.

118. See note 115, p. 39.

119. Bakunin, *Philosophie der Tat,* Cologne, 1968, p. 317.

120. Stendhal's aphorism is appropriate in this context: "The best way for a ruler to gain the approval of the masses is the thorough extermination of that element of public opinion which used to be called Jacobinism."

121. Karl Marx, *Der 18. Brumaire des Louis Bonaparte,* Frankfurt, 1965, p. 10.

122. This structure is treated in the catalog under the name "Galeries de Bois."

123. Title of the famous story by Edgar Allen Poe.

124. Walter Benjamin, "The Flâneur," in *Charles Baudelaire: A Lyric Poet in the Era of High Capitalism,* London, 1973.

125. This was true of the following Parisian arcades: Passage des Panoramas, Passage du Caire, Passage Choiseul, Passage Montesquieu, and Galerie Véro-Dodat.

126. See note 31, entry on *ponts.*

127. See note 88, entry on *Trottoirs.*

128. Marie-Louise Biver, *Le Paris de Napoléon,* Paris, 1963, pp. 54–56.

129. Louis-Sebastian Mercier, *Paris am Vorabend der Revolution,* Karlsruhe, 1967, p. 47.

130. Quoted from 88a.

131. Quoted from: *Ansichten der Hauptstadt des Französischen Kayserreiches vom Jahre 1806 an,* 2 volumes, p. 188, "Die Strassen von Paris."

132. Quoted from 131, pp. 214–217, "Apologie des Kothes und der Cabriolets."

133. See note 128.

134. See note 127.

135. See note 17, pp. 92f.

136. See note 17, p. 113.

137. See Kolloff's comment.

138. Henri Besmard, *L'Industrie du Gaz à Paris depuis Ses Origines,* Paris, 1942, p. 17.

139. See note 138, p. 18.

140. To my knowledge this is the first direct reference of an architect to his models. Ware makes the reference in a manuscript document which contains the cost list for the Burlington Arcade project. See catalog.

141. See the text by Pizzala in the catalog (Milan, Galleria de Cristoforis).

142. See James Marston Fitch, *American Building: The Historical Forces That Shaped It,* Boston, 1966.

143. Paul Saintenoy, "J. P. Cluysenaar, Architecte des Galeries Saint-Hubert," *Académie Royale de Belgique, Bulletin de la Classe des Beaux-Arts,* 26, 1944, pp. 125f.

144. G. H. Dumont, "Comment Bruxelles fut dotés des Galeries Saint-Hubert," *Les Cahiers Leopoldiens,* série II, no. 9, Sept./Oct. 1961, p. 88.

145. Dolf Sternberger, *Panorama oder Ansichten zum 19. Jahrhundert,* 3d edition, Hamburg, 1955, pp. 175f.

146. See works mentioned in the catalog.

147. Asa Briggs, *Victorian Cities,* London, 1963, p. 16.

148. F. Engels, *Die Lage der arbeitenden Klasse in England,* Dietz, 1923, 8th edition, pp. 46f.

149. Helmut Böhme, *Prolegomena zu einer Sozial- und Wirtschafts-geschichte Deutschlands im 19. und 20. Jahrhundert,* Frankfurt, 1968, p. 62.

150. Quoted from 149, pp. 67f.

151. For a more detailed account see *Berlins Aufstieg zur Weltstadt,* Berlin, 1929, pp. 109f.

152. Arthur Fürst, *Das elektrische Licht,* Munich, 1926, p. 69.

153. Roger Shattuck, *The Banquet Years*, New York, Alfred A. Knopf, Vintage Books, 1968.

154. Ebenezer Howard, *Garden Cities of To-Morrow*, London, 1898.

155. Rudolf Hartog, *Stadterweiterungen im 19. Jahrhundert*, Stuttgart, 1962, pp. 114f.

156. See note 109b, p. 4.

157. *Bauausführungen der Berliner Terrain-und Bau-Aktiengesellschaft*, "Passage-Kaufhaus," Berlin, undated, pp. 19f.

158. Valeriy Bressov, *Die Republik des Südkreuzes*, in *Russland erzählt*, Fischer vol. 298, pp. 23–40; quote, p. 23.

159. *The Architectural Review*, December 1967, pp. 447f.

160. Vincent Scully, *Frank Lloyd Wright*, New York, 1960, figs. 29–32.

161. P. Berlage, *Amerikaansche Reisherinneringen*, Rotterdam, 1908.

162. Werner Hegemann, *Otto Kohtz*, 1930, figures, pp. 9–10.

163. *Zodiac*, vol. 18 (Great Britain).

164. On Sauvage: *Werk*, February 2, 1965, pp. 45–48; Stanislaus von Moos, *Aspekte der neuen Architektur in Paris, 1912–32*.

165. See note 164, p. 47.

166. Le Corbusier, *Ausblick auf eine Architektur*, 1922, Bauwelt Fundamente, p. 186.

167. *Probleme des Bauens, der Wohnbau*, Fritz Bloch, 1928, p. 63.

168. See note 55, p. 15.

169. See note 55, p. 18.

170. *Zodiac*, vol. 18 (Great Britain).

171. See note 166, p. 58.

172. The Museum of Modern Art, New York, catalog of the exhibition "The New City," March 1967, p. 18.

173. See note 172, pp. 30–35.

174. Walter Hantschk, "Geschäfte in Etage und Passage," *Stadtbauwelt* 20, Dec. 23, 1968, pp. 1591–1595.

175. *Zodiac*, vol. 17 (USA Architecture).

176. *Zodiac*, vol. 18 (Great Britain).

177. See the design by Prof. Böhm for the University of Dortmund (*Bauwelt* 42, 1968, p. 1308), and the design by Prof. Ungers and J. Sawade for the museums at the zoo in West Berlin. In both designs the arcade is more a quotation than a necessity, let alone a matter of the relationship between spatial proportions and number of visitors.

178. Scene from the Beatles film "Yellow Submarine."

179. Walter Benjamin, *Illuminationen*, 1961, p. 242, note 6 to "Über einige Motive bei Baudelaire."

180. Préfecture de Police, Ordonnance concernant les Passages ouverts au public sur des Propriétés particulières, Article 2: "The owner or leaser of shops in arcades which are 2-3 meters wide or wider may in no case employ fixed or moveable displays, show windows, clocks, lanterns, pictures, or signs which project more than 16 centimeters over the building. None of the presently standing show windows which projects more than 16 centimeters may be repaired. All displays and moveable projections must be removed immediately."

181. See: E. Paneth, *Entwicklung der Reklame*, 1926, pp. 44f.

182. *Building News*, 49, 1885, p. 351.

183. Baedeker, *Le Nord-Ouest de la France*, 1898, city plan of Amiens.

184. *Handbuch der Architektur*, 2d ed., IV, 9, p. 66.

185. H. J. F. De Roy van Zuydewijn, *Amsterdamse Bouwkunst, 1815–1940*, undated, p. 131.

186. Baedeker, *Belgium and Holland*, 1885, city plan of Amsterdam.

187. H. Hymans, *Une famille d'artistes, Les Cluysenaar*, Brussels, 1928. In its list of works, the Cité is listed under 1840 as a project, and under 1842 as a construction. Hence, the plan for this arcade is later than the first plans for the Galeries Saint-Hubert.

188. G. v. Cauwenberg, *Gids voor Oud Antwerpen*, Antwerp, 1973, p. 333.

189. I am grateful to Herr Hagen of Athens for this information.

190. Baedeker, *Mittelmeer* (The Mediterranean), 1934, city plan of Athens.

191. Peter Blake, "Shopping Streets under Roofs of Glass," *Architectural Forum*, vol. 124, no. 1, 1966, pp. 68–75.

192. C. Boell, *Promenades historiques à travers la paroisse Notre Dame*, Autun, n.d., pp. 150–153.

193. The arcade at Autun has been an especially frequent subject of countless letters and souvenirs I have received. I still cannot understand why I did not notice it in the first place. I would like here to thank the observant readers who have traveled and gotten in touch with me since 1969.

194. Brian Little, *Bath Portrait*, Bristol, 1961; and *Official Guide Book*, 1966.

195. "The Corridor," *Bath Chronicle*, May 29, 1965, p. 20; also Sept. 20, 1962, p. 7; and Dec. 1, 1962, p. 7.

196. Wolzogen, *Aus Schinkels Nachlass*, part 3, p. 129.

197. See note 196, part 1, p. 156.

198. See note 196, part 2, p. 150.

199. See note 196, part 3, p. 27.

200. Illustrated in Schinkel, *Sammlung architektonischer Entwürfe*, 1841–1843, p. 108. Building history in Rave, *Schinkel*, Berlin II, 1948, pp. 48–62.

201. Dehio, *Friedrich Wilhelm IV of Prussia*, pp. 54f. The book also includes reproductions of hand sketches.

202. *Gostinny dvor* is the name for the great trading halls which existed in almost every Russian city. According to the eastern model the shops were located in the arcaded promenades of the ground floor while the offices and storerooms were in the upper stories. One of the largest is in Leningrad. It has been renovated and contains 250 shops.

203. The original designs are located in the Schinkel Museum at the Nationalgalerie in East Berlin, Blatt 3: perspectives, ground plans, sections (23b/52, 53, 54).

204. *Berlin und seine Bauten*, 1877, p. 318.

205. Plan collection of the Technische Universität Berlin, *Monats-Konkurrenz-Entwürfe des Architekten-Vereins Berlins*, vol. 6, p. 5.

206. See note 205, vol. 11, pp. 30f.

207. P. Wallé, *Eduard Knoblauch*, Berlin, 1902, p. 30.

208. Kunstbibliothek Berlin, not yet catalogued.

209. See note 205, inventory number 18031–18043.

210. Max Osborn, *Berlin's Rise. . .*, Berlin, 1929, p. 108f.

211. Ernst Friedel, *Die Deutsche Kaiserstadt Berlin*, Leipzig, 1882, p. 78 and fig., p. 20.

212. The polygonal corner motif with two small towers can be found in Schinkel's *Sammlung*, p. 106, in the design for alteration of the city hall in Berlin, dated 1817. There, however, it is developed more connectedly and cubically out of the entrance.

213. See note 210, pp. 109f. He discovered the ebullient praise of the Kaisergalerie to be typical of Germany and Berlin.

214. August Orth, *Bauliche Reorganisation der Stadt Berlin*, Berlin, 1875, p. 13.

215. Information from 204, pp. 314–317.

216. Hugo Licht, *Die Architektur Berlins*, Berlin, Wasmuth, 1877, pp. 35–38. There also additional facts on the sculptor.

217. Information from 204, pp. 314–317.

218. *Die Gartenlaube*, 1874, p. 781.

219. *Der Bär*, 1898, p. 155. This source also reprints the letter of thanks from the emperor for the invitation to the arcade opening.

220. Julius Faucher in *Vergleichende Culturbilder*, 1877, p. 35.

221. Hach, *Kunstgeschichtliche Wanderungen durch Berlin*, Berlin, 1897, p. 45.

222. Satyr, *Lebeweltnächte der Friedrichstadt*, *Grossstadtdokumente*, vol. 30, Berlin, undated, p. 39.

223. See note 219, p. 781.

224. See note 157, p. 69.

225. See note 219, p. 155.

226. See note 210, p. 120.

227. The arcade panopticon (Passage-Optikon) should not be confused with Castan's Panopticon, which was located in the arcade at an earlier date and moved in 1888 to the corner opposite the Passage-Panoptikon, Friedrichstrasse 165. Sources on this subject are (a) Jonas Geist, script for radio broadcast on NDR-SFB, 3. Programm, March 6, 1972; (b) P. Letkemann, "Das Berliner Panoptikon," in *Mitteilungen des Vereins für die Geschichte Berlins*, vol. 69, no. 11, July 1, 1973, pp. 319–326.

228. *Illustrierter Catalog des Passage-Panoptikums*, Berlin, undated, many editions.

229. (a) Franz Hessel, *Spazieren in Berlin*, 1929, pp. 264–267; (b) Karl Kraus, *Beim Wort genommen*, *Werke*, vol. 3, 1955, p. 428; (c) Siegfried Kracauer, *Das Ornament der Masse*, 1963, pp. 326–332; (d) Egon Erwin Kirsch, "Das Geheimkabinett des anatomischen Museums," *Der rasende Reporter*, Berlin, 1925, pp. 164–167.

230. Alfred Grenander, *Neue Werkkunst*, Berlin, 1930, proposal for the reconstruction of the Galerie unter den Linden.

231. *Deutsche Bauzeitung*, 1874, pp. 339f. This great exhibition, with twenty sections, included a photographic exhibition on the Kaisergalerie and a design by Ende & Böckmann for a bazaar on the Friedrichstrasse modeled on the Palais-Royal.

232. On the Lindengalerie: (a) *Deutsche Bauzeitung*, 1892, pp. 553–557; (b) *Berlin und seine Bauten*, 1896, part 2, pp. 505–507; (c) H. C. Hoffman, *Die Theaterbauten von Fellner und Helmer*, Munich, 1966, pp. 89f.

233. *Passage-Kaufhaus Friedrichstrassenpassage*, *Bauausführungen der Berliner Terrain und Bau Aktiengesellschaft*, monograph with no date or publisher. Besides the text and photographs it contains floor plans of all stories, sections, and facades, scales of 1:500 and 1:200.

234. Sources on the Friedrichstrassenpassage include (a) *Architektonische Rundschau*, 1909, no. 7; (b) *Armierter Beton*, 1909, nos. 3–6; (c) *Beton und Eisen*, 1911, nos. 1–17; (d) *Zeitschrift für Bauwesen*, nos. 1–2, pp. 324–331 and 476f; (e) *Berliner Architekturwelt*, 1909, pp. 324–331 and pp. 467–477; (f) *Handbuch für Eisenbetonbau*, Berlin, 1924, "Gebäude für bes. Zwecke I," pp. 142–146; (g) *Handbuch der Architektur*, III, 2, 4, 3d edition, pp. 446–449. The last two books deal in particular with the construction of the dome.

235. Process described in note 233.

236. See Willy Lesser, *Die baulichen und wirtschaftlichen Grundlagen der Geschäftsstadt Berlin*, 1915.

237. See note 236, p. 104.

238. See note 236, chapter 4, "Die Zwangsversteigerungen der Geschäftsgebäude."

239. In 234d, p. 36, one reads: "The conveyor mechanism is a unique innovation. Its purpose is to convey the merchandise as quickly as possible to the shipping department, from which goods can be forwarded to customers. The chutes mentioned earlier serve to carry the merchandise from the different floors to the conveyor belt in the cellar. These chutes, which are at six locations in the building, have a slide that varies in slope so that the openings will be in the appropriate places, namely, lined up under each other. The packages glide down this slide onto the electrically driven conveyor belt, which then carries them automatically down to the collection room under the dome. The belts, which come together in this room, dump the packages onto a slowly revolving table, around which men are seated waiting for packages from their assigned areas. Express packages or goods which are to be taken immediately are conveyed onto a different belt and are carried from there to the appropriate collection site."—This description offers a glimpse into the workings under the great rotunda, a system which certainly never functioned.

240. For a more detailed account, see E. G. Ermisch, and K. K. Weber, *Richard Ermisch*, Berlin, 1971, p. 64, and *Neue Bauwelt*, vol. 50, 1947, pp. 787ff. On the history of urban planning, see Frank Werner, *Stadtplanung Berlin*, part 1, 1900–1960, pp. 102ff.

241. This description from Martin Geiger, "Das nicht zentrische Zentrum Bern," *Werk*, no. 5, 1966, pp. 94–96.

242. Besides the Von Werth Passage Bern also contains the following arcades, which do not have glass roofs: the Marktpassage, Neuengassenpassage, Spitalgassenpassage.

243. *Birmingham Mail*, March 8, 1882; quoted in B. Fineberg, "The History and Design of

Notes

Shopping Arcades," manuscript, Regional College of Art Library, Manchester, 1953, p. 69.

244. On the Great Western Arcade: (a) *The Architect*, 1974, p. 157; (b) *The Builder*, vol. 33, 1875, p. 183; (c) *The Builder*, vol. 34, 1876, pp. 862, 1192, and 1194 (woodcut).

245. John Summerson, *Georgian London*, Harmondsworth, 1962, pp. 65f.

246. *The Architect*, vol. 25, 1881, p. 115, with all ground plans, sections and facades.

247. *The Builder*, vol. 41, 1881, p. 526.

248. To my knowledge, the Royal Arcade in Hyde and the Metropole Arcade in Melbourne are the only examples of this kind of arcade besides the Imperial Arcade in Birmingham.

249. *Building News*, vol. 46, 1884, p. 69.

250. *Building News*, vol. 43, 1882, p. 706; and vol. 45, 1883, p. 744.

251. The earliest arcade in Leeds (1878) is likewise built in the Gothic style and is still standing.

252. *The Builder*, vol. 47, 1884, p. 340.

253. The ten-page prospectus, "The City Arcades, Birmingham, Limited" can be found in the Reference Library, Birmingham (243102) L/P 47.14.

254. *The Builder*, vol. 73, 1897, pp. 486f; *The Birmingham Magazine*, vol. 1, no. 4, new series, 1904, pp. 116f (two reproductions).

255. Colored glazed terra cotta can also be found in the arcades in Leeds.

256. I found in the Reference Library of Birmingham the contemporary photograph of the interior of the City Arcades that is reproduced in the plates. It shows better than almost any other picture the congruence of architecture, decor, and costume, a congruence which can no longer be achieved.

257. *The Builder*, vol. 73, 1897, pp. 486f.

258. *Building News*, vol. 42, 1882, p. 123.

259. *L'Indicateur*, April 2, 1834, p. 3.

260. According to the concierge, this corner apartment on the Rue Ste. Cathérine was used by the SS during the occupation in World War II for interrogation and torture of the captured members of the resistance. Later it was the residence of the directors of the Communist Party in Bordeaux.

261. Merill Ferms, *Feuillets Bordelais* 2, "La Galerie Bordelaise."

262. See note 259, p. 3.

263. On the Bazar Bordelais: (a) Bernadau, *Le Viographie Bordelais*, 1844, p. 170; (b) *Nouveau Guide de l'Etrangers*, 1871, p. 84.

264. Desgraves, *Évocation du Vieux Bordeaux*, 1960, pp. 301f.

265. N. Pevsner, *Buildings of England: Hampshire*, 1967, pp. 132f.

266. See note 265.

267. *The Builder*, 1877, p. 937.

268. I am grateful to Mrs. Bruce of Bradford for this information.

269. Information from the Stadtarchiv Braunschweig.

270. *The Builder*, vol. 23, 1865, pp. 209f.

271. N. Pevsner, *Europäische Architektur*, Munich, 1957, fig. 170, Lincoln Cathedral, interior elevation.

272. On the arcades: *Arrowsmith's Dictionary of Bristol*, entry on arcades. On the architect Thomas Foster: (a) Walter Ison, *The Georgian Buildings of Bristol*, pp. 29–34; (b) H. Colvin, *Dictionary of British Architects*.

273. "Old Bristol," no. 47, *Western Daily Press*, March 14, 1930.

274. Reece Winstone, *Bristol, 1950–1953*, June 4, 1950.

275. (a) Henri Hymans, *Brüssel*, Leipzig, 1910; (b) Fritz Stahl, *Brüssel*, 1910; (c) Touring Club Royal de Belgique, *Guide Illustré de Bruxelles*, 1958.

276. See note 275b, pp. 199f.

277. Henri Beyaert, *Projet d'un Ensemble de Rues Destinées a Faciliter les Communications entre le Haut er le Bas de la Ville de Bruxelles*, Brussels, 1861.

278. City Archive, Brussels: Dossier Passage de la Monnaie, 16964. I am grateful to Mlle. Maertens, head archivist of the city of Brussels, and to her assistants for their great help.

279. See note 278.

280. Henri Hymans, *Une Famille d'Artistes, les Cluysenaars*, Brussels, 1928, p. 29.

281. Jean Pierre Cluysenaar came from a Tyrolean family named Klausener. He was born in 1811 in Kampen, Holland, and died in 1880 in Brussels. He moved to Brussels when he was six, studied at the Académie Royale des Beaux-Arts in Brussels, and became the student of the well-known architect T. J. Suys (1783–1861), builder of the great glass house in the Botanical Garden. He later studied under Percier and Fontaine. Besides countless private homes, châteaux, and city palaces, Cluysenaar also built the train stations on the line from Dendre to Waes, the Marché de la Madeleine, the conservatory in Brussels (1876–1877), the hospital for the blind in Brussels, the bath house in Bad Homburg, the church of Sainte-Devoté in Monte Carlo, and the arcades dealt with here. And this is only a part of his oeuvre. Cluysenaar was famous for the speed with which he worked, for staying within estimates, and for his wealth of ideas. He was architect and engineer in one.

282. See note 187.

283. J. P. Cluysenaar, *Plans et Description des Deux Galeries Couvertes a Construire à Bruxelles*, Brussels, Société Belge de Librairie, 1840, pp. 1–12 text, p. 13 appendixes ("Cahier des Charges"), pp. 19f "Explication du Plan." Plan of the arcade 1:500, facade, interior, and city plan with arcades marked in red.

284. *Les Cahiers Léopoldiens*, 9, série II, 1961, p. 88. It must have been on Mengoni's journey to Brussels and London in 1864.

285. See note 295, text 1.

286. Sources for this history, not cited individually: (a) *Les Cahiers Léopoldiens*, 9, série II, 1961, pp. 79–88, G. H. Dumont, "Comment Bruxelles fut dotée des Galeries Saint Hubert, les Premières en Importance de l'Occident"; (b) *Festschrift zum Centenaire des Galeries St. Hubert*, June 1947; (c) see note 280, pp. 19–50 on the Galeries St. Hubert, and pp. 92–96 on Cluysenaar; (d) Henri Hymans, *Bruxelles à travers les Âges* (Brussels Through the Ages), 3 volumes, Brussels, 1882–1884, vol. 3, pp. 267–275; (e) see note 275c, p. 99.

287. *Projet de Communication entre le Marché aux Herbes et la Montaigne aux Herbes Potagères à Bruxelles*; presented to the presiding council by Messieurs Ad. Hauman, Brugelman, Jan de mot, Baron de Wykersloot de Weerdesteyn, Brussels, January, 1838, pp. 1–12 text. Contains one facade and one city plan showing the site of the arcade.

288. City Archive of Brussels: folder with 12 plans (421.1–424 6/6) (44925). Volume with the financial statement of the Société and photographs. Drawings: (a) From 1838, facades, longitudinal sections, site plan; (b) from 1839, ground floor and first floor plans, 1:250; (c) from 1845, part of the drawings, floor plans, sections, facades (which already contain the Galerie des Princes), 1:100. Unfortunately a series of the drawings is missing, so that it was impossible to reproduce completely all of the stories.

289. Cahier des Charges (account books), contained in note 283.

290. Aimé de Saint Ferreol, *Les Proscrits Français en Belgique.*

291. See note 277.

292. The statues in the niches represent Belgium, Brabant, and the City of Brussels.

293. The statues in the staircase bays represent Flora, Pomona, Industry, Mercury. All of the statues are by Jacques.

294. See note 286d, vol. 3, pp. 275–278.

295. See note 286e.

296. See note 286c.

297. City Archive of Brussels, Dossier Travaux Publics, 940/1–3.

298. See note 297, 1964.

299. Documents on the construction of the Galerie du Commerce, in the City Archive of Brussels, Dossier Travaux Publics, 6681/21796; and documents of the firm Sarma, photocopies owned by the author.

300. See note 286e, p. 313.

301. Plans published in *Chronique des Travaux Publics*, June 27, 1880, no. 26, supplement.

302. City Archive of Brussels, Dossier Travaux Publics, 6139, 12 drawings at 1:100 and 1:50.

303. See note 286e, p. 313.

304. *Wiener Bauindustriezeitung*, vol. 2, p. 125/126, 180.

305. *Wiener Bauindustriezeitung*, vol. 1, p. 98.

306. *Die Architektur des 20. Jahrhunderts*, vol. 2, 1902, part 1, pp. 15–16, figs. 21–22.

307. I am grateful to Eva Bodnar of Budapest for this information.

308. Elisabeth Toth-Epstein, *Historische Enzyklopädie von Budapest*, Budapest, NP, 1974, p. 152.

309. *Revista Architectura*, January 1948, pp. 13–32, galleries in Buenos Aires.

310. Julio Cortazar, "L'autre Ciel" in *Tous les Feux le Feu*, Paris, 1970, pp. 169ff.

311. See note 297.

312. See note 774.

313. Dates of the following arcades are from Fineberg (see note 85).

314. *The Builder*, vol. 52, 1897, p. 250.

315. Information from the Schlossber-Museum in Karl-Marx-Stadt.

316. H. M. Mayer and R. C. Wade, *Chicago: Growth of a Metropolis*, Chicago, 1969, p. 189.

317. On the Cleveland Arcade: (a) Ada Louise Huxtable, "Cleveland Arcade, 1888–90," *Progressive Architecture*, Sept. 1956, pp. 139f. (b) Mary-Peale Schofield, "Cleveland Arcade," *Journal of the Society of Architectural Historians*, vol. 25, Dec. 1966, pp. 281–291. (c) Mary-Peale Schofield, "Cleveland Arcade," *Architectural Forum*, 1967(?), pp. 60–66. (d) Detailed material and drawings can be obtained from the Cleveland Arcade Company. However, I was unable to use them.

318. See note 317b, pp. 288–291, for biographies of the two architects. Eisenmann could have seen European arcades, since he studied in Germany in 1876–1878.

319. See note 317a.

320. The roof construction was published in: (a) *Engineering Record*, March 21 and 28, 1891, pp. 256f and 274–276; (b) *La Construction Moderne*, June 10, 1891, pp. 436–438.

321. See note 317b, p. 289, note 16.

322. The engineer K. J. Bollenbeck is presently writing a biography of Weyer. He published an article in the *Kölner Stadt-Rundschau* on the arcade (Dec. 14, 1963).

323. Catalog of the exhibition "Vom Dadamax bis zum Grüngürtel" on Cologne in the twenties, Artists' Union, 1975, p. 203.

324. Vogts, *Köln, Bauliche Entwicklung 1888–1927*, Cologne, 1927, p. 18.

325. I am grateful to the city curator Dr. H. Adenauer for the photocopies of these documents, which he made available to me. They include: (a) ground floor plan; scale is the Rhenish foot; date probably pre–1846; (b) ground floor plan; scale is the Prussian foot; dated August 1846; (c) cross section, no scale, probably belongs with (b); (d) longitudinal section and street perspective; scale, Rhenish foot; probably pre–1846; (e) facade facing Hohe Strasse; scale 1:50; photograph, 1939; (f) facade facing Brückenstrasse; scale 1:50; photograph, 1939.

326. Karl Josef Bollenbeck, "Der Kölner Stadtbaumeister Johann Peter Weyer," Dissertation, Technische Hochschule Aachen, 1969, vol. 1, pp. 147–152, and vol. 2, plans and photographs.

327. Baedeker, *Nord-Westdeutschland* (Northwest Germany), 1914, city plan of Cologne.

328. Ground plans and perspectives in *Handbuch der Architektur*, 4, 2, 2, 1923, pp. 154–158.

329. See note 328, 4, 2, 2, 1923, p. 114.

330. *Bauwerkzeitung*, vol. 31, 1899, p. 1449.

331. Drawing in: *Two Hundred Summers in a City, Edinburgh, 1767–1967*, exhibition catalog.

332. Johanna Schopenhauer, *Reise durch England und Schottland*, Stuttgart, 1965, p. 76.

333. See note 331.

334. *Edinburgh, An Architectural Guide*, The Edinburgh Architectural Association, 1964, building catalog.

335. For a more precise account, see A. J. Youngson, *The Making of Classical Edinburgh, 1750–1850*, Edinburgh, 1966, pp. 169–173.

336. See note 335, pp. 170f.

337. Archibald Elliot (1761–1823) had three sons who exhibited plans for Edinburgh buildings in the London Royal Academy between 1816 and 1820.

Notes

338. Floor plan and elevation reproduced in note 335, pp. 172f.

339. Quoted from note 335, p. 171.

340. *Building News*, vol. 30, 1876, p. 181.

341. Baedeker, *England*, 1906, site plan, Exeter.

342. N. Pevsner, *Buildings of England: South Devon*, 1952, p. 197.

343. Albert, *Rückblicke auf mein Leben im Jahre 1847*, Frankfurt, 1909, p. 30.

344. Eulogy for Daube in a Frankfurt newspaper.

345. *Frankfurt und seine Bauten* (Frankfurt and Its Buildings), 1886, pp. 297 and 337.

346. There are two small illustrations of the arcade in *Frankfurt und Umgebung*, 1908, p. 21.

347. Information from the prospectus and company files of the Main-Gaswerke AG.

348. Baedeker, *Schweiz* (Switzerland), 1913, city plan of Geneva.

349. The information is taken from the private notebooks of a deceased archivist. I was unable to confirm it. The material is kept in the Palazzo Rosso in Genoa.

350. Carroll Meeks, *Italian Architecture, 1750–1914*, New Haven, 1966, p. 292.

351. V. Fris, *Les Accroissements et les Transformations de la Superficie bâtie de Gand au XIXe Siècle*, Ghent, 1920, p. 19, p. 57.

352. I am grateful to Mr. Gomme of Stoke on Trent for all information and photographs. He is presently doing research on Glasgow's architecture.

353. I was able to study the voluminous town maps (on a surprisingly large scale of 1:500) in the British Museum. I would like to thank the staff there for their assistance.

354. Reproduced in *Glasgow at a Glance, an Architectural Handbook*, Glasgow, 1965, no. 42. Oddly enough, this guide does not mention the Argyle Arcade.

355. Quoted from an article in *Glasgow's Treasure Chest*, undated, pp. 66–72.

356. *Building News*, 32, 1874, p. 564.

357. *Führer durch Görlitz*, Verkehrsverein undated, p. 79, figure; p. 18, announcement.

358. A. J. Servaas von Rooijen, "De Nieuwe Passage te 's-Gravenhage," *Het Leeskabinet*, June 1885, pp. 164–173; also, "De Nieuwe Doorgang (Passage) te 's-Gravenhage," *Eigen Haard*, 1885, pp. 164f. With a reproduction of the design for the entrance on Buitenhof.

359. *Bouwkundig Weekblad*, March 21, 1885, pp. 69–72, article by the architects van Wijk and Wesstra, "De nieuwe Passage te 's-Gravenhage." It includes a longitudinal section, 1:200; a view of Buitenhof, 1:200; a ground plan, 1:333⅓. The ground plan and longitudinal section are dated November 1883.

360. I obtained the photocopies of a ground plan and the two perspectives on a scale of 1:200 (showing the structure as built) from the Gemeente Archief of The Hague, where documents on the construction of the arcade are stored. The ground plan is included in an exact redrawing.

361. See note 358.

362. See the site plans, which show the different versions.

363. The numbers in parentheses refer to fig. 193.

364. *The Builder*, vol. 89, 1910, p. 50.

365. *Försters Allgemeine Bauzeitung*, vol. 13, 1848, pp. 162–164; glass roof detail, p. 67; atlas, page 190, ground plan and sections.

366. On the urban context: (a) J. Faulwasser, *Der grosse Brand und der Wiederaufbau von Hamburg*, Hamburg, 1892; (b) Fritz Schuhmacher, *Wie das Kunstwerk Hamburg nach dem grossen Brand entstand*, Hamburg, 1920; (c) Günther Lange, *Alexis de Châteauneuf, ein Hamburger Baumeister*, Hamburg, 1965.

367. On the architect Averdieck: (a) *Hamburgisches Künstlerlexikon*, vol. 1, *Die bildenden Künstler*, Hamburg, 1854; and (b) Rump, *Lexikon der bildenden Künstler*, Hamburg, 1912, entries on Averdieck.

368. *Zeitschrift für Bauwesen*, 1855, p. 171, article on the Galerie Colbert in Paris and a critique of the bazaar in Hamburg. Also, quote from *Der Freischütz* (weekly Hamburg newspaper), no. 23, June 7, 1845, article on the opening.

369. Announcement of the opening of the hotel in *Privilegierte wöchentliche gemeinnützige Nachrichten für Hamburg*, no. 67, March 3, 1845.

370. *Der Freischütz*, no. 29, July 19, 1845, p. 230, and no. 20, July 26, 1845, p. 238.

371. See note 366a, p. 102.

372. *Hamburgs Vergangenheit und Gegenwart*, Hamburg, 1896, p. 170.

373. (a) W. Melhop, *Historische Topographie der Freien und Hansestadt Hamburg von 1880–1895*, Hamburg, 1895, p. 167; (b) *Hamburg und seine Bauten*, 1890, p. 681.

374. See note 366a, b.

375. Proposal by Wimmel and Châteauneuf, December 1842; permission from the authorities, March 1843.

376. See note 366c, "Alsterarkaden," p. 24.

377. See note 366c, figs. 17 and 18.

378. Quoted from 366c, p. 22.

379. "Die Georgspassage in Hannover," in *Baugewerks-Zeitung*, March 16, 1964, no. 22, pp. 273–275.

380. "Unter blinkender Glasglocke," *Hannoversche Allgemeine Zeitung*, Dec. 8, 1961.

381. "Die Passage," *Hannoversches Tageblatt*, no. 129, May 11, 1901.

382. I am grateful to Mr. Stuffins of the Public Library, Harrogate, for this information.

383. *Arkkitehti*, vol. 5, 1868, p. 33, fig. 23, 24. Figure 24 shows a reconstruction of the arcade with a glass roof.

384. David Lloyd, "Notes about Halifax and Hudderfield," Paper of the Victorian Society.

385. I am grateful to Mr. Aldridge of the Huddersfield Public Library for this information.

386. *Deutsche Bauzeitung*, April 10, 1897, pp. 181–182, 184; plans and view.

387. Illustrated in J. Gloag, *A History of Cast Iron in Architecture*, London, 1948, fig. 304.

388. Weinreb Ltd., Catalogue 20, no. 126: Walter Macfarlane & Co., *Illustrated Examples of Macfairlane's Architectural Iron Work*, Glasgow, undated.

389. I am grateful to the Staatliches Amt für Denkmalspflege, Karlsruhe, for the information on the history of the Kaiserpassage. Other sources: (a) *Chronik der Haupt- und Residenzstadt Karlsruhe für das Jahr 1887*, Karlsruhe, 1888; (b) Kick, *Neubauten Süddeutschlands*, vol. 1, 1894, fig. 24, portal.

390. Parts of the construction documents for the Kaisergalerie can be found in the Bauordnungsamt, Karlsruhe: drawings at 1:100 and reconstruction proposals from 1914–1951.

391. Sylvain Malfroy, "Un modèle de passage piétonnier: Les Galeries du Commerce à Lausanne," "Vom Abriss bedroht," in *Bauwelt*, no. 17, May 1978, pp. 660–664.

392. I am grateful to Mr. Craven of the Central Library, Leeds, for information on the individual arcades.

393. *Building News*, vol. 56, 1889, p. 87: a short article on the Queen's Arcade and reports on the projects for two other arcades on Kirkgate.

394. *Building News*, vol. 73, 1897, p. 904.

395. I am grateful to Mr. Collinson of the Archives Department, Leeds, for this information. He wrote to me about the company: "Subscribers being Charles Watson, Mary Ann Watson and Joseph Watson, Elizabeth Ann North and John North and Walter Battle. The Watsons were Leeds soap manufacturers, the Norths solicitors. They bought up a very large area in Central Leeds and developed it, building new streets and a large restaurant (the latter opened 1904). A theatre was built on part of the site but this appears to have been sold by the company at quite an early stage." The name of the architect is written in on the plan from 1902, but is otherwise nowhere to be found. I obtained the plan from the archive.

396. Derek Linstrum, *Historic Architecture of Leeds*, Newcastle upon Tyne, 1969, pp. 92–93.

397. *Building News*, vol. 77, 1900, p. 510.

398. Fineberg, list following text; see note 85.

399. See (a) "Auerbachs Keller 1530–1930," jubilee paper by Paul Daehne; (b) Dietrich, *Beiträge zur Entwicklung des bürgerlichen Wohnhauses in Sachsen*, Leipzig, 1904, p. 39, p. 75 (on walk-through houses); (c) Werner Starke, *Die Leipziger Messehäuser*, Leipzig, 1962. I am also grateful to Mr. Starke for information on some particular points.

400. For a more detailed account see note 399c, pp. 48–53.

401. See note 399a, pp. 12–18.

402. See note 399e, p. 73.

403. Werner Starke, personal communication.

404. G. Hallmann, *Leningrad*, Leipzig, 1967.

405. The large two-storied trade halls (*gostinny dvor*), built in 1785, are located opposite the arcade.

406. Erich Mendelsohn, *Russland-Europa-Amerika*, Berlin, 1929, pp. 86f.

407. Compare the photographs of the two arcades.

408. The dates given in the following account have been taken from a short section on the Passage Lemonnier in Théodore Gobert's book *Les Rues de Liège*.

409. Louis Désiré Lemonnier, who was born in Mons in 1800 and died in Brussels in 1862, was chief engineer with the administration of the national railways.

410. At the center of Covent Garden Market is a true arcade. The Leadenhall Market, which probably has the Milan arcade as its model, and many other London markets are built as arcades into the street system, the only difference being that the individual shops are open structures which are shuttered at night.

411. Quoted from Asa Briggs, *Victorian Cities*, London, 1963, pp. 332f.

412. *The Builder*, vol. 138, 1930, pp. 184f, "The Revival of the Arcade."

413. Additional literature: (a) *Survey of London*, vol. 29/30, pp. 240–249. Plates 38–39: facades, sections and ground plan of the Royal Opera Arcade. (b) B. Fineberg, "The History and Design of Shopping Arcades," thesis, Regional College of Art, Manchester, 1953, pp. 25–35: The Royal Opera Arcade, Pall Mall.

414. Detailed account in Terence Davis, *John Nash*, London, 1966, chapter 5: "London Transformed," pp. 63–82.

415. See note 413a, p. 241.

416. John Nash (1752–1835); see 414. George Stanley Repton (?–1858), son of Humphrey Repton, student of Auguste Pugin, assistant to Nash.

417. London, RIBA, Drawing Collection, K2/2 3/2/1; Repton: London Opera House, Haymarket. (1) ground plan; (2) front; (3) south front.

418. The following English arcades are modeled on the Royal Opera Arcade: Lowther Arcade, London; London Bridge Arcade, London; Piccadilly Arcade, London; Royal Arcade, Newcastle upon Tyne.

419. See 413a. Quotation from *Bohn's Pictorial Handbook of London*, 1854.

420. See 413a for the plans.

421. Quoted from Alison Adburgham, *Shops and Shopping, 1800–1914*, London, 1964, preceding title page.

422. The history of the Burlington Arcade is covered in detail in the *Survey of London*, vol. 21/22, pp. 430–434, figs. 50, 51, 74.

423. Quoted from *The Builder*, vol. 108, 1915, p. 352.

424. Samuel Ware, who wrote extensively on vaulting, spent the major part of his career doing building alterations for the Dukes of Devonshire and Northumberland. He was active until 1840.

425. Quoted from a copy of Ware's report, for which I am grateful to Mr. Hutchinson of the Royal Academy of Arts.

426. The drawings include (a) site plan (reproduced in the plates); (b) drawing with ground plans, perspectives, and sections; (c) longitudinal section through the intershops; (d) entrance facade, Piccadilly (arches). In *Survey of London* (see note 422) the plans are said to date from 1815 (see p. 433).

427. See note 422, p. 430 for more precise figures.

428. Quoted from note 422, p. 430.

429. See note 422, p. 430.

430. Henry Mayhew, *London Labour and the London Poor*, 1862, vol. 4, pp. 217–222, quoted in note 422, p. 431.

Notes

431. *The Architectural Review,* July 1931, p. 32.

432. *The Builder,* September 1954, pp. 450–452; detailed account with plans of this last phase of the Burlington Arcade.

433. See note 422, p. 432.

434. See note 422, p. 432.

435. The stairs have for the most part been altered. In shop no. 70 evidently one can still find an original staircase with a mahagony bannister around an iron pillar.

436. There are many prints of the Burlington Arcade, including some by Sheppard.

437. The facades are shown in note 426b.

438. See note 426d and note 422, fig. 74a.

439. See note 422, fig. 74b, c, d.

440. Appendix 23 of *Fifth Report of the Commissioners of His Majesty's Woods, Forests, and Land Revenue,* 1826, scale 1:1000.

441. Nash is named as the architect in *Survey of London,* vol. 28, p. 125.

442. Terence Davis, *John Nash,* London, 1966, p. 74.

443. Among others, Robert Smirke, Decimus Burton, Witherden Young.

444. See note 419, p. 101.

445. "Plan Showing the Arcade and New Streets at the West End of the Strand and Improvements at Charing Cross," William Herbert, 1830. British Museum, Grace Collection, XVII, Views 33.

446. RIBA Drawing Collection, Lowther Arcade, 1902, John. Mac. Vicar Anderson, Arc III 457–464. The collection also includes a drawing by David Mocatta. In pink wash, it is dated 1839 and includes a longitudinal section, ground plan, cross section, and facade.

447. On the construction history: (a) *Survey of London,* vol. 28, part 2, p. 125; (b) *Old and New London,* 1873–1878, vol. 3, p. 132; (c) E. B. Chancellor, *Annals of the Strand,* London, 1912, pp. 40f.

448. The design is attributed to Young and the execution to Herbert.

449. John Timbs, *Curiosities of London,* London, 1885, p. 20.

450. *Illustrated London News,* 1870, Christmas. Quoted from Fineberg (see note 413b).

451. A painting from the Victorian period showing the interior of the arcade with a toy market is reproduced in Leslie Daiken, *Children's Toys throughout the Ages,* London, 1953, p. 163.

452. Reginald Colby, "Shopping off the City Streets," *Country Life,* Nov. 1964, p. 1346.

453. On the tearing down of the Lowther Arcade: *The Builder,* vol. 80, 1901, p. 552.

454. John Tallis, *London Public Streets,* London, 1850(?), no. 81, Lowther Arcade.

455. British Museum, Grace Collection, 3495 (43), Plan of the Proposed City of London Arcade.

456. *Civil Engineer and Architects Journal,* vol. 7, 1844, pp. 305, 306, New Exeter Change.

457. *The Builder,* vol. 108, 1915, p. 352.

458. Illustration in *Illustrated London News,* 1844.

459. *The Builder,* Dec. 15, 1855, pp. 603f.

460. "A Railway Arcade," *Civil Engineer and Architects Journal,* vol. 8, 1950, p. 368.

461. Harold P. Clunn, *The Face of London,* p. 340.

462. *Old and New London,* 1876, vol. 4, p. 487.

463. W. and A. Moseley were the architects of the 1860 Westminster Palace Hotel on Victoria Street. With its 400 rooms, it was the first great luxury hotel in London.

464. Metropolitan Communications, Minutes of evidence taken before Select Committee, Report, 1855, pp. 52–57, plan V–VIII.

465. See note 464, p. 52, question 420.

466. The works of Sir Joseph Paxton (1803–1865) include the Great Stove in Chatsworth (1836–1840); the Crystal Palace, Hyde Park, London (1850–1851); design of the Crystal Palace, New York (1851); Crystal Palace, Sydenham (1852–1856); project for the Great Victorian Way (1855).

467. Metropolitan Communications, Report 1855, pp. 78–96, Plan XV, Victorian Way.

468. A cross section of the Great Victorian Way, drawn by Paxton in 1855, is owned by G. I. Larkin, Esq., London. Mentioned in the exhibition catalog *Paxton,* 1965, Victorian Society.

469. See G. F. Chadwick, *The Works of Sir J. Paxton,* London, 1961, pp. 208–212.

470. *Civil Engineer and Architects Journal,* vol. 18, 1855, p. 247, Paxton Arcade.

471. *Survey of London,* vol. 32, pp. 454f.

472. *The Builder,* vol. 22, 1864, pp. 132f.

473. *Survey of London,* vol. 31/32, p. 431.

474. See note 452, pp. 1346–1352.

475. See the two prints in *Modern London, 1887: The World's Metropolis, Historical, Statistical, Biographical Business Man and Commercial Interests,* p. 56, Royal Arcade.

476. *The Builder,* vol. 138, 1930, p. 184.

477. For a more detailed account see note 412.

478. *Building News,* 96, 1909, p. 753, ground plan. A number of designs for the arcade, which were awarded prizes by the RIBA, are also published in the same volume.

479. *Survey of London,* vol. 29–30, p. 265, Piccadilly Arcade.

480. Mentioned in note 476.

481. The other arcades are the Galerie Bordelaise in Bordeaux and the Passage Pommeraye in Nantes.

482. All dates are from (a) Louis Maynard, *Dictionnaire de Lyonnaiseries,* 1932; (b) Ad. Vachet, *A travers les Rues de Lyon,* Lyon, 1902, p. 43.

483. Vincent Farges, born in Givors, 1788, died in Lyon, 1847. In 1828, together with Falconnet, he built the Théâtre Provisoire, Place de Terreaux; in 1830 he began the construction of the Rue de la Préfecture in Lyon.

484. See note 482a.

485. See note 482a, entry on Passage de l'Hôtel Dieu.

486. See note 482b, p. 347.

487. I am grateful to Mrs. Mary Lemmon of the Local History Library and Mr. Fineberg,

whom I visited in Manchester, for the most important information and pictures.

488. See note 413b, pp. 69f.

489. *The Builder,* 1871, pp. 625–627; the ground plan is taken from the article.

490. *The British Architect and Northern Engineer,* Sept. 22, 1876, p. 189.

491. *The Builder,* July 25, 1885, pp. 136f.

492. *The Architect,* April 10, 1857, p. 216, and November 1878, p. 284.

493. *Manchester City News,* March 26, 1927.

494. *Manchester City News,* Dec. 30, 1899.

495. I am grateful to Arthur Gibbon, President of the Manchester Society of Architects, for the negative of the plans.

496. Mrs. Mary Lemmon provided me with the elevation photographs.

497. The site plan and all facts on the arcades in Melbourne are taken from: Janet Garside and Deborah White, "Arcades of Melbourne," in *Australia Architecture,* June 1963, pp. 80–86.

498. Information on the development of Melbourne is from Asa Briggs, *Victorian Cities,* London, 1963, Chapter VII.

499. Quoted from note 498, p. 96.

500. Galleria de Cristoforis in Milano del Architetto Andrea Pizzala, Milan, 1832, 6 leaves: (a) title page; (b) acknowledgments by Pizzala; (c) longitudinal section and ground plan; (d) façade of the Galleria; (e) details of the capitals, doors, etc.; (f) interior, lithograph.

501. See Text 1.

502. Information from Luigi Tatti, *Milano e il suo territorio,* Milan, 1844, p. 420.

503. See note 502.

504. Giulio Ferrario, *Memorie per servire alla storia dell'architettura Milanese,* Milan, 1843, p. 142.

505. P. Degen, *Descrizione accurata e critica della Galleria de Cristoforis,* Milan, 1832; citation from Gianni Mezzanotte, "Edilizia e politica," *Casabella* 338, July 1969, pp. 42–53.

506. The most important sources on the history of the Galleria Vittorio Emanuele II are (a) G. Barigazzi, "Cento Anni in Galleria," Milan, 1957, city *Festschrift* for the centennial of the arcade; (b) P. J. J. V. Smyth, "The Galleria Vittorio Emanuele II, Milano," dissertation for the Diplom in Architecture, Cambridge University, 1963; (c) Günther Bandmann, "Die Galleria Vittorio Emanuele II in Mailand," *Zeitschrift für Kunstgeschichte,* vol. 29, no. 2, L966, pp. 89–110; (d) Ferdinando Reggiori, "Milano 1800–1943," Milan, 1947, pp. 109f; (e) "Milano tecnica dal 1859–84," Milan, 1885, pp. 195–220; (f) G. Guilini, "La Piazza del Duomo di Milano," undated, pp. 100–126; (g) G. Rici, *La Vita e le opere dell'architetto Giuseppe Mengoni,* Bologna, 1930; (h) Commune di Milano, *Annuario-Storico-Statistico, 1919* (City of Milan, Historical and Statistical Yearbook), Milan, 1921, pp. xxii–xxxvii.

507. See *The Builder,* vol. 10, May 1856, pp. 264–265.

508. This expansion of the square in front of the Palazzo Reale led to schematic comparisons with the Piazza S. Marco and to the idea of building a similar campanile. See note 491a, p. 146.

509. See note 506a, p. 22; 506b, p. 85, fig. 4; 506h, p. xxvi.

510. See note 506a, p. 22; 506h, p. xxviii.

511. See note 506a, p. 22; 506h, pp. xxvii–xxviii.

512. See note 506a, p. 34.

513. See note 506a, p. 35.

514. (a) See note 506a, p. 27.; (b) Milan, Raccolta delle Stampe A. Bertarelli (Collection of Prints, A. Bertarelli), leaf 2.

515. See note 506a, p. 39.

516. See note 506a, p. 40.

517. See note 514a, OP, Q, 38.

518. See note 506a, p. 43; plan of the commission: note 514b, PV.8–68.

519. See note 506a, p. 43.

520. See note 506a, p. 43.

521. Giuseppe Mengoni, 1829–1877. For his biography see note 506g; autobiographical account in 506a, pp. 10–13.

522. See note 506a, p. 44.

523. Giuseppe Mengoni: "Progetto della Nuova Piazza del Duomo di Milano e della Via Vittorio Emanuele, fatto per Commissione des Consiglio Communale dall'Ingegnere Architetto Giuseppe Mengoni di Bologna." (Project for the new Piazza del Duomo in Milan and for the Via Vittorio Emanuele, made on commission from the Consiglio Communale by the Engineer-Architect G. Mengoni), Milan, 1863, 10 pages with 1 plan. I obtained a photocopy from the Biblioteca Nazionale, Brindisi.

524. See note 506a, p. 586, note 23.

525. See note 506a, pp. 86 and 92f. Bandmann makes particular reference to the Palazzo del Podestà in Bologna, located at what was the intersection of *cardo* and *decumanus* at the ancient city center.

526. Raccolta delle Stampe A Bertarelli, Castello Sforzesco (urban history collection).

527. D. Joseph, *Geschichte der Architektur Italiens* (History of Italian Architecture), Leipzig, 1907, p. 442.

528. See note 506c, p. 89.

529. See note 506a, p. 54.

530. *The Builder,* vol. 26, 1868, pp. 297, 493.

531. *Catalogue Officiel des Collections du Conservatoire National des Arts et Métiers,* Paris, 1910; 13571–1837, Combles en fer du Passage Victor-Emanuel, à Milan, construits par M. Joret, Montataire (5 plates). The Galleria also attracted international news coverage. Even during its construction, many German-speaking countries reported on its progress. See, for example, *Leipziger Illustrierte Zeitung,* no. 1135 (April 1, 1865), pp. 211–212, and no. 1277 (Dec. 1, 1867), pp. 432–434.

532. See note 506g, p. 41, letters from London and Paris.

533. See note 506a, pp. 28f.

534. Raccolta delle Stampe A. Bertarelli, Albo G 107, H. Heyland.

535. See note 506a, p. 73.

536. See note 506c, p. 82.

537. See note 506a, p. 87.

538. See note 506g, p. 73.

539. *The Architectural Review,* vol. 140, Nov. 1966, pp. 373–375.

Notes

540. Bernard Rudofsky, *Streets for People,* New York, 1969, pp. 86–96; Mark Twain, *A Tramp Abroad,* 1880; Ernest Hemingway, *A Farewell to Arms,* 1929.

541. See note 506a, p. 25; the original drawings of the triumphal arch are in the Archivio Civico of Milan, number 285; the Raccolta delle Stampe A. Bertarelli, vol. AA 406, contains the estimates and details. I was unable to see the plans in the Archivio Storico of the Castello Sforzesco, since they had been loaned out for the centennial. I found the ground plan and elevation in the Milan Officio Tecnico del Commune. I am grateful to Ingegnere Gambetta for the copy.

542. *Handbuch der Architektur,* II, 2, 5, pp. 658–660.

543. See note 506c, p. 82.

544. The statues depicted Giovanni Battista Vico, Volta, Canzone da Corte, Giovanni da Procida, C. Beccaria, Vincenzo Monti, Ferruccio, Michelangelo, Dante, Raphael, Savonarola, Foscolo, Marco Polo, Machiavelli, Capponi Romagnosi, Cozzadini, Christopher Columbus, Galeazzo Visconti, Vittor Pisoni, Fillbesto Cavour, Arnaldo di Brescia. They were probably destroyed by bombing.

545. See note 542, p. 344.

546. Theodor Fontane, *Aufsätze zür bildenden Kunst,* part 2, Munich, 1970, p. 82.

547. Bunin, *Geschichte des Russischen Städtebaues* (History of Russian City Planning), Berlin, 1961, p. 139.

548. See note 547, p. 153; see plate in *Das XIX. Jahrhundert in Wort und Bild,* vol. 1, pp. 328–329.

549. The ground plan and information for the following section are from *Centralblatt der Bauverwaltung,* Sept. 14, 1895, pp. 396f.; 1887, p. 361; 1889, p. 8.

550. Aleksandr Nikanorovitch Pomerantsev (1849–1918) studied at the St. Petersburg Academy. In 1894, after the construction of the Upper Trade Halls, he became a professor in St. Petersburg.

551. For information on its present condition, see (a) *Die Welt,* Nov. 29, 1966; (b) *Merian,* Moscow, 1967.

552. Shokov was one of the first engineers to build suspension structures. He also built a radio tower in Moscow and, with the architect Melnikov, a garage.

553. Today the old city is traversed by numerous attached arcades. See the chapter on "The Arcade as Project and Utopia."

554. M. Hauptmann and H. Karlinger, *München,* Munich, 1922, p. 71.

555. Stadtarchiv, Munich, documents on Kaufingerstrasse 9, Signatur Lokalbaukommission no. 906 and 10, 079.

556. (a) A. Pieyre de Mandiargues, *Le Musée Noir,* Paris, 1946, pp. 81–104, Le Passage Pommeraye; (b) Marcel Schneider, *Aux Couleurs de la Nuit,* A. Michel, Paris, 1955, pp. 207–220, "Le Coeur-Mystère."

557. The Passage Pommeraye is a focus of the Jacques Demy film "The Umbrellas of Cherbourg."

558. See note 556a. Excerpts from the first part of the story that relate directly to the arcade are reprinted here with the texts.

559. Information on the history of the arcade is taken from (a) *Société Archéologique et Historique, Nantes 1943,* 1945, pp. 66–69, Le Passage Pommeraye; (b) *Bulletin de la Vie Artistique Nantaise,* 2d trimester 1943, pp. 2–3, Le Centenaire de l'Ouverture du Passage Pommeraye, 1843–1943.

560. Quoted from 559a.

561. Planat, *Encyclopédie de l'Architecture et de la Construction,* Paris, 1888–1892, vol. 1–6, entry on "Passages," including a small woodcut of the Passage Pommeraye.

562. The Galerie Vivienne was published by Thiollet in 1840.

563. The medallions depict Abélard, Rabelais, Cassard, Du Guesclin, Olivier de Caisson, and others.

564. The ironwork was produced by the Vorus & Lotz workshop. See note 559b.

565. Arnaldo Venditti, *Architettura Neoclassica a Napoli,* fig. 43.

566. See note 565, n. 21.

567. *Bolletino del Collegio degli Ingegneri ed Architetti in Napoli,* Sept. 1, 1885, p. 130.

568. Illustrations in note 567, pp. 129–133, and in Giuseppe Russo, *Il Risanamento e l'Ampliamento della Città di Napoli,* figs. 294–296.

569. See note 567 and note 568, figs. 296, 298 (model).

570. See note 569.

571. See note 567.

572. See (a) Malaparte, *Die Haut;* (b) Robles, *Der Vesuv;* (c) John Horne Burns, *The Gallery,* 1947.

573. See note 527, pp. 448–449.

574. H. R. Hitchcock, *Architecture: Nineteenth and Twentieth Centuries,* 1958, pp. 119–120.

575. Quoted from Ross, *Architectural and Picturesque Views in Newcastle upon Tyne,* 1841, p. 64.

576. John Dobson, 1787–1865, studied first under Boniface Moss and then under the watercolor painter John Vorley. He traveled as a young man through England and France. He went to London on the urging of Sydney Smirke. In 1810 he settled in the north, in Newcastle, as one of the first architects. See Margret Jane Dobson, *Memoir of John Dobson,* London, 1885, which includes as number 119 the drawing of the Royal Arcade which is dated: "designed 1826."

577. (a) *The Journal of the Society of Architectural Historians of Great Britain,* vol. 2, 1959, pp. 81–93: The Royal Arcade. Including photographs; (b) Wilkers and Gordon Dodds, *Tyneside Classical,* London, 1964, pp. 45–50, Royal Arcade.

578. Richard Turley, "Early Victorian City Planning, The Work of John Dobson and Richard Grainger at Newcastle," *Architectural Review,* May 1946, pp. 141–146.

579. See note 578.

580. *Newcastle Journal,* May 19, 1832; quoted from note 577b.

581. *The Penny Magazine of the Society for the Diffusion of Useful Knowledge,* April 11, 1840. Quoted from note 577a.

582. B. Fineberg, "The History and Design of Shopping Arcades," thesis, Regional College of Art, Manchester, 1953, p. 48.

583. This project was designed by Matthew, Johnson, Marshall and Partners, who also built the New Zealand House next to the Royal Opera Arcade in London. Illustrated in *The Victorian Society Annual Report*, 1966, pp. 10–12.

584. *The Builder*, 1906, p. 327.

585. Robert Alexander, "The Arcade in Providence," *Journal of the Society of Architectural Historians*, 1953, nos. 2–3, p. 13.

586. "Young Consuela was . . . in the arcade at Times Square before she became converted to nonviolence. . . ." Ed Sanders, "The Gobble Gang Poem," *Underground Poems*, Darmstadt, 1968, p. 80.

587. Nathan Silver, *Lost New York*, 1971, pp. 178–179.

588. I am grateful to Jürgen Sawade of Berlin for the photograph and information.

589. From the overwhelming amount of literature on this topic I will mention only one title: H. Specker, *Paris, Städtebau von der Renaissance bis zur Neuzeit*, Munich, 1964.

590. The first uniform structure in Paris was the reconstruction of the Pont Notre Dame by the Italian architect Fra Giocondo.

591. P. Patte, *Monuments Érigés en France à la Gloire de Louis XV*, Paris, 1765.

592. Paris had in 1807, for example: 1109 streets, 120 culs-de-sac, 13 *enclos*, 40 *cours*, 82 *passages,* 75 squares.

593. Victor Louis, 1731–1800, studied under Loriot; architect of the Théâtre de Bordeaux; court architect of Louis Philippe of Orléans after 1780; in 1781–1786 he built the colonnades of the Jardin du Palais Royal, in 1782–1783 the Salle de Beaujolais (today the Théâtre du Palais Royal), and 1787–1790 the Théâtre Français (damaged by fire in 1900, today remodeled).

594. See note 593.

595. Begun in 1801 from the plans of the architects Percier and Fontaine. Since the state was the owner of the property it could prescribe the form of the facades down to the slightest detail and determine the use of the individual buildings. The three-meter-wide arcaded walk became, after the Palais Royal, the favorite Parisian promenade.

596. The population of Paris was 500,000 in 1800, 700,000 in 1817, 900,000 in 1836, and 1,000,000 in 1940.

597. For example, the Passage des Panoramas.

598. Passage Choiseul, Galerie Vivienne, Passage Véro-Dodat.

599. Passage Jouffroy, Passage Verdeau.

600. Passage Choiseul, Passage des Panoramas, Passage de l'Opéra.

601. Passage du Caire, Passage du Ponceau, and others.

602. See the introductory text, section on the bazaar.

603. The first large department store building followed the first small Bon Marché in 1862–1863.

604. I will cite here the most recent literature on the Paris arcades by date of publication: (a) *Architectures, Paris, 1848–1914*, catalog, 1972, Arcades, pp. 15–16; (b) Dominique Desanti, "Les Refuges du Piéton de Paris," *Le Monde*, October 9, 1973; (c) H. G. Puttnies, "Pariser Passagen," *Frankfurter Allgemeine Zeitung*, January 25, 1975; (d) Marc Gaillard, "Rues Piétonnières à Paris," in "Les Passages," *Renovation*, no. 2, February/March, 1975, pp. 23–32; (e) "Les Passages de Paris," *L'Immédiate*, 5, 1975, photo by Lazarevsky; (f) "Les Passages Couverts dans Paris," *Paris Project*, nos. 15 and 16, 1976, pp. 110–151. Detailed analysis by Laura Wodka of the individual arcades and their occupational uses in *Atelier Parisien d'Urbanisme* (APU); (g) Yvette Gloague, "Les Passages Couverts à Paris, Les Effets Réciproques du Parcellaire et de la Typologie," typescript, undated, Paris (dissertation). The "Physiologies" Walter Benjamin describes in his essay "The Flaneur" (see "Literature on the Arcade") may be found in chapter 13, "Les quais et les Passages," and "Paris ou le Cent-et-un," vol. 11 of Les Passages de Paris, 12 vols., Stuttgart, 1831.

605. On the Palais-Royal, see (a) Victor Champier and G. Roger, *Le Palais-Royal*, vols. 1–2, Paris, 1900; (b) *Dictionnaire de Paris*, Larousse, 1964, entry on the Palais-Royal; (c) Pierre Fontaine, *Palais-Royal*, volume in the series Domaines de la Couronne, Paris, 1829.

606. See note 593.

607. The Duke of Chartres took the name Philippe-Egalité in 1787. It did not protect him, however, from the guillotine, where he met his death on Nov. 6, 1793.

608. See the figure in note 605b.

609. See note 608.

610. The date of construction cannot be fixed without doubt. Construction accounts exist for the years 1786–1788.

611. See note 608.

612. Bibliothèque Nationale, Cabinet d'Estampes, Va 231 c IV, I.Arr., 2 drawings (ground plan, view of the roof, section), color wash, unsigned; it is doubtful that these are design sketches.

613. In 1795 there were 15 restaurants, 20 cafes, and 18 gambling tables in the Palais Royal. The prostitutes lived in the apartments above the shops, from which they descended after eight o'clock in the evening to claim their territories. There were three spatially distinct classes among the prostitutes of the Palais Royal: (a) *demi castor*, whose domain was the *alleés* and the Galeries de Bois; (b) *castor*, who occupied the stone galleries; (c) *castor fine*, who resided on the terrace of the Café du Caveau. One could purchase catalogs with pictures of all the ladies and brief summaries of their talents, types, and so on. Today these are rarities of the first order.

614. On the habitués of the Palais Royal, see 599a.

615. The expression was coined by Loweet.

616. Bibliothèque Nationale, Cabinet d'Estampes, Va 419j, Paris, Seine, Nr.7/2.Arr. I would like to thank Madame Villa, print curator, for her assistance during my investigations in Paris.

617. Marchant, *Le Conducteur de l'Etranger à Paris*, Paris, 1815, p. 295.

618. Bildarchiv Marburg, 181 038.

619. See note 617, pp. 185–186.

620. Félix Pigeroy, *Les Monuments de Paris au XIX. Siècle*, Paris, 1849, p. 654.

Notes

621. The Passage du Caire was originally called the Passage de la Foire-du-Caire. Durand published his arcade-like designs under the heading "foire" as well. See the part of the introduction related to fairs.

622. See Eduard Kolloff, *Paris, ein Reisenbuch*, 1849, p. 117.

623. L. Hautecoeur, *Histoire de l'Architecture Classique en France*, Paris, 1952–1957, vol. 6, pp. 285–286.

624. C. Bandmann, "Das Exotische in der europäischen Kunst," in *Der Mensch und die Künste, Festschrift* for Heinrich Lützeler on his sixtieth birthday, 1962, pp. 327–354.

625. In his *Dictionnaire des Rues de Paris*, Hillairet says of this glass roof: ". . . and then the rain, for the majority of them were glassed over under the Second Empire." This comment could lead to the assumption that the arcade was covered only later. However, the structural description of its cross section speaks against this conclusion. Furthermore, Möller comments on page 33 of his 1823 *Paris und seine Bewohner*, "I must mention a unique kind of street, namely the so-called arcade. It is a passageway which contains a series of markets. Some arcades have the most splendid shops after the Palais Royal. One of these is the Passage Delorme, between the Rue St. Honoré and the Rue de Rivoli. It was built not long ago by Herr Delorme. It is lighted from above like the Passage du Caire, running between the square of the same name and the Rue St. Denis. Along with the street and the square of the same name it was built in 1789 on the former site of the cloister and garden of the Filles-Dieu. The Passage des Panoramas was built between the Rue St. Marc and the Boulevard Montmartre."

626. On the history of the Passage des Panoramas: (a) Dumolin, "Les origines du Passage des Panoramas," Commission de Vieux Paris, 1929, pp. 83–86; (b) Gustave Pessard, *Nouveau Dictionnaire Historique de Paris*, Paris, 1904, entry on Passage des Panoramas; (c) *Dictionnaire de Paris*, Paris, 1904, pp. 401–403, entry on *Passages*, including a color reproduction of the Carnavalet painting. All these texts have different information, varying dates, etc. Mistakes are passed along from one source to another. The name of the architect cannot be ascertained.

627. On panoramas: (a) *Handbuch der Architektur*, 3d edition, IV/4/2, section 7, pp. 272–288, "Panoramen"; (b) Dolf Sternberger, *Panorama oder Ansichten zum 19. Jahrhundert*, 3d edition, 1955, n. 1, pp. 215–218.

628. See the engraving by Opitz from 1814 and the engraving of the ground plan of the Théâtre des Variétés with a partial ground plan of the arcade.

629. Reproduced in 626c.

630. The relationship can be seen not only in the form of the glass roof, but also in the spatial proportions and the circumstances of construction.

631. Bibliothèque Nationale, Cabinet d'Estampes, Collection topographique, v a 239f, leaf 1.

632. See note 622, p. 118.

633. (a) Montigny, *Le Provincial à Paris*, 2d edition, 1825, vol. 1, chapter 19, pp. 158–172; (b) Emile Zola, *Nana*, trans. F. J. Vizetelly, New York, The Heritage Press, 1948, p. 176.

634. Thiollet and Roux, *Nouveau recueil du menuiserie et décorations intérieures et extérieures*, Paris, 1837, plates 40, 50.

635. J. F. Wittkop, *Der Boulevard*, Zurich-Stuttgart, 1965, chapter on arcades, pp. 115–119. Wittkop refers to the short work by Georges Cain, "Le Passage des Panoramas où fût fondée la Maison Susse Frères," Paris, 1910. This four-page paper, which appeared as a result of the purchase of the painting in the Carnavalet (mentioned above), provides a detailed history of the shop owned by the Susse family.

636. August Lewald, *Gesammelte Schriften*, Leipzig, 1844, vol. 6, letter 57, winter 1831–1832.

637. See note 622, pp. 115–116.

638. Gustave Pessard, *Nouveau Dictionnaire Historique de Paris*, Paris, 1904, entry on the Passage Delorme.

639. Lanzac de Laborie, *Paris sous Napoléon*, Paris, 1905, vol. 2, pp. 97–98.

640. Emmanuel de Montcorin, "Paris qui s'en va La Passage Delorme," poem, *La Revue d'Europe et des Colonies*, 1906.

641. "Les Passages Couvertes," Commission de Vieux Paris, 1916, pp. 270–273.

642. Simon, *La Vie Parisienne aux XIX. Siècle*, Paris, 1900–1901, 3 vols., under the year 1811.

643. Hillairet, *Dictionnaire Historique des Rues de Paris*, 1965, entry on Montesquieu.

644. Bibliothèque Nationale, Cabinet d'Estampes, Va 419j, Nr.6, I.Arr. (floor plans for all stories).

645. See Henri Besmard, *L'Industrie du Gaz a Paris depuis Ses Origines*, Paris, 1942, p. 17.

646. Louis Aragon, *Le Paysan de Paris*, Paris, 1926, pp. 17–134, chapter on Le Passage de l'Opéra.

647. Double arcades: Galeries de Bois, Paris; Passage Montesquieu, Paris; Passage de l'Opéra, Paris; Philadelphia Arcade, Philadelphia; GUM and Petrovsky Arcade, Moscow.

648. On the history of the Paris opera see note 605b, entry on the Opéra.

649. François Debret (1777–1850), student of Percier and Fontaine, who built the Ecole des Beaux-Arts and the Théâtre des Nouveautés in Paris.

650. See note 638, entry on Passage de l'Opéra.

651. See note 641.

652. Mr. Fenner was kind enough to place the photograph at my disposal.

653. See note 605b, p. 402.

654. Bibliothèque Historique de la Ville de Paris, 1384, *Le Guide des Acheteurs ou Almanach des Passages de l'Opéra*, Paris, 1826.

655. See note 622, p. 118.

656. On Blanqui see: Auguste Blanqui, *Instruktionen für den Aufstand*, Frankfurt, 1968, pp. 28–29.

657. See note 635, p. 118. I am grateful to the author Wittkop for this valuable reference.

658. See note 605b, p. 403.

659. Quoted from Louis Aragon, *Nightwalker (Le Paysan de Paris)*, trans. Frederick Brown, Englewood Cliffs, N.J., Prentice-Hall, 1970.

660. Pessard and the Commission de Vieux Paris give 1825 as the date of construction, whereas the Larousse *Dictionnaire de Paris* states that it was opened in 1823.

661. Emile Zola, *Thérèse Raquin*, trans. Leonard Tancock, Harmondsworth, Penguin Books, 1962, pp. 31–33.

662. See note 638.

663. I am grateful to Mr. Fenner for the reference.

664. See note 643.

665. See note 638.

666. See note 622, p. 118.

667. Thiollet, *Choix de Maisons, Edifices et Monuments Publics de Paris et de ses Environs*, 3 vols., Paris, 1829. Volume 3 contains, as figures 49–52, a ground plan of the Galerie Colbert and Galerie Vivienne; as figures 53–54, Galerie Vivienne, 3 longitudinal sections; as figures 57–58, Galerie Vivienne and Galerie Colbert, portals and facades, all accompanied by explanations.

668. François Jacques Delannoy (1755–1835); student of Antoine; received the Prix de Rôme in 1778; converted the palace of the Duchess of Toulouse into the Bank of France in 1812.

669. *Souvenirs de la Vie et des Ouvrages de F. J. Delannoy, Architecte*, Paris, 1839; figures 17 and 18 are ground plans of the Passage Vivienne.

670. See notes 638, 643, and 605b.

671. See note 670. In 1823, however, Marchoux merely purchased the buildings.

672. See note 669.

673. The transverse buttresses describe a semicircle and determine the spatial profile of the building. The same motif appears later in the Passage du Saumon and in a section of the Passage Pommeraye in Nantes.

674. Quoted from note 605b, entry on *Passagen*.

675. See note 634, fig. 61, elevation of the Galerie Vivienne.

676. J. Billaud, *Galerie Colbert d'après les Plans et Dessins de J. Billaud, Architecte de la Galerie*, Paris, 1828.

677. See note 667, plates 49–52 (ground plan), plates 55–56 (sections), plates 57–58 (facades).

678. G. Borstell and Fr. Koch, "Mitteilungen über bauliche Tätigkeit und die neueren Bau-Unternehmungen in Paris," *Zeitschrift für Bauwesen*, 1855, p. 171, atlas, leaf 23, ground plan and sections.

679. This is especially clear in the original lithograph by Billaud, which is in the Musée Carnavalet, topographic collections, 45F.

680. For example: S. Paolo fuori le Mura in Rome, or S. Apollinare in Classe near Ravenna. There are perspectives of these churches in D. Joseph, *Geschichte der Architektur Italiens*, Leipzig, 1907, pp. 129–130.

681. Thiollet, *Serrurerie et Font de Fer*, Paris, 1832, plate 42, dome of the Galerie Colbert.

682. See note 675, plate 61 and accompanying explanation.

683. This staircase construction, with two intertwining spirals, appears in Leonardo's works. In modern architecture I have only seen it in the Instituti riuniti Marchiondi by Vigano in Milan.

684. All historical information from note 638.

685. See note 675, plates 21 and 62, Galerie Véro-Dodat, shop facades; text, p. 4.

686. The motif of the tall, narrow, show window is a precursor of the large undivided windowpane and can be found in many shops of the Empire. Thiollet and Roux reproduced a similar shop on the Rue St. Honoré (pl. 21). Mr. Fenner assumes that the architect of the arcade also built the short stretch of arcade in the Cour St. André des Arts (1823), which has the same style of window.

687. Mirror facing with lamps in front of it can also be found in the Galerie d'Orléans and Galerie Bordelaise, Bordeaux.

688. See note 641.

689. Tavernier, who built the Galerie de Fer in 1830 (see the introductory section on the bazaar), is mentioned in all works as the architect. Thieme-Becker mentions F. Mazois, the builder of the Passage Choiseul and the Passage Saucède. Since Mazois died in 1826 one can assume that Tavernier finished the work which he had begun.

690. See note 638 and note 605b.

691. Huvé, a student of Percier, built the theater in 1826–1829. Later it became the Salle Ventadour. It was then partially destroyed by the great fire. After 1838 it was the Théâtre de la Renaissance. Now it serves as an annex of the Bank of France.

692. Bibliothèque Nationale, Cabinet d'Estampes, Collections Topographiques, Fol Va 236a.

693. Siegfried Kracauer, *Pariser Leben*, Munich, 1962, pp. 153 and 164.

694. See note 642.

695. Louis-Ferdinand Céline, *Death on the Installment Plan (Le Mort à Credit)*, trans. Ralph Manheim, New York, New Directions, 1966, p. 70.

696. *Elle*, May 1966, p. 1063.

697. See note 638, p. 204.

698. See note 622, p. 117.

699. See note 283, p. 7.

700. See notes 638 and 643.

701. Hubert Rohault de Fleury, son of Charles (1777–1846), student of Durand.

702. *Paris dans Sa Splendeur*, Paris, 1863, 3 vols., vol. 2, p. 33.

703. See note 675, pl. 62.

704. In contrast to the Galerie Vivienne, the springing point of the arches was covered by projecting moulding; hence the arches do not logically follow the development of the facade.

705. See note 643.

706. See note 622, p. 117.

707. Musée Carnavalet, Collections Topographiques, 51C, photograph from 1917.

708. See note 641.

709. See notes 638 and 641.

710. "Entrée du Passage du Bourg l'Abbé, M. Blondel, Arch.," *Moniteur des Architects*, 1879, pl. 55.

711. See note 622, p. 117.

712. See note 605c.

713. See note 605a.

714. Börne, *Pariser Briefe*, no. 8.

715. See note 605b.

716. See note 506c.

717. See note 605c.

718. See note 681, plates 22, 23.

719. The cellar is shown in note 605c.

Notes

720. See the description of the plates cited in note 718.

721. Hülsen, *Forum und Palatin*, 1926, plate 58.

722. See note 638.

723. See note 638.

724. See notes 638 and 641.

725. See notes 638 and 643.

726. See note 623, vol. 6, pp. 67–68, list of arcades.

727. Hans Wachenhusen, *Das Neue Paris*, Leipzig, 1855, p. 42.

728. A panopticon was a feature of the Berlin Kaisergalerie as well. On the Musée Grévin, see Claude Cézan, *Le Musée Grévin*, Paris, undated.

729. *Allgemeine Bauzeitung*, Vienna, 1849, pp. 5–6, atlas, leaf 235: "Eisenkonstruktionen an der Passage Jouffroy zu Paris"; Karl H. Wittek, *Die Entwicklung des Stahlhochbaus* (The Development of the Steel Skyscraper), Düsseldorf, 1964; on Vaux, p. 23.

730. See notes 638, 641, and 643.

731. See note 641.

732. See note 641.

733. See note 638.

734. In *Recueil des Lettres Patentes, Ordonnances Royales, Decrets et Arrêtés Préfectoraux Concernant les Voies Publiques*, M. Alphand, 1886, p. 321.

735. See note 643.

736. On the Philadelphia Arcade: (a) Mathew Baigell, "John Haviland in Philadelphia, 1818–26," *Journal of the Society of Architectural Historians*, vol. 25, 1966, pp. 197–208; (b) B. Tatum, *Penn's Great Town*, Philadelphia, 1961, fig. 63, pp. 68–71 and 174–175.

737. See note 736a, pp. 206–207.

738. *Atkinson's Casket*, vol. 3, 1828, p. 551; also vol. 7, 1832, p. 560. I am grateful to Mrs. Tafel of the Free Library of Philadelphia for photocopies of the articles.

739. *Building News*, vol. 55, 1888, p. 224.

740. I am grateful to Mr. Frecot for the information on the arcades in Prague.

741. *Arkkitehti*, vol. 5, 1968, p. 33, fig. 21.

742. Fineberg, list; see note 413b.

743. Robert Alexander, "The Arcade in Providence," *Journal of the Society of Architectural Historians*, vol. 12, 1953, pp. 13–16. I am grateful to Mr. Alexander and Mr. Gomme for the photographs.

744. Alexander points out that these capitals were also used in St. Paul's church in Boston.

745. See note 413b.

746. Fr. Otto Schulze, "Die Galerie der Piazza Colonna in Rom," *Centralblatt der Bauverwaltung*, 1885, pp. 21–23. In particular, the article describes the Mazzanti project.

747. The planning stages of the Galleria Piazza Colonna are presented in detail in Annibale Sprega, "La sistemazione della Piazza Colonna in Roma," *Estratto dagli Annali della Società degli Ingegneri e degli Architetti Italiani*, Feb. 1, 1912, 24 pages. This paper does not deal with the Mazzanti project.

748. Bibliotheca Hertziana, Rome, W 8647/8649.

749. See note 743 and Ferdinando Mazzanti, *La Galleria in Piazza Colonna*, Rome, 1884, 8 pages.

750. Quoted from note 746, which is practically a literal translation of note 749.

751. The Y-shaped ground plan, which presumes a completely independent building block, is nowhere else to be found. The Galerie Bordelaise in Bordeaux is the only arcade which crosses a block diagonally.

752. *Sistemazione di Piazza Colonna, Galleria-Roma*, Eng. A. Petrignani, architect; project by Deserti & Caffoni, Rome, 1895, 7 pages with 3 plates. See also note 747, fig. 3 and text.

753. *La Tribuna*, April 14, 1895.

754. Pietro Via, "Progetto di Sistemazione di Piazza Colonna in Roma," *Estratto dagli Annali della Società degli Ingegneri e degli Architetti Italiani*, Rome, vol. 3, 1900, 20 pages.

755. Marc Aurelio Boldi, "Progetto di Massima par la Sistemazione de Piazza Colonna," *Estratto dagli Annali della Società degli Ingegneri e degli Architetti Italiani*, Rome, Oct. 31, 1894, 32 pages.

756. See note 747, fig. 8, ground plan; fig. 9, perspective and text.

757. Illustrated in Carroll Meeks, *Italian Architecture, 1750–1914*, London, 1966, figs. 194a and 196.

758. See note 747, figs. 7 and 17 and text.

759. See note 747, fig. 10 (first project), 1910; figs. 14 and 15 (second project), 1912. Carbone also published his projects in a small pamphlet, *La Questione di Piazza Colonna*, Rome, 1912, 30 pages with 5 plates. In 1910 two temporary structures were built on the site, which had been undeveloped since 1889: a cafe with a terrace overlooking the piazza and a cinema. See illustrations in note 747, figs. 11–13.

760. I am grateful to Herr Renting of the Gemeentarchief, Rotterdam, for this information and for the reproductions.

761. Numerous articles in the *Rotterdamsch Nieuwsblad*, 1879.

762. The journal *Eigen Haard*, 1879, no. 48, pp. 477–480: article by Erasianus, "De Rotterdamsche Passage."

763. See note 760.

764. Victorian Society, Annual Report, 1965–1966, p. 16.

765. Baedeker, *Spanien und Portugal*, 1912, city plan of Seville.

766. *Building News*, vol. 75, 1898, p. 45, perspective and ground plan.

767. Talbot Hamlin, *Greek Revival, Architecture in America*, 1944, p. 179.

768. Baedeker, *USA*, 1904, city plan of St. Paul.

769. *Building News*, vol. 58, 1890, pp. 164 and 166.

770. All information and the site plans of the arcades in Sydney are taken from Tom Heath and Tony Moore, "Sydney's Arcades," *Architecture in Australia*, June 1963, pp. 85–90.

771. Maria Walcher, *L'Architettura a Trieste della fine del settecento agli inizi des novecento*, Trieste, 1967, pp. 26–27, on Antonio Buttazoni; figs. 54–58.

772. See note 771. The exact dates are taken from a paper incorporating the ground plans which I have redrawn here, published by Butta-

zoni under the title *Progetto di un fabricato con galleria coperta a vetrata compilato dal sotto-scrito architetto fino dall'anno 1836. . . .*

773. Buttazoni was born in 1800 in Trieste. He studied first under Pertsch in Trieste, and then completed his studies at the Accademia Brera in Milan. After 1821 he worked for twenty years as an architect in Trieste; he designed in the neo-classical style and built a series of palaces. In 1845 he moved to Lubiana and became the technical director of the company which built the railroad between Trieste and Vienna. He died in 1848 in Lubiana.

774. Attilo Tamaro, *Storia di Trieste* (The History of Trieste), vol. 2, Rome, 1924, p. 581.

775. Remodeling plans are in the Archivio Edilicio in Turin.

776. L. Frassati, *Torino come era 1880–1915,* pp. 105–106.

777. Archivio dell'Commune, Turin, Correspondence, 1866.

778. The history of the arcade is recounted in (a) *Cenni sulla Galleria dell'Industria Subalpina,* Turin, Dec. 10, 1874, 7 pages of text and 1 lithograph; (b) *L'Ingegneria Civile,* Feb. 1, 1876, pp. 17–20, ground plans and sections; (c) Mario Vicary, "Relazione della Visita fatta dagli Allieri della R. Scuola d'A. per gl. Ingegneri alla Galleria dell'Ind. Subalpina . . . ," dissertation, 30 pages. Text, plans, and investigation of the vaulting of the cellar.

779. 1873, Biblioteca di Torino, 261, LD, 6.

780. *Ricordi di Architettura,* vol. 1, series 2, 1890, figs. 28, 33, plans and photographs.

781. See note 776, p. 105. From the advertisement reprinted there one can see that a theater, a concert hall, and a music hall were also located in the Galleria Nazionale.

782. Archivio dell'Commune, Turin, Correspondence, 1888–1889.

783. *Guida Touristica di Touring Club,* Milan, 1962.

784. *Building News,* vol. 48, 1885, p. 810, perspective and ground plan.

785. Bruno Carl, *Winterthurer Baurisse 1770–1879,* p. 7.

786. Illustrated in note 784, p. 23.

787. On the history of the town hall: *Die Kunstdenkmäler der Schweiz,* vol. 6, *Die Stadt Winterthur and Zürich,* pp. 78–79.

788. Richard Zürcher, *Alt-Winterthur, ein Architekturführer,* undated, pp. 13–14.

789. Described and partly illustrated, note 785, pp. 72–75.

790. *The British Builder,* Sept. 1925, pp. 414–415.

791. Information over the entranceway.

792. Baedeker, *Belgien und Holland,* 1885. I am grateful to Mr. Hekker of The Hague for the reference.

Illustration Credits

Numbers are illustration numbers.

Archival and Photographic Sources

Author's collection, 27–29, 66, 67, 70, 71, 86, 89, 100–102, 106, 110–114, 121–123, 137, 138, 140–146, 149, 160, 162–164, 183–186, 187, 195–197, 210, 211, 218, 221, 223, 225a, 225b, 226, 230, 232, 241, 244, 254, 255, 265, 273–276, 287, 318–322, 326–333, 335–341, 343, 344, 350–353, 357, 359, 361, 368, 377, 385, 398, 404, 405, 411, 412, 416, 417, 426, 431–433, 458–460, 464, 465

Atlanta, Benzur, 65

Berlin, Technische Universität, drawings collection, 74–77, 80, 81

Berlin, Kunstbibliotek, 78, 79

Berlin, Landesbildstelle, 87, 89, 90

Berlin (East), Schinkel Archiv, 72, 73

Berlin, Muthesius, Stefan, 360

Berlin, Ermisch, 103, 167

Birmingham, Free Library, 108

Bradford, Bruce, 117, 118

Brussels, Andry, 145

Brussels, Bibliothèque Royale, 233, 234

Cleveland, Cleveland Arcade Company, 168–170

Cologne, Rheinisches Bildarchiv, 177, 178

Florence, Alinari, 182, 348, 349, 443, 457

The Hague, Gemeente Archief, 198, 199

Hamburg, Museum für Hamburgische Geschichte, 206

Hamburg, Staatsarchiv, 207–209

Hamburg, Meyer-Veden, 392

Hannover, Historisches Museum, 213, 214

Karlsruhe, Archiv, 217

Leeds, Gilchrist, 222, 227, 228

Leeds, *Yorkshire Evening Post*, 229

Leipzig, Dick Foto Verlag, 231

Liège, Musée de la Wallonnie, 235

London, British Museum, Grace Collections, 268

London, County Council Library, 270–272

London, National Buildings Record, 105, 125–127, 220, 242, 243, 266, 356, 358

London, RIBA, 239, 240

Marburg, Bildarchiv, 8, 406

Manchester, Public Library, 280–283, 286, 292, 293

Milan, Collectione Bertarelli, 298, 299, 306–314

Paris, Bibliothèque Nationale, 32, 115, 363, 369–371, 374, 375, 378, 383, 387, 388, 413b, 417

Paris, Giraudon, 379

Paris, Monuments Historiques, 376

Paris, Musée Carnavalet, 376, 380, 381, 386, 397, 403, 408–410, 415, 419, 420, 430

Paris, Roger Viollet, 367, 428

Rotterdam, Gemeente Werken, 450, 451

Stoke-on-Trent, Dr. Gomme, 189, 190, 436

Zurich, Meyer, 323

Zurich, Bruell, 324

Books and Periodicals

The British Architect and Northern Engineer, 288

The Builder, 107, 119, 284, 452

Centralblatt der Bauverwaltung, 441, 442

Cento Anni in Galleria, 315–317

Coste, 1

Fontaine, *Domaine de la Couronne*, Palais Royal, 364–366

Gloag, *A History of Cast Iron in Architecture*, 215

Journal of the Society of Architectural Historians (U.S.A.), 435, 437, 438

Krafft, *Choix des Maisons*, 401, 402

Wiener Bauindustrie Zeitung, 161

Zeitschrift für Bauwesen, 98, 99

Index of Arcades